THE CLASSICAL PAPERS
OF A. E. HOUSMAN

VOLUME III

D1103725

THE
CLASSICAL PAPERS
OF
A. E. HOUSMAN

COLLECTED AND EDITED BY

J. DIGGLE & F. R. D. GOODYEAR

Volume III 1915–1936

CAMBRIDGE
AT THE UNIVERSITY PRESS
1972

Published by the Syndics of the Cambridge University Press
Bentley House, 200 Euston Road, London NW1 2DB
American Branch: 32 East 57th Street, New York, N.Y. 10022

Library of Congress Catalogue Card Number: 74-158552

I S B NS:

0 521   08243   9   Vol. I
0 521   08511   X   Vol. II
0 521   08479   2   Vol. III

Printed in Great Britain
at the University Printing House, Cambridge
(Brooke Crutchley, University Printer)

CONTENTS

[v]

APPENDIX

108

REVIEW: S. G. OWEN, *P. OVIDI NASONIS TRISTIVM LIBRI QVINQVE**

Little in this volume is new, for seven-eighths of it consist of the *ex Ponto*, which Mr Owen has edited once already, and the *Tristia*, which he has edited twice. His first edition of the *Tristia* had value, which it still retains, as furnishing full collations of the principal manuscripts; but its reader was repeatedly jolted out of his chair by collision with obstacles in the text. Picking himself up from the hearthrug, and feeling his neck to make sure it was not broken, he would find that what he had encountered was either a lection which no other editor had ever admitted or a conjecture which no other editor could easily have made. The disfigurement inflicted upon Ovid's text by Mr Owen's recension is not a matter of dispute, for it is tacitly acknowledged by its author, whose labours on the *Tristia* for the last quarter of a century have chiefly consisted in removing his own corruptions and reinstating the comparatively pure text of his pre-decessors. For example, of more than thirty original conjectures which he printed in 1889, only eight remain in 1915. That is six or seven too many; but Augeas failed to clean out his own stables, and it is no wonder if Mr Owen's similar task is even yet unfinished and will need a fourth edition to complete it. The notes are sometimes inaccurate and often defective. To take the first elegy only, they state that Bentley and Madvig read *hi quoque* at 112, which is not only untrue but incredible, and they omit to state that all or almost all good manu-scripts have *carmina* for *crimina* at 23, *dictata* for *deducta* at 39, and *latori* for *laturo* at 126. The verses I. 2. 74, I. 10. 7, II. 542, IV. 4. 4, IV. 5. 29, V. 6. 35, V. 12. 23, are not printed as the Editor meant that they should be; and all seven miscarriages may be traced by the curious to a single cause.

In the *ex Ponto* Mr Owen had displayed less originality and consequently has less to repent of. Most of the changes in this edition are made in pursuance of orders issued by R. Ehwald in his *Kritische Beiträge* of 1896; but let it be counted to Mr Owen for righteousness that at III. 7. 37 and IV. 15. 42 he has refused to execute the sanguinary mandates of his superior officer.

To the *Tristia* and *ex Ponto* Mr Owen has added the 134 lines of the *Halieutica*.

* [P. Ouidi Nasonis Tristium libri quinque, ex Ponto libri quattuor, Halieutica, fragmenta. Recognouit breuique adnotatione critica instruxit S. G. Owen. Clarendon Press, Oxford, 1915. *Cambridge Review*, 37 (1915), 60]

There has been some dispute in the past about the authorship of this fragment, but that is now happily set at rest, for Mr Owen assures us that the genuineness of the work is fully established by the testimony of Pliny. He says this once on p. iii and twice on p. xi, so that no further doubt is possible; for, in the words of another Student of Christ Church, 'What I tell you three times is true.'

Another poem, more than 600 lines long, was written by Ovid in his exile and has come down to our own times. Its name is not upon Mr Owen's title-page, but under cover of this silence it has been slipped into the middle of the book, – *medio tutissimus Ibis*, as its author himself observed, – apparently in the hope that it may escape notice. Well, so it shall.

109

OVID, *IBIS* 512 AND *TRISTIA* III 6 8*

Ib. 511 sq. lapsuramque domum subeas, ut sanguis Aleuae,
  stella Leoprepidae cum fuit aequa uiro.

'May you perish by the fall of a house, as Scopas did, when Simonides escaped.' The story is told in various places collected by Micyllus and subsequent editors, Suid. pp. 757–9 Bernh. [vol. IV p. 362 Adler] (= Callim. *fr.* 71 Schn. [64 7–14 Pfeiffer]), Cic. *de or.* II 352 sq., Val. Max. I 8 ext. 7, Phaedr. IV 23 [22], Quint. *inst.* XI 2 11–16: how Simonides, dining at the table of Scopas, was called to the door by two young men, who were none other than Castor and Polydeuces; how he went out and found no one there, and meanwhile the roof fell and all within doors were crushed.

In 1894, in a recension of the *Ibis* published in the *corpus poetarum Latinorum*, I changed the *uiro* of u. 512 to *Iouis*, citing Hor. *carm.* II 17 22–4 'te Iouis impio | tutela Saturno refulgens | eripuit'; and editors of Ovid cannot imagine why. Mr Ehwald in 1902 (Bursian's *Jahresbericht* CIX p. 287) enquired 'aber was hat Horat. II 17 22 mit unserer Stelle zu thun?', and Mr Owen in 1914 (*C.Q.* VIII p. 258) 'but what has the star of Jupiter to do with Simonides?'. When these scholars ask me these questions, they are not beseeching me to lighten their darkness; nothing is further from their desire. They hope and believe that they are asking me awkward questions, questions which I in my precipitancy have forgotten to ask myself; and accordingly, like Pilate of old, they do not stay for an answer. They assume without more ado that there is no answer, and that my conjecture is therefore wrong.

The first and indeed the only comment on this pentameter which bewrays any serious attention to its language and meaning is Merkel's in his edition of 1889. Merkel, who had access to the manuscript notes of Schrader, writes as follows: 'in librorum scriptura... *Leoprepidae uiro* iure displicebat Schradero, temptabat *dei*... maxime uero improbabile illud, quod etiam Schraderus habet, "*stella* pro Tyndaridis", quamquam adiecto "modo sit locus sanus".' There are two problems: what sense can be given to *stella*, and what excuse can be found for *uiro*?

'The son of Leoprepes' is *Leoprepides*, not *Leoprepides uir*. When Ellis

* [*CQ* 9 (1915), 31–8]

writes '*uiro* cum *Leoprepidae* coniunctum patris laudem laudi filii adnectit' he appears to mean, if anything, the opposite of what he says; but his translation ‖ is 'Leoprepes' famous son'. Hundreds and thousands of times are famous sons mentioned by patronymic in Ovid and other Latin poets, and where else is that notion conveyed by the bare addition of *uir*? I know but a single apparent instance; and that will vanish as soon as it is approached.

Of Lucr. III 370 sq. 'illud in his rebus nequaquam sumere possis, | *Democriti* quod sancta *uiri* sententia ponit' I should not venture to say with Mr Heinze 'die Verbindung *Democriti...uiri* wäre ohne die prädicative Bestimmung *sancta* nicht möglich': I agree rather with Lobeck at Soph. *Ai.* 817 that *uiri* is 'honoris causa additum' with the pregnant force of 'worthy wight' as a formal civility to a respected antagonist. But there is no similar reason why Simonides should be singled out from the multitude of his peers to be designated as Ovid never designates anyone else. The solitary parallel of which I spoke is to be found in Silius *Pun.* XIII 800. Scipio, having descended to the Elysian fields, sees the spirit of Homer pacing along: 781–3 'dic, ait, hic quinam, uirgo? nam luce refulget | praecipua frons sacra uiro, multaeque secuntur | mirantes animae et laeto clamore frequentant.' Autonoe* answers his question, and his next question is about the admiring throng which follows at Homer's heels, 798–802:

> sed, quae tanta adeo gratantum turba, requirens
> heroum effigies maiorisque accipit umbras.
> ire *uiro* stupet *Aeacide*, stupet Hectore magno
> Aiacisque gradum uenerandaque Nestoris ora
> miratur etc.

But this cannot be construed; and if the text is corrupt, *uiro* may be part of the corruption, as the latest editors assume when they write '*inuicto* stupet Aeacide' with Thilo. The text however is not corrupt, but only the punctuation.

> heroum effigies maiorisque accipit umbras
> ire uiro. stupet Aeacide etc.

He learns (from Autonoe*) that those approaching him (Homer) are the mighty shades of heroes. 'ire *uiro*' for *ad uirum* is in Prop. I 15 8, and Silius himself has 'Daunius *huic* robur iuuenis iacit' for *in hunc* at II 244 and '*huic* procul ardentem iaculatus lampada Cimber | conicit' at XIV 305 sq.

The *uiro* of *Ib.* 512 seems therefore to be an unexampled redundancy, and its presence is the more surprising because its place is wanted for something else.

stella means simply a star; and when the commentators explain it as *stella Dioscurorum* Merkel has every right to reject their gloss. But if we let them have their way it will help them nothing, for Simonides was not rescued by the *stella Dioscurorum*. That *stella*, mentioned by Horace *carm.* I 12 28 and described by

* ⟦Corrected by Housman to 'the Sibyl' in *JPh* 35 (1920), 287 (this edition p. 1018)⟧

Pliny *n.h.* II 101 and Seneca *n.q.* I 1 13, was a marine phenomenon promising fair weather to sailors, and never came anywhere near || Pharsalus or Crannon, in whichever of those two towns the house of Scopas stood. Interpreters who mistake *stella* for the constellation Gemini, the third sign of the zodiac, make the matter even worse. For, first, it was no sign of the zodiac that came to the door and called for Simonides, any more than it was a form of electricity; it was a pair of travel-stained young men on horseback. And, secondly, *stella* does not mean a constellation: the examples alleged in the dictionaries are all false. Verg. *georg.* I 222 'Cnosiaque ardentis decedat *stella Coronae*' is not the constellation of the Crown but the bright star in its centre signalised by Manilius I 319–22 'at parte ex alia claro uolat orbe Corona | luce micans uaria; nam *stella* uincitur una | circulus, in media radiat quae maxima fronte | candidaque ardenti distinguit lumina flamma', whose rising was separately noted in the calendars: Colum. XI 2 73 sq. 'tertio Non. Octobris *Corona* incipit oriri...octauo Id. Octobris *Coronae clara stella* exoritur...tertio et pridie Id. Octobris *Corona tota*', Plin. *n.h.* XVIII 313 'VIII Id. Oct.... *fulgens in Corona stella* exoritur,... Idibus *Corona tota*'. Again, Hor. *carm.* III 29 19 'stella uesani *Leonis*' is not the constellation Leo but '*stella regia* appellata Tuberoni *in pectore Leonis*' (Plin. *n.h.* XVIII 235 and 271, schol. Germ. Breys. p. 132 14), the star we now call Regulus, the Βασιλίσκος or Καρδία Λέοντος of the Greeks. In Ovid himself, *amor.* II 16 4 'Icarii *stella* proterua *Canis*' is not the constellation Canicula but the star Sirius; *fast.* V 112 '*stella*...in cunas officiosa Iouis' is a perfectly correct description of Capella, which is a single star and not a constellation. As for *fast.* III 793 sq.,

> *stella* Lycaoniam uergit declinis ad Arcton
> *Miluus*: haec illa nocte uidenda uenit,

the fact that Ovid called the *miluus* a *stella* shows that he believed it to be a star; and no writer mentions any constellation of that name. But in truth the *miluus* was neither a constellation nor a star but a bird of passage, the Greek ἰκτῖνος, which made its appearance about the same time as the swallow; and Ovid or his informant, finding the words ἰκτῖνος φαίνεται in a calendar (they occur for instance in Geminus ed. Manit. p. 228 1 and 11, Ptolemy ed. Heib. II p. 41 11, Clodius Tuscus ap. Lyd. *de ostent.* ed. Wachsm. p. 123 5), supposed them to signify the rising of a heavenly body.

That the Dioscuri might be called *stellae* I would not deny, for Callimachus plainly calls them ἀστέρες in *lau. Pall.* 23–5 δὶς ἑξήκοντα διαθρέξασα διαύλως, | οἷα παρ᾽ Εὐρώτᾳ τοὶ Λακεδαιμόνιοι | ἀστέρες, and is imitated by Statius *Ach.* I 180 sq. 'Eurotae qualis uada Castor anhelo | intrat equo fessumque sui iubar excitat astri'; but what we have here is the singular *stella*, and that question does not arise.

It appears then that the star which rescued Simonides must be sought in the heaven not of mythology but of astrology. But there can be no allusion to that astrological entity which is called in English the natal star. 'Natal star' is a translation of *natale astrum* or *sidus natalicium*, and it means one of the || twelve signs of the zodiac. But *stella*, as I have said, does not mean a sign of the zodiac; and moreover the signs of the zodiac are neither *aequa* nor *iniqua* and do not rescue anybody from anything. A man's natal sign determines his character and pursuits, but for accidents or escape from accidents he must thank the planets, and to these are the epithets *aequus* and *iniquus* applicable: Sen. *dial.* VI 18 3 'uidebis *quinque sidera* diuersas agentia uias et in contrarium praecipiti mundo nitentia; ex horum leuissimis motibus fortunae populorum dependent, et maxima ac minima proinde formantur, prout *aequum iniquumue sidus* incessit.' And 'planet' is what *stella* most often means in astrology, and what it means in another astrological passage of the *Ibis*: 209–16 'natus es infelix, ita di uoluere, nec *ulla* | commoda nascenti *stella* leuisue fuit. | non *Venus* affulsit, non illa *Iuppiter* hora, | *Luna*que non apto *Sol*que fuere loco. | nec satis utiliter positos tibi praebuit ignes | *quem peperit* magno lucida *Maia* Ioui. | te fera nec quicquam placidum spondentia *Martis* | sidera presserunt *falciferique senis*.' It is therefore to be presumed that *stella* means a planet in verse 512.

But what planet of the seven? for Simonides (even if *stella* were *stella sua*) had no planet of his own. No planet was singly assigned to a man at his birth, to control his destiny: he was subject to the influences of all, according to their aspects. But if *stella* means simply 'a planet', some one or other of the choir, there was no cause or excuse for introducing astrology at all; it is as if he had said vaguely *deus* when he meant the Tyndarids. If he wished to profess ignorance of the planet's name, there were ways of professing it, as Persius V 51 says *nescioquod...astrum*, or as Hermione enquires 'quod...mihi miserae *sidus* obesse querar?' in *her.* VIII 88, or Ovid himself 'quod...putem *sidus* nostris occurrere fatis?' in *amor.* III 12 3: even *stellarum una* might have been sufficient. But he knew the planet's name well enough, and the wonder is that he should conceal his knowledge.

This verse therefore combines redundancy in phrase with deficiency in sense; and it needs no training in any art of criticism, it needs nothing but sincerity and mother-wit, to recognise that these two phenomena, found in conjunction, are not to be considered separately. It is not for us to set our teeth and accept *Leoprepidae uiro* for *Leoprepidae*, and then to take a breath, set them again, and accept *stella* for *stella Iouis*. The superfluity provides the material for repairing the defect, and *uiro* is a corruption of a word defining *stella*.

Two of the planets, Mars and Saturn, are specifically baneful, κακοποιοί, *maleuoli*, and two, Venus and Jupiter, are specifically benign, ἀγαθοποιοί, *beneuoli*; and it is the office of the two latter to contend against the two former in mankind's behalf: *C.C.A.G.* v iii p. 100 6 sq. οἱ ἀγαθοποιοὶ ὅτε ὁρῶσι τοὺς κακοποιοὺς ἐλαττοῦσι τὴν κακίαν αὐτῶν. Venus is naturally the special antagonist of Mars, and Jupiter of Saturn: ibid. p. 101 2–5 ὁ Ζεὺς ἀναλύει τὰ ὑπὸ τοῦ Κρόνου δεσμούμενα καὶ μεταβάλλει τὴν κακίαν αὐτοῦ, ὅτε συσχηματίζεται αὐτῷ· ἡ δὲ Ἀφροδίτη λύει τὴν κακίαν τοῦ Ἄρεως, Ouid. *amor.* 1 8 29 sq. '*stella* tibi oppositi nocuit contraria *Martis.* | illa ⟦Mars⟧ abiit, signo nunc *Venus* apta ‖ suo',[1] Pers. v 50 '*Saturnum*que grauem nostro *Ioue* frangimus una', Hor. *carm.* 11 17 22–5 'te *Iouis* impio | tutela *Saturno* refulgens | eripuit uolucrisque fati | tardauit alas', where Porphyrion says 'aiunt Saturni stellam infestam esse hominibus, Iouis autem e contrario saluberrimam, Saturno pericula adferri eaque tamen euinci si perfulget Iouis stella.' But Jupiter, not Venus, is the saviour star κατ' ἐξοχήν, the stronger and more active of the two: *C.C.A.G.* v iii p. 100 sq. ὁ Ζεὺς ἐὰν ὁρᾷ κακοποιὸν ἀστέρα μεταβάλλει τὴν κρᾶσιν αὐτοῦ ἐπὶ τὸ ἀγαθόν· ἡ δὲ Ἀφροδίτη οὐ δύναται μεταβαλεῖν τὴν κακίαν τοῦ κακοποιοῦ ὥσπερ ὁ Ζεύς, εἰ μήπω ἐφορᾷ τὸν Δία. His pre-eminent goodwill and potency may be judged from what Firmicus says in *math.* 11 13 6: 'unum tamen sciendum est, quod, licet beniuola sit Iouis stella, tamen contra impugnationem Martis et Saturni, si eam uiolenti radiatione constringant, resistere sola non possit; *essent enim immortales homines, si numquam in genituris hominum Iouis benignitas uinceretur.* sed quia sic artifex deus hominem fecit, ut substantia eius transacto certo uitae spatio solueretur, necesse fuit ut detento *Ioue, per quem uitae confertur hominibus salutare praesidium,* in extinguendo homine maliuolarum stellarum malitiosa uel perniciosa potestas cum augmento malitiae permaneret, ut maliuolis radiationibus inpugnata compago corporis solueretur'; and so Cicero calls him 'hominum generi prosperus et salutaris ille fulgor, qui dicitur Iouis' *de r. p.* VI 17, and Ausonius 'stella salutigeri Iouis' 332 26 (Peip. p. 25).

The malignant planets to some extent divide their provinces of evil: death by the sword and perils of warfare are naturally assigned to Mars, but some dangers to life and limb, including many maladies, are in the gift of Saturn. The peril incurred and escaped by Maecenas is not known and cannot be discovered from Horace; but Porphyrion says it was an illness, and his statement is generally and perhaps rightly accepted. Maecenas, as Pliny tells us in *n. h.* VII 172, suffered all his life long from fever, and if on this occasion his fever was an ague, ῥιγοπύρετος, it would fall within Saturn's department. Help, if it came, would come, as Horace says it did, from one of the benignant planets: Firm. *math.* III 2 26 'in duodecimo loco Saturnus ab horoscopo constitutus... faciet... maximas aegritudines, sed et ualetudines non modicas, praesertim si... nulla beniuola stella in geniturae cardinibus fuerit collocata. nam si sic posito Saturno beniuola

---

[1] Ovid knows too much astrology for his editors, and this phrase is misinterpreted by Heinsius and Némethy and not interpreted at all by any other commentator whom I have read. It means 'Venus is now favourably situate in a sign of her own', that is in one or other of the two signs Taurus and Libra, which are the houses (οἶκοι, *domus, domicilia*) of the planet Venus.

stella in quocumque geniturae cardine fuerit inuenta, haec mala, quae diximus, ex parte aliqua mitigantur', IV 19 7–8 'facit (Saturnus) pleumonicos hydropicos podagricos caducos spasticos...quodsi eum beniuolae stellae habentem dominium sic, sicut diximus, positum bona radiatione conueniant, istas ualetudines *uel praesidium dei alicuius uel sollers medicina* curabit.' I have italicised these words with a purpose. For an astrologer the stars are supreme; || physicians and even gods are only their ministers. Maecenas may think that the doctors cured him, and Simonides may ascribe his rescue to the Heavenly Twins; but astrologers know that the true cause was higher and mightier than the sons of Aesculapius or of Leda.

But it is time to be telling Messrs Ehwald and Owen exactly how the planet Jupiter was concerned in the rescue of Simonides; and I begin with Firm. *math.* IV 20 5–6: 'si...in opportunis geniturae locis Iuppiter et Venus fuerint inuenti in horoscopo,...minaces periculorum impetus salutari beniuolarum stellarum praesidio subleuantur et homines ex inminentibus periculis liberantur. periculorum autem non una substantia est; aut enim ex...aegritudinibus... aut *ex ruinis*...periculorum discrimen adfertur.' Falling houses are thus among the perils from which men are saved by benignant stars. And both in ancient and in medieval astrology the fall of houses is laid to the account of Saturn. Manetho VI 611 sq.

εἰ δέ τε καὶ Φαίνων ὀλοὴν ἀκτῖνα βάλῃσιν
ἄχθεσιν ἢ λάεσσι δόμων τ' ὀροφῇσιν ἔθλιψεν.

Chaucer *Knightes Tale* 1605–8:

Myn is the ruine of the hye halles,
The falling of the toures and of the walles
Up-on the mynour or the carpenter.
I slow Sampsoun in shaking the piler.

Jupiter, as Saturn's especial foe, is the planet to mitigate the calamity: *C.C.A.G.* II p. 123 12–16 ὁπηνίκα ὁ Κρόνος συνοδεύῃ μετὰ τοῦ Διός, δηλοῖ παντοίων οἰκοδομημάτων κατάλυσιν · ... εἰ δὲ συμβαίνει ἐν τῷ τοῦ Κρόνου οἴκῳ (Capricorn or Aquarius) τοῦτο γίνεσθαι, τότε ἔτι μᾶλλον τὰ τῆς κακίας αὔξει · εἰ δὲ ἐν τῷ τοῦ Διός (Sagittarius or Pisces), ἔλαττον ὑπάρχει τὸ κακὸν ὡς τούτου ὑπερνικῶντος. Sometimes Saturn is reinforced by Mars: Firm. *math.* VI 19 20 'si Saturnus in horoscopo partiliter fuerit constitutus et Martem habeat in occasu, id est in diametro, partiliter constitutum,...ista coniunctio graue ac miserum mortis decernit exitium. aut enim ferarum morsu consumpti artus miseris lacerationibus dissipantur...aut *corpus cadentium culminum ruinis opprimitur*.' But Jupiter may yet be a match for the pair of them: ibid. VI 15 8–9 'si uero in quadrupedibus signis fuerint constituti (Mars et Saturnus) uel unus eorum in signo quadrupede inuentus alium diametra radiatione respexerit,...*graui ruinarum pondere oppressi* (homines) *et dissipati corporis laceratione confecti aut moriuntur aut uicina mortis coguntur subire discrimina*. sed haec omnia infortunia tunc forti calamitatis cumulo conualescunt, cum hos sic positos nullis *Iuppiter* radiationibus mitigarit.' That is, if Jupiter does not intervene, the threatened men *moriuntur*, like Scopas; if he intervenes, then, like Simonides, *uicina mortis coguntur subire discrimina*, and no more.

When a noun is distant from the word to which it is grammatically ‖ related, and adjacent to a word possessing or governing a different case, its case is often altered by copyists who mistake its construction. Thus in *Ib.* 375 sq., 'ut quorum Aeacides misit uiolentus in altum | corpora cum senis altera sena *rogum*', more than half the MSS have *rogis* because of *cum senis*; and in the same way *Iouis*, because of *aequa*, might here be changed to *Ioui*. The letters *i* and *r* are sometimes mistaken for one another in minuscules (even as early as the MSS of Lucr. VI 210, *iubeant* for *rubeant*), and the word *Ioui*, which at *Ib.* 214 appears in the Vindobonensis as *roim*, might here by a slighter error become *roui*; while the transposition of syllables which converts the meaningless *ro-ui* into *ui-ro* is one which I have illustrated in my edition of Manil. I pp. lvii sq. and in the *Journal of Philology* XXX pp. 229 sq. [this edition pp. 711–12]: add here Stat. *silu.* I praef. l. 28 Klotz ed. 2 [l. 23 Phillimore] *bi-du*-o *du-bi*-o, Seru. *georg.* I 149 *br-um*-as *um-br*-as. But in the works of Ovid himself there is another verse in which I find, not a similar error, but the very same.

trist. III 6 1–8 foedus amicitiae nec uis, carissime, nostrae
    nec, si forte uelis, dissimulare potes.
donec enim licuit nec te mihi carior alter
    nec tibi me tota iunctior urbe fuit.
isque erat usque adeo populo testatus, ut esset   5
    paene magis quam tu quamque ego notus, amor.
quique est in caris animi tibi candor amicis
    cognita sunt ipsi, quem colis, ista uiro.

The last couplet means 'so generous a friend are you that you have not disguised our intimacy even from that man "quem colis"'. But 'ipsi uiro, quem colis' designates nobody, for there were dozens of men whom Ovid's friend 'colebat'. The relation between man and man described by the verb *colere*, with its synonyms *diligere* and *obseruare*, pervaded all society: 'utque ego maiores, sic me coluere minores' says Ovid in *trist.* IV 10 55, and again in *amor.* III 4 45, 'et cole, quos dederit (multos dabit) uxor, amicos'. The phrase does not even imply of necessity that *is qui colit* is inferior to *is qui colitur*: Seru. *Aen.* I 16 'ueteres *colere* dicebant etiam cum maior minorem diligeret', and such is its sense in Ter. *ad.* 925–7 'ego uero iubeo et hac re et aliis omnibus | quam maxime unam facere nos hanc familiam, | *colere* adiuuare adiungere.' But it is evident and admitted that the person here meant must be the emperor; and Heinsius accordingly says 'puto *ipsi*...*deo*, hoc est Augusto'. For when a subject 'colit Caesarem', he 'colit deum' and not 'uirum'. Let Ovid himself be witness: *ex Pont.* II 2 123–5 〚121–3〛 'quoniam patria toto sumus orbe remoti | nec licet ante *ipsos* procubuisse *deos*, | quos *colis*, ad *superos* haec fer mandata sacerdos', IV 8 22 sq. '*quos colis*, exora supplice uoce *deos*. | *di* tibi sunt *Caesar* iuuenis', 15 23 sq. 'quod quoniam in *dis* est, tempta lenire precando | *numina*, perpetua *quae* pietate *colis*'. And in the ‖ only other verse of our poem where Augustus is signified he is called a god: 23 'numinis...laesi'. But the change of *deo* to *uiro*, though not impossible, is unlikely; and the same sense will be given by

> cognita sunt ipsi, quem colis, ista Ioui.

In the *tristia* alone there are eight verses where oblique cases of *Iuppiter* denote Augustus: 1 1 81, 4 26, 5 78, III 1 38, 5 7, 11 62, IV 3 69, V 2 46: the nominative, for some reason or other, is not thus abused.

   It may spare editors of Ovid some little trouble if I suggest to them how they had better defend the MS reading. The defence is one which would sooner or later occur to them spontaneously, even if I now said nothing; but I can save them time by foretelling it, as my acquaintance with their habits of thought enables me to do. I advise them then to ignore my objection and to set about proving what is not in dispute: that Augustus was a man and was so called by Ovid. I will even provide examples for them: *trist.* v 2 50 'o *uir* non ipso, quem regis, orbe minor', *ex Pont.* I 2 89 〚87〛 'ira *uiri* mitis', 120 〚118〛 'aequandi superis pectora flecte *uiri*'. This defence ought to satisfy quite a large number of their readers; for there are millions of mankind who can no more detect *ignoratio elenchi* than if they were editors of Ovid.

110

CATULLUS LXIV 324*

O decus eximium magnis uirtutibus augens,
Emathiae tutamen opis, carissime nato,   324
accipe quod laeta tibi pandunt luce sorores
ueridicum oraclum.

It neither is nor need be doubted that *tutamen opis*, preserved like many another
true lection in the margin of G and R, is what Catullus wrote. The *tutū opus*
which OGR present in their texts is a simple error arising from the abbreviation
of *tamen* as *tn̄*. But the verse still fails to satisfy and is universally esteemed
corrupt. The description of Peleus as dear exceedingly to his yet unborn and
unbegotten son is so absurd a form of address that all editors now adopt from
the interpolated MSS the conjecture '*clarissime* nato'. This description is
neither absurd nor untrue, but it is yet untimely, and sorts ill with the bride-
groom's other titles. The 'decus eximium', the 'magnae uirtutes', the 'tutela
Emathiae', all are already his: the glory reflected from his heroic son belongs to
the future and is part of that prophecy to which in the next two verses he is
bidden to give ear. *clarissime nupta* would be appropriate, and would resemble
25 'eximie taedis felicibus aucte' and Ouid. *met.* XI 217 sq. 'coniuge Peleus |
clarus erat diua'; but 'most illustrious in thy son' breaks away from the rest of
this prelude and forestalls what is to come in 338 and the following verses.
There is therefore an undercurrent of feeling that even now all is not well: 'de
coniectura illa dubitari potest, cum propriae Pelei ipsius uirtutes hic prae-
dicentur' says Baehrens, and Schwabe even proposes so wretched an alternative as 'carissime *fato*'.

The other half of the verse, 'Emathiae tutamen opis', seems to trouble
nobody; and yet it is strange. The singular *opis*, beside its usual sense of 'aid',
can mean resources proffered or procured, as in Hor. *serm.* I 2 74 'diues *opis*
natura suae', Ouid. *trist.* I 3 10 'aptae profugo uestis *opis*ue (legendae cura)';
or power to aid, as in Hor. *epist.* I 9 9 'dissimulator *opis* propriae, mihi commodus uni'; or even simply power and might: Verg. *Aen.* I 600 sq. 'grates
persoluere dignas | non *opis* est nostrae', VIII 376 sq. 'non arma rogaui |
artis *opis*ue tuae', Ouid. *met.* VI 700 'hac *ope* debueram thalamos petiisse', IX 125
'*ope* fidis equina', *fast.* I 269 'oraque, qua pollens *ope* sum, fontana reclusi',

* [[CQ 9 (1915), 229–30]]

III 22 'sua diuina furta fefellit *ope*'. But the might of Emathia did not want protecting: it was itself a protection. Peleus could || well be said to protect the wealth or prosperity of Emathia, but then it should be *Emathiarum opum*. Baehrens indeed adduces Enn. *Andr. aechm.* [89 Jocelyn] ap. Cic. *Tusc.* III 44 'o Priami domus,...uidi ego te adstante *ope barbarica*'; but that means 'with the might of Asia marshalled by', and is so interpreted by Virgil, *Aen.* VIII 685 'hinc *ope barbarica* uariisque Antonius armis', 'with the forces of the East to aid him'. In Plaut. *capt.* 15, where commentators explain *ope* as *opibus* without citing any parallel, the context suggests that it means assistance rendered to the actor by members of the audience who sit still and do not interrupt.

But my difficulty in the first half of the verse is only a consequence of the editors' attempt to remove their difficulty in its last half. The reading of the MSS offers no difficulty in either, and stands in need of no help from anyone except the printer:

Emathiae tutamen, Opis carissime nato.

Opis carissime nato is διίφιλε, an epithet unknown indeed to Stephanus and consequently to Passow and Pape and Liddell and Scott, but applied by Homer to Achilles and other heroes, and applicable also to Peleus: Πηλέϊ, ὃς περὶ κῆρι φίλος γένετ' ἀθανάτοισιν, *Il.* XXIV 61. See Pind. *Ol.* II 23 [12] ὦ Κρόνιε παῖ 'Ρέας, *frag.* 144 Bergk [144 Snell] (schol. Ar. *eq.* 624) ἐλασίβροντα παῖ 'Ρέας, *anth. Pal.* IX 645 4 υἷα 'Ρέης, Auson. 343 2 (Peip. p. 161) 'Rhea, quae Latiis Ops', Plaut. *Pers.* 251 sq. 'Ioui opulento, incluto, | Ope gnato', *mil.* 1082 'Iuppiter ex Ope natust'. Designation by metronymic recurs in Catullus at 66 44, 'progenies Thiae' for Sol. The verse is much like 26 sq. 'Thessaliae columen, Peleu, cui Iuppiter ipse, | ipse suos diuum genitor concessit amores'.

111

MERGERE AND PRIAP. 65*

Hic tibi qui rostro crescentia lilia mersit
caeditur e tepida uictima porcus hara.
ne tamen exanimum facias pecus omne, Priape,
horti sit facias ianua clausa tui.

The first volume of Buecheler's collected opuscula has just been published, and
it includes the celebrated 'uindiciae libri Priapeorum' from *Rhein. Mus.* XVIII
pp. 381–415, written at the age of twenty-six, but inferior to none of its author's
work in his special characteristic of patient ingenuity. The note upon the first
verse of this poem runs as follows (*Rh. M.* p. 405, *kl. Schr.* 1 p. 352, where
there are two misprints):

> 'oscitantia incredibili propagabatur *qui rostro lilia mersit,* Heinsius tamen
> *carpsit* uel *rasit* uel *rosit* proposuerat. nimirum Ouidius *rode caper uitem*
> dixit, Martialis *uite nocens rosa hircus.* at *rostro rodere* dedecet poetam. hic ut
> ego emendaui sic Ouidius *uite caper morsa,* Iuuenalis *haedulus inscius herbae*
> *necdum ausus uirgas humilis mordere salicti,* Vergilius *signata admorso in*
> *stirpe cicatrix.*'

His emendation, as he calls it, was *morsit*. This he had printed already in his
smaller Petronius of 1862, he repeated it in 1871 and 1882 and 1904, and it is
piously preserved by Mr Heraeus in the 5th edition. Yet all that Buecheler has
to say for it is said above: there is no defence of the form; no sign of any
suspicion that defence is needed; not even a reference to Gellius VI 9 7. And then
it is others who are charged with 'oscitantia incredibilis'. It is incredibilis
oscitantia to believe for forty years and more that in the age of Ovid (for that is
the age to which Buecheler assigned the Priapea) they said *morsit* for *momordit*. ||

The verb *mordere* is not even suitable. Goats, it is true, damage vegetation by
nibbling it; but the devastation spread by M. Grunnius Corocotta, soliuertiator,
when he and his snout get into the garden, consists much rather in routing up
and in breaking down, and is much better described by *mersit*, which means
obruit, afflixit, perdidit, pessum dedit. This use begins with cases where the
metaphor is still clearly discernible and the disaster in which a thing is whelmed

* ⟦*CR* 29 (1915), 173–4⟧

is expressed by the presence of an ablative: Verg. *Aen.* VI 429, XI 28 '*funere mersit* acerbo', VI 512 'me fata mea et scelus exitiale Lacaenae | his *mersere malis*' (compare Liu. III 16 4 'superantibus aliis ac *mergentibus malis*'), Liu. VI 17 2 '*mersam* et *obrutam fenore* partem ciuitatis', Plin. *n.h.* VII 132 'quam multos accepta *adflixere* imperia! quam multos bona *perdidere* et ultimis *mersere suppliciis*!' Flor. I 47 (III 12) 8 'illae opes atque diuitiae *adflixere* saeculi mores, *mersam*que *uitiis* suis quasi sentina rem publicam *pessum dedere*'. Then this ablative disappears and *mergere* by itself means *ruin, crush*; and if an ablative is present it expresses that *by* which, not *in* which, the thing is whelmed: Liu. IX 18 1 'Alexandro nondum *merso* secundis rebus', Ouid. *trist.* III 11 38 'carnifici fortuna potest mea flenda uideri, | te tamen est uno iudice *mersa* parum', Vell. II 91 3 'cum esset omni flagitiorum scelerumque conscientia *mersus*, nec melior illi res familiaris quam mens foret', Sen. *ep.* 55 3 'quotiens aliquos amicitiae Asinii Galli, quotiens Seiani odium, deinde amor *merserat*', Luc. I 159 'publica belli | semina, quae populos semper *mersere* potentes', VI 8 'placet alea fati | alterutrum *mersura* caput', VII 655 'trahere omnia secum | *mersa* iuuat gentesque suae miscere ruinae', VIII 509 'regesque timet, quorum omnia *mersit*', anth. Lat. Ries. 472 1 'non satis est quod nos *mergit* furiosa iuuentus | transuersosque rapit fama sepulta probris', Sil. VIII 285 'cernebat Paulus . . . labi, *mergente* sinistro | consule, res *pessum*que *dari*', Iuu. X 57 'quosdam *praecipitat* subiecta potentia magnae | inuidiae, *mergit* longa atque insignis honorum | pagina' (compare Cic. *pro Sull.* 87 'rei publicae *praecipitanti* subueni, patriam *demersam* extuli'), XIII 8 'ut mediocris | iacturae te *mergat* onus', Plin. *n.h.* IX 67 'nullusque prope iam mortalis aestimatur pluris quam qui peritissime censum domini *mergit*'; Verg. *Aen.* VI 615 'ne quaere doceri . . . quae forma uiros fortunaue *mersit*' is not easily intelligible but appears to contain another example. So *mersare* in Lucr. V 1008 'tum penuria deinde cibi languentia *leto* | membra *dedit*, contra nunc rerum copia *mersat*'; so *demergere* in Hor. *carm.* III 16 13 'concidit auguris | Argiui domus ob lucrum | *demersa* exitio', Sen. *Med.* 528 'his adice Colchos, adice et Aeeten ducem, | Scythas Pelasgis iunge: *demersos* dabo'; and so βαπτίζειν and καταποντίζειν in Greek, Lobeck Soph. *Ai.* pp. 357 sq.

It will be noticed that in these examples the metaphor signifies ruin of fortune or health or character; Priap. 65 1 is singular, so far as I know, in extending it to material destruction, such as laying a row of lilies flat. The French *abîmer* has acquired and often enjoys this meaning, as in Hugo *Les Misérables* V 13 'j'ai eu tort d'abîmer le chapeau de ce monsieur'.

112

OVIDIANA*

TRIST. I 7 5–8

hoc tibi dissimula, senti tamen, optime, dici,   5
   in digito qui me fersque refersque tuo
effigiemque meam fuluo complexus in auro
   cara relegati, quac potes, ora uides.

This is the way to say in Latin 'you see my face, though you cannot see the rest of me'. So *her.* X 53 'tua, *quae* possum, pro te *uestigia* tango', 135 'non oculis sed, *qua* potes, aspice *mente*', *art.* II 633 'corpora si nequeunt, *quae* possunt, *nomina* tangunt', *trist.* IV 2 57 'haec ego summotus, *qua* possum, *mente* uidebo', 3 17 sq. 'esse tui memorem... *quod*que potest, secum *nomen* habere tuum', 10 112 'tristia, *quo* possum, *carmine* fata leuo', *ex Pont.* IV 4 45 'absentem, *qua* possum, *mente* uidebo'.[1] But that is not what Ovid seeks to say: he means 'you see my face in such fashion as you can', not in the flesh but in counterfeit presentment; and Latin expresses this meaning otherwise. As Ovid here speaks of his own likeness on a ring, so in *ex Pont.* II 8 55 he speaks of the likenesses of Augustus Tiberius and Liuia on a medal; and he says 'nos quoque uestra iuuat quod, *qua* licet, *ora uidemus*'. Arellius Fuscus in Sen. *suas.* 4 1 puts the same thought in the same way, 'cur non ab infantia *rerum naturam deosque, qua* licet, *uisimus*, cum pateant nobis sidera et interesse numinibus liceat?' In *her.* XIII 41 sq. '*qua* possum, squalore tuos imitata labores | dicar' many MSS have changed the adverb into *quo* agreeing with the substantive hard by; and similarly here the 'quae potes' of the text has come from 'qua potes'.

And so read three of Heinsius' MSS, and so, with his usual rightness of instinct, did Heinsius, though he might have found it hard to formulate his reason, for his faculty of analysis was slight. The lection was adopted by Burman and remained the vulgate till in 1837 it collided with the density of Merkel, who thought he disposed of it by citing *trist.* I 1 16 'contingam certe *quo* licet illa *pede*'. That is a play upon two senses of the word *pes*; it means 'non meo pede sed uersuum meorum pede siue metro'. To realise the futility of the parallel, try the experiment of substituting *qua* for *quo* in that verse. All

---

* [[CQ 10 (1916), 130–50: some of these notes are summarized in *PCPhS* 1915, 16–17]]

[1] Sometimes *solus* is added, *met.* I 731 '*quos* potuit *solos*, tollens ad sidera *uultus*', *ex Pont.* II 10 47 'te tamen intueor *quo solo pectore* possum'.

sense will vanish, for *quo licet* is necessary to the definition of *pede*: if *quo* were removed, *pede* must be removed; if *qua* were substituted, it must be || substituted for *quo pede* and not for *quo*; and in fact 'contingam illa *quo licet pede*' is parallel, not to the 'uides cara relegati ora, *quae potes*' which Merkel was defending, but to the 'uides . . . ora, *qua potes*' which he was trying to set aside.

TRIST. II 275–80

275   sic igitur carmen, recta si mente legatur,
              constabit nulli posse nocere meum.
          [at quasdam uitio. quicumque hoc concipit, errat
              et nimium scriptis arrogat ille meis.]
           ut tamen hoc fatear, ludi quoque semina praebent
280   nequitiae: tolli tota theatra iube.

277 *uicio* L, *uitiat* HPV, *quaedam uitia* AG. The sense is 'but it may be thought that I corrupt a matron here and there': *uitio* is 1st pers. sing. pres. indic. of *uitiare*. 'Who could mistake it for anything else?' asks the reader. A modern editor of Ovid. He would mistake it for the dative or ablative of *uitium*; he would enclose the words *at quasdam uitio* between inverted commas and put them into the mouth of Ovid's adversary; and he would explain the construction by an ellipse of *afficit* or of *uertisse meos libros arguunt*.

There is no reason to doubt that the couplet 277 sq. now stands as its author wrote it; but its author was not Ovid. Bentley's proposal to eject it was founded on the false readings current in his day; and when he adds 'quibus sublatis uide ut pulchre cohaerent reliqua', that, though a just observation, is not a compelling argument. But an argument which I find compelling is this: the point here raised, – that Ovid's *artes* may pervert individuals though not the whole class, – is a point which Ovid has met by anticipation. He has already said (257 sq.) 'quodcumque attigerit, *si qua est studiosa sinistri*, | ad uitium mores instruet inde suos' and (275 sq.) 'carmen, *recta si mente legatur*, | constabit *nulli* posse nocere meum': the virtuous will not be corrupted, the vicious will find corruption everywhere, in neither case is the poet a corrupter. The diction too is not above suspicion. *hoc concipit* may be defended by *met.* II 76–8 'forsitan et lucos illic urbesque deorum | concipias animo delubraque ditia donis | esse'; but the verb *arrogare* occurs neither in Ovid elsewhere nor in any poet except Horace, and the figurative use of *uitiare*, which properly means 'ravish' or 'seduce', is not Ovidian either. The distich was intruded, like 263 sq. 'persequar inferius, modo si licet ordine ferri, | posse nocere animis carminis omne genus', by a reader who could not follow Ovid's argument and flattered himself that he was making it clearer.

TRIST. III 2 23 sq.

ei mihi, quod totiens nostri pulsata sepulcri
ianua sed nullo tempore aperta fuit.

The construction 'ei mihi, quod' occurs in Ovid half a dozen times, as at
trist. I 6 29 'ei mihi, non magnas quod habent mea carmina uires'; the sense ||
is perfect, 'alas that death's door has never been opened to me though I have
knocked at it so often'; the text stands thus in almost all the MSS; and thus it
stood, I suppose, in every edition down to 1889.

But a little before that date Providence played the editors of Ovid a cruel
trick; it put into their hands a 'best MS', and that was giving gunpowder to a
child. In this passage L has *et* for *ei* and *quo* for *quod*. Not even the editors of
Ovid were beguiled by the first of these corruptions, but the second they
promptly accepted because they saw no reason why they should not: 'ei mihi,
quo...fuit?' And how do they defend it? Mr Owen says 'cf. Ehwaldium, *Burs.*
nunt. annal. XLIII p. 269'; thither we turn only to find Mr Ehwald saying 'cf.
Vahlen, *Sitzungsber. der Berl. Akad.* 1883 S. 89'; and there at last we learn what
is the matter, for Vahlen there cites four passages in which, if we take his word
for it, *quo* means *cur*.

That *quo* means *cur* is an ambiguous proposition; for *cur*, like *why* in English,
has more meanings than one. It means 'to what end', 'quo fine proposito', and
it also means 'from what cause', 'qua causa efficiente'. The first of these senses
is one which *quo*, originally 'whither', might be expected to acquire; and
expectation is not disappointed: Verg. *buc.* VI 23 '*quo* uincula nectitis?', *Aen.* II
150 '*quo* molem hanc immanis equi statuere?', XI 735 '*quo* ferrum quidue haec
gerimus tela inrita dextris?', XII 879 '*quo* uitam dedit aeternam?', Hor. *carm.*
II 3 9–11 '*quo* pinus ingens albaque populus | umbram hospitalem consociare
amant | ramis?', Prop. II 13 45 'nam *quo* tam dubiae seruetur spiritus horae?',
Ouid. *met.* XIII 516 sq. '*quo* ferrea resto | quidue moror?'. But it would be
strange if *quo* acquired so alien a sense as 'qua causa efficiente'; and it did not
acquire it. Where are the examples? I know that '*quo* querimur flammas totum
saeuisse per orbem?' is the reading of G at Manil. I 744; but L has *quod* and M
has *quid*, a word which really does mean *cur*. Again at II 534 sq., in a sentence
which I take to be interrogative, G has '*quo* mirer...nascentis...superari
posse'; but L again gives *quod* and M *qd*, which the addition of a stroke corrects
to *quid*. Apart from these I find one example only; and I find it, where you
expect to find such things, in printed texts of Ovid: *amor.* III 7 19 sq.

a, pudet annorum! *quo* me iuuenemque uirumque
nec iuuenem nec me sensit amica uirum?

That *quo* must mean 'from what cause' is here a minor wonder: the sentence is unconstruable: look at the two *me*'s! Riese put everything to rights by a proper punctuation:

> a, pudet annorum! quo me iuuenemque uirumque?
> nec iuuenem nec me sensit amica uirum.

The construction is that of Val. Max. IX 13 ext. 2 'quo tam late patens imperium? quo tantum liberorum numerum?'

The reader should now be able to judge whether *quo* in *trist.* III 2 23 can mean, as it must if it is to be sense, '*what has brought it to pass* that death is ‖ denied me though I have provoked it so often?' If it is to be Latin it must mean 'to what purpose is it'; and then it will not be sense. That Ovid stood in peril of robbers and shipwreck was an incident of exile; that he escaped them was a perversity of chance: there is no place for the notion of purpose.

TRIST. III 4 71 sq.

> nec meus indicio latitantes uersus amicos
> protrahit: occulte, siquis amabit, amet.

amabit scripsi, *amauit* GHPV cum plerisque, *amabat* L cum paucis. When the best MS gives *amabat* and the four next best *amauit*, nothing so well accounts for the facts as the hypothesis that the archetype had *amabit*. But the bond-servants of a best MS are not concerned to account for facts, and L's reading is their reading. The case is the same at Iuu. VI 660: P gives *praegustabit*, and so consequently do the editors, but most other MSS have *praegustaret*: this divergency is best explained by Markland's conjecture *praegustarit*, which is now found in cod. Monac. 14466 and is supported by the *manducauerit* of the ancient scholia, whose authority is higher than P's.

The imperfect *amabat* is bad sense, since it implies that the persons in question have ceased to love. I do not pretend that *amabit* is better sense than *amauit* (I 9 26 'cum quis in aduersis, siquid *amauit*, amat'), but certainly it is no less good, for *occulte amet* can refer only to those friends whose friendship continues in the future. But Merkel and Ehwald so little understand what the sense is that they join *occulte* with *amabat*.

TRIST. III 8 11 sq.

> stulte, quid haec frustra uotis puerilibus optas,
> quae non ulla tulit fertque feretque[1] dies?

'Fool, why idly and childishly yearning for what never was nor is nor will be?' The preceding context is this, 1–10: 'nunc ego Triptolemi cuperem consistere curru,...nunc ego Medeae uellem frenare dracones,...nunc ego iactandas

---

[1] *refertque* most MSS, but the correction is recognised as certain.

optarem sumere pennas | siue tuas, Perseu, Daedale, siue tuas, | ut tenera nostris cedente uolatibus aura | aspicerem patriae dulce repente solum | desertaeque domus uultus memoresque sodales | caraque praecipue coniugis ora meae.' The ensuing context is this, 13–16: 'si semel optandum est, Augusti numen adora | et, quem sensisti, rite precare deum. | ille tibi pennasque potest currusque uolucres | tradere. det reditum, protinus ales eris.' Nothing therefore can be clearer than the sense of 'haec...quae non ulla tulit fertque feretque dies': it signifies the flying cars of Triptolemus and Medea and the wings of Perseus and Daedalus. And to make assurance doubly sure we have the parallel of *amor*. III 6 13–18 'nunc ego quas habuit pinnas Danaeius heros, | terribili densum cum tulit angue caput, | nunc opto currum de quo Cerealia primum | semina uenerunt in rude missa solum. | || prodigiosa loquor ueterum mendacia uatum: | nec tulit haec umquam nec feret ulla dies.' When I add that *tulit* in u. 12 is given by Ovid's best MSS and was printed by Ovid's best editor, the reader will surely wonder why it should be altered, and why, except for natural affinity, the inferior editors of our own day should print in its stead the *tibi* of the inferior MSS.

The cause appears to be Burman, for he, when *tulit* had been restored by Heinsius, expelled it again with this note: 'certe *tulit* aliquando dies ut uideret coniugem sodales etc., sed iam non fert nec feret dies.' Indeed? non *feret* dies ut uideat coniugem sodalesque? if Ovid says so, how can he look forward, as in 19 sq. of this very poem he does, to begging that very boon of Augustus? The future tense is alone enough to show that Burman was wrong in referring *haec* to the contents of the final clause 7–10: and from that mistake springs all the trouble. Merkel however, in accepting *tibi* from Burman, reveals another misunderstanding, which is his own: 'spectant ad illud (*tibi*) e sequentibus uerba *quem sensisti* (14). debilis esset ea ratio, si sibi opponerentur uanitas illa fabularum et sensus praesentioris numinis.' The opposition is not between 'uanitas fabularum' and *quem sensisti* but between 'uanitas fabularum' and *ille... pennas...potest...tradere* 15 sq.

TRIST. III 11 61 sq.

crede mihi, si sit nobis collatus Vlixes,
Neptunique minor, quam Iouis, ira fuit.

This couplet, at present unconstruable, would become grammatical and yield a just sense if the conjunction *que* were removed from the pentameter; and how to remove it without wrecking the metre is the problem to which critics have hitherto addressed themselves. The violent effort of the inferior MSS, *Neptuni minor est*, will give a wrong sense unless it is subjected to a still more violent punctuation, 'Neptuni *minor*, *est* quam Iouis, ira fuit'. Karl Schenkl's 'Neptuni *minor, a*!' is only fit for a schoolboy. Mr Owen has printed in three successive editions, spread over a space of 26 years, the distich 'crede mihi, si sit nobis collatus Vlixes, | Neptun*ine* minor quam Iouis ira fuit?' Crede mihi, Owenine peior ceteris coniectura est? The only proposal worth considering was made in 1890 by Robinson Ellis (*Hermathena* vol. VII p. 212) and again in 1894 by Mr I. Hilberg (*Wortstellung im pent. des Ovid* p. 198), 'Neptuni *leuior*, quam Iouis, ira fuit'. The sense is right but the change not easy to explain: Mr Hilberg supposes that some reader wrote *minor* over *leuior*; but why?

I believe that all these shots are aimed at the wrong target; that the pentameter is sound and the hexameter will prove much more amenable to treatment. Our present text may easily have arisen from this:

si sit
crede mihi, felix, nobis collatus, Vlixes,
Neptunique minor, quam Iouis, ira fuit. ||

si sit is an elucidation, like the *o* sometimes written over vocatives to show that they are not nominatives, and warns the reader that the participle *collatus* is equivalent to the protasis of a conditional sentence. So it often is: Prop. I 5 7 'non est illa uagis similis *conlata* puellis' (but I 4 9 '*si* leuibus *fuerit collata* figuris'), Varr. *l. L.* IX 28 'non bos ad bouem *collatus* similis?', X 36 'unaquaeque ratio, *collata* cum altera, aut similis aut dissimilis', Mart. XI 72 I sq. 'drauci..., *conlatus* cui Gallus est Priapus', Liu. XXIX 17 5 'quid illa sunt, *conlata* cum eis quae hodie patimur?' and especially XLV 43 2 '*minor* ipse imperator...Anicius cum Aemilio...*conlatus*': Ovid himself *fast.* III 825 sq. has 'licet, antiquo manibus *conlatus* Epeo, | sit prior'. Pliny *ep.* III 5 19 uses the two modes of speaking side by side, '*si comparer illi*, sum desidiosissimus' and 'quis...*collatus illi* non erubescat?' The counterpart of Ovid's *felix nobis collatus* occurs in Quint. *inst.* VI 2 22 'quam miser enim casus Andromachae, si, *comparata ei, felix* Polyxena'; and the same use of *felix* is found in *ex Pont.* I 2 29 'felicem Nioben' and *fast.* III 597 'Dido felix est dicta sorori'.

There is another verse of the *tristia* where an explanatory note has supplanted a word of the text: in III 13 I, 'quid enim fuit utile *gigni*', two of the best MSS, A and V, have *nobis* instead, which comes from *utile gigni*. The usual correction of *remed.* 492 involves the same assumption. All MSS of any authority have

quamuis infelix media torreberis Aetna,
frigidior dominae fac uideare tuae.

It is plain that 'frigidior' needs an ablative of comparison, and Heinsius borrowed from a couple of copies the reading

frigidior ⟨glacie⟩ fac uideare tuae.

dominae must then have been an explanation added to *tuae*. This correction however is not certain. It is true that 'frigidior glacie' occurs at *her.* I 22, X 32, and *ex Pont.* III 4 33 sq.; but in the last of these three places another comparison is found beside it, '*niuibus* glacieque. . .*frigidiora*', and Ovid may well have written

> frigidior dominae fac uideare niue.

He ends a pentameter with *niue* at *amor.* III 7 8 and *ex Pont.* II 5 38, and in the *remedia* and *artes* he so places *boue* (twice), *ope, pede* (twice, for I omit I 560), *dare, date, fuge, ego* (twice), *aquă* (three times), *togă*, and *foră*.

TRIST. III 14 47–50

> Threicio Scythicoque fere circumsonor ore
> et uideor Geticis scribere posse modis.
> crede mihi, timeo ne sint inmixta Latinis
> inque meis scriptis Pontica uerba legas.   50

The order of words in the last clause is a permissible equivalent for 'ne Pontica uerba sint inmixta Latinis inque meis scriptis (ea) legas'; but neither ‖ the one nor the other is the diction of Ovid or of any Latin poet, even in exile among savages. A Latin would have inserted neither *sint* nor *que*, but would have said 'ne inmixta Latinis in meis scriptis Pontica uerba legas'. Where *sint* now stands there once stood an epithet of *uerba* which was joined with *Pontica* by *que*; and perhaps it is recoverable.

Geticus (48) is the adjective by which Ovid is accustomed to describe the immediate neighbourhood of Tomis. *Threicius* and *Scythicus* (47) describe the surrounding peoples. *Ponticus* (50) is a synonym of *Scythicus* (*Scythicus Pontus* III 4 46 and IV 1 45), and under *sint* (29) we may expect to find a synonym of *Threicius*.

Love of synecdoche impels Ovid, like other Latin poets, to use in a wide sense geographical terms whose proper meaning is narrow. When in speaking of his overland journey from Tempyra to Tomis at *ex Pont.* IV 5 35 he says 'sanguine *Bistonium* quod non tepefecerit ensem', he is not far from fact, for the Bistones were not far from Tempyra. But when ib. I 3 57–60 in describing his life at Tomis he says 'hostis adest dextra laeuaque a parte timendus, . . . altera *Bistonias* pars est sensura sarisas, | altera Sarmatica spicula missa manu', and when ib. I 2 108–10 in foreboding his death he says 'ossa nec a Scythica nostra premantur humo, | nec. . . *Bistonii* cineres ungula pulset equi', he is transferring the Bistones from the extreme south to the extreme north of Thrace. So again at *trist.* III 10 5 'Sauromatae cingunt, fera gens, *Bessi*que Getaeque', IV 1 67 'uiuere quam miserum est inter *Bessos*que Getasque', when he says *Bessi* he means simply *Thraces*, not the Bessi proper, who dwelt south of Haemus. Now adjacent to the Bessi dwelt the Sinti on the Strymon. Strab. p. 331 fr. 36

[p. 466 Meineke] ὁ Cτρυμὼν ἐξ Ἀγριάνων...διὰ Μαίδων καὶ Cιντῶν εἰς τὰ μεταξὺ Βισαλτῶν καὶ Ὀδομάντων ἐκπίπτει, fr. 46 [p. 468 Meineke] Cιντοὶ ἔθνος Θρᾳκικόν, p. 549 [p. 772 Meineke] Cίντιες... ἐκαλοῦντό τινες τῶν Θρᾳκῶν, εἶτα Cιντοί, Arist. *mirab. ausc.* 115 τὴν τῶν Cιντῶν καὶ Μαίδων χώραν καλουμένην τῆς Θρᾴκης. The name of this people seems to have been elsewhere mentioned by Ovid and again corrupted by his scribes. In an allusion to his journey across Thrace, *trist.* IV 1 21 sq., the best MSS have 'sola nec insidias *inter* nec militis ensem | nec mare nec uentos barbariamque timet', where Mr Ehwald following a suggestion of Iac. Gronouius has proposed 'Sinti nec militis'; and this conjecture gains support from a very similar error in Liu. XLII 51 7 'ab Heraclea ex *intris* (*Sintiis* Grynaeus, *Sintis* Drakenborch)'.[1]

The adjective is regularly Cιντικός and the district is thence called ἡ Cιντική, but Stephanus Byzantius has Cιντία, πόλις Μακεδονίας πρὸς τῇ Θρᾴκη...λέγεται καὶ Cίντιοι καὶ Cίντιον τὸ οὐδέτερον; and though Aeschylus ‖ says Μαιωτικός, Virgil says *Maeotius*. I suppose then that Ovid wrote what differs by one letter only from the MS text,

> crede mihi, timeo ne Sintia mixta Latinis
> inque meis scriptis Pontica uerba legas.

in meis scriptis ἀπὸ κοινοῦ, like *met.* XII 109 sq. 'Tenedonque *suo*que | Eetioneas inpleui *sanguine* Thebas'.

TRIST. V 2 23–7

> litora quot conchas, quot amoena rosaria flores
> quotue soporiferum grana papauer habet,
> 25 silua feras quot alit, quot piscibus unda natatur,
> quot tenerum pennis aera pulsat auis,
> tot premor aduersis.

amoena rosaria, though printed by all editors, is written only in the vulgar MSS: the better class, AGHPV (for L is absent), have *amoenos hostia* (*postia* A) instead. Now there are indeed many places where the worse MSS give a true reading and the better MSS a false one; but in those places we can generally find a cause for the error. Here there is no explaining how *amoena rosaria* can be the origin of anything so different and so difficult as *amoenos hostia*; whereas *amoenos hostia* would be corrected without scruple by the interpolators to

---

[1] Ellis in *Hermath.* vol. VII pp. 191–3 absurdly confuses these Cιντοί with the Cίνδοι dwelling in Asia on the eastern shore of the Euxine. There were other Cίνδοι on the Hister, but apparently far inland, half way between the Euxine and the Adriatic, schol. Apoll. Rhod. IV 321 κατὰ δὲ τὸ τῶν Cίνδων πεδίον σχίζεται ὁ ποταμὸς Ἴστρος, καὶ τὸ μὲν αὐτοῦ ῥεῦμα εἰς τὸν Ἀδρίαν, τὸ δὲ εἰς τὸν Εὔξεινον πόντον εἰσβάλλει; and I only mention them in order to bring together a pair of ἅπαξ εἰρημένα which ought to merge in one: Apoll. Rhod. IV 320–2 οὔτ' οὖν Θρήιξιν μιγάδες Cκύθαι, οὐδὲ Cίγυννοι, | οὔτ' οὖν Γραυκένιοι, οὔθ' οἱ περὶ Λαύριον ἤδη | Cίνδοι ἐρημαῖον πεδίον μέγα ναιετάοντες and Steph. Byz. Τραυχένιοι, ἔθνο περὶ τὸν πόντον τὸν Εὔξεινον, ὅμορον Cίνδοις.

whom the inferior MSS owe their inferiority, and *amoena rosaria* may very well be their correction. What I propose is less a correction than an interpretation of the more authentic text:

> quot amoenos Ostia flores.

The neighbourhood of Ostia, which Minucius Felix 2 3 calls 'amoenissima ciuitas', is still very gay with flowers in spring; and that this is no recent effort of Nature's we learn from a document of the 6th century, the anonymous *cosmographia* printed on pp. 71–103 of Riese's *geographi Latini minores*. There, p. 83 24–30, the island formed by the mouth of the Tiber is described in language as flowery as itself: 'insula uero, quam facit inter urbis portum et *Ostiam* ciuitatem, tantae uiriditatis *amoenitatis*que est, ut neque aestiuis mensibus neque hiemalibus pasturae admirabiles herbas dehabeat; ita autem uernali tempore *rosa uel ceteris floribus* adimpletur, ut pro nimietate sui odoris et *floris* insula ipsa libanus almae Veneris nuncupetur.' The *cosmographia* is edited by Riese from two MSS, one of the 8th and one of the 10th century: the latter, both in the passage just quoted and again at l. 22 of the same page, writes *Ostiam* as *hostiam*; and Ovid's MSS, none of them older than the 13th century, have misspelt the word in the same way. Indeed the error is found in much more ancient authorities, at Min. Fel. 2 3 in the Parisinus (saec. IX), at Liu. XXII 11 6 in the Puteaneus (saec. V).

It may perhaps be thought that in this series of comparisons the common nouns *litora, papauer, silua, unda, aera*, should not be varied by a proper name, *Ostia*. But see *trist.* V 1 31 sq. 'quot frutices *siluae*, quot flauas *Thybris* harenas, | ‖ mollia quot *Martis* gramina *Campus* habet', 6 37–40 'quam multa madidae celantur harundine *fossae*, | florida quam multas *Hybla* tuetur apes, | quam multae gracili *terrena* sub *horrea* ferre | limite formicae grana reperta solent', *ex Pont.* II 7 25–8 '*Cinyphiae segetis* citius numerabis aristas | altaque quam multis floreat *Hybla* thymis, | et quot aues motis nitantur in *aere* pinnis | quotque natent pisces *aequore* certus eris'.

TRIST. V 8 1 sq.

> non adeo cecidi, quamuis abiectus, ut infra
> te quoque sim, inferius quo nihil esse potest.

Lachmann at Lucr. I 159 remarked that three times in Ovid the last syllable of *nihil* is shown by metre to be long: *trist.* V 14 41 and *ex Pont.* III 1 113 'morte *nihil* opus est', *met.* VII 644 'in superis opis esse *nihil*. at in aedibus ingens'. He proposed to introduce a fourth example at *met.* X 520; but he might with better reason have cited and examined XIV 23 sq.,

> nec medeare mihi sanesque haec uulnera mando;
> fineque nil opus est; partem ferat illa caloris.

The attachment of *que* to *ĕ* is not Ovidian, and the conjunction itself is both unnecessary and undesirable: Heinsius quotes from some MSS the reading *fine nihil opus est*, and this has in its favour the 'morte nihil opus est' of the *tristia* and *ex Ponto*, where such variants as *morteque nil opus est*, *at nece nil opus est*, *nil opus est leto*, are found in the MSS.

Lachmann further implies in his note on Lucretius and states explicitly in *Kl. Schr.* II p. 59 that there is no place in Ovid where the last syllable of *nihil* is shown by metre to be short: denying that Ovid wrote the epistle of Hero, he says 'hic uersus, si Nasonis est, in XIX, 170, *Exiguum, sed plus quam nihil, illud erat*, aut spondeum aut Creticum habet ubi non debet, quoniam hic poëta aliter non dixit quam aut *nil* una syllaba aut *nihil* altera producta'. Merkel in his Ovid, vol. I p. x, pointed out that Lachmann had overlooked *trist.* v 8 2 above; and Lucian Mueller, *d. r. m.* p. 47, added an example overlooked by both, *trist.* IV 8 38:

mitius inmensus quo nihil orbis habet.

This latter verse contains nothing suspicious unless *nihĭl* itself is so; though the transposition

inmensus quo nil mitius orbis habet

might be supported by *trist.* v 2 38 'Caesare *nil* ingens *mitius orbis habet*' and 8 25 sq. '*nil* ingens ad finem solis ab ortu | illo, cui paret, *mitius orbis habet*' and the error of the MSS, if error it is, might be compared with that of the cod. Erfurtanus at *ex Pont.* I 5 78, 'res *nihĭl* ista iuuat' for 'res iuuat ista nihil'. But the couplet *trist.* v 8 1 sq., apart from its *nihĭl*, is suspicious on general grounds. The unity of the poem would gain by its removal and is impaired by its presence; for the vehement contempt of these two verses is not explained, nor even continued, in the sequel. What follows is quite in another || vein: 3 sqq. 'quae tibi res animos in me facit, improbe, curue | casibus insultas quos potes ipse pati, | nec mala te reddunt mitem placidumque iacenti | nostra, quibus possint illacrimare ferae?' Instead of anything like 'non adeo cecidi...ut infra te...sim' we come to 10 'imposito calcas quid mea fata pede?' Instead of disdainful affronts we read appeals to considerations of prudence and humanity. The expostulation is bitter, but its tone is not heated or contumelious. Verse 3 is well fitted to be the first of the poem; and verses 1 and 2 are such as might have been added by the obtuse reader who added so many to the Second book.

Mr Isidor Hilberg, by way of showing that 'Lachmann's Behauptung, Ovid gebrauche diese Silbe niemals als Kürze, widerspricht den Thatsachen', is good enough to cite on p. 745 of his *Wortstellung im pent. des Ovid* about a dozen such passages as *art.* II 280 'si *nihĭl* attuleris' and *fast.* VI 177 '*nihĭl* in pauone placebat'. He might easily have cited a dozen more: there are nine in the *tristia* alone. If Mr Hilberg means to learn prosody from the spelling of MSS, it will teach him terrible things. He will be dismayed to find that the last syllable of *nihil* is short even when the next word begins with a consonant. This verse, Verg. *buc.* VIII 103,

> adgrediar; nihil ille deos, *nihĭl* carmina curat,

reposes on far surer testimony than any verse of Ovid, for it reposes on MPγac: the only one of Ribbeck's MSS which has *nil* is *b*. None of Ovid's works is preserved in MSS so good as those which impute to Horace the verses 'Piplea dulcis *nihil* sine te mei', '*nihil* interest an pauper et infima'; 'ab dis plura feret: *nihil* cupientium'. Mr Hilberg's observations are not merely infantile: they are the observations of an infant who has not read Lachmann's note. From Lachmann's note he might have learnt that Lucretius, if the spelling of MSS is evidence, wrote not only 'praeterea *nihĭl* est' but '*nihĭl* semine egeret', 'quorum *nihĭl* fieri', 'quia *nihil* est', and began hexameters with '*nihil* tamen' and '*nihil* igitur'.

Some editors even thrust *nihĭl* upon Ovid when the MSS do not. At *Ib.* 284 the MSS have

> cui *nil rethei* profuit ara Iouis.

So FGHVX, *nil etherei* T, *nichil ethei* P. Most of those who adopt the correction *Hercei* have seized the opportunity of importing *nihil*. Yet the rhythm of *cui nil Hercei* is quite good and common: 26 'pro tam mansueto', 37 'et uer autumno', etc.

TRIST. V 13 1–6

> hanc tuus e Getico mittit tibi Naso salutem,
>   mittere si quisquam, quo caret ipse, potest.
> aeger enim traxi contagia corpore mentis,
>   libera tormento pars mihi nequa uacet,
> perque dies multos lateris cruciatibus uror,   5
>   saeua quod inmodico frigore laesit hiemps. ||

On the ground that *Getico* is everywhere else an adjective Daniel Heinsius proposed

> hanc tuus e Getico mittit tibi Naso salutem
> litore, si quisquam, quo caret ipse, potest.

Gronouius *obs.* II c. 3 rejects the proposal: 'nam *Geticum* dixit, ut *Illyricum, Vindelicum, Noricum, Celticum*...dicebant'. But that is just what is not likely. Ovid uses no such form elsewhere, and these territorial names in -*icum* belong to the language of prose; they are not even found, where it would be less strange to find them, in the satirists. The *Illyricum* of Manil. IV 611 is an adjective in the MS text and was only turned into a substantive by the editors; and Claudian and Ausonius I do not count. On the other hand Ovid has '*Getico litore*' *trist.* III 12 14, '*Getici litoris*' I 10 14 and *ex Pont.* IV 4 8, '*litore ab Euxino* Nasonis

epistula ueni' *trist.* v 4 1, 'haec mihi *Cimmerio* bis tertia ducitur aestas | *litore*'
ex Pont. IV 10 1 sq., and the close parallels *ex Pont.* 1 1 2 'hoc tibi *de Getico litore
mittit* opus' and *trist.* v 1 1 sq. 'hunc quoque *de Getico*, nostri studiose, libel-
lum | *litore* praemissis quattuor adde meis'. The substitution of *mittere* might be
prompted by an untimely recollection of *ex Pont.* 1 10 1 sq. 'Naso suo profugus
mittit tibi, Flacce, *salutem*, | *mittere* rem *si* quis, qua *caret ipse, potest*'; and such
a reminiscence has in fact caused the change of *si quisquam quo* to *rem si quis qua*
or *si quis rem qua* in several of the inferior MSS. This sort of error is common in
the *tristia* as elsewhere: thus at III 1 62, 'stricto *barbarus* ense pater', some MSS,
among them one of the best, have *stat ferus* from *art.* 1 74. There can be no
difficulty in supplying the infinitive *mittere* from the preceding *mittit* when
claudere is supplied from the following *clausit* in *art.* II 53 'aera non *potuit*
Minos, alia omnia *clausit*'.

The emendation of u. 6, *saeua quod immodico* for the *sed quod in immodico* or
sed quod non modico of the MSS, is mentioned in his ed. of 1837 by Merkel, who
ascribes it to Heinsius; in 1890 it was again proposed by Arthur Palmer, and in
1891, for the third time, by a German, to whom Mr Owen, after ignoring it in
his first and second editions, now attributes it. But this conjecture does not
destroy the continuity of a sentence nor deprive a transitive verb of its object;
so Mr Owen still prefers his own conjecture *scilicet inmodico*, which does.

EX PONT. I 2 99–102 [97–100]

di faciant igitur, quorum iustissimus ipse est,
100 [98]   alma nihil maius Caesare terra ferat,
utque diu sub eo sic sit sub Caesare terra,
perque manus huius tradita gentis eat.

The rules of criticism are a very inadequate outfit for the practice of emendation,
which is mainly an affair of natural aptitude and partly even of mere luck; but
problems will now and then present themselves which the rules of criticism, with
no aid from genius or fortune, are competent to solve. Such a problem is
verse 101 [99], and it ought therefore to have been solved by this time, ‖ not
molested by haphazard alterations of *diu* into *fuit* or *sub eo* into *saluo* or *sic sit
sub Caesare terra* into *sit publica sarcina rerum*.

This verse not only suffers from the internal malady of making no sense, but
also from an outward and visible disfigurement. Ovid cannot have meant to
repeat the two words *Caesare terra* from the verse above, because the repetition
serves no purpose; and he cannot have repeated them without meaning it,
because the repetition could not be overlooked. Here then is the seat of the evil;
and the field of enquiry can be further narrowed till all suspicion converges on
the one word *terra*. First, it is useless: take it away, and neither grammar nor

sense (or nonsense rather) is affected. Secondly, the presence of *Caesare* in both verses explains how *terra* got into the second, just as at *trist.* I 6 I sq.

> nec *tantum Clario* Lyde dilecta poetae
> nec *tantum Coo* Bittis amata suo est

the presence of *tantum* in both verses explains how it is that four of the five best MSS have *Clario* for *Coo* in the pentameter.

The injury, thus located by rule, can also be mended by rule. There is no room for the quackery which calls itself palaeographical emendation: to fill this gap,

> utque diu sub eo sic sit sub Caesare – ◡
> perque manus huius tradita gentis eat,

ask yourself only what sense and what part of speech the pentameter suggests and the rest of the hexameter requires. The lost word is an abverb answering *diu*:

> utque diu sub eo sic sit sub Caesare ⟨semper⟩.

ut and *sic* are μέν and δέ: Ovid prays that earth may be ruled for many a year by Augustus himself and for all time by some one or other of his name, even as he augured in *trist.* IV 2 9 sq. 'qui Caesareo iuuenes sub nomine crescunt, | perpetuo terras ut domus illa regat'. This sense of the word *Caesar* has been missed by the commentators on Lucan at III 167 sq.

> tristi spoliantur templa rapina
> pauperiorque fuit tunc primum Caesare Roma,

which they interpret as meaning that never till he robbed the treasury had C. Iulius been wealthier than the state: C. Iulius, whose debts and prodigality were a byword! What it does mean is that a spectacle grown familiar in Lucan's day, the spectacle of a Caesar richer than the commonwealth, was then witnessed for the first time.

It is the practice, or rather the instinct, of 'palaeographical emendators' to misrepresent scientific emendations; and their first impulse will be to describe this correction as a change of *terra* into *semper*, and to add a note of exclamation. Ignorant or unsuspicious readers, seeing no likeness between the two words, will then infer, as they are meant to infer, that the error was improbable and that the correction is violent. To spoil this game I subjoin a pair of examples. In Luc. V 192 the oldest MS, the Vienna palimpsest, instead of *tum maestus*, has *tum primum* from the *tum primum* of 190; and in Lucr. I 1023, ‖ instead of *quaeque darent motus pepigere profecto* which Marullus restored from V 421, all MSS have *quaeque sagaci mente locarunt* from 1022. Again, *semper* has no more likeness to *ferto* than to *terra*; yet at *trist.* III 3 81, where the majority of good MSS have rightly *semper*, most MSS, including one of the best, have *ferto* in its place. There, as here, the error was due to no resemblance between word and word, but to a cause unconnected with palaeography.

Ex Pont. I 6 21–4

nec breue nec tutum, peccati quae sit origo,
    scribere: tractari uulnera nostra timent.
qualicumque modo mihi sint ea facta, rogare
    desine: non agites, siqua coire uelis.

Since *qualiscumque* is not an interrogative word, the clause which it here introduces must be relative and must mean 'no matter how I got my wounds'; and
then not only strict rule but Ovidian usage will require the indicative mood.
Mr Ehwald *Krit. Beitr.* pp. 69 sq. accordingly changes *sint* to *sunt*. But interrogation, if forbidden by *qualicumque*, is demanded by *rogare*, which, now that
the clause is relative, has neither a grammatical object nor an appropriate sense:
the appropriate sense would be that of *tangere*, 'no matter how I got my
wounds, let them alone'. I infer then that *sint* is right and *qualicumque* wrong.
Now the best MS, the Hamburgensis A, three centuries older than the rest, has
not *qualicumque* but *qualiacumque*, from which I elicit

        qualia quoque modo mihi sint ea facta, rogare
        desine:

'ask not the nature of those wounds nor how I got them'. A similarly ungrammatical *cumque* is corrected to *quoque* by Lucian Mueller at Priap. 68 31
and to *quaeque* by me at Lucr. vi 85 and Manil. ii 745 in my note on the latter
verse.

Ex Pont. ii 2 31–6

tuta petant alii: fortuna miserrima tuta est,
    nam timor euentus deterioris abest.
qui rapitur
    porrigit spinas dura quae saxa
35   accipitremque timens pennis trepidantibus ales
    audet ad humanos fessa uenire sinus.

Verses 33 sq. are shown thus mutilated in A; B and C omit them altogether, and
C covers the traces of this omission by altering *accipitremque timens* in 35 to
accipitrem metuens; the inferior MSS on the other hand offer various completions
of the distich. Most of these are absurdly wide of the required sense – that men
will incur a lesser evil in the hope of escaping a greater; but two 13th-century
copies, Lips. and Erfurt., present the verses thus,

    qui rapitur ⟨spumante salo (*Lips.*, freto *Erf.*), sua brachia tendens⟩
    porrigit ⟨ad⟩ spinas duraque saxa ⟨manus⟩. ‖

In the pentameter the supplements are probably true, but were easy to find by guessing: in the hexameter they are certainly false. What decisively condemns them is not the superfluity of *sua*, nor even the uselessness of *bracchia tendens* beside *porrigit manus*, but the word *salo* or *freto*. When a man is drowning at sea, the only *spinae* to which he can stretch out his hands are those which grow on the backs of fishes: if he finds thorns to clutch at, he must be drowning in a river. And this is the picture drawn in a parallel passage, apparently an imitation, adduced by Korn from Sen. *ep.* 4 5: 'hoc cotidie meditare, ut possis aequo animo uitam relinquere, quam multi sic complectuntur et tenent, quomodo, *qui aqua torrente rapiuntur, spinas et aspera*'. Hence I conclude that the sense of what Ovid wrote was this:

> qui rapitur ⟨praeceps torrenti fluminis unda⟩
> porrigit ad spinas duraque saxa manus.

In u. 32 the two best MSS have *euentu*, which, though less natural than the genitive, may be defended as ablative of cause: 'euentus facit ut timor deterioris fortunae absit'. *trist.* 1 9 16 'sunt tamen euentu uera fatenda meo' is not unlike.

Ex Pont. II 5 8–12

> diceris exiliis indoluisse meis,
> missaque ab Euxino legeres cum carmina Ponto
>   illa tuus iuuit qualiacumque fauor,   10
> optastique breuem salui mihi Caesaris iram,
>   quod tamen[1] optari si sciat ipse sinat.

Early and late, conjectures have been showered on verse 11. For *salui* some inferior MSS offer *saluo*, others *fieri*; one scholar proposes *sancti*, another *statui*, a third *breui solui*; till anyone would think there really were something wrong. Yet all is well, and the conjectures are all aimed at the one word which must on no account be altered.

If *salui* is an obstacle, remove it, and mark the consequence. Ovid's friend will then have prayed that Caesar's anger against Ovid might be short; and this prayer contains not merely an ambiguity but a dangerous ambiguity. Even Virgil's innocent phrase 'tuque adeo, quem mox quae sint habitura deorum | concilia incertum est' did not escape malicious interpretation: Seru. *georg.* 1 24 'male quidam culpant Vergilium, dicentes eum auiditate laudandi citum interitum Augusto optasse': and 'optasti breuem mihi Caesaris iram' is much more like high treason, for one way to shorten Caesar's anger is to shorten Caesar's life. This implication is excluded by the addition of *salui*, which is part

---

[1] Since *tamen* is a word so often misunderstood, I had better say that the construction is 'si sciat, tamen sinat', 'would permit, even if he knew'.

of the prayer: 'optasti breuem mihi Caesaris iram, ita tamen ut ipse saluus esset'. The exile took the same precaution at *trist.* III 1 57 sq., where his book, arrived before the house of Augustus, is made to say 'quandocumque, precor, nostro placata parenti | *isdem sub dominis* aspiciare domus': || he does not wish to purchase pardon and recall at the price of the emperor's decease. The passage cited by Heinsius, *ex Pont.* II 3 97 sq. 'precabor | ut tibi sit saluo Caesare salua parens', though no parallel in point of sense, is similar in expression, for it is a way of saying 'ut et Caesar et parens tua salua sit'.

Perhaps we shall now be able to defend what is right and amend what is wrong in the MS tradition of *met.* XV 838, where the prophecy of Augustus' reign concludes with these words:

> nec nisi cum senior similes aequauerit annos
> aetherias sedes cognataque sidera tanget.

Neither *similes* nor *aequauerit* has any sense, for there is nothing in the context to which the years of Augustus' life can either be likened or equalled. Heinsius, comparing *ex Pont.* II 8 41 sq. 'sic pater in Pylios, Cumaeos mater in annos | uiuant' and *trist.* V 5 61 sq. 'Caesar dis accessure, sed olim, | aequarint Pylios cum tua fata dies', altered *similes* to *Pylios*; and this conjecture, despite its violence, is adopted by the latest editors. But what then possessed the poet to add *senior*? If a man is to die as old as Nestor and outlive three generations of his fellows, what need to tell us that he will then be well stricken in years? Ovid added *senior* because he was using a phrase which without *senior* would have been ambiguous: *similes* has usurped the place of a dative, probably

> nec nisi cum senior meritis aequauerit annos.

To foretell that Augustus will quit the earth only when his years are as many as his good deeds is not necessarily to foretell him a long life: the number of his good deeds may be matter of opinion, and if T. Labienus heard that prophecy and put faith in it he would expect Augustus to drop down dead on the spot. Ovid therefore takes care to preclude all suspicion of a double meaning. *meritis* differs in two letters only from *mesilis*, which differs from *similes* only in the order of letters: compare such changes as *met.* XIII 624 *patrem* (*patlem*) *templa*, XIV 233 *lami* (*sami*) *imas*.

EX PONT. II 6 19–24

> turpe erit in miseris ueteri tibi rebus amico
> 　　auxilium nulla parte tulisse tuum.
> turpe referre pedem nec passu stare tenaci,
> 　　turpe laborantem deseruisse ratem:
> turpe sequi casum et fortunae accedere amicum
> 　　et, nisi sit felix, esse negare suum.

So I punctuate, with a full stop after 20 and a colon after 22. Heinsius put full stops in both places, and then proposed, no wonder, to delete 23 sq.; Merkel ended both 20 and 22 with colons, which makes no difference and leaves 23 sq. no less intolerable. Korn placed a colon after the first distich, a full stop after the second, and deleted the third; and Guethling, rejecting the || deletion and yet accepting the punctuation, reduced the passage to the worst plight in which it has yet been seen.

What Guethling conceived I cannot guess, but it seems clear that the other editors repeat *erit tibi* from 19 with the *turpe*'s of 21 and 22 and 23, so that the three distichs form a series in which each member stands on an equal footing: then, to be sure, the third distich is flat after the second and futile after the first, and the *suum* of 24 ought to be *tuum*, which some MSS accordingly substitute.[1] With my punctuation the passage ought to interpret itself. *turpe* in 21 and the following verses is not *turpe tibi erit* but *turpe est*; verse 21 is to be introduced with μὲν γάρ and verse 23 with δέ. 'It will be shame to you if you do not help an old friend in his trouble; *for, even as* it is shame to retire in battle or to abandon a labouring ship, *so* is it shame to be led by luck, to transfer one's friendship to fortune, and to disown a comrade except he be prosperous.' The verses 21–4 are a general reflexion enforcing the personal monition of 19 sq.; and the distich 21 sq. is related to the distich 23 sq. as 'triste lupus stabulis, maturis frugibus imbres, | arboribus uenti' to 'nobis Amaryllidos irae' in Verg. *buc.* III 80 sq. The subject of *sit* and *esse* in 24 is the other party whose existence is necessarily implied when the talk is of friendship: similarly *diligit* has no expressed subject in Cic. *de inu.* II 166 'amicitia (est) uoluntas erga aliquem rerum bonarum illius ipsius causa, quem *diligit*, cum eius pari uoluntate'.

Ex Pont. II 7 1–4

> esse salutatum uult te mea littera primum
>   a male pacatis, Attice, missa Getis.
> proxima subsequitur, quid agas, audire uoluntas,
>   et si, quidquid agis, sit tibi cura mei.

For *uoluntas* in u. 3 the best MSS give *uoluptas*, which Heinsius brought into the text without a word of explanation, which Merkel, merely because of the MSS, retained, and which his followers accepted merely because of Merkel. Vahlen in 1881, *über die Anfänge der Heroiden des Ovid* p. 33 n. 1, justly observed '*uoluptas* giebt keinen Sinn, *uoluntas* den besten'; but there he would have been

---

[1] Mr Owen, who has Merkel's punctuation, says 'sed cf. 1 3 2'. In another editor one would suppose this to be a slip of the pen for *trist.* 1 5 2, which is less obviously irrelevant; but Mr Owen probably means what he has written, *ex Pont.* 1 3 2, 'qui miser est, ulli si suus esse potest', for he has similar notes elsewhere: at 1 4 46 he refers to 5 28, at 1 10 22 to *Ib.* 150 (152), at III 5 29 to 50, at IV 6 15 to Liu. XXII 4 4, and at *trist.* IV 1 10 to Verg. *georg.* IV 313.

wise to stop. When he went on to explain what he supposed this best of senses
to be, he showed that he did not comprehend it: 'das erste ist mein Gruss (*salus*),
das zweite mein Wunsch (*uoluntas*) zu erfahren, wie es dir geht und ob du
meiner eingedenk bist.' That this is not the sense, and that no contrast exists
between *salutatum* in the one verse and *uoluntas* in the other, Ovid has tried to
make plain by mentioning his *uoluntas* in both verses; for *uult primum* is the
same as *prima uoluntas est*, and *proxima subsequitur uoluntas* is the same as
secundo loco uult. The contrast is between *te salutatum esse* and ‖ *audire quid agas
et si sit tibi cura mei*; and the sense is 'primum te salutatum uolo, deinde uolo
audire quid agas'.

Ex Pont. ii 8 71–6

aut ego me fallo nimiaque cupidine ludor
　　aut spes exilii commodioris adest.
nam minus et minus est facies in imagine tristis
　　uisaque sunt dictis adnuere ora meis.
75　　uera precor fiant timidae praesagia mentis,
　　iustaque quamuis est sit minor ira dei.

The proposal, now generally approved, of Mr Hilberg in his *Wortstellung im
pent. des Ovid*, p. 4, to corrupt the last verse thus,

iustaque, quam uisa est, sit minor ira dei,

is one of those false conjectures which have more luck in the world than most of
the true. The metre of the verse as it stands is said to be objectionable. Suppose
that the objection is just: it is a pity if the metre cannot be mended without
spoiling the sense.

Ovid has received from his friend Cotta a silver medal or other work of art
representing Augustus, Tiberius, and Liuia. He finds in the face of Augustus a
trace of anger, 21 sq. 'fallor, an irati mihi sunt in imagine uultus | toruaque
nescioquid forma minantis habet?'; but now, 73 sq., the graven countenance
seems to grow milder, 'minus est facies in imagine tristis' etc. Mr Hilberg will
have it that the *quam uisa est* of his pentameter looks back to 21 sq. It cannot
possibly look back to anything but the *uisa sunt adnuere ora* of the immediately
preceding couplet 73 sq.; and it therefore gives a false sense: sense requires *sicut
uisa est*, not *quam*. If *quam* is right, *uisa est* will be wrong, and sense will
require *quam fuit*, as in iii 1 98 'sit ut iratum, quam fuit ante, minus'.

And what fault has the metre that must thus be cured at the cost of the
meaning? A second foot consisting of a single spondaic word, says Mr Hilberg.
It is true that such verses as

hanc tibi *cuius* me magnus edebat amor

are not found between Catullus and Paulinus; but this is not such a verse, for *quamuis* is not a single word. Ordinarily it counts as one, and so does *internos*, as in Ouid. *art.* II 612 'sed sic *internos* ut latuisse uelint'; but *internos* likewise, being two words, is once treated as two, in Mart. *spect.* 18 6 'postquam *internos* est, plus feritatis habet'. *nequis* again, by the punctuation of the oldest inscriptions, is not two words but one, and accordingly the poets do not scruple to place it in the fifth foot of the hexameter and before the last iambus of the pentameter, as at Verg. *Aen.* II 606 '*nequa* parentis', III 473 '*nequa* ferenti', VIII 205 '*nequid* inausum', Ouid. *trist.* V 13 4 '*nequa* ‖ uacet';[1] but it is two words in Prop. IV 5 60 'utere, *nequid* cras libet ab ore dies'. *uis* and *libet* stand apart from their relative in Cat. *agr. cult.* 52 2 'quod genus *uis* propagabis', 158 2 'unum quod eorum *uis*', and Sall. *Cat.* 5 4 'cuius rei *libet* simulator'; and here in Ovid, under stress of metre, the compound remembers its composition and resolves itself into its components. The MSS even offer another example, *trist.* V 9 25 sq.

> nunc quoque, *quamuis* est iam iussa quiescere, quin te
> nominet inuitum, uix mea Musa tenet.

Here however something is wrong, for *tenet* requires an object. Editors write *se quamuis est iussa* with Naugerius: in some respects there is more to be said for Mr Owen's suggestion that *tenet* has come from the end of 28 and has ousted *potest*; but it must be allowed that *iam* in the hexameter is devoid of force.

The fact that *postquam*, like *quamuis*, is two words renders just endurable the rhythm of *her.* XV 113

> *postquam* se dolor inuenit, nec pectora plangi,

which otherwise would be harsher even than *ex Pont.* IV 9 99 'illi me, quia uelle uident, discedere malunt' and without a parallel in Ovid. But even so it is harsh, much beyond *her.* II 37 'perque tuum mihi iurasti', *amor.* III 1 25 'materia premis ingenium', 9 53 'cumque tuis sua iunxerunt'.

Ex Pont. III 4 17–20

> spectatum uates alii scripsere triumphum:
> est aliquid memori uisa notare manu.
> nos ea uix auidam uulgo captata per aurem
> scripsimus, atque oculi fama fuere mei.   20

20 *scripsimus* edd.; but most MSS, including C, the best here legible, have *uidimus*, and B, the best here extant, shows *scripsimus* written by the second

---

[1] So also *amor.* III 4 32 'siqua potest', *art.* III 466 'siqua negat', *rem.* 330 'siqua proba est'. There are in Ovid only two pentameters where a pair of monosyllables stands in this position, *rem.* 306 'non dat habet' and *ex Pont.* I 1 14 'non sit amor'; to which the spurious epistles add two more, *her.* XVIII 170 'qua sit iter' and XX 62 'par sit opus'.

hand in an erasure. *uidimus* is plainly corrupt, but it is not plainly nor even probably a corruption of *scripsimus*; while *scripsimus* may easily be a correction of *uidimus*, suggested by *scripsere* in 17. I propose no*uimus* instead. If the first two letters were lost in the margin, *uimus*, especially with *uisa* standing in 18, might be expanded into *uidimus*, just as *ueri* (*u̅i̅*) in *trist.* IV I 66 has been expanded into *uidi*, or, to take an instance yet more similar, as *iu-uit* at the beginning of *Ib.* 488 has been changed in most MSS to *uidit*.

EX PONT. III 4 63 sq.

quid mirum, lectis exhausto floribus horto,
si duce non facta est digna corona suo?

Ovid has indited a poem on Tiberius' triumph of January A.D. 13, but ‖ other poets, less remote from the scene, have forestalled him; they have stripped the garden of flowers and left him none from which to twine a worthy wreath. Instead of *duce...suo* Merkel in 1884 printed *uice...sua*: this made Messrs Owen and Ehwald suppose that something was amiss, and they both conjectured, as they naturally would, *duce...tuo*. 'Die Elegie ist an Rufinus gerichtet' says Mr Ehwald 'und handelt vom Triumph des Germanicus', – he means Tiberius, but no matter, – 'also ist zu schreiben: *quid mirum...si duce non facta est digna corona tuo? tuus dux* ist eben Germanicus.' A pretty description of Tiberius, or Germanicus either, to call him *dux Rufini*, the chief of one civilian! Let *suo* be as false as you will, *tuo* cannot be true; but why is *suo* false? Mr Ehwald, *Krit. Beitr.* p. 40, says that the text is impossible 'da *suo* absolut beziehungslos steht: denn der *dux suus* kann doch unmöglich durch den *lectis exhaustus floribus hortus* erklärt werden...der *hortus* ist...kein Besitzstück des *dux*, sondern gehört den Dichtern.' Of course it does: what belongs to the *dux* is the *corona*, and it is to *corona* that *suo* refers. Better critics than Mr Ehwald have before now proposed alterations just as false and needless, because they have not rightly conceived the nature and observed the usage of the Latin possessive pronoun. The relation which it signifies is a mutual relation, for which possession is often no appropriate name: two objects may so appertain to one another that *suus* can properly be attached to either of them. At *her.* XIV 67 we find 'lacrimae *sua uerba* sequuntur'; at XX 76 on the contrary 'liceat *lacrimis* addere uerba *suis*', whereupon most MSS substitute *meis* and one editor *sua*; but the tears suit the words just as the words suit the tears. Virgil *georg.* IV 190 has 'fessosque *sopor suus* occupat artus', Ovid *met.* VI 489 'placido dantur *sua corpora* somno'; sleep and the body are joined in a natural union and each is apportioned to the other. We speak in English of crime and its punishment, not of punishment and its crime; but Ovid *trist.* II 578 says 'ut par *delicto* sit mea poena *suo*'. We speak of the leek and its leaves, not of leaves and their leek; but Martial XI 52 6 says *'porris fila resecta suis'*. We speak of the face and its beard, not of the beard and its face; but Martial IX 76 4 says 'gaudebatque *suas* pingere barba *genas'*. So again he has I 111 1 sq. 'cum tibi sit sophiae par fama et cura deorum, | *ingenio* pietas nec minor ipsa *suo'*, i.e. to which it is linked; so Manilius IV 912 'trepidaeque *suo* sub *pectore* fibrae', the breast which is their seat, where Bentley conjectured *boum*; so Ovid *ex Pont.* III 9 22 'cumque *suo* crescens *pectore* feruet opus', the heart or brain from which the poem issues forth. Finally in *ex Pont.* III 8 14 'nulla premunt *ramos* pondere poma *suos'* some MSS and editors substitute *suo*; but *ramos suos* means the boughs where the fruit should rightly grow. And even so with III 4 64: 'the flowers are plucked and the garden rifled; what marvel then if I have twined no garland worthy of the victor for whose brows it was meant?' ||

EX PONT. IV 16 31–4

cum Varus Graccusque darent fera dicta tyrannis,
            Callimachi Proculus molle teneret iter,
Tityron antiquas Passerque rediret ad herbas,
            aptaque uenanti Grattius arma daret, . . .

'Verdorben und noch nicht geheilt ist *Pont.* IV 16 33 *Tityron antiquas passerque rediret ad herbas'* says Teuffel's *Gesch. d. Röm. Lit.* §252 12 even in the last edition (1910); and so, even in the last edition (1911), says Schanz's, §314. Yet Riese emended the verse in 1874 by simply printing *passer* with a capital. The name is known to us from Varr. *r.r.* III 2 2 'N. Petronius Passer', and this bearer of the name is as well known to us as Proculus in the line above, Numa in 10, Marius in 24, Lupus in 26, Turranius in 29, Fontanus in 35, or Capella in 36: he is mentioned only in this elegy, and so are they. He wrote bucolics, or, as Ovid puts it, he went back to Tityrus and the pastures of old, the traditional shepherd and the country life of a bygone age: Paul. Fest. p. 99 [88 Lindsay] 'antiquae et pastoralis uitae indicium'. The only difficulty is the order of the words; and this Riese failed to defend, because he did not analyse its complexity. His examples *ex Pont.* III 6 48 and *Ib.* 576 illustrate nothing but the postponement of the conjunction, and *trist.* IV 5 31 sq. 'sic iuuenis similisque tibi sit natus et illum | moribus agnoscat quilibet esse tuum' does not even illustrate this, for *que* and *et* must there answer one another like τε and καί.

The construction is 'cum Passer rediret ad Tityron antiquasque herbas'. Propertius would have written

Tityron antiquasque rediret Passer ad herbas,

as he wrote 'cum te iussit habere puellam cornua Iuno' and 'et grauiora rependit iniquis pensa quasillis'; but Ovid disliked this rhythm more than he disliked entanglements of words. Here he has resorted to no fewer than three artificial dislocations, each of them legitimate, but not perhaps elsewhere assembled in a single verse.

For the delay of the preposition, 'Tityron antiquasque ad herbas' for 'ad Tityron antiquasque herbas', see such examples as Verg. *Aen.* V 512 'illa *notos* atque alta uolans *in nubila* fugit', Ouid. *her.* VI 107 sq. 'illa sibi *Tanai* Scythiaeque *paludibus* udae | quaerat et *a ripa* Phasidis usque uirum', *met.* VII 708 '*pectore* Procris erat, Procris mihi semper *in ore*', Val. Fl. I 716 sq. 'non Scythicas ferus ille *domos* nec *ad ostia* Ponti | tendit iter', Sil. XIV 2 'Ortygiae *pelagus* Siculique *ad* litoris *urbes*'.

The postponement of the conjunction, 'antiquas...que', is commoner; but take for instance Hor. *carm.* IV 2 21 sq. 'flebili sponsae iuuenem*ue* raptum | plorat', Ouid. *met.* XIV 30 'poteras certe*que*', *Ib.* 451 'uulnera tot*que* feras', *fast.* IV 609 sq. 'indoluit...maesta parens, longa uix*que* refecta mora est', *ex Pont.* II 1 5 sq. serenum | uidi, fortunae uerba dedi*que* meae': one example, *ex Pont.* III 6 48 'cesserat omne nouis consilium*que* malis', is || especially significant, since Ovid could have avoided the postponement if he had cared by writing 'consiliumque nouis cesserat omne malis'.

The construction 'Tityron antiquas *Passer*que *rediret* ad herbas' for '*Passer rediret* Tityron antiquasque ad herbas' or 'Tityron antiquasque ad herbas *Passer rediret*' is of the sort called ἀπὸ κοινοῦ and typified by Hor. *carm.* II 19 32 'pedes *tetigit*que crura'. Most commonly it is the verb alone which is thus dislocated; but sometimes the subject, as in Lucr. V 214 'frondent atque *omnia* florent', Tib. I 6 81 sq. 'hanc animo gaudente uident *iuuenum*que *cateruae* | commemorant merito tot mala ferre senem', Ouid. *her.* II 70 'tauri *mixta*que *forma* uiri', XVIII 32 'aut uidet aut *acies nostra* uidere putat', Sen. *H.f.* 1213 sq. 'in se coibunt *saxa*que in caelum expriment...mare'; and sometimes, as here, the verb with its subject or object or both: Hor. *carm.* I 11 4 'seu pluris hiemes seu *tribuit Iuppiter* ultimam', Manil. II 325 sq. 'summa prioris | et *pars confertur* subiuncti prima', V 479 'tacito gestu *referet*que affectibus *orsa*', Tib. I 2 39 sq. 'is sanguine natam, | is *Venerem* e rabido *sentiet* esse mari', Ouid. *amor.* III 7 20 'nec iuuenem nec *me sensit amica* uirum'.

The combination of the construction ἀπὸ κοινοῦ with the postponement of a conjunction is natural and simple enough in such an example as Tib. I 3 56 'Messallam terra *dum sequitur*que mari', where both the two words preceding the *que* are ἀπὸ κοινοῦ and pertain equally to *terra* and to *mari*. A complication is added if one word is ἀπὸ κοινοῦ and the other is not, as may seem to be the case with our '*antiquas Passer*que'. But this too has parallels: Tib. II 3 12 'nec cithara *intonsae profuerunt*que comae', Ouid. *trist.* V 1 46 'barbariam *rigidos effugiam*que Getas', *ex Pont.* IV 9 42 'praetextam *fasces aspiciam*que tuos'. And possibly, nay probably, *antiquas* itself is ἀπὸ κοινοῦ. Epithets are often thus placed: Verg. *catal.* 13 5 'ualent mihi ira et *antiquus* furor', Hor. *epist.* I 17 57 'nulla fides damnis *ueris*que doloribus adsit', Ouid. *art.* II 108 'quod tibi non facies *sola*ue forma dabit'; and this position is present, and softens the postponement of the conjunction, in Tib. II 5 22 'Ilion *ardentes respiceret*que deos' (ardentem Ilion ardentesque deos), 86 'dolia *dum magni deficiant*que lacus' (magna dolia), 111 sq. 'uersus mihi nullus | uerba potest *iustos* aut *reperire* pedes' (iusta uerba). Similarly Ovid may here be saying 'Passer rediret ad antiquum Tityron antiquasque herbas'.

Madvig *adu.* II p. 104 started the opinion, afterwards taken up by Bergk and by some editors of Ovid and historians of literature, that the hexameter as well as the pentameter refers to Grattius, and alludes to his Bucolics. The Bucolics of Grattius belong to the same category as his Georgics and his Aeneid. To blot out the name of a bucolic poet which is extant in Ovid's MSS, and to bestow his Bucolics on a poet who is not recorded to have written any, is robbery and murder in one.

113

VÜRTHEIMIANVM*

me sene necdum mortuo etiamtum apud Batauos meos supererant, quae nunc perisse intellego, Pindari exemplaria Ὀλυμπιονίκας complectentia, quorum in prima pagina haec habebantur:

ἄριστον μὲν ὕδωρ,
ὁ δὲ χρυσὸς αἰθόμενον πῦρ
ἅτε διαπρέπει νυκτί.

νυκτί autem rectius *noctu* quam *coctum* Latine reddi putabam.

D. Erasmus

Camp. Elys.
X m. Mai. 1916

* ⟦*CR* 30 (1916), 128: and see p. 72 of this same volume. We ascribe the item to Housman on the authority of A. S. F. Gow, *A. E. Housman*, Cambridge 1936, p. 73⟧

114

THE *THYESTES* OF VARIUS*

One day towards the end of the eighth century the scribe of cod. Paris. Lat.
7530, a miscellany to which we owe the *carmen de figuris* (anth. Lat. Ries. 485,
P.L.M. Baehr. III pp. 273–85), began to copy out for us, on the 28th leaf of the
MS, the *Thyestes* of Varius. He transcribed the title and the prefatory note, which
run thus: *INCIPIT THVESTA VARII. Lucius Varius cognomento Rufus
Thyesten tragoediam (traged...cod.) magna cura absolutam (absoluto cod.)
post Actiacam uictoriam Augusti (aug... cod.) ludis eius in scaena edidit, pro qua
fabula sestertium deciens accepit.* Then he changed his mind: he proceeded with
a list of the *notae* employed by Probus and Aristarchus, and the masterpiece of
Roman tragedy has rejoined its author in the shades.

This testimony is cited, though not always fully or accurately, in the ordinary
books of reference; and if for any reason I wished to confer the *Thyestes* on
another than L. Varius, my first business would be to impugn the credit of this
testimony. If I could not, I must renounce my design. Simply to say nothing
about it, and hope that nobody else would say anything either, is an alternative
which would not occur to me.

Mr Garrod 'would fain know who wrote the tragedy *Thyestes*', and in *C.Q.*
x pp. 206–21 he sets forth the process by which he has persuaded himself that
its true author was the Varus of Virgil's *bucolics*, whom Donatus and others call
Alfenus Varus and whom some have identified with the consul suffectus of
39 B.C. and the eminent jurist. He began his enquiry, he says, in a very natural
and obvious fashion.

'I asked myself, Who is the first person who mentions the *Thyestes?* and
"It would be strange", I said, "if Horace, who so often mentions Varius,
says nothing of the *Thyestes*." Let us see. In the *Odes* (I 6 1–2) Varius is the
"bird of Maeonian song"...Varius is an epic poet; and wherever else
Horace mentions him, it is as an epic poet, or at any rate in company with
epic poets.'

Horace's words are 'scriberis Vario fortis et hostium | uictor Maeonii carminis
alite', and I do not find it strange that he says nothing of the *Thyestes*. I think
that Agrippa's wars were an epic rather than a tragic theme, and that Varius'

* [[CQ 11 (1917), 42–8]]

chief qualification for putting them into verse was not the success with which he had portrayed a cannibal banquet. Horace's allusion to the *Thyestes* of Varius comes in more aptly and gracefully at verse 8, 'nos, Agrippa, neque haec dicere...nec *saeuam Pelopis domum* | conamur tenues grandia'.

'*Sat.* I 10 43–4 is significant: "forte epos acer | ut nemo Varius ducit". Not a word about Varius' tragedy. But worse than that. Varius is mentioned here not only as an epic poet, but as the epic poet *par excellence*: while in the very sentence before Pollio is mentioned as the tragic poet *par excellence* – as though Ben Jonson, say, had left it on record that Marlowe was the prince of tragedians; but for sonnets one must go to Shakespeare.'

The first book of Horace's satires was published about the year 35 B.C.; the *Thyestes* of Varius was produced in the year 29. In these circumstances Mr Garrod ‖ deems it significant that there is not a word about Varius' tragedy in *serm.* I 10 43 sq.

'Nor do I think that the chagrin, which might well be forgiven here to Varius, was much likely to be appeased if he had turned from *Sat.* I 10 43–4 to *Ars Poetica* 90–91, where "The Banquet of Thyestes", Horace writes, "resents a narration in bourgeois (*priuatis*) verse about fit for the comic stage." The author of Rome's greatest tragedy could hardly have read that without some feeling of uneasiness.'

He could hardly have read it at all to judge from Mr Garrod's next sentence:

'(A *Thyestes* of Varius could not have been unknown to Horace, had it ever existed: for Varius was already dead when Horace wrote II *Epp.* III 55.)'

II *Epp.* III is the same poem which Mr Garrod, with elegant variety, called *Ars Poetica* a moment before and will call 'The Epistle to the Pisos' a moment later. If Varius was already dead when Horace wrote the 55th verse of it, we need not consider how he would have felt 'if he had turned from *Sat.* I 10 43–4' to the 90th and 91st. But why Horace's just remark that Thyestes is no theme for treatment in a mean style should cause uneasiness to a dear friend whom he had often praised and whose own *Thyestes* must have been executed in a style the reverse of mean, Mr Garrod leaves us guessing. He goes on to observe that the *ars poetica*, though mainly concerned with tragedy, contains no mention of the *Thyestes* of Varius. It contains no mention of any work by a Latin author.

Fortified by the silence of Horace, Mr Garrod proceeds to passages where either Varius or Varus is named as the author of the *Thyestes* or at any rate as a writer of tragedy. He ranges them in order of date; but it will conduce to clearness if I divide the examples of *Varius* from those of *Varus*, and take the former, as the more numerous, first.

The *Thyestes* is ascribed to Varius in Tac. *dial.* 12 ⟦6⟧ 'Medea Ouidii aut

Varii Thyestes' and Quint. *inst.* x 1 98 'iam *Varii* Thyestes cuilibet Graecarum comparari potest'. Mr Garrod wishes to set aside the first example on the plea that the MSS of the *dialogus* are late and imperfectly known, and the second because he thinks it can be made quite certain that Quintilian himself wrote *Vari* in the genitive whether the nominative were *Varus* or *Varius*. He says that he examined the first six books of the *inst. orat.* in order to find out for himself how often Quintilian preferred *-ii* to *-i* in the genitive of proper names in *-ius*; and he has drawn up a list containing three false references and omitting one of the few examples relevant to his contention, vi 3 61 *Fabi*. Examining MSS of the 10th and 11th centuries is no very likely way to find out the spelling of the 1st; and moreover it is not for 'names in *-ius*' that he must prove his point, but for names in *-ius* which are tribrachs. Such forms as a gen. *Vări* from a nom. *Vărius* are common and indeed usual in inscriptions, but the only classical authors known to have employed them are Propertius, who has *Deci Mari Tati*, and Ovid in one place (*fast.* 1 260 *Tati*) where he is echoing Propertius: when Horace makes *Capri* from *Căprius* he scans it *Cāpri*; and editors have no right to assume that *Titi* (al. *Titus*) in Nouius [[67 Ribbeck]] ap. Non. p. 455 [[729 Lindsay]] is the gen. of *Titius*, nor to elicit *Noui* from *nouit Ianus* in Lucilius [[117 Marx]] ib. p. 25 [[37 Lindsay]]. In Quintilian's own time Lucan, who under metrical compulsion has *Domiti Minici Hortensi Sertori*, wrote *Marii* where the metre left him free, and Silius, like Propertius himself, wrote *Fabii*; from common nouns of the same termination and scansion Ovid and Lucan have *gladii*, Statius Silius Lucan and even Virgil *fluuii*, nobody *fluui* nor *gladi* nor *geni* nor *modi* nor *radi*. None of Mr Garrod's examples are pertinent but v 9 13 *Spuri* and 11 15 *Mari*. He thinks that the Ambrosian MS, if we had it at x 1 98, would there give *Vari* for *Varii*; but at v 11 15 it gives *Marii*, and at 9 13 its original reading seems to have been neither *Spurii* nor *Spuri*. ||

Next we come to passages where the *Thyestes* itself is not named but where Varius is mentioned as a tragedian. In the first four centuries Mr Garrod (p. 209) can find only two, Quint. iii 8 45 'Atreus apud *Varium*' and Mart. viii 18 7 '*Vario* cessit Romani laude coturni (Maro)'; but since he includes commentators and means to cite Philargyrius he should also cite Porphyrion ad Hor. *carm.* 1 6 1 'fuit autem *L. Varius* et epici carminis et tragoediarum et elegiorum auctor', for this example at least is no error of transcription, and he cannot substitute *Varus* as he substitutes *Varum* in Quintilian and *Varo* in Martial. 'The evidence of MSS' he says 'is, in this matter, utterly untrustworthy', and he begins his paper (p. 206) with remarks, which I will now examine, on the frequent confusion of these two names.

'The name of Varus occurs five times in Vergil: and twice (*Ecl.* vi 12, ix 35) out of these five times the oldest Latin MSS which we possess have confounded it with that of Varius.'

The five verses in which *Varus* occurs are VI 7, 10, 12, IX 26, 27, and consequently IX 35 is not one of them. The true statement of facts is the following. *Varus* occurs in five places, and only in one has a capital MS substituted *Varius*. *Varius* occurs only in one, and in that place a capital MS has substituted *Varus*. The proportion of errors to instances is therefore 20 per cent in the one case, cent per cent in the other.[1]

> 'In the *Vitae Vergilianae*, recently edited with an adequate Apparatus Criticus, the names Varus and Varius are found, I think, twenty-eight times; and twenty-two times out of these twenty-eight all, or most, of our MSS have confused them.'

The fullest apparatus criticus is in J. Brummer's edition of 1912, where the names are found in 29 places and confused in 16. Mr Garrod apparently uses E. Diehl's edition of 1911, which admits the interpolated Donatus and excludes the abridgment: if so, his count of examples is still rather too low and his count of confusions too high. My present concern however is not with his arithmetic but with the phrasing by which he has obscured the true state of affairs. The state of affairs, in Brummer's collection, and with little difference in Diehl's, is this. *Varus* occurs in 14 places, and only once does any MS corrupt it to *Varius*. *Varius* occurs in 15 places, and in every one of them it is corrupted to *Varus* by some or most or all of the MSS.

The reader wonders, and Mr Garrod, whom I should not judge to be skilled in self-analysis, must also wonder, why he has huddled away this salient contrast, so material to the question at issue, under a counterpane of indeterminate language. But I have long dwelt among men and I see the reason plain enough. It is because coming events cast their shadows before. Mr Garrod is going to say on the next page, in support of his thesis, 'Bear in mind...how much greater for a scribe was the temptation to change *Varum* to *Varium* than to make the inverse change'; and if he now allows himself to notice how scribes really behaved, he will be unable to cherish this delusion or to bid us bear it in mind. Instinct, more sensitive to danger than the conscious intellect, takes alarm betimes; and the pen automatically glides into a form of words which will help the truth to escape detection.

After some inexact observations on Quintilian and Martial he adds that 'the MSS of Horace tell a like tale'. They tell a tale like mine and unlike Mr Garrod's. *Varus* occurs in two verses of Horace, and none of Keller's MSS corrupt it to *Varius* in either. *Varius* occurs in eleven verses, and in eight of them a large number of MSS corrupt it to *Varus*. Mr Garrod himself on p. 209 makes the innocent ‖ remark that in Philargyrius' note on Verg. *buc.* VIII 6, though the

---

[1] In Seruius' notes on these passages *Varus* occurs 14 times and is never corrupted in any of Thilo's MSS to *Varius*: *Varius* occurs 5 times and is always corrupted to *Varus* in one or more MSS; and that though Seruius is inculcating the distinction.

name *Varus* occurs nearly a dozen times, the MSS, 'oddly enough', never blunder into *Varius*.

I have said enough to show that where MSS give *Varius* we must hesitate before changing it to *Varus*, but that where they give *Varus* we may change it to *Varius* without much scruple. Mr Garrod inverts this principle. He contends that at Quint. III 8 45 and Mart. VIII 18 7 the scribes have written *Varius* for *Varus*, which they hardly ever do, and he will refuse to allow that at *laud. Pis.* 239 they have written *Varus* for *Varius*, though it is their usual habit.

Now follow the examples of *Varus*, and the first passage is one where no question of clerical error arises. Philargyrius at Verg. *buc.* VIII 6 makes mention of Alfenus Varus and adds 'eiusdem autem *Vari* est tragoedia Thyestes omnibus tragicis praeferenda, aliud nihil eius habetur'. The Seruius Danielis at *buc.* IX 35 is diametrically adverse, 'Varius poeta fuit... Varus dux fuit, cui supra blanditur, qui nulla carmina scripsit. nonnulli sane Alfenum Varum uolunt, qui licet iurisconsultus et successor Seruii Sulpicii esset, etiam carmina aliqua[1] composuisse dicitur'; but Mr Garrod cannot hesitate an instant which to believe. Philargyrius has given the correct answer; he is a good boy, and goes to the top of the class.

'Let no one tell me that Philargyrius did not know what he was saying. He knew perfectly well. And he knew that, when he said "Varus", there were people about – already in the fourth century as to-day – who would exclaim at once, "The fool has confused Varus and Varius".'

This is on p. 210: turn over one leaf and look at p. 213. O the heavy change! Philargyrius has been naughty, he has refused to say what Mr Garrod wished to hear; so now he stands in the corner with his face to the wall. 'Philargyrius has muddled his notes – or we have the notes of some unintelligent student who attended his lectures.' And it is not upon two different annotations of Philargyrius' that Mr Garrod pronounces these two different judgments; it is upon the same annotation, *buc.* VIII 6. Ebal and Gerizim are one mount. Far be it from me to say that the words 'eiusdem autem Vari est tragoedia Thyestes' are the note of some unintelligent student who attended Philargyrius' lectures; but if anyone does care to say so, Mr Garrod cannot object. For my own part I think that Philargyrius was quite unintelligent enough to write the note himself: you can hardly expect a man to know Varius from Varus when he does not know Daphnis from Daphne.

---

[1] Mr Garrod, when the fit is on him, thinks it likely that *carmina aliqua* means the most famous of Latin tragedies; and 'in support of this view' (p. 210) he cites the story of Donatus and Seruius that the *Thyestes*, though published under Varius' name, was composed by Virgil. *In support of this view?* Yes, so Mr Garrod says: these passages 'furnish evidence that at an early date the ascription of the *Thyestes* to Varius was called in question'; and therefore it is likely that the *carmina aliqua* ascribed to Alfenus Varus were the *Thyestes*.

The next passage is *laud. Pison.* 237–42:

> nec sua Vergilio permisit carmina soli.
> Maecenas tragico quatientem pulpita gestu
> erexit *Varum*, Maecenas alta Thoantis
240   eruit et populis ostendit nomina Grais,
> carmina Romanis etiam resonantia chordis
> Ausoniamque chelyn gracilis patefecit Horati.

A list of poets who owed their rise to Maecenas. Virgil and Horace are two; a third is a Greek not otherwise known to us, with a romantic name; the fourth, according to the MSS, is a tragedian named Varus. Alfenus Varus, if we believe ‖ Philargyrius, wrote one tragedy; but the Varus of *laud. Pis.* 239 cannot be the Varus of the *bucolics*, who, far from finding, like Virgil, a patron in Maecenas, anticipated Maecenas in patronising Virgil, and was employed almost as early as he in the public service. Mr Garrod at any rate ought to have some difficulty in identifying the two, for he opines, or will opine on p. 214, that Varus was *senex* (Hor. *epod.* V 57) by the year 30 B.C. or thereabouts, and therefore probably a good deal older than Maecenas: I say nothing yet of a much more terrible surprise which he has in store for himself on pp. 215 sq. Editors have hitherto assumed that this verse is one of the innumerable places where scribes have written *Varus* for *Varius*. Varius is known to have been a tragic poet, Maecenas is known to have been his patron, and just as he and Maecenas and Virgil and Horace are here conjoined by the laudator Pisonis, so are they by Martial XII 4 〚3〛 1 sq. 'quod Flacco Varioque fuit summoque Maroni ǀ Maecenas'.

But Mr Garrod does identify, at any rate for the nonce, this Varus of *laud. Pis.* 239 with Virgil's; and further he has no doubt (p. 207) 'that Ovid IV *Pont.* 16 31 is a reference – and an almost contemporary reference – to the same poem and poet'. I have very grave doubt; but the doubt of Mr Garrod, if he had known at p. 207 what he was going to write on p. 215, would have been much graver than mine. In a long list of poets contemporary with himself Ovid has the line

> cum *Varus* Gracchusque darent fera dicta tyrannis.

Gracchus is known from Priscian and Nonius as the author of an *Atalanta*, a *Peliades*, and a *Thyestes*. The best MSS and most of the editors give *Varus*, and there is no advantage in writing *Varius*, for L. Varius Rufus cannot well be the tragedian meant. Of all the other poets here enumerated none is known to have been much older than Ovid, except Domitius Marsus, who heads the roll; none of them is known to have died very long before this poem was written; and a catalogue which excludes even Propertius is not likely to have included Varius. But when Mr Garrod identifies this Varus, Ovid's contemporary, with the Varus of Virgil, he reminds me of a story in Suetonius about the emperor

Claudius: 'inter cetera in eo mirati sunt homines et obliuionem et inconside-
rantiam, uel ut Graece dicam μετεωρίαν et ἀβλεψίαν. occisa Messalina, paulo post
quam in triclinio decubuit, cur domina non ueniret requisiit.' Virgil's Varus, it
will shortly transpire, was put to death by Mr Garrod's orders when Ovid was
quite a boy. Ovid's Varus may be one of the many poets in this list who are
otherwise unheard-of; or perhaps he is heard of once again. Philargyrius at
Verg. *buc.* II 70 quotes an anapaestic fragment, 'et frondosam et semiputatam |
queritur uitem', from an author whom the MSS call *auarus* but the editors *Varus*.

Here ends all mention of Varus as the writer of a *Thyestes* or of any tragedy, so
Mr Garrod now goes in quest of allusions; and he finds one in Verg. *buc.* VIII 10
'sola Sophocleo tua carmina digna coturno', referred by most commentators to
Pollio, who, as Mr Garrod on p. 207 himself observed, is mentioned in Hor.
serm. I 10 42 sq. 'as the tragic poet *par excellence*'. He contends (p. 212) that in
this passage, *buc.* VIII 6–10, Virgil says of the person addressed precisely what in
buc. VI 6–9 he had said of Varus: (1) he is a victorious general, (2) Virgil has
promised him a poem in honour of his warlike achievements, (3) the eclogues
were undertaken at his bidding. Of these three alleged correspondences only the
first exists. There is nothing in either place about having promised a poem in
honour of achievements, and the 'non iniussa cano' of VI 9 cannot possibly
signify the bidding of the person addressed. But 'it can be shewn beyond
dispute' (p. 213) that Philargyrius in his note on VIII 6 identifies the person
there addressed with Varus, as an alternative to Pollio or Gallus. Of that note
Mr Garrod gives an account which readers who turn to Philargyrius will not
be able to verify. A ‖ sentence which they expect to find in one context they will
find in another, a 'biography of Varus' they will not find at all.

'It is perhaps worth noting' he adds 'that if Vergil, at VIII 10, has in mind
the *Thyestes* of Varus – as I believe he has – then in the phrase *Sophocleo
cothurno* he chose his epithet well. Of the three great Attic tragedians Sophocles
alone wrote a *Thyestes*.' It is perhaps also worth noting that Mr Garrod does not
reckon Euripides one of the three great Attic tragedians; but more noteworthy
still is his belief that Virgil at *buc.* VIII 10 has in mind 'the *Thyestes* of Varus'.
The date to which on p. 217 he assigns this eclogue is the unusually late[1] date of
35 B.C.; and in that year, he believes, Virgil had in mind a tragedy which did not
make its appearance till six years afterwards.

Next comes an allusion to this allusion to Varus, Hor. *art.* 90 sq. 'indignatur

---

[1] Mr Garrod admits this, but says, as if by way of defence, 'we have already seen reason to
suppose that in Vergil's first arrangement of the *Eclogues* it stood last'. We have seen it at p. 213:
Philargyrius on VIII 6 says that Virgil speaks of Gallus in the last eclogue, 'ultima ode'; and Mr
Garrod, finding nothing about Gallus in the tenth eclogue, supposes that Philargyrius must have
meant the eighth, in which I find a good deal less about Gallus.

> ego sedulo hunc dixisse credo; uerum itast:
> quot homines tot sententiae: suos cuique mos.

item priuatis ac prope *socco* | *dignis carminibus* narrari cena Thyestae': 'does it
not look as though Horace had deliberately taken Vergil's phrase in order to
direct a sharp criticism at Vergil's patron?' It appears that Horace could not
utter a truth unless he had a discreditable motive: if his words are not a stab at
a friend (Varius, p. 207), they are a stab at a friend's benefactor (Varus, p. 213).
Where Mr Garrod sees a sharp criticism others, with equal reason (for o = o),
have seen a compliment; but that would not suit Mr Garrod's conception of
Horace's character. Hic niger est, hunc tu, Romane, caueto.

There are two more poems of Horace, *epod.* 5 and *carm.* 1 16, where Mr
Garrod suspects allusion to 'the *Thyestes* of Varus', p. 214.

> 'Consider first the titulus to *Epode* v: "Puerum praetextatum defossum
> inducit a Canidia: quo necato Alpho (*v.l.* Aleio) Varo daret potionem de-
> linimentorum". *Alpho* here is commonly corrected to *Alfio*. But though
> *Epode* ii has in some MSS the titulus *Oratio Alfii*, and though Horace speaks
> at 67 of "fenerator Alfius", we know of no Alfius Varus, and a more probable
> correction is surely *Alpheno Varo*. In the text Horace calls him simply Varus
> (73 *Vare*).'

Alfio is in ΑαΟγu, five out of the eight of Keller's MSS which contain this
titulus; B has *Alphio*, which is the same name; the MS from which Orelli quotes
Alpho is of no importance. However, in verse 86 of this epode Mr Garrod finds
'Thyesteas preces', and in verse 87 the words 'fas nefasque non ualent', which
remind him of Sen. *Thy.* 138 sq. 'fas ualuit nihil | aut commune nefas'; and
these he interprets as allusions to a tragedy on Thyestes by Canidia's Varus.
Further, in *carm.* 1 16, which has been taken for a palinode addressed to Canidia,
he finds 17 sq. 'irae Thyesten exitio graui | strauere', and thinks Thyestes 'an
apt example to offer to the mistress of the Varus who wrote the tragedy *Thyestes*'.
Now the odes of Horace may no doubt contain allusions to the *Thyestes*; but
that his epodes contain one is a proposition on which judgment must be
suspended till Mr Garrod has completed his reforms in the chronology of
Augustan literature.

One of those reforms awaits us on the next pages, 215–17. Seruius at *buc.* v 20
says that some supposed the Daphnis whose death is there celebrated to be
Quintilius Varus. 'It can, I fancy', says Mr Garrod, 'be shown that Seruius is
right about Varus, but has blundered over the gentile name: that Vergil's
Daphnis is Alphenus Varus.' How he fancies it can be shown I need not now
relate, for I ‖ am concerned only with the consequences of this identification.
This fifth eclogue, in common with the rest, is generally thought to have been
published about 39 B.C. Mr Garrod, for reasons which he sets forth on p. 217,
assigns it a date 'in or after 35 B.C.'. If 'after' means six years after, when Virgil
is usually supposed to have finished the *georgics*, I have no remark to make on

that. But 'in' perplexes me; because, if Varus was dead, 'extinctus crudeli funere', in the year 35 B.C., I do not see how he could produce the *Thyestes* in the year 29.

Yes, perhaps I do see. Mr Garrod has not given a full and consecutive account of Varus' career, but has left something to the intelligence of his readers. By putting together his scattered utterances, dotting his *i*'s and crossing his *t*'s, I think I have constructed what is surely the most eventful history in the annals of literature: the life, death, and resurrection of Alfenus Varus.

Varus was living when Virgil wrote *buc.* VI and IX, and also when he wrote VIII (pp. 212 sq.), which was in 35 B.C. (p. 217). He was living, in old age and unreverend profligacy (his mother, who according to Virgil *buc.* V 23 survived him, must have been a venerable figure), when Horace wrote *epod.* 5 (p. 214), to which no precise date is assigned. But when Virgil wrote *buc.* V, that is 'in or after 35 B.C.' (p. 217), he was dead (pp. 215 sq.). Then there is silence for a while; and then in the August of 29 B.C. is produced the *Thyestes*, which was no posthumous work, for its author was rewarded with a gift of a million sesterces.

The explanation of this seeming inconsistency will be found in a passage already cited by Mr Garrod, *laud. Pis.* 238 sq.

> Maecenas tragico quatientem pulpita gestu
> erexit Varum.

Mr Garrod did not translate these words, but I now see how he understands them: 'Maecenas erexit Varum' means that Maecenas raised Varus from the dead. And no public man of the time was more competent to do so. Eques Etrusco de sanguine regum, imbued with the traditions of an ancient and religious folk much given to the worship of infernal deities, he possessed the further and exceptional advantage of a house on the Esquiline. There, from the *turris Maecenatiana*, most likely built for the purpose, he commanded a view of the adjacent graveyard and could observe the nocturnal sorceries of Canidia. If the moon blushed and withdrew, as would sometimes happen, he sent out Horace as a spy. The zeal with which the grateful poet discharged his mission has left its literary record in *serm.* I 8, and his inquisitorial supervision of her rites provoked Canidia to describe him as 'Esquilini pontifex uenefici'. 'crematos excitare mortuos' was one of the accomplishments on which this good lady prided herself, and we may believe that she practised it often; Maecenas was an apt though furtive pupil; and never did the black art subserve a better end than when, no doubt at Virgil's request, he resuscitated Alfenus Varus, enriching the literature of Rome with its loftiest tragedy and the late deceased with more than £10,000.

'It is the moderns', says Mr Garrod on p. 217, 'who rush into print.' Well, perhaps some of them do.

115

ANTH. LAT. RIES. 678*

This poem, first printed by Scaliger in his *Ausonianae lectiones*, lib. II c. 29, from a MS in the possession of Cuiacius, will also be found in Burman's anthologia Latina, vol. II p. 321, in Meyer's, no. 1032, and in Baehrens' poetae Latini minores, vol. V p. 350. In date, combining as it does the prosody of *plānetae* with the syntax of *sex* (for *sexiens*) *denos*, it can hardly be earlier than Prudentius and may easily be much later. It is edited by Riese from eight MSS better than the Cuiacian, three of the 9th century, three of the 10th, one of the 11th, and one of the 12th: the best of these, and the only one of which he professes to give a full collation, is C, Aug. 167 at Karlsruhe.

The texts of Scaliger, Burman, and Meyer are corrupted by the false readings of the Cuiacian MS, and all five texts are corrupted by conjecture. All of them desert the MSS in two verses, some of them in more; in every one of these cases the MS reading is true or at least unimpeachable, the alteration useless or even false; and the editors' explanations, where they make bold to give any, are no more serviceable than their conjectures.

The text which I present below contains nothing but what is found in the MSS or at least in some one MS: my own innovations are merely typographical, a comma in verse 5 and a capital letter in verse 10. This text is intelligible from beginning to end, and every detail of its astronomy, even when false, can be confirmed from other sources.

> bis sex signiferae numerantur sidera sphaerae,
> per quae planetae dicuntur currere septem.
> Polluris proles ter denis uoluitur annis.
> fulmina dispergens duodenis lustrat aristis.
5   bellipotens genitor, mensum pensare bilibri.
> in medio mundi fertur Phaethontia flamma
> ter centum soles, sex denos, quinque, quadrantem.
> ter senas partes ex his, Cytherea, retorques
> lustrando totum praeclaro lumine mundum;
10   terque dies ternos puro de Vespere tollens
> sermonis domini completur circulus anni.

* ⟦*CQ* 12 (1918), 29–37: some of the main points in this paper are briefly outlined in *PCPhS* 1917, 11–12⟧

> horas octo, dies ternos seruato nouenos,
> proxima telluri dum curris, candida Phoebe.

The verses purport to give the times occupied by the Sun and Moon and the five planets in performing their revolutions. For antiquity in general the ‖ times of the five planets were fixed by Eudoxus, whose figures are recorded by Simplicius in his commentary on Aristotle's *de caelo*, ed. Heiberg. p. 495 ll. 26–8: Saturn 30 years, Jupiter 12 years, Mars 2 years, Venus 1 year, Mercury 1 year. They reappear, for example, in Theon Smyrnaeus *astr.* c. 12 (p. 136 Hiller), Achill. *isag.* 18, Stob. *ecl.* 1 8 42ᶜ ⟦1 p. 107 Wachsmuth⟧, Plut. *placit.* 11 32 ⟦892 B⟧, Cic. *n. d.* 11 52 sq., Macr. *somn. Scip.* 1 19 3. For Venus and Mercury they are correct; for Saturn and Jupiter and Mars the round numbers are somewhat in excess of the truth.

The seven planets are usually ranged in the order of their supposed distances from the earth, and the order here assigned them is the Chaldaean order, which, though disturbed by the earliest Greek astronomers, regained authority later and is observed in most of the ancient accounts, as for instance Gemin. 1 24–30, Cleom. 1 3 (16 sq.), Cens. *de d. nat.* 13, Claud. III *cons. Hon.* 164–8, Apoll. Sid. *carm.* 15 61–6, anth. Lat. Ries. 786ᵇ and 798; Saturn, Jupiter, Mars, Sun, Venus, Mercury, Moon.

1. If *sphaerae* here meant the zodiac it would be incorrectly used, for the zodiac is not a sphere but a circle. There is however no need to give the word this sense, nor yet to adopt the *sperae* of some MSS and interpret it as *spirae*. *sphaera* is simply the sky: the words which mean the zodiac are *signifera sphaera*, that is *sphaerae pars signifera*. Lucan has *signifer polus* in the same sense at III 254, and Ammianus at XXVI 1 8 interprets the phrase, '*polo* percurso *signifero*, quem ζῳδιακόν sermo Graecus appellat': it is like *pomifero anno* for *anni parte pomifera*, the autumn, in Hor. *carm.* III 23 8. The word *signum*, though applicable to any constellation, is often appropriated to the twelve constellations of the zodiac, as is *stella* to the five (or seven) planets: Seneca for example in *dial.* XII 6 7 says 'sol...per omnes *signorum* partes discurrit', which is true only of the zodiacal signs; and the adjective *signifer* is subject to the same restriction of meaning.

3. The theme of this verse must be the first planet, Saturn, and the time which it mentions, 30 years, is the time of Saturn's revolution; but in place of Saturn's name the greater part of the MSS and all the editors give *Pollucis proles*. Hereupon Meyer says 'i.e. Saturnus', and Riese says 'Saturnum dicit', and they say no more; and neither Burman nor Baehrens says anything. But how can *Pollucis proles* signify Saturn? Saturn indeed was no model of the domestic virtues; he was a bad son, a bad husband, and a bad father; but he is not on that account to be charged with the unheard-of enormity of being his own great-grandchild.

Well might he devour his offspring, if this was to be the consequence of letting them live. Scaliger refers us to Fulgentius *myth*. 1 2, and there indeed we find 'Saturnus *Pollucis* filius dicitur,...*Pollucis*...filius siue a pollendo siue a pollucibilitate quam nos humanitatem dicimus,...*Pollucis* quasi poli filium dicunt', but we find it only in the less good and ancient of the two families of MSS: the other in all three places has *Polluris*. And so in our verse *Polluris* is the reading of the best MS and of one or two more. Again in Mai's mythographi Vaticani (*class. auct*. vol. III) we have 1 102 'Saturnus *Pollucis* filius dicitur', III 1 9 'Saturnum *Pollucis* filium ‖ refert Fulgentius', 2 6 'Saturnum...*Pollucis* filium...dicunt', but in each case with the variant *Polluris*; and in II 1 we have 'Saturnus Caeli uel *Polluris* filius' without the variant *Pollucis*.

If *Polluris* has eight times supplanted *Pollucis* it is very strange: strange not merely because *Pollux* and its cases are familiar words, but because only the genitive case is thus corrupted, and only in a certain connexion. It is always dependent on a word meaning 'son', and that son is always Saturn. But what then is this name *Polluris*, unknown to lexicographers and existing only in the genitive? It is a name like *Boadicea*, a name never borne by the person whom it is meant to designate, and owing its origin simply to a chance corruption of two letters in a MS. Who were Saturn's parents? His father was Caelus and his mother was Terra, whose name is also Tellus and whose genitive is then *Telluris*. In some MS of some author who called Saturn *Telluris filius* the name was ill written or defaced, and was deciphered as *Polluris* by some reader who was himself an author and who therefore had good opportunity to propagate his error. This has already been half-perceived by Mai and Bode at myth. Vat. 1 102: 'scriberem *Telluris* nisi alibi scirem dictum filium Pollucis'; 'error satis antiquus est, quo *Pollucem* pro *Tellure* acceperunt'.

4. 'The scatterer of thunderbolts (Jupiter) makes the circuit in twelve summers.' *bis sex sidera* is perhaps to be supplied from above as object to the verb; but even to take *lustrat* absolutely would be better than to adopt with Burman and Meyer Scaliger's proposal *duodenas...aristas*, which yields no proper sense.

5. *bellipotens genitor* is *Mars pater*; and then follows *mensum pensare bilibri*. The *thes. ling. Lat*. II p. 1986 8 calls this 'uersus corruptus', and none of the editors can interpret it. Scaliger writes *bilibre*, which makes no difference;[1] Burman and Meyer accept *mensem* from a cod. Petauianus and then pronounce the words corrupt, Burman in his addenda proposing *pensatque*, which is unintelligible to me in default of explanation; Riese marks the loss of two half-verses after *genitor*, but does not suggest what they contained. Baehrens, adopting the conjectures of Burman and of Scaliger, wrote 'bellipotens genitor

---

[1] *bilibre* is the ablative used by the other writers (all of them late) who make *bilibris* a substantive; but *bilibri* cannot be deemed incorrect in view of *bipenni* and *biremi*.

mensum *pensatque bilibre*': if he meant *bilibrem*, that would be capable of the required sense; but *que* is thus three places removed from its proper seat and superfluous into the bargain, and the required sense is already given by the reading of the MSS.

bellipotens genitor is vocative, like *Cytherea* in 8 and *Phoebe* in 13; *pensare* is 2nd pers. sing. pres. indic. passive; and the words literally mean 'father Mars, you weight a couple of pounds of months', which signifies that the time of the revolution of Mars is two years. The brachylogy by which a planet is mentioned instead of a planet's revolution will recur in verse 10 and is exactly like the use of *sol* for *annus* in Manil. III 547 and Nemes. *cyn.* 122. *pensari* ‖ with the ablative signifies equivalence whether literal or figurative: Sen. *ep.* 73 5 'auro pensanda', Ouid. *met.* XIII 372 'titulum meritis pensandum...nostris'. The analogy between the pound with its 12 ounces and the year with its 12 months is a subject of remark in the metrological writers, Isid. *orig.* XVI 25 20 'libra duodecim unciis perficitur, et inde habetur perfecti ponderis genus quia tot constat unciis quot mensibus annus', *carm. de pond.* (anth. Lat. Ries. 486) 28 'unciaque in libra pars est quae mensis in anno'; and they even declare that *libra* can stand for *annus*, Hultsch. metrol. script. II p. 139 19–21 (Lach. gromat. uet. p. 374 6–8) 'libra dicitur quicquid per duodenarii numeri perfectionem adimpletur. nam libra dici potest annus, qui constat ex IV temporibus et XII mensibus', Auson. 368 27 sq. (Peip. p. 95) 'ponderis et numeri morumque operumque et aquarum | libra; nec est modulus, quem non hoc nomine signes'. *bilibris mensum* therefore is two years, as many months as there are ounces in two pounds.

6. *in medio mundi* describes the position of the Sun in this arrangement of the planets: he is fourth, and therefore midmost of the seven. Cleom. I 3 (17) ὑπὸ τοῦτον (τὸν τοῦ Ἄρεως) ὁ Ἥλιος ὑπονοεῖται, μέσος ὑπάρχων τῶν ἄλλων, Cic. *de r. p.* VI 17 (4) 'mediam fere regionem Sol optinet'. *Phaethontia flamma*, though the Sun is *Phaethon* in Verg. *Aen.* V 105 and *ora Phaethontia* means the Sun's countenance in Sil. X 110, is not here a well-chosen name for the Sun; for *Phaethon* is likewise the name of the planet Jupiter, and *Phaethontius ardor* has that sense in anth. Lat. Ries. 786ᵇ 7. Still less happy is the use of *soles* for *dies* in the next verse, when the Sun himself is the theme of discourse.

7. *sex denos*, sexaginta. Two examples of this solecism, cardinal number for numerical adverb, are cited in Neue's *Formenlehre* vol. II p. 342 ed. 3, and there is a fourth in anth. Lat. Ries. 761 2 'in septem quinis...signis' (where by the way *quinis* should be corrected to *senis*, since the constellations are 42, not 35). In this connexion I have a word to say on the *thesaurus linguae Latinae*. That lexicon is not unacquainted with this poem, which it calls by no fewer than three different names: '*anth.* 678' in vol. II p. 1986 7, '*carm. de* XII *signis* (it should be *VII planetis*) *poet. min.* V p. 350 3' ibid. p. 580 45, and, stranger still, '*Maxim.*

eleg. 3' in vol. v p. 1408 49, though it is neither Maximian's nor an elegy. In the article on *deni*, vol. v pp. 525 sq., the last section, 2 c, is headed 'multiplicatiue, plerumque cum *bis, ter, quater*': examples (with two wrong references) are given of all three, and then we are bidden to note two instances of *nouies denos* and one of *uicies milies dena*, all of which are quite normal; but this much more noteworthy instance of *sex denos* is not registered. At the beginning of the article, p. 525 58–60, there is a profession of enumerating the examples of the singular number: 'singularis: Diom. *gramm.* 1 498 24, Ambr. *hymn.* 67 3, *anth.* 680ᵃ 15, 798 5, Veg. *mil.* 3 15, Cypr. Gall. *Ios.* 438, *gloss.* (ter).' This list omits at least five instances, and among them the earliest, though they are all cited by Neue vol. II p. 335 ed. 3: Sil. xv 259 'ter dena boue', Stat. *silu.* v 5 24 'ter dena luce', Ser. Samm. 1065 'bis denum rutae folium', C.I.L. VI 504 (carm. epigr. Buech. 264 1) 'uota ‖ Fauentinus bis deni suscipit orbis', IX 4756 (carm. epigr. 409 3) 'bis deno circite solis'. Furthermore it includes, jumbled up with the rest, two examples of a usage which the article nowhere mentions or recognises, *denus* as an ordinal; for *denam* in anth. 680ᵃ 15 means *decimam* and *denus* in Cypr. Gall. *Ios.* 438 means *decimus*.

Professor Lindsay says in *C.Q.* XI p. 41 that with the help of the *thesaurus* Latin scholarship is now becoming easy, and that textual emendation will become equally easy when certain advances have been made in palaeography. No advance in palaeography will ever make textual emendation easy, because textual emendation depends much less on palaeography than on several other things, the chief of which is the textual emendator; and for a like reason Latin scholarship will never be made easy by any dictionary,[1] much less by such a dictionary as this. In present circumstances I think it right to add that the article on *deni* is not of German manufacture and might be better if it were: it is contributed to the *thesaurus* by its American editor.

8. *ter senas partes his Cytherea retorques* in the MS tradition, but *Cȳthērea* is a scansion of which even this poet can hardly have been guilty: the Oxford MS (saec. XI) gives ⟨*ex*⟩ *his*, and this, though probably a conjecture, is probably true: Riese's *his* ⟨*tu*⟩ is inferior, and the ⟨*plus*⟩ *his* of the Cuiacian MS is absurd.

What the words must convey is the time of the revolution of Venus; and hereupon Meyer observes 'Venus conficit orbem diebus 224. uersus corruptus.' This wise remark is echoed by Riese, who augments its wisdom from his own store: 'corruptus: possis *ter quinas his partes*; nam Venus circiter in ⅔ temporis Terrae (224 diebus) Solem circuit.' On the metre of this conjecture I say nothing, as *his partes* is probably a slip of the pen for *partes his*; and on its Latinity I only observe in passing that the Latin for ⅔ is *tres quintas*, and that

---

1 'I will allow the publisher of a dictionary to know the meaning of a single word, but not of two words put together' said Pope.

ter quinas is Latin not for ⅗ but for 15. The point on which I dwell is the statement of both scholars that the time of Venus' revolution is 224 days. 224 days,
as Riese in his innocence blurts out, is the time of her revolution round the Sun.
These well-intentioned but ill-instructed editors, in hopes of finding out what
number this verse might be expected to contain, have resorted to some handbook
of modern astronomy: modern, and therefore Copernican and heliocentric. The
astronomy of this poem is ancient astronomy, Ptolemaic and geocentric, and
with Venus' revolution round the Sun it has no concern: this verse contains the
time of her revolution round the Earth. Now the mean time of Venus' revolution, and of Mercury's too, is necessarily the same as the Sun's, 365¼ days,
though a single and particular revolution of either may exceed that time or fall
short of it within certain limits; and this, as I have already said, was the teaching
of Eudoxus and the general opinion of antiquity. The case is perhaps best put
by Theon p. 136 Φωσφόρος δὲ καὶ Στίλβων καθ' ἕκαστα μὲν ἀνωμάλως (τὸν τῶν
ζῳδίων κύκλον διέρχονται), ὀλίγον παραλλάττοντες ‖ τοῖς χρόνοις, ὡς δὲ τὸ ὅλον
εἰπεῖν ἰσόδρομοι Ἡλίῳ εἰσίν, ἀεὶ περὶ τοῦτον ὁρώμενοι. But Meyer and Riese are
not alone in their confusion: Cornewall Lewis in his *Astronomy of the Ancients*
p. 155 says of Eudoxus' figures 'the error with respect to Venus and Mercury
is considerable', and thinks to show the magnitude of that error by giving the
Copernican figures, 224 days 16 hours and 87 days 23 hours; W. Ramsay and
A. S. Wilkins in Smith's *Dictionary of Antiquities* vol. II p. 433 ed. 3 repeat the
blunder and the slander; and Joseph Mayor in his note on Cic. *n. d.* II 52 p. 154
compares Eudoxus' and Vitruuius' figures with Herschel's, as if they could be
expected to agree.

But the true opinion concerning the times of Venus and Mercury, though
general in antiquity, was not universal, and evidently it was not held by the
author of this poem. Let us see then what other opinions were in circulation.
The time of Venus is 336 days in schol. Arat. 455, 300 days and a few over in
Mart. Cap. VIII §882, while Vitruuius IX 1 9 gives the ample sum of 485 days:
none of these can be reconciled with the wording of our verse. But there was
another false opinion more widely diffused than any of them: that the time of
Venus was 348 days and the time of Mercury 339. This is stated by Pliny *n. h.*
II 38 sq. and repeated in schol. Germ. Breys. pp. 184 and 228, and it reappears
in anth. Lat. Ries. 798 9 sq., though the number for Mercury has there been
corrupted either by the scribe or by the poet. These, it appears, are the times
given by our author. Subtract 18 days from the solar year, says he, and you have
the time of Venus; subtract 9 from that, and you have the time of Mercury.
Now he has stated the solar year as 365¼ days, and if he is subtracting from the
nearest round number, 365, his figures for Venus and Mercury will be one less
than Pliny's, 347 and 338: the number first subtracted should have been 17.
But 17 is a much less easy number to mention in Latin hexameters than 18, and

it seems that instead of subtracting 17 from the nearest round number to $365\frac{1}{4}$ he takes leave to subtract 18 from the next nearest, the 366 days of leap-year. If so, his figures for Venus and Mercury both will be those of Pliny.

ter senas ex his retorques must signify 'you subtract 18 from this number': the literal translation is 'you turn back (or away) 18 out of these', so that the total is shortened by that amount. The usual names for subtraction are *demere deducere detrahere*, often with *ex* c. abl. added, but compounds of *re* are also employed: *remouere* by Horace *art.* 327 sq. 'si de quincunce *remota* est | uncia, quid superat?', *retrahere* by Ausonius 396 14 (Peip. p. 250) 'Priamidae quot erant, si bis deni *retrahantur*' (i.e. 50—20 = 30). *retorquere* itself is given an arithmetical sense in verse 23 of the same epistle, 'in se *retortas* explicabo summulas', where the 'summulae in se *retortae*' are various artificial modes of saying *triginta*, such as 'duc binas decies semelque denas', though only one of them involves subtraction, 'octonas quater, hinc duae *recedant*'.

10. The only editorial comment on this verse is Riese's: 'cum Mercurii cursus sit 87 dierum, *dies terni* fortasse intellegendi sunt cuiusque mensis kalendae nonae idus.' That Mercury's revolution of 87 days round the Sun has ‖ nothing to do with the matter I have already said; and what shadow of sense has 'circulus Mercurii tollens kalendas nonas idus puro de uespere'? *uespere* should be *Vespere*: *puro Vespere* is the clear evening star, as in Hor. *carm.* III 19 26 '*puro* te similem, Telephe, *Vespero*'; and Vesper is identical with the Cytherea of verse 8. The words mean 'subtracting nine days from Venus', that is from Venus' revolution: 348—9 = 339. Pliny states the time of Mercury just in the same way, by subtracting 9 from 348: *n.h.* II 36-9 'sidus... Veneris... signiferi...ambitum peragit *trecenis et duodequinquagenis diebus*...proximum illi Mercurii sidus... inferiore circulo fertur *nouem diebus ociore ambitu*.'

11. This verse is altered by every editor except Burman. Scaliger wrote *Semonis dii* for *sermonis domini* and *anno* for *anni*. *anno* would be plausible if the verse had no context, for Mercury does in fact complete his circle in a year; but this poet thought otherwise, and has said so in the verse above. *Semonis* is accepted by Meyer, Riese, and Baehrens, though they prefer *diui* to Scaliger's *dii*; and they seem to take on trust his assertion that *Semo* can mean Mercury, though he makes no more than a feint of supporting it: 'Semo autem uocatur Mercurius, quia fere in infimis collocatus est; quemadmodum Semones uocabant eos deos qui in infimis censebantur, maiores scilicet hominibus, minores deis.' On the other hand *sermonis dominus*, lord or master of language, does properly designate Mercury, who in C.I.L. VI 520 (carm. epigr. 1528) is twice called 'sermonis dator', and says of himself 'sermonem docui mortales'. See also Diod. Sic. I 16 1 ὑπὸ γὰρ τούτου πρῶτον μὲν τήν τε κοινὴν διάλεκτον διαρθρωθῆναι καὶ πολλὰ τῶν ἀνωνύμων τυχεῖν προσηγορίας, V 75 2 εὑρετὴν τῶν ὀνομάτων καὶ λεξέων γενόμενον, ὥς τινές φασιν, Nonn. *Dion.* XXVI 284 γλώσσης ἡγεμονῆα,

σοφῆς ἰθύντορα φωνῆς, Orph. *hymn.* XXVIII 4 λόγου θνητοῖσι προφῆτα, Hor. *carm.* I 10 1–3 'Mercuri facunde,... qui feros cultus hominum recentum | uoce formasti', Ouid. *fast.* v 668 'quo didicit culte lingua docente loqui', schol. Germ. Breys. p. 229 'Mercurii stella, a qua se linguam et sapientiam percipere arbitrabantur'. The translation is therefore 'the complete circle of the year of the lord of language is formed by taking away nine days from that of the evening star'.

ἐνιαυτός in Greek is used to signify the circuit of a planet, e.g. Plut. *placit.* II 32 1 ⟦892 B⟧ ἐνιαυτός ἐστι Κρόνου μὲν ἐνιαυτῶν περίοδος τριάκοντα, and so is *annus* in Latin. As the *thesaurus* (with whose help Latin scholarship is becoming easy to Mr Lindsay) ignores this usage totally, I give examples. Cic. *Arat.* 232 'haec (quinque stellae) faciunt magnos longinqui temporis annos' (= Arat. 458 μακροὶ δέ σφεων εἰσιν ἑλισσομένων ἐνιαυτοί), Lucr. v 643 sq. 'stellae...quae uoluunt magnos in magnis orbibus annos', Macr. *somn. Scip.* II 11 5 'singulorum seu luminum seu stellarum emenso omni caeli circuitu a certo loco in eundem locum reditus annus suus est', 6 'sic mensis Lunae annus est', 7 'Martis uero annus fere biennium tenet', 11 'annus Lunae mensis est et annus Solis duodecim menses et aliarum stellarum hi sunt anni quos supra rettulimus', *Sat.* I 14 4 'lunaris annus mensis est... Lunae annus ‖ breuis', Seru. *Aen.* III 284 'lunarem annum triginta dierum': in one MS the title of our poem is 'uersus de annis planetarum'. Not all these references are absent from the *thesaurus*: some of them will be found in a wrong place and under a false interpretation, I 6 *annus magnus, maximus, mundanus* (*ca.* 25800 *anni*). The peculiar and technical use of *annus* in Firm. *math.* II 11 was sure to escape lexicographers, as the corresponding use of ἔτος in Greek has escaped them.

12. The time of the Moon's revolution (sidereal of course, not synodic[1]) is given as 27 days 8 hours by Geminus I 30, Theon p. 136, Pliny *n. h.* II 44, and this is only 17 minutes in excess of the truth. Since *terni deni* is 13, *terni noueni* should by rights be 12 if it were anything; but it is clear that the distributive *ternos* is here misapplied like the cardinal *sex* in verse 7 and stands for the adverb *ter*. Neue cites no example of this particular abuse, and I have observed no other; for in Plaut. *Bacch.* 1050 '*binos ducentos* Philippos iam intus ecferam' the meaning is not 400, *bis ducentos*, but separate sums of 200 each, as the next words show: 'et militi quos dudum promisi miser | et istos'.

I append a still worse poem on the same subject, anth. Lat. Ries. 798 (poet. Lat. min. Baehr. vol. v p. 382), which also stands in some need of annotation. It is preserved in one MS of the 13th century, Paris. 7461, and was printed first by L. Angeloni in 1811 and again by Orelli on p. 242 of his Phaedrus in 1832.

---

[1] This parenthesis is not unnecessary, for Sir Norman Lockyer in his *Primer of Astronomy* confounds the two, and says on p. 61 that the Moon is overtaken by the Sun every 27⅓ days. The mean synodic time is in truth more than 29½ days.

> signifer aethereus, mundus quo cingitur omnis,
> astra tenet tantum se sede mouentia septem,
> caetera nam proprio stant semper in ordine fixa.
> Saturni sidus summa concurrit in arce
> 5　ter denoque suus completur tempore cursus.
> inde Iouis cursus bis senis uoluitur annis
> et Mars quingentis rubeus quadraginta diebus.
> ast uno Solis completur circulus anno.
> trecentis Venus octo et quadraginta diebus,
> 10　Mercurius centum triginta nouemque diebus,
> bis denis septemque diebus Luna peragrans
> octo horisque simul proprium sic conficit orbem.

The times here assigned to Saturn, Jupiter, Venus, and the Moon are the same as in the other poem, and when Orelli in verse 11 alters *septemque diebus* into *septem atque duobus* he substitutes an incorrect statement of the synodic revolution for a correct statement of the sidereal. The *concurrit* of verse 4, unless the metre has forced it on a poetaster who only wanted to say *currit*, may be meant for *una currit* (cum fixis astris); for though it is not true that Saturn actually keeps pace with the fixed stars, it is true that he falls behind them much less rapidly than the other planets: Mart. Cap. VIII §853 ‖ ‘Saturnus nimia cum mundo celeritate concertans uix exiguis cursibus superatur’. The *thes. ling. Lat.*, – ecce iterum Crispinus, – quotes the verse in company with Manil. 1 613 ‘(alter limes) aduerso concurrit rursus in axe’, which it misconstrues as the editors of Manilius used to do, not perceiving that *aduerso* is dative, and with Filastr. 133 3 ⟦p. 102 Marx⟧ ‘concurrere atque discurrere sidera’, where *concurrere* has a plural subject and means *concurrere inter se*.

But the times assigned to Mars and Mercury are new and strange. In verse 7 the word *rubeus* is neither to be altered with Baehrens and Ziehen nor marked as corrupt with Riese, for the Latin scholia in Maass' *comm. in Arat.* p. 274 I have ‘tertia autem Mars, *rubea*’ where the Greek of Erat. *catast.* 43 is ὁ δὲ τρίτος Ἄρεως· Πυρόεις δὲ καλεῖται. But 540 days is a long way short of the two years commonly attributed to Mars by the ancients. Two years are 730 days, and this number might be obtained by writing

> Mars septingentis rubeus triginta diebus.

Ciphers are so easily confused that the change of the numerals is much less violent than it seems; the initial *et* has *sic* for a variant, and both may be metrical interpolations. But first let us look round for other estimates of this planet's time. The modern calculation is 687 days, and Vitruuius IX 1 10 comes very near it with 683; 720 is the figure in Hyg. *astr.* IV 14 (p. 117 Bunte), 724 in Cic. *n. d.* II 53, 2 years 5 months (about 882) in Cleom. 1 3 (17), 2½ years (say

913) in Gemin. 1 26, and 9 years in schol. Germ. Breys. pp. 183 and 222, which is so extravagant that it probably arises from a scribe's error of IX for II. But a contrast to these excessive rates is presented by schol. Arat. 455 (Maass pp. 427 sq.) τὸν δὲ Ἄρεα εἰς ἕκαστον ζῴδιον (ποιεῖν φασιν) ἡμέρας με′ καὶ τὸν πάντα κύκλον ἀνύειν εἰς ἐνιαυτὸν καὶ μῆνας δ′. This is both false and self-contradictory, for the proposition that 45 × 12 = 485 (or thereabouts) is not arithmetically sound. A rough correspondence may be brought about either by changing the 45 days to 40 (με′ to μ′) or the 4 months to 6 (δ′ to ϛ′), and the latter is the better because the less remote from fact. 45 × 12 = 540; and 540 is the number given in our verse. The coincidence may be a pure accident, but it puts a scruple in the way of altering the text.

In verse 10 the time of Mercury is said to be 139 days, which is nowhere near the truth and was not even, so far as I am aware, among the false opinions of antiquity. Now the time assigned to Venus in the verse above is the time of Pliny and the other poem, 348 days: the time which they assign to Mercury is 339 days; and it is natural to suspect that in our number of 139 the 1 ought to be 3. Perhaps then *Mercurius* is a gloss on some shorter name of the planet and has ousted the adverb from a verse of this sort,

Stilbon (*or* Arcas) ter centum triginta nouemque diebus.

But it is hard to prescribe limits to the ignorance or error of such a poet as this, and it deserves note that he calls all the other planets by the names which we ourselves usually attach to them.

116

JESTS OF PLAUTUS, CICERO, AND TRIMALCHIO*

Plaut. *rud.* 766–8

> L. ibo hercle aliquo quaeritatum ignem. D. quid quom inueneris?
> L. ignem magnum hic faciam. D. quin inhumanum exuras tibi?
> L. immo hasce ambas hic in ara ut uiuas comburam, id uolo.

On *inhumanum*, which he marks as corrupt, Leo observes 'quid fuerit apud medicos quaerendum'; Professor Lindsay refers his readers to *C.R.* XVIII p. 402, where he cites the verse as evidence for the pronunciation of *gn* in Latin and says 'Clearly this strange reply is due to the resemblance of *ignem magnum* in pronunciation to *inhumanum*.'[1] That hardly diminishes any strangeness it may have; and I believe that the problem can be solved without researches in the abyss of ancient medicine or hypotheses about the pronunciation of *gn*.

When one speaker announces his intention of going about to make a great fire, and the other thereupon enquires 'What for? to burn the churlishness (or something of that sort) out of you?' this insult at first sight appears to have two incongruous faults: it is both clumsy and mild. It does not seem to arise naturally, as a good insult should, from the previous conversation, and it is not nearly so offensive as a bad insult, unconfined by any requirements of neatness, might easily be. Why should the proceedings of Labrax suggest the notion of burning any element out of anybody? and why should the particular element be *inhumanum*? ||

Because men once went about to make a great and famous fire which had for its purpose to burn out of a certain person the element of *humanity*; and that person's name was casually and inadvertently mentioned by Labrax when he made use of the interjection *hercle*. Minuc. *Oct.* 22 [23] 7 'Hercules, ut hominem exuat, Oetaeis ignibus concrematur', Ouid. *met.* IX 250–3 (Jove is the speaker)

---

* [CR 32 (1918), 162–4]

[1] In the same note he cites for the same purpose Cic. *de rep.* IV 6 (Non. p. 24 [35 Lindsay] 'censoris iudicium nihil fere damnato obfert nisi ruborem. itaque, ut omnis ea iudicatio uersatur tantummodo in nomine, animaduersio illa ignominia dicta est', and comments 'So Cicero pronounced *ignominia* more or less as "innominia".' Non sequitur: the only inference which can be drawn from Cicero's words is that he derived *ignominia*, quite rightly, from *nomen*: there is no indication that he made the mistake of deriving it from *in nomine*.

'omnia qui uicit, uincet, quos cernitis, ignes | nec nisi materna Vulcanum parte potentem | sentiet: aeternum est, a me quod traxit, et expers | atque inmune necis nullaque domabile flamma', 262–5 'interea, quodcumque fuit populabile flammae, | Mulciber abstulerat, nec cognoscenda remansit | Herculis effigies, nec quicquam ab imagine ductum | matris habet tantumque Iouis uestigia seruat', Sen. *H.O.* 1966–8 (Hercules to Alcmena) 'quidquid in nobis tui | mortale fuerat, ignis euictus tulit: | paterna caelo, pars data est flammis tua.' Fire was used with the same intent though not with the same effect by Thetis on Achilles, Apollod. *bibl.* III 171 ὡς δὲ ἐγέννησε Θέτις ἐκ Πηλέως βρέφος, ἀθάνατον θέλουσα ποιῆσαι τοῦτο, κρύφα Πηλέως εἰς τὸ πῦρ ἐγκρύβουσα τῆς νυκτὸς ἔφθειρεν ὃ ἦν αὐτῷ θνητὸν πατρῷον, Apoll. Rhod. IV 869 sq. ἡ μὲν γὰρ βροτέας αἰεὶ περὶ σάρκας ἔδαιεν | νύκτα διὰ μέσσην φλογμῷ πυρός, and by Demeter on Demophon or Triptolemus, Apollod. *bibl.* I 31 βουλομένη δὲ αὐτὸ ἀθάνατον ποιῆσαι τὰς νύκτας εἰς πῦρ κατετίθει τὸ βρέφος καὶ περιῄρει τὰς θνητὰς σάρκας αὐτοῦ, Ouid. *fast.* IV 553 sq. 'inque foco corpus pueri uiuente fauilla | obruit, humanum purget ut ignis onus'. Labrax therefore may be making a bonfire with a view to such self-improvement as the nature of his case allows. Burning him alive will not indeed turn him into a god, but it may perhaps turn him into a human being.

Both interlocutors are at home in mythology: Daemones at 604 recalls that swallows are the descendants of Philomela; Labrax at 509 is expected to know who Tereus and Thyestes were, and with the life of Hercules he seems to have been thoroughly familiar, for we owe to him our knowledge of a detail recorded by no other authority, 489 sq.:

> edepol, Libertas, lepida es, quae numquam pedem
> uoluisti in nauem cum Hercule una imponere.

Macrob. *Saturn.* II 3 16 Cicero...cum Piso gener mollius incederet, filia autem concitatius, ait filiae 'ambula tamquam uir', ⟨at genero 'ambula tamquam femina'⟩. et cum M. Lepidus in senatu dixisset patribus conscriptis ⟨'ego non tanti fecissem simile factum'⟩, Tullius ait 'ego non tanti fecissem ὁμοιόπτωτον'.

These supplements of the defective text are those of early editions, and they are approved by the latest editor Eyssenhardt. The second, though manifestly quite uncertain, is not manifestly false; for *fecissem...factum* would seem to come within Quintilian's definition of ὁμοιόπτωτον *inst.* IX 3 78, though ib. 80 he refers 'non minus *cederet* quam *cessit*' to a distinct and different figure 'qua nomina mutatis casibus repetuntur'. But it is so inconspicuous and inoffensive a specimen of its class that it can hardly have elicited Cicero's raillery; and from the emphasis of 'patribus conscriptis' following upon 'in senatu' I should infer that Lepidus had slipped into some expression unfit for the ears of his audience, like that cited in *ad fam.* IX 22 2 'memini in senatu disertum consularem ita eloqui, "hanc culpam maiorem an illam dicam?" potuit opscenius?' This however is likewise uncertain: about the first of the two witticisms there should be no similar doubt. The supplement above given is wrong, and Cicero's own words can be recovered.

Piso had a mincing gait and Tullia a rapid stride: Cicero, displeased with these peculiarities, is supposed to say to his daughter 'walk like a man' and to his son-in-law 'walk like a woman'. That is what they did already and what he wished to break them of doing; and the form of εἰρωνεία which consists in saying the opposite of what one means is much too common and simple to constitute a pleasantry or to win a place among the *dicta Ciceronis*. The contrast between the pair suggested to ‖ their sprightly relative a whimsical way of conveying his reproof. When he said to his daughter 'ambula tamquam uir', what he meant was 'walk like *your husband*'. And what he said to his son-in-law was 'ambula tamquam *uxor*'.

Petron. 41 6–8 dum haec loquimur, puer speciosus, uitibus hederisque redimitus, modo Bromium, interdum Lyaeum Euhiumque confessus, cala-thisco uuas circumtulit et poemata domini sui acutissima uoce traduxit. ad quem sonum conuersus Trimalchio 'Dionyse' inquit 'LIBER esto.' puer detraxit pilleum apro capitique suo imposuit. tum Trimalchio rursus adiecit: 'non negabitis me' inquit 'habere LIBERVM patrem.' laudauimus dictum Trimalchionis et circumeuntem puerum sane perbasiamus.

I print this passage as Trimalchio would have wished it to be read. Our current texts, with their 'liber esto' and 'Liberum patrem', would show him that half his labour had been lost and half his wit wasted; and if he could consult the translators and commentators he would be grievously disappointed with most of them and thoroughly satisfied with none.

It is likely that many readers have understood the pun in 'me habere LIBERVM patrem', and it is not impossible that many translators have done so; but only two or three of them give proof that they understand it, and a larger number give proof that they do not. Trimalchio is happier dead than if he had lived to see such interpretations as 'dass Bacchus mein Sohn sey', 'the god of liberation is my father', 'I have freed him who frees us from care', 'on ne peut pas nier qu'à présent Bacchus ne dépende de moi (iocus inter Liberum Patrem et seruum liberum)'. But as to 'LIBER esto', few even suspect that it contains a pun; few of those who suspect it can explain what the pun is; and nobody, not even W. K. Kelly, explains it in terms which would assure Trimalchio that he had not been casting pearls before swine.

There comes in a boy, Dionysus by name, as the sequel tells us, wearing a wreath of vine and ivy, handing round grapes, and declaring himself now Bromius, now Lyaeus, now Euhius. 'Dionysus', says Trimalchio, 'LIBER esto': that is, assume the character of the indigenous wine-god; be, not Bromius nor Lyaeus nor Euhius, but our Italian Liber. The boy, instructed beforehand, feigns to take the proper name for an adjective and to recognise the formula of manumission; he snatches the cap of liberty from the head of the lately en-franchised boar and claps it on his own. By this pun in action he has performed his master's bidding to the letter: LIBER est, and by logical consequence also *pater*: Seru. *georg.* II 4 '*pater* licet generale sit omnium deorum, tamen proprie Libero semper cohaeret, nam Liber pater uocatur.' Trimalchio's way is now clear to his next pun, 'non negabitis me habere LIBERVM patrem': in the words' first sense as they fall on the ear, 'father Liber is of my household', – and there stands Dionysus with his cap on to prove it; in their after-meaning, as they reach the mind, 'I am a freeman's son', – false within the knowledge of the whole company, and yet not deniable.

117

JUVENAL AND TWO OF HIS EDITORS*

The following remarks are occasioned by Mr S. G. Owen's paper on 'The Phillipps manuscripts of Juvenal' in the last number of this Journal, pp. 238–64, and more especially by the six paragraphs in which my name occurs. The particular questions at issue are mostly trifles and mostly incapable of decision; but their discussion will have a more general interest as showing how differently it is possible for two scholars to conduct their mental operations. The causes which render me unintelligible to Mr Owen and Mr Owen unintelligible to me are probably many and various, but perhaps it is not difficult to distinguish and isolate one. I am accustomed to reach conclusions by reasoning and to commend them by argument. How Mr Owen reaches conclusions I have no means of knowing except by observing how he commends them; and I observe that argument is not his favourite method. His favourite method is simple affirmation, which he applies to the settlement of disputed questions with the utmost freedom and confidence. For this confidence I see so little ground that I infer it has some ground which I cannot see; and the less evidence of reason I find in Mr Owen's writing the more am I forced to the hypothesis that he has access to a higher and purer source of illumination.

III 236 sq. (p. 246)   raedarum transitus arto
                              uicorum inflexu.

'The reading *in flexu* was adopted by Housman from the editiones ueteres. But though it is true that the substantive *flexus* is common, while *inflexus* is rare (it is quoted, besides ‖ this passage, only from Sen. Breu. Vit. 12 4 and Arnob. 2 p. 57 by Forcellini), this is clearly one of the cases in which the vocabulary of later Latin appears first or nearly first in Juvenal. The word is doubtless colloquial.'

'Clearly', for revelation makes all clear. 'Doubtless', for revelation dispels all doubt. But if one is a simple ζῷον λογιστικόν, not entitled to use adverbs in lieu of argument, one cannot talk in that style. Whether Juvenal meant INFLEXV for one word or for two, *inflexu* or *in flexu*, is a question which only Mr Owen and the Pope are competent to decide: all that I can do is to balance probabilities. The way I went to work was this: it is certain, I said to myself, that

* [*JPh* 34 (1918), 40–6]

the substantive *flexus* existed in Juvenal's time, and it is not certain that *inflexus* did. For I was not content to take my text of Seneca from Forcellini; I went to dial. X 12 4 itself, and I found that the best MS and the last edition had not *inflexu* but *in flexus*. I further observed what seemed to be some support for *flexu* in a similar passage of Tacitus, ann. XV 38 4 [3] 'obnoxia urbe *artis* itineribus hucque et illuc *flexis* atque enormibus *uicis*'. But when Mr Owen says 'In *inflexu* I recognise the signature of Juvenal' I can make no counter-proclamation that I recognise Juvenal's signature in *in flexu*: the rushlight of reason sheds much too faint a ray.

VII 184 sq. (p. 247)

> ueniet qui fercula docte
> conponat, ueniet qui pulmentaria condit.

> *conponat* P and most MSS, *conponit* GT.
> *condit* P and most MSS, *condat* LOU.

'In order to regularise the moods Leo follows Housman in retaining *condit* and accepting *componit* from G. "artifices dicit, inde indicatiui" says Leo. But we have here an instance of variation of construction, the consecutive subjunctive *componat* being followed by a relative indicative clause.'

If this piece of dialectic occurred in the writings of an uninspired author it would be called by the harsh name of petitio principii; for the very question at issue is whether we have or have not a variation of construction here. But we ‖ have, for Mr Owen has said so. We have another, by the by, in Pers. III 60, 'est aliquid quo *tendis* et in quod *dirigăs* arcum'; at least, one would have thought so, for this also is the reading of P; but I see that Mr Owen prints *derigis*, so it appears that not even P can be trusted in this matter, but only Mr Owen.

I 168 (p. 248)   inde irae et lacrimae.

'Here for *irae* GO *Val.* and a few other MSS have *ira*, a reading which is adopted by no editor except Housman, who defends it because "the singular *ira*, not the plural *irae*, is the just and proper counterpart to the plural *lacrimae*, which is of another nature". This justification fails because it does not take account of Latin usage.'

Mr Owen then proceeds to teach me Latin usage, a thing I am always anxious to learn. He says that 'the Latin plural very early underwent a weakening, so that it ceased to differ from the singular in meaning', and that 'as time went on this weakening tendency increased', and that 'with the word *ira* this is conspicuously the case: singular and plural are used indifferently with identical sense'. Exactly so; and therefore, as I said, the plural *irae* is not a just and proper counterpart to the plural *lacrimae*, which is of another nature.

But assume that my objection to *irae* fails: now let us hear Mr Owen's objection to *ira*. 'It is clear that not *ira* but *irae* is the correct reading.' It is clear to him, and that must suffice. It is also clear, he says, that *irae* is 'the reading which Cyprian had before him, as appears from his imitation Heptat. Genes. 895 *inde irae et lacrimae*'. What Cyprian had before him, and what he wrote, has been disclosed to nobody but Mr Owen: the three MSS differ, none of them gives what Mr Owen gives, and the only one whose reading is metrical has *inde ira et lacrimae*.

XIII 49 sq. (p. 251)

> nondum aliquis sortitus triste profundi
> imperium aut Sicula toruos cum coniuge Pluton.

49 *aliquis* om. P.   50 *aut* om. LO. ||

On the ground that *triste* is applicable to Pluto's empire and inapplicable to Neptune's I proposed

> nondum ⟨imi⟩ sortitus triste profundi
> imperium Sicula toruos cum coniuge Pluton.

See Luc. VI 341 'imi...habitator Olympi', Stat. Theb. IV 476 'imi...regia mundi', Sil. V 241 'deus ima colentum', VII 688 sq. 'aeternae regnator noctis, ad imos | cum fugeret thalamos'. Leo, following me, preferred '⟨atri⟩', which perhaps is no less probable. But Mr Owen says that 'there are two insuperable objections to the conjecture'; and they are these. '(1) it leaves Neptune unmentioned in this full catalogue of the gods.' This full catalogue of the gods already omits Apollo, Diana, Mercury, Mars, Venus, Vesta, Ceres, and Minerva, not to mention Amphitrite; but if it also omitted Neptune it would cease to be a full catalogue; and this is an insuperable objection. Mr Owen and I do not even speak the same language: he uses the word 'full' to express the idea which I express by the word 'defective'. Pass to the second insuperable objection: '(2) it assigns to *profundum* the meaning of "hell", a meaning which as far as I know is unparalleled.' It assigns to *profundum* its proper meaning, 'the deep'; and *imum profundum* is what Milton calls 'the lowest deep'. There are half a dozen verses in the Aetna alone where *profundum* signifies the subterranean world; for example 578 'septemque duces raptumque profundo' (Amphiaraum). So 'insuperable' is another of the English words to which Mr Owen and I attach different notions. But even after surmounting two insuperable objections I cannot escape defeat, for Mr Owen now brings up his 42 centimetre gun: '*aliquis* is unquestionably right.' Nil ultra quaero plebeius.

I 150 sq. (p. 254)   dices hic forsitan 'unde
> ingenium par materiae?'

dices PBO, *dicas* most MSS.

'I see no reason why *dicas* should be preferred to *dices*, as it is by Mr Housman followed by Leo.' – When Mr Owen says || 'followed by Leo' he appears to mean 'preceded by Jahn, Hermann, Friedlaender, and Buecheler'. – 'Two reasons are given for preferring it: "(1) because *forsitan* in Juvenal regularly takes the subjunctive, and (2) because, apart from *forsitan*, the subjunctive is usual when no definite person is addressed" (Housman, pref. p. xix).'

'As to (1)' begins Mr Owen, and then, instead of invalidating my reason, he substantiates it. He obligingly cites the facts upon which my statement was founded, and shows that Juvenal elsewhere has four examples of *forsitan* with the subjunctive and only one with the indicative. The subjunctive therefore, as I said, is the rule, and the indicative the exception.

'As to (2), the passages where the subjunctive undoubtedly occurs are v 156 *forsitan...credas*, viii 113 *forsitan...despicias*, xi 162 *forsitan expectes*, xiv 34 *forsitan...spernant*, and with *forsan* vi 14 *forsan...extiterint*. Of these v 156, viii 113, xi 162 are not cases of subjunctive "where no definite person is addressed".' Very true; they are cases of subjunctive due to *forsitan*, which, as I said, regularly takes the subjunctive. But why is Mr Owen making this remark 'as to (2)', i.e. as to my argument that 'apart from *forsitan*, the subjunctive is usual when no definite person is addressed'? What sense, if any, does he attach to the word 'apart'? 'Moreover', says he, 'the statement that "the subjunctive is usual when no definite person is addressed" is in direct conflict with the conclusion at which Dr Roby arrives in his exhaustive essay on this particular point (Latin Grammar ii, preface, pp. ci–cvii), where after a long collection of instances Dr Roby decides that "the indicative is the ordinary use" (p. ciii).' If so, Dr Roby is wrong. But Mr Owen does not know what Dr Roby's exhaustive essay is about, and apparently has not even perused its title, which is 'Of the expressions *dicat aliquis, dixerit aliquis*'. To the use of verbs in the second person it contains only one allusion, which I will transcribe; and I wish Mr Owen joy of it: p. ciii 'the indicative...is exceedingly frequent in the second person, *when a definite person is meant*'.

I repeat then that when the person addressed is not a definite person the subjunctive and not the indicative is usual. ‖ I did not say that it was invariable, nor is it. The indicative, though very rare, does sometimes occur; and Mr Owen will be more than ever assured that *dices* is right when I refer him to Catull. 89 6 'quantumuis quare sit macer *inuenies*'.

I 155 sq. (p. 255)

> pone Tigellinum, taeda lucebis in illa
> qua stantes ardent qui fixo pectore fumant.

pectore PBAO, *gutture* most MSS.

'The reading *gutture* is absurd. It is defended by Mr Housman on the ground that to fasten a victim by the throat would involve less trouble.' It was defended by me on four grounds; but this is the only one of them which Mr Owen can remember. 'As if the object of torturers was to save themselves trouble! Such people are prepared to take infinite trouble.' If necessary. I had better quote what I actually said: '*gutture*...is on every count superior: superior palaeographically, as the less common word, and superior in sense, because to fasten a victim by the throat involves less trouble, consumes less material, *and causes more discomfort*, than to fasten him by the chest.' Mr Owen however dissents: 'And consider what the result of fastening the victim by the throat would be. The swift result would be throttling and consequent death, the last thing desired by the torturer, whose object is to prolong the pain.' If the torturer were so misguided as to use a slipknot, throttling, I imagine, would indeed be the result; but not otherwise: we do not hear that throttling was of frequent occurrence in the pillory. *fixo* moreover, properly 'nailed', implies nothing so loose as a slipknot, and will indicate rather a collar clamped to the stake. But the torturer's object, says Mr Owen, 'would be better attained by fastening by the chest: then the victim while being roasted could not struggle, so far from stopping his anguish by throttling himself he could not even show it.' I cannot struggle either: I feel like the queen of Sheba when she had seen all Solomon's wisdom and there was no more spirit in her. Is there in all the wide world a single person except Mr Owen who conceives that to fasten || a man by the chest will prevent him from moving his arms and legs? Does Mr Owen himself conceive it? Does his mind know that this is the meaning of the words which his hand has written?

His final stroke is now impending. 'So the scholiast understood it: "ut lucerent spectatoribus, cum fixa essent illis guttura, ne se curuarent".' The dispute is whether Juvenal wrote *fixo pectore* or *fixo gutture*; and when the scholiast says 'cum *fixa* essent illis *guttura, ne se curuarent*', Mr Owen quotes those words as showing how the scholiast understood *fixo pectore*. Am I awake or asleep?

118

TRANSPOSITIONS IN THE *IBIS* OF OVID*

In my recension of the Ibis, published in 1894 as part of Postgate's corpus poetarum Latinorum, tom. I fasc. 2, I transposed four distichs, 135–40[1] and 459 sq., and suggested the transposition of three more, 181 sq., 203 sq., 409 sq. Perhaps, after two-and-twenty years, it is time to unravel the mystery of this behaviour, and disclose my inscrutable reasons for resorting to the most unpopular of all methods of emendation.

One of the causes why any proposal to correct a verse or sentence alarms and distresses the natural man is that it makes an unusual demand upon his intellect and entails the weary work of reading and considering the context. That form of correction which consists in transferring a verse or sentence from one place to another is in consequence doubly discomposing, because the mental fatigue which it involves is twice as heavy. There are two contexts to be read and considered, not only one.

Disrelish for excessive and unwonted labour will often put on disguises, and much is sometimes said on these occasions about the respect due to the authority of MSS. But that is a cloak which does not always fit; and whatever may be the reason why Ovid's editors, in the passage which I shall first examine, maintain the arrangement of verses which I propose to disturb, it cannot be their respect for MS authority. MS authority is here divided, and the weight of it is adverse.

For more than 400 years the editors of the Ibis, with the single exception of myself, have printed the two verses 338 'ultores rapiant turpe cadauer equi' and 339 'uiscera sic aliquis scopulus tua figat ut olim' in juxtaposition; and so they mean to print them still. Their authority? one, only one, and that ‖ not the best nor the next best, of the seven[2] MSS possessing independent value. Only in X, Parisinus 7994 saec. XIII, does 339 immediately follow 338: in two MSS there is one distich between them, in one MS there are two distichs, and in three there are three. So much do the editors here respect MS authority: what they really respect is editorial tradition. The true reason why 338 and 339 are still

---

* ⟦*JPh* 34 (1918), 222–38⟧

[1] I follow the numeration of Ellis and of Merkel's last edition: in other texts the numbering is sometimes two verses out.

[2] The seven are TGXPVFH, and this order is roughly their order of merit.

printed together is that Iacobus Rubeus printed them so in his text of 1474, which became by chance a parent of the vulgate.

I will set out the verses with their surrounding context, and add in the margin a guaranty of the MSS.[1]

	331	utque uel Eurydamas ter circum busta Thrasylli
		est Larisaeis raptus ab hoste rotis,
		uel qui quae fuerat tutatus moenia saepe
		corpore lustrauit non diuturna suo, ‖
	335	utque nouum passa genus Hippomeneide poenae
		tractus in Actaea fertur adulter humo,
		sic, ubi uita tuos inuisa reliquerit artus,
F G H P T V X	338	ultores rapiant turpe cadauer equi.
F G H P V	637	denique Sarmaticas inter Geticasque sagittas
	638	his precor ut uiuas et moriare locis.
F H T V	439	utque ferox Phalaris lingua prius ense resecta
	440	more bouis Paphio clausus in aere gemas.
	461	aut, ut Cassandreus domino non mitior illo,
	462	saucius ingesta contumuleris humo.
F G H P T V X	339	uiscera sic aliquis scopulus tua figat, ut olim
		fixa sub Euboico Graia fuere sinu.

Now to investigate the true seat of the six verses thus interposed.

About the distich 637 sq. there can be no question: its only possible place in the poem is after 636; and there it is found in GTX. Since G presents it in both places, the conflict is between TX on the one hand and FHPV on the other: TX are in general the more trustworthy, and in this instance they do not belie their character.

[1] Statements touching the two MSS G and T I make on my own responsibility: of F and V we get our reports from Merkel and Ellis, of H and P and X from Ellis alone, so we must expect contradictions and inaccuracy. The page of V now reproduced by photography in Chatelain's Paléographie des class. lat., part II pl. CI 2, displays their negligence, or that of their informants, in a disgraceful light; and neither is better or worse than the other.

That V presents the verses 637 sq. 439 sq. 461 sq. between 338 and 339 is the statement of Ellis, who said on p. lv of his edition 'usus sum apographo quod rogatu meo exscribendum curauit Iosephus Hauptius', though to me he gave two different accounts, consistent neither with this nor with one another: (1) that the transcript was Haupt's own, (2) that it was a 'collation with Merkel's edition' (and therefore not a transcript). Merkel, who used a collation made by Moriz Haupt, reports on the contrary that V does not contain these six verses at all, either in that place or in the places indicated by their numeration. When I brought this discrepancy to Ellis's notice in 1891, he asseverated that he had accurately reproduced the testimony of Josef Haupt; and it is to be noted, as some confirmation, that in 439 he cites a variant from V, utue for utque, so that this verse at least would seem to be present in the MS.

That F presents the verses 439 sq. 461 sq. both before 339 and in the places indicated by their numeration is the statement of Ellis, who had seen the MS. Merkel on the contrary reports from the collation of Heinsius that F does not present these four verses in either position. This discrepancy also I brought to Ellis's notice, and he again assured me that his report was true; and it is in some measure confirmed by his citation from F of the readings Cassandreus and dominus in 461.

Next comes the distich 439 sq.; and we will seek it in its usual context.

	et tua sic latos spargantur membra per agros,	435
	tamquam quae patrias detinuere uias.	
	aere Perilleo ueros imitere iuuencos	
F G H P T V X	ad formam tauri conueniente sono.	438
F G P X	utque ferox Phalaris lingua prius ense resecta	439⎫
	more bouis Paphio clausus in aere gemas.	440⎭
F G H P T V X	dumque redire uoles aeui melioris in annos	441
	ut uetus Admeti decipiare socer.	

Since F presents the two verses in both places, the conflict is between GPX and HTV. T is the best MS, GXP are the three next best, so that authority is nearly balanced and the cause must be tried on its merits. And every shallow and careless and hasty judge will instantly cry out that here the couplet is at home, because it has the same theme as 437 sq., the brazen bull of Agrigentum. ‖

That is a reason why shallow and careless and hasty scribes should put 439 sq. in this place, even if its proper place was elsewhere: I have given examples of rearrangement so caused in the Classical Quarterly VIII p. 155 ⟦this edition pp. 884–5⟧. But I aver that 437 sq. and 439 sq. could not have been placed in juxtaposition either by Ovid or by any respectable practitioner of the art of verse. Both couplets are quite well written, and anyone capable of writing them would have taken great care to keep them apart, because of their phraseology. If he had written them to stand side by side, he would have written them otherwise, avoiding repetition and conferring point; not allowing *aere Perilleo* to be followed by *Paphio...in aere* nor *imitere iuuencos...sono* by *more bouis...gemas*. How Ovid manages such things may be seen in 365–8 (Oenomaus' victims and Oenomaus) 'ut iuuenes pereas quorum fastigia uultus | membraque Pisaeae sustinuere foris, | ut qui perfusam miserorum saepe procorum | ipse suo melius sanguine tinxit humum', 397–400 (Thrasius and Busiris) 'ut qui post longum, sacri monstrator iniqui, | elicuit pluuias uictima caesus aquas, | frater ut Antaei, quo sanguine debuit, aras | tinxit et exemplis occidit ipse suis'. Placed where T places it, between 337 sq. and 461 sq., the couplet 439 sq. is without offence. There is no reason why Phalaris and his victims should occupy consecutive distichs: the Minotaur's victims are cited in 373 sq., the Minotaur himself in 408. And there is no reason why persons burnt in the brazen bull under different circumstances should all be mentioned together: persons torn to pieces by dogs are mentioned separately in 477 sq. and 595 sq.

So now let us proceed to the couplet 461 sq. in its usual context of 457–64.

inque pecus subito magnae uertare parentis,	457
uictor ut est celeri uictaque uersa pede.	

solaque Limone poenam ne senserit illam

F G H P T V X   460   et tua dente fero uiscera carpat equs.

F G   P   X   { 461   aut, ut Cassandreus domino non mitior illo,

                         462   saucius ingesta contumuleris humo.

F G H P T V X   463   aut ut Abantiades aut ut Cycneius heros

                              clausus in aequoreas praecipiteris aquas. ||

The MSS are divided just as before, GPX on one side, HTV on the other. Who is meant by *domino*[1] ... *illo* in 461? The punctuation of most editors is ambiguous, but Merkel in his last recension clearly refers *non mitior* to Ibis himself and *domino illo* to *Cassandreus*. Such a comparison has no parallel in all this long series of examples, and so far Saluagnius is better advised in referring *mitior* to *Cassandreus* and *illo* to Hippomenes, implied in the mention of his daughter Limone at 459: the four words will then be meant as a clue to the identity of 'the Cassandrean'. But Hippomenes was no tyrant, *dominus*. He was one of the house of Codrus, king of Athens say some, archon say others, εἷς τῶν πολιτῶν says Aeschines Timarch. 182, who visited a domestic offence with a punishment which public opinion justly condemned as inhuman, but which Aeschines lauds as an example of antique severity, and which, if we may trust Heraclides Ponticus, was meant to repel the charge of softness and luxury which his family had incurred. And 'non mitior Hippomene' is an incredible way to describe that monster of tyranny Apollodorus of Cassandrea: Polyaen. strat. VI 7 Ἀπολλόδωρος ὁ Κασσανδρεὺς ... τύραννος ἐγένετο φονικώτατος καὶ ὠμότατος πάντων ὅσοι παρ᾽ Ἕλλησιν ἢ παρὰ βαρβάροις ἐτυράννησαν. The person whom the ancients couple with Apollodorus is Phalaris: Polyb. VII 7 2 μήτε Φάλαριν μήτ᾽ Ἀπολλόδωρον, Plut. cum princ. phil. 3 5 〚778 E〛 Ἀπολλο- δώρου τοῦ τυράννου καὶ Φαλάριδος, Dio Chrys. II 76 Φάλαρίν τε καὶ Ἀπολλό- δωρον, Cic. n. d. III 82 'at Phalaris, at Apollodorus poenas sustulit', Sen. dial. IV 5 1 'qualis fuit Apollodorus aut Phalaris', de ben. VII 19 5 'qualis Apollo- dorus aut Phalaris'. Ovid himself brings the two together at ex Pont. II 9 43 sq. 'non tibi *Cassandreus* pater est gentisue Pheraeae | *quiue repertorem torruit arte sua*', and in the Ibis, according to HTV, he brought them together again; for these MSS make 461 sq. follow 439 sq., so that *domino* ... *illo* signifies Phalaris.

The best position then for 439 sq. and 461 sq. is that in which they are placed by the best MS. Standing together || between 338 and 339 they are in accord with one another and are not in disaccord with their context.

But the place immediately after 338, now occupied in FGHPV by 637 sq., is the best place in the poem for another distich, which in FGPX is immediately followed by 461 sq. The verses 459 sq.,

___
[1] *dominus* FPX, but no editor now prefers this reading, and it would not mend matters.

> solaque Limone poenam ne senserit illam
> et tua dente fero uiscera carpat equs,

are indeed explicable where they stand in the MSS, immediately after 458. But, since neither 458 nor the verses preceding it contain anything to which *poenam ...illam* can refer, it is necessary to interpret these words as looking forward to the pentameter; and this, though possible, is not natural, and is contrary to the analogy of *domino...illo* in 461. If 459 sq. as well as 461 sq. are placed in the gap between 338 and 339, *poenam...illam* will refer to the *nouum...genus...poenae* of 335; and nothing could be more apt and harmonious. Ovid first imprecates on Ibis the doom of Limone's paramour, and then the doom of Limone herself. To mention a person first by patronymic (*Hippomeneide*) or some other periphrasis, and then directly afterwards by his or her proper name (*Limone*), is an artifice in which Latin poets take no less delight than Gibbon himself: Hor. carm. IV 8 22–4 'quid foret *Iliae* | *Mauortisque puer*, si taciturnitas | obstaret meritis aemula *Romuli*?', Ouid. trist. I 9 27 sq. 'de *comite* Argolici postquam cognouit *Orestae*, | narratur *Pyladen* ipse probasse Thoas', Ib. 393–5 'ut iacet Aonio *luctator* ab hospite fusus | qui, mirum, uictor, cum cecidisset, erat, | ut quos *Antaei* fortes pressere lacerti'. The whole passage then will originally have stood as follows:

> utque nouum passa genus Hippomeneide poenae   335
> tractus in Actaea fertur adulter humo,
> sic, ubi uita tuos inuisa reliquerit artus,
> ultores rapiant turpe cadauer equi.   338
> solaque Limone poenam ne senserit illam   459
> et tua dente fero uiscera carpat equs.   460
> utque ferox Phalaris lingua prius ense resecta   439
> more bouis Paphio clausus in aere gemas. || 440
> aut, ut Cassandreus domino non mitior illo,   461
> saucius ingesta contumuleris humo.   462
> uiscera sic aliquis scopulus tua figat, ut olim   339
> fixa sub Euboico Graia fuere sinu.

All the omissions and transpositions may be explained by the following history. The scribe has written the last word of 336, *humo*, and should now proceed to 337. But his eye descends to the *humo* which is the last word of 462, and he proceeds instead to 339, omitting 337 sq., 459 sq., 439 sq., and 461 sq. These omissions he discovers at a later stage. There is not room in the margin to insert the eight missing verses at the proper place, but there is room for two; so he there inserts the first two, 337 sq., which are closely and evidently connected with 335 sq.; the other six, 459 sq., 439 sq., 461 sq., he subjoins at the end of the whole series of imprecations, after 638, and adds marks to show whither they should be transferred. But these marks are in part obliterated or misunderstood. The couplet 459 sq. (Limone daughter of Hippomenes) is referred, by a reader who knows too much and yet too little, to 457 sq. (Hippomenes husband of Atalanta). In some copies it carries 461 sq. with it, while the couplet 439 sq. is attached to 437 sq. because the bull of Phalaris is in both. In other copies the marks of transposition are so far understood that 439 sq. and 461 sq. are restored to their right place before 339, or so far misinterpreted that 637 sq. are removed thither likewise or instead.

I daresay that those who accept as true the order of verses found in X may be able to frame an hypothesis explaining how the arrangement in T, which they think false, was brought about; but they will then be confronted with the further difficulty of explaining how it is that the false arrangement is so much more appropriate than the true. At present however they do not think it their business to explain anything, nor even to acquaint their readers or themselves with the facts of the case: their authority is the printed vulgate, and if MSS order the verses otherwise, that is transposition. Hear Mr Ehwald talk in Burs. Jahresb. vol. 109 p. 286: 'Am wenigsten kann ich || mich mit dem von Housman vorgeschlagenen Versumstellungen befreunden': he mentions some of these, and then proceeds 'noch unglaublicher ist die Anordnung, nach der nach v. 338 gelesen werden soll 459. 460. 439. 440. 461. 462'. No argument is vouchsafed, for none is needed; it matters not that this position of 439, 440, 461, 462 is their position in the best MS; the numeration of current editions is Mr Ehwald's norm, and anything which disturbs it is 'Umstellung'. Mr Owen goes even further: he has taken upon himself, in the interests of the commonwealth, to withhold from his readers what he regards as pernicious knowledge, and has contrived his apparatus criticus, not to instruct, but to edify. He prints 339 immediately after 338, and lets his readers suppose that he is obeying the MSS, when in truth he is obeying one MS and disobeying six. He places 439 sq. between 438 and 441, and lets his readers suppose that the MSS do so, when in truth half the MSS place them elsewhere. He places 637 sq. between 636 and 639, and never tells his readers that most of the MSS do not. Only at 461 sq. does he fail to shield our innocence from contact with the truth. There he confesses '459–460 (461–462) hic om. BHTV'; but even this tiny dose of fact is diluted with fiction, for he adds 'in quibus post 336 (338) ponuntur'. Not one of these four MSS places the distich after 338: they all place it after 440.

The verses which I shall next consider are 135–40. These are placed by the seven MSS, without variation, immediately before 141; and not only by the MSS but by the independent deflorationes Atrebatensis 65 and Parisina 17903 (saec. XIII).

> certe ego, quae uoueo, superos motura putabo
> speque tuae mortis, perfide, semper alar.   130
> et prius hanc animam nimium tibi, saeue, petitam
> auferet illa dies quae mihi sera uenit,
> quam dolor hic umquam spatio euanescere possit,
> leniat aut odium tempus et hora meum.
> pugnabunt arcu dum Thraces, Iazyges hasta,   135
> dum tepidus Ganges, frigidus Hister erit,
> robora dum montes, dum mollia pabula campi,
> dum Tiberis liquidas Tuscus habebit aquas, ||
> tecum bella geram; nec mors mihi finiet iras,
> saeua sed in manis manibus arma dabit.   140

dabit in 140 is Heinsius' correction of *dabo*; but if *dabo* is retained, though the phrase will be foolish, 'dabo arma (meis) manibus', the main sense of the verse will not be affected; and that sense is unmistakable. Ovid declares that his warfare with Ibis will persist even when both of them are dead. The situation contemplated is that Ibis and Ovid are a pair of ghosts in the world below and are there continuing their ancient combat. Bear this in mind, and read on.

> tum quoque, cum fuero uacuas dilapsus in auras,   141
> exanguis mores[1] oderit umbra tuos.
> tum quoque factorum ueniam memor umbra tuorum,
> insequar et uultus ossea forma tuos.
> siue ego, quod nolim, longis consumptus ab annis,   145
> siue manu facta morte solutus ero,
> siue per inmensas iactabor naufragus undas
> nostraque longinqus uiscera piscis edet,
> siue peregrinae carpent mea membra uolucres,
> siue meo tinguent sanguine rostra lupi,   150
> siue aliquis dignatus erit supponere terrae
> et dare plebeio corpus inane rogo,
> quidquid ero, Stygiis erumpere nitar ab oris
> et tendam gelidas ultor in ora manus.
> me uigilans cernes, tacitis ego noctis in umbris   155
> excutiam somnos uisus adesse tuos.
> denique quidquid ages, ante os oculosque uolabo
> et querar, et nulla sede quietus eris.

What is all this? It is no combat between two ghosts: it is no combat at all. A ghost is haunting a living man: Ovid is still dead, but Ibis has come to life again. Such phrases as 143 *ueniam...umbra*, 144 *insequar...uultus ossea forma*

---

[1] *manes* FT; but editors rightly disregard this, as a mere repetition from 140.

tuos, 154 *tendam gelidas...in ora manus*, 155 *me uigilans cernes*, 156 *excutiam somnos uisus adesse tuos*, 157 sq. *ante os oculosque uolabo* | *et querar et nulla sede quietus eris*, are merely comical ‖ if they describe one spectre trying to haunt another spectre; whose form is no less bony, whose fingers are no less cold, and whose capacity for flitting and shrieking is no whit inferior. These are the phrases used when the living are haunted by the dead: Tibull. 1 5 51 sq. 'hanc *uolitent* animae circum sua fata *querentes* | semper', Verg. Aen. IV 386 '*omnibus umbra locis adero*', Stat. Theb. III 74–7 'te series orbarum excisa domorum | *planctibus adsiduis*, te diro horrore *uolantes* | quinquaginta animae circum *noctesque diesque* | adsilient', Amm. Marc. XIV 11 17 'sauciabantur eius sensus *circumstridentium* terrore *laruarum*', Hor. epod. 5 91–6 'quin, ubi perire iussus expirauero, | *nocturnus occurram* furor | *petam*que *uultus umbra curuis unguibus*, | quae uis deorum est manium, | et *inquietis* assidens praecordiis | pauore *somnos auferam*'. But put all this aside and look simply at verse 153: *Stygiis erumpere nitar ab oris.* If Ibis as well as Ovid is dead, this can only mean that Ovid's ghost will turn tail on Ibis' ghost and make a bolt for the upper air. More marvels yet: we proceed with 159 sq., 'uerbera saeua dabunt sonitum nexaeque colubrae: | conscia fumabunt semper ad ora faces': – that is, Ovid's ghost will have a Fury to help him, as Valerius Flaccus writes III 386–90 'patet ollis (animis) ianua leti | atque iterum remeare licet; comes una sororum | additur, et pariter terras atque aequora lustrant. | quisque suos sontes inimicaque pectora poenis | implicat, et uaria meritos formidine pulsant': – and then we come to 161 sq. 'his uiuus furiis agitabere, mortuus isdem, | et breuior poena uita futura tua est'. *uiuus agitabere* and *uita futura est*, and in verse 140 he was already dead and disembodied. O grave, where is thy victory?

Before I edit a work, I read it; and a quarter of a century ago I read the Ibis and consequently noticed this discrepancy. I am the first editor who ever did read the Ibis, and down to this year 1916 I am the last; but it may have been read by some persons other than its editors, and this passage at any rate was read by one scholar before me. Karl Schenkl in 1883, Zeitschr. f. d. oest. Gymn. p. 264, stated briefly the repugnancy which I have just set forth at length: 'v. 142 (140) *saeua sed in manis manibus arma dabo* ist *in manis* auffällig; denn dies setzt voraus, dass der Gegner des Ovid auch als bereits gestorben ‖ gedacht wird, was aber nach den folgenden Versen nicht anzunehmen ist.' The truth of this remark was recognised by Guethling and Merkel, and in their texts of 1884 the offence is removed, but at heavy cost. Guethling writes with Schenkl '*inde meis* manibus arma dabo'; Merkel prefers to maltreat the verse in his own fashion, '*innocuis* manibus arma dabit'. I proposed, not to enfeeble and disfigure a good pentameter, but to put it where it could do no mischief; and I transferred the six verses 135–40 to another seat, leaving 141 sq. to follow upon 134. All inconsistency is thus removed: Ovid says in 131–4 that while his life lasts he will hate his adversary, in 141–58 that when dead he will haunt him as a ghost; the death of Ibis is not contemplated till 161; his funeral follows in 163–72, and only in 173 does he reach the world below.

But who will convey an apprehension of such matters as these to the mind of Mr Ehwald or Mr Owen? They find three editors in succession, Guethling, Merkel, and me, arrested by the same invisible obstacle; and our behaviour inspires them, not with curiosity, not with a wish to read the passage instead of skimming it, but with the impatient wonder of Balaam when his ass persisted in seeing the angel of the Lord. If transposition is proposed, they must of course resist it, but they resist in the dark and have nothing more apposite to urge than the automatic objection, always ready to be reached down from the shelf, that the verses to be separated are inseparable. Mr Ehwald, Burs. Jahresb. vol. 109 p. 286, alleges that the removal of 135–40 is discountenanced by 'der Umstand, dass v. 141 sich eng an v. 140 anschliesst'; and Mr Owen, reddens dictata magistro, writes as follows in the Classical Quarterly VIII p. 254: 'These two couplets (139 sq. and 141 sq.) are closely connected in sense, and should not be separated from one another by such transposition as Mr Housman has introduced into the text in the *Corpus Poetarum Latinorum*. In the first couplet Ovid says that death will not end his wrath, but will furnish his spirit with merciless arms against the spirit of his enemy. This idea is repeated in the next couplet with redundancy characteristic of Ovid.' And that is all: 'the next couplet' is the critics' horizon, and if they read as far as the ‖ third couplet they would lose sight and memory of the first. But to this pretence, – that the couplets 139 sq. and 141 sq. are too closely connected in sense to be separated, – I make the following answer. The couplet 141 sq. cannot be more closely connected with anything in the world than with the verses 131–4 to which I have joined it: if that were its place in the MSS, Messrs Ehwald and Owen would assert, and with better cause, that this bond also was indissoluble, and they would appeal, and very plausibly too, to the apt correspondence between *odium* in 134 and *oderit* in 142. And the other couplet, 139 sq., cannot be more closely connected in sense with 141 sq. or with anything else than with the context which I have found for it elsewhere.

That context is one to which I was led by two guides: consideration of the sense, and observation of displacements still to be traced in the MSS. The six verses which I have excised, 135–40, depict Ovid and Ibis as engaged in combat; and the context from which I have excised them, 131–4 and 141–62, exhibits no such picture. But there is a passage which does: 29 sq. *tibi . . . hostis ero*, 39 *positis, quae sumpsimus, armis*, 43 *pax*, 45 *proelia*, 46 *bella*, 49 *ferro*, 50 *hasta*. And in our MSS the same couplet, 'quam dolor hic umquam spatio euanescere possit, | leniat aut odium tempus et hora meum' is found in both of these two contexts: it is both 41 sq. and 133 sq. In HTX it stands before 135 and also before

43; in F before 135 and also before 39; in V only before 43;[1] in GP only before
135. The last is its true seat, for it is needed to complete the sentence begun in
131 'et prius'; in the earlier place it is superfluous and even detrimental. But
the near neighbourhood of the one place is the most appropriate seat in the
poem for the verses which in the other place immediately follow it, 135–40;
and I set them between 44 and 45.

<blockquote>
43   pax erit haec nobis, donec mihi uita manebit,
44   cum pecore infirmo quae solet esse lupis. ‖
135   pugnabunt arcu dum Thraces, Iazyges hasta,
           dum tepidus Ganges, frigidus Hister erit,
        robora dum montes, dum mollia pabula campi,
           dum Tiberis liquidas Tuscus habebit aquas,
        tecum bella geram; nec mors mihi finiet iras,
140   saeua sed in manis manibus arma dabit.
45   prima quidem coepto committam proelia uersu,
46   non soleant quamuis hoc pede bella geri.
</blockquote>

Mr Ehwald, contradicting, as before, in haste and at random, has been so
unlucky as to say, Burs. Jahresb. vol. 109 p. 286, 'v. 135–140 nach v. 49' – he
means 44 – 'zu stellen muss schon die enge Zusammengehörigkeit von 43 f. und
45 widerraten'. There exists no 'enge Zusammengehörigkeit' between 43 sq.
and 45: they were quite happy together, but they are equally happy apart, and
lose nothing by separation. On the contrary, they gain. 'Enge Zusammengehörigkeit' is the name for what my transposition has brought about: the
correspondence of 43 with 139 and of 139 with 46; of donec mihi uita manebit
with nec mors mihi finiet iras and of bella geram with bella geri. But close correspondence is visible to Mr Ehwald where it does not exist and invisible where
it does, because not his opinions only, but even his perceptions, are led in
chains behind the pen of the copyist.

The three distichs whose place in the poem remains to be considered I will take
in their numerical order.

181 sq.

<blockquote>
175   Sisyphus est illic saxum uoluensque petensque
           quique agitur rapidae uinctus ab orbe rotae,
        quaeque gerunt umeris perituras Belides undas,
           exulis Aegypti, turba cruenta, nurus.
        poma pater Pelopis praesentia quaerit et idem
180   semper eget liquidis semper abundat aquis.
</blockquote>

---

[1] So says Merkel; Ellis is silent. Mr Owen's note on 40 contains two mis-statements.

iugeribusque nouem summus qui distat ab imo
uisceraque assiduae debita praebet aui.
hic tibi de Furiis scindet latus una flagello... ‖

In the texts of Burman and Ellis the couplet 181 sq. is enclosed, as above, between full stops. Then it cannot be construed, for it is not a sentence; it is only a conjunction and a relative clause. But Burman and Ellis are used to that: they print as sentences more than forty similar collections of words whose grammatical structure is fragmentary. Sometimes, as here or in 257 sq. 'quique decidit', it is *que* with a *qui*-clause; sometimes *que* with a noun, as 277 sq. 'sollertique uiro'; sometimes *que* with an *ut*-clause, which may contain a verb, as 331–4 'utque Eurydamas est raptus', or may not, as 345 sq. 'utque Dryantiadae'; sometimes an *ut*-clause without *que*, whether containing a verb, as 347 sq. 'ut fuit Oetaeo', or containing none, as 407 sq. 'ut Sinis'; sometimes a *quam*-clause, with a verb, as 489 sq. 'quam periit Cacus', or without, as 491 sq. 'quam qui tulit'.

Other editors join the couplet to the preceding sentence. It then ceases to be ungrammatical and becomes absurd, for it visits Tityus with the punishment of Tantalus: the construction is 'isque, qui iugeribus nouem summus ab imo distat, poma praesentia quaerit'. It is therefore necessary that 181 sq. should be placed before 179, so that the construction may be 'isque, qui...distat, illic est' (175); but whether the right place for the verses is immediately before 179 or immediately after 176 I see no way to determine. I have therefore said in my note '181 sq. ponendi uidentur inter 176 et 179', and have made no change in my text.

Mr Ehwald, p. 287, accepts my transposition; but I expect the advent of a genius who will remove all difficulty by the simple and brilliant device of surrounding 179 sq. with marks of parenthesis.

203 sq.

nec mortis poenas mors altera finiet huius,   195
        horaque erit tantis ultima nulla malis.
inde ego pauca canam, frondes ut siquis ab Ida
        aut summam Libyco de mare carpat aquam.
nam neque, quot flores Sicula nascantur in Hybla
        quotue ferat, dicam, terra Cilissa crocos, ‖   200
nec, cum tristis hiemps Aquilonis inhorruit alis,
        quam multa fiat grandine canus Athos.
nec mala uoce mea poterunt tua cuncta referri,
        ora licet tribuas multiplicata mihi.
tot tibi uae misero uenient talesque ruinae,   205
        ut cogi in lacrimas me quoque posse putem.

In the preceding verses, 173–94, Ovid has described the torments awaiting Ibis after death in the world below. In 195 sq. he adds that these ills will be endless, because there is no second death. And then in 197 he says that he will relate a few of them. He has already related a few of them, and he never relates any more. The ills which he proceeds to relate, and which fill the greater part of the poem, are ills which Ibis is to suffer in this world, not in the next. If the sketch of Ibis' sufferings in the next world had been preceded by a general prophecy of his sufferings in this, it would have been possible, though awkward, to include these in the reference of *inde*. But now it is not even possible, for the only woes in this world yet prophesied to Ibis are his persecution by Ovid's ghost (if Ovid dies before him) and the maltreatment of his dead body; and the catalogue filling 251–638 is no selection from these.

The couplet 203 sq. '*nec* mala...mihi' is quite well suited to its present place, after the couplet 201 sq. '*nec* cum...Athos'; but it is not needed there, for the comparisons may close the period, as in Verg. georg. ii 105–8, Ouid. ex Pont. iv 2 7–10, Mart. xii 57 15–17. If placed before 197, after the couplet 195 sq. '*nec* mortis...malis', it will provide *inde* with the reference it requires: *mala...tua cuncta*. An editor who, like Ellis, divides the poem into paragraphs, should begin a new paragraph not only after 126 and 250 but after 196, and should begin it with 203.

Merkel wrote in 1837 'nescio quid Heinsium commouerit, ut in schedis tentaret: *Iliaca canas frondes* et *Laomedontea frondes ut si quis*'. But with advancing years he grew less obtuse, and by 1884 his eyes had been opened to Heinsius' motive: 'offendor disticho 197–198. *Inde* quod legimus, ‖ referri non potest ad *tanta mala* quae dicuntur v. 196 et enarrantur inde a v. 161: non sunt ea *cuncta*, quae indicantur v. 203, unde partem deprompturus est poeta.'

409 sq.

405   ut pronepos, Saturne, tuus, quem reddere uitam
       urbe Coronides uidit ab ipse sua,
    ut Sinis et Sciron et cum Polypemone natus
       quique homo parte sui parte iuuencus erat,
    quique trabes pressas ab humo mittebat in auras
410   aequoris aspiciens huius et huius aquas,
    quaeque Ceres laeto uidit pereuntia uultu
       corpora Thesea Cercyonea manu.

'May you perish' – *pereas* in 365 is the principal verb of the sentence – 'like Periphetes, like Sinis and Sciron and Procrustes with his father Polypemon and the Minotaur and Pityocamptes and Cercyon.' But Sinis and Pityocamptes were one and the same, Cίνις ὁ καὶ Πιτυοκάμπτης. So we are assured, not only by many authors in many places, but by Ovid himself in a similar catalogue of the male-factors slain by Theseus, met. VII 440–2 'ille Sinis, magnis male uiribus usus, | qui poterat curuare trabes et agebat ab alto | ad terram late sparsuras corpora pinus'. There is indeed one passage where a Christian writer of the 12th century has taken the two names for two persons, Eustath. ad Iliad. p. 158 αἱ ἱστορίαι . . . περιᾴδουσαι καὶ αὐτόν (Cίνιν), καθὰ καὶ τὸν Cκείρωνα καὶ τὸν Πιτυοκάμπτην καὶ τὸν Κάκον καὶ τὸν Λίβυν 'Ανταῖον καὶ τοὺς τοιούτους; but the error was evidently rare, and we have seen that Ovid did not share it.

For this reason I proposed to place 409 sq. after 396:

> ut iacet Aonio luctator ab hospite fusus   393
>   qui, mirum, uictor, cum cecidisset, erat,
> ut quos Antaei fortes pressere lacerti,
>   quosque ferae morti Lemnia claua dedit   396
> quique trabes pressas ab humo mittebat in auras   409
>   aequoris aspiciens huius et huius aquas. ‖   410

The construction will then be 'quos ferae morti dedit Lemnia claua deditque is qui trabes mittebat in auras': may you perish like the victims of Antaeus, of Periphetes, and of Sinis. The next distich, 397 sq., likewise ends with *aquas* (as do 142 and 144 with *tuos*, 610 and 612 with *manus*), and this may have had something to do with the omission and consequent transposition of 409 sq.

119

NOTES ON MARTIAL*

i 68

Quidquid agit Rufus, nihil est nisi Naeuia Rufo.
 si gaudet, si flet, si tacet, hanc loquitur.
 cenat, propinat, poscit, negat, innuit: una est
 Naeuia; si non sit Naeuia, mutus erit.
5 scriberet hesterna patri cum luce salutem,
 'Naeuia lux', inquit, 'Naeuia lumen, haue.'
 haec legit et ridet demisso Naeuia uoltu.
 Naeuia non una est: quid, uir inepte, furis?

The old interpretations of the last line are fairly represented by Nisard's version, 'Névia n'est pas à toi seul; pourquoi donc, sot amant, une passion si folle?' They suppose that *una* can mean 'uno contenta', and so put themselves out of court. Friedlaender explains thus: 'Der Sinn scheint zu sein: Naeuia liest das Epigramm und lacht, aber Rufus ist thöricht sich zu ereifern, wenn er dies hört. [He is indeed, incredibly so.] Es giebt ja mehr als eine Naeuia, ich kann also auch eine andere meinen. [No, Martial cannot mean any other Naeuia than the one whom Rufus loves.] Zugleich giebt M. wol zu verstehen: Jedes andere Mädchen kann ihm die Stelle des ihn verschmähenden ersetzen.' Zugleich! Mr G. Friedrich may well say in *Rhein. Mus.* 1907 p. 367 'Friedländer hat das Epigramm nicht verstanden'; but he himself proceeds to weave out of nothing a fabric which is not worth the trouble of tearing to pieces: suffice it to say that he forgets to give any interpretation whatsoever of the words *Naeuia non una est*.

All commentators assume that the vocative *uir inepte* is addressed to Rufus. Most of them simply treat *uir* as if it were *homo*; a smaller number see that it ought to mean *marite*, but of these some say that for present purposes it means *adulter*, while others commit the crowning absurdity of supposing that Rufus and Naeuia were man and wife. *uir* means, quite straightforwardly, 'husband'; any husband whose wife's name happens to be Naeuia. The contents of the epigram are the following. Rufus is distraught with love of Naeuia; so distraught that yesterday he began a letter to his father with 'Naeuia darling'. Naeuia peruses this anecdote, so flattering to the vanity of her sex, with a

* [[CQ 13 (1919), 68–80]]

demure smirk of self-complacency. At this point readers who are married to ladies of the name of Naeuia begin to fume and chafe, because it is intolerable that their wives should be represented as taking ‖ pleasure in a lover's passion. 'Be calm' says Martial; 'there is more than one Naeuia in the world: why assume that the beloved of Rufus is your wife?'

I subjoin two illustrative parallels. From book III: 8 'Thaida Quintus amat. quam Thaida? Thaida luscam. | unum oculum Thais non habet, ille duos', 11 'si tua nec Thais nec lusca est, Quinte, puella, | cur in te factum distichon esse putas?...tu tamen es Quintus. mutemus nomen amantis: | si non uult Quintus, Thaida Sextus amet.' From book IX: 95 'Alphius ante fuit, coepit nunc Olphius esse, | uxorem postquam duxit, Athenagoras', 95B 'nomen Athenagorae credis, Callistrate, uerum. | si scio, dispeream, qui sit Athenagoras. | sed puta me uerum, Callistrate, dicere nomen: | non ego sed uester peccat Athenagoras.'

III 20 1–5

> dic, Musa, quid agat Canius meus Rufus.
> utrumne chartis tradit ille uicturis
> legenda temporum acta Claudianorum,
> an quae Neroni falsus adstruit scriptor
> an aemulatur improbi iocos Phaedri?   5

The difficulty of explaining this last verse has been somewhat exaggerated. It is true that both *improbus* and *iocus* have associations (see for instance III 86 4 'non sunt haec mimis *improbiora*' and I 35 13 sq. 'parcas lusibus et *iocis* rogamus | nec castrare uelis meos libellos') which, when the two words are thus brought together, suggest the notion of lascivious poetry; and true that among the extant fables of Phaedrus there is not one lascivious piece, and many moral. But Phaedrus himself describes his fables as *ioci*, I *prol.* 7 'fictis *iocari* nos meminerit fabulis', IV 7 1 sq. 'tu qui, nasute, scripta destringis mea | et hoc *iocorum* legere fastidis genus'; and *improbus*, which is capable of meaning 'disrespectful', as in Hor. *epist.* I 7 63 and elsewhere, may allude to those hits at the high and mighty which are supposed to have provoked the displeasure of Seianus.

iocos however is not the MS text, but *locos* γ, *locus* β; and these lections are just as near to *logos*, which is less misleading and leaves *improbi* freer to mean what it ought. *logi* are fables: Ar. *pac.* 129 ἐν τοῖσιν Αἰσώπου λόγοις, Quint. *inst.* V 11 20 'αἶνον Graeci uocant et Αἰσωπείους, ut dixi, λόγους et Λιβυκούς', Sen. *dial.* XI 8 3 'fabellas quoque et Aesopeos *logos* (*longos* MSS)'. The MSS of Plautus give *locos* for *logos* at *Men.* 779 and *Stich.* 221 (some of them at 383 and 393), and perhaps the same error occurs in Phaedrus himself, III *prol.* 34–7:

> seruitus obnoxia,
> quia quae uolebat non audebat dicere,
> affectus proprios in fabellas transtulit
> calumniamque fictis elusit *locis*. ||

Editors print *iocis*, which gets support from the *iocari* of the similar verse
I *prol.* 7 quoted above; but its *fictis...fabulis* gives equal support to '*fictis*
elusit *logis*'.

The *locus* of β perhaps points to *logus*, for it is possible that Martial gave the
Greek word its Greek inflexion, as he did, if we may trust his MSS, in the
genitive *Praxitelus* IV 39 3. Neue's examples of the acc. plur. -*us* for -ους in
vol. I p. 209 ed. 3 may be augmented from Lucian Mueller *Lucil.* p. 256; and
the palimpsest of Fronto p. 148* Nab. ⟦140 Van Den Hout⟧ has 'ceratinas et
soritas et *pseudomenus*'.

V 16 5–8

> nam, si falciferi defendere templa Tonantis
> sollicitisque uelim uendere uerba reis,
> plurimus Hispanas mittet mihi nauta metretas
> et fiet uario sordidus aere sinus.

falciferi templa Tonantis must mean, as Gronouius says, the aerarium in the
temple of Saturn. And why should it not? why does Haupt say in *opusc.* III
p. 500 'adparet ineptissimum esse *tonantis*', and why do Friedlaender and Duff
affix the obelus? Saturn, it is very true, was not the Thunderer, but neither was
Propertius Callimachus nor Domitian Nero; yet Juvenal calls Domitian *caluus
Nero* and Propertius calls himself *Romanus Callimachus*. The Latin poets, with
Hom. *Il.* IX 457 Ζεύς...καταχθόνιος to lend them countenance, will often take
the name of Jove in vain and attach to it an epithet explaining what person they
really mean: Verg. *Aen.* IV 638 (Ouid. *fast.* V 448, Sil. I 386) *Ioui Stygio* (Diti),[1]
Sen. *H. f.* 47 *inferni Iouis*, 608 *diro ... Ioui, H.O.* 1705 (Sil. VIII 116, Stat. *Theb.*
II 49) *nigri...Iouis*, Val. Fl. I 730 (Sil. II 674) *Tartareo...Ioui*, III 384 sq.
tremendi...Iouis, Stat. *Theb.* I 615 sq. *profundo...Ioui*, Auson. 250 8 *Iouis
Elysii*; Stat. *Ach.* I 48 sq. *secundi Iouis* (Neptuni), Claud. XVII 282 *Iouis aequorei*,
Apoll. Sid. *carm.* 22 158 *tridentiferi Iouis*; Stat. *silu.* III 4 18 *Iuppiter Ausonius*
(Domitianus), Mart. XIV 1 2 *nostrum...Iouem. Tonans*, being a synonym,
suffers the same usage: Stat. *Theb.* XI 209 *inferno...Tonanti* (Diti), Mart.
IX 39 1 *Palatino...Tonanti* (Domitiano). In Sen. *Med.* 59 *sceptriferis...
Tonantibus* (Ioui et Iunoni) the word signifies only 'sovereign of heaven';
and by *falciferi Tonantis* Martial means no more than what he says in XII 61 1
'antiqui rex magne poli mundique prioris'.

---

* ⟦146: so corrected by Housman in *CQ* 24 (1930), 12 (this edition p. 1165)⟧
[1] So Proserpine is called *Iuno Stygia, Auerna, Aetnaea, inferna, infera, profunda*.

This calls to my mind a misinterpreted passage of Statius, *silu.* 1 6 39–42.

> i nunc saecula compara, Vetustas,
> antiqui Iouis aureumque tempus:
> non sic libera uina tunc fluebant
> nec tardum seges occupabat annum.

'*antiqui Iouis* das erste, silberne Zeitalter Iuppiters (Ou. *met.* 1 113 ff.)' says ||
Mr Vollmer. It was not in the silver age that wine flowed all abroad: Jove's
accession put a stop to that, 'et passim riuis currentia uina repressit'. *antiquus
Iuppiter*, like *falcifer Tonans*, is Saturn, 'aureus...Saturnus' Verg. *georg.* II 538.
So already F. Morellus.

v 66

> saepe salutatus numquam prior ipse salutas.
> sic eris aeternum, Pontiliane, uale.

In the days before Schneidewin editors used to read *erit* with inferior MSS; the
present text is expounded thus: 'The poet says that...he will have no more to
do with him: he shall be to the poet *aeternum uale*, a goodbye for ever' (Paley
and Stone, 1868). Such words have no meaning. By saying goodbye to a person
you do not transform him into a goodbye. Munro punctuated 'sic eris aeternum, Pontiliane? uale'; but nobody would use *aeternum* here instead of *semper*,
and Verg. *Aen.* XI 97 sq. 'salue aeternum mihi...aeternumque uale' dis-
countenances or even forbids this divorce of the verb and adverb. I should
write therefore
> sic eris? aeternum, Pontiliane, uale.

'Is that how you mean to behave? then farewell for ever (you are to me as dead).'
IX 7 ⟦6⟧ 4 'non uis, Afer, hauere: uale'. *sic*, as in Munro's punctuation, stands
for *talis*: Ter. *Phorm.* 527 'sic sum; si placeo, utere', Cic. *pro. Q. Rosc.* 29 'sic
est uulgus', Tib. 1 10 43 'sic ego sim', Hom. *Il.* XI 762 ὣς ἔον.

VI 14

> uersus scribere posse te disertos
> adfirmas, Laberi: quid ergo non uis?
> uersus scribere qui potest disertos,
> non scribat, Laberi: uirum putabo.

For *non scribat* Schneidewin in his second edition wrote *conscribat*; Friedlaender Gilbert and Lindsay follow him, and Duff marks *non scribat* as corrupt.
conscribat I suppose will mean something like 'make a book of them'; but
nothing of this sort will accord with *uirum putabo*. The force of *uirum* may be
seen from II 69 'inuitum cenare foris te, Classice, dicis:...en rogat ad cenam

Melior te, Classice, rectam. | grandia uerba ubi sunt? si *uir* es, ecce nega.' If a person can write accomplished verse, he gives no proof of stoutness or manfulness by indulging his faculty: to refrain from indulging it, *non scribere*, may at any rate be held to argue strength of will and contempt of fame. But I imagine that Schneidewin's difficulty was this: *non scribat* evidently must suggest the pursuit of a course which Laberius did not pursue, and yet 'quid ergo non uis?' implies that 'non scribere uersus disertos' was the course which he did pursue. Yes, but there are two ways of not writing accomplished verse. One is to write nothing, *non scribere*; and || if the epigram ended with line 2 we should perhaps infer that this was what Laberius did. Line 4 lets us know that it was not: scribebat ille quidem uersus, sed non disertos.

The phrase *uirum putabo* recurs in a passage of Cicero, *ad Q. frat.* II 9 (= 10 = 11) ⟦II 10⟧ 3, which does not reflect much credit on its critics, whether radical or conservative.

> Lucreti poemata, ut scribis, ita sunt, multis luminibus ingenii, multae tamen artis. sed, cum ueneris. uirum te putabo, si Sallusti Empedoclea legeris, hominem non putabo.

After suffering various changes in the past from Ernesti, Orelli, Lachmann, Bergk, Munro, and others, it is now printed as above by Messrs Tyrrell and Purser and the last editor Mr Sjoegren; and they are quite satisfied with it and with themselves. 'Lucretius' books of poetry, as you say in your letter, have many scintillations of genius, yet much art as well': *tamen* is explained, after Munro in the introduction to his commentary on Lucretius, as implying that there is almost an incongruity between genius (like that of Ennius) and art (like that of Catullus and Caluus), and that Lucretius combined two virtues which might be thought irreconcilable. 'But more on that matter when you are here':[1] *cum ueneris* has this sense in *ad Att.* II 3 1 'quid sit sciemus, cum ueneris' and elsewhere, and the principal verb is similarly omitted ibid. XII 21 2 'sed coram', 'but more of this when we meet'.

Very well: and now what of the last sentence? 'I shall think you a stout-hearted man if you get through Sallust's Empedoclea, I shall not think you a human being.' That the same person under the same conditions should be *uir* and should not be *homo* is a contradiction in terms. If one is not a human being, one cannot be a stout-hearted man nor a man of any sort; one is either above or below humanity, a god or a beast; and *uir* is not Latin for a stout-hearted god nor for a stout-hearted beast. Applied to any creature not human, it means

---

[1] 'Diese Ansicht hat zuerst F. Marx (*Berl. phil. Woch.* 1891 Sp. 834) vorgebracht' says Schanz *Gesch. d. röm. Litt.* I ii p. 43 ed. 3. It was put forward by Tyrrell in 1886. There is another false attribution in the next epistle, II 10 1, where the emendation *pipulo* for *populi*, ascribed by Mr Sjoegren in his edition to Housmanius and in his *commentationes Tullianae* p. 158 to Housmannus, is due to neither of those critics, but again to Tyrrell.

either a male or a husband; and here it can mean neither. Yet Vahlen *opusc.* I p. 154, far from perceiving the discrepancy, maintains in opposition to Bergk that *uirum te putabo* and *hominem non putabo* are inseparably associated; and to defend this sentence, where the same person is *uir* and yet not *homo*, he quotes, if you will believe me, sentences where the same person is both *homo* and *uir*: Cic. *ad fam.* V 17 3 'ut et *hominem* te et *uirum* esse meminisses, id est, communem incertumque casum...sapienter ferres et dolori fortiter ac fortunae resisteres', 'in other words, that you should bear philosophically the changes and chances which are our common portion (as *homo*), and show a bold face to pain and misfortune (as *uir*)'; *Tusc.* II 53 'Marius et tulit dolorem, ut *uir*, et, ut *homo*, maiorem ferre sine causa necessaria ‖ noluit'; Sen. *dial.* XI 17 2 'nam et non sentire mala sua non est *hominis*, et non ferre non est *uiri*', – you are both *homo* and *uir*, and you therefore both feel and endure. The effect of these passages is to enhance by contrast the strangeness of what we find in the letter to Quintus. And when Vahlen has concluded his very untoward citations and comes to the definite explanation of the words before us, he is obliged to invent for *homo* a sense which belongs to it neither in the citations nor anywhere else: he says it means a man of taste, possessing 'pulchri sensum et decori'. Another and very different defence of the text is essayed by Tyrrell and Purser, who rely chiefly upon elegant mistranslation. *hominem esse* they interpret 'to be subject to the ordinary weaknesses of humanity': correct 'ordinary' to 'universal' and the attempt collapses.

So long as these words are left in their present condition, to say with Mr Sjoegren that the passage is 'locus iniuria temptatus' is to holloa before you are out of the wood. The correction of this sentence may, for aught we know, involve some change in the preceding sentences, like the conjectures of Bergk and Munro. I think it probable however that the true correction is one which does not. A second protasis may have fallen out thus: 'uirum te putabo, ⟨si...⟩; si Sallusti Empedoclea legeris, hominem non putabo', 'if you can read through..., you are a man indeed; if you can read through Sallust's Empedoclea, you are more or less than human.'

VI 29 7 sq.

inmodicis breuis est aetas et rara senectus.
quidquid ames, cupias non placuisse nimis.

ames is read by Scriuerius and some other of the older editors, but *amas* by Schneidewin and all the moderns except Mr Duff. According to Mr Lindsay's apparatus criticus *ames* is the reading of β and *amas* of γ; but his collations in *Ancient editions of Martial* p. 82 show that E, the best MS of the latter family, gives *ames* in agreement with the former. *ames* therefore has much the better

authority to uphold it; and it is also upheld by something much better than any
authority, the sense. This poem is addressed to no individual, and there is
nobody for the 2nd pers. indic. to refer to. The words must mean 'whatever
one loves', and the subjunctive is then the proper mood, as in Ouid. *art.* I 741
'non tutum est, *quod ames*, laudare sodali', *her.* XX 31 sq. 'sit fraus huic facto
nomen dicarque dolosus, | si tamen est, *quod ames*, uelle tenere dolus', Lucr.
IV 1061 sq. 'nam, si abest *quod ames*, praesto simulacra tamen sunt | illius',
Cic. *de sen.* 27 'quod est, eo decet uti et, *quidquid agas*, agere pro uiribus'.

In this passage of Cicero Dr Reid prints *agis* for *agas* and has the following
note:

> '*quidquid agis*: all MSS and editions hitherto have *agas*, which I have un-
> hesitatingly altered because (1) the subjunctive does not occur in Cicero after
> *quisquis*, || *quicumque, ubi* and the like unless in *oratio obliqua* or by the attrac-
> tion of the indicative into the mood of a neighbouring subjunctive, (2) *agas*
> would be doubly peculiar after *quod est*. See a valuable note by Kühner on
> *Tusc.* I 110, whose conclusions are entirely confirmed by my own reading.
> Thus in *de or.* III 201 the clause *quibuscumque uerbis uti uelis* is parallel with
> and influenced by the preceding conditional clause *si uerba mutaris*.'

Cicero employs the subjunctive where the sense requires that mood, *quisquis* or
no *quisquis*; and the sense requires it here. Cato's meaning is not 'quidquid tu,
Scipio, agis' but 'quidquid agimus', 'whatever one does'. This construction,
whose occurrence in Cicero Dr Reid denies, recurs at *de off.* III 57 'neque enim
id est celare, *quidquid reticeas*, sed cum, quod tu scias, id ignorare emolumenti
tui causa uelis eos quorum intersit id scire', and also, though the eye alone
cannot there detect it, at *de amic.* 22 'amicitia res plurimas continet; *quoquo* te
uerteris, praesto est'. Even in the passage cited by Dr Reid, *de or.* III 200 'inter
conformationem uerborum et sententiarum hoc interest, quod uerborum
tollitur, si uerba mutaris, sententiarum permanet, *quibuscumque* uerbis uti *uelis*',
the mood is due to no external influence but to inherent propriety, and *uelis*
would remain *uelis* if there were nothing but indicatives in the neighbourhood.
As for *agas* after *quod est*, far from being doubly peculiar, it is both logical and
regular, like Lucr. II 850 'quoad *licet* ac *possis* reperire' or Ouid. *amor.* III
14 7 sq. 'quis furor est, quae nocte *latent*, in luce fateri | et, quae clam *facias*,
facta referre palam?'

VIII 56 [[55]] 17–20

excidit attonito pinguis Galatea poetae
    Thestylis et rubras messibus usta genas:
protinus Italiam concepit et ARMA VIRVMQVE
    qui modo uix culicem fleuerat ore rudi.

Schneidewin and all his successors print ITALIAM or indicate by other means that they regard this word, like ARMA VIRVMQVE, as a quotation. But whence is it quoted? not surely from *Aen.* I 2. *Italiam* in that line is not an object of *cano* but merely one of a dozen words in a relative clause; it signifies no conception or design of Virgil's; and in any case it would be perverse to cite the opening of the second line before the famous and symbolic opening of the whole epic.

Schrevel and other of the earlier editors give the verse as I do. *Italiam* means the theme of Italy. Whether this also refers to the *Aeneid*, especially book VII and verses 641–4 'pandite nunc Helicona, deae, cantusque mouete, | qui bello exciti reges, quae quemque secutae | complerint campos acies, quibus Itala iam tum | floruerit terra alma uiris, quibus arserit armis', or whether to the *georgics* and especially to the laudes Italiae in III 136–76, it is possible to doubt. ||

IX 20 5 sq.

hic steterat ueneranda domus quae praestitit orbi
　　quod Rhodos astrifero quod pia Creta polo.

The birthplace of Domitian is equalled to Crete, the birthplace of Jove, and to Rhodes, the birthplace of whom? Of Neptune, say the commentators; for Posidon, though not indeed born in Rhodes, was reared there by the Telchines, Diod. Sic. v 55 I. Neptune however has no particular connexion with *astrifer polus*, and the god meant is Sol, who according to one story was born in his own chosen island. Cic. *n. d.* III 54 'Soles ipsi quam multi a theologis proferuntur! unus eorum Ioue natus, nepos Aetheris, alter Hyperione, tertius Vulcano, Nili filio, cuius urbem Aegyptii uolunt esse eam quae Heliopolis appellatur, quartus is quem heroicis temporibus Acantho Rhodi peperisse dicitur', Ampel. 9 3, Arnob. *nat.* IV 14, schol. Bern. ad Luc. VIII 248.

Tiberius is likened to the Sun by Manilius IV 765 sq. and by Antiphilus *anth. Pal.* IX 178; and the shepherd in buc. Einsidl. I 27 is uncertain, as Martial seems to be, whether his emperor more resembles the supreme deity or the chief light in the firmament: 'seu caeli mens illa fuit seu Solis imago'.

IX 99

Marcus amat nostras Antonius, Attice, musas,
　　charta salutatrix si modo uera refert,
Marcus, Palladiae non infitianda Tolosae
　　gloria, quem genuit pacis alumna quies.
tu, qui longa potes dispendia ferre uiarum,　　　　5
　　i, liber, absentis pignus amicitiae.

uilis eras, fateor, si te nunc mitteret emptor;
grande tui pretium muneris auctor erit.
multum, crede mihi, refert a fonte bibatur
10   quae fluit an pigro quae stupet unda lacu.

4. The singularly unintelligent conjecture *quam* for *quem*, proposed long ago
by Scriuerius, has been repeated by Friedlaender and adopted by Gilbert. 'Das
überlieferte *quem* ist unhaltbar' says Friedlaender, 'denn der Friede könnte nur
den Ruhm des Antonius...erzeugen, aber nicht ihn selbst.' *gloria* does not
mean 'der Ruhm des Antonius', and would make nonsense if it did: it means
Antonius himself, who was the glory of Toulouse. The conjecture therefore
does not alter the sense, it only corrupts the Latin. *quam* is not grammatical: no
more grammatical than *quae* would be in IV 55 1–3 'Luci, *gloria* temporum
tuorum, | *qui* Caium ueterem Tagumque nostrum | Arpis cedere non sinis
disertis'; no more grammatical than the *deuoraturam* which Geppert fancied he
had found in the palimpsest at Plaut. *rud.* 543 sq. 'iam postulabas te, impurata
belua, | totam Siciliam *deuoraturum* insulam'. 'Wer von Grammatik und
Sprachgebrauch nur eine mäszige Kenntniss hat, ‖ sieht auf den ersten Blick,
dass...*deuoraturam*, wenn es auch im Palimpsest stünde, nichts als ein zu-
fälliger Schreibfehler sein würde' said Ritschl *opusc.* II p. 226; and so say I of
quam. That Antonius should be called the child of tranquillity is quite in keeping
with x 23 'iam numerat *placido felix* Antonius *aeuo* | quindecies actas Primus
olympiadas, | praeteritosque dies et *tutos* (βγ, *totos* α) respicit *annos*...nulla
recordanti lux est ingrata grauisque; | nulla fuit, cuius non meminisse uelit.'
It is clear from the whole tenour of the three or four poems in which Martial
celebrates him that this Antonius Primus of Tolosa is wrongly identified by
Friedlaender and Klebs *prosop. imp. Rom.* I p. 103 and Pauly-Wissowa *Real-
encycl.* I pp. 2635–7 with his namesake and townsman the soldier and politician,
whose turbulent character and eventful career we know from the *histories* of
Tacitus, and whose praenomen we do not know to have been Marcus.

8. The gross blunder committed by the Delphin editor, and apparently not
by him alone, of mistaking *tui* for an adjective in agreement with *muneris*, is
avoided by Nisard and Stephenson, who translate 'ce qui te donne du prix,
c'est que tu es un présent de l'auteur', 'as a present from the author, your
value will be indefinitely enhanced'. These versions give the substance of the
thought, but I cannot help wondering if the translators have avoided another
error, committed by the *thes. ling. Lat.* II p. 1211 14. There this verse is cited
among passages in which *auctor* is 'auctor carminis, eum significans qui fecit'.
Martial was indeed the author of the book which he sent to Antonius, but no
allusion to that fact is contained in the word *auctor*. If the 'emptor' imagined in
the verse above had been the sender, he would have been *muneris auctor*

instead of Martial, though Martial would still have been author of the book. *muneris auctor* is a regular phrase, illustrated in the *thesaurus* p. 1202 64–9 and meaning simply 'is qui dat': see for instance Mart. VIII 51 ⟦50⟧ 22 '*auctor* enim tanti *muneris* (phialae) ille mihi', and add V 52 7 sq. 'quamuis ingentia, Postume, dona | *auctoris* pereunt garrulitate sui', IX 49 6 '(toga) *auctoris* nomine digna sui'. The verse means only 'the giver will make you precious', and the closest parallel is Ouid. *her.* XVII 71 sq. 'acceptissima semper | *munera* sunt, *auctor* quae *pretiosa* facit', where Heinsius says 'unice haec illustrat epigr. 99 lib. IX apud Martialem'.

X 24

natales mihi Martiae kalendae,
lux formosior omnibus kalendis,
qua mittunt mihi munus et puellae,
quinquagensima liba septimamque
uestris addimus hanc focis acerram.　　　　　　　　　　5
his uos, si tamen expedit roganti,
annos addite bis, precor, nouenos,
ut nondum nimia piger senecta ||
sed uitae tribus areis peractis
lucos Elysiae petam puellae.　　　　　　　　　　　　　10
post hoc Nestora nec diem rogabo.

It is Martial's 57th birthday, and his prayer is for 18 years more of life, that so he may die at 75, not in extreme old age but 'uitae tribus areis peractis'. *tribus areis* is explained as meaning *tribus spatiis*, though *area* has not that sense elsewhere; and the three courses run are said to be *pueritia, iuuentus, senectus*. But Martial's own words, 'nondum nimia piger senecta', show that *senectus* is not to be *peracta*. *area* therefore must somehow mean a period of 25 years; and neither Scriuerius here nor Scaliger at Manil. III 560 succeeds in showing how it can.

But though *areis* stands in the text of all modern editions it is only a conjectural alteration of *aureis*. This word itself is more capable of the required meaning, since the aureus was reckoned equivalent to 25 denarii. But it is not apparent why the denarius rather than the sestertius or the as should be taken to symbolise a year, and *peractis* is not suitable to this noun.

Now 75 is $\frac{3}{4}$ of 100, and a century was in popular opinion the utmost span of human life: Varr. *l. L.* VI 11 'saeclum spatium annorum centum uocarunt, dictum a sene, quod longissimum spatium senescendorum hominum id putarunt', Seru. *Aen.* VI 325 'centum autem annos ideo dicit quia hi sunt legitimi uitae humanae'. The sense therefore will be satisfied if the place of *aureis* is taken by a word which can mean a quarter. And although Mr Lindsay's apparatus criticus says only '*areis* Ald.: *aureis* codd.', his collations (*Anc. ed. of*

Mart. p. 101) disclose the very important fact that L has *auribus*. L is the best
MS of the better family, and the only MS of that family which has not been
invaded by lections derived from the other; and its authority is therefore about
equal to that of all the remaining MSS put together. This variant leads me to the
conjecture 'uitae tribus *arcubus* peractis'. The Latin *arcus* means the same as the
English *arc*, a portion of the circumference of a circle, in Germ. *phaen.* 572
'orbis perfecti diuisus tollitur *arcus*', in Manil. III 212 sq. 'cursibus aeternis
mundum per signa uolantem | ut totum lustret curuatis *arcubus* orbem', and in
II 853, to be cited anon. In Germanicus the portion signified is half, in Manil.
III 213 the size of the arc cannot be determined from the context, but in II 853
it is a quarter. Astrologers divide the circle of the zodiac, by means of the four
κέντρα or *cardines* at which the horizon and meridian intersect it, into four arcs
or τεταρτημόρια, and to these they assign the governance of four stages of
human life. Manilius describes them thus, II 844–55, 'quidquid ab exortu
summum curuatur in orbem | aetatis primae nascentisque adserit annos. | quod
summo premitur deuexum culmine mundi | donec ad occasus ueniat, puerilibus
annis | succedit teneramque regit sub sede iuuentam. | quae pars occasus aufert
imumque sub orbem | descendit, regit haec maturae tempora uitae | perpetua
serie uarioque exercita cursu. | at, qua perficitur cursus redeunte sibimet, | tarda
supinatum lassatis uiribus || *arcum* | ascendens, seros demum complectitur
annos | labentemque diem uitae tremulamque senectam.' In Paul. Alex. fol. D 3
ed. 1586 [[p. 20 Boer]] the first arc corresponds to τὴν πρώτην ἡλικίαν, λέγω δὲ
τὴν νεότητα, the second to τὴν μετὰ τὴν νεότητα ἡλικίαν, ἥτις ἐστὶ μέση, the
third to τὴν τοῦ γήρως ἡλικίαν, and the fourth to τὴν πρεσβυτικὴν ἡλικίαν ἕως
τῆς τοῦ θανάτου τελευτῆς; and this appears to be the distribution which Martial
has in view. There are other passages of Latin poetry which possibly or probably refer to this astrological scheme of κέντρα and τεταρτημόρια: Luc. VII
380 sq. 'ultima fata | deprecor ac turpes extremi *cardinis* annos', Sen. *Tro.* 52
'mortalis aeui *cardinem* extremum premens'.

XII 59

tantum dat tibi Roma basiorum
post annos modo quindecim reuerso
quantum Lesbia non dedit Catullo.
te uicinia tota, te pilosus
5　　hircoso premit osculo colonus,
hinc instat tibi textor, inde fullo,
hinc sutor modo pelle basiata,
hinc menti dominus periculosi,

hinc $\begin{cases} \text{dexiocholus et } \beta \\ \text{dexiocolus } \gamma \end{cases}$ inde lippus

fellatorque recensque cunnilingus.   10
iam tanti tibi non fuit redire.

Although some MSS of the family γ offer *desiocolus* and *desioculus*, whence the impossible word *defioculus* was coined and issued in the old editions, it is plain from a comparison of the two stocks that *dexioc(h)olus* was in the archetype. But *dexiocholus* (if ever there was such a word) is no better sense than metre. Neither leg, so far as I have noticed, is much used in kissing; and it therefore does not appear how lameness can lend horror to a kiss, nor what difference it makes if the lame leg happens to be the right one. The conjectural substitutes for the letters between *hinc* and *inde* are either violent or absurd: *defioculusque et, caecis oculis et* (with *lippis*), *luscusque oculis et, factus modo luscus, de fornice luscus, et dexiocholus, rex unoculus uel.*[1] If anyone proposed *hinc cui dest oculus, set inde lippus*, I should think it less open to objection, but no truer than the rest; for they all leave the poem labouring under a defect which they do not even aim at repairing. ||

There are in Martial many epigrams addressed to persons whom he does not call by name. Some of these, II 85 and IV 19 and many in books XIII and XIV, are *xenia* or *apophoreta*: the person is merely the recipient of a gift, and his name and address were on the parcel. In one poem, V 60, the name is designedly withheld. There remains a large class, comprising I 66, II 39, 61, 76, III 23, 49, IV 41, 47, 76, 88, VI 64, VII 25, 75, VIII 14, 34, 47, 74, X 45, 59, 100, XI 22, 44, XII 26 〚29〛, 37, 47 〚46〛, 48, 50, 86, in which the persons addressed are chosen as types or invented for the occasion. From that class this epigram is excluded, if by nothing else, by the touch of personal detail in u. 2, 'post annos modo quindecim reuerso': it is addressed at a particular time to a living and breathing acquaintance of Martial's, and in view of Martial's practice we expect to have his name. And we have it: *Dexi*. The gens Dexia survives in several inscriptions collected by W. Schulze *Gesch. lat. Eigennamen* p. 272: *C.I.L.* VI 16824 *L. Dexio Ilo*, VIII 2858–60 *Q. Dexius Licinianus*, IX 6078 73 *C. Dexi Staberiani*, X 411 *C. Dexius*, 534 *Dexio Decumino*, XI 949 *Dexsia*, 4206 sq. *C. Dexius*: add Cic. *ad fam.* VII 23 4 'est enim profectus in Hispaniam *Dexius*'. The name of the person addressed is most commonly put near the beginning of an epigram, but it may be deferred till the last line, as at III 82 33, or the last but one,

---

[1] This last conjecture is Mr Birt's, and very like him. In the same place, *Rhein. Mus.* 1916 pp. 274–6, he corrupts the *menti* of u. 8 into *uenti*, of all things in the world, because *menti periculosi* 'ist offenbar Unsinn'. I therefore cite Plin. *n. h.* XXVI 2 'grauissimum ex his (nouis faciei morbis) lichenas appellauere Graeco nomine, Latine, quoniam a *mento* fere oriebatur, . . .*mentagram*', 3 'non fuerat haec lues apud maiores patresque nostros, et primum Ti. Claudi Caesaris principatu medio inrepsit in Italiam quodam Perusino equite Romano quaestorio scriba, cum in Asia adparuisset, inde *contagionem* eius importante. nec sensere id malum feminae aut seruitia plebesque humilis aut media, sed proceres *ueloci transitu osculi* maxime.'

as at VIII 61 8, or the last but two, as here and at X 73 8, or may stand in the middle, as at VIII 38 8.

Before proceeding further we must ask whether *et* has been wrongly added in β or wrongly subtracted in γ. The parallel of u. 6 is against the conjunction, and no motive for its omission is apparent, whereas it may have been inserted by some one who was at least metrist enough to know that the line ought to have eleven syllables. It seems therefore that criticism has now to deal only with the letters *oc(h)olus*.

De Rooy and Munro and Gilbert have all wished to introduce the word *luscus*, and naturally. Martial couples it with *lippus* in VI 78 1 sq. 'lumine uno | *luscus* Phryx erat alteroque *lippus*', VIII 9 1 sq. 'soluere dodrantem nuper tibi, Quinte, uolebat | *lippus* Hylas, *luscus* uult dare dimidium', 59 1–6 'cuius | *lippa* sub adtrita fronte lacuna patet...oculo *luscus* utroque uidet', and its appropriateness to this epigram is well shown by II 33 3 'cur non *basio* te, Philaeni? *lusca* es.' *lus* then is probably the surviving half of *lus-cus*, and it only remains to find a pyrrhic which will complete the verse. The sense does not require, and hardly even admits, any addition, so I should expect here the cognomen of Dexius, for Martial often calls his friends by two of their names: I 107 *Luci*... *Iuli*, IV 71 *Safroni Rufe*, VI 85 *Rufe Camoni*, VII 41 *Semproni Tucca*, 47 *Licini*... *Sura*, 68 *Instanti Rufe*, X 33 *Munati Galle*, 44 *Quinte*...*Ouidi*, XI 52 *Iuli Cerialis*, XII 4 ⟦3⟧ *Prisce Terenti*. The nearest to the letters will be the rare cognomen *Colo*: *C.I.L.* VI 32764 *L. Cassio Coloni*, VIII 15472 *Q. Numisius C. f. Arn. Colo Heluacianus*, X 3395 *Camurius Colo, Antonius Colo*.

hinc, Dexi Co*lo*, lus*cus*, inde lippus. ‖

A slip from *ol* to *ol* and from *us* to *us* reduces *dexicololuscus* to *dexicolus*, which is, as it happens, the original reading of E. The additional *o* in *dexiocolus* may be that *o* which is often written over a vocative to indicate the case, and which to most readers would be a welcome signpost when the vocative was so unfamiliar as *dexi colo*.

Although this conjecture accounts for every letter in the corrupt text of the MSS, it is not for that reason true, and the truth may be something which is further away from the letters and will not account for them. *Dexi* is the MS reading and *luscus* a probable change, but *Colo*, having nothing better than palaeography to rest on, is quite uncertain, and indeed there is no actual proof that its first syllable is short.

XII 95 1–4

Musseti pathicissimos libellos,
qui certant Sybariticis libellis,
et tinctas sale pruriente chartas,
Instanti, lege, Rufe.

Musseti codd., *Musaei* edd. And who is this Musaeus? 'Ein sonst unbekannter Autor' says Friedlaender. But, if you know nothing else about him, how do you know his name? who told you it was Musaeus and not, as the MSS say, Mussetius? The latter exists in *C.I.L.* XIV 2982 *Musseti*, and with variations of spelling in XI 5702 and 5718 *L. Musetio*, VIII 6236 *Musetia*, ib. *suppl.* 19168 *Musaetiae*. Martial's Mussetius has as much right to his place in the text, and to a mention in lexicons and histories of literature, as Ovid's Turranius or half-a-dozen other poets out of *ex Pont.* IV 16. But instead of him we find in De Vit's *onomasticon* 'Musaeus, poeta, auctor carminum nefandi argumenti, teste Martial. 12, 95', and in Teuffel's *Gesch. d. röm. Lit.* §329 4 'Mart. 12, 95 *Musaei pathicissimos libellos* (griechisch?)'.

The reading of L is *Musetis*, but this is rather *Musseti* with an *s* out of place than a token of the spelling *Museti*.

120

SIPARVM AND SVPPARVS*

A student who looks out *siparum* in the dictionary is sent on to *supparum*. Forcellini: '*sĭpărum* et *sīpărus* et *sīphărum*, v. *supparum*'; '*suppărum*, i, n. et *supparus*, i, m....scribitur autem et *sifarus* et *siparum* et *siparus* et *sipharum*'. Georges:[1] '*sīpărum, sīphărum (sīphărus*), s. *supparum*'; '*suppărum (sĭpărum* u. *sĭphărum*), i, n., u. *suppărus (sĭphărus*), i, m. (σίφαρος)'. Lewis and Short: '*sĭpărum* or -*us*, i, v. *supparum*'; '*suppărum (sĭpărium, sĭpărum, sĭphărum*), i, n. and *suppărus (sĭphărus*), i, m.'. This then is one word, rejoicing in no fewer than eleven forms (most of which I have never met anywhere outside a dictionary);[2] *supparum, supparus, sīparum, sĭparum, sīpharum, sĭpharum, siparus, sifarus, sīpharus, sĭpharus, sĭpharium*. And to this one word the lexicographers assign two meanings: (1) a topsail (or in military use a sort of banner), (2) a linen garment mostly worn by women. Similar opinions are forthcoming from all quarters: Studniczka *Beitr. ʒ. Gesch. d. altgr. Tracht* p. 90 '*supparus*...bezeichnet ein linnenes Obergewand der Männer und Frauen, zugleich aber eine Art Segel und segeltüchtige Vorhänge, wie sie im Theater und anderwärts verwendet wurden'; Vaniček *Fremdwörter* p. 79 '*supparus* m., *supparum* n., ursprünglicher Name eines Segels...dann ein Frauengewand' (a description taken word for word from Hehn *Kulturpfl. u. Hausth.* p. 154 ed. 2); Pauli in Kuhn's *Zeitschrift* XVIII p. 5 '*supparus, supparum*, leinenes gewand, frauenhemde, toppsegel'; Weise *Griech. Wört. im Lat.* p. 181 'nächst der Tunika und Stola ist das am frühesten in der Litteratur auftretende Frauengewand das *supparum*. Sein Name (= σίφαρον) ist ein uraltes Lehnwort des Seewesens und bezeichnet ursprünglich ein linnenes Segel'; Marquardt *Privatl.* pp. 484 sqq. ed. 2 'das linnene Frauenkleid, welches zuerst in Mode kam, war das *supparum*. Das Wort ist...identisch mit *siparum* oder σίφαρος (das Segel)'; Lindsay *Lat. Lang.* p. 29 '*supparum*, with byform *siparum*'; Walde *Lat. etym. Wörterb.* '*supparum*, Toppsegel, Bramsegel, auch *siparum, sipharum*, aus gr. σίπαρος, σίφαρος entlehnt'; Keller *Lat.*

---

* [CQ 13 (1919), 149–52]

[1] Georges' article on *supparum* is reproduced, false quantities and all, in Saalfeld's *tensaurus Italograecus*.

[2] Not even Greek is copious enough for our etymologers, who enrich it with the forms σίπαρος and σίφαρον: Schuchardt *Vokal. d. Vulgärlat.* II p. 228, Ernout *Élém. dial. Lat.* p. 234, Keller *Lat. Volksetym.* pp. 106, 168, 175, Saalfeld *Italograeca* II p. 26, Weise *Griech. Wört. im Lat.* pp. 69, 181, 293, 517, Walde *Lat. etym. Wörterb.* s. u. *supparum*.

Volksetym. p. 106 'das Toppsegel heisst lateinisch *supparum* und *supparus*, griechisch σίφαρος, σίπαρος'.

Facts tell another tale. These are two words, distinct both in form and in significance, and one of them makes its appearance more than two centuries ‖ earlier than the other. The word for a topsail is *sīpărum* or *sīphărum*: although its Greek name is σίφαρος in Arr. Epict. III 2 18 βυθιζομένου δὲ τοῦ πλοίου σύ μοι παρελθὼν ἐπαίρεις τοὺς σιφάρους and presumably also in Hesych. ἐπίδρομον...τὸ ἱστίον τὸ ἐν τῇ πρύμνῃ κρεμάμενον, ὃ καλοῦσι σίφαρον καὶ ἔλασσον (if this conjecture of Casaubon's for φᾶρον is true), its Latin name is neuter; for *sifarus* in *not. Tiron.* IV 4, tab. 109 88 ed. Schmitz., has no more right to count as Latin than *primna* or *bieris* on the same page. The word for the garment is *supparus*, masculine, which possesses, like *carbasus* and *sibilus*, a poetical neuter plural, *suppara*. For a neuter singular *supparum*[1] I can find no evidence but unsupported statements of the stupid and ignorant Nonius, the not very learned or intelligent Priscian, and certain scholiasts at Luc. II 364: Non. p. 540 [866 Lindsay] '*supparum* est linteum femorale usque ad talos pendens, dictum quod subtus appareat', Prisc. G.L.K. II p. 169 '*supparus* περιώμιον et hoc *supparum*', schol. Luc. '*supparum* genus est indumenti', 'hoc *supparum* et haec suppara', '*supparum* est uestimentum puellare lineum' etc. (borrowed and corrupted from Paul. Fest. p. 311 [407 Lindsay] *supparus*). Priscian and the scholiasts cite no example; Nonius is less discreet and cites four, one of which is visibly masculine, while the others, of which none is perceptibly neuter, include a verse cited by Festus as an example of *supparus*. It is however quite likely that in the decline of Latin, earlier than Nonius, a neuter singular was fabricated by false inference from the neuter plural, as *sibilum* was from *sibila* and *carbasum* from *carbasa*. The upstart has prospered amazingly: not only has it ousted both *supparus* and *siparum* from their place in the modern lexicons, but it has thence redounded upon the ancient, and in filling the gap at Fest. p. 340ᵃ 20–2 [458 Lindsay] it is thrice introduced by Mueller and Lindsay, once for *supparus* and twice for *siparum*.

The facts of which I speak are the following texts. Wherever the MSS have any variant worth mentioning, I mention it; but in every such case the balance of their authority is in favour of the form which I adopt.

siparum or sipharum

Sen. *ep.* 77 1 'omnis in pilis Puteolorum turba constitit et ex ipso genere uelorum Alexandrinas quamuis in magna turba nauium intellegit. solis enim licet *siparum* intendere, quod in alto omnes habent naues'...2 'ceterae uelo iubentur esse contentae: *siparum* Alexandrinarum insigne est'. *siparum* utrobique VPb, *supparum* V ex corr.

[1] The lateness of this form is recognised, though not to the full, by Studniczka l.c.

Sen. *Med.* 327 sq. 'alto rubicunda tremunt | *sipara* uelo'. *sipara* E, *suppara* A.

Sen. *H.O.* 698 sq. 'rates quaerit in alto | quarum feriunt *sipara* nubes'. *sipara* E, *suppara* A.

Luc. v 427–9 'flexo nauita cornu | obliquat laeuo pede carbasa, summaque pandens | *sipara* uelorum perituras colligit auras'. *sipara* MZPC, Isid. *orig.* || XIX 3 4, *supara* U, *suppara* VG and all editors, '*sippera* uela sunt minora, unde et pantomimorum uela sic dicuntur, "siphario c. a. u." (Iuu. VIII 186)' schol. Bern.

Stat. *silu.* III 2 27 'uos summis adnectite *sipara* uelis'.

Auien. *Arat.* 760 sq. 'cum portum tenuere, auidi uolitantia raptim | *sipara* conuertunt'.

Isid. *orig.* XIX 3 2 'genera uelorum: acation, epidromos, dolo, artemo, *siparum*, mendicum'. . . . 4 '*siparum*[1] genus ueli unum pedem habens, quo iuuari nauigia solent in nauigatione quotiens uis uenti languescit. de quo Lucanus (v 429 above) "summaque tendens | *sipara* uelorum perituras colligit auras"; quod ex separatione existimant nominatum.'

Front. *ep. ad Anton.* I 2 p. 97 Nab. ⟦90–1 Van Den Hout⟧ 'quod nunc uides prouenisse, et, quamquam non semper ex summis opibus ad eloquentiam uelificaris, tamen *sipharis* et remis tenuisse iter, atque, ut primum uela pandere necessitas impulit, omnis eloquentiae studiosos, ut lembos et celocas, facile praeteruehi'.

Tert. *apol.* 16 '*siphara* illa uexillorum et cantabrorum stolae crucum sunt'.

Tert. *ad nat.* I 12 'sic etiam in cantabris atque uexillis. . .*siphara* illa uestes crucum sunt'.

supparus

Plaut. *Epid.* 232 '*supparum* (A and Non. p. 540 ⟦866 Lindsay⟧, *subparum* P) aut subnimium, ricam, basilicum aut exoticum'.

Afran. *epistula* (Non. p. 540 ⟦866 Lindsay⟧, Paul. Fest. p. 311 ⟦407 Lindsay⟧, Ribb. *frag. com.* 122 sq.) 'tace: | puella non sum, *supparo* si induta sum?'

Nou. *paedio* (Non. p. 540 ⟦866 Lindsay⟧, Ribb. *frag. com.* 70) '*supparum* purum belliensem (Veliensem coni. Lipsius) interim, escam meram'.

Varr. *Eumenidibus* (Non. pp. 540 ⟦867 Lindsay⟧ and 549 ⟦881 Lindsay⟧, Buech. *sat. Menipp.* 121) 'aurorat ostrinum hic indutus *supparum*'.

Varr. *l. L.* v 131 'indutui alterum quod subtus, a quo subucula; alterum quod supra, a quo *supparus*'.

Paul. Fest. p. 311 4 ⟦407 Lindsay⟧ '*supparus* uestimentum puellare lineum, quod et subucula, id est camisia, dicitur'.

Fest. p. 310ª 10–23 ⟦406 Lindsay⟧ (I do not try to show the dimensions of the

---

[1] Mr Lindsay has *siparum* in his text but *supparum* in his index, or rather Otto's index, which he has taken over without adapting it duly to his own recension or eliminating its misprints and other errors.

gaps) 'supparus ⟨puellare dicebatu⟩r uestimen⟨tum lineum quod et s⟩ubucula ap⟨pellabatur. Titinius i⟩n fullonia…omne quod…⟨sup⟩parum puni…cat Naeuius de ⟨bello Puni⟩co. et in nautis…⟨u⟩estem consec…nunc *supparos*… na iam crucem…detur puella…⟨Afra⟩nius ait "puella ⟨non sum, supparo si in⟩duta sum?".'

Tert. *pall.* 4 'stolam et *supparum*'.

C.G.L. v p. 623 27 'subucula uel *supparis* (read *supparus*) est camisia'.

Luc. II 363 sq. 'umerisque haerentia primis | *suppara* nudatos cingunt || angusta lacertos'. schol. Bern. '*subpara* pro amiculis. *suppara* genus uestis quod alii stolam dicunt, alii thoracem uel amiculi genus.'

Arnob. *nat.* II 19 'subuculas, *suppara*, laenas'.

Apoll. Sid. *carm.* II 326 'pendula gemmiferae mordebant *suppara* bullae'.

C.G.L. IV p. 180 1 '*suppara*…tunicae quae et subuculae dicuntur'.

The confusion between *sipara* and *suppara*, which has ended in confounding *siparum* with *supparus*, perhaps began in the fifth century, the earliest date which can well be assigned to a poem exhibiting such prosody as *măluit, nēque, mentēque, Thersitěs, Deidamiam* − ∪ ∪ − , and such grammar as *comes esse placet*. The 'uerba Achillis in parthenone' (anth. Lat. Ries. 198, P.L.M. Baehr. IV pp. 332 sqq.) contain the verse, 23, 'arma tegant nostrum potius quam *sipara* corpus'.

121

NIHIL IN OVID*

In the *Classical Quarterly* for 1916, vol. x pp. 138f. ⟦this edition pp. 925–7⟧,
I considered Lachmann's doctrine of the Ovidian prosody of *nihil* together
with the evidence alleged against it, and concluded that judgment on the controversy must be held in suspense. Before proceeding further let me rehearse the
facts and contentions. It is Lachmann's precept, delivered in *Kl. Schr.* II p. 59
and at Lucr. I 159, that Ovid used only *nil* and *nihīl*, not *nihĭl*. For *nihĭl* he
adduced

> *met.* VII 644 in superis opis esse *nihil*. at in aedibus ingens,
>
> *trist.* V 14 41 morte *nihil* opus est pro me sed amore fideque,
>
> *ex Pont.* III 1 113 morte *nihil* opus est, n(ih)il Icariotide tela; ‖

to which I added

> *met.* XIV 24 fine *nihil* opus est; partem ferat illa caloris,

where the main tradition of the MSS is corrupt and gives *fineque nil* or rather
et neque nil. The one instance of *nihĭl* which he found,

> *her.* XIX 170 exiguum, sed plus quam *nihil*, illud erat,

he reckoned among the features assigning that epistle to another hand than
Ovid's. Merkel opposed him with

> *trist.* V 8 2 te quoque sim, inferius quo *nihil* esse potest,

and Lucian Mueller with

> *trist.* IV 8 38 mitius inmensus quo *nihil* orbis habet;

but I remarked that the distich containing the former of these two examples is
on other grounds suspect, and that the latter could, if need were, be removed
by an easy and even plausible transposition. Wherever else in Ovid's text the
form *nihil* is followed by a vowel, the metre allows *nil*; and the spelling of MSS,
which often offer *nihil* where only *nil* is metrical, has no claim to represent the
spelling or pronunciation of the author.

I can now settle the question by means of an observation which I ought to
have made before, and so indeed ought Lachmann. I have collected all the verses

* ⟦*CR* 33 (1919), 56–9⟧

in which this word, call it *nil* or *nihil*, constitutes the latter half of the first foot. There are twenty examples, or, if a suspected epistle is included, twenty-one; and they are these.

> *her.* XVII 127 sed *nihil* infirmo.
> *art.* I 519 et *nihil* emineant.
> *art.* II 280 si *nihil* attuleris.
> *remed.* 410 et *nihil* est.
> *met.* VI 465 et *nihil* est.
> *met.* VII 830 quod *nihil* est.
> *met.* IX 628 ut *nihil* adiciam.
> *met.* X 520 et *nihil* est.
> *met.* XIII 266 at *nil* inpendit.
> *fast.* I 445 sed *nil* ista.
> *trist.* I 8 8 et *nihil* est.
> *trist.* V 5 51 si *nihil* infesti.
> *trist.* V 14 26 et *nihil* officio.
> *ex Pont.* II 2 56 an *nihil* expediat.
> *ex Pont.* II 3 33 te *nihil* ex.
> *ex Pont.* II 7 46 et *nihil* inueni.
> *ex Pont.* III 1 47 ut *nihil* ipse.
> *ex Pont.* III 1 127 qua *nihil* in.
> *ex Pont.* IV 8 15 at *nihil* hic.
> *ex Pont.* IV 14 23 sed *nihil* admisi.
> *Ib.* 284 cui *nil* rethei.

Eighteen where the MSS have *nihil*, three where they have *nil*. But, with the single exception of the last instance, the word, however spelt, is always followed by a vowel; and that exception is of the sort which proves a rule. In the couplet

> nec tibi subsidio praesens sit numen, ut illi
> cui nil rethei profuit ara Iouis,

rethei, which can only be interpreted *Rhoetei*, is rejected by the sense, which demands *Hercei*; and so vanishes the consonant. Now this perpetually attendant circumstance can be no result of chance. Words having the metrical properties of *nil* are often placed by Ovid in this part of the verse with a consonant after them: *remed.* 138 'haec *sunt* iucundi', 426 'non *sunt* iudiciis', 507 'nec *dic* blanditias', 694 'nec *dic* quid', 701 'nec *nos* purpureas'. *nil* itself is so placed by other poets: Lucr. II 7 'sed *nil* dulcius', 673 ⟦674⟧ 'si *nil* praeterea' (in both of which instances the MSS have *nihil*), Hor. *serm.* I 1 49 'qui *nil* portarit', Mart. I 98 2 'sed *nil* patrono', III 61 2 'si *nil* Cinna'. Ovid must have had a motive for saddling himself with this restriction; but if he meant the word for a monosyllable he can have had none. His only imaginable motive was to procure a dactyl instead of a spondee for the first foot. *nihil* therefore in the eighteen verses where it occurs is a pyrrhic, and *nil* in the three others should be changed to *nihil*. This may be done without scruple; for although scribes are less prone to write *nil* for *nihil* than *nihil* for *nil*, the error is both common and early: B and R are two of Horace's best and oldest MSS, yet the one at *carm.* I 28 12 and the other at IV 2 37 gives *nil* where the metre proves that Horace wrote *nihil*. And *nihil* was printed in all our three verses by Heinsius, who carried into practice the rule which Seruius tried and failed to formulate at Virg. *Aen.* VI 104,[1] and ‖ read *nihil* wherever metre gave him the chance, without regard to the spelling of the MSS. Merkel's practice on the other hand was to preserve the spelling of the MSS unless metre forbade him; and at *met.* XIII 266 and *fast.* I 445 he has been followed by all subsequent editors in retaining *nil*, which Guethling and I retained also at *Ib.* 284 when changing *rethei* to *Hercei*, because it was irrational to introduce *nihil* in this verse and not in the other two. But the facts which I have just set forth put a new complexion on the case, and show that Ovid wrote *nihil* in all three places.

In the second and third and fourth foot of the hexameter the case stands otherwise, and Ovid unquestionably admitted *nil*, as at *met.* XV 92 'terra creat, *nil* te nisi tristia mandere saeuo', *amor.* II 1 19 'Iuppiter, ignoscas: *nil* me tua tela iuuabant', *ex Pont.* I 1 7 'a quotiens dixi: certe *nil* turpe docetis'. But yet verses where a vowel follows and leaves the form of the word in doubt are much more numerous: *met.* VII 567 'utile enim *nihil* est', XV 177, *trist.* II 195, III 4 51, *ex Pont.* I 2 65; *amor.* III 8 29 '*nihil* esse potentius auro', *art.* II 365, 599, *met.* V 221, VI 25, 305, VII 67, XIII 100, XIV 730, XV 165, 629, *fast.* VI 177, *trist.* I 2 23, 11 23, II 259, III 1 9, 13 23, *ex Pont.* III 1 113, *her.* XX 99; *met.* III 590 '*nihil* ille reliquit', V 273, VI 685, IX 148, *ex Pont.* I 1 21, 7 25. The MSS or the best part of them (except that at *met.* XV 165 authority is about equally divided) give *nihil* in all these verses, and so does Heinsius; Merkel and his followers diverge at one place only, *trist.* III 13 23 '*nihil* exorantia diuos', where all of them except Guethling print *nil*, though four out of the five best MSS have *nihil*. In two verses *nihil* is certainly to be preferred, *met.* V 273 'sed (uetitum est adeo sceleri *nihil*) omnia terrent' and VI 685 'ast, ubi blanditiis agitur *nihil*, horridus ira', where *nil* would create a rhythm less acceptable to Ovid. Some might say that at three other places we have guidance for our choice: that in *met.* XIII 100 'luce *nihil* gestum, *nihil* est Diomede remoto' and XV 629 'temptamenta *nihil*, *nihil* artes posse medentum' the one *nihil* defends the other, and that in *art.* II 365 '*nil* Helene peccat, *nihil* hic committit adulter' *nil* in the first place re-

---

[1] 'si pars sequens orationis a uocali inchoet, *nihil* dicimus, ut (II 402) "heu *nihil* inuitis fas quemquam fidere diuis"; si autem a consonante inchoet, *nil* ponimus, ut Iuuenalis (IV 22) "*nil* tale expectes: emit sibi. multa uidemus".' One sees what he wants to say, though he has not said it: he does not really mean that he writes or pronounces 'te sine *nihil* altum mens incohat' in *georg.* III 42, nor 'ille *nil*, nec me quaerentem uana moratur' in *Aen.* II 287.

commends *nil* in the second. But any such expectation of uniformity is shown to be fallacious by Catull. 17 21 '*nil* uidet, *nihil* audit', 42 21 'sed *nil* proficimus, *nihil* mouetur', 64 146 '*nil* metuunt iurare, *nihil* promittere parcunt', Virg. *buc.* 11 6 f. 'o crudelis Alexi, *nihil* mea carmina curas? | *nil* nostri miserere?', Sen. *Med.* 163 'qui *nil* potest sperare, desperet *nihil*', Mart. 11 3 1 'Sexte, *nihil* debes, *nil* debes, Sexte', Iuu. VI 212 f. '*nil* umquam inuita donabis coniuge, uendas | hac opstante *nihil*'; and it is manifest that nothing, neither *nihil* nor *nil*, can bring about uniformity in *ex Pont.* III 1 113 'morte *nihĭl* opus est, *nihil* Icariotide tela'.

Ovid's practice in respect of the first foot appears to be that of most dactylic poets later than Lucretius. Even in Horace and Martial, who allow a consonant to follow, a vowel is much more frequent, and it is invariable in Catullus, Virgil, Tibullus, Propertius, Manilius, Persius, Calpurnius, the Aetna, Lucan, Silius (if I can trust a rapid examination[1]) and Juvenal, though in many of them the number of examples is too small to establish a rule.

About Juvenal I have a short story to tell. The disputed word forms the latter half of the first foot in three verses, VI 331 'si *nihil* est', VII 54 'qui *nihil* expositum', XIII 18 'an *nihil* in melius'. In all three the MSS, or most of them, give the form *nihil*, and so did the editions down to 1886. In that year Buecheler introduced *nil* from the Pithoeanus at VII 54, leaving *nihil* in the two other verses; and his sheep followed him as their tails did them. He was disregarding authority as well as reason, for *nihil* is given at VII 54 not only by the most and best of the inferior MSS but by the lemma ‖ of the ancient scholia, which is as good a witness as the Pithoeanus itself; but reason and authority together are no match for that passion of love which is inspired in modern scholars by MSS whose names begin with a P. In my edition of 1905 I made a brief remark on the circumstances and restored *nihil*. The result of my action deserves to be put on record as exemplifying the customs of classical scholarship in the twentieth century. Buecheler, though placing *nil* in his text, had exhibited in his apparatus criticus and in his excerpts from the scholia the facts which I have stated, '*nihil* S ω', 'qui nihil expositum'. It was safe to print this evidence so long as nobody took any notice of it; but as soon as I gave it effect by promoting *nihil* to the text, the case was altered. The fetish was in danger, the facts must be suppressed, and Leo in his edition of 1910 suppressed them.

---

[1] In Valerius Flaccus and Statius I have noticed no example of *nihil* or *nil* in this situation.

122

REVIEW: I. BYWATER, *FOUR CENTURIES OF GREEK LEARNING IN ENGLAND**

This lecture, which Bywater probably thought too slight for publication, has been found among his notebooks and is issued from the press of his University. It is the business-like performance of a good scholar who did not aspire to be an indifferent man of letters; and readers who wish to hear about the Greek spirit may leave it alone.

The greatest part of it is occupied with matter of the least importance. The renascence of learning in England is history in which Bywater was at home, and he collects a large number of details which I presume to be accurate and which have some interest of a purely antiquarian sort. But those were the years when we were learning Greek and were not yet in case to teach it: our contribution to the European fund begins with the seventeenth century. In Bywater's account of this period there is nothing which I can gainsay of my own knowledge; though I should have thought that Pearson, of whom Bentley said that the very dust of his writings was gold, and Porson that he would have equalled even Bentley as a critic in Greek if he had not muddled his brains with divinity, deserved more prominence than is given him. The two pages on Bentley himself are excellent; and laymen who wonder at the fame of this tasteless and arbitrary pedant, and the reverence paid him by every competent judge, will hardly find elsewhere in so small a compass so clear a definition of his unique originality and greatness.

But in Bywater's sketch of Greek scholarship after Bentley there are places where I find his judgment or his knowledge defective. He says with truth that Bentley's chief successors, excepting Taylor and in some measure Toup and Tyrwhitt, were mostly occupied, like Bentley himself, with the poets; and I surmise that for this very reason they were not familiar to Bywater.

'The school of Bentley, if the expression may be hazarded, Markland, Dawes, Musgrave, Warton, and the rest, allowed itself to be absorbed in the study of the Greek poets. If I were asked who was the strong man and chief figure in this company, I should say with little hesitation, Richard Dawes.'

* [*Four Centuries of Greek Learning in England.* Inaugural Lecture delivered before the University of Oxford on March 8, 1894. By Ingram Bywater. Pp. 20. Oxford: at the Clarendon Press, 1919. *CR* 34 (1920), 110–11]

Warton makes a strange appearance here, though far be it from me to blame Bywater or anyone else for ignorance of his large and empty Theocritus; and I should have liked to watch Bentley from a safe distance in Elysium when he heard the expression hazarded that Warton was one of his school. Although the preeminence assigned to Dawes is disputable, I will not dispute it, and I grudge him no praise; but *strong* is not the right word to praise him with. His special virtue was a preternatural alertness and insight in the two fields of metre and grammar, the more extraordinary because his mere learning was not profound. The *strong* man of the company was Markland, devoid of these peculiar qualities, but superior in range and vigour and general activity of mind. || It is probable that Englishmen are right in counting Porson the second of English scholars, but many judges on the Continent would give that rank to Markland. He is the only one except Bentley who has been highly and equally eminent in Greek and Latin; and I believe that Bentley did him the honour, extravagant I admit, to be jealous of him.

> 'Porson...is...a model of caution and patience, not an impetuous genius like Bentley or Dawes.'

Certainly Porson had less genius and less impetuosity than Bentley, but he had as much genius as Dawes, and Dawes had not much more impetuosity than Porson: those who think he had are misled by the effervescence of his style, and its unlikeness to Porson's constraint. There may have been impetuosity, or at least some lack of caution, in Dawes's canon about ὅπως μή with the 1st aor. subj. active and middle and his alteration of Ar. *Ach.* 633 and *Pac.* 918, but so there was in Porson's pronouncement on the form of the 2nd pers. sing. pres. indic. passive and his destruction of the metre of Eur. *Med.* 629.

> 'The Porsonian school, Blomfield, Monk, and Elmsley, if I may include him among them, continued Porson's work on the dramatists, though with little of Porson's freshness or felicity of touch.'

This is true of Monk, if not of Blomfield, but of Elmsley it is false and unjust. Elmsley no doubt was distinctly inferior to Porson as an emendator, though still a good one, but he was not much inferior as an observer and discoverer in grammar and metre, and his writing has a candour and a pleasant irony which are graces not easily to be matched. See how Nauck and Wilamowitz speak of him, or hear the words of his great antagonist Hermann:

> 'Est enim P. Elmsleius, si quis alius, uir natus augendae accuratiori Graecae linguae cognitioni, ut cuius eximia ac plane singularis in peruestigandis rebus grammaticis diligentia regatur praeclaro ingenio, mente ab auctoritatibus libera, animo ueri amantissimo, neque aut superbia aut gloriae studio aut

obtrectandi cupiditate praepedito. his ille uirtutibus id est consecutus, ut, cum doctrina eius maximi facienda sit, non minus ipse sit amandus atque uene-randus.'

And this one slighting mention is all that the Regius Professor of Greek at Oxford could spare for the most famous scholar that Oxford ever produced. He continues: 'if the mantle of the master descended on anyone, it was rather on Dobree'. It is very hard to decide between the merits of Dobree and Elmsley: I should say that the mantle came in two and half of it fell on each; Dobree was the shrewder emendator and Elmsley the subtler grammarian.

The statement on p. 15 that 'Porson edited Photius' is not strictly true, and on p. 18 the death of Badham is post-dated by five years.

123

REVIEW: J. P. POSTGATE, *PHAEDRI FABVLAE AESOPIAE**

Dr Postgate's is a purer text of Phaedrus than Lucian Mueller's and could hardly fail to be a purer than Mr Havet's; and the reason of its superiority is partly that he has used better judgment in choosing among the lections at his disposal and partly that he has imported fewer novelties of his own. A simple way to purify the text still further would be to remove those novelties: not that all of them are improbable or injurious, but most of them are, like most of Mueller's and Mr Havet's; and although Dr Postgate's conjectures do less harm than the former's and much less than the latter's, they also do less good. These fables are not a field in which anyone at this date can make 60 restorations, and Dr Postgate was not the critic most likely to make them. The matter and manner of Phaedrus are so plain and lucid that his correctors ‖ have not been baffled or distracted by difficulties inherent in the author; they have been able to concentrate their scrutiny on his textual condition, and the scrutiny of Mr Havet has been uncommonly minute. The consequence is that most errors which can be set right with certainty have been set right already: there remains a vast deal of damage which is beyond repair. The licence of scribes who neither understood nor regarded the metre has bred such disorder that the words in the MSS are often far away from anything that the poet can have written, and editors accordingly have a large choice of possible corrections, few of which, for that very reason, will be probable. To handle a text of this sort is a business which calls for diffidence and flexibility: Dr Postgate is both sanguine and stubborn, and if once he gets hold of the stick by the wrong end he does not soon let go.

He has amended the punctuation of I 27 7; in III *epil.* 28 'excedit animus quem *proposuit* terminum' his *proposui* is an improvement; in IV 18 25 *odorem mixto* his *odore* is a slighter change than *mixtum* or *odores mixtos*; and in V 9 4 his *tu quam* for *quam* gives a better emphasis than *quam tu*. His *grana* in IV 24 14 is almost required by *congero*, though his derision of *granum* is beside the mark and shows that he has mistaken the author's meaning. *Mulum* in II 7 8 was justly

---

* ⟦*Phaedri Fabulae Aesopiae cum Nicolai Perotti prologo et decem nouis fabulis. Recognouit breuique adnotatione critica instruxit* Iohannes Percival Postgate. Pp. xxviii, no further pagination. Oxonii e typographeo Clarendoniano, 1920. *CR* 34 (1920), 121–4⟧

condemned by Riese, and Dr Postgate's *ditem* is probably the best substitute that can be found. With the help of the medieval paraphrasts he has detected gaps after 1 7 1 and *app. Perott.* 1 1, and has filled them with something very like what Phaedrus must have written.

In the following passages a variety of corrections are propounded by different critics, and each prefers his own: I will quote alternatives without interposing any judgment, and the reader shall try to pick out Dr Postgate's conjectures from the rest by their superiority. 1 16 2 'fraudator homines cum aduocat sponsum improbos, | non rem expedire sed *malauidere* expetit': *malum inferre* or *ingerere* or *ordiri.* III 3 2 'usu peritus hariolo ueracior | uulgo *causa fertur* sed non dicitur': *esse fertur, causa* or *perhibetur, causa.* III *epil.* 11 'et hoc minus *ueniet* ad me muneris': *perueniet* or *redibit.* IV 9 1 '*homo simul ac uenit in magnum periculum* (with title *in periculum simul ac uenit callidus*), | reperire effugium quaerit alterius malo': *homo in periclum simul ac uenit callidus* or *homo magnum ut uenit in periclum callidus* or *magnum in periclum simul ac uenit callidus.* IV 24 19 'aestate me lacessis; *cum bruma est* (PR, *cur bruma* NV) siles': *cum brumast* or *cum bruma. App.* 11 9 'ferendus esses, arte si te diceres | superasse *qui esset melior* uiribus': *qui te melior esset* or *quam tu qui esset m.* or *eum qui te esset m. App.* 16 6 'postquam *esurire coepit fera societas*': *e. societas coepit fera* or *fera esurire coepit s. App.* 29 1 'papilio uespam *preteruolantem* uiderat': *praeuolantem* or *prope uolantem.*

Similar cases, less handy to cite, may be found at 1 5 7, 30 7, III *prol.* 22, III 10 2, 13 13, IV 6 2, and several places in the *appendix Perottina.* But there are others where Dr Postgate's expedient is quite evidently inferior. 1 3 6–9, where he spoils the natural flow of the narrative, and II 4 19 cannot be dealt with briefly; but take the following examples.

III *prol.* 20 'quamuis in ipsa natus sim *pene* schola'. Heinsius mended nothing but the metre with his transposition *paene sim natus*: Mr Havet saw that *schola* needed definition, and altered *pene* to *Phoebi*: so *Phoebus* in Manil. IV 728 is corrupted to *Poenus* and *Paenus*, and *Phoebigenam* in Verg. *Aen.* VII 773 to *Poenigenam*. But Dr Postgate conceives the project of saving the letter *n*, and apparently with that single aim he writes *Paeanis*. This is not so apt a name as *Phoebi*, it is certainly no nearer to *pene*, and instead of mending the metre it requires the transposition of another word; 'doch die Katze, die Katz' ist gerettet'.

IV 2 4 'sed diligenter intuere has nenias: | quantam *subtilis* utilitatem reperies!' Pithoeus wrote *sub illis*, which procures unimpeachable sense by the irreducible minimum of change. Mr Havet's egotism forced him to prefer *sub titulis*, poor though it was; and against *sub illis* he said the first thing that came into his head, 'quod || post *has* nefas'. Dr Postgate knows that this is false, that *hic* and *ille* are referred to one object by writers so pure as Plautus and so elegant as

Ovid; but the hunt is up and he cannot sit idle, he must venture *in pusillis*. Suppose that I were the author of this conjecture: does Dr Postgate think he would print it instead of Pithou's?

IV 17 8 'factus *periculosis tum* gubernator sophus: | "parce gaudere oportet et sensim queri".' *periclis tum* Orelli, *periclo sic* Dr Postgate, who says that Orelli's reading does not account for the *-os-* (as if his own accounted for the *tum*), and that the plural is inappropriate. The singular is inappropriate: the pilot, who had seen many a storm before, is contrasted with his less experienced and more impressionable shipmates.

These however are places where the tradition is corrupt: there are others where it is sound and where Dr Postgate vitiates it by alteration. His text of III *prol.* 45–8 checked me and threw me out as I read it, and before I had time to look at the note I had hit by conjecture on what I there found to be the MS reading; but not every corruption is so slight.

III 2 5 gives not only a good sense but exactly the right sense. A panther had fallen into a pit, and the country-folk came and threw stones at it; a few however were sorry for the poor creature, sure to die even if nobody molested it, *periturae quippe, quamuis nemo laederet*, and they threw it food instead. The panther after all made its escape in the night, and a day or two later it returned and fell with tooth and claw upon man and beast. When the soft-hearted few implored it to spare their lives, it answered them 'memini quis me saxo petierit, | quis panem dederit: uos timere absistite, | illis reuertor hostis *qui me laeserunt*', 17–19. In spite of this fingerpost the meaning of *quamuis nemo laederet* was beyond the medieval paraphrasts, and they substituted *qui neminem laesit*, as if the beast of prey were an injured innocent; and upon this hint Dr Postgate writes *quamuis nullum laederet*, in which even the tense is wrong. That he cites the *qui me laeserunt* of verse 19 as bearing him out, and says that *nemo* injures the purpose of the story, and exclaims 'what a reason for compassion!' all serves to indicate his frame of mind; and so does his charge of 'more than questionable Latinity' against *periturae...quamuis...laederet* (for *laesurus esset*), which is the same construction as *dabunt quamuis redeant* in Hor. *carm.* IV 2 39. There is a fable in Phaedrus about a wolf and a lamb, written for those 'qui fictis causis innocentes opprimunt'.

IV *epil.* 7–9 'si non ingenium, certe breuitatem adproba, | quae commendari tanto debet iustius | quanto poetae sunt molesti ualidius.' Phaedrus says that his brevity is the more to his credit because he is one of a tedious tribe. This plain and excellent sense Dr Postgate somehow manages to miss; to fortify himself in error he calls *poetae* stupid and intolerable and says it completely stultifies the poem; and to have his own way he writes *cantores* instead. Such iron resolve may be a good thing in its proper place, but in criticism it is less desirable than perception and consideration.

v 10 6. The old hound 'obiectus hispidi pugnae suis | arripuit aurem, sed cariosis dentibus | praedam dimisit. *hic tunc* uenator dolens | canem obiurgabat'. *hic tunc* is both appropriate and idiomatic; but modern editors of Phaedrus are much too full of themselves to find that out, and when Mueller had conjectured *hoc tunc* and Mr Havet *dimisit hietans* it was more natural for Dr Postgate to write *rictus* in emulation than to bethink himself of Hand Turs. III p. 79 or Mayor on Iuu. III 21. What he says against *hic tunc* is that it 'has no friends'.

At the end of *app.* 27 the medieval paraphrasts, not understanding what they read, have added *sic uerbis mutuo se deluserunt* or similar absurdities. Dr Postgate makes this into a verse, *sic uerbis illi se luserunt inuicem*, marks the poem as mutilated, and calls it 'an ironical composition in which the mutual insincerities of a pair of lovers are transfixed'. It treats of no such matter: all the insincerity is on one side.

I think that Dr Postgate is rather || too fond of these paraphrasts. Their *altitonans* or *Iuppiter intonans ab aethere* at I 2 28 does not justify him in writing *Tonans* for *deus*: it seems to be merely a poetical gewgaw like the others in Mr Havet's notes on I 3 11 and 12 9. At I 21 5, instead of *ad eum*, which is in the MSS and the paraphrasts as well, he writes *spumans*, which is only in the paraphrasts. A more plausible and certainly ingenious conjecture is '*quae* (better *cui*) *dorsum* cum *tutudisset inuitae* diu', based on their *tundens dorsum eius*, for the '*quam dorso* cum *tulisset inuita et* diu' of the MSS at *app.* 24 2. In the attempt to reconstruct lost fables of Phaedrus from the prose of the paraphrases he has taken more pains that his predecessors and practised more self-restraint.

Dr Postgate has shown on other occasions that his ear for the Latin iambic is not perfect, and some of his conjectures here are metrically insecure or vicious. Phaedrus has no such verses as the *illius se miscere antidoto toxicum* and the *Demetrius rex qui Phalereus dictus est* which he offers at I 14 8 and v 1 1, nor as the *ego illius pro semita feci uiam* which he adopts from Johnson at III *prol.* 38; and *fab. nou.* 8 1 is astonishing. At *app.* 12 4 he fills out the verse by inserting *ea* before *ait*: there are probably more than two such elisions in Latin poetry, but I have only noticed two, and neither is in Phaedrus.

The preface gives a clear and comprehensive account of the MSS and the other sources of the text, and the papers in British and American journals of the last two years to which the reader is constantly referred contain matter of value. An orderly and intelligible apparatus criticus, as several volumes of this series have shown, is a gift not always to be expected from an English editor. Dr Postgate's notes on I 19 7, 28 5, IV 9 5, 17 8 and 10, 18 14, 20 15, V 5 1, *app.* 13 25, 14 10, 15 10, appear to have been written before he knew what his text was going to be, or after he had forgotten what it was. Some of them, *e.g.* 1 28 5, are merely wrong-end-foremost and cause nothing worse than annoyance and delay. Others tell us things which we could infer for ourselves and hide from us things which we cannot: that P has *catulos posset* in I 19 7 might have been said by silence, but who is to know that D has *posset catulos*? The MS reading is not discoverable from the notes on III *prol.* 12 and *app.* 9 2, nor the source of the text from those on III 19 8, IV 17 10, V 5 1, *app.* 9 2, 15 10. The note on III *prol.* 20 contains a wrong statement, and those on III 6 2 and *app.* 4 22 must inevitably mislead. Such particulars as '*xystum* Salmasius, *xistum* P' and '*umor* Havet, *humor* NV' could better be spared than the information that *ni* in *app.* 15 8 is a correction of Mueller's and the MSS have *nisi*. A part of the notes on IV 17 belongs to 16, and there are misprints or other slips in the apparatus at I 12 1, 21 2, 22 8, 26 4, II 3 2, 9 18, IV 1 6, 15 13, *app.* 20 3, and in the text (apart from errors of punctuation) at *app.* 25 2. The name of Heinsius is missing at I 13 13 sq., and Jannelli's rather than Mueller's should appear at *app.* 7 4. The conjecture *logis* ascribed to me at III *prol.* 37 had been anticipated, though I cannot say by whom; and I do not remember proposing *frondosum* in *app.* 6 2.

124

DE NIHILO*

In *C.R.* XXXIII pp. 56–9 [this edition pp. 1000–3] I investigated the prosody of *nihil* in Ovid and determined to some extent his principle of choice between *nihil* and *nil*. I showed that in the latter half of the first foot of the verse this word, *n(ih)il*, is always[1] followed by a vowel; I said that Ovid's only imaginable motive for maintaining this restriction was to procure ‖ a dactyl; and I concluded that in this place he always wrote *nihil*, though in 3 out of 21 examples the MSS give *nil*. I further showed that in the latter half of the second and third and fourth foot of the hexameter the word is sometimes followed by a consonant, so that in these three feet the case stands otherwise than in the first.

This was the best I could do without the guidance of Dr Postgate, which he has now vouchsafed me in *Hermathena* XLII pp. 54 sq. After reminding a forgetful world that in 1892 he quoted against Lachmann the same two instances of *nihil* which Lucian Mueller had quoted in 1861, he attempts to give the Irish an account of my investigations, but does not succeed. My observation about the invariably following vowel he omits altogether, not having grasped its significance; and he describes me as holding the opinion that to procure a dactyl instead of a spondee for the first foot was Ovid's motive for reading *nihil* with Heinsius in *met.* XIII 266, *fast.* I 445, and *Ib.* 284. This of course is not what he was trying to say, but the pen is mightier than the wrist. The statement to which in his following remarks he takes exception appears to be the statement which I really made but which he has not communicated to his readers – that Ovid's only imaginable motive for making a vowel follow the first foot in all the 21 verses which I cited was to procure for that foot a dactyl instead of a spondee. Dr Postgate observes that I adduced not only 18 instances where *nihil* precedes a vowel in the latter half of the first foot, but also 30 where it does so in the latter half of the second or third or fourth, and he proceeds

'By needlessly restricting his imagination Mr Housman has failed to perceive the connexion between his two series of instances, and to divine the significance of the poet's behaviour, who was not pursuing a dactyl, but avoiding *nil.*'

* [CR 34 (1920), 161–4]
[1] Except in one verse where the sense is faulty, and to correct the sense removes the consonant.

My imagination, I must confess, is restricted by my knowledge of facts. Ovid did not avoid *nil*: he admitted it everywhere in the first four feet except, as I have established, in the latter half of the first: in the latter half of the third foot he admitted it at least 5 times, *amor.* II 1 19, *met.* VIII 440, IX 626, *fast.* III 623, *ex Pont.* III 6 9. Dr Postgate goes on to explain the connexion, which I have failed to perceive and he has succeeded in perceiving, between the 18 instances of *nihil* in the first foot and the 30 instances elsewhere. Instead of attending to the difference between Ovid's employment of *n(ih)il* in the first foot and his employment of it in the second and third and fourth – the circumstance that only in the first foot does he always contrive to let a vowel follow – I ought to have ignored it, and treated all four feet alike. I ought to have imagined, although the propensity of scribes to write *nihil* for *nil* is notorious,[1] that the spelling of the MSS is a guide in the 48 places where they give *nihil* as the latter half of the first or second or third or fourth foot; and for expelling *nil* from *met.* XIII 266 and *fast.* I 445 and *Ib.* 284 I ought to have relied not, as I did, on reasoning, but on the imposing size of this rickety regiment, as if 48 precarious examples were less precarious than one. But suppose that they were so, what then? why should the three examples of *nil* be altered? Because Dr Postgate tacitly assumes the very thing which he is trying to prove, that Ovid did not use both *nil* and *nihil* under the circumstances in question, as modern editors hold that he did.

These methods enable him to formulate the following 'Ovidian rule' in italics: '*nil may be used in the "rise" of a foot before both vowels and consonants, but in the "fall" before consonants only.*' Has Dr Postgate any news from the sick bed of our beloved sovereign Queen Anne? This opinion, as I mentioned in my paper, was apparently held by Seruius in the 4th century and certainly by Heinsius in the 17th; it was held by Ovid's editors in general down to the time of Merkel, and I was taught it at school. It may be true, but it may be ‖ false: it is a mere opinion, like the contrary opinion of Lucian Mueller *de r. m.* p. 296 ed. 2, 'usque ad Augusti finem potiores fuisse existimo formas breuiores (*nil, nilum* etc.) easque restituendas ubiuis, quando metro id permittitur'; and Dr Postgate supports it by no stronger argument than announcing that he holds it. What I did was to remove from the domain of opinion the question between *nil* and *nihil* in the fall of the first foot. It is now ascertained that in this place Ovid used only *nihil*, which gave him what he liked in the first foot, a dactyl. Beyond the first foot certainty does not extend. That in the third foot, where dactyls are much less common than spondees and where *nil* in the fall is

---

[1] 'The preponderance of *nihil* in our MSS (of Phaedrus) does not really need explanation when we consider that it has ousted *nil* almost entirely from the MSS of Lucretius' says Dr Postgate on p. 58, when he has left Ovid a safe distance behind him. In Phaedrus he twelve times alters *nihil* to *nil*, in Lucretius everyone alters it scores of times.

5 times followed by a consonant, Ovid always used *nihil* instead if the following letter was a vowel, is neither ascertained nor intrinsically probable; though the preponderance (about 4 to 1) of following vowels over following consonants lends countenance to the opinion.[1]

Dr Postgate's willingness to teach is great and obvious, yet I do not find him very instructive. An air of ripe and penetrating judgment is never absent from anything that he writes, but I sometimes miss the substance, and I cannot reconcile the strength of his anxiety to seem superior with the faintness of his endeavour to be so.

On pp. 56 sq. Dr Postgate proceeds to Juvenal, of whom I also spoke in *C.R.* xxxiii pp. 58 sq. [[this edition p. 1003]], and whom I have edited. Juvenal's MSS, or the best part of them, give *nihil* as the latter half of a foot with a vowel following in 15 verses. But in two verses where a vowel followed I found them favouring *nil*:

VI 58　　　　quis tamen adfirmat *nil* actum in montibus aut in
　　　　　　　(*nil* PFOU, *nihil* AGLT),
XV 88　　　　sustinuit, *nil* umquam hac carne libentius edit
　　　　　　　(*nil* PAFOT, *nihil* GLU);

and at VI 58 I wrote '*nihil* AGLT ut solet Iuuenalis in altero semipede ante uocalem; hic tamen et XV 88 Pithoeanus sequendus uidetur propter numeros, VII 54 non item.' Dr Postgate says on p. 57 'I cannot divine what are the "numeri" supporting *nil* to the overthrow of those conceded to support *nihil* "ut solet", etc.' I gather that because he cannot divine it he thinks that I was contradicting myself; and as I am sure that this suspicion cannot be agreeable to him I will try to dispel it.

These were the only two verses in Juvenal where *nil*, under the conditions

---

[1] In a footnote on p. 54 Dr Postgate takes occasion to say that in the *Classical Quarterly* for 1916, pp. 143 sq. [[this edition pp. 931–2]], I handled *ex Pont.* II 5 11 sq. with odd negligence or perversity. This means that I had the misfortune to tread on one of Dr Postgate's chickens. In the couplet

　　　　　optastique breuem salui mihi Caesaris iram,
　　　　　quod tamen optari si sciat ipse sinat,

I upheld the MS text against a troop of conjectures one of which, alack, was *breui solui*. Parental affection is strong in Dr Postgate, and danger to his offspring has a tendency to discompose his thoughts. Here, by way of defending his conjecture from the charge of treasonable ambiguity which I brought against all the conjectures, he goes about to show, citing *met.* IX 273 sq., that it admits an innocent interpretation, as if that were in dispute. The task of a defender is to show that it does not admit a sinister interpretation; but this he is not calm enough to see. He even argues against himself: 'one might suppose from this' – my charge of dangerous ambiguity – 'that no pentameter followed the hexameter, or that this too contained a dangerous ambiguity, as Caesar *might* approve of a prayer for his own demise.' In other and plainer words, Ovid's pentameter implies that Ovid's hexameter was innocent. Which hexameter then is the more likely to be Ovid's: that of the MSS, which is innocent, or that of Dr Postgate, which, as he does not and cannot deny, is ambiguous? When, in this troubled atmosphere, he calls my handling of the passage perverse or negligent, I am not very much upset: I suppose it was less confused than could have been wished.

described, was better[1] supported by the MSS than *nihil*, and in both verses the rhythm of *nihil* struck me as unfamiliar and unwelcome. I have little faith in MSS and still less in my own ear, but as they here gave the same counsel I thought there might be something in it; I made investigation, and there was.

In those verses of Juvenal which have ‖ the normal caesura, and in which the fourth foot is a spondee consisting of a single word, the latter half of the third foot is often a monosyllable, seldom a word of pyrrhic scansion. Of the monosyllable there are 11 examples in *sat.* I alone, of the pyrrhic word there are only 12 in all Juvenal: III 134 *super illam*, 202 *ubi reddunt*, IV 60 *ubi quamquam*, VII 195 *modo primos*, VIII 47 *tamen ima*, X 154 *tamen ultra*, 155 *nisi Poeno*, 194 *ubi pandit*, 323 *habet illic*, XIII 150 *minor extat*, 216 *uelut acri*, XIV 22 *duo propter*. And 10 of the 12 are due to what may be called compulsion, for the rhythm could not be avoided by a different arrangement of the words. The two exceptions are X 155 and XIV 22, where he might have written *Poeno nisi milite* and *propter duo lintea*. Wherever else he can avoid the rhythm, he does, as in XI 122 *latos nisi sustinet*.

When the spondee of the fourth foot is composed of an elided disyllable followed by a monosyllable, there is a similar preference for a monosyllable over a pyrrhic word in the third foot – for the rhythm *nil actum in* over *nihil actum in*. The monosyllables are to the pyrrhics as 7 to 1: monosyllables III 30 *qui nigrum in*, 83, 148, 210, 216, 311, IV 14, 47, 84, VI 178, VIII 128, IX 81, X 356, XI 29, XII 60, XIII 51, XV 42, 43, 78, 166, XVI 53; pyrrhics X 112 *sine caede ac*, XI 146, XIII 221.

So much then for *nil* rather than *nihil* in the third foot of VI 58: now for the second foot of XV 88. In verses where the caesura in the third foot is procured by eliding a disyllable, and the latter half of the second foot consists of a single word, that word is a monosyllable on 10 occasions, IV 35 *res uer(a)*, 102, VI 277, 281, VII 5, 95, X 77, 284, XIII 217, XIV 206, a pyrrhic only on 3, VI 390 *stetit ant(e)*, 596, XII 24: the monosyllables therefore are more than 3 to 1. In verses where the caesura is not procured by elision the proportion of monosyllables to pyrrhics is only 3 to 2. The elision therefore made a difference, and *nil umqu(am)* is preferable to *nihil umqu(am)* in XV 88.

---

[1] Since Paris. 8072 (Π or B) is now found to give *nihil* in VI 58, the support for *nil* in that verse is no longer better, but only equally good.

125

TRISTE PROFVNDI IMPERIVM*

Iuu. XIII 49 sq.

nondum *imi* sortitus triste profundi
imperium Sicula toruos cum coniuge Pluton.

I will transcribe first the notes on these lines in my edition of 1905, and then Mr Owen's remarks in J. P. xxxv p. 144.

'**49 imi***, om. **P, aliquis** Ψ, uide Ouid. met. IV 444 *imi tecta tyranni* **50 imperium LO, imperium aut P**Ψ; at de Neptuno sermonem non esse demonstrat *triste* adiectiuum, uide Hor. carm. III 4 46 *regnaque tristia*, Sen. Med. 11 *dominumque regni tristis*, Stat. Theb. VIII 80 *regia tristis*.'

'I naturally inferred from Mr Housman's note "IMI*, om. P, ALIQVIS Ψ" that his surprising conjecture *imi* for *aliquis* was due to the supposed loss of a word for which *aliquis* found in the manuscripts other than P was a stopgap conjecturally supplied. Therefore I showed by examples that the omission of a word such as *aliquis* is a slip common in P, and affords no basis for conjecture. But Mr Housman now' – i.e. an. 1918, J. P. xxxiv p. 43 ⟦this edition p. 966⟧ – 'says that his objection to the text is that "*triste* is applicable to Pluto's empire and inapplicable to Neptune's".'

When Mr Owen confesses that he 'naturally' behaved in this manner, – naturally left my notes unread, naturally inferred, from having done so, that I, in spite of my record, was a palaeographical emendator like himself, – he lays bare with great simplicity the root of the trouble. That such proceedings are natural to him, and almost unimaginable to me, is a fact which accounts for most of our dissensions; and when he says on p. 142 'Mr Housman is dissatisfied that I disagree with him' his divination is far astray.

But although he has not even yet read my notes of 1905 he has read at least one sentence in my article of 1918, '*triste* is applicable to Pluto's empire and inapplicable to Neptune's'; ‖ and he replies that *triste* is equally applicable to either. Because there are occasions when the sea deserves and receives the epithet *tristis*, he thinks that Neptune's empire can be called *triste profundi imperium*. Neither I nor anyone else can explain to Mr Owen that this is not so, and I shall make no endeavour of the sort. The way to refute such reasoning, as

* ⟦*JPh* 35 (1920), 201–3⟧

Burke said, is not to answer it, but to use it. The sky, as well as the sea, is called *tristis* on appropriate occasions, Sen. dial. 1 4 14 'perpetua illos hiemps, *triste caelum* premit', n.q. IV [b] 4 3 'niualem diem, cum altum frigus et *triste caelum* est'; and Mr Owen says (J. P. XXXIII p. 252) that *profundum* means the sky in Manil. V 721 [720]. Therefore Jove's empire, as well as Neptune's, can be called *triste profundi imperium*. The only one of Saturn's sons whose empire, according to Mr Owen, cannot be called so, is the lord of hell, called *dominus regni tristis* by Seneca.

And why? Because Mr Owen, casting about for something definite to say against my surprising conjecture, discovered, to his relief and joy, that there is no example in the dictionaries of *profundum* meaning the deep of hell. That the adjective *profundus* is attached to *Acheruns, manes, Dis, Erebus, Tartara*, that Pluto is called *Iuppiter profundus* and Proserpine *Iuno profunda*, are not considerations which, under the circumstances, would weigh with Mr Owen. Nor, from the fact that *profundum* means the deep of heaven in Manil. V 720, did Mr Owen infer that a fortiori it could mean the deep of hell: quite the contrary. J. P. XXXIII p. 252 'The same word could hardly mean both heaven and hell in so precise a language as Latin. Considering the quantity of theological literature that has been written in this language, if this were so, it would lead to confusing results' (it is horrible to think what confusion must have been caused by using *spiritus*, as theologians did, of both God and the Devil). Now I do not myself care whether the substantive *profundum* occurs elsewhere in the required sense or not; but for Mr Owen's sake I turned to the first author whom I thought likely to furnish an example, and I cited an allusion to Amphiaraus' descent into the underworld from Aetn. 578 'septemque duces raptumque profundo'. Mr Owen however says that *profundum* here means merely 'the abyss', || which is a comparatively shallow affair: hell is too deep to be called *profundum*; and he still requires a passage where the realm of Pluto is un-mistakably so entitled. Well, here are two: Sen. Phaed. 147 sq. 'teneri crede Lethaeo abditum | Thesea profundo' and Oed. 577 sq. 'temptari abditum | Acheron profundum mente non aequa tulit'. But I suspect that Mr Owen will still find my conjecture as surprising as ever, and that his dislike of it is based upon something much more solid than any erroneous opinion about the sense of *profundum*.

At the three other places, III 236 sq., VII 184 sq., I 168, Mr Owen un-ostentatiously abandons, in deference to my unfair criticism, the attitude which I criticised: this surely is very handsome conduct on his part. I will only add that what he calls on p. 142 'the attack which has been made by Mr Housman (J. P. XXXIV 40 foll. [this edition pp. 964–8]) on certain conclusions of mine' was a reply to an attack which had been made by Mr Owen (J. P. XXXIII pp. 246–55) on certain of my conclusions.

THE *IBIS* OF OVID*

In 1894, when my recension of the Ibis had been published in Postgate's corpus poetarum Latinorum, I intended to put together a paper discussing various problems which the poem presents, and in particular defending and explaining my alterations of its text. From this design I was led away by other interests, and the editors of Ovid were left staring at a set of very puzzling objects, – conjectures which I had proposed because I had read the Ibis with attention, and whose cause and aim were obscure to those who had not. Within the last few years I have published two articles upon some of my proposals: one in this Journal, xxxiv pp. 222–38 [[this edition pp. 969–81]], on my transposition of certain distichs, the other in the Classical Quarterly, ix pp. 31–8 [[this edition pp. 905–12]],[1] on my correction of verse 512. I will now take leave of the poem by adding a series of remarks, general and particular, upon matters which may still seem to need explanation or discussion. But first I will correct one error in my text, and mention four other places where I should now alter it.

praesidio in 283 is a slip of the pen for *subsidio*. In order to force myself to think about every detail, I made a manuscript copy of the whole poem, which I sent to the printer; and this is one of those errors of transcription which are caused by anticipating a coming word, here *praesens*.

In the same verse, knowing what I now know of the MSS (see pp. 291 sq.), I should write *praesens sit* for *sit praesens*; in 284 I should write *nihil* instead of *nil*, for the reason which I gave in the Classical Review xxxiii pp. 57 sq. [[this edition pp. 1001–2]]; in 415 I should write *Achaemenidis* for *Achaemenidae* (see p. 314); and in 470 I should write *Dexithoes* or rather *Dexitheae* for *Dexiones* (see pp. 300–4). ||

I

The first editor to furnish the Ibis with an apparatus criticus was Merkel in his recension of 1837. His collations, 18 in number, are mostly derived from the unpublished papers of Heinsius, among them the collation of F, called C in his edition; V, called A in his edition, was collated by Moriz Haupt; the rest of the 18 MSS are without importance.

---

* [[*JPh* 35 (1920), 287–318]]

[1] In this paper, on p. 32 [[this edition p. 906]] (where I twice wrote 'Autonoe' by mistake for 'the Sibyl'), the *ire uiro* which I restore at Sil. xiii 800 may be supported by the *ire sorori* of xv 327.

Ellis in 1881 gave, or rather professed to give, collations of 10 MSS, including F (as he chose to call it, though Merkel had attached this letter to another MS) and V (as he chose to call Merkel's A). Only seven of them are worth anything: FG (again a letter to which Merkel had given a different meaning) H (another yet) PTVX. As for the remainder, M is merely a copy of H, and neither Vat.[1] nor Parm. contains anything of merit which is not to be found in one or more of the seven.

The same is true of certain excerpts from a Florentine 'exemplar ex Marcia bibliotheca' made by Politian in the Bodleian copy of the ed. Parmensis 1477. The Zamoscianus saec. xv adduced by R. Foerster in Rhein. Mus. 1900 p. 453 contains only verses 1–37 and in them nothing of importance or even of interest except the *audiat* 27 which it shares with G. The corrupt and corrected Bodleian cod. Canonicianus 20, of 1500 or thereabouts, collated by Mr Winstedt in Class. Rev. 1899 pp. 395 sq., has one lection of note, *thaleceae* 502 for the *paphegee* etc. of the other MSS; but this only shows that some scholar of the renascence had anticipated Heinsius in conjecturing *Phalaeceae*.

The florilegia excel the complete MSS in two readings, 109 *calidus* Atr. Par. Brit. Bodl. for *clarus*, and 135 *iaziges* Atr., *iatiges* Par., for *iapiges* and worse. The repertorium uocabulorum exquisitorum of Conradus de Mure preserves *astacide* at 515, where the MSS have various corruptions, and slightly excels them in *theudocus* 466 and *Euenus* 513. The late MSS and early editions provide many corrections: 36 *quem*, 84 *chao*, 145 *nolim*, 178 *egypti*, 229 *imbuerunt*, 249 *accedent*, 256 *armati...inermis opem*, ‖ 272 *Demodoci*, 284 *ercei*, 323 *Aleuas*, 348 *Tisameni...Calliroes*, 357 *facit*, 366 *foris*, 391 *sex bis ut*, 412 *cercionea*, 434 *Threicius*, 463 *cygneius*, 466 *Theudotus*, 483 *Hypsipyles*, 500 *quae*, 545 *Harpagides*, 569 *acerno*, 571 *Anaxarchus*, 573 *Psamathes*, 600 *Orpheos*, 615 *obstructo*. But the MSS on which we depend for the tradition of what Ovid wrote are the seven which I selected in my recension of 1894.

F = Francofurtanus. G = Galeanus, in Trinity College, Cambridge. H = Holkhamicus. P = Phillippicus, now at Berlin. T = Turonensis. V = Vindobonensis. X = Parisinus. The date of one or two is not settled, and is not worth settling: none is much earlier than 1200, and none perhaps much later than 1300.

An apparatus criticus constructed by Ellis is never complete and never completely intelligible. This I already knew when I undertook to edit the Ibis, and even if I had not known it I should have begun to learn it in the course of my task. But I did not yet know, what subsequent experience taught me, that he never in his life collated a MS nor even grasped the meaning of the word *collation*. I consequently supposed that he knew the readings of his MSS even

---

[1] A possible exception is the *nichil arcei* of Vat. in 284, which is nearer than the *nil rethei* of most MSS to the true reading *nihil Hercei*; but it may be merely a corruption of a correction.

where he did not report them, and that his reports themselves were true except where they were self-contradictory; and I contented myself with asking him to supplement them or to clear them up. Sometimes he could, sometimes he could not. 418: text *qui*; note (wrong end foremost, as often) '*que* FHMPVX, *quē* Vat., *qui* G Conr. bis'. What has T? I asked him, and he said *que*. 137: text *mollia pabula*; note '*mollia pabula* FTV Paris. Atrebat., *pabula mollia* PX, *mitia pabula* G'. What has H? I asked him, and he could not tell. 345: text *Dryantiadae*; note '*driantides* P, *driantide* TV, *drianthide* Conr. bis, *driantiade* G unde *Dryantiadae* scripsi cum Riesio et ed. Rubei'. What have FHX? I asked him, and he replied 'no entry for HF: *driantide* X: *Dry(?i)antiadae* may be inferred for F'. 362: text *sua uel Pterelae*; note '*sua* GPVX, *tua* FT Conr., *tibi* M. *pterele* P, *pterere* Vat., *pteleri* F, *sterole* T, *terele* HV, *cherele* X, *cerele* M, *terei* G, *therele* Contr.'. What has H for *sua*? I asked him, and he said *tibi*, and he added (contradicting his own note) that it had *cerele* for *Pterelae*, which is not true. ‖

The defects which my enquiries revealed in Ellis's knowledge of F and V I could repair, or thought I could, from the apparatus criticus of Merkel: to repair the defects in his knowledge of H, which were most conspicuous, I applied to Lord Leicester's librarian, Mr A. J. Napier. But no defects, or hardly any, were perceptible in Ellis's knowledge of the best and most important MSS GPT; and there I thought I might trust him. Trust however was not encouraged when Chatelain in 1894 published a photographic reproduction of the first page of V, which furnished the following additions to Ellis's apparatus: 2 *carmen*] *tempus*. 10 *manus*] *meas* corr. in *manus*. 17 *meae* om. 24 *melius* (after *nostras*) expunged. 29 *at*] *ft*. 30 *quod licet hei*.[1] And mistrust was so confirmed by the progress of my acquaintance with Ellis's publications that I have now thought it advisable to ascertain for myself the readings of the two most important MSS G and T. G is in the library of my own college, and of T I possess photographs given me by Prof. D. A. Slater. To these I have added the much less important H, which I have been able to examine, by the kindness of Lord Leicester, in the Cambridge University Library. The following corrections or additions (I omit a few mere trifles) are to be made in Ellis's reports of these three MSS.

21 *profugae*] *nostre* H. 24 *noluit* (not *uoluit*) T. 42 *et*] *aut* H. 49 *nondum ferro*] *ferro nondum* T. 60 *iudicii*] *inditii* G. 65 *calendis* H. 84 *chao*] *chori* T. 95 *ibin* T. 99 *ades*] *adest* G. 107 *amnis*] *pontus* T. 120 *quum*] *cum* GHT (and doubtless FPVX). 137 *mollia pabula* H. 141 *tunc* G (Ellis contradicts himself), *tum* T. 142 *mores* H. 177 *quaeque*] *atque* H. 189 *monimenta* G. 194 *aues* H. 198 *aut*] *et* GHT (also F according to Merkel, and very likely PX in spite of Ellis's silence).

[1] But at 22 the reading is *ipse*, as it should be from Ellis's silence, not *ille*, as Merkel states and as I stated in reliance on him.

220 *ibī* T. 233 *uinxerunt* or perhaps *iunxerunt* H. 247 *disces*] *disce* T. 259 *amin-torides* H. 272 *ut*] *et* H. *Demodoci*] *democii* H, *demophodi* (not *demodofi*) T. 275 *melior tumidis* H (Ellis contradicts himself). 277 *sollertique* H. 280 *aquis* (misprint)] *equis* GH. 283 *sit praesens*] *praesens sit* HT. 290 *humor* H. 294 *im-mensum*] *inmensum* if not rather *inmersum* G. *proiciare*] *praecipitere* H. 331 *euri-damas* H. 345 *driantide* H. 350 *tideus* H. 351 *uenerem iuncxit*] *iuncxit* ‖ (or *uincxit*) *uenerem* H. 359 *thesti* H (Ellis contradicts himself). 362 *sua*] *tibi* H. 383 *Therodomanteos* T. 388 *ut*] *aut* T. 389 *penus* H. 391 *ycaridos* H. 407 *cum* H 418 *qui*] *que* T. 426 *conficiare*] *destituare* H. 454 *frigios* H. 467 *Abdera*] *addera* G (which Ellis cites from X). 471 *martertera* G. 488 *driops* H. 497 *eadem*] *eadem et* G. 500 *quod* GT. 510 *cressia* T. 515 *Astacidaeque*] *t̄acide quo* G, *Hyrcacideque* T. 546 *caesus*] *scelus* (not *sectus*) H. 549 *utue*] *utque* H. 552 *habent*] *habet* T. 571 *anaxarnis* (not *-arrus*) H. 581 *fr̄s* H. 596 *dilaniet*] *dilaceret* H. 606 *sic tua uirus*] *corpora uirus* G. 611 and 612 are not omitted by G. 611 *tuis laedaris*] *datus ladaris* G (whence Ellis would have conjectured *datis* if he had noticed it). 615 *lumine*] *limine* G. 617 *Mineruae*] *diane* G. 628 *eat*] *erat* corr. in *erit* G. 639 *sint* H. 641 *dii* H. 643 *post modo* H.

These errors and oversights,[1] however discreditable to Ellis, have done little harm to Ovid; and there are only four verses on which it is necessary to make any remark. In 49 the order of words

> sic ego te *ferro nondum* iaculabor acuto,

preferred by Heinsius, conforms to Ovid's usual practice of balancing sub-stantive and adjective in the verse, and now that T as well as FP is found to support it the contrary evidence of GHVX for *nondum ferro* is not superior: there may however be some force in what Merkel says, or rather seems struggling to say in his usual inarticulate fashion, that the latter lays the right stress on *nondum*. In 283 the rhythm of

> nec tibi subsidio *praesens sit* numen, ut illi ‖

is more Ovidian than *sit praesens* and was preferred by Merkel and Riese; but from the silence of Ellis's apparatus it appeared that the *sit praesens* of his text was in all his MSS.[2] It is in G, but it is not in T nor H, and we must now doubt

---

[1] Mr Owen's report of H in the tristia, though he says 'contuli diligentissime', appears to be no more accurate. I have checked it by the MS for book II, and I find that the following additions or corrections are needed. 61 *quid*] *quod*. 65 *illic*] *illis*. 67 *fit*] *sit*. 111 *patrio*] *toto* with *uel patrio* superscript. 113 *ut...nec*] *et...et*. 114 *sit*] *fit*. 122 *non*] *tamen*. 137 *in illo*] *ab urbe*. 143 *honeratam*] *hornatam*. 150 *continuasse*] *continuisse*. 175 *et*] *es*. 176 *dimidio*] *dimidioque*. 203 *ister*. 213 *pectora*] *numina*. 226 *metum*] *metu*. 235 *non*] *nec*. 251 *submouimus*] *sūmouimus*. 261 *genitrix*. 262 *genetrix*] *genitrix et*. 291 *adoranti*] *adorande*. 379 *indicio*] *iudicio*. 397 *tetrice*] *tretrice*. 411 *qui*] *quod*. 419 *monimentis*. 433 *Memmi*] *memi*. 447 *tibulus*. 476 *deceat*] *deceat et*. 493 *hic* (misprint)] *his*. 495 *de scribentibus*] *describentibus*. 523 *uarios uenerisque*] *ueneris uariosque*. 547 *credas opus*] *tempus credas*.

[2] The other editors subsequent to Ellis have overlooked this, and are lucky in their oversight.

whether it is in any other of the seven, for Merkel certainly implies that F and V have *praesens sit*: this reading therefore I should now adopt. In 500

> dixerat inuiso *quod* mala uerba deo,

now that Ellis's report of G is found to be false, there is no authority for *quae* in any good MS; but I still prefer it, as Heinsius and Merkel did. Similarly in 198

> inde ego pauca canam, frondes ut siquis ab Ida
> *aut* summam Libyco de mare carpat aquam,

aut is better than *et*, even though it proves to have less authority.

After my corrections and supplements to Ellis's reports of GHT, the text of these three MSS is at length fully known to the public, but not the text of any of the other four. As regards F and V there are contradictions between Ellis and Merkel; and although, when two scholars in succession report upon a MS, the second usually keeps the report of the first before his eyes, and means his own report, where it differs, to be taken as correcting the other, this is not what happens when the second scholar is Ellis; and on occasions when I called his attention to discrepancies between Merkel's apparatus and his own, it appeared that he had not previously noticed them. As regards P and X we have no witness but Ellis, and what that means we know by this time. But though a fresh examination of these MSS would certainly disclose omissions and errors in his report of them, I do not suppose that here, any more than in GHT, the corrections would render any appreciable service to the text of Ovid. I do not intend to collate the MSS myself, nor do I urge any other scholar to that undertaking, unless he thinks he can find nothing better to do.

I subjoin a list of the changes and additions required in my apparatus criticus by my present knowledge of the MSS; I also ‖ repair three errors (404, 470, 540) and two omissions (61, 431) of my own, and I add at 211 a lection which perhaps deserves to be recorded.

22 *ille* GHVX] delete V. 49 *fer. non.* FP] add T. 61 *qui* PVX] add F ex sil. Ell. et Merk. 98 et 99 *ades* GX] G in 99 has *adest.* 107 add 'amnis. pontus T, potus...unda F'. 198 add 'aut V, et FGHT, de PX siletur'. 211 add 'non. nec in FTV'. 256 after *inermis opem* insert ʃ. 281 delete 'redemi C bis' on the authority of Anton Meyer, Die quellen zum Fabularius des Konrad von Mure p. 119. 283 add 'praesens sit HT et ex Merkelii silentio FV, sit praesens G, de PX siletur'. 348 *callirices* C] *callirces* teste Meyero. 351 *iun. uen.* TV] add H. 383 *Therodomanteos* GHV] add T. 388 add 'ut GPX, aut FHTV'. 404 *temporibus* GHTV] delete HV and add PX.[1] 431 *repetas* H] add V on Merkel's authority. 434 delete 'tu cereique C' and add C after *tu tereique.* 470 delete

---

[1] *temporibus* has the better authority, but *diuersis uulneribus* is more expressive, and resembles met. v 141 'matre satos una *diuerso uulnere* fudit'.

'sicut coni. Kinkel'. 497 *et* om. GH] delete G. 500 *quae* G, *quod* cett. (de TX siletur)] *quae* 5, *quod* O (de X siletur). 515 *Tacideq.*] *Tacide quo.* 540 fort. *urbis*] *urbis* 5. 572 add '*tritaq.* (al. *circaq.*) C'. 596 *dilaceret* FV] add H. 611 sq. om. G] delete. 617 add '*diane* FG'.

The relations of the seven MSS to one another may be represented thus:

$$G...XP..T..F.H.V$$

The nearest akin are X and P; next in closeness is the tie between H and its two neighbours F and V; T stands more apart, and G still more. G and V are the most unlike to one another, and G's next neighbour X is further away from it than are the next neighbours of other MSS from them.

Before asking which is the best MS we must determine what we mean by goodness. The MS whose readings are oftenest right is P: both Ellis and I, though our texts[1] differ in more than 80 places, follow P more frequently, – I only a little more frequently, – than any other MS. Second, by the same test, comes T; then || begins divergency, and G compares very differently with our two recensions; tried by Ellis's it is third or fourth, tried by mine it is seventh.

Ellis		Housman	
1.	P	1.	P
2.	T	2.	T
3.	{ F	3.	V
	{ G	4.	F
5.	V	5.	X
6.	X	6.	H
7.	H	7.	G

But if the best MS is that which oftenest is right when all the rest are wrong, or nearer the truth when all the rest are further away, then P descends to the third place, and the first and second are occupied respectively by G and T according to Ellis, by T and G according to me.

There is one place where, beyond all question, G alone of the seven MSS is right, 488 *iuuit*. There are three where, though not certainly right, it is preferred to the rest by all the latest editors, from Ellis onwards, 139 *tecum bella geram*,[2] 443 *aut*, 470 *Dexiones*; and five more where it is preferred by most of those editors, 27 *audiat*, 30 *qua*, 159 *colubre*, 293 *ethreclides*, 625 *uiscera*. There are six where only a minority prefers it, 16 *uiui*, 211 *illuxit*, 285 *a*, 316 *ossa*, 365 *uestigia*, 434 *tu Teleique*; one where nobody prefers it but Ellis, 492 *nomine fecit* (though Merkel builds a conjecture on this reading); and one, 173 *uocabere*, where

---

[1] Of the other editors since 1881, Guethling (1884) generally follows Ellis, and Mr Owen (1915) generally follows me; Merkel's text of 1884 is more independent but less satisfactory than either.

[2] Calp. buc. 1 50 *secum bella geret*.

nobody prefers it but Merkel. Altogether Ellis prefers it in thirteen places, I in eight (now seven only), and three of my seven are places where Ellis does not prefer it.

The places where I prefer T alone to the six other MSS are thirteen: 76 *netis*, 85 *canentur*, 135 *iapiges*, 142 *exanguis*, 233 *uinxerunt* (but here H perhaps agrees), 293 *uictus*, 329 *leneus*, insertion between 338 and 339 of 439 sq. and 461 sq. without 637 sq., 366 *membraque*, 380 *quos*, 387 *demisit*, 449 *et*, 472 *ut*. Of these places there are seven where all recent editors share my preference, 76, 135, 233, 329, 387, 449, 472; two more, 142 and 293, where I am in the majority; and yet two more, 366 ‖ and 380, where one other editor agrees with me. Ellis prefers T in eight places out of my thirteen.

The two MSS therefore compare as follows:

G	T
preferred by all in 4 places	preferred by all in 7 places
preferred by most in $4 + 5 = 9$	preferred by most in $7 + 2 = 9$

But now let us turn from their peculiar merits to their peculiar faults. These are so much more numerous that it is impossible to give them all; but out of each MS I have made what I hope is a fair and representative collection of readings somewhat conspicuously different from those of the other MSS and rejected by the consent of recent editors.

G: 24 *non sinit*, 34 *gelido tepidus*, 58 *quamuis non soleam*, 61 *nondum quis sis*, 65 *festo*, 103 *mortales*, 110 *lumina*, 126 *deserat* (for *torqueat*), 131 sq. om., 153 *erit*, 174 *impia*, 189 *monimenta*, 191 *credas*, 205 *tot ue tibi uenient misero*, 264 *clarus . . . sumptus*, 267 *postquam*, 308 *matre parante*, 311 *gratissima*, 325 *roma*, 362 *terei*, 375 *artis*, 407 *de*, 409 *in humum*, 420 *sepe*, 437 *perille tuo*, 439 *ore*, 459 *ne penam*, 538 *oculos*, 606 *sic tua . . . corpora*, 637 *sciticas*, 641 *tibi*, 644 *sub*.

T: 56 *quoque*, 98 *precor*, 201 *inhorreat*, 275 *tumidi tibi sit melior*, 276 *uise*, 287 *yrioni*, 355 *necem miseris*, 385 *rapax*, 406 *ipse . . . urbe*, 430 *consternati*, 443 *utque*, 493 *ad*, 555 *fauniadum*, 586 *et . . . ut*.

These readings are not all necessarily false, and a partisan of either MS could cram a good many of them into the text. But readings certainly false are much commoner in G than in T, and T has none so bad as some of G's, 103 *mortales*, 205 *tot ue tibi*, 325 *Roma*, 362 *Terei*, which are deliberate interpolations.

In our preferences of P there is little disagreement between Ellis and me and the other recent editors. All of us regard it as right or nearest the truth in five places, 256 *armatis*, 362 *pterele*, 502 *paphegee*, 545 *arpacides*, 559 *aniti* (though in 256 and 502 its superiority is very slight), and most of us in one more, 335 *ypomenida*. Further in 30 *et* it is preferred by two editors, in 181 *qui distat summus* by Ellis alone.

Its singularities are universally rejected in 12 *suo*, 15 sq. ‖ post 18, 28 *potior*,

30 *quam*, 48 *uelitis*, 54 *dicta*, 98 *rogo*, 408 *una*, 457 *magnae subito*, 523 *que* om., 562 *tua* (for *sic*); but two of these, 12 and 457, are possibly or even probably true. It thus has fewer errors peculiar to itself than any other of the seven MSS, and, as I have said, it is the MS with which modern texts most closely agree; only it has less singularity in merit than T and G.

The remaining MSS are singly assigned preeminence in the following places:

F: by all in 272 *ut*, 461 *Cassandreus*, 615 *obstructus*, 631 *Rutulo*; by most in 190 *manibus* and 551 *derepta*.

H: by all in 200 *cylissa*, 470 *ypponoo*, 525 *utque*, 539 *conditor*...*tardae*, 555 *Potniadum*; by most in 515 *decisa*.

V: by all in 199 *nascantur*, 256 *uulnus*, 270 *thelemus*, 511 *aleue*, 531 *lico-phrona*; by most in 444 *fati* and 478 *Thaso*.

X: by all in 99 *ades* and 391 *sexus ut*.

They are single in somewhat conspicuous errors, or readings deemed erroneous by the editors, as follows: F in 12 places, H in 18, V in 23, X in 16.

The upshot of these investigations is that T emerges as the best MS on the whole, while the next best is P or G, according as general correctness or singularity in merit is the more esteemed. I was trusting too much to memory and impression when I said in J. P. xxxiv p. 223 [[this edition p. 969]] that the order was roughly TGXPVFH. This puts X a good deal too high: in spite of its affinity to P and G it is much less correct than the one and much less important than the other.

II

Consideration of a question which concerns the poem as a whole, and affects the criticism or interpretation of several verses, may take its start from the couplet 291 sq.

$$\text{utque parum} \begin{Bmatrix} \textit{mitis} \text{ GHPTVX} \\ \textit{fidus} \text{ F} \end{Bmatrix}, \text{ sed non inpune, Prometheus}$$

$$\text{aerias uolucres} \begin{Bmatrix} \textit{sanguine} \text{ GPTX} \\ \textit{corpore} \text{ FHV} \end{Bmatrix} \begin{Bmatrix} \textit{fixus alas} \text{ PT} \\ \textit{pasce tuo} \text{ FGHV} \end{Bmatrix}.^{1} \parallel$$

The same thing is said over again in 543 sq.

> fixus et in duris carparis uiscera saxis
> ut cui Pyrrha sui filia fratris erat;

and the earlier distich was condemned by Saluagnius and Bentley. Schrader in lib. emend. c. XIII, approving its deletion, takes occasion to say on p. 230 'in his Diris poeta bis idem non dicit', and again on p. 233 'Ouidius iisdem exemplis in breui carmine non utitur'. Merkel on the other hand, professing to contradict

---

¹ The reading of X is not given by Ellis and cannot be inferred from his silence; he told me he had 'no entry'.

him, says on p. ix of his edition of 1884 'fabularum argumenta aliquot mutata paulum elocutione iterata esse a poeta nemo dubitat'. Assertion and counter-assertion are equally wanting in precision: I will show what Ovid's practice actually was; and it will prove to be just what might have been expected, the practice of a reasonable man.

He would not have been reasonable if, after saying at 347 'may you run mad like Hercules', he had scrupled to say at 605 'may you be consumed by venom like Hercules', or if anywhere he had shrunk from mentioning one person twice in connexion with two of his misfortunes. But he would have been unreasonable and indeed ridiculous if he had twice imprecated on his enemy the same misfortune of the same person; and he has not done so.

The persons whom he twice mentions or unmistakably signifies are the following. Adonis: 503 as killed by a boar, 565 as expiating by death an incestuous origin. Astyanax: 496 as hurled from a height, 563 as witnessing the fall of his city. Hercules: 347 as plagued with madness, 605 as consumed by venom. Lycaon: 431 as setting human flesh before Jove, 473 as struck by lightning. Macareus: 357 as having an incestuous sister, 562 as bereft of his love. Orestes: 348 as plagued with madness, 527 as killed by a serpent. Thyestes: 359 as having an incestuous daughter, 429 as frightening away the Sun. Ulysses: 277 as shipwrecked, 567 as killed with the sting of a ray. There is no repetition, not even in the case of Adonis: for the stain of his birth might have been expiated by many other deaths than the death which he actually died.

But the two imprecations in 291 sq. and 543 sq. are identical: ‖ not only is the same person mentioned but he is mentioned for the same reason. This is not merely absurd but unique in its absurdity, and is therefore to be got rid of. Which of the two couplets is spurious nobody can doubt, and the cause of its interpolation is not obscure. In this long catalogue of pains and penalties the interpolator could find no reference, such as anyone would expect, to the famous sufferings of Prometheus, whom he did not recognise under the title of 'Pyrrha's paternal uncle'. He therefore wrote 291 sq. somewhere in the margin: in most of our MSS the couplet stands after 290, but in H after 288, and it was absent from Saluagnius' 'membranae San-Victorianae'.[1]

At any rate repetitions ought not to be imported by conjecture; and Ellis's conjecture at 327 will import one. The MSS have

> quaeque in *Adimantum Phillesia* (*Phylesia* sim.) regna tenentem
> a Ioue uenerunt te quoque tela petant.

---

[1] In what form the verses were written by their author, and whether in any of the various forms which they wear in the MSS, is another and a minor question. *sanguine* (*corpore*) *fixus alas* in the pentameter is not so bad as *sanguine* (*corpore*) *pasce tuo* with its impossible imperative; and in the hexameter *fidus* is evidently no more than an attempt to amend *mitis*. I suppose that *parum mitis* is a rendering of Aesch. Prom. 944 τὸν πικρῶς ὑπέρπικρον.

Nothing is known of Adimantus[1] or his kingdom, but that is no reason for altering a verse in this poem, much less for altering it into '*Aphidantum Phylacesia* (or *Phyllesia* or *Phialesia*) regna tenentem' and explaining it of Lycaon; for Lycaon is instanced as struck by lightning in 473 sq.

> ut ferus Aeolides, ut sanguine natus eodem,
>   quo genita est liquidis quae caret Arctos aquis.

I at least cannot interpret this couplet otherwise than Sanctius and Desselius did, 'like Salmoneus, and like his cousin, who was Callisto's father' (the genealogy is Zeus, Hellen, Aeolus, Salmoneus; Zeus, Pelasgus, Lycaon). I do not see how *quo* can be referred to *eodem* and *natus* made to signify a brother of Callisto's, for all her brothers, or all with one exception, were struck by ‖ lightning, and it will be necessary to write *eodem sanguine nati* with MSS of no authority.

That there is no repetition involved in the mention of Lycaon at 431 for one reason and at 473 for another I have already said; and bearing this in mind let us approach the verses 617 sq.

> illius exemplo uioles simulacra Mineruae
>   Aulidis a portu qui leue uertit iter.

Of the three who sailed from Aulis and profaned an image of Athena, neither Ulysses nor Diomed could be indicated by '*leue* iter': this is Aiax Oilei, who tore Cassandra from the goddess's statue, and who appears in Homer's catalogue of the ships as small and nimble and lightly armed, ᾿Οιλῆος ταχὺς Αἴας, | μείων, οὔ τι τόσος γε ὅσος Τελαμώνιος Αἴας, | ἀλλὰ πολὺ μείων· ὀλίγος μὲν ἔην, λινοθώρηξ. And it is no hindrance to this interpretation that Aiax recurs at 341

> utque ferox periit et fulmine et aequore raptor,

since punishment for the violation of the statue might take many other forms than death by thunderstroke and drowning.

The same holds good of 447 sq., upon which there is more to be said.

> et quae *Penthides* fecit *de fratre* Medusae
>   eueniant capiti uota sinistra tuo.

penthides FV, *pentides* GHPX, *pentelides* T. *de fratre* FHTV, *fraterque* GPX.

Saluagnius, apparently in ignorance of the variant *de fratre*, explained *frater Medusae* as Eurystheus; but his statement that Eurystheus 'multa uota sinistra in Herculis exitium fecit' is an impudent and comical fiction: antiquity never heard of these vows, and would have laughed at the notion; Eurystheus him-

---

[1] The fiction of Mr C. Zipfel must be sought on pp. 51 sq. of his dissertation 'quatenus Ouidius in Ibide Callimachum...secutus sit', Lips. 1910: I will give it no further publicity.

self would have laughed at it. Even if we had to abandon the distich without hope of explaining it, *de fratre* would be preferable to *fraterque*, because it is more likely that Ovid defined the vows of one person than that he left the vows of two persons undefined. Nothing has ever been made of *Penthides*; but in a scholium on 577 (Ellis p. 97 [[181 La Penna]]) *ponthei* appears as a corruption of *Pitthei*, and here Saluagnius 'cum aliquibus editionibus' proposed *Pitthides* (though he spelt it *Pittheides* because he knew no better, like || the modern editors who give *Tereides* in 434). This conjecture will draw support from *de fratre Medusae*, and in its turn will confirm that reading against *fraterque*. We know at least of one imprecation uttered by Theseus with terrible consequences: its object was Hippolytus, and Hippolytus by one account was *frater Medusae*. Medusa was daughter of Phorcus, and Phorcus according to Seruius at Verg. Aen. v 824 was 'Thoosae nymphae et Neptuni filius'; Neptune therefore was the common grandfather of Medusa and Hippolytus, and Hippolytus was her *frater patruelis*, in which sense the simple *frater* is used at met. XIII 31 and her. VIII 28. The far-fetched description is quite in the manner of this poem, and it has its purpose, since the curse of Theseus on Hippolytus was fulfilled by Neptune, the ancestor whom he shared with Medusa; and Theseus, in keeping with this allusion, is called *Pitthides* and not *Aegides*. This reading and interpretation meet with no obstacle in 577 sq.

> utque nepos Aethrae Veneris moriturus ob iram
> exul ab attonitis excutiaris equis;

for the imprecation of Theseus on Hippolytus was not that he might be thrown from his chariot, and it could have been fulfilled in many other ways: there is no more repetition here than in the two introductions of Aiax Oilei at 341 and 617 or of Adonis at 503 and 565.

This is also the place to consider two distichs on which much light has fallen since 1894.

469 sq.   aut Iouis infesti telo feriare trisulco

ut satus Hipponoo $\begin{Bmatrix} Dexithoes \\ Dexiones \end{Bmatrix}$ que pater

dexithoes HT, *dexitoes* P, *desithoes* X, *dexithoos* F, *desithoos* V, *dexiones* G. 475 sq.

ut $\begin{Bmatrix} Macelo \\ Macedon \end{Bmatrix}$ rapidis $\begin{Bmatrix} iacta\ est \\ ictus \end{Bmatrix}$ cum coniuge flammis
sic precor aetherii uindicis igne cadas.

macelo FT, *machelo* G, *macedo* HPV, *macedon* X. *iacta est* FGHPV, *ictus* TX, *icta est* ς. ||

To clear the way, I had better begin with the *Dexiones* of G in 470, adopted, though doubtfully, by Ellis and all succeeding editors. *Dexiones pater* is supposed to be Aesculapius, a notable example of death by lightning, and not elsewhere mentioned in the Ibis. But the statement in Ellis's note 'Dectionen siue Dexionen nomen tertiae Aesculapii filiae esse recte intellexit Kinkel Lycophr. p. iv' is false,[1] and 'sicut coni. Kinkel' in my note is an expansion of the falsehood. Kinkel is there commenting on etym. magn. 434 15 sqq., where Aesculapius is said to have had a wife named Ἠπιόνην, ἐξ ἧς αὐτῷ γενέσθαι Ἰάσονα, Πανάκειαν· Δεκτίων ἐν ὑπομνήματι Λυκόφρονος, and what he says is simply 'Dectionem hunc nullum esse uocabulumque hoc nomen tertiae Aesculapii filiae expulisse, inter uiros doctos iamdudum constat': that is, the true reading may be something like Ἰασώ, Πανάκειαν, Ἀκεσώ (or Αἴγλην)· ὡς Θέων ἐν ὑπ. Λυκ. All that can be said for *Dexiones* in Ib. 470 is that the name of a daughter of Aesculapius would be appropriate, and that in etym. magn. 434 15 sq., where we expect the name of a daughter of Aesculapius, we find a word beginning with Δεκ.

The scholia on the Ibis, which are much more fabulous than the poem itself, inform us that *satus Hipponoo* (in whom they do not recognise Capaneus) was named Demeus or Procrustes. This does not prepare us to believe them when they proceed to say that *Dexithoes* or *Dexiones pater* was one Pantacrita (or Acrita or Pactama or Pauacurta), struck by lightning for no fewer than three reasons, (1) 'pro nequitia sua', (2) as 'contemptor deorum', (3) 'quia filiam suam interfecerat quia Iouem cum ea concubuisse audierat'. But two of them agree on another story: P 'Telchinum princeps fulmine periit cum tota sua domo excepta filia cuius erat Iupiter usus hospitio', Conradus de Mure 'Telchinon princeps periit cum tota familia eius fulminatus excepta *Dexithoe*, a qua Iupiter quadam uice fuerat hospitatus.'

This legend reappears in a scholium cited at 475 sq. by ‖ Saluagnius in his edition of 1661 [[pp. 130–1 La Penna]]: 'Nicander dicit *Macelon* filiam Damonis cum sororibus fuisse. harum hospitio Iupiter susceptus, cum Thelonios (i.e. Telchinas), quorum hic Damo princeps erat, corrumpentes uenenis successus omnium fructuum, fulmine interficeret, seruauit eas. sed *Macelo* cum uiro propter uiri nequitiam periit. ad alias seruatas cum uenisset Minos, cum *Desitone* concubuit, ex qua creauit Eusantium, unde Eusantiae fuerunt.' Otto Schneider at Nicand. fr. 116 in 1856 and at Callim. fr. 504 in 1873 corrected *Desitone* to *Dexithea*, *Eusantium* to *Euxantium*, and *Eusantiae* to *Euxantiadae*, comparing Apollod. bibl. III 1 2 Μίνως... παῖδας μὲν ἐτέκνωσεν... ἐκ δὲ Δεξιθέας Εὐξάνθιον

---

[1] Equally false is his statement 'Sophocles, teste eodem Etymologo 256 6, cum Aesculapium hospitio excepisset, post mortem ἡρῴῳ sub nomine Dexionis colebatur, *quasi filius ac Dexiones frater.*' The words of the etym. magn. are ὠνόμασαν αὐτὸν Δεξίωνα ἀπὸ τῆς τοῦ Ἀσκληπιοῦ δεξιώσεως· καὶ γὰρ ὑπεδέξατο τὸν θεὸν ἐν τῇ αὐτοῦ οἰκίᾳ.

and schol. Apoll. Rhod. I 185 Εὐξαντίου τοῦ Μίνωος, passages which make it clear that the scholium is no mere figment. Next, in 1876, Rohde on p. 506 of his Griechische Roman brought this Macelo into relation with Nonn. Dion. XVIII 35–8 Ζῆνα καὶ Ἀπόλλωνα μιῇ ξείνισσε Μακελλώ | (here there is a verse or more wanting) καὶ Φλεγύας ὅτε πάντας ἀνερρίзωσε θαλάσσῃ | νῆσον ὅλην τριόδοντι διαρρήξας Ἐνοσίχθων | ἀμφοτέρας ἐφύλαξε καὶ οὐ πρήνιξε τριαίνῃ. Ellis in 1881 printed scholia resembling that of Saluagnius from P (which corrects Thelonios to Telchinas, as Rohde had conjectured) and from Conr. de Mure: the former has *Macedo filia Damonis*, the latter *Macedon Dānethis filia*; the former *Dexione*, the latter *Dexithoe*; the former does not say that 'Macedo' was destroyed, the latter says that 'Macedon' was destroyed because 'successus omnium fructuum inuidia corrupit'.

At this stage the question stood as follows. There was no evidence, except some MSS and scholia at this verse 475, that any person named Macelo had ever been struck by lightning, nor even that Macelo was the name of any person. A person with the similar name of Macello was mentioned by Nonnus, but mentioned, as was pretty clear despite the mutilation of the passage, not as incurring punishment but as exempted from punishment incurred by her folk. On the other hand Macedon was at any rate a Greek name, and death by thunderstroke might conceivably have befallen either the Μακεδόνα γηγενῆ of anon. descr. orb. 620 in Muell. geogr. Gr. min. I p. 220 or τὸν εἰκημάχον Μακεδόνα cited from Caesarius Mign. bibl. Gr. patr. ‖ uol. 38 p. 993 by Lobeck Agl. p. 575 and Ellis p. 181. It therefore seemed to Guethling and me that the safest course was to accept provisionally the lections *Macedon*[1] (or *Macedo*) from HPVX and *ictus* from TX.

But then came the successive publication of Bacchylides in 1897, Pindar's Paeans in 1907, and, more important than either for these verses of the Ibis, some 90 lines of the aetia of Callimachus in 1910. These furnished the following evidence.

Bacchyl. I (for Argius of Ceos) 3–17 [[113–27 Snell]] Μίνως…βαθύзωνον κόραν Δεξιθέαν δάμασεν…δεκάτῳ δ' Εὐξ[άντι]ον [μηνὶ τέ]κ' εὐπλόκ[αμος νύμφα], 73 [Μακ]ελὼ δὲ…[φιλ]αλάκατος (Blass).

Pind. Paean. (Oxyrh. pap. v 841) IV (for the Ceans) 40–5 (Euxantius speaks) τρέω τοι πόλεμον Διὸς Ἐννοσίδαν τε βαρύκτυπον· χθόνα τοί ποτε καὶ στρατὸν ἀθρόον πέμψαν κεραυνῷ τριόδοντί τε ἐς τὸν βαθὺν Τάρταρον, ἐμὰν ματέρα λιπόντες καὶ ὅλον οἶκον εὐερκέα.

Callim. aet. (Oxyrh. pap. VII 1011) [[fr. 75 Pfeiffer]] 64–9 (Xenomedes wrote

---

[1] The form *Macedon* derives no strong support from X, in which the words are transposed *ut Macedon ictus rapidis*; but *Macedo* is a form which Ovid would not use. Horace used it, though not as a proper name, and Seneca might have used it; but in Ovid there are 40 examples certified by metre of Greek nominatives in *-ōn*, and not one of the Latin form.

the history of Ceos) ἐν δ' ὕβριν θάνατόν τε κεραύνιον, ἐν δὲ γόητας | Τελχῖνας μακάρων τ' οὐκ ἀλέγοντα θεῶν | ἠλεὰ Δημώνακτα γέρων ἐνεθήκατο δέλτοις | καὶ γρηῦν Μακελὼ μητέρα Δεξιθέης, | ἃς μούνας, ὅτε νῆσον ἀνέτρεπον εἵνεκ' ἀλιτρῆς | ὕβριος, ἀσκηθεῖς ἔλλιπον ἀθάνατοι.

This settles the reference and reading of Ib. 470. The man there signified as struck by lightning is the father of Dexithea of Ceos, whose name, it appears from Callimachus, was Demonax; and the *dexithoes* etc. of the MSS should be corrected, as Jurenka at Bacchyl. 1 5, following Otto Schneider's hint, proposes, to *Dexitheae*. Δεξιθέα is evidently ἡ δεξαμένη θεούς (Ζῆνα καὶ 'Απόλλωνα Nonn.), and Δεξιθόη would be meaningless. That the error is not Ovid's but the scribes' I infer from what happens to the similar name Λευκοθέα in Latin MSS. Ouid. fast. VI 501 and 545 *Leucothea* codd. opt. aliique, -*oe* dett., Ciris 396 *Leucothea* A¹R, -*toa* H, -*thoe* A² dett., Stat. Theb. VI 12 *Leucothea* P ‖ (saec. IX) ceterique, IX 402 *Leucothean* idem, -*oan* man. rec. in P, Cic. n. d. III 39 *Leucotheam* V (saec. X) aliique, -*toe* Harl. (saec. XV), 48 *Leucothea* omnes: I omit writers like Seruius and Hyginus. On the other hand the MSS of Propertius, being late and bad, give *Leucothoe* II 26 10 and *Leucothoen* 28 20, and so do the earlier if not better MSS of Ovid met. IV 542, but there the scribes were fresh from the Leucothoe of verses 196, 208, 220, who is a different person, like the Aurelia Leucothoe of C.I.L. II 1694: *Leucothoe* in Claud. nupt. Hon. 156 may be Claudian's own mistake. Such forms as *Leucothee* and *Dexithee* in Latin have neither authority nor probability.

But at 475 sq. increase of knowledge has brought no diminution of perplexity. Macelo is now a person, not a mere name, but the more we learn about her the less does she fit this place. Far from being struck by lightning, with or without her husband, she escaped the stroke which slew him and all her people excepting only her daughter Dexithea. Perhaps the best way out of the trouble is to trust yet further those scholia which have been shown to deserve at least some trust. Nicander, whom they give as their authority, may have told the tale otherwise than Callimachus and Nonnus: to him Macelo may have been, as the scholiasts call her, the daughter and not the wife of Damon (or Demonax), and she may have perished 'cum uiro propter uiri nequitiam', whoever her husband was.

Either way, there is no repetition in 469 sq. and 475 sq.: *Dexitheae pater* and *Macelonis coniunx* are not the same person. If we believe Callimachus, the Macelo whose husband was Dexithea's father did not perish with him by lightning: if we believe the Nicander of the scholia, the husband with whom Macelo perished by lightning was not Dexithea's father but her brother-in-law.

III

My correction of *uiro* to *Iouis* in 512, and my transposition of the verses 135–40, 181 sq., 203 sq., 409 sq., and 459 sq., as I said on p. 287, are defended elsewhere; so I will now proceed to the other verses on which I have remarks to make, and I will take them in their numerical order. ||

11–12   ille relegatum gelidos Aquilonis ad ortus
     non sinit exilio delituisse meo.

This couplet is cited by Eutyches G.L.K. v p. 475 in the following form:

    ille relegatum *gelidas* Aquilonis ad *oras*
     non sinit exilio delituisse *suo*.

Although Eutyches and even his MSS are much older than the MSS of the Ibis, these divergencies from our text are of little weight, because his sole concern is with the conjugation of *relēgo*, and grammarians do not trouble to be exact in such particulars as are foreign to the matter they have in hand. *oras* is less exquisite than *ortus*, and as two of Eutyches' best MSS give *legidos* and *agelidos*, it may be that *ortus* is what Eutyches himself had written. But the *suo* of Eutyches is the reading also of P and several inferior MSS in the Ibis; and this agreement between two independent authorities is noteworthy and may be significant. Though Ovid speaks of himself, the pronoun of the 3rd person in this sentence is not impossible nor even incorrect.

25–8   huic igitur meritas grates, ubicumque licebit,
     pro tam mansueto pectore semper agam.
    audiet hoc Pontus. faciet quoque forsitan idem
     terra sit ut propior testificanda mihi.

In this text of most MSS and editions the sense of *audiet hoc Pontus* is 'audiet me grates Augusto agentem'; and quite good sense it is if you read no further. But if you do, Ovid is found hoping for the day when he will 'call to witness' some region less remote than Pontus; and what is the point or meaning of that? he has said nothing of calling Pontus to witness anything, nothing of any *testificatio*. The missing notion is supplied by the jussive *audiat hoc Pontus* of G and two inferior MSS: that is 'audiat hoc quod modo dixi, grates me semper acturum esse'. In these words he 'testificatur Pontum'; and he hopes that some day Augustus will transfer him to a region nearer home, || and enable him to say, for instance, 'audiat hoc Phrygia', when he repeats his declaration.

audiat was first adopted by Guethling and Merkel in 1884, but I doubt if they understood its necessity or were moved by anything but the same heedless partiality for G with which they accepted its highly inappropriate *uiui* for *miseri* in 16. There is no similar doubt about Mr Ehwald: when he writes in Burs. Jahresb. vol. 43 p. 262 'ich halte den Conjunctiv hier für ebenso unpassend wie *sentiat* trist. I 1 14 und *experiare* Ibis 250 (248)', he shows that he has no apprehension of the problem.

131–2　　　　et prius hanc animam, nimium tibi saepe petitam,
　　　　　　　auferet illa dies quae mihi sera uenit.

saepe, still more *nimium saepe*, is at variance with Ovid's account of the circumstances. Ibis had shown him no enmity before his banishment, and since his banishment he can hardly have found opportunity for *frequent* attacks: what he did, according to verses 11–22, was to bring a lawsuit against Ovid laying claim to some of his property. I have therefore accepted Heinsius' conjecture *saeue*, so that *nimium* belongs to *petitam*. The two words are confused at Mart. XIV 211 2, Stat. Theb. XI 379, and elsewhere; and the vocative is like 29 *uiolente*, 40 *improbe*, 130 *perfide*.

187–90　　　noxia mille modis lacerabitur umbra, tuasque
　　　　　　　　Aeacus in poenas ingeniosus erit.
　　　　　　　in te transcribet ueterum tormenta uirorum:
　　　　　　　　omnibus antiquis causa quietis eris.

uirorum in 189 is not merely a vague but an inappropriate word; the *reorum* of Heinsius is accepted by Merkel and Riese and supported by the following parallels: Sen. H.f. 579–81 'qui fronte nimis crimina tetrica | quaerunt ac *ueteres* excutiunt *reos* | deflent iuridici Threiciam nurum', Claud. in Ruf. II 494 sq. 'dum lites Stygiique negotia soluit | dura fori *ueteresque reos* ex ordine quaerit', Drac. Orest. 499 'non sat erunt quaecumque *reis tormenta* paratis'. It may have shrunk to *rorum* and then have been expanded to *ui-rorum*, or perhaps *deorum* was the ‖ corruption and *uirorum* its correction. At Prop. III 5 39 'sub terris sint iura deum et *tormenta gigantum*', where the last word is hardly apposite and the Neapolitanus omits it, I proposed *tormenta reorum* in J. P. XXI pp. 165 sq. [[this edition pp. 280–1]].

In 190 almost all MSS have *omnibus* and almost all editors *manibus*, the reading of F. This is not, like *uirorum*, inappropriate, but it is still somewhat vague, and we have no assurance that it is more than a conjecture. Heinsius' conjecture *sontibus* is nearer to *omnibus*, and *ueterum...reorum* supports and is supported by *sontibus antiquis*. Perhaps it is worth while to quote Sen. H. f. 1222 sq. 'inferorum carcer et *sonti* plaga | decreta turbae' and Claud. in Ruf. II 478 '(Minos) iustis dirimit *sontes*'.

It may not sound credible, but it is true, that Mr Owen defends *uirorum* by citing ex Pont. I 3 61 sq. 'i nunc et ueterum nobis exempla uirorum, | qui forti casum mente tulere, refer', and *omnibus* by citing Rutil. Nam. II 57 'omnia

Tartarei cessent tormenta Neronis'. The former of these citations helps to show that the *uirorum* of Ib. 189 is corrupt, and the latter lends support to *sontibus* in 190.

217–20
> lux quoque natalis, nequid nisi triste uideres,
> turpis et inductis nubibus atra fuit.
> haec est, in fastis cui dat grauis Allia nomen,
> quaeque dies Ibin, publica damna, tulit.

The last couplet is thus punctuated by most editors, and is interpreted accordingly by such commentators as do interpret it. It means then 'this (the birthday of Ibis) is the dies Alliensis and the birthday of Ibis'. This nonsense would be converted into sense if *haec est* were changed to *est eadem*; but there would remain the absurdity of *publica damna* in apposition with Ibis, who was nothing of the sort: the meaning of the phrase may be seen from cons. Liu. 200 cited by Ellis, 'consulis erepti publica damna'.

That Heinsius punctuated the distich otherwise,

> haec est, in fastis cui dat grauis Allia nomen;
> quaeque dies Ibin publica damna tulit, ||

is probably a fact of no significance; for he often used the semicolon instead of the comma (as in 579 sq. 'propter opes magnas ut perdidit hospes alumnum; | perdat ob exiguas te tuus hospes opes'), and omitted the commas which serve to indicate apposition (as in 81 'uos quoque plebs superum Fauni'). But his punctuation nevertheless is right, and answers to the true construction. The pentameter means 'eaque dies, quae Ibin tulit, publica damna tulit' and repeats in another form what has been said in the hexameter, that the birthday of Ibis and the dies Alliensis are the same: compare rem. 220 'damnis Allia nota suis'. The *haec est* of the hexameter resembles trist. IV 10 11–14 'Lucifer amborum natalibus affuit idem; | una celebrata est per duo liba dies. | *haec est* armiferae festis de quinque Mineruae | quae fieri pugna prima cruenta solet.'

221–6
> qui simul inpura matris prolapsus ab aluo
> Cinyphiam foedo corpore pressit humum,
> sedit in aduerso nocturnus culmine bubo
> funereoque graues edidit ore sonos.
> protinus Eumenides lauere palustribus undis
> qua caua de Stygiis fluxerat unda uadis.

Ovid causes Ibis to be born in Africa, the native continent of savage beasts and venomous reptiles, and in the region most infested by serpents, *Cinyphiam humum*, the neighbourhood of the Syrtes. The exact spot is near a *palus*[1] and a

---

[1] The *palus* is recognised as lake Tritonis by Mr A. Rostagni, Contr. al. sc. dell'antich. vol. III. pp. 21 sq.

river which issues from the world below; and this spot can be identified by comparing the following passages. Apoll. Sid. carm. 15 6 *Cinyphio Tritone*. Strab. XVII p. 836 〚1167 Meineke〛 ἔστι δὲ ἄκρα λεγομένη Ψευδοπενιάς, ἐφ' ἧς ἡ Βερενίκη τὴν θέσιν ἔχει παρὰ λίμνην τινὰ Τριτωνιάδα, ἐν ᾗ μάλιστα νησίον ἐστὶ καὶ ἱερὸν τῆς Ἀφροδίτης ἐν αὐτῷ· ἔστι δὲ καὶ λιμὴν Ἑσπερίδων, καὶ ποταμὸς ἐμβάλλει Λάθων. Luc. IX 347–56 'torpentem *Tritonos . . . paludem . . .* quam iuxta *Lethon* tacitus praelabitur amnis | *infernis*, ut fama, trahens obliuia *uenis*'. Solin. 27 54 'circa extimum Syrtium cornum Bernicen ciuitatem adluit ‖ *Lethon* (*Leton* Plin. n. h. v 31) amnis *inferna*, ut putant, *exundatione* prorumpens.'

'illa uerborum constructio, *Eumenides lauere palustribus undis qua caua unda de Stygiis uadis fluxerat*, plane est inelegans' says Saluagnius. The repetition is hardly worse than 627 sq. *agebat . . . acta* and others which can be cited from Ovid or at least from Ovid's MSS; but if any change were to be made I should think Saluagnius' *paludibus udis* less likely than *palustribus antris*. The MSS of Claudian 12 35 are divided between *antris* and *undis*, and some of Ovid's have *undis* for *antris* at mct. II 269 and *antris* for *undis* at v 48; *antra* means valleys in Prop. I 1 11, 2 11, IV 4 3, and perhaps also in Sil. II 59 sq. 'Phorcynidos *antra* Medusae | *Cinyphiumque* Macen', since the Gorgons are not usually represented as dwelling in a cave.

282   a duce Puniceo.

Here I said '*Puniceo* non Ouidianum'. *punicus* is used in both senses, 'red' and 'Carthaginian'; but the only other example of *puniceus* in the latter which Lachmann could produce at Lucr. II 829 was from the lex Thoria; and though Georges cites *Punicea religio* from 'Liv.', what I find in Liu. XXII 6 12 is *Punica religione*. There is however one other place in Ovid where this form seems to have this meaning, met. v 536 '*puniceum* curua decerpserat arbore pomum'; for although the adjective might describe the colour of the pulp of the pomegranate, it cannot easily be dissociated from the name *punica malus*, which indicates the country whence the fruit came to Italy. But the *Cinyphio* (*cinifeo, cinyphis, cenifeas, cinisso*) of a few late MSS, though probably no more than a conjecture, may yet be a true one: for this epithet is extended to things Carthaginian in Stat. silu. IV 3 90 sq. 'qualis *Cinyphius* tacente ripa | *Poenos* Bagrada serpit inter agros', and to Iuba, who has less right to it, by Ovid himself in met. XV 755.

365–6   ut iuuenes pereas, quorum fastigia uultus
                  membraque Pisaeae sustinuere fores. ‖

365 *fastigia* FHPTX et corr. in *uestigia* G, *proiecta cadauera quorum* V. 366 *membraque* T, *brachia* FGH, *oraque* V, *quorum* PX, *olim* ϛ. *fores* FGHPTVX, *foris* ϛ.

Saluagnius Heinsius and Burman printed *fastigia . . . olim . . . foris*, Merkel and

Riese *proiecta cadauera quorum* | *oraque. . .fores*, both of which may be set aside as disregarding the best MSS: Ellis's 'quorum *uestigia*, uultus, | *brachia. . .fores*', though accepted by Guethling, may be set aside for another reason, that Oenomaus was not at all likely to nail up the *feet* of his victims; and Ellis himself in his note is evidently repentant. That *fastigia* should be kept is certain: the chief question is what should be read at the beginning of the penta-meter. *quorum* is impossible and seems to be only an accidental repetition from above, but either *bracchia* (with asyndeton) or *membraque* would satisfy the sense. I have preferred *membraque* because both *brachia* and *oraque* would arise much more easily from *(mem)braque* than it could arise from either of them, or than either of them could arise from the other. *membra* may be compared with Luc. II 162–5 'scelerum non Thracia tantum | uidit Bistonii stabulis pendere tyranni, | postibus Antaei Libye, nec Graecia maerens | tot laceros *artus Pisaea* fleuit in *aula*'. I doubt however if this completes the restoration of the couplet: Ellis indeed says 'ut ad fores brachia (membra), ita uultus in fastigiis merito proponendi erant', but to me this separation is artificial and surprising, especially in view of fast. I 557 'ora super postes affixaque bracchia pendent' and Verg. Aen. VIII 196 sq. 'foribusque adfixa superbis | ora uirum. . .pendebant', and I think that *foris* is a true correction. Ovid has half-a-dozen examples of the singular in the sense of the plural, such as fast. II 738 'custos in fore nullus erat'.

379–80   ut qui Bistoniae templo cecidere Mineruae,
        propter quod facies nunc quoque tecta deaest.

380 *quod*] *quos* T, Conr. de Mure. *tecta*] *torta* HT. ||

This couplet alludes, it is generally agreed, to the history told in Iust. xx 2 3–5 'Metapontini cum Sybaritanis et Crotoniensibus pellere ceteros Graecos Italia statuerunt. cum primum urbem Sirim cepissent, in expugnatione eius *L iuuenes amplexos Mineruae simulacrum* sacerdotemque deae uelatum orna-mentis *inter ipsa altaria trucidauerunt*.' The Minerua of Siris, according to Strabo VI p. 264 [362–3 Meineke], had been brought from Troy: if Ovid calls her *Bistonia* or Thracian it may be because of some story connecting Siris in Italy with Siris in Paeonia, which lay on the Thracian side of the Strymon and not very far from the Bistones, or with the Cίρες (Cἶρες Lobeck) ἔθνος Θρᾴκης ὑπὲρ τοὺς Βυζαντίους of Stephanus Byzantius. But this goddess did not veil her face at the murder and sacrilege; she closed her eyes: Lycophr. 988 γλήναις δ' ἄγαλμα ταῖς ἀναιμάκτοις μύσει, schol. διὸ ἡ Ἀθηνᾶ ὀργισθεῖσα ἔμυσεν, Strab. VI p. 264 [362 Meineke] τὸ τῆς Ἀθηνᾶς τῆς Ἰλιάδος ξόανον..., ὅπερ κατα-μῦσαι μυθεύουσιν ἀποσπωμένων τῶν ἱκετῶν...δείκνυσθαι δὲ καὶ νῦν καταμῦον τὸ ξόανον. I believe therefore that the *quod facies* and *quos facies* of Ovid's MSS arise from *quofacies*, that is

        propter quos acies nunc quoque tecta deaest.

Compare Gratt. 97 *caecas aciem* A, *caeca faciem* B, Ouid. met. IV 464 *omnes acie meliores libri, omnes facie* deteriores, Val. Fl. III 502 *Perses faciem* V for *Perses aciem*; Cic. n. d. II 142 '*acies* ipsa, qua cernimus, quae pupula uocatur, . . . palpebrae, quae sunt *tegumenta oculorum*', Ouid. her. XXI 199 '*tecto* simulatur *lumine* somnus'. And this, *quos acies*, appears to have been read by the scholiast of P, who is the best scholiast: '*quos* ne Minerua uideret, fecit sua *lumina operiri*' (see Iuu. VI 433 '*oculis* bilem substringit *opertis*').[1]

395–8   ut quos Antaei fortes pressere lacerti
           quosque ferae morti Lemnia turba dedit,
           ut qui post longum, sacri monstrator iniqui,
           elicuit pluuias uictima caesus aquas. ‖

The principal verb of the sentence, which extends from 365 to 412, is *pereas* in its first verse. At 396 Ellis was unusually attentive, and enquired 'unde hic Lemniades?' The victims of Antaeus go before, the first victim of Busiris follows after; the context is full of deaths inflicted by violent oppressors and suffered in turn by themselves; and the wives of Lemnos, as they steal in on tip-toe to murder their husbands in their beds, are incongruous intruders. The epithet *Lemnia* carries my mind to a person who would be more at home in this verse and who actually appears in a couplet not far away, 405 sq., 'ut pronepos, Saturne, tuus, quem reddere uitam | urbe Coronides uidit ab ipse sua'. This is Periphetes the son of Hephaestus, called Corynetes from his club: Apollod. bibl. III 16 2 (Θησεύς) Περιφήτην τὸν Ἡφαίστου καὶ Ἀντικλείας, ὃς ἀπὸ τῆς κορύνης ἣν ἐφόρει Κορυνήτης ἐπεκαλεῖτο, ἔκτεινεν ἐν Ἐπιδαύρῳ. πόδας δὲ ἀσθενεῖς ἔχων οὗτος ἐφόρει κορύνην σιδηρᾶν, δι' ἧς τοὺς παριόντας ἔκτεινε. ταύτην ἀφελόμενος Θησεὺς ἐφόρει, Plut. Thes. 8 1 ἐν τῇ Ἐπιδαυρίᾳ Περιφήτην ὅπλῳ χρώμενον κορύνῃ καὶ διὰ τοῦτο Κορυνήτην ἐπικαλούμενον, ἁπτόμενον αὐτοῦ καὶ κωλύοντα προάγειν συμβαλὼν ἀπέκτεινεν· ἡσθεὶς δὲ τῇ κορύνῃ λαβὼν ὅπλον ἐποιήσατο καὶ διετέλει χρώμενος . . . τὴν κορύνην ἐπεδείκνυεν ἡττημένην μὲν ὑπ' αὐτοῦ, μετ' αὐτοῦ δὲ ἀήττητον οὖσαν, Diod. IV 59 2 ἀνεῖλε τὸν ὀνομαζόμενον Κορυνήτην, χρώμενον τῇ προσαγορευομένῃ κορύνῃ, ὅπερ ἦν ὅπλον ἀμυντήριον, καὶ τοὺς παριόντας ἀποκτείνοντα, Paus. II 1 4 Περιφήτην Ἡφαίστου νομιζόμενον κορύνῃ χαλκῇ χρώμενον ἐς τὰς μάχας, Ouid. met. VII 436 sq. 'tellus Epidauria per te | *clauigeram* uidit *Vulcani* occumbere *prolem*'. That his victims should be first mentioned in 396 and then he himself in 405 sq. is like the mention of Diomed's victims in 381 sq. and Diomed in 401 sq., or the Minotaur's in 373 sq. and the Minotaur in 408. *turba* then I take to be a corruption of *claua*. The change could be traced through changes of letters from *claua* to *truba* and so to *turba*;

---

[1] Some of the other scholiasts seem to have had before them the *torta* of HT, which they try to interpret with 'oculos suos retorsit', 'uultu retorto', 'facie uersa'. *torta* is not capable of these senses: it might mean, as Ellis says, 'distorta'.

but I should rather suppose that *turba* is due to the frequency of this noun with an attendant epithet at this place in the pentameter: *noxia turba* 174, *Cresia turba* 510, *ebria turba* 612, *barbara turba* her. VIII 12, rem. 594, fast. VI 374, trist. V 10 28, and so forth. *Lemnius* is Vulcan in met. IV 185, and here *Lemnia* is *Vulcania* as ‖ *Amphrysia* is *Apollinea* in Verg. Aen. VI 398 *Amphrysia uates* and as *Paphia* is *Veneria* in Stat. silu. v 4 8 sq. *Paphia lampas*.

407   ut Sinis et Sciron et cum Polypemone natus.

That this verse must contain a mention of Procrustes was always pretty clear from the similar passages her. II 69 sq. and met. VII 433–45; and a comparison of Paus. I 38 5 ληστὴν Πολυπήμονα ὄνομα, Προκρούστην δὲ ἐπίκλησιν, Plut. Thes. II 1 Δαμάστην τὸν Προκρούστην, Apollod. epit. I 4 Δαμάστην, ὃν ἔνιοι Πολυπήμονα λέγουσιν, appeared to show that Procrustes was the person here called Polypemon. But then arose the question, who could be meant by Polypemon's son. Sinis is his son in Apollod. bibl. III 16 2 and Sciron in Prob. ad Verg. georg. I 399 ⟦III p. 366 Thilo–Hagen⟧, but nothing was known of any other. This difficulty however is now removed, and the verse is elucidated by Bacchyl. XVIII 27–30, with which I compared it in the Athenaeum of Dec. 25, 1897 ⟦see this edition p. 453⟧: Πολυπήμονός τε καρτερὰν σφῦραν ἐξέβαλεν Προκόπτας, ἀρείονος τυχὼν φωτός. *cum Polypemone natus* means 'Procrustes and his father Polypemon'. Although Pausanias regards the two as one, and although Procrustes (whom Bacchylides calls Procoptes and others Damastes) is said by Hyginus fab. 38 to have been the son of Neptune, it is evident that Bacchylides and Ovid followed another story.

415–18   qualis Achaemenides Sicula desertus in Aetna,
                    Troica cum uidit uela uenire, fuit.
               qualis erat nec non fortuna binominis Iri,
                    quique tenent pontem, quae tibi maior erit.

In editions earlier than mine these four verses have no construction. The punctuation here given, which is that of Saluagnius, Heinsius, Burman, and Ellis, is not improved nor even really altered by Merkel and Riese and Guethling when they place a colon instead of a full stop at the end of 416. For the two distichs are simply a pair of relative clauses dangling ‖ from the sky: when the apodosis ought to arrive, there arrives in its stead a third and subordinate relative clause, *quae tibi maior erit*. This was perceived by Schrader, who proposed to delete 417 sq. and assume the loss of a couplet before 415, and after him by Merkel, who marked 418 as corrupt. Ellis, who marked as corrupt the single and probably genuine word *maior*, perceived nothing of the sort, and it would have been strange if he had, for in his text of the Ibis there are some 40 passages with no more construction than this; passages not ungrammatical in themselves, but rendered so by his punctuation.

Corruption however is not here confined to verse 418, and before I approach the main difficulty I will deal with another. The construction, so far as it goes, is 'qualis fuit Achaemenides, nec non qualis erat fortuna Iri (qualis)que (est[1] fortuna eorum[2]) qui tenent pontem'. But the destitution foretold to Ibis, if it resembles the destitution of Irus and of beggars on the bridge, will resemble the destitution of Achaemenides, not Achaemenides himself. *Achaemenides* therefore should be a genitive depending on *fortuna*, which should be supplied from below as the subject of *fuit*; and the words should be written and punctuated thus:

> qualis Achaemenidis,[3] Sicula desertus in Aetna
>   Troica cum uidit uela uenire, fuit,
> qualis erat nec non fortuna binominis Iri etc.

Such alterations by copyists who cannot stay an instant to learn the construction of a word are very frequent: in Catull. 64 136 sq. 'nullane res potuit *crudelis* flectere *mentis* | consilium?' the scribe has written *crudeles...mentes* without even waiting for the next line. ||

In 418 the MS reading is *que*, for the *qui* of G is merely an accommodation to the gender of *pontem*. This is the one word which must be altered; there is no other word which need. To restore a construction and a sense without regard for likelihood is easy enough: for example, '*uel* tibi *peior*[4] erit', that is 'talis, uel peior, tibi fortuna erit'; or '*uae*, tibi *talis* erit'.[5] But *maior*, since *fortuna* in this passage means *opes*, possessions,[6] is too appropriate an adjective to be altered without necessity; and change should be confined if possible to the one word which neither sense nor construction admits. These would be satisfied by '*nec* tibi maior erit', that is 'talis, nec maior, tibi erit fortuna'; but a much lighter alteration, considering how often *p* and *qu* are confused, is '*spe* tibi maior erit': 'such beggary as that of Achaemenides, of Irus, of mendicants on the bridge, shall be more wealth than you can hope for'. The scruple which I feel about this is that *spe maior*, to judge from the general use of *spe* with comparatives (met. VII 648 *spe...maiora*, trist. I 11 36 *inferiora*, fast. IV 606 *citius*, Sall. Iug. 75 8

---

[1] For *est* thus supplied from *erat* compare e.g. trist. I 5 78 'illum Neptuni (premebat ira), me Iouis ira premit'.

[2] For the omission of *eorum* compare e.g. Nep. x 9 5 'quam...sit...miseranda uita (eorum) qui se metui quam amari malunt'.

[3] As I said in J. P. xxxi pp. 249 sq. [this edition pp. 826–7], there is no metrical evidence to determine with certainty whether a poet would write *Achaemenidis* or *Achaemenidae*. In my edition I printed *Achaemenidae*, and that is the gen. of the patronymic; but as to the proper name the MSS of the poets, Hor. epist. II 2 184 and Pers. v 180 *Herodis*, Phaed. IV 23 [22] 20 *Simonidis*, bear out, so far as they can, the statement of Priscian G.L.K. II p. 246 that the termination *-is* was usual.

[4] *peior* Heinsius; and this word is corrupted to *maior* in most MSS at trist. I 1 26.

[5] This improbable conjecture has also occurred to Mr Owen, who has put it straight into his text.

[6] That Ellis should explain *fortuna Iri* as 'ut mendices *et a fortiore aliquo pugnis caesus humi impingaris*' is quite in the natural order of things. It was easier for him to write these words, or any number of words, than to consider the context for one instant of time.

amplior, hist. II fr. 79 Maur. *celerius*, Liu. I 53 4 *lentius*, II 3 1 and XXVI 26 4
serius, III 38 13 *frequentior*, XXI 6 5 and XXXV 45 7 and XLIV 28 16 *celerius*),
should mean 'greater than expectation' rather than 'too great for hope'. But as
Ovid himself often says *res fide maior* (met. III 106, 660, IV 394, VII 648, XII 545,
XIII 651, fast. II 113) in the sense of 'maior quam ut ei fidem habeas', there
seems to be no reason why he should not say *spe maior* in the sense of 'maior
quam ut eam speres'. Still one would perhaps expect *quae* rather than *qualis* in
415 and 417.

> 539–40   conditor ut tardae, laesus cognomine, Myrrhae,
>   orbis in innumeris inueniare locis.

In 1883, in J. P. XII p. 167 [this edition p. 9], I explained this couplet as an ||
allusion to the fate of the poet C. Heluius Cinna. This appeared to involve an
error on Ovid's part, since it was then believed that the poet lived on later than
44 B.C. and ought not to be identified with the tribune torn to pieces at Caesar's
funeral. But Kiessling in 1887, in comment. Mommsen. p. 353, showed that this
belief had no sufficient ground; and Schanz and the successors of Teuffel in
their histories of Latin literature agree in regarding the poet and the tribune
(ποιητικὸς ἀνήρ Plut. uit. Brut. 20 4) as one.

When in my recension I suggested *urbis* for *orbis*, I had not observed that it
was cited from two MSS by Heinsius and Merkel. I do not think it necessary, but
it is favoured by parallels in the neighbourhood, 533 'lacer *in silua* manibus
spargare tuorum' and 535 '*per*que feros *montes* tauro rapiente traharis'.

IV

Who was Ibis? Nobody. He is much too good to be true. If one's enemies are
of flesh and blood, they do not carry complaisance so far as to choose the dies
Alliensis for their birthday and the most ineligible spot in Africa for their
birthplace. Such order and harmony exist only in worlds of our own creation,
not in the jerry-built edifice of the demiurge. Nor does man assail a real enemy,
the object of his sincere and lively hatred, with an interminable and incon-
sistent series of execrations which can neither be read nor written seriously. To
be starved to death and killed by lightning, to be brayed in a mortar as you
plunge into a gulf on horseback, to be devoured by dogs, serpents, a lioness,
and your own father in the brazen bull of Phalaris, are calamities too awful to
be probable and too improbable to be awful. And when I say that Ibis was
nobody I am repeating Ovid's own words. In the last book that he wrote,
several years after the Ibis,[1] he said, ex Pont. IV 14 44, 'extat adhuc nemo
saucius ore meo'.

---

[1] The Ibis, with its 'lustris bis iam mihi quinque peractis', cannot be later than A.D. 12, and is not
likely to be so late.

It appears from trist. I 6, III 11, IV 9, and V 8, that Ovid had, or pretended to have, more enemies than one. In IV 9 the ‖ enemy's offence is left unknown, 'nomen facinusque tacebo', and probably neither it nor he existed; in V 8 it is vaguely described by the phrases 'casibus insultas' and 'nostra laetere ruina'. The two other passages are more precise. In I 6 some person or persons have tried to lay hands on Ovid's property and have been defeated by his wife and friends: 7 sq. 'tu facis ut spolium non sim nec nuder ab illis | naufragii tabulas qui petiere mei', 13 sq. 'mea nescioquis, rebus male fidus acerbis, | in bona uenturus, si paterere, fuit'. In III 11 the enemy is an orator and his offence is speech: 19 sq. 'est aliquis qui uulnera cruda retractet | soluat et in mores ora diserta meos'. These two characters are put together to make Ibis: 13 sq. 'uulneraque inmitis requiem quaerentia uexat | iactat et in toto nomina nostra foro' (232 'latrat et in toto uerba canina foro'), 18 'naufragii tabulas pugnat habere mei', 20 sq. 'praedam medio raptor ab igne petit. | nititur ut profugae desint alimenta senectae'. But they do not make him black enough; and there-fore, whereas one of them is 'nescioquis', I 6 13, and Ovid says of the other, III 11 69 sqq., 'fieri quod numquam posse putaui, | est tibi de rebus maxima cura meis', Ibis is represented as a person bound to Ovid by ties of duty, 19 'qui debuerat subitas extinguere flammas'.

The two halves of the poem, 1–250 and 251–644, derive their origin from two quite different motives. In the poems of his exile Ovid often laments the mono-tony of his theme. But in III 11 and IV 9 and V 8 he hit on a new subject, remon-strance with a persecutor; and it proved no bad variation, for IV 9 contains some of his best lines. A longer effort, treating the same matter in another vein, was a promising enterprise; for the vein itself, though new to Ovid, was congenial to the Roman fibre, and Roman poets had excelled in it. The 91st poem of Catullus and the 5th and 17th epodes of Horace, however little accor-dant with modern fashions, are masterpieces without which no anthology of Latin poetry is complete or representative. And the first 250 lines of the Ibis are another masterpiece: Ovid has written no passage of equal length which has equal merit.

From that point onward the poem is merely a display of ‖ erudition. Ovid, at the date of his exile, was bursting with information rather recently acquired. In his young days he had been by no means a learned poet; and Propertius, in the season of their sodality, must often have exhorted him to lay in a larger stock of those examples from mythology with which his own elegies are so much embellished or encumbered. But by the time he was fifty he had at his disposal more examples from mythology than he knew what to do with. His studies for the metamorphoses and some of his studies for the fasti (notably in the aetia of Callimachus) had furnished him with a far greater number of stories and histories than could be crowded into those two poems; and he felt the craving of the ὀψιμαθής to let everyone know how learned he had become. Here was his chance: history and mythology alike are largely composed of misfortunes as bad as one could wish for one's worst enemy; and he could discharge a great part of his load of knowledge through the channel of imprecation.

There is no reason to think that he took any of these examples from the Ibis of Callimachus, and there is some reason to think that he took none. All he says about imitating that poem is this, 55–60 'nunc quo Battiades inimicum deuouet Ibin | hoc ego deuoueo teque tuosque modo. | utque ille historiis inuoluam carmina caecis, | non soleam quamuis hoc genus ipse sequi. | illius ambages imitatus in Ibide dicar | oblitus moris iudiciique mei.' The new Ibis, like the old one, is to be an imprecation wrapped in obscurely worded allusions to history or legend: no further likeness is professed. And when in 448–50 he says 'eueniant capiti uota sinistra tuo . . . quibus exiguo uolucris deuota libello est | corpora proiecta quae sua purgat aqua', – that is 'may Callimachus' imprecations on his Ibis fall upon you' – this will constitute a tautology if he has translated those imprecations in other verses of his poem; and so Otto Schneider has remarked in his Callimachus vol. II p. 274.

127

LUCAN VII 460–5 *

460 ut rapido cursu fati suprema morantem
1 consumpsere locum, parua tellure dirempti,
463 quo sua pila cadant aut *quam* sibi fata minentur
462 inde *manum*, spectant. *tempus, quo noscere possent*
4 facturi quae monstra forent. uidere parentes
465 frontibus aduersis fraternaque comminus arma.

463 ante 462 VGP et ante corr. ut uidetur U, item adnotator super Lucanum ed. Endtii p. 276 et Statii scholiastes ad *Theb.* vi 760, qui 462 et 464 coniunctos legerunt. 462 ante 463 MZ et ex corr. U. 463 *quam* MZPGV, *qua* ex corr. U. 462 *manum* VGP, lemma schol. Bern., Statii schol., *manus* Z et ex corr. U, de M non liquet. *tempus quo noscere possent* VGP et ut uidetur M, adn. sup. Luc., Z (*poss͡s*), Statii schol. (*possint*), *tempus = q.t.i.r.n.p.* lemma schol. Bern., *uultusque agnoscere quaerunt* ex corr. U, Z² G², *uultus* etiam V².

The text printed above is the reading of Gronouius, Cortius, Heitland, and a few old editors of the days before Grotius; it is one of the only two readings yet adopted which require any consideration, and of those two it is by far the better authenticated and moreover the better. It is paraphrased by Gronouius thus: 'paullulum stant defixi in contemplando, quae in corpora (nempe cognatorum) pila essent missuri, aut quam ex aduerso manum consanguineorum, tamquam fatalem, haberent metuendam: erat id tempus sufficiens ad intelligendum, quae monstra essent facturi. uidere namque et agnouere parentes et fratres.' Sense and expression are perfect, except for the doubt whether *tempus* can well stand, as the Bernese scholiast says, for 'tempus erat': in the one parallel cited by Cortius (for he cites only one) the noun has an epithet, Plin. *ep.* ii 13 2 'tibi...*longum* ...*tempus*...quo amicos tuos exornare potuisti', and this may make a difference.[1]

The incoherent order of verses traditional among editors, 462 463, I will not even consider. It is a pure accident, injurious to sense and even to grammar: if

---

* [[CQ 15 (1921), 172–4]]
[1] Mr Hosius in *Neue Jahrb. f. Phil.* 1893 p. 348 says 'zu *tempus* ist wie so häufig *erat* zu ergänzen'. Out of the seven examples which he pretends to add to Kortte's there is not a single one where *erat* is to be supplied: the time is always the present, and the sense of *tempus* is always ὥρα ἐστίν, as at Catull. 62 3 'surgere iam *tempus*'.

readers care to see what editors make of it, here are two specimens, the texts of
Grotius and of Mr Hosius.

parua tellure dirempti,

462   inde *manum* spectant, *uultusque agnoscere quaerunt,*
463   quo sua pila cadant, aut *qua* sibi fata minentur,
       facturi quae monstra forent.[1] ||

parua tellure dirempti

462   inde *manum* spectant: *tempus, quo noscere possent,*
463   quo sua pila cadant, aut *qua* sibi fata minentur,
       facturi quae monstra forent.[2]

The variants *qua* and *manus* may equally be set aside. It ought to be recognised
that the line and a half

463   quo sua pila cadant aut *quam* sibi fata minentur
462   inde *manum*, spectant

are securely established, and that all uncertainty is confined to what follows.

The only reading which stands over against the text of Gronouius as a rival
tradition, not a mere blunder of scribes, is that elicited and recommended by
Weber,

spectant, *uultusque agnoscere quaerunt,*
facturi, quae monstra forent:

that is 'facturi res monstrosas'. It cannot compete with the other, but it robs it
of security. If Lucan wrote *tempus quo noscere possent*, there was nothing to
provoke such an interpolation as this.

Hitherto I have cited only the medieval MSS, of the 9th century or later, on
which we mainly depend throughout. But verses 458–537 of this book, much
defaced and mutilated, survive in Π, the Vatican fragmenta Palatina, assigned to
the 4th or 5th century. The authority of this palimpsest, despite its antiquity, is
not greater than the joint authority of the medieval MSS, but it is equal; and
where they dissent among themselves its intervention must needs be weighty.
It gives verses 462–4 as follows:

463   quo sua pila cadant aut *quam* sibi fata[
462   inde *manum* spectant *uultus quo no*[
       facturi quae monsta forent uidere pa[.

---

[1] 'ubi propius hostem uentum est, aspiciunt quos petant uultus, quae ipsis minentur manus,
quae denique facturi essent scelera.'

[2] 'die truppen einander nahe gerückt schauen die schar sc. der feinde; es ist die zeit, wo sie ein
ziel für ihre geschosse zu suchen beginnen, wo sie gegen das von den gegnern drohende geschick
vorkehrungen zu treffen suchen, aber auch die zeit wo sie noch einsehen können was für frevel sie
zu begehen im begriff sind.'

It thus confirms the majority of the younger MSS in the ordering of the lines and, so far as it reaches, in every other particular, except that instead of *tempus* it has *uultus* with the minority.

If now we simply write out in succession the several words which possess most MS authority, they will give us this:

> uultus quo noscere possent
> facturi quae monstra forent uidere parentes.

And this is a source from which the two variants would easily and naturally spring. It was unintelligible, and had to be altered somehow. One corrector made the bold but intelligent change of *uultus* to *tempus*, which was good enough even to satisfy Gronouius. The other, bolder still and not quite so intelligent, wrote *uultusque agnoscere quaerunt*, which was good enough to satisfy Weber. But try again.

> uultus, quo noscere possent
> facturi quae monstra forent, uidere parent*um*
> frontibus aduersis fraternaque comminus arma.

Π, as I have said, retains only *pa-*, and we do not know whether it had *parentes* or *parentum* or *paternos*. I mention *paternos* because it will promptly be conjectured ‖ and stoutly preferred if I do not. I reject it because it is less elegant, as *fraterna* follows, and was less likely to be changed. The last word of a verse is especially liable to have its inflexion altered by scribes who do not at once perceive its construction and who seek to bring it into false grammatical connexion with the word immediately preceding. Hence such corruptions as v 19 *ab urbe* for *ab urbis*, VII 310 *respexerit hostem* for *r. hoste*, Verg. *georg.* II 274 *metabere campos* for *m. campi*, 467 *fallere uitam* for *f. uita*, *Aen.* XI 605 *hastasque reductas* for *h. reductis*, Hor. *serm.* I 1 118 *tempore uitae* for *t. uita*. The whole passage, as thus amended, may be compared with IV 169–72 *postquam spatio languentia nullo | mutua conspicuos habuerunt lumina uoltus, | deprensum est ciuile nefas* and v 470–2 *posse duces parua campi statione diremptos | admotum damnare nefas; nam cernere uoltus | et uoces audire datur.*

It once occurred to me that the common origin of *possent* and *quaerunt* might be sought in *quirent*, as *queo* is regularly explained in glossaries by *possum*. But the imperfect subjunctive is not found between *ciris* 5 and Stat. *silu.* v 3 60; and Lucan, whose vocabulary is as commonplace as his versification, was not likely to use it.

128

THE CODEX LIPSIENSIS OF MANILIUS*

Professor J. van Wageningen has sent me a review of my fourth volume of Manilius which he has published in *Museum* vol. 28 pp. 173–7. I never contradict the taradiddles usual in reviews, because, if the reader thinks it worth his while, he can find out for himself whether they are true or no, and if he chooses to believe them without enquiry, it serves him right. But when he is fed with false information about a MS which is out of his reach, he can do nothing to help himself, and may fairly claim to be protected.

In the edition of Manilius which he published in 1915 Mr van Wageningen misreported the readings of L, cod. Lips. 1465, in a great number of places. He did so in the following twenty-seven verses of book IV alone: 44, 104, 114, 126, 164, 169, 205, 228, 275, 369, 412, 489, 510, 523, 583, 585 (titulus), 614, 622, 640, 685, 729, 748, 759, 804, 818 (titulus), 889, 907 (for I omit 508 and 553 and 670 where his errors are merely slips of the pen or misprints); and further at 179 and 350 and 469 and 698, without actually misreporting the MS, he wrote notes which force the reader to draw false conclusions. Sixteen of his twenty-seven errors had already been committed by Breiter in his edition of 1907. Some of these, such as '*mensurae et* L' at 205, are errors which both Breiter and Mr van Wageningen were sure to commit, and which might indeed be committed by almost any collator who was not on the alert.[1] But others, notably those at 169, 585, 640, 818, 889, are such blunders as no two persons could make independently; and I stated the truth of the matter when I said of Mr van Wageningen in my note on 169 'multis locis falsa Breiteri testimonia exscribere maluit quam ipsum librum sua causa Groningam missum inspicere'.

Mr van Wageningen, bent on retaliation, believes that he has found three places where my reports of L are wrong. They are the following. To win credence for his testimony he tells us that he possesses a photographic reproduction of L; but it is no use possessing photographs of MSS unless you can read them.

1. At IV 44 Mr van Wageningen's note was '*adice* ML¹G, *adice et* L² (ss. *et* inter *ciuilia* et *bella*)'; mine was '*adice et* L nisi fallor et cod. Cusanus, *adice* GM, *et adice* L²'.

---

* ⟦*CQ* 15 (1921), 175–6⟧

[1] The reading of L, as of M, is *mensura et*: L² has very carefully and cleverly altered the final *a* into the ligature *æ*, which L does not use.

Except for one detail which I will mention presently, the verse stands in the MS thus:

et
Pugnantē menbris. adice ciuilia bella.

The superscript *et* is in the neat and rather pretty hand of L²; the two pairs of dots, which Mr van Wageningen appears to regard as meaningless ornament, signify that this word is to be inserted after *menbris*; and therefore the reading of L² is, as I said, *et adice*, and not, as he said, *adice et*. Between *adice* and *ciuilia*, much too faint and blurred for Mr van Wageningen to notice it, there is something which seemed to me as if it might once have been that abbreviation of *et*, resembling the Arabic numeral 7, which is used by L in a few other places; and I further observed that the cod. Cusanus, which was copied from L in the 12th century, was ‖ cited as giving here *adice et*. I therefore wrote with due caution '*adice et* L nisi fallor'. Mr van Wageningen begs the reader to believe – 'uix credideris, lector, sed crede'[1] – that this was a mistake which had been made by Breiter. Breiter either made the same mistake as Mr van Wageningen, the mistake of thinking that the superscript *et* was meant for insertion at this point, or else he thought that the faint sign was a caret, as indeed it may be, though not from the hand which wrote the *et*.

2. At 350 Mr van Wageningen's text was *ingratus* and his note was '*ingrati* M'; my text was *ingrati* and my note was '*ingrati* LM cod. Venetus, *ingratus* GL²'. He asseverates that the reading of L is simply *ingratus*.

The reading of L is *ingrati*. Between that word and the next, as often happens in this MS, there is a rather wide space, where L² found enough room to make the correction *ingratus*. It accordingly expanded the final *i* to *u* by a supplementary stroke, and it added the tall free springing *s* which is characteristic of L² and which differentiates it more than anything else from L. How L writes the syllable *-tus* may be seen in the *receptus* of the next line. The truth was stated, before my time, by Jacob; Mr van Wageningen presumes to contradict us both, relying on his own defective eyesight or superficial observation or inexperience in reading MSS.

3. At 369 Mr van Wageningen's text was *cunctisque* and his note was '*cunctisque* L, *cunctis* G, *iunctisque* MC'; my text was *iunctisque* and my note was '*iunctisque* M, *coniunctisque* L cod. Venetus, *cunctisque* L², *cunctis* G'. He asseverates that the reading of L is simply *cunctisque*.

The reading of L is this:

Inq. alio querendo mali.   qđ c̄iunctisq. sequendū.

The preposition (*con-*), as often in this MS, stands a little apart from the rest of the compound. There has been drawn through *qđ* and *c̄* a horizontal stroke of

---

[1] He calls this 'het Latijn van Housman', but it seems to be his own improvement of the Latin of Ovid, 'uix mihi credetis, sed credite', which I borrowed in my note on IV 141.

deletion, which makes $\bar{c}$ look something like $\bar{e}$ and has deceived all my pre-decessors, and the initial *i* of *iunctis* has been converted into *c* with a clumsiness which ought to deceive nobody.

If Mr van Wageningen wishes to know of errors in my writings he had better address enquiry to me. I am more interested in discovering them than anyone else can possibly be, and consequently I discover more of them. Here are two: II 79 '*minusque* GLM' should be '*minusque* GL, *mimusque* M', and II 394 '*adsumpto* L², *assumpto* L' should be '*adsumpto* L, *assumpto* L²'.

REVIEW: A. ROSTAGNI, *IBIS**

It is said by Ovid in *Ib.* 55 and by Suidas s.u. Καλλίμαχος that Callimachus wrote a poem against an enemy of his, one Ἴβις. Mr Rostagni contends that they were wrong. There existed a poem of that name and nature, but its author was not Callimachus. This he proves as follows.

He begins by assuming that Ovid's *Ibis* is substantially a translation of the Greek Ἴβις. Now not only is there no support for this assumption in Ovid or anywhere else, but there is one couplet of the *Ibis*, 449 sq., which conflicts with it. That couplet therefore Mr Rostagni declares to be interpolated, alleging further that it contradicts Suidas. It does not necessarily contradict him at all, but what if it did? must nobody contradict Suidas except Mr Rostagni? And why not rather declare the sentence in Suidas to be interpolated, on the ground that it contradicts Ovid?

He then remarks that the *Ibis* contains in 299 sq. a reference to an event of the year 213 B.C., too late for Callimachus, and that it contains no reference to any event of later date: the author of the Ἴβις therefore belonged to the first part of the second century. But the *Ibis* contains in 631 sq. a reference to the ninth book of Virgil's *Aeneid*, which is too late not only for Callimachus but for Mr Rostagni's pseudo-Callimachus. Ovid himself must have inserted it; and even if the *Ibis* is a copy of the Ἴβις, why cannot Ovid have inserted also the reference to Achaeus in 299 sq.? Because it is Greek, says Mr Rostagni, who tacitly assumes that the Ἴβις was the only Greek book which Ovid had ever read. For instance, many of the stories to which Ovid in his *Ibis* makes allusion are known to have been told by Callimachus in his αἴτια, a work which might be perused, one would think, by the author of the *fasti*; but Mr Rostagni will not allow the αἴτια to be Ovid's source for these stories: they must have been in the Ἴβις too, and ‖ that is how Ovid came to know of them.

It is thus demonstrated, by assumption piled on assumption, that Callimachus wrote no Ἴβις. But Mr Rostagni will also investigate the personality of Ovid's enemy. He says that Ovid did not know who he was. But Ovid knew his birthplace. Oh, he took that from the Ἴβις. But Ovid also knew his birthday, which he could not take from the Ἴβις, for it is a date in the Roman calendar. Oh, he

* ⟦*Ibis*. A. Rostagni (Contributi alla Scienza dell'Antichità, vol. III). Pp. 123. Florence: Felice le Monnier, 1920. *CR* 35 (1921), 67–8⟧

made that up out of his own head. Cannot Mr Rostagni see that if Ovid specified the birthday and birthplace of an enemy whose very identity was unknown to him he was ensuring that his invective and execrations should miss their mark? Unless this real and unknown person was actually born in Libya on the dies Alliensis, which would be a miracle, the *Ibis* does not apply to him; and Ovid may curse till he is black in the face without doing him the slightest injury in this world or the next. And where did Mr Rostagni pick up his extraordinary notion? He says that Ibis is the person spoken of in *trist.* 1 6 7–16 as defeated by Ovid's wife and friends in an attempt to lay hands on some of his property. Then Ovid must have known who he was: if his wife was such a Mrs Nickleby that she omitted the enemy's name in relating his actions, Ovid would have written to ask for it; he would not have sat down in easily remediable ignorance to pen 600 lines of verse and discharge them at the circle of the horizon. But in *trist.* 1 6 13 he contemptuously calls this person *nescioquis*, an insignificant creature; and that has done the mischief: Mr Rostagni takes this word to mean that Ovid really did not know whom he was talking about. His Latin scholarship indeed is not of the best: in the verse 'siue idem simili pinus quem morte peremit' he construes *idem* with *pinus* and translates 'il medesimo albero'.

Mr Rostagni has also much to say upon the scholia of Ovid's *Ibis*. These often offer us explanations which we know to be figments, because we understand Ovid's allusions, which the scholiasts did not. But wherever we do not understand his allusions Mr Rostagni is prepared to believe that the scholiasts did, and listens with eager credulity to convicted liars. More yet. These scholiasts, except the most respectable of them, the scholiast of the cod. Phillippicus, enrich their notes with Latin elegiacs and hexameters, redolent of the middle ages, which they ascribe to persons whose names they found in Ovid and Fulgentius; not merely to Roman poets like Tibullus and Propertius and Gallus but to Greek poets like Arion and Callimachus and to mere vocables like Lupercus and Menephron. Mr Rostagni will have it that these concoctions, many of them made out of Ovid's own words, are translations of Greek verses preserved in Greek scholia on the Ἶβις. Greek verses of Tibullus and Propertius and Gallus? Well, not exactly; but *Gallus* is a corruption of *Callimachus* (as also are *Darius* and *Clarus* and *Calixto* and *Calmethes* and even *Promptius*), and *Tibullus* and *Propertius* are corruptions of the names of other Greek poets whom Mr Rostagni has not yet decided to identify. There is a certain *Battus* (*Batus, Bacus, Bachus, Bacchus*) to whom Latin verses are imputed at 259 and 299; and for Mr Rostagni he is Callimachus again, *Battiades*. In truth he is nothing of the sort: he recurs in a similar imposture, *L. Caecilii Minutiani Apuleii de orthographia* § 43, as '*Battus* iambicus poeta Ouidii contubernalis', and his birthplace is Ouid. *trist.* IV 10 47, where the MSS present 'Ponticus heroo, *Battus* (*Batus, Bacus, Bachus, Bacchus*) quoque clarus iambis', and editors read *Bassus* with Scaliger.

Worse argument and vainer conclusions than make up the staple of this treatise are not often met with; but the pains which Mr Rostagni has wasted on it are considerable, and so is his knowledge of recent literature relevant to the subject. One would think however that at pp. 56–8 he must have quoted *Oxyrh. pap.* 1011, published in 1910, if he had ever read it.

130

ATTAMEN AND OVID, *HER.* I 2*

What the nineteenth century knew of *attamen* or *at tamen* it did not learn from dictionaries. The two last revisions of Forcellini, Corradini's and De-Vit's, provided eight examples between them, of which three were false. Klotz added one, Georges two, Smith two: one of these five was false, and two more lie under much suspicion. Freund gave no instance whatsoever. In preparing his first volume, which appeared in 1834, he turned, like a good compiler, to the first volume of Hand's *Tursellinus*, published in 1829. What he found there, on p. 450, was 'de AT TAMEN uide in TAMEN'; so he sat down quickly and wrote 'attamen *adv.*, s. tamen'. But Hand's *Tursellinus*, which never reached *tamen*, had proceeded no further than *multum* when Freund in 1840 produced the last volume of his dictionary; so he did not redeem his promise, and when you got there the cupboard was bare. This perfidy was faithfully imitated by the English and American dictionaries of Andrews, White and Riddle, Lewis and Short. To all intents and purposes one was left to depend on one's own reading and on the observations of Madvig at Cic. *de fin.* pp. 286 and 425 and *opusc.* I p. 491.

Since 1903 the usage of *attamen* can be studied[1] in the *thes. ling. Lat.* II pp. 1010 sq., and there is no longer any excuse[2] for the ignorance which would retain it in the text of Ovid *her.* I 2:

hanc tua Penelope lento tibi mittit, Vlixe:
nil mihi rescribas, attamen ipse ueni.

* [[*CQ* 16 (1922), 88–91]]

[1] A column and a half of the *thes. ling. Lat.*, chosen at random, will generally contain a good many errors, and this specimen is no exception to the rule. Val. Fl. II 151 and Cic. *Font.* 37 should be subtracted, for there the MS readings are respectively *ac tamen*, which is right, and *at de*, which points rather to *at certe*. Germ. *phaen.* 626 should be added, for it is peculiar. In *Ciris* 74 the best MS, not alone, gives *ast tamen*, and Heinsius restored *has*. In Ouid. *met.* x 724 all good MSS have *et* or *est*; in Sil. VII 114 the MSS are divided between *at* and *et*. If Pers. v 159 is cited, where P has *at* and α has *et*, II 48 should be cited also, where *at* is in α and *et* in P; but probably *et tamen* is right in both verses. The statement at p. 1010 45 sq. that the MSS give *attamen* in Cic. *de fin.* II 85 is not true, whereas it would be true of *de or.* I 241, which is not mentioned; and p. 1010 57 sq. '*attamen* (Madvig, *tamen* codd.)' is the contrary of the fact. At p. 1010 39 the reference '634' should be 637; p. 1011 1 '2, 79' should be simply 79; p. 1011 20 '1, 459' should be 2, 459.

[2] But the blind affection with which so many scribes and editors persisted in substituting *attamen* for *ac tamen* and *et tamen* is not even now extinct. So late as 1908 I notice Mr P. H. Damsté in *Mnemos.* 36 p. 207 corrupting Tib. III 4 11 in the old fashion; and the particle is a great favourite with young German scholars in their doctoral dissertations, where they use it as equivalent to *uerum enimuero.*

attamen means 'yet even so' or 'yet at least'; and its absurdity in this verse will be best apprehended by observing that the word would become suitable if the thought were inverted thus: 'si ipse uenire non potes, attamen rescribe'. The old but quite untrustworthy Etonensis has *sed tamen*, which is no better, || and which Mr Birt did not defend, as Sedlmayer states, in *Goett. gel. An̄*. 1882 p. 854: what Mr Birt there said, and said truly, was that the sense requires *sed* instead of *attamen*. Heinsius felt in his bones that something was amiss, but when he changed the punctuation to 'nil mihi rescribas attamen: ipse ueni', that was only St Laurence turning on his gridiron. Gronouius in *obs.* I c. 22 with much clearer perception proposed 'nil mihi rescribas *ut* tamen: ipse ueni', 'scribit quidem marito, non tamen ut rescribatur: quin potius ut ipse ueniat'; and it cannot be said that such an order of words is unlike Ovid. The conjecture of Bentley in his manuscript notes is still better, 'nil mihi rescribas *tu* tamen: ipse ueni'; for the pronoun, 'you on your part', has force, and *tu*, if absorbed by the following *ta*, would leave a gap which might be variously filled, whether with the *at* of most MSS or the *sed* of E.

But all this while the editors and critics are not pushing beyond the MSS of Ovid, the oldest of which are E, of the eleventh century, and G, of the twelfth. This verse is extant, and for our present purpose virtually four times over, in two MSS of the ninth century, Palatinus 1753 and Parisinus 7539 of the metrical treatise of Aelius Festus Apthonius now going by the name of *Marii Victorini ars grammatica* and printed in Keil's *grammatici Latini* VI pp. 31–173.

p. 109 29–35:
'in scandendo autem pentametro non nulli dissentiunt, quidam enim eum in duo diuidunt cola et percussis utriusque partis binis pedibus semipedes, qui supersunt, coniungunt et ex his spondeum quintum uersui adnectunt, tamquam *nil mihi rescribas attinet ipse ueni*, sic *nil mihi rescri attinet ipse ueni bas*.'

p. 111 21–4:
'traditur etiam elegius scazon talis ut primum colum, id est penthemimeres, integrum habeat, secundo uero contra legem suam non una sed duabus syllabis terminante, ut *nil mihi rescribas* primum colon, secundum *attinet ipsa ueni*, scazon *attinet ut ueniatis*.'

Keil does not refer this verse to its place and author either in his notes or in his index,[1] and therefore the citation is unknown to modern editors of the *heroides*. Heinsius knew of it, as might be expected; but his knowledge was of no use to him, because Camerarius, the first editor of the treatise, doubtless also recognising the verse, had everywhere changed *attinet* to *attamen* in conformity with

---

[1] Similar omissions on his part, which I will here make good, are the following. p. 109 15 = Quint. *inst.* VIII 3 29. p. 109 18 (p. 112 15 and 19, p. 640 9) = Ouid. *art.* I 8. p. 136 27 = Hor. *epod.* 2 5. p. 137 29 = Verg. *catal.* 13 16. p. 139 6 = Hor. *epod.* 2 34. p. 149 4 = Verg. *Aen.* IX 525.

the current text of Ovid, and Keil's was the first edition in which the MS reading was restored.

The MSS do not vary, except that in one place one of them has *ati Ti et*; and it is impossible to believe that the scribes have four times ‖ written *attinet* where Apthonius wrote *attamen*, even though on pp. 166 sq., after once writing *constiterunt* (with one of Horace's own best MSS) for *constiterint* in Hor. *carm.* 1 9 4, they have persisted in repeating that small mistake. This testimony therefore comes to us not from the ninth century, the date of the scribes, but from the fourth, the date of the metrist. Nor can *attinet* easily have taken its origin from him. It is true that grammarians, especially Seruius, citing passages to prove some single point and having their attention concentrated on that, are often inaccurate in those words of the citation which are not relevant to their purpose. But a metrist citing verses for their metre has his attention equally distributed, and Apthonius is generally exact. *dicor* for *dicar* in Ouid. *art.* 1 8 at p. 109 18 is only a copyist's error, for *dicar* is given rightly at p. 112 15 and 19; *miserorum* for *miserarum* in Hor. *carm.* III 12 1 at p. 53 3 is another, for *miserarum* is given in five other places. The errors *recreetur umbra* for *recreatur aura* in Hor. *carm.* I 22 18 at p. 157 4 and *incaluisse* for *caluisse* in III 21 12 at p. 159 33 may be Apthonius' own; the misquotation of Plaut. *mil.* 103 on p. 147 occurs in an unintelligible passage and its history is obscure. There remains a notable variant on p. 38: 'eadem metri lege etiam consonantes geminantur, ut *relliquias Danaum* et *rettulit Argolico fulgentia poma tyranno* et *redduxere retro longe capita ardua ab ictu*.' Virgil's MSS in *Aen.* v 428 have '*abduxere* retro' etc.; and as it is incredible that Apthonius should blunder in the very word for whose sake he was citing the verse, Lucian Mueller and Ribbeck suppose that his MS of Virgil gave *redduxere*. I doubt if he was citing Virgil at all: he does not say so, and the preceding verse is Lucan's. This verse may belong to some poet from whom Virgil borrowed it with the change of one word, not liking to lengthen, as Lucilius and Lucretius and Horace did, the first syllable of *reduco*; and *redduxere retro* reminds one of *retro reccidit* in the verse cited at *G.L.K.* VI p. 613 17 and ascribed with probability to Ennius.

In all this I can find nothing to encourage a suspicion that Apthonius in citing Ouid. *her.* 1 2 wrote *attinet* four times by mistake for *attamen*. Nor would he make the change deliberately, as he does make some changes, when he is engaged in deriving one form of verse from another or in establishing relationship between them: for instance, when he cites Ouid. *art.* 1 8 rightly with *amoris ego* on p. 109 but substitutes *amore potens* on p. 112 because a long syllable is necessary for his purpose.[1] *attinet* serves no purpose either on p. 109 or on p. 111 which would not equally be served by *attamen*.

---

[1] His motive in most of these changes is metrical, but in *negotio* for *negotiis* p. 137 10 and apparently in *dedit* for *procul* p. 117 15 and p. 125 it is syntactical. In *recuruo* for *canoro* p. 122 32 and p. 125 23

Ovid therefore, according to the best evidence in our possession, wrote thus:

nil mihi rescribas attinet: ipse ueni. ‖

'It is no good your sending me an answer', says Penelope, 'come yourself.' This construction puzzled the scribes, so they wrote *attamen*, which puzzles only scholars. Ovid has *attinet* with its usual infinitive in *her.* XII 207 sq. 'sed quid praedicere poenam | attinet?': the subjunctive seems to be unique, though as lexicographers have overlooked this instance they may also have overlooked others. It is supported by the analogy of *oportet* and *necesse est* and more particularly of *opus est*, which usually takes, like *attinet*, the infinitive, but the subjunctive here and there, as in Plaut. *merc.* 1004 'nil opust *resciscat*', Cic. *ad Att.* XI 8 1 '*contendas* opus est', *pan. Messall.* 101 'seu sit opus quadratum acies *consistat* in agmen', Plin. *ep.* IX 33 11 'non est opus *adfingas* aliquid aut *adstruas*'. Equally unique and equally consonant to analogy is the construction of *her.* VI 3 sq. '*hoc* tamen *ipsum* | debueram scripto *certior esse* tuo'. Whether *nil* belongs, as often, to *attinet*, or whether it should here be broken up into *non* and *quicquam*, *non* with *attinet* and *quicquam* with *rescribas*, I cannot determine.

he is following Terentianus Maurus 1855, and the object of this change may be seen in Ter. Maur. 1912 sq. and p. 125 25.

131

HERODAS II 65–71*

65

δεῦρο, Μυρτάλη, καὶ σύ·
δεῖξον σεαυτὴν πᾶσι· μηδὲν αἰσχύνευ·
νόμιζε τούτους οὒς ὁρῆς δικάζοντας
πατέρας ἀδελφοὺς ἐμβλέπειν. ὁρῆτ᾽, ἄνδρες,
τὰ τίλματ᾽ αὐτῆς καὶ κάτωθε κἄνωθεν

70

ὡς λεῖα ταῦτ᾽ ἔτιλλεν ὡναγὴς οὗτος,
ὅθ᾽ εἷλκεν αὐτὴν κἀβιάζετο.

'Come here, Myrtale – it's your turn. Show yourself to all; don't be ashamed. Consider that those whom you see trying the case are your fathers and brethren. Look, gentlemen, up and down, at her rents, how threadbare these were rent by this villain, when he mauled and tousled her.'

This is the translation of Mr A. G. Knox in his recently published completion of Walter Headlam's work; and it is at any rate faithful enough to Headlam's commentary, which represents that the outrage here alleged against Thales by Battarus is damage to Myrtale's clothing. I cannot find that any editor has ever made this mistake before. It is one which argues some innocence of mind and not much attention to the context or to the meaning of Greek words.

Headlam is of course unable to cite any passage where τίλλειν or its cognates signify the rending or mauling of garments, and he is obliged to invent an instance: 'the τιλμοί with which the Herald threatens the Danaids in Aesch. *Suppl.* 852 [839] include the πολυμίτων πέπλων ἐπιλαβάς they apprehend in *v.* 439 [432].' On the contrary, the τιλμοί (which he himself rightly translated 'plucking of hair') distinctly exclude the πέπλων ἐπιλαβάς (which he translated 'rude clutchings of robes'): τιλμοὶ πέπλων would mean shredding robes for lint. When he comes to λεῖα he says that it means 'plain' as distinguished from ὑφαντά 'embroidered' (Thuc. II 97 3), and that Myrtale's garments, originally ὑφαντά, had been made λεῖα by the rough handling of her assailant. Rough handling will not unpick embroidery.

And what, by this interpretation, is the ordeal which Myrtale's modesty is summoned to face? Tattered and torn as she may be, she is already present || in court, where anyone could stare at her as he liked: simply to stand forth in her

* [CR 36 (1922), 109–10]

rags is nothing that calls for the encouragement μηδὲν αἰσχύνευ or for assurances that the jury have minds as chaste as a father's or a brother's. Such language means that she is required to show ἃ κρύπτειν ὄμματ᾽ ἀρσένων χρεών; and this is necessary in order that the jury may see for themselves

τὰ τίλματ᾽ αὐτῆς, καὶ κάτωθε κἄνωθεν
ὡς λεῖα ταῦτ᾽ ἔτιλλεν ὠναγὴς οὗτος,

uolsuras eius, quam glabra haec (quae iam nudata digito demonstrat) *et infra et supra euolsis pilis reddiderit.*

The mere sense of the words is rightly understood by Buecheler, whose punctuation I have given, and by others if not by all; but I find no sign that anyone sees the joke, which for Herodas and his first readers was the best joke in the mime. When Crusius *Unters.* p. 42 says 'der Schlaukopf spekuliert wohl nicht nur auf das Mitleid, sondern auch auf die Sinnlichkeit der Herrn Geschworenen', and Hense *Rhein. Mus.* 1900 p. 230 repeats that explanation, they are far astray.

Had Myrtale been induced to surmount her bashfulness under the eyes of a British jury, they might have believed, at least for the moment, that they had ocular evidence of shocking maltreatment; and their horror at the ruffian's brutality would have been equalled or surpassed by their amazement at his thoroughness. The λειότης revealed was complete. But that was no surprise or mystery to burghers of Cos. It was none of Thales' handiwork, but an ordinary feature of the feminine toilet, *munditiae muliebres*, perpetuated in marble and still imposed as a convention on sculptors and painters of the nude by the prestige of antiquity. Any woman of Myrtale's trade who was careful of her person and solicitous to please her customers would be παρατετιλμένη. Battarus achieves the height of his impudence when he offers in proof of outrage a piece of evidence which really shows that the particular outrage alleged was an impossible and a proverbially impossible feat: φαλακρὸν τίλλειν, *nudo detrahere uestimenta*, taking the breeks off a Highlander.

132

THE APPLICATION OF THOUGHT TO TEXTUAL CRITICISM*

In beginning to speak about the application of thought to textual criticism, I do not intend to define the term *thought*, because I hope that the sense which I attach to the word will emerge from what I say. But it is necessary at the outset to define *textual criticism*, because many people, and even some people who profess to teach it to others, do not know what it is. One sees books calling themselves introductions to textual criticism which contain nothing about textual criticism from beginning to end; which are all about palaeography and manuscripts and collation, and have no more to do with textual criticism than if they were all about accidence and syntax. Palaeography is one of the things with which a textual critic needs to ‖ acquaint himself, but grammar is another, and equally indispensable; and no amount either of grammar or of palaeography will teach a man one scrap of textual criticism.

Textual criticism is a science, and, since it comprises recension and emendation, it is also an art. It is the science of discovering error in texts and the art of removing it. That is its definition, that is what the name *denotes*. But I must also say something about what it does and does not *connote*, what attributes it does and does not imply; because here also there are false impressions abroad.

First, then, it is not a sacred mystery. It is purely a matter of reason and of common sense. We exercise textual criticism whenever we notice and correct a misprint. A man who possesses common sense and the use of reason must not expect to learn from treatises or lectures on textual criticism anything that he could not, with leisure and industry, find out for himself. What the lectures and treatises can do for him is to save him time and trouble by presenting to him immediately considerations which would in any case occur to him sooner or later. And whatever he reads about textual criticism in books, or hears at lectures, he should test by reason and common sense, and reject everything which conflicts with either as mere hocus-pocus.

Secondly, textual criticism is not a branch of mathematics, nor indeed an exact science at all. It deals with a matter not rigid and constant, like lines and numbers, but fluid and variable; namely the frailties and aberrations of the

* [*PCA* 18 (1922), 67–84]

human mind, and of its insubordinate servants, the human fingers. It therefore is not susceptible of hard-and-fast rules. It would be much easier if it were; and that is why people try to pretend that it is, or at least behave as if they thought so. Of course you can have hard-and-fast rules if you like, but then you will have false rules, and they will lead you wrong; because their simplicity will render them inapplicable to problems which are not simple, but complicated by the play of personality. A textual critic || engaged upon his business is not at all like Newton investigating the motions of the planets: he is much more like a dog hunting for fleas. If a dog hunted for fleas on mathematical principles, basing his researches on statistics of area and population, he would never catch a flea except by accident. They require to be treated as individuals; and every problem which presents itself to the textual critic must be regarded as possibly unique.

Textual criticism therefore is neither mystery nor mathematics: it cannot be learnt either like the catechism or like the multiplication table. This science and this art require more in the learner than a simply receptive mind; and indeed the truth is that they cannot be taught at all: *criticus nascitur, non fit*. If a dog is to hunt for fleas successfully he must be quick and he must be sensitive. It is no good for a rhinoceros to hunt for fleas: he does not know where they are, and could not catch them if he did. It has sometimes been said that textual criticism is the crown and summit of all scholarship. This is not evidently or necessarily true; but it is true that the qualities which make a critic, whether they are thus transcendent or no, are rare, and that a good critic is a much less common thing than for instance a good grammarian. I have in my mind a paper by a well-known scholar on a certain Latin writer, half of which was concerned with grammar and half with criticism. The grammatical part was excellent; it showed wide reading and accurate observation, and contributed matter which was both new and valuable. In the textual part the author was like nothing so much as an ill-bred child interrupting the conversation of grown men. If it was possible to mistake the question at issue, he mistook it. If an opponent's arguments were contained in some book which was not at hand, he did not try to find the book, but he tried to guess the arguments; and he never succeeded. If the book was at hand, and he had read the arguments, he did not understand them; and represented his opponents as saying the opposite of what they had said. If another scholar had already removed a corruption || by slightly altering the text, he proposed to remove it by altering the text violently. So possible is it to be a learned man, and admirable in other departments, and yet to have in you not even the makings of a critic.

But the application of thought to textual criticism is an action which ought to be within the power of anyone who can apply thought to anything. It is not, like the talent for textual criticism, a gift of nature, but it is a habit: and, like other habits, it can be formed. And, when formed, although it cannot fill the place of an absent talent, it can modify and minimise the ill effects of the talent's absence. Because a man is not a born critic, he need not therefore act like a born fool; but when he engages in textual criticism he often does. There are reasons for everything, and there are reasons for this; and I will now set forth the chief of them. The *fact* that thought is not sufficiently applied to the subject I shall show hereafter by examples; but at present I consider the causes which bring that result about.

First, then, not only is a natural aptitude for the study rare, but so also is a genuine interest in it. Most people, and many scholars among them, find it rather dry and rather dull. Now if a subject bores us, we are apt to avoid the trouble of thinking about it; but if we do that, we had better go further and avoid also the trouble of writing about it. And that is what English scholars often did in the middle of the nineteenth century, when nobody in England wanted to hear about textual criticism. This was not an ideal condition of affairs, but it had its compensation. The less one says about a subject which one does not understand, the less one will say about it which is foolish; and on this subject editors were allowed by public opinion to be silent if they chose. But public opinion is now aware that textual criticism, however repulsive, is nevertheless indispensable, and editors find that some pretence of dealing with the subject is obligatory; and in these circumstances they apply, not thought, but words, to textual criticism. They get rules by rote without grasping the realities of which those ‖ rules are merely emblems, and recite them on inappropriate occasions instead of seriously thinking out each problem as it arises.

Secondly, it is only a minority of those who engage in this study who are sincerely bent upon the discovery of truth. We all know that the discovery of truth is seldom the sole object of political writers; and the world believes, justly or unjustly, that it is not always the sole object of theologians: but the amount of sub-conscious dishonesty which pervades the textual criticism of the Greek and Latin classics is little suspected except by those who have had occasion to analyse it. People come upon this field bringing with them prepossessions and preferences; they are not willing to look all facts in the face, nor to draw the most probable conclusion unless it is also the most agreeable conclusion. Most men are rather stupid, and most of those who are not stupid are, consequently, rather vain; and it is hardly possible to step aside from the pursuit of truth without falling a victim either to your stupidity or else to your vanity. Stupidity will then attach you to received opinions, and you will stick in the mud; or vanity will set you hunting for novelty, and you will find mare's-nests. Added to these snares and hindrances there are the various forms of partisanship: sectarianism, which handcuffs you to your own school and teachers and associates, and patriotism, which handcuffs you to your own country. Patriotism has a great name as a virtue, and in civic matters, at the present stage of the world's history, it possibly still does more good than harm; but in the sphere of intellect it is an unmitigated nuisance. I do not know which cuts the worse figure: a German scholar encouraging his countrymen to believe that 'wir Deutsche' have nothing to learn from foreigners, or an Englishman demonstrating the unity of Homer by sneers at 'Teutonic professors', who are supposed by his audience to have goggle eyes behind large spectacles, and ragged moustaches saturated in lager beer, and consequently to be incapable of forming literary judgments. ||

Thirdly, these internal causes of error and folly are subject to very little counteraction or correction from outside. The average reader knows hardly anything about textual criticism, and therefore cannot exercise a vigilant control over the writer: the addle-pate is at liberty to maunder and the impostor is at liberty to lie. And, what is worse, the reader often shares the writer's prejudices, and is far too well pleased with his conclusions to examine either his premises or his reasoning. Stand on a barrel in the streets of Bagdad, and say in a loud voice, 'Twice two is four, and ginger is hot in the mouth, therefore Mohammed is the prophet of God', and your logic will probably escape criticism; or, if anyone by chance should criticise it, you could easily silence him by calling him a Christian dog.

Fourthly, the things which the textual critic has to talk about are not things which present themselves clearly and sharply to the mind; and it is easy to say, and to fancy that you think, what you really do not think, and even what, if you seriously tried to think it, you would find to be unthinkable. Mistakes are therefore made which could not be made if the matter under discussion were any corporeal object, having qualities perceptible to the senses. The human senses have had a much longer history than the human intellect, and have been brought much nearer to perfection: they are far more acute, far less easy to deceive. The difference between an icicle and a red-hot poker is really much slighter than the difference between truth and falsehood or sense and nonsense; yet it is much more immediately noticeable and much more universally noticed, because the body is more sensitive than the mind. I find therefore that a good way of exposing the falsehood of a statement or the absurdity of an argument in textual criticism is to transpose it into sensuous terms and see what it looks like then. If the nouns which we use are the names of things which can be handled or tasted, differing from one another in being hot or cold, sweet or sour, then we realise what we are saying and take care what we say. But || the terms of textual criticism are deplorably intellectual; and probably in no other field do men tell so many falsehoods in the idle hope that they are telling the truth, or talk so much nonsense in the vague belief that they are talking sense.

This is particularly unfortunate and particularly reprehensible, because there is no science in which it is more necessary to take precautions against error arising from internal causes. Those who follow the physical sciences enjoy the great advantage that they can constantly bring their opinions to the test of fact, and verify or falsify their theories by experiment. When a chemist has mixed sulphur and saltpetre and charcoal in certain proportions and wishes to ascertain if the mixture is explosive, he need only apply a match. When a doctor has compounded a new drug and desires to find out what diseases, if any, it is good for, he has only to give it to his patients all round and notice which die and which recover. Our conclusions regarding the truth or falsehood of a MS reading can never be confirmed or corrected by an equally decisive test; for the only equally decisive test would be the production of the author's autograph. The discovery merely of better and older MSS than were previously known to us is *not* equally decisive; and even this inadequate verification is not to be expected often, or on a large scale. It is therefore a matter of common prudence and common decency that we should neglect no safeguard lying within our reach; that we should look sharp after ourselves; that we should narrowly scrutinise our own proceedings and rigorously analyse our springs of action. How far these elementary requirements are satisfied, we will now learn from examples.

At the very beginning, to see what pure irrelevancy, what almost incredible foolishness, finds its way into print, take this instance. It had been supposed for several centuries that Plautus' name was *M. Accius Plautus*, when Ritschl in 1845 pointed out that in the Ambrosian palimpsest discovered by Mai in 1815, written in the ‖ fourth or fifth century, and much the oldest of Plautus' MSS, the name appears in the genitive as *T. Macci Plauti*, so that he was really called *Titus Maccius* (or *Maccus*) *Plautus*. An Italian scholar, one Vallauri, objected to this innovation on the ground that in all printed editions from the sixteenth to the nineteenth century the name was *M. Accius*. He went to Milan to look at the palimpsest, and there, to be sure, he found *T. Macci* quite legibly written. But he observed that many *other* pages of the MS were quite illegible, and that the whole book was very much tattered and battered; whereupon he said that he could not sufficiently wonder at anyone attaching any weight to a MS which was in such a condition. Is there any other science, anything calling itself a science, into which such intellects intrude and conduct such operations in public? But you may think that Mr Vallauri is a unique phenomenon. No: if you engage in textual criticism you may come upon a second Mr Vallauri at any turn. The MSS of Catullus, none of them older than the fourteenth century, present at 64. 23 the verse:

> heroes saluete, deum genus! o bona mater!

The Veronese scholia on Vergil, a palimpsest of the fifth or sixth century, at *Aen.* v. 80, 'salue sancte parens', have the note: 'Catullus: saluete, deum *gens*, o bona *matrum* | progenies, saluete iter[um]' – giving *gens* for *genus*, *matrum* for *mater*, and adding a half-verse absent from Catullus' MSS; and scholars have naturally preferred an authority so much more ancient. But one editor is found to object: 'the weight of the Veronese scholia, imperfect and full of lacunae as they are, is not to be set against our MSS'. There is Mr Vallauri over again: because the palimpsest has large holes elsewhere and because much of it has perished, therefore what remains, though written as early as the sixth century, has less authority than MSS written in the fourteenth. If however any-one gets hold of these fourteenth-century MSS, destroys pages of them and tears holes in the pages he ‖ does not destroy, the authority of those parts which he allows to survive will presumably deteriorate, and may even sink as low as that of the palimpsest.

Again. There are two MSS of a certain author, which we will call A and B. Of these two it is recognised that A is the more correct but the less sincere, and that B is the more corrupt but the less interpolated. It is desired to know which MS, if either, is bettei than the other, or whether both are equal. One scholar tries to determine this question by the collection and comparison of examples. But another thinks that he knows a shorter way than that; and it consists in saying 'the more sincere MS is and must be for any critic who understands his business the better MS'.

This I cite as a specimen of the things which people may say if they do not think about the meaning of what they are saying, and especially as an example of the danger of dealing in generalisations. The best way to treat such pretentious inanities is to transfer them from the sphere of textual criticism, where the difference between truth and falsehood or between sense and nonsense is little regarded and seldom even perceived, into some sphere where men are obliged to use concrete and sensuous terms, which force them, however reluctantly, to think.

I ask this scholar, this critic who knows his business, and who says that the more sincere of two MSS is and must be the better – I ask him to tell me which weighs most, a tall man or a fat man. He cannot answer; nobody can; every-body sees in a moment that the question is absurd. *Tall* and *fat* are adjectives which transport even a textual critic from the world of humbug into the world of reality, a world inhabited by comparatively thoughtful people, such as butchers and grocers, who depend on their brains for their bread. There he begins to understand that to such general questions any answer must be false; that judgment can only be pronounced on individual specimens; that everything depends on the degree of tallness and the degree of fatness. It may well be that an inch of girth ‖ adds more weight than an inch of height, or vice versa; but that altitude is incomparably more ponderous than obesity, or obesity than altitude, and that an inch of one depresses the scale more than a yard of the other, has never been maintained. The way to find out whether this tall man weighs more or less than that fat man is to weigh them; and the way to find out whether this corrupt MS is better or worse than that interpolated MS is to collect and compare their readings; not to ride easily off on the false and ridiculous generalisation that the more sincere MS is and must be the better.

When you call a MS *sincere* you instantly engage on its behalf the moral sympathy of the thoughtless: moral sympathy is a line in which they are very strong. I do not desire to exclude morality from textual criticism; I wish indeed that some moral qualities were commoner in textual criticism than they are; but let us not indulge our moral emotions out of season. It may be that a scribe who interpolates, who makes changes deliberately, is guilty of wickedness, while a scribe who makes changes accidentally, because he is sleepy or illiterate or drunk, is guilty of none; but that is a question which will be determined by a competent authority at the Day of Judgment, and is no concern of ours. Our concern is not with the eternal destiny of the scribe, but with the temporal utility of the MS; and a MS is useful or the reverse in proportion to the amount of truth which it discloses or conceals, no matter what may be the causes of the disclosure or concealment. It is a mistake to suppose that deliberate change is always or necessarily more destructive of truth than accidental change; and even if it were, the main question, as I have said already, is one of degree. A MS in which 1 per cent of the words have been viciously and intentionally altered and 99 per cent are right is not so bad as a MS in which only 1 per cent are right and 99 per cent have been altered virtuously and unintentionally; and if you go to a critic with any such vague inquiry as the question whether the 'more sincere' or the 'more || correct' of two MSS is the better, he will reply, 'If I am to answer that question, you must show me the two MSS first; for aught that I know at present, from the terms of your query, either may be better than the other, or both may be equal.' But that is what the incompetent intruders into criticism can never admit. They *must* have a better MS, whether it exists or no; because they could never get along without one. If Providence permitted two MSS to be equal, the editor would have to choose between their readings by considerations of intrinsic merit, and in order to do that he would need to acquire intelligence and impartiality and willingness to take pains, and all sorts of things which he neither has nor wishes for; and he feels sure that God, who tempers the wind to the shorn lamb, can never have meant to lay upon his shoulders such a burden as this.

This is thoughtlessness in the sphere of recension: come now to the sphere of emendation. There is one foolish sort of conjecture which seems to be commoner in the British Isles than anywhere else, though it is also practised abroad, and of late years especially at Munich. The practice is, if you have persuaded yourself that a text is corrupt, to alter a letter or two and see what happens. If what happens is anything which the warmest good-will can mistake for sense and grammar, you call it an emendation; and you call this silly game the palaeo-graphical method.

The palaeographical method has always been the delight of tiros and the scorn of critics. Haupt, for example, used to warn his pupils against mistaking this sort of thing for emendation. 'The prime requisite of a good emendation', said he, 'is that it should start from the thought; it is only afterwards that other considerations, such as those of metre, or possibilities, such as the interchange of letters, are taken into account.' And again: 'If the sense requires it, I am pre-pared to write *Constantinopolitanus* where the MSS have the monosyllabic interjection *o.*' And again: 'From the requirement that one should ‖ always begin with the thought, there results, as is self-evident, the negative aspect of the case, that one should not, at the outset, consider what exchange of letters may possibly have brought about the corruption of the passage one is dealing with.' And further, in his oration on Lachmann as a critic: 'Some people, if they see that anything in an ancient text wants correcting, immediately betake themselves to the art of palaeography, investigate the shapes of letters and the forms of abbreviation, and try one dodge after another, as if it were a game, until they hit upon something which they think they can substitute for the corruption; as if forsooth truth were generally discovered by shots of that sort, or as if emendation could take its rise from anything but a careful consideration of the thought.'

But even when palaeography is kept in her proper place, as handmaid, and not allowed to give herself the airs of mistress, she is apt to be overworked. There is a preference for conjectures which call in the aid of palaeography, and which assume, as the cause of error, the accidental interchange of similar letters or similar words, although other causes of error are known to exist. One is presented, for instance, with the following maxim: 'Interpolation is, speaking generally, comparatively an uncommon source of alteration, and we should therefore be loth to assume it in a given case.'

Every case is a given case; so what this maxim really means is that we should always be loth to assume interpolation as a source of alteration. But it is certain, and admitted by this writer when he uses the phrase 'comparatively uncom-mon', that interpolation does occur; so he is telling us that we should be loth to assume interpolation even when that assumption is true. And the reason why we are to behave in this ridiculous manner is that interpolation is, speaking generally, comparatively an uncommon source of alteration.

Now to detect a *non sequitur*, unless it leads to an unwelcome conclusion, is as much beyond the power of ‖ the average reader as it is beyond the power of the average writer to attach ideas to his own words when those words are terms of textual criticism. I will therefore substitute other terms, terms to which ideas must be attached; and I invite consideration of this maxim and this ratiocination:

'A bullet-wound is, speaking generally, comparatively an uncommon cause of death, and we should therefore be loth to assume it in a given case.'

Should we? Should we be loth to assume a bullet-wound as the cause of death if the given case were death on a battlefield? and should we be loth to do so for the reason alleged, that a bullet-wound is, speaking generally, comparatively an uncommon cause of death? Ought we to assume instead the commonest cause of death, and assign death on a battlefield to tuberculosis? What would be thought of a counsellor who enjoined that method of procedure? Well, it would probably be thought that he was a textual critic strayed from home.

Why is interpolation comparatively uncommon? For the same reason that bullet-wounds are: because the opportunity for it is comparatively uncommon. Interpolation is provoked by real or supposed difficulties, and is not frequently volunteered where all is plain sailing; whereas accidental alteration may happen anywhere. Every letter of every word lies exposed to it, and that is the sole reason why accidental alteration is more common. In a given case where either assumption is possible, the assumption of interpolation is equally probable, nay more probable; because action with a motive is more probable than action without a motive. The truth therefore is that in such a case we should be loth to assume accident and should rather assume interpolation; and the circumstance that such cases are comparatively uncommon is no reason for behaving irrationally when they occur.

There is one special province of textual criticism, a large and important province, which is concerned with || the establishment of rules of grammar and of metre. Those rules are in part traditional, and given us by the ancient grammarians; but in part they are formed by our own induction from what we find in the MSS of Greek and Latin authors; and even the traditional rules must of course be tested by comparison with the witness of the MSS. But every rule, whether traditional or framed from induction, is sometimes broken by the MSS; it may be by few, it may be by many; it may be seldom, it may be often; and critics may then say that the MSS are wrong, and may correct them in accordance with the rule. This state of affairs is apparently, nay evidently, paradoxical. The MSS are the material upon which we base our rule, and then, when we have got our rule, we turn round upon the MSS and say that the rule, based upon them, convicts them of error. We are thus working in a circle, that is a fact which there is no denying; but, as Lachmann says, the task of the critic is just this, to tread that circle deftly and warily; and that is precisely what elevates the critic's business above mere mechanical labour. The difficulty is one which lies in the nature of the case, and is inevitable; and the only way to surmount it is just to be a critic.

The paradox is more formidable in appearance than in reality, and has plenty of analogies in daily life. In a trial or lawsuit the jury's verdict is mainly based upon the evidence of the witnesses; but that does not prevent the jury from making up its mind, from the evidence in general, that one or more witnesses have been guilty of perjury and that their evidence is to be disregarded. It is quite possible to elicit from the general testimony of MSS a rule of sufficient certainty to convict of falsehood their exceptional testimony, or of sufficient probability to throw doubt upon it. But that exceptional testimony must in each case be considered. It must be recognised that there are two hypotheses between which we have to decide: the question is whether the exceptions come from the author, and so break down the rule, or whether they come from the scribe, and are to be corrected by it: || and in order to decide this we must keep our eyes open for any peculiarity which may happen to characterise them.

One of the forms which lack of thought has assumed in textual criticism is the tendency now prevailing, especially among some Continental scholars, to try to break down accepted rules of grammar or metre by the mere collection and enumeration of exceptions presented by the MSS. Now that can never break down a rule: the mere number of exceptions is nothing; what matters is their weight, and that can only be ascertained by classification and scrutiny. If I had noted down every example which I have met, I should now have a large collection of places in Latin MSS where the substantive *orbis*, which our grammars and dictionaries declare to be masculine, has a feminine adjective attached to it. But I do not therefore propose to revise that rule of syntax, for examination would show that these examples, though numerous, have no force. Most of them are places where the sense and context show that *orbis*, in whatever case or number it may be, is merely a corruption of the corresponding case and number of *urbs*; and in the remaining places it is natural to suppose that the scribe has been influenced and confused by the great likeness of the one word to the other. Or again, read Madvig, *Adu. Crit.*, vol. I, book i, chap. iv, where he sifts the evidence for the opinion that the aorist infinitive can be used in Greek after verbs of saying and thinking in the sense of the future infinitive or of the aorist infinitive with ἄν. The list of examples in the MSS is very long indeed; but the moment you begin to sort them and examine them you are less struck by their number than by the restriction of their extent. Almost all of them are such as δέξασθαι used for δέξεσθαι, where the two forms differ by one letter only; a smaller number are such as ποιῆσαι for ποιήσειν, where the difference, though greater, is still slight; others are examples like ἥκιστα ἀναγκασθῆναι for ἥκιστ' ἂν ἀναγκασθῆναι, where again the difference is next to nothing. Now if the MSS are right in these cases, and the Greek authors did use this || construction, how are we to explain this extraordinary limitation of the use? There is no syntactical difference between the first and second aorist: why then did they use the 1st

aorist so often for the future and the 2nd aorist so seldom? why did they say
δέξασθαι for δέξεσθαι dozens of times and λαβεῖν for λήψεσθαι never? The mere
asking of that question is enough to show the true state of the case. The bare
fact that the aorists thus used in the MSS are aorists of similar *form* to the future,
while aorists of dissimilar form are not thus used, proves that the phenomenon
has its cause in the copyist's eye and not in the author's mind, that it is not a
variation in grammatical usage but an error in transcription. The number of
examples is nothing; all depends upon their character; and a single example of
λαβεῖν in a future sense would have more weight than a hundred of δέξασθαι.

In particular, scribes will alter a less familiar form to a more familiar, if they
see nothing to prevent them. If metre allows, or if they do not know that metre
forbids, they will alter ἐλεινός to ἐλεεινός, οἰστός to ὀϊστός, *nil* to *nihil*, *deprendo*
to *deprehendo*. Since metre convicts them of infidelity in some places, they
forfeit the right to be trusted in any place; if we choose to trust them we are
credulous, and if we build structures on our trust we are no critics. Even if
metre does not convict them, reason sometimes can. Take the statement,
repeatedly made in grammars and editions, that the Latins sometimes used the
pluperfect for the imperfect and the perfect. They did use it for the imperfect;
they used it also for the preterite or past aorist; but for the perfect they did not
use it; and that is proved by the very examples of its use as perfect which are
found in MSS. All those examples are of the 3rd person plural. Why? We must
choose between the two following hypotheses:

(*a*) That the Latins used the pluperfect for the perfect in the 3rd person
plural only.

(*b*) That they did not use the pluperfect for the perfect, and that these
examples are corrupt. ‖

If anyone adopted the former, he would have to explain what syntactical
property, inviting the author to use pluperfect for perfect, is possessed by the
3rd person plural and not by the two other plural or the three singular persons:
and I should like to see some one set about it.

If we adopt the latter, we must show what *external* feature, inviting the *scribe*
to write pluperfect for perfect, is possessed by the 3rd person plural exclusively:
and that is quite easy. The 3rd person plural is the only person in which the
perfect and the pluperfect differ merely by one letter. Moreover in verse the
perfect termination -*ĕrunt*, being comparatively unfamiliar to scribes, is altered
by them to the nearest familiar form with the same scansion, sometimes -*erint*,
sometimes -*erant*: in Ovid's *Heroides* there are four places where the best MS
gives *praebuĕrunt, stetĕrunt, excidĕrunt, expulĕrunt,* and the other MSS give
-*erant* or -*erint* or both. Accordingly, when the much inferior MSS of Propertius
present pluperfect for perfect in four places, *fuerant* once, *steterant* once,
exciderant twice, Scaliger corrects to *fuĕrunt, stetĕrunt, excidĕrunt.* Thereupon

an editor of this enlightened age takes up his pen and writes as follows: 'It is quite erroneous to remove the pluperfects where it can be done without great expenditure of conjectural sagacity (*steterunt* for *steterant* and the like), and not to trouble oneself about the phenomenon elsewhere.' I ask, how is it possible to trouble oneself about the phenomenon elsewhere? It does not exist elsewhere. There is no place where the MSS give *steteram* in the sense of the perfect *steti*, nor *steteras* in the sense of the perfect *stetisti*. Wherever they give examples of the pluperfect which cannot be removed by the change of one letter – such as *pararat* in I 8 36 or *fueram* in I 12 11 – those are examples where it has sometimes the sense of the imperfect, sometimes of the preterite, but never of the perfect. And the inference is plain: the Latins did not use the pluperfect for the perfect.

Scaliger knew that in the sixteenth century: Mr ‖ Rothstein, in the nineteenth and twentieth, does not know it; he has found a form of words to prevent him from knowing it, and he thinks himself in advance of Scaliger. It is supposed that there has been progress in the science of textual criticism, and the most frivolous pretender has learnt to talk superciliously about 'the old unscientific days'. The old unscientific days are everlasting; they are here and now; they are renewed perennially by the ear which takes formulas in, and the tongue which gives them out again, and the mind which meanwhile is empty of reflexion and stuffed with self-complacency. Progress there has been, but where? In superior intellects: the rabble do not share it. Such a man as Scaliger, living in our time, would be a better critic than Scaliger was; but we shall not be better critics than Scaliger by the simple act of living in our own time. Textual criticism, like most other sciences, is an aristocratic affair, not communicable to all men, nor to most men. Not to be a textual critic is no reproach to anyone, unless he pretends to be what he is not. To *be* a textual critic requires aptitude for thinking and willingness to think; and though it also requires other things, those things are supplements and cannot be substitutes. Knowledge is good, method is good, but one thing beyond all others is necessary; and that is to have a head, not a pumpkin, on your shoulders, and brains, not pudding, in your head.

133

DOROTHEUS ONCE MORE*

In the last instalment of the *catalogus codicum astrologorum Graecorum*, vol. VIII part iv (1922), Mr Cumont publishes from cod. Paris. Gr. 2425 two fragments of hexameter verse, one of three lines and the other of seven or eight, which he attributes,[1] perhaps rightly, to Dorotheus of Sidon, on whose remains I have written in *C.Q.* 1908 pp. 47–61 [[this edition pp. 740–55]] and 1911 pp. 249 sq. [[this edition pp. 840–1]]. The scribe, who makes a practice of suppressing names, assigns the shorter piece to no author, and the longer he introduces with the circumlocution φησί τις τῶν σοφῶν.

The citations occur in the geniture[2] of a Θηβαῖος γραμματικός printed on pp. 221–4. The first is given on p. 222 12–14. The Moon was in Taurus, which is the house of Venus, and Venus herself was in the opposite sign of Scorpius; and accordingly

φυγὰς ἐν πολλοῖς τόποις ἐγένετο διὰ τὸ διαμετρεῖσθαι τὴν Σελήνην ὑπὸ τοῦ ἰδίου οἰκοδεσπότου· φησὶ γὰρ

> τὴν Μήνην καθόρα τίνος ἀστέρος ἐν οἴκῳ ἐστίν
> καὶ ἢν εὕρης τοῦτο φωλευόμενον διάμετρον
> καὶ φυγάς ἐστι δὲ καὶ ἄσιμος (ἄτιμος m. 2) καὶ μετανάστης.

Mr Cumont corrects the metre of verse 1 to ἐστὶν ἐν οἴκῳ; in verse 2 he writes κἄν, which should of course be κἤν, and διαμέτρῳ, which is needless and useless, διάμετρος being commonly and properly an adjective; in verse 3 he adopts from Mr Delcourt the conjecture ἔσται δή, which, if right, forbids the ascription of the verse to Dorotheus, and prints κἄσημος, which ought at any rate to be καὶ ἄσημος, though in fact the καὶ ἄτιμος of the second hand is the true reading, as can be shown without difficulty. For Mr Cumont has not observed that these

---

* [[CQ 17 (1923), 53–4]]

[1] On p. 118, n. 2, Mr Cumont says that the verses printed in *C.C.A.G.* 1 pp. 108–13 'Dorothei esse uidentur'. I showed in *C.Q.* 1908 p. 62 [[this edition p. 755]] that this is on metrical grounds impossible.

[2] The text says, p. 221 10, that at the time of birth the 24th degree of Aquarius was on the eastern horizon and the 6th degree of Sagittarius in the mid-heaven. If this measurement of the arc is not quite correct for the latitude of Thebes at the date, whatever it was, of his nativity, it is very near so: Mr Cumont's substitution of Ταύρῳ for Τοξότῃ, with the note ' si horoscopus est in Aquario, medium caelum est in Tauro', is an extraordinary blunder, and so is his conjecture ὑπεργείου for ὑπογείου at p. 222 5.

three lines are substantially identical with lines 222–4 of that jumble of scraps which is called the 5th book of Manetho's *apotelesmatica*:

τὴν Μήνην σκέπτου εἰ τίτανός ἐστιν ἐν οἴκῳ,
κἢν εὕρῃς τοῦτον φωλευόμενον διάμετρον
καὶ φυγάδας σὺ νόει καὶ ἀτίμητον διὰ πάντων.

The second verse is thus established securely, 'if you find that planet lodging opposite', and the end of the first should pretty clearly be τίνος ἀστέρος ἐστὶν ἐν οἴκῳ in both places: for the third verse the parallel gives less help.

The other fragment is cited on p. 223 13–19 to show that the position of Mercury and Mars in this nativity explains why the native was a traitor. Mercury was in Libra and Mars in Capricorn. Libra and Capricorn are angular signs of the same square, and Libra's angle is technically said to be δεξιὸν καὶ προηγούμενον with respect to Capricorn's, which is εὐώνυμον καὶ ἑπόμενον; and the relation of the two planets when thus situate is expressed by saying καθυπερτερεῖ ὁ Ἑρμῆς τὸν Ἄρη κατὰ τετράγωνον (Heph. Theb. I 16, Porph. *isag.* p. 188 ed. Basil. 1559, *C.C.A.G.* I p. 157 4–6).

περὶ τοῦ εἶναι αὐτὸν προδότην. ὅμα τὸν Ἑρμην καθυπερτεροῦντα τὸν Ἄρη κατὰ τετράγωνον. φησὶ γάρ τις τῶν σοφῶν·
εἰ δὲ νῦν τετράκληρος ἐων τὸν ἀνώτερον ἴσχυ ερμῆς βαίον δὲ τόπον μαίνει φυλώτ(α)τ(ος) ἄρης δυνὸς ἐξετέλεσε πανούργων ετὴ μέλλων τὰς ἁρπαγὰς καὶ ἀλλοτρίων σερητ(ως) εἰς ἕτερον ‖ δὲ ἐξ ἑτέρου μετάνασιν ἄπανερο ἄνδρα ἀλοτ' (or αὐλοτ') εὕροιμεν καὶ τὸ λοιπὸν ἐνίσκηψουσιν ὀδόντος φικακομηχανία κτεανῶν δὲ γυμνῶσουσι.

'Nonnulla ab amico Iosepho Bidez adiutus corrigere dubitanter tentaui' says Mr Cumont; and this is the result:

εἰ δὲ τόπον τετράκληρος ἐων τὸν ἀνώτερον ἴσχει
Ἑρμείας, βαιὸν δὲ τόπον ναίει φιλότητος ὁ Ἄρης,
δεινῶς ἐξετέλεσσε πανούργων ἦτε μέλοντας
ἁρπακτὰς ἦτ' ἀλλοτρίων...στερητάς,
εἰς ἕτερον δ' ἑτέρου μετανάστασιν ἀνέρος ἄνδρα   5
†ἀλοτ' εὕροιμεν κτλ.
.   .   .   .   . ἐνισκήψουσι προδόντες
σφῇ κακομηχανίη κτεάνων δ' ἀπογυμνώσουσιν.

I say nothing of the heptameter and its digammated Ἄρης, but it may not be amiss to remark that στερητάς is a word which Dorotheus would not admit into his verse, and that he would not scan τετράκληρος as ∪ ∪ – ∪. The passage should be corrected somewhat as follows:

εἰ δέ νυ τετράπλευρος ἐὼν τὸν ἀνώτερον ἴσχει
Ἑρμείας, βαιὸν δὲ τόπον μενεφύλοπις Ἄρης,
οὐρανὸς ἐξετέλεσσε πανουργείην μελετῶντας,
ἅρπαγας, ἀλλοτρίων θηρήτορας· εἰς ἕτερον δὲ
5   ἐξ ἑτέρου μεταβᾶσιν ἀπ᾽ ἀνέρος ἄνδρα ἀλόντα
εὕροιμέν ⟨κε⟩ κτλ.

. . . . ἐνισκήψουσιν ἑλόντες
σφῇ κακομηχανίῃ κτεάνων δέ ⟨ἑ⟩ γυμνώσουσιν.

'If Mercury in quartile aspect holds the superior place, and the stout warrior
Mars a humble one, heaven creates such as practise villainy and rob and pursue
after their neighbours' goods; and as they pass from one to another we shall
find man after man entrapped by them...When they have snared him with
their evil arts they will pounce on him and strip him of all his substance.'

1. εἰ δέ νυ occurs in Dor. 211 (his fragments are collected in *C.C.A.G.* VI
pp. 91–113). I do not see how τετράκληρος (a word not otherwise known) could
earn the required sense of τετράγωνος, quartile, which τετράπλευρος possesses
in Dor. 271 sq. Ζεὺς δ᾽ ὅτε τετράπλευρος ἄνω χθονὸς οὖσαν ἴδηται | ἠύκερον
Μήνην. With τὸν ἀνώτερον supply τόπον from the next clause, which is quite
in the manner of Dorotheus: so 36 sq. μοίρας, 98 δέμας, 158 sq. ζῴῳ κακοδαι-
μονέοντι.

2. The ornamental epithet is like Dor. 11 and 38 θοῦρος Ἄρης, 101 πτολι-
πόρθιος Ἄρης, 268 ὀλοφώιος Ἄρης.

3. The singular verb requires a subject, and δυνός points to ο̅υ̅ν̅ο̅ς̅, the regular
abbreviation of οὐρανός. The form πανουργείην is like Dor. 122 κακοεργείην,
225 δυσεργείην, *C.C.A.G.* II p. 202 16 (= VI p. 91 17) and VIII p. 125 15
ἀεργείην.

4. The scansion ἀλλŏτρίων has the same excuse as its only parallel in Dorotheus, τε̆τράγωνος, 181, 196, 261, – that the word cannot be brought into the
verse without this licence.

5. The construction of μεταβᾶσιν ἀλόντα is that of δάμεν Ἕκτορι in *Il.*
XVIII 103.

8. δέ ἑ has shrunk to δέ also in Dor. 236 κακὸς δέ ⟨ἑ⟩ μῆτις ὁράτω; but perhaps
in our verse the lost word is τε.

It is probable that most of my corrections have been made independently
and simultaneously by Mr Kroll, and it may be that he has already published
them, living as he does in a country where opportunity for publication is
ampler and more frequent than in England.

134

NOTES ON SENECA'S TRAGEDIES*

These minute annotations, put together for a paper read to the Cambridge Philological Society on February 15, are mostly taken from jottings which I made some thirty years ago in the margin of Leo's edition. There they would have stayed, but for the appearance in 1918 of the Illinois *index uerborum* compiled by Messrs Oldfather, Pease, and Canter, which is not merely what its title promises, but also aims at recording the conjectures of the present century, and has enabled me to cancel three or four proposals which I found anticipated. Other people, from Dr U. von Wilamowitz-Moellendorff downward, so often print emendations of mine as their own, or indeed as anyone else's, that I am even more anxious than I otherwise should be to avoid printing as mine the emendations of other people.[1]

The criticism and interpretation of these tragedies now suffer chiefly from two causes; and I will give one example of the operation of each. First *Herc. Oet.* 1170–6:

> sine hoste uincor, quodque me torquet magis   1170
> (o misera uirtus!) summus Alcidae dies
> nullum malum prosternit, inpendo, ei mihi,
> in nulla uitam facta. pro mundi arbiter
> superique quondam dexterae testes meae,
> pro cuncta tellus, Herculis uestri placet   1175
> mortem perire?

These last words, if not what the author wrote, are what he ought to have written; nothing fitter or better could be invented; and they are the reading of A. Editors were once contented with this, as well they might be; but the reading of E is '*Herculem uestrum* placet | *morte ferire*'; and because in many places the truth has been found underlying the corruptions of E and obliterated by the corrections of A, therefore critics here also turn their backs on A and try their hands at correcting E for themselves. Some of their efforts have probably escaped me, but I have collected more than enough: 'Herculem uestrum

---

* [[CQ 17 (1923), 163–72: summarized in *PCPhS* 1923, 3–4]]

[1] So I take this opportunity of saying that the conjecture *logos* at Mart. III 20 5, which I published in *C.Q.* 1919 p. 69 [[this edition p. 983]], had been published by G. Thiele in *Philol.* 1911 p. 548; and that *logis* in Phaed. III *prol.* 37, which I proposed in the same place, is at any rate not mine, as it was mentioned two months earlier by Mr Vollmer in his *Lesungen und Deutungen* III p. 10.

placet | *morte feriari*' (this, alas, is Gronouius), '*morte hac perire*', '*hac* placet | *morte interire*', '*perire inertem*', '*morbo perire*', '*inertem obire*', '*mortis pudere*'. Now these are bad conjectures: the reading of A, if likewise a conjecture and nothing more, is a good one. It accounts better than any of them for the corruption in E, – *mortem perire* first changed by inadvertence to *morte ferire*, and then *Herculis uestri* changed to the accusative for grammar, – and its sense is uniquely appropriate. But I daresay few readers of the nineteenth and twentieth centuries have understood what its sense is; so I had better cite the parallels *Ag.* 519 *perdenda mors est*, Sil. IV 605 *perdere mortem*, Luc. III 706 *perdere letum*.

This brings me to the second cause and to *Tro.* 766–70:

> o dulce pignus, o decus lapsae domus
> summumque Troiae funus, o Danaum timor,
> genetricis o spes uana, cui demens ego
> laudes parentis bellicas, annos aui
> 770   medios precabar, uota destituit deus. ||

So speaks Andromache to Astyanax. When Seneca had written *medios* in 770 he felt a pleasant glow of pride: it was worthy of himself, at once smart and subtle, and he knew that none of his contemporaries would miss the point. The seventeenth century, could he have foreseen it, was to prove no less quick of apprehension than the first, and the passage was rightly explained by Farnaby and rightly translated by Marolles. The nineteenth century arrived, and the silver age of Latin became unintelligible to a breed of men who have no natural affinity with its ways of speech and thought and who do not think it worth their while to learn them; so *medios* is supposed to be unsound, and up starts a crop of conjectures, each worse than the other, *demens, toties, melius*, I know not what besides.

HERC. FVR. 448–58

	Lyc.	mortale caelo non potest iungi genus.
	Amph.	communis ista pluribus causa est deis.
450	L.	famuline fuerant ante quam fierent dei?
	A.	pastor Pheraeos Delius pauit greges.
	L.	sed non per omnes exul errauit plagas.
	A.	quem profuga terra mater errante edidit.
	L.	num monstra saeua Phoebus aut timuit feras?
455	A.	primus sagittas imbuit Phoebi draco.
	L.	quam grauia paruus tulerit ignoras mala?
	A.	e matris utero fulmine eiectus puer
		mox fulminanti proximus patri stetit.

Lycus and Amphitryon are wrangling over the divinity of Hercules, Lycus alleging circumstances which should argue a mortal origin, and Amphitryon replying with parallels from the history of other sons of Jove. What, in verse 456, are the heavy ills which Hercules endured in infancy, *paruus*? The serpents which assailed him in his cradle when he was eight months old endured heavy ills of their own, but the worst which even Lycus could pretend that they did to Hercules was to give him a fright; and that falsehood has already been insinuated in the 'monstra timuit' of 454. Amphitryon's reply in 457 sq. points in another direction, and shows that Lycus had here made allusion to the prolonged labour of Alcmena and her son's retarded birth, εἰργούσης τῆς Ἥρας τῷ Ἡρακλεῖ τὴν ἐκ τῆς γαστρὸς ἔξοδον, as the story is told after Nicander by Ovid *met.* ix 281–323 and Antonius Liberalis 29. But nobody designates a babe unborn as *paruus*: these were 'partus...mala', the ills attendant on his birth; and Amphitryon answers the taunt by recalling the yet more terrible childbed in which Semele was delivered of Bacchus.

In this verse the allusion has to be restored by conjecture: in Val. Fl. iii 514–16 it is preserved in the text and editors have erased it. Iuno speaks:

> en ego nunc regum soror; et mihi gentis
> ullus honos? iam tum indecores iussaeque dolorum
> primitiae et tenero superati protinus angues.

That is, 'the pangs in which at my bidding his life began, and the serpents which he quelled in first infancy, redounded even then to my discredit': *que* and *et* are corresponsive. To spoil this sense, and to make 'dolorum primitiae' absurdly signify the exhilarating adventure of the serpents, they have struck out *et* or changed it to *ut* or *a*; and *iussae* they have altered into all sorts of things, *cassae, missae, iustae, lusae, miserae.* ‖

TRO. 386–90

quo bis sena uolant sidera turbine,
quo cursu properat uoluere saecula
astrorum dominus, quo properat modo
obliquis Hecate currere flexibus,
hoc omnes petimus fata.

For *quo bis* in 386 the cod. Etruscus has *bis quos*, that is, apart from the accidental repetition of *s*, *bis quo* as a late hand has corrected it (Leo vol. 1 p. 20). There are many places, as I have already intimated, where undue preference is now given to this best MS, but there are some where it has been unduly disregarded, and here *bis quo* is probably right. No rule ordains that the relative in anaphora shall stand first in every clause: compare *Oed.* 251 sq. 'bis sena cursu signa *qui* uario regis, | *qui* tarda celeri saecula euoluis rota', *Ag.* 515 sq. 'cadere *qui* meruit manu, | *quem* terra seruat, uicta *quem* tellus tegit', *Tro.* 353–5 '*qui* Pelasgae uincla soluisti rati | morasque bellis, arte *qui* reseras polum, | *cui*' etc. And separation of the numerical adverb from its numeral is frequent, occurring not only where metre needs it, as Lucr. V 1300 '*bis* coniungere *binos*', *moret.* 18 'quae *bis* in *octonas* excurrit pondere libras', Ouid. *met.* V 50 '*bis* adhuc *octonis* integer annis', VIII 242 sq. 'natalibus actis | *bis* puerum *senis*, animi' etc., *fast.* II 196 '*ter* cecidere *duo*', VI 768 '*quintus* ab extremo mense *bis* ille dies', *trist.* IV 10 4 'milia qui *nouies* distat ab urbe *decem*', 10 'qui *tribus* ante *quater* mensibus ortus erat', Manil. II 727 'numeris hanc *ter* dispone *quaternis*', Mart. X 24 7 'annos addite *bis*, precor, *nouenos*', *carm. epigr. Buech.* 1071 1 (saec. I P.C.) 'iam *bis* ut *octonos* Spendon compleuerat annos', but also where metre allows free choice, Ouid. *met.* III 351 sq. 'namque *ter* ad *quinos* unum Cephisius annum | addiderat', VIII 500 'et quos sustinui *bis* mensum *quinque* labores', *Ib.* 1 'lustris *bis* iam mihi *quinque* peractis', Manil. I 588 '*bis*que iacet *binis* summotus partibus', Mart. I 15 3 '*bis* iam paene tibi consul *tricesimus* instat', *carm. epigr.* 55 18 (saec. I A.C.) '*bis* hic *septeni* mecum mortales dies | tenebris tenentur', Plin. *n.h.* IV 81 '*bis* ad *decies centum* milium passuum'. As inferior MSS have changed the order in this verse of Seneca's, so have they in Ouid. *met.* VIII 500 (*mensum bis quinque*) and *Ib.* 1 (*mihi iam bis quinque*).

Again in *Tro.* 1123 the best MS is wrongly abandoned:

1120   idem ille populus aliud ad facinus redit
        tumulumque Achillis; cuius extremum latus
        Rhoetea leni uerberant fluctu uada,
        auersa cingit campus et cliuo leui
        erecta medium uallis includens locum
1125   crescit theatri more. concursus frequens
        impleuit omne litus.

Leo's perverse punctuation of 1124–6 is consigned to limbo by Richter, so I let it be; but both of them in 1123 accept *aduersa* from the inferior MSS (A), though Gronouius had adopted and defended the *auersa* of E: 'recte: nam frons promontoriorum respicit mare: altera igitur pars auersa et tergi instar.' If you mention first one side of a valley and then the other, the latter is *aduersus*, because the two sides of a valley are face to face. But if you mention first one and then the other side of a hill, the latter is *auersus*, because the two sides of a hill are back to back.[1]

There are several places besides *Tro.* 386 where minute corrections of the text can be gleaned from readings of E which are themselves erroneous. Thus at ‖

---

[1] I cite here Sall. *Iug.* 93 2 'haud procul ab *latere* castelli *quod auorsum* proeliantibus erat' because the *thes. ling. Lat.*, being a dictionary, misconstrues it at II p. 1323 66 and refers *quod* to *castelli*.

Ag. 298 for *subripere doctus* it gives *sub rupe reductus*, that is, as Munro observed at Lucr. III 1031, *subrupere*, a spelling frequent in the MSS of Plautus, established by Ritschl *opusc.* IV p. 67 upon the inscription *C.I.L.* I 603 14, and illustrated by Buecheler *opusc.* I p. 410 from Fronto, Martial, and the elder Seneca.[1] It has also been recognised that E points to the forms *turpis Tro.* 504, *qum H.O.* 208, *exserit* 255. At *H.f.* 1198 A have 'neruum uix recedentem mihi' and E has *neruos*, that is *neruom*. But its lection at *H.O.* 1608 has a little more importance:

> effare casus, iuuenis, Herculeos, precor,
> uoltuque quonam tulerit Alcides necem.

uoltuque A, *uoltune* E. There are places – Luc. X 542 ought to be recognised as one of them – where *que*, though so much the commoner word, has been corrupted into *ne*; but naturally there are not many, and a better way to explain the variants here is to suppose that their common origin was *uoltuue*. That disjunctive particles often lose their disjunctive force when they couple interrogatives was shown for Virgil by Wagner *quaest. Verg.* XXXVI 5, 'ut uel tum *ue* inueniatur, ubi is, qui uaria quaerit, ad omnia sibi responderi cupit, non ad partem tantum'; and so it is in Seneca: *Thy.* 423 sq. 'quid, anime, pendes *quidue* consilium diu | tam facile torques?', *Tro.* 477, *Phaed.* 1157, *Oed.* 866, *Oct.* 788, 899. The present passage, in which the first clause is not formally interrogative, is parallel to Verg. *Aen.* X 149 sq. 'regi memorat nomenque genusque (*i.e.* quis sit) | *quidue* petat quidue ipse ferat', where Seruius remarks 'multi...dicunt...*que* coniunctione opus fuisse, *ue* enim proprie *uel* significat'; and so thought the writer of the archetype of A.

Med. 652–69

> Idmonem, quamuis bene fata nosset,
> condidit serpens Libycis harenis;
> omnibus uerax, sibi falsus uni
> concidit Mopsus caruitque Thebis.   655
> ille si uere cecinit futura,
> exul errauit Thetidis maritus;
> igne fallaci nociturus Argis
> Nauplius praeceps cadet in profundum

---

[1] At Manil. III 355, where the MSS give *eruptis* in the sense of *ereptis*, I said I had no second example of that form; but there exists one in Appul. *apol.* 28 'curae meae *eruptum*'. I doubt however if any trust is to be put in MSS when they present *-ruptus* for *-reptus* in compounds other than *subripio*. When for instance at Luc. VI 35 and Stat. *Theb.* VII 316 the most and best MSS have *direpta* and *abreptis*, and a few offer *dirupta* and *abruptis*, I regard these as mere blunders; and I do not advise editors of Phaedrus to retain the *corruptus* of the MSS in *app. Per.* 13 18, nor editors of Catullus to interpret *abrupto* as *abrepto* in 68 84. As somebody will some day cite in this connexion the *abruptum* of Manil. V 107, which all editors change to *abreptum*, I give warning that it is the participle of *abrumpo* and means ἀπότομον, *praefractum*, as in Sil. VII 219.

660 patrioque pendet crimine poenas
  fulmine et ponto moriens Oileus;
  coniugis fatum redimens Pheraei,
  uxor, impendes animam marito.
  ipse qui praedam spoliumque iussit
665 aureum prima reuehi carina
  ustus accenso Pelias aeno
  arsit angustas uagus inter undas.
  iam satis, diui, mare uindicastis:
   parcite iusso. ‖

The theme of this chorus, 579–669, is the price paid by the Argonauts for their invasion of the sea. Seven Sapphic stanzas of the Horatian type are followed by seven others, in which the adoneus is preceded not by three but by eight hendecasyllables. Of these seven the first five and the last are intact; but the sixth, 652–60, has a line too much and half a line too little. The adoneus, *crimine poenas*, is visible in 660, but *patrioque pendet* is only half a line; and if that is completed with another half, the lines preceding the adoneus will be nine instead of eight.

Leo appears to be right in ejecting 657 as the intruder. About Peleus Seneca may have thought it wise to say nothing, because Peleus was a type of felicity (Pind. *Pyth.* III 86 sqq.); and an interpolator may have missed him and thrust him in at a point where neither verse nor sense will receive him. Because some of the Argonauts have not encountered calamity yet, the chorus professes to extract from the prophecies of Mopsus calamities still in store for Nauplius, Oileus, and Admetus.[1] The future tense is preserved by E in 660 *pendet*, but corrupted, as it so often is, to the present by A; in 659 the corruption *cadit* is in all MSS, and had to be removed by Gruter; in 663 *impendes*[2] is Gronouius' emendation for the ungrammatical *impendens* of E and the unmetrical *impendit* of A. In this context the past tense *errauit* of 657 is absurd, and Gruter's *errabit*, though a very easy change and perhaps even a true one, is absurd in another way, for Peleus had already suffered both his exiles.[3]

It remains to make good the loss of half a line at 660. The nominative *Oileus*[4] in 661 must be false, for it was not he but his son who met the death described;

---

[1] The proposal of W. R. Hardie in *Journ. Phil.* XXXIII p. 99 to expel 656 instead of 657 is only of interest as showing how bad a critic a good scholar may be. It ruins the passage through and through. If that verse goes, 658–61 go with it, and no writing *cadit* and *pendit* will save them.

[2] *impendes* in 663, not *redimes* or anything else in 662, is of course the true correction. The blow which fell on Admetus was not that Alcestis saved his life, but that she lost her own.

[3] For murdering Phocus in his early youth, and for killing Eurytion at the Calydonian hunt, which has been mentioned in 643 sq.

[4] Apollinaris Sidonius *carm.* V 197 transfers the father's name to the son, but Seneca cannot have made that blunder in a passage where he was speaking of both.

and the defective verse must be so repaired as to mention Aiax. This is most simply done as follows:

> patrio ⟨gnatus proprio⟩que pendet
> crimine poenas
> fulmine et ponto moriens Oilei.

The cause of the omission is evident; and the genitive, having lost its construction, was changed to the nominative, which *pendet* and *moriens* now required.[1]

I observe that this is the only one of the seven long stanzas which does not end with the end of a sentence. But a conjecture which removed that singularity would have to be a violent one, like the transpositions and excisions of Peiper and Richter.

PHAED. 989–90

> sed quid citato nuntius portat gradu
> rigatque maestis lugubrem uultum genis?

Leo, followed by Richter, changes *portat* to *properat*, because, says he in vol. 1 p. 212 n. 1, 'ferri non potest *quid portat rigatque?*'. But there he is wrong. The interrogation runs no further than the first verse; the second is predication, and *rigatque* is the same as *rigans*. Adjuncts of this sort are more familiar in relative ‖ clauses, such as Manil. IV 694 sq. 'Italia...quam rerum maxima Roma │ inposuit terris *caeloque adiungitur ipsa*', where the last member is similarly an independent statement, whose connexion with *quam inposuit* is only formal. But they are found with interrogatives also, as in Sil. XIV 117 sq. 'quantos Arethusa tumores │ concipiat *perstetque suas non pandere portas*'.

PHAED. 1201–12

> pallidi fauces Auerni uosque, Taenarii specus,
> unda miseris grata Lethes uosque, torpentes lacus,
> impium rapite atque mersum premite perpetuis malis.
> nunc adeste, saeua ponti monstra, nunc uastum mare,
> ultimo quodcumque Proteus aequorum abscondit sinu,   1205
> meque ouantem scelere tanto rapite in altos gurgites.
> tuque semper, genitor, irae facilis assensor meae,
> morte facili dignus haud sum qui noua natum nece
> segregem sparsi per agros quique, dum falsum nefas
> exsequor uindex seuerus, incidi in uerum scelus.   1210
> sidera et manes et undas scelere compleui meo:
> amplius sors nulla restat; regna me norunt tria.

---

[1] It would be mere trifling to pretend that *Oileus* is Ὀιλεῦς, a genitive like the Ὀδυσεῦς of Hom. *Od.* XXIV 398. Hardie's vocative *Oileu*, impossible with his own reading of 660, '⟨tum suoque Aia⟩x patrioque', where Aiax is called Aiax, becomes possible, though not commendable, with mine, where *gnatus* gives it something to cling to.

In this punctuation, which seems to be that of all editions, the *tu* of 1207 must be vocative. To that in itself there is no objection, for clear examples of the vocative occur at *Med.* 71, *Phaed.* 960, and *Ag.* 368; but I take occasion to remark, for the remark wants making, that the vocative of the second personal pronoun is not common in Latin, and much rarer than some suppose. For instance, in Schwabe's index to Catullus there are sixteen examples of it, but in Schwabe's text there is only one, if one. The Illinois *index uerborum* to these tragedies exhibits on p. 245 no fewer than forty-five examples of a vocative *tu*. Thirty-nine of these are nominatives in regular construction with verbs, and two more (*Med.* 1 and 4) are possibly also nominatives, disappointed of their verb by the anacoluthon in which that long sentence loses its way. On the same page it presents fourteen examples of a vocative *uos*. Of these at least eleven are nominatives, and one, *Ag.* 754, is an accusative.

The objection to the vocative *tu*, and *genitor* also, at *Phaed.* 1207 is that in this sentence there is no occasion or excuse for a vocative. The substance of lines 1208–10 is not specially addressed to Neptune, still less to Neptune as 'irae facilis assensor'. Moreover the conjunction *que* is not suited for linking together the prayer 'rapite me in altos gurgites' and the statement 'morte facili dignus haud sum': the suitable conjunction would be *nam*. The full stop should be transferred from the end of 1206 to the end of 1207:

> nunc adeste, saeua ponti monstra, . . .
> meque ouantem scelere tanto rapite in altos gurgites,
> tuque, semper, genitor, irae facilis assensor meae.

That is 'tuque rape'. His prayer to be whelmed in the sea is addressed to the monsters and the waves of the sea and to the god of the sea himself; and the words 'semper irae facilis assensor meae' give a reason why Neptune should grant this second prayer no less readily than he granted the first.

Bentley saw what was wrong, and mended it by placing 1207 before 1206. I prefer the MS order, which gives Neptune due dignity by setting him apart from the 'monstra' and the 'mare'. There is no reason why all the vocatives should stand before the imperative: see for instance Ouid. *Ib.* 72 sq. 'ipse meas, aether, accipe, summe, preces, | sideraque' etc. ||

OED. 952–6

> subitus en uultus grauat
> profusus imber ac rigat fletu genas.
> 'et flere satis est? hactenus fundent leuem
> oculi liquorem: sedibus pulsi suis
> lacrimas sequantur.'

I have placed a colon after *liquorem* with Bothe. The full stop of Gronouius and older editors is not incorrect, but gives the reader less help; and modern editors in consequence have missed the sense, which neither Gronouius nor Farnaby explained, and have spoilt it thoroughly with a note of interrogation. The paraphrase 'oculine satis habebunt nunc etiam inutilem liquorem fundere?' is sheer mistranslation; and 'only thus far shall mine eyes o'erflow with some few drops?' is a question so framed that one cannot tell whether *yes* or *no* should be the answer, and is in either case ridiculous after 'uultus grauat profusus imber'.

leuem liquorem signifies *lacrimas* as opposed to what Shakespeare calls the jelly of the eyes themselves, and the sentence means 'my eyes shall shed tears no more': the next sentence tells what is to be done instead. This pregnant use of *hactenus* for *non amplius* is, or ought to be, well known: Verg. *Aen.* VI 62 '*hac* Troiana *tenus* fuerit fortuna secuta' (where Seruius explains 'id est hic sit finis'), Ouid. *trist.* I 10 22–4 '*hac* dominum *tenus* est illa (nauis) secuta suum. | nam mihi Bistonios placuit pede carpere campos, | Hellespontiacas illa relegit aquas', Tac. *ann.* XII 42 [3] '*hactenus* Vitellius uoluerat' (desired no more vengeance), Suet. *Dom.* 16 2 'dum exulceratam in fronte uerrucam uehementius scalpit, profluenti sanguine, "utinam" inquit "*hactenus*"'. It occurs again in Sen. *Ag.* 27–30, where Thyestes says 'uiscera exedi mea. | nec *hactenus* Fortuna maculauit patrem, | sed maius aliud ausa commisso scelus | natae nefandos petere concubitus iubet.' *Thy.* 744 is not parallel.

AG. 726–33

ubi sum? fugit lux alma et obscurat genas
nox alta et aether abditus tenebris latet,
sed ecce gemino sole praefulget dies
geminumque duplices Argos attollit domus.
Idaea cerno nemora? fatalis sedet   730
inter potentes arbiter pastor deas?
timete, reges, moneo, furtiuum genus:
agrestis iste alumnus euertet domum.

I have set notes of interrogation in 730 and 731, and they will clear up a passage which has caused much perplexity: 'post 733 intercidisse uersus aliquot de Troiae fatis et Atridarum sceleribus coniecit de Wilamowitz, mihi uu. 730–733 spurii esse uidentur' says Leo. Against this last suspicion the verses are defended by the occurrence of *Idai cernu nemura* at Pompei in *C.I.L.* IV 6698; and when rightly punctuated they yield good sense. 'What do I behold?' cries Cassandra at Mycenae, 'Paris again, compassing the overthrow of Troy? No, but something very like: another *furtiuum genus*, another *agrestis alumnus*; Aegisthus, compassing another overthrow.' Aegisthus, like Paris, was smuggled away at birth to perish on the hills, and saved and reared by shepherds; and the issue in his case too was disastrous. The parallel is drawn again by Dracontius *Orest.* 469 sq. 'nonne laborasti, Helenam ne pastor haberet? | ecce tuam (Clytaemestram) nunc pastor habet.' ||

THY. 976–9

hic esse natos crede in amplexu patris.
hic sunt eruntque; nulla pars prolis tuae
tibi subtrahetur. ora quae exoptas dabo
totumque turba iam sua implebo patrem.

In 978 Leo punctuates 'ora; quae exoptas dabo'. America hears and obeys: she translates the words as 'ask, and whate'er thou wishest I will give' in verse, and as 'make request; what thou desirest will I give' in prose; and in the Illinois *index uerborum* this *orā* will be found registered under the verb *oro* and not under the noun *os*.

Leo again violates the metre at *H.f.* 20 by adopting Buecheler's 'Thebana tellus sparsa nuribus impiis'. That Mr Garrod should propose 'et nube maestum squalida exerit iubar' at *Oed.* 2 is less surprising; and that Mr Damsté should propose 'ueteresque fagi ubi iuuat aut amnis uagi' at *Phaed.* 510, and 'pretia mouebunt hinc uetus regni furor' at *Thy.* 302, and 'hinc raptum animos grauius incertos tenes' *ib.* 638, and 'medios in ignes solis eieceram malum' at *H.O.* 725, and 'pars est et ipsa uestis in uice est cutis' *ib.* 831, and should crown these senarii with the Sapphic line *Phaed.* 305 'perque fratris non sua regna fluctus', belongs to the natural order of things.

HERC. OET. 1176–86

dirus o nobis pudor,
o turpe fatum! femina Herculeae necis
auctor feretur: morior Alcides quibus!
iniusta si me cadere feminea manu
1180   uoluere fata, perque tam turpes colus
mea mors cucurrit, cadere potuissem tamen
Iunonis odio: feminae caderem manu
sed caelum habentis. si nimis, superi, fuit,
Scythico sub axe genita domuisset meas
1185   uires Amazon: feminae cuius manu
Iunonis hostis uincor!

Here in 1179 I have received Bentley's *iniusta*, which is as apt as the MS *inuicta* is aimless; and in 1181, where E has *potuisset mihi*, A *potuissem mihi*, and editors adopt from Lipsius *ei mihi* (a quite inappropriate outcry at this juncture, as may be seen from its proper use in 1024, 1172, 1205, 1402, 1784), I have written *potuissem tamen*, which probably was first corrupted to *potuisset a me*. But I cite the passage in order to punctuate it rightly by substituting exclamation for the interrogation of the editors in 1178 and 1186. 'feminae cuius manu uincor?' is an absurd question: he knew the hand was Deianira's, and he knew, or thought he knew, what manner of woman she was. *cuius* is exclamatory, and means 'quam despectae!', οἴας γυναικός, not ποίας; and again in 1178 *quibus* means 'quam ignauis!'

The very existence of the exclamatory *quis* and *qui* is unknown to the lexicons of Georges and of Lewis and Short. To editors, whose trade brings them into contact with reality, it is not unknown, but they often overlook it, and print exclamations as questions; not merely when the exclamatory word is *quis*, but when it is *quot, quotiens, quotus, quantulus, quantillus*, even *quantus* or *qualis*: the only word beginning with *qu* which they can be trusted to recognise as exclamatory is the adverb *quam*. In Seneca (leaving aside passages where the interjections *o* and *pro* made mistake impossible, *Thy.* 449, *H.O.* 61, 93, 1201, 1760) I find the right sign used at *Phaed.* 651 *quis!*, 1035 *quis!*, *Oed.* 7 *quantum!*, *Ag.* 253 *quanto!*, 512 *quid!*, *H.O.* 56 ‖ *quanta!*, 57 *quot!*, 649 *quantos!*, 1685 *quanta!*, 1913 *quotiens!*, *Oct.* 503 *quantum!*, 506 *quot!*, but the wrong one at *H.f.* 1191 *quota?* (where 'cladis tuae pars ista quam nosti quota est?' would be a ridiculous question from Amphitryon, who knows the answer, to Hercules, who does not), at *Phoen.* 8 *quantulum?* (where the sense is 'how little!'), at *H.O.* 322 *quot?* (where 'una *quot* poenas dabis!' means *innumerabiles*), 1840 *quot?* ('*quot* misera in uno condidi natos parens!'), and 1852 *quot?* ('gregibus aequari meus | *quot* ille potuit!').

HERC. OET. 1696–704

> quacumque parte prospicis natum, pater,
> te te pater quem nocte commissa dies
> quaesiuit unus, si meas laudes canit
> utrumque Phoebi litus, ...   1699
> . . . . spiritum admitte hunc, precor,   1703
> in astra.

1697 *te te* E, *iste est* A. The latter is a plain interpolation, and the ungrammatical *te te* which provoked it is all we have to build on. Sense, and the required sense, can be brought about by combining Richter's *precor* for *pater* with Leo's *cui . . . quieuit* for *quem . . . quaesiuit*:

> te, te precor, cui nocte commissa dies
> quieuit unus.

But this is a sprawling conjecture, and postulates diverse and unrelated errors: the text shows no sign of corruption beyond the beginning of 1697, and the phrase *dies quaesiuit unus* is a clue to its emendation. The object of *quaesiuit* cannot be *quem*, i.e. Iouem, for then the subject must be *caelum* or the like: compare Prop. II 22 25 sq. 'Iuppiter Alcmenae geminas requieuerat Arctos | et caelum noctu bis sine rege fuit'. The occasion when Alcmena's lover 'commisit noctes in sua uota duas' was an occasion when, because of his action, 'unus dies quaesiuit' – what?

> Titana per quem nocte commissa dies
> quaesiuit unus:

'quaesiuit neque inuenit', as in Prop. I 17 18 'optatos quaerere Tyndaridas'. *Titan* is corrupted to *tetit* in the Bernese scholia of Lucan VIII 159.

OCT. 806–10

> quid fera frustra bella mouetis?
> inuicta gerit tela Cupido:
> flammis uestros obruet ignes
> quis extinxit fulmina saepe
> captumque Iouem caelo traxit.

Richter has rightly returned to the *quis* of the principal MSS and the older editors; but as Peiper and Leo, who seldom agreed, agreed here in accepting *quibus*, with Bothe, from inferior MSS, and as Leo, in his half-hearted attempt at collecting examples of *quīs* from the poets, vol. I pp. 213 sq., overlooks this verse and scarcely touches the question which it raises, I note the following facts.

Most of those poets who use *quīs* use it only where metre excludes *quibus*. Horace is hardly an exception when in *epod*. II 9 he writes 'in *quis* amantem'; for though a pyrrhic is shown to be allowable by 2 33 and 67, 5 85 and 91, II 27, 15 24, 17 12 and 78, he employs that resolution sparingly. The true exceptions are found in Manil. I 488 'e *quis* et maria', Val. Fl. III 505 '*quis* arma uolens, *quis* agmina iungat', Sil. XIII 422 '*quis* abdita uates', XIV 373 '*quis* excitus aequore Triton', || XV 77 'at *quis* aetherii', XVI 338 'at *quis* interior', Sen. *Oed*. 680 'in utrumque *quis* est liber etiamnum status', and finally *Oct*. 621 'poenasque *quis* et Tantali uincat sitim'. The MSS may probably be trusted in these cases; for although *quib;* undeniably might be corrupted to *quis*, yet *quis* is so much the less familiar form that such corruption was not likely and could not be frequent. It appears therefore that the author of the *Octauia* wrote *quis* not only in 621 but in 809, where the spondee gives a rhythm which he prefers to the other. Again in 964, where Bothe and Leo read '*quibus* inuisa es numina diuum', most MSS seem to have *quis*, and that is the form which has just been used in 961.

135

ALLOBROGA*

The nominative singular of *Allobroges* is *Allobrox* in Horace and seems to occur nowhere else in classical literature, though the same form is found in *G.L.K. suppl.* p. 119, in Herodian ap. Steph. Byz., and as a cognomen in *C.I.L.* XII 3109. Probus *G.L.K.* IV p. 124 enquires, in apparent ignorance, whether it should be *Allobrogus* or *Allobroges*, and decides for the latter because the former would be anomalous. He says nothing about another anomalous nominative, *Allobroga*, of which the *thes.ling.Lat.* I p. 1690 16 professes to cite two examples: '*Allobroga* gloss. V 590 24, 652 11'.

The second of these glosses is no example of the nominative. It runs '*Adlobroga* Graece declinauit quod Gallus erat Rufus', and is a ‖ note on Iuu. VII 213 sq., 'sed Rufum atque alios caedit sua quemque iuuentus, │ Rufum, quem totiens Ciceronem *Allobroga* dixit', written by some one who rightly understood that *Allobroga* was accusative and who sought to explain why Juvenal had used that form instead of the Latin *Allobrogem*. A nominative *Allobroga* would not be Greek. The other example, *corp. gloss. Lat.* V p. 590 24, '*Allobroga* Gallus Rufus', is drawn from the same passage; and the nominative has no existence except in the writer's inability to construe Juvenal's words.

The plural corresponding to this fictitious nominative is cited by the *thesaurus* ib. l. 23 from the ancient scholium on Iuu. VIII 234, which I transcribe entire: '*ut bracatorum p.*: Gallos significat, et deest "teneant". *Allobrogae* Galli sunt. ideo autem dicti *Allobrogae*, quoniam "brogae" Galli agrum dicunt, "alla" autem aliud. dicti autem *Allobroges*, quia ex alio loco fuerant translati.' Now Juvenal's lines are these, 'arma tamen uos │ nocturna et flammas domibus templisque paratis, │ ut bracatorum pueri Senonumque minores': not a word about *Allobrogae* or *Allobroges*, whom indeed it would have been absurd to mention. The Allobroges are not heard of in history till the time of Hannibal; they certainly took no part, as the Senones did, in the sack of Rome; and their ambassadors actually helped to save Rome from Catiline and Cethegus, the persons here addressed. The fact therefore that in Juvenal's best MS the letters after *Sen-* are written over an erasure is no sign that anything like *Senonum Allobrogumque* once stood in the text; and moreover the last letters of the original reading, still visible, are *-nores*. Besides, this scholium cannot be a note

* [[CR 37 (1923), 60–1]]

even on *Allobrogum*: if it were, it would not contain the form *Allobrogae*; for the writer was evidently accustomed to call them *Allobroges*, and relapses into that form at the end of his comment. This is a note on some passage which presented, or seemed to present, a form of the first declension and not of the third: in other words it is a note on VII 214. That is the only place in Juvenal, except perhaps VIII 13, where a note about the Allobroges would not be impertinent; and there stands *Allobroga* to account for *Allobrogae*. The only scholium now extant at that spot is the curt and unintelligible '*Allobroga dixit m*. Gallia'; and here at VIII 234 we have what ought to be there. Neither nominative, the singular *Allobroga* nor the plural *Allobrogae*, has any other origin than misinterpretation of Iuu. VII 214.

The so-called *glossae Iuuenalianae* printed in the *corp. gloss. Lat.* V pp. 652–6 from cod. Paris. 7730 include some fifty or sixty which have nothing to do with Juvenal: for instance, 656 21 *Ergenna sacerdos* is from Persius and 652 7 *acer lignum coloribus impar* is from Ovid; but many of these are nevertheless now twisted into connexion with him under the most threadbare pretences. If the γλῶσσα is not to be found in Juvenal, the γλώσσημα will suffice. 653 9 *monoptalmus luscus* (a regular item in bilingual glossaries, recurring at II 373 14, III 181 12, 252 67, 339 41) is to be a gloss on Iuu. X 158 *ducem*...*luscum*: even if it were *luscus monoptalmus* (as it is at II 125 25 and III 445 20), it could not be that. So too they refer 655 15 *pantomimus histrio* to Iuu. VII 90 *dabit histrio*, and 655 19 *pastillus crustula* to Iuu. IX 5 *lambenti crustula*: it is therefore mere negligence, not common sense, which prevents them from referring 652 6 *abiuro abnego* to Iuu. XIII 94 *abnego nummos*, and 652 12 *agagulis lenonibus* to Iuu. VI 216 *lenonibus atque lanistis*. The worst of this craze is that it diverts attention from serious business and delays the progress of correction. At 655 12 we have the gloss *taberna ubi uestes ponuntur aut quodlibet aliud*. Friedlaender's index provides four instances of *taberna* in Juvenal, and therefore Mr Goetz *thes. gloss. emend.* II p. 323 refers this to the least inapposite of them, II 42 *ne pudeat dominum monstrare tabernae*, where however *taberna* is not a place in which clothes or anything else is deposited but *unde opobalsama emuntur*. If Mr Goetz would turn to p. 432 of his own volume, he would find these same words, *ubi uestes ponuntur aut quodlibet aliud*, cited from *corp. gloss.* V 104 14 and, with trifling variants, from five other places; and the word which they explain is not *taberna* but *zaberna*. The next gloss, 655 13, is *tomo luscello*. Friedlaender cannot furnish his clients with *tomo*, but any word beginning with the same letters, however different its meaning, will satisfy their simple needs; so we read in the *thes. gloss. emend.* II p. 354 '*tomo uiscello* (corr. W. Heraeus: *luscello* cod.) V 655 13 (cf. Iuuenal. X 355)': and X 355 is 'candiduli diuina *tomacula* porci'! The true correction is *zomo iuscello*, as may be seen from IV 198 3 *zomos* (*zonos* cod.) *ius*, III 470 23 *ius* ζωμός, 24 *iuscellarius* ζωμοποιός, 219 2 διὰ ζωμοῦ *iuscellatas* (*luscellatas* cod.).

136

HORACE, *EPODE* XIII 3*

horrida tempestas caelum contraxit, et imbres
  niuesque deducunt Iouem; nunc mare, nunc siluae
Threicio Aquilone sonant. rapiamus, amici,
  occasionem de die, dumque uirent genua
et decet obducta soluatur fronte senectus.   5
  tu uina Torquato moue consule pressa meo;
cetera mitte loqui: deus haec fortasse benigna
  reducet in sedem uice.

Verse 3 is usually printed thus, and anyone who reads it imagines for the moment that the poem is addressed to a company of friends, as *carm.* I 27 and 37 are addressed to 'sodales'. At verses 6 sq. he is undeceived: it is addressed to a single person. True, the words *tu uina moue* would not in themselves be irreconcilable with the plural *amici* if a distribution of offices were indicated, and if there followed another *tu* with another injunction, such as *ligna super foco repone*. But *cetera mitte loqui* is not a command which can be restricted to one of a company; the person so addressed is the only other person present.

Bentley therefore wrote *amice*, Baxter removed the two commas and made *amici* nominative; both have had several followers, yet neither can be right. For in none of his poems does Horace omit to name the friend whom he addresses, unless in a very different one, *carm.* II 5, where he is probably addressing himself. Scheibe accordingly suggested that *amici* was the corruption of some proper name such as *Apici*. But no corruption needs to be assumed: a proper name is there already, *Amici*. *C.I.L.* X 1403 *d* 3 22 provides *L. Amicius Fortunatus* (from Herculaneum), and XIII 6385 adds *L. Amicius Donatus*. The quantity of the second syllable is visible in *C.I.G.* 3665 15 Ἀμεικιανός (the inscription is consistently correct in this particular), and as for the first, no name or word in Latin is known to begin with a long *am-* excepting compounds of the preposition *a*; for *amentum* is but a later spelling of *ammentum*.

* [[*CR* 37 (1923), 104]]

REVIEW: C. HOSIUS, *SEX. PROPERTII*
ELEGIARVM LIBRI IV *

This edition follows the first at an interval of eleven years. In the apparatus criticus Mr Hosius has made some 70 or 80 changes, attended by misprints at I I 30, II 32 23, and III 22 9. Some of the additions are details derived from a fresh examination of N and A, but others were already to be found in Baehrens and might have been given in the 1st ed. if they were to be given at all. Most of them are quite useless and so trivial as to be out of place in an apparatus which does not pretend to furnish full collations; it is however worth knowing that AFDV all four of them have *quantus* I 14 6 and *sunt* ib. 16, that A, and perhaps N, has *uota* I 16 2, and that in II 1 47 the first reading of A was *uni*, which is the conjecture of Bosscha. The new proposals ‖ recorded are about 25, which is far too many. The apparatus of the 1st ed. was already full enough of rubbish: at I 3 20 three conjectures, *ignotae, in notis, in natis*, all intolerable and all arising from simple ignorance, which Mr Hosius must be deemed to share, of what *ignotis* means. He still does not distinguish sensible suggestions from foolish ones, nor cite those in preference to these. If any substitute for *creditur* IV 8 10 was to be mentioned, it should have been Mr Birt's *conditur*, not Cornelissen's *raditur*.

In the attribution of conjectures to their authors Mr Hosius' Propertius is less untrustworthy than his Lucan, but the following corrections are required. I 16 38 *tanta* not Hailer but Vat. 5. I 19 19 *mixta* not Otto but Baehrens (*cum mixta mea possim*). II 1 37: Vulpius placed no lacuna before this verse. II 2 11 *et* not Butler but Scaliger. II 6 35 sq. before 27 not Heydenreich but Kuinoel. II 8 8 *sic in* not Rasi but Palmer (1874, *Ouid. her.* p. xxxvi). II 12 6 *haud uano* not Housman but Nodell. II 16 23 *cubares* not Palmer but codd. recc. II 19 5 *ulla* not Guyet but Commelini liber. II 20 8 *in* not Enk but Vat. 5. II 28 62 dist. not Gebhardus but Gebhardi codd. II 34 31 *Musis meliorem* not Fuerstenau but Scaliger. II 34 83 *hic* not Lachmann but the printer of his 2nd ed. III 5 6 *misera* not Broukhusius but Acidalius (at Vell. Pat. I 14). III 6 29 *tacentia* not Palmer but Palmerius. III 15 21 *componunt* not Marx but Doruilii cod. 2. III 18 21 *manet*

---

* ⟦*Sex. Propertii Elegiarum* libri IV. Iterum edidit Carolus Hosius. Pp. xxii + 190. Leipzig: Teubner, 1922. *CR* 37 (1923), 120–1⟧

not Palmer but Keil. IV 3 11 *gaudia* and *noctis* not Rothstein and Bury but
L. Mueller. IV 3 55 *Craugidos* not Buecheler but Bergk.[1] IV 7 27 *furuum* not
Heinsius but Passerat. IV 11 97 *sumpta* not Havet but Baehrens (with *matri*).
Conjectures of my own attributed to others I do not reclaim.

Mr Hosius says that he has made few changes in the text, and apart from the
correction of misprints in II 1 68, 24 24, and 26 35, I have noticed only three:
I 16 2 *uota* for *nota*, II 28 56 *omnes* for *omnis*, and IV 1 71 *fata* for *facta*. The
medieval orthography of the MSS, *humor, humidus, iocundus, soboles, nequic-
quam* II 4 5 (though N has the true form, which is printed in III 17 23), *Alcidem,
Cybellem, Aganippeae, Ephyreae*, is still ascribed to Propertius; and so are other
false spellings which have been imported by conjecture: *siccine* III 6 9, *Theioda-
manteo* I 20 6, *Perimedeae* II 4 8, *Philitaeis* IV 6 3 (but *Philitea* correctly
III 3 52). The hexameter II 34 39 *Amphiareae non prosint tibi fata quadrigae* still
bears its witness to Mr Hosius' knowledge of metre. So correct and normal does
it appear to him that he makes no remark upon it in his *index metricus et
prosodiacus*.

---

[1] I have said this before, and as scholars educated at Bonn are loth to believe it I now give chapter
and verse. Buecheler proposed *Craugidos* in 1888 (*Rhein. Mus.* XLIII p. 297): Bergk had already
proposed it, not for the first time, in 1873 (*Augusti rer. u se gest. ind.* p. 124).

138

REVIEW: E. T. MERRILL, *CATVLLI VERONENSIS LIBER**

The publisher asked Professor Merrill to make his notes as short as possible; 'quam ob rem' says he 'uarias lectiones meliorum codicum Catullianorum neque omnes (uel fere omnes), ut olim mihi proposui, neque multas in calce paginarum exhibere possum.' That is not so: there is ample room in his notes for every MS variant which a student really needs to know; but this room is otherwise occupied, and half the ship's cargo has been thrown overboard to save the bilge-water.

By his own rule the apparatus criticus of Catullus is to be constructed 'ex O (O^2 raro) GRR^2 solis, neglectis quae uaria MM^2G^2 et omnes alii intulerint'; yet I have counted some 30 occurrences of G^2 alone. Again, he will squander his precious space at this rate: 75 3 '*uelle queat tibi* La. *uelleque tot tibi* V *uelle queam tibi* ω': *tibi* three times where it should not appear at all and *uelle* where it need not; '*queat* La., *queam* iam ω, *-que tot* V' would tell all that wants telling. But his main purpose in withholding indispensable information || and deceiving the reader by silence is to find room for a long record of conjectures which dishonour the human intellect. A brilliant and celebrated emendation like Schrader's *Eous* at 62 35 he cannot mention, nor such shrewd and thoughtful proposals as *deprendis* ibid., *Africis* 48 5, *saluete bonarum* 64 23 b, *acta* 116 7; he prefers the worst conjectures of the worst critics. When I say that more than 60 proceed from Robinson Ellis and nearly 30 from his disciples, their average quality can be imagined. At 64 359 'iter caesis angustans corporum aceruis' there should either be no note or this note, '*cessis* O, *celsis* Bae.': what we find instead is '*caecis* (coll. Ou. *met.* I 24) Ell.', a conjecture whose proper place is not the pillory but the grave; and at 64 207 more than a line is sacrificed to registering a proposal of the same character and authorship. It would have been better to leave a blank at 98 6 than to fill it with Mr Hendrickson's conjecture, 'if you want to be the death of us all you need only split'. The notes on 80 are these: '4 *e* V *de* Ell. (ex *te* D). 7 *fictoris* Ell. (coll. Non. 308)'. In both verses the text is faultless; the one conjecture is based on nothing but a preference for bad MSS, and the absurdity of the other is not redeemed by its obscenity; yet for their

* [*Catulli Veronensis liber.* Recensuit Elmer Truesdell Merrill. Pp. viii +92. Leipzig and Berlin: Teubner, 1923. *CR* 38 (1924), 25–7]

sweet sake we must forgo the knowledge that in 8 the MSS have *ille te mulso*, and the critics who restored *ilia et emulso* must be robbed of the credit due to them. The difficulties of 10 9 sq. can be removed by writing 'nihil neque ipsis | *nunc* (Westphal) *quaestoribus* (Muretus) esse nec cohorti': the corrections are not certain, but they are sensible. Mr Merrill quotes instead – no, he misquotes, as Ellis did before him[1] – Traube's slapdash conjecture '*mihi* neque *ipsi* (thus much is Estaço's) | *hoc praetore* fuisse nec cohorti', which is shown to be false by verses 12 sq., and he adds two more which are not much better. At 10 33 'sed tu insulsa male et molesta uiuis' he has no room to say what the MSS give instead of *insulsa*, yet room for such frivolity as '*niuis* O *cuiuis* Monse *abibis* Busche'. At 64 273 'leuiterque sonant' he neither mentions that G omits *que* nor tells us whether or no R omits it, but cites three conjectures, one of them impossible. At 66 12 'uastatum finis iuerat Assyrios' his note is '*iuerat ante Syros* Ow.' instead of '*uastum* V'. At 64 89 he prints the conjecture *progignunt*, and in the note, instead of the MS reading, another conjecture.

The book teems with suggestio falsi. A bare text without notes is not deceptive, because the reader knows his ignorance and suspends belief; but these notes perpetually encourage him to wrong conclusions. At 1 8 he finds *habe tibi* in the text and '*tibi habe* V' in the note. When therefore at 23 13 and 39 3 and 64 334 and 66 85 and 68 160 he finds *magis aridum* and *orator excitat* and *tales unquam* and *dona leuis bibat* and *dulce mihi* in the text and nothing in the notes, how can he fail to infer that the MSS give the words in this order? how can he suspect that they really give *aridum magis* and *excitat orator* and *unquam tales* and *leuis bibat dona* and *michi dulce*? When at two of the three places where Tethys occurs he is told that the MSS call her Thetis, what inference but a false one can he draw from the silence of the note at 64 29? When at 4 3 'neque ullius natantis impetum trabis' he reads '*illius* V', how can he help concluding that if V had *tardis* for *trabis* he would be warned of it? When such a trifle as the variant *tum* for *tunc* is recorded at 64 56, how can he conceive that this editor has left him ignorant in places where the MSS have *tamen . . . est* for *tum . . . es*, *uocare cura* for *uocaret aura*, *posse* for *se*, *inimica* for *minuta*, *luci* for *iugi*, *adlenire* for *aduenere*, *nicenis a* for *moenia*, *Pharsaliam* for *Pharsalum*, *tum* for *nunc*, *tuos* for *talos*, *currus* for *tauros*, *pro* for *me*, *numula* for *lumina*, *deficeret* for *desideret*, *corpore* for *torpor*, *inquam* for *ni quem*? At 66 50 'ferri fingere duritiem' the only note is '*fingere* O *fringere* GR *stringere* Hey.'. The reason ‖ why Heyse made his conjecture, and why most editors accept it, is that the MSS have not *ferri* but *ferris*. Such deficiency in craftsmanship or care or sense is not distinguishable by its consequences from malice aforethought and an intent to deceive.

[1] Mr Merrill's dependence on Ellis is almost ludicrous. 64 23 'dein spatium quinquaginta fere litterarum (Ell.)': our informant is Keil, and Ellis merely substituted a round number for Keil's 'quadraginta octo'. When Ellis appropriates the conjectures of others, 31 5, 55 9, 64 273, 350, Mr Merrill repeats the false ascription.

The editor's own conjectures at 55 9 and 68 118 call for no remark except that the one is violent and that half of the other is not his; but at 64 16 he relegates to the note proposals of Lachmann's and Friedrich's which yield reasonable sense, and prints in the text his own, which is 'illa (*ecquanam* alia?) uiderunt luce...mortales...nymphas'. The answer to this injudicious question is *yes*: Hom. *Il.* XVIII 35–145, Ap. Rh. IV 930–67, etc.

Mr Merrill has special disqualifications for editing a poet. At 62 63 he prints an hexameter beginning 'tertia patri pars', and boasts in his note 'sic scripsi'. At 52 2 'sella in curuli struma Nonius sedet' he says '*nouius* V fortasse recte'; and therefore, though he does well to keep *Fuficio* out of the text at 54 5, he will not be suspected of knowing the quantity of its second syllable. Whatever his partiality for the Ellisian type of conjecture, he would hardly have cited *fraglans* 6 8 and *tablam* 63 9 if he had been aware that they are unmetrical. On p. VII, under the heading *prosodia Catulli*, he says 'diastole bis apparet (64 360 *tepēfaciet*; 90 6 *liquēfaciens*: sed cf. 68 29 *tepĕfactet*)': the *ē* was original and *tepĕfactet* is systole. He adds to his preface a couple of pages on *metra Catulli* 'quae tironibus auxilio sint'. German tiros can learn metre from experts; it is in Mr Merrill's country and mine that tiros are instructed by their fellow-tiros. On the continent of Europe even a tiro may smile to see the Galliambic chopped up into trochees and tribrachs diversified with dactyls and μακραί τρίχρονοι. 'Versus Galliambicus' says Mr Merrill 'ex origine tetrameter Ionicus a minore catalecticus esse adfirmatur.' *adfirmatur* indeed! It *is* Ionic, and no metrist mistakes it for anything else; it is as thoroughly known as the dactylic hexameter and much simpler than the iambic senarius. Competent authority speaks with one voice, and provokes a babel of dissent from the Anglo-Saxon race, which will not study metre and yet presumes to have opinions upon it. Error by its very nature is manifold, and the dissenters dissent from one another: where Mr Merrill finds trochees and dactyls, Dr Postgate (*Prosodia Latina* p. 104), who calls the verse composite, finds iambi and anapaests, and R. Y. Tyrrell (*C.R.* 1893 p. 44), who calls it antispastic, finds all four. To Catullus the Phalaecean hendecasyllable was probably also Ionic, as it was to Varro and Quintilian and as it evidently is in Soph. *Ai.* 634 and 645. Mr Merrill scans it on Hermann's system, which is already discarded by Hermann's compatriots; but Parisian fashions have a second life in Bayswater, and this scansion, congenial to British and American notions, is sure of a refuge under the Union Jack and the Stars and Stripes. Mr Merrill's scheme of the iambic scazon is another obsolete piece of apriorism, to which he adds an error of his own by allowing a long syllable in the ninth place.

There is given a *conspectus editorum*, including Bentley, Bergk, Buecheler, Burman, and many more who never edited Catullus in their lives; Rossbach, who did, is omitted, and *Ro.* stands for Mr K. Rossberg.

139

REVIEW: A. C. PEARSON, SOPHOCLIS
FABVLAE*

After his edition of Sophocles' *fragments* in 1917 Dr Pearson was marked out as the English scholar best qualified to undertake the recension of the seven tragedies; and in discharge of the duty very properly laid upon him by the Oxford Press he has produced what is ‖ much the best critical edition of Sophocles now in existence; the most complete and the most judicious. It is good fortune which many authors have never encountered, and Sophocles has often missed, to be edited by one who unites the characters of an acute grammarian, a vigilant critic, and an honest man.

So much it is bare justice to say; and if most of what follows is adverse criticism of details, that should not be misunderstood by the reader, for it certainly will not be misunderstood by Dr Pearson himself.

The opinion, especially upheld in the last century by Dindorf, that Laur. XXXII 9 was the parent of Sophocles' other MSS, withstood the arguments of J. H. Lipsius and Nauck, but succumbs to authority now that ancient papyri are found concurring with the later copies. Neither alone nor in conjunction with Par. 2712 can L now be made the foundation for a text of Sophocles; and Dr Pearson's edition is the first to reflect faithfully the changed situation. Perhaps he leans even too much towards the codd. recc., of which he mentions more than forty; and certainly his apparatus criticus is in excess of our needs, embracing as it does unmetrical or ungrammatical readings from this source which throw no light on the text, such as *Ai.* 127 ὑπέρκομπον, 1170 περιστελοῦντες, *El.* 1222 προσβλέψουσα, *Tr.* 1092 βουκόλον.

Among the papyri, Oxy. 22 is too little heeded. If Oedipus in *O.t.* 378 had asked Κρέοντος ἢ σοῦ ταῦτα τἀξευρήματα; the irritable and angry Tiresias would not have replied as he does: from the papyrus we obtain ἢ τοῦ. In 430 the detached interrogation οὐχὶ θᾶσσον; seemed to me so silly that I conjectured θᾶσσον αὖ (for οὐ) πάλιν, and so did G. Wolff before me: this is now offered by the papyrus, yet not received.

It should not be praise, but in England it is, to say that the apparatus is

* [*Sophoclis fabulae.* Recognouit breuique adnotatione critica instruxit A. C. Pearson. Pp. xxiv, no further pagination. Oxonii e typographeo Clarendoniano, 1924. *CR* 39 (1925), 76–80]

workmanlike; that the editor knows how to put himself in the reader's place, and how not to be ambiguous or unintelligible or misleading. At *O.t.* 493 we are left ignorant of something which we ought to be told, and the note on *Ph.* 1407 f. contains a misstatement; but beyond these I have noticed only the most trifling flaws, as at *Ai.* 991 and *Ant.* 362. This is not to say that there are no inequalities and inconsistencies. The fortunes of ἀνήρ for ἀνήρ and ηὗρ- for εὗρ- are very various: compare for instance *Ai.* 9, 228, 878, *Ph.* 40, or *O.t.* 68, 546, 1050, 1213, *Ph.* 283. There are irregularities also in the text: ἀνακαλεῖν is changed to ἀγκαλεῖν only at *Tr.* 910; *El.* 1155 λάθρα and 1405 ἔρημοι are at variance with the practice observed elsewhere; and I do not understand the accentuation προσθεῖναι τινά *El.* 933 compared with 1107 Αἴγισθόν τινες, where the pronoun is less indefinite, nor ἀκτὰν παρὰ βώμιον *O.t.* 184 beside ἀστῶν ὕπο πάντων *O.C.* 737 f.

Much more than usual care has been taken in assigning emendations to their true authors, and I can make few corrections: *Ai.* 420 εὔφρονες (a very precarious conjecture) Hermann, 1032 δωρειάν A. von Bamberg, *El.* 686 δρόμον Thiersch, *Ant.* 241 στιχίζῃ nescioquis ante 1888, *O.C.* 1212 πάρεκ Badham (Plat. *Euthyd.* p. 93). The rectification of a false accent no more demands the mention of its author at *Ai.* 407 μώραις, *El.* 901 νεώρη, *Tr.* 751 τροπαῖα, 1224 προσθοῦ, than at *Ai.* 551 ὁμοῖος or 1100 λεών or 1228 αἰχμαλωτίδος. εἰκαθεῖν is more than a mere correction of accent, but it would have been enough to mention Elmsley once instead of six times in that connexion, and once instead of eight times as writing ἦ for ἦν, and Brunck once instead of thrice as restoring ἤδη; and Wecklein's name accompanies σέσωμαι either too often or too seldom.

About fifty of Dr Pearson's own conjectures stand in the text. Three which appear evidently true are *Ant.* 1247 γόου (the note does not make it clear whether the chief credit is Dr Pearson's or Dr Postgate's), *Tr.* 520 ἀμφίπλικτοι (see Cobet *V.L.* p. 135), and 940 'μβάλοι. Others having various claims to consideration are *Ai.* 802 ὁ τούτῳ, 1268 ἐπὶ σμικρὸν λέγων, *O.t.* 971 προδόντα, *Ant.* 966 κυανέαιν σπιλάδοιν, 1301 ἦ δ' ὀξύπληκτος ἡ⟨μένη⟩ δὲ βωμία (this hardly accounts for πέριξ, but is the only effective attempt to rescue βωμία), *Ph.* 1192 προφαίνεις. Some do not seem ‖ preferable to older conjectures: *Ai.* 886, *El.* 221, *O.t.* 494, *Tr.* 220 (προσφέρων Margoliouth), 654, *Ph.* 850, 1407–8 ⟨σοὶ τὸ⟩ δρᾶν τάδ' (I suggest ἀλλ' εἰ ⟨θέλεις⟩ | δρᾶν σὺ ταῦθ' ὅπωσπερ), *O.C.* 1164, 1702 (περ ὦδ' Meineke). Others are unattractive in themselves. *Ant.* 674 τ' ἐν for σύν: the conjunction is better away. *Tr.* 837 νήματι: the νῆμα was not the hydra's, only the βάμμα. *Ph.* 1099 λῴονος ἔκ for τοῦ λῴονος is not easy and perhaps not metrically necessary. *O.C.* 1057 ἀντάρει is a false Doricism, notwithstanding *fr.* 681 N (747 P), which is unintelligible and presumably corrupt. *O.t.* 665–7 thus restored to metre: ἀλλά μοι δυσμόρῳ γᾶ φθίνουσα τρύχει λῆμα καὶ τάδ' εἰ κακοῖς [κακὰ] προσάψει τοῖς πάλαι τὰ πρὸς σφῷν: the omission of κακά spoils the rhetoric, and the substitution of λῆμα for ψυχάν takes all meaning away, for a λῆμα is not sentient and capable of affliction.[1] *Tr.* 267 f. φωνῇ (for φώνει) δέ, δοῦλος ἀνδρὸς ὡς ἐλευθέρου, | ῥαίοιτο: punctuated thus, but rendered (*C.R.*, vol. xxxix p. 2*b*) 'he was like a slave ever crushed by a free man's voice'. Slaves are not so crushed: it is their master's voice that crushes them; to other free men they are as insolent as you please. A just sense is given by Mr Margoliouth's φωνὴν...αἴροιτο. *Ph.* 984 ὦ κακῶν κάκιστε καὶ τόλμης πέρα (for τολμήσατε): ὦ τόλμης πέρα is a strange use of the adverb, and the phrase is quite unlike δεινὸν καὶ πέρα δεινοῦ, which might perhaps defend ὦ τολμηρὲ καὶ τόλμης πέρα. I am not wedded to my own conjecture τόλμης τέρας (τέρας τι κάλλους Damox. [3 9 Kock] ap. Ath. p. 15 B, θαῦμ' ἰδεῖν εὐκοσμίας Eur. *Bacch.* 693), and the truth may be πέρας (see Cobet *N.L.* p. 72).

The worst that I can find to say of Dr Pearson's conjectures is that they are sometimes mechanical and not methodical, and that like so many of his countrymen he is apt to approach emendation from the palaeographical rather than the critical side; though he knows better, and accepts at *O.t.* 943 Nauck's bold, prudent, and happy restoration of the Sophoclean stroke Οἰδίπου πατήρ. Conjectures which stick close to the MSS are neat if true, but if not true they are not even neat. Nor is a small change necessarily an easy one; it may be improbable even palaeographically. It would have been hard for δρόμον, which Dr Pearson writes in *El.* 684, to become δρόμου in that context. At *O.C.* 220 the ἀπόγονον of the MSS would spring much more readily from mere interpolation than from ἔκγονον. The two half-lines which he ejects at *Ai.* 841 f. would far less easily make their way into the text than the two whole lines ejected by others. At *O.C.* 380 f. ὡς αὐτίκ' Ἄργος ἢ τὸ Καδμείων πέδον | τιμῇ καθέξον ἢ πρὸς οὐρανὸν βιβῶν he writes, partly following others, τιμῆς καθέλξον. But κατέχειν πέδον is much more natural than καθέλκειν, and all that spoils it is τιμῇ, which should be transferred to a clause where it is actually needed and has caused doubt and error by its absence: καθέξον ἢ τιμῇ πρὸς οὐρανὸν βιβῶν (or ἢ π. οὐ. τιμῇ β.). At *Tr.* 910 f. αὐτὴ τὸν αὑτῆς δαίμον' ἀνακαλουμένη | καὶ τὰς ἄπαιδας ἐς τὸ λοιπὸν οὐσίας he changes the last word to οἰκίας, 'referring to the future existence of Deianira in Hades', and further suggests παρ' Ἅιδην for ἄπαιδας. οὐσίας is the last word that should be tampered with, the very cornerstone on which to build emendation; it fits the context so exactly. But it cannot be plural, and is therefore genitive; and ἄπαιδας, which is perfectly irrelevant, should furnish another genitive: καὶ τῆς παλαιᾶς ἐς τὸ λοιπὸν οὐσίας, 'the future lot of herself and of the substance that was hers'. ἄπαιδας is a rearrangement of

---

[1] τρύχει λῆμα is no better than a piece of scholars' slang which usually crops up in prefaces and will be found on p. xv of Dr Pearson's, *indoles codicum*. Codices have no *indoles*, a term implying capacity of growth and development: Plautus' use of the word in *rud.* 423 is playful, and he means you to connect it with *olere* and *odor*.

the letters ΠΑΔΑΙΑC, τάς is an accommodation to the apparent accusative, ἐς τὸ λοιπόν is attached to δαίμονα by the construction called ὑφ' ἕν, and is placed next to παλαιᾶς for effect.

But it is not by his own emendations that an editor of Sophocles will at this date bring most healing to the text: that will depend on his choice among earlier conjectures and the variants of ‖ the MSS; and Dr Pearson's choice is generally sagacious, as for example, within a small compass, at *Ant.* 211, 223, 235, 368. To find errors of judgment one must cast the net wider, but at *O.t.* 525 there is a grave one: πρὸς τοῦ would never have been changed to τοῦ πρός, and both alike ask a question which is not answered; if τοῦπος is a conjecture, as Dr Pearson seems to think, it is none the less true for that. Again at *Tr.* 88 he expels two verses rather than transpose one letter;[1] and intelligent proposals like *Ai.* 630 σχήσει, 775 ἐκλήξει, 1141 τοῦθ' ἕν, 1353 πιθοῦ are consigned to the oblivion which ought to swallow 516 ἀλαῇ, *Ant.* 593 δόμων, 927 μείω, and several more. He accepts without visible qualms the forms στράψαντα (in iambic dialogue), κατέστειψας, and ἠνσχόμην, the last on poor authority and the first on none; περιίδῃς, which Jebb and Mr Masqueray foist on their readers as MS tradition, has less luck.

Lest these judgments should seem curt and disrespectful, I will speak more at length on four passages: two lections which should not be retained, and two conjectures which should not be admitted.

O.t. 794–6 τὴν Κορινθίαν ‖ ἄστροις τὸ λοιπὸν ἐκμετρούμενος χθόνα ‖ ἔφευγον. This can only be defended by the usual defence of false readings, mistranslation. Jebb's 'measuring from afar by the stars the region of Corinth' and 'wotting of its region by the stars alone' are translations not of ἐκμετρεῖσθαι, which never means anything of the sort (and how could it?), but of τεκμαίρεσθαι. The phrase ἄστροις τεκμαίρεσθαι is explained, with reference to some such passage as this, by Suidas Bernh. 1 p. 813 ⟦1 p. 393 Adler⟧, ἐπὶ τῶν μακρὰν καὶ ἔρημον ὁδὸν πορευομένων καὶ ἄστροις σημειουμένων τὰς θέσεις τῶν πατρίδων, and the very words of Sophocles are borrowed by Libanius *decl.* 12 11 (Reisk. IV p. 184 ⟦V p. 540 Foerster⟧) τὴν ἐκκλησίαν καὶ τὸ βῆμα καὶ τοὺς ἐνταυθοῖ θορύβους ἄστροις, τοῦτο δὴ τὸ τοῦ λόγου, τὸ λοιπὸν τεκμαιρόμενος. Nauck therefore wrote τεκμαρούμενος, which is the change of one letter and the transposition of another.

Ant. 126 ἀντιπάλου δυσχείρωμα δράκοντος. δυσχείρωμα is no more Greek than τηλέγραμμα, and Musgrave long ago observed 'contra analogiam peccare uidetur'. Jebb gathered that something was wrong, but did not know what, and tried to guess as follows: 'The form of the word is in one respect unique. Every similar neuter noun compounded with δυσ is from a verb so compounded': he cites δυστύχημα and the like, and proceeds, 'But there is no such

---

[1] I understand his reason, but it is insufficient: see for instance *Ai.* 852 f.

verb as δυσχειρόω, *to subdue with difficulty.*' A verb δυσχειρόω meaning *to subdue with difficulty* would be just as unique and as barbarous as δυσχείρωμα itself. No verb was ever compounded with δυσ till Greek was in decay:[1] verbs beginning with that particle are formed without composition from compound adjectives. A substantive δυσχείρωμα could only be formed from a verb δυσχειρόω formed in its turn from an adjective δύσχειρ: this, on the analogy of εὔχειρ, would mean *clumsy*, δυσχειρόω would therefore mean *render clumsy*, and δυσχείρωμα would signify the result of this process. As a compound of δυσ and χείρωμα meaning χαλεπὸν χείρωμα it is Greek of the same sort as εὔπραξις in Aesch. *Ag.* 255 and the other monsters collected by Lobeck *Phryn.* p. 501; and Jebb's declaration 'The noun has been boldly coined to express δυσχείρωτον πρᾶγμα' would come with more authority from a better grammarian. The MSS and scholia favour ἀντιπάλῳ...δράκοντι, and Moriz Schmidt corrected πάταγος ¨Αρεος...δοὺς χείρωμα, 'that gave him for a conquest to his adversary the dragon'.

The conjecture which Dr Pearson adopts from Jebb in *O.t.* 1219, ὥσπερ ἰάλεμον χέων, is unmetrical. If synaphea existed where this conjecture creates it, the final syllable of πατρί in 1209 could not be *anceps*, as it is. Wecklein censured ‖ the error in his review of Jebb's first edition, but Jebb in his British ignorance did not even understand what was meant, and calumniously replied that Wecklein's own proposal was open to the same objection. In Jebb's text of *Ph.* 187 f., not in Dr Pearson's, the metre is violated by a similar blunder.

O.C. 534 f. edited from Jebb's conjecture thus: σαί τ' εἶσ' ἄρ' ἀπόγονοί τε καὶ – κοιναί γε πατρὸς ἀδελφεαί. That such a proposal should ever have been made is strange, but that it should deceive anyone who did not make it is stranger. Let Dr Pearson try to construe it. Jebb could not; he translated 'these then are at once thine offspring, and...yea, very sisters of their sire', the Greek for which is σαί εἶσ', etc.: the τ' which saves the metre must be ignored in order to save the grammar and sense. Schoolboys more prudently use γ' on such occasions.

It would be turning from the ἴδιον to the κοινόν and straying outside this particular text of Sophocles if I asked such questions as why the prepositions in *Ai.* 1029, 1231, *El.* 554, *Ant.* 1012, *Tr.* 744, 854, *Ph.* 334, 343 should suffer anastrophe contrary to grammatical precept, or why ἦμαρ should be changed to ἄμαρ at *O.t.* 199 and *Ph.* 1089, retained at *O.C.* 682 and 688, and imported by conjecture at *O.C.* 1455 into a context where μάτην is changed to μάταν. But there is one vulgar error which ought to be rooted out. Dr Pearson prints

---

[1] δυσθνῄσκω is no verb: Euripides compounded δυσ with θνῄσκων, treating the participle as an adjective, which certainly was reprehensible enough; and it seems that someone played the same trick with δυσ and τοπάζων, misled by δυστόπαστος. The derivation of δυσοίζω is unknown, but its meaning shows that it is not from οἴζω.

θἠμέρᾳ θοὔρμαιον χαἰ χἀρπάσαι χἀτέρας χαὔτη χαὑτοῦ χἠ χἠμεῖς χοἱ χοῦτος χοῦτως χὠ χῶνπερ χὠπόσοι χὤπου χὤπως χὠς χὦτε χὦτι. The Greeks had a sign, the right-hand half of a circle, which they called ἀπόστροφος or κορωνίς and employed to indicate, among other things, elision and crasis; and the sign of the smooth breathing, originally the right-hand half of H, assumed in the course of centuries a like form. Dindorf, whom Mekler and Masqueray follow, knew that the present identity of the two symbols is an accident, but Wilamowitz and contemporary scholars in general do not. When they look at τοὐμόν they fancy that what they see is the smooth breathing, a thing which belongs to initial vowels and would be as foolish in τοὐμόν as in μετἐλθεῖν; and under this delusion they substitute the rough breathing after aspirate consonants, and print θοὑμόφυλον and χὑμεῖς and the like, which are as foolish as καθόρᾶν or δεχἤμερος. But false doctrine is tempered by inconstancy: Wilamowitz prints χὦτι Aesch. *sept.* 197, Jebb θοὔρμαιον *Ant.* 397, and Dr Pearson himself χοῦτος *Ph.* 1078.

I have observed misprints in the text at *Ai.* 865, 1226, *El.* 69, *Tr.* 575, *O.C.* 1673, so I fear there may be more; and there are faults of one sort and another in the notes at *El.* 84, *O.t.* 1242, *Tr.* 530–4 and 893.

140

REVIEW: W. HERAEUS, *M. VALERII MARTIALIS EPIGRAMMATON LIBRI**

Students of Martial now live in an age which was begun by Professor Lindsay's edition of 1903, one of those works which are such boons to mankind that their shortcomings must be forgiven them. All that energy could do in the investigation or skill and industry in the collation of MSS was done, and the fruits of this labour were condensed in an apparatus criticus of the most admirable lucidity. It is true that one was obliged to form one's text for oneself, but without Mr Lindsay that would not have been possible. Mr Duff produced a more critical recension in 1905, and here is another[1] from Professor Heraeus, who is probably better qualified for editing Martial than anyone else in the world. He has used no new MSS, only correcting faults and omissions in Mr Lindsay's apparatus; but he adds the *testimonia*, which Mr Lindsay generally ignored, and the more important imitations, and prefixes 50 pages of critical notes. ||

Mr Heraeus makes choice among the lections of the MSS with a judgment which I am bound to regard as good because it so often coincides with my own. All the following changes of Mr Lindsay's text (I omit such as are merely orthographical), I 51 4 *uelint*, 76 3 *que chorosque*, II 55 2 *coleris*, III 24 2 *focis*, 68 12 *leges*, 100 4 *iste*, IV 49 2 *ista*, V 16 13 *iuuat*, 58 6 *possit*, VI 29 8 *ames*, 45 4 *turpius*, 51 4 *inquis*, 71 4 *sollicitare*, 88 3 *constet*, VII 56 1 *pia*, VIII 4 1 *conuentus*, 6 1 *Eucti*, 56 [[55]][2] 23 *ero*, IX 67 2 *nemo*, 73 3 *regna*, 92 1 *sint*, 94 1 *Santonica*, XI 70 6 *inspicitur*, 79 3 *uiae*, 99 5 *gemina*, XII 3 [[2]] 12 *Hyanteae*, 17 3 *pariterque*, 55 13 *non*, 82 5 and 12 *colliget*, XIV 121 2 *uocer*, 197 2 *paene*, are changes which I had made myself. Others too seem right or probable, as III 93 23 *exigis*, IV 59 2 *gutta*, VI 21 3 *aurem*, IX 54 7 *fringuillarum*, X 10 8 *ire*, 48 24 *facient*, XI 7 10 *paras*, 42 2 *quid*, 98 22 *dabit et*, XIV 81 2 *tetrico*; but some are certainly wrong. III 42 4 'quod tegitur, *maius* (βγ, *magnum* α) creditur esse *malum* (αβ,

* [*M. Valerii Martialis epigrammaton libri*. Recognouit W. Heraeus. Pp. lxviii + 417. Lipsiae in aedibus B. G. Teubneri, 1925. *CR* 39 (1925), 199–203]

[1] Mr Giarratano's edition is negligible.

[2] I quote everywhere according to Schneidewin, Friedlaender, Gilbert, and Duff, and ignore the nuisance of changed and duplicated numeration which Mr Lindsay introduced and Mr Heraeus aggravates. On p. 8 he is caught in his own snare, and has unwittingly transferred to the poem he calls xxviii (xxvii) a distich of the poem he calls xxx (xxviii).

nefas γ)': if this is compared with 72 2 'nescioquod *magnum* (αβ, *maius* γ) suspicor esse *nefas*', it will appear that single families have corrupted each verse from the other. Mr Heraeus rightly rejects the singular *nefas* and *maius*, yet prefers the singular *magnum* in 42 4: but if Martial wrote *magnum* in both verses, why did *maius* intrude into either? IV 67 8 'quod non *uis* (β, *das* γ Heraeus) equiti, uis dare, praetor, equo': *das* was introduced by some one who did not see the construction of *equiti*. XIV 130 2 *nusquam* α Lindsay, *numquam* β Heraeus (see too IX 27 7 *usquam* β Duff, *umquam* γ uulgo). Editors should make it a rule, where MSS offer them this choice and sense allows it, to take (*n*)*usquam*, because scribes change it into the commoner word: see for instance Virgil's MSS at *georg.* IV 185, *Aen.* II 142, 620, V 633, IX 420. Other lections which Mr Heraeus prefers while I side with Mr Lindsay are IV 35 5 *animae*, VII 17 9 *dedicata*, X 12 9 *cognoscendus*, 77 3 *fuisset*.

Mr Heraeus discards in favour of MS readings the following conjectures admitted by Mr Lindsay, who, like conservative editors in general, has a kindness for bad conjectures: *spect.* 21 b 2 *mersa*, I 69 1 *qui*, III 82 26 *fusus*, VI 14 4 *conscribat*, IX 22 15 *ac*, XI 90 4 *situst*, 99 6 *Minyas*, XII 82 11 *tropin*, 95 1 *Musaei*, XIV 46 1 *mobilibus*, 106 1 *panda*. So far I am with him, but not in refusing VII 96 4 *male*, still less in the two following cases. IV 58 2: to adopt *iam* from α is short-sighted and not even really conservative, for it does not account for the *non* of βγ, while *nam* accounts for both: compare the MS variants in III 22 4, 47 6, VI 23 4, VIII 36 4, 52 4, 70 1, IX 54 10, X 37 18. The point of the epigram will perhaps be understood if I say that *uirum* means *marem*. XI 90 3 'et tibi Maeonio *res* carmine *maior* habetur | LVCILI' etc. β, *quod*...*maius* γ, *quoque*... *maius* Lachmann. 'Wenn eine Stelle in der Ueberlieferung so einwandsfrei ist wie unser *Maeonio res carmine maior*, ist es unzulässig, sie durch eine andere Lesart ersetzen zu wollen, die erst durch Konjektur Sinn erhält' quoth Mr Friedrich. Critics know that the contrary is true, and that in such a case the intelligible reading lies under suspicion, unless it can be shown how the unintelligible reading arose from it. This Mr Heraeus tries to do: he supposes that *maior* was accidentally corrupted to *maius* (a change which he illustrates), and that *res* was then altered by an interpolator to *quod*. But what interpolator would behave so strangely, instead of simply altering *maius* back again into *maior*?

Emendations rejected by Mr Lindsay and accepted by Mr Heraeus are these: II 14 7 *hic*, VII 34 8 *quid tu tot*, IX 54 10 *miluus astra*, X 48 20 *trima*, XI 56 11 *modo qui dum*, XII 3 ⟦2⟧ 4 *amnes quos*, 8 *tecta*, 88 1 *nego*, XIII 116 2 *sistant*, XIV 24 1 *madidi*, 158 1 *nata*. Two more, *sp.* 28 10 *Caesar io* and 11 *diri*, are hardly emendations; much less what has been done at XII 59 9. There the MSS mention, among persons by whom it is disagreeable to be kissed, those who are ‖ lame of the right leg. Does it not seem incredible that this should be defended? yet Mr Heraeus defends it thus: 'δεξιόχωλος mihi est *rechtsseitig gelähmt*, cuius

nimirum indecens amplexus est.' Scilicet, qui *linksseitig gelähmt* est, eius amplexus minus est indecens. And this ridiculous reading is also unmetrical; but
Mr Heraeus, instead of finding in that any cause for suspicion, rebuilds the verse
as a shelter for the cripple by prefixing a worse than superabundant *et*.

He places eight of his own conjectures in the text. The best of these is the
excellent emendation x 13 ⟦14⟧ 1 'cum *cathedrata litos* portet tibi raeda minis-
tros' for *cathedratalios* or *cotathedratos*: he cites καρρίον καθεδρωτόν from a
glossary, and for *litos* Mart. x 68 3 and Sen. *ep.* 123 7. At *sp.* 27 9 his 'si *uetus*
(for *situs*) aequorei reuocetur fabula monstri' is probable, and better than
Heinsius' *sit ut*. *Catacisse* IX 93 3 is just a trifle nearer the MSS than *Calocisse*;
but Lobeck, to whom he refers, did not and could not object to the latter forma-
tion in a proper name. He admits his own conjectures on easier terms than
anyone else's, reading *caede deos* at VI 21 10 and *Cadilla* at VII 87 7 while con-
fessing that the *parce tuo* of Heinsius and the *Gadilla* of β may be right and that
the prosody of *Cadilla* is unknown. At *sp.* 15 8 he prints something which
I need not mention, for it makes Martial say 'ferret (Meleagros)' in an epigram
which begins 'summa tuae, Meleagre'. At 19 3 he writes *cornuta mole* for
cornuto adore; but who will prefer '*mole* petitus'[1] to *cornu* (*potiore* or *maiore*)?
At 27 2 he has plucked up courage to eject Buecheler's obviously and necessarily false conjecture *Parthaoniam*, tamely accepted by five editors in succession
just because it was Buecheler's; and perhaps in his next edition of the *Priapea*
he will eject *morsit*, which has been repeated with equal servility, from 65 1.
But his own supplement '⟨monstra quibus fudit⟩ barbara terra fera' is also false:
barbara even so has no legitimate sense, and the only pentameter in Martial
ending with an epithet of the metrical form *feră* is XII 94 6, where *noua* carries
emphasis.[2] Two conjectures proposed only in the notes, *sp.* 21 b 1 *Orphei* and
XI 52 9 *leni*, have more to be said for them. The punctuation is amended at
VII 38 1, and everyone ought to be ashamed that it was not done before. The
propin of the MSS in XII 82 11 was vindicated ten years ago by Mr Heraeus in
Rh. Mus. LXX 1 ff., and he now successfully defends the reading of αβ in XIV
29 2 as *Mandatus*, the name of an official like *Leitus* V 8 12 and *Oceanus* III
95 10: Heinsius had already scented a proper name, but did not know that
Mandatus was such. The explanations of I 15 7 *catenati* and v 44 6 *conclauibus*
are true but not new; the interpretation of II 66 8 is pointless.

Perhaps the best novelty in the book, strange to say, comes from Mr Gustav
Friedrich, who at III 32 1 f. thus punctuates the text of βγ: '*non* (*an* α) possum
uetulam. *quereris* (*quaeris* α), Matrinia? possum | et uetulam, sed tu mortua,
non uetula es.' Editors had obtained grammar and sense by writing 'an *possim*

---

[1] *petitus*, however, does not suit the context, *cornuto...ore* is too good to be an accident, and
Martial probably wrote 'cornuto *optritus ab ore*'.
[2] Possessive pronouns are allowed, and the numeral *duo*; *proba* 1 4 8 is predicate.

uetulam quaeris'; Mr Lindsay composed from *non* and *quaeris* a text untainted by conjecture and punctuated it so as to make Matrinia ask 'non ego femina possum uetulam?'

Mr Heraeus' morality, if I may say so, is good. He is no friend to *liuidas obliuiones*, and duly records what his predecessors have done in the important matter of punctuation. He also respects property, and would rather be right than wrong in naming the author of an emendation; but at *sp.* 23 1 ⟦22 7⟧ and XI 43 3 he attributes to himself corrections which were quietly made by Mr Duff twenty years before. At VII 72 6 he says '*seu quid* Gilbert': in my margin I have 'Markland', but I cannot supply the reference. Some things I miss: to pass over in silence Munro's perfect completion of II 73 and Mr Duff's necessary correction of IX 3 14, while mentioning three or four of the light-hearted guesses of Mr Lindsay, is not fair to the reader. ‖

There are valuable notes on II 27 3 *cito*, V 37 8 *nitelam*, VI 70 6 *Alconti*, 94 1 *Calpetiano*, VII 26 4 *haec* fem. plur., IX 22 15 *ac*. But the learned illustration of *uissit* at XII 32 17 is futile, because no such noun as *aura* can be the subject of this verb: uissitur aura, non uissit. It is quite right to exclude *haud* from IX 2 8, but what is the use of saying 'sciendum est *haud* proprium heroici uersus esse' and 'in elegiacis semper uitatum est' when there are six examples in Propertius and more than forty in Seneca's tragedies? It is also right to reject *cubiclo* at X 30 17, but not right to add 'quali syncopa M. abstinet', for he has *tomacla* in I 41 9.

I subjoin some miscellaneous criticisms.

I 48 6 'nec *caueae* tanta conditur ille fide' is rightly read but mistaken for locative: it is genitive, as I explained at Manil. III 305: see Appul. *met.* IX 18 'fide tenebrarum contectus atque absconditus', Liu. I 26 11 'tanta foeditate supplicii' (tam foedo supplicio).

II 2 5 'editores ubique *Thule*': quite untrue.

II 36 3 *mitratarum* in the note should be *mitratorum*.

III 13 2 'plus quam *patri*, Naeuia, parcis apro': Mr Heraeus hankers after Heinsius' *putri*, which is foreign to the sense, but timidly suggests that *patri* may mean 'seni', which is equally so. The construction, explained by Raderus, is 'plus apro parcis quam patri', you show the boar more than filial consideration.

III 15 1 '*quam tota*...quod...lex Marxii...falsum coarguit'. Marxii forsooth! see Cortius on Luc. IV 476, where this verse is cited.

III 80 1 'de nullo loqui' and VII 18 1 f. 'de facie dicere' in the sense of 'male loqui (dicere)' are illustrated by Prop. IV 7 42 'de facie siqua locuta mea est': but there the sense is the opposite.

IV 31 10 'morem dicendi et faciendi obscene' is both a strange and false description of a perfectly definite σχῆμα which could be practised by the deaf and dumb.

IV 61 12 text and note conflict, and again XIV 189 2.

V 16 5 the reference to *C.L.E.* 253 1 is irrelevant, for Hammon is one with Iuppiter and Saturn is not.

V 22 7 *uincere* is probably an attempt to emend *mulorumpere*.

VI 64 3 'hirsuta peperit *deprensa* (α, *rubicunda* βγ) sub ilice coniunx'. Mr Heraeus prefers *rubicunda* and says '*deprensa* α, fortasse pudice, ut solet', as if 'sunburnt' were an indecent word or 'overtaken with travail' were more delicate. *depren-sa* may have been swallowed up between *peperit* and *su-*. I take occasion to say that what is termed modesty in α by Mr Heraeus and elegance by Mr Lindsay (who thinks *monstrum* a 'suitable euphemism' to signify what Burke calls the fount of life itself) is mere monkish horror of woman: α will copy down the grossest and filthiest words, such lines as III 71 1 and VII 10 1, if only they do not call up thoughts of the abhorred sex.

VIII 6 7 *chrocos* β is much better explained by Mr Lindsay as from *Rhoecos*: this was the Centaur's true name, which is to be learnt, not from Latin MSS, where *c* and *t* are much confused, but from Greek, where κ and τ are not.

VIII 45 4 '*facta minor* = decollata Buech.'. If that were so, *centeno consule* would have to mean 'centesimo', a solecism on which I discoursed at Manil. IV 451: it means 'centum consulibus', and therefore *amphora* means the contents of the jar (Fest. p. 153 ⟦138 Lindsay⟧ metonymia), as indeed *splendescat turbida lino* should be enough to show, and *facta minor* means 'shrunken' (Plin. *n.h.* XIV 55).

IX 44 3 '*solet hoc*, sc. ridet Hercules poculum tenens'. If so, if the statuette had a fixed smile on its face (which, by the way, *solet* is incapable of meaning), it could not smile in answer to Martial's question, non risit uerum ridebat; it must therefore have been Vindex who smiled and was wont to smile, and *Alcides*... *Vindicem* must be read. What a world is this, in which such truths have to be enunciated ! Mr Heraeus, I may add, makes *poeta* vocative, though Mr Lindsay removed that error.

X 80 6 the note is confused: it is Scriuerius who puts a comma after *ridet*. ‖

XI 99 Mr Heraeus rightly reads *gemina* in 5 and refuses both *Minyas* and *minias* in 6, but adds 'tamquam parum sit lusus ex Argonautis aut ex colore podicis μελαμπύγου (*cyaneas*, non *Cy.*)'. Ergo femina μελάμπυγος? et quid id ad rem?

XI 100 4 'uariauit modum metro cogente': immo sensu. I warned scholars against that error in my note on Iuu. VII 185. The subjunctives *cingant radat pungat* are conditional, 'cingant anuli lacertos si induantur, clune radat amica genuque pungat si amplecti uelis'; 'serra lumbis *eminet*' is absolute. So Luc. VI 436 f. 'ficti quas nulla licentia monstri | *transierit* (si fingatur), quarum quid-quid non creditur ars *est*', X 456 f. 'hic, cui Romani spatium non *sufficit* orbis | paruaque regna *putet* (si dentur, quod non fit) Tyriis cum Gadibus Indos'.

XIII 74 1 (on the false form *Tarpeĭa*) 'Prop. IV 10 31 *Veius dux astitit* pro *dux Veius ast.* legerim.' That would be a pity. The gentile name *Veius* is of course disyllabic (Hor. *epod.* 5 29), but the poetical adjective formed from *Vei* on the analogy of *Troius*, which occurs again *G.L.K.* VI p. 563 6 ('corruptum uidetur' says Mr Heraeus), is and ought to be a dactyl.

XIV 131 1 '*qui c. sumis* γ prob. Markland, at cf. ad XI 42 2', where it is observed that Martial has not the adverb *qui*: but here *qui* will be the relative pronoun.

XIV 216 ⟦217⟧ 2 *decipit* would be better defended by the single citation *paraphr.* Dionys. ὀρνιθ. III 5 than by Mr Heraeus' vague reference to Hehn and by his totally inapposite references to the *thes. ling. Lat.* and Columella. He cannot really think that 'accipitres decipiuntur' supports 'accipiter decipit', nor that hawks catch birds with birdlime.

I have found some errors in numerals, and on p. vii there are four.

141

MARTIAL XII 59 9*

I can now provide *dexiocholus* with a stouter defence than the imprudent improvisation of Mr Heraeus. Men lame of the right leg were to be dreaded because it was unlucky to meet them. Lucian *pseudol.* 17 ἡμεῖς δὲ καὶ τοὺς χωλοὺς τῷ δεξιῷ ἐκτρεπόμεθα, καὶ μάλιστα εἰ ἕωθεν ἴδοιμεν αὐτούς, Pliny *n. h.* xxviii 35 'despuimus comitiales morbos...simili modo et fascinationes repercutimus dextraeque clauditatis occursum', wrongly explained in *thes. ling. Lat.* iii p. 1306 17 and v p. 922 9.

The metre and the missing vocative, about which I wrote in *C.Q.* xiii p. 79 ⟦this edition pp. 993–4⟧, may now be restored thus:

hinc ⟨, Rex,⟩ dexiocholus, inde lippus.

Cicero's correspondent in *fam.* xiii 52 is addressed solely by this cognomen, 'Cicero Regi s.', 'fac igitur, mi Rex, ut intellegat'.

* ⟦*CR* 40 (1926), 19: and see this edition pp. 1100–1⟧

142

REVIEW: U. KNOCHE, DIE ÜBERLIEFERUNG JUVENALS*

Mr Knoche's object is to make clear the relations between the several MSS and groups, and so to reconstruct the archetype; and with this aim he wishes to enlarge our apparatus criticus and build recension upon a broader base. He complains that Leo and I use too few MSS and despise most of those which Mr Hosius collated and which Jahn professed to collate. We despise them because we find them despicable. If such MSS as Hosius' VBM are to be included in an apparatus, no MS can well be shut out; for they contain nothing good or seemingly ancient which is not also to be found in other MSS which contain more of it.

His attempt fails, and was doomed to failure, because he misconceives the problem and does not properly define his terms in his own mind. According to him there were two ancient recensions, Π, whence P and its relatives descend, and ω, whence descend the vulgar MSS; and he aims at separating these two strains, at tracing them back beyond our MSS, and at so drawing near to the archetype. But the sign ω, as he uses it, is ambiguous and delusive. The readings in which the vulgar MSS differ from P are of three distinct sorts: wrong readings where P is right, as I 52 *Herculeias* (*Heracleas* P); right readings where P is wrong, as xv 26 *haec* (*his* P); readings where either may be wrong and either right, as IX 148 *uocatur* (*rogatur* P). Mr Knoche, without discriminating these three sorts, sets forth in quest of MSS containing the largest number of all of them together, believing that such MSS will present the text of ω in its most original form. They will not: those MSS which contain most readings of the first sort (which is much the most plentiful) will present the least original form of the text of ω. These false lections were not all invented at once by a single malefactor: they are the gradual deposit, century after century, of human ignorance and conceit; and if any large number of them are derived from a recension, it was probably Carolingian, whether or no we father it on Heiric of Auxerre. The ancient fragments, though often dissenting from P, possess but few of them. Bob. in the fourth century has xv 25 *deduxerat*, but not 20 *Cyanes*,

* [*Die Überlieferung Juvenals*. Von Ulrich Knoche. Pp. 75. (Klassisch-Philologische Studien, Heft 6.) Berlin: Ebering, 1926. *CR* 40 (1926), 170–1]

27 *Iunio*, 36 *uulgi*;[1] Ambr. in the sixth has XIV 289 *uda*, but not 270 *pingui*, 287 *lacertis*, 315 *sed te*; and Vind. even in the ninth has only eight out of forty. Seruius knows none but XV 168 *nescirent. . .extundere*, and Priscian only three, VI 329 *dormitat* (if that is wrong), XIV 30 *moechos*, 121 f. *illam. . .uiam*. The readings (other than certainly true ones) for which a common ancient origin may be sought with some hope of success are those of the third sort, such as I collected on p. xxv of my edition. At present Mr Knoche is seeking what he will never find, because it never existed.

And he has turned his face in the wrong direction. What we need are MSS in which the Carolingian vulgate has not thoroughly overlaid an older substratum; and my seven, AFGLOTU, are selected as being such. What Mr Knoche wants are MSS completely smothered; and when he finds one he calls it an almost pure representative of ω. If an older substratum emerges – *e.g.* *libis* III 187 in L, – he assigns it (p. 27) to the Π-stem and not the ω-stem. He argues, after Mr Hosius, thus (p. 25): 'A ist aus einer Π-quelle ursprünglich hergeleitet; A hat aber dieselbe vorlage wie MLHVB; also stammt diese auch aus Π'; but his minor premiss is false. What A is we know exactly: it was copied from a MS almost identical with P which had been corrected by a hand much resembling P[2]. But L is something far different: its alliances with A are almost always alliances with A's second and superimposed element; it seldom sides with A where A sides with P. In other words, A and L have not the same substratum. The substratum of A is virtually P; that of L is nothing similar and is not definitely known; for many true readings, such as XV 26 *haec*, which in A belong to the added element, may belong to the substratum in L, and probably do.

I note some errors of detail.

P. 11 *autem* in VII 217 is said to be 'sinnwidrig': it is the most appropriate word in the whole Latin language (*thes. ling. Lat.* II p. 1592 58–81).

P. 14 the *si dormit* of Par. 8072 (and P[2]) in VI 329, which Mr Knoche like Leo accepts, is quite obviously an attempt to correct the metre of *si iam dormit*; and Pithou's *iam dormit* is a better one, because it accounts for the intrusion of *si*, while the other does not account for the intrusion of *iam*. The anaphora to which Mr Knoche appeals does not exist: he has overlooked *abstuleris*.

On the same page the absurd *egeum* of the same MS in VI 93, a bad conjecture for the *igneum* of P, is said to be 'gestützt durch Σ'. The *Adriacum* and *Aegaeum* of Σ are a paraphrase, of course erroneous, of *late sonantem Ionium*, which extended from the one to the other and was thought by some (Seru. *Aen.* III 211) to include both.

P. 18 'G nicht eine einzige evidente conjectur aufweist.' G has never been collated: Jahn only pretended to collate it, and I did not pretend.

---

[1] Mr Knoche says on p. 38 that Bob. has an ω-text: if so, ω was something very different from the ω which he is seeking.

P. 19 X 310 *i nunc et* GU, *inunget* PS, ‖ *nunc ergo* P²ω: 'γ (= GU)[1] hat allein das richtige, das, wie der vergleich mit PS zeigt, sich nur im Π-strang erhalten hatte.' PS no more show this than P²ω show the contrary. *i nunc et* is the common original, diversely corrupted in PS and P²ω, each tradition preserving something which the other has lost.

P. 21 'cod. class. lat. 41 Bodleian.' is not the name of T nor indeed of any other MS.

P. 23 an argument is built on the belief that *nolet* VI 213 is the reading of flor. Sang. 870, which does not even contain the verse. This mistake has arisen from a hasty glance at my note, where I cite *nolet* from another St Gall MS. On the same page Leo's note at VII 185 has been misunderstood with no more excuse.

P. 35 XIV 310 '*atque* ist hier sicher falsch.' It gives excellent sense and is explained by Munro and Friedlaender. *aut* is equally good in itself, but may have been introduced by a reader who was puzzled by *atque* as Mr Knoche is.

The treatise is laborious, minute, and methodical in design and construction; and although it contains a good deal of bad reasoning, notably on pp. 17, 18, 36, 37, 38, it may be regarded as marking a stage in the slow improvement of Juvenalian criticism since the early years of the century. Mr Knoche is at least delivered from the yoke of P, and has an open mind with respect to spurious verses. At VI 373 (pp. 54 f.) he defends the order 'tonsoris *tantum damno*' against the *damno tantum* of P by the good observation (though he does not state it correctly) that in Juvenal the adverb *tantum* is always in contact with the word to be emphasised.

---

[1] P. 17 'Leo hat schon erkannt, dass G und U auf eine gemeinsame quelle...zurückgehn.' Leo did not say so, I did, *corp. poet. Lat. Postg.* fasc. v p. ix 'sunt...inter se cognati U et G'.

143

THE MICHIGAN ASTROLOGICAL PAPYRUS*

Mr Robbins' commentary on this treatise shows thorough knowledge of the subject, provides sufficient information, and affords in the arithmetical portion a great deal of assistance. The text itself he has evidently transcribed with scrupulous care, and most of his supplements are either certain or appropriate. But in particulars much remains to do, not only of completion but of correction and interpretation. There are also inconsistencies in Mr Robbins' practice. For his readers' convenience he has freely inserted colons and full stops, but in many places where they are no less necessary and their necessity is no less obvious he allows sentences to mix. It was quite right, in printing a document for the first time, to preserve the vulgar interchanges of certain vowels and diphthongs, ε and η, ο and ω, ι and ει, η and οι (1 G 19), and so forth; and where they are likely to cause difficulty Mr Robbins points them out (1 H 8, 1 I 20), though perhaps not everyone will immediately recognize λυποῦνται in 6 11. But inflexions violating syntax he sometimes corrects and sometimes lets alone: he restores ἐκπρεπῆ (1 F 15), τό (1 H 24), ὡροσκόπος (1 I 11 f.), Κρόνῳ (3 A 18), but not ἀρτηρίας (1 D 12), Αἰγόκερῳ (2 A 31 and 3 B 5), Λέοντος (3 B 14). He accepts in his commentary the form νοερεον, and even ventures to accentuate it; and his own supplements present a genitive Αἰγόκερως (twice), ἀποέχοντες (three times), ἐστὶ ἡμέρας, and δυνάμεσι ἐναντίοι.

I have inclosed with brackets, so far as may be, only what is my own; what stands immediately outside is not always the text of the papyrus but sometimes a satisfactory supplement of Mr Robbins.

1 A 5 f. π[αθ]ῶν ὅσα νεφ[ρικὰ] καὶ ἀπόκρυφά ἐστιν ἐπαίτια. See Valens, p. 2, 15 f.: νεφρῶν καὶ τῶν ἐντὸς ἀποκρύφων.

1 A 8–11 τῶν μὲν ἔμπροσθεν [μερῶν τὸ] 'Ηλίου πρῶτ[ον καὶ ὀλίγιστον. οὗτο]ς γὰρ ὀλιγίστην δια[τρέχει σφαῖραν τοῦ] πλάτους. This, σφαῖρα, is the term used below, and the ἡ of 13 looks hither. The subject ‖ of columns A–F is a planetary μελοθεσία of the human body, and the calculations in A and B are subsidiary to this end. The seven planets take possession of fourteen parts, seven ἔμπροσθεν and seven ὄπισθεν, of what this author calls the ἀνδριάς (1 B 35, C 19, E 40), which I suppose to be the body of man considered as an image of the universe. See 1 B 34 f.: τῶν ἔμπροσθεν μερῶν τοῦ ἀνδριάντος.

---

* [[CPh 22 (1927), 257–63: and see pp. 5–26 of this same volume]]

1 A 23 ἐν [ἦ]ι. If there is not room for θέ[ουσα], θεός must be the planet Venus herself.

1 A 25 f. τοσαύτη μὲν ἡ περί[οδος τῶν] κύκλων αὐτῶν.

1 B 29 f. ὥστε ὀξύτερον τοῦ Ἡλίου [αὐτὴν] φέρεσθαι. The diphthong ει is written for short ι in 1 E 27, 3 A 16, and elsewhere.

1 B 31–3 τοιαύτας οὔ[ν ἔ]στ[α]ι κατὰ τοὺς ἐπικύκλους ἑκάστου αὐτῶν λαμβάνειν. Supply μοίρας, which is often left unsaid.

1 C 18–24 καταντήσει δὲ ἕως ἄκρ[ου γενείο]υ. καὶ ἔστιν ἡ ὄψις τὸ θαῦμα τοῦ ἀνδρι[άντος], ὥστε ὅλην μὲν τὴν κεφαλὴν τὴν σ[ὴν ? Ἡλίου] καὶ Σελήνης εἶναι, ἀλλ' ἔχειν [τὸν] μὲν [τὸ γνωμ]ονικόν, [αὐτὴν] δὲ τὸ μεταβολικὸν καὶ [παθητι]κόν. καὶ ἀπὸ μὲν Ἑρμοῦ τὸ νοερὸν [καὶ ? λόγ]ου ἡγεμονικὸν πρόσεστιν. See 30 below, and 1 F 38: ἡ μὲν γὰρ κεφαλὴ ὅλη Ἡλίου καὶ Σελήνης.

1 C 28–31 ἔστιν οὖν, ὡς ἐν ἀνθρώπῳ τὸ πρόσωπον μάλιστα θαυμαστὸν διὰ τὰς μεταβολὰς καὶ τὰ προσπίπτοντα [πά]θη, οὕτως καὶ ἡ Σελήνη θαυμαστὸν ἐν [κόσμῳ]. See 22 above.

1 D 17 Διὸς μέρος. [λαμβάνει] δὲ [σ]τῆ[θος]. ἕως στομάχου καὶ ἧπα[ρ. Διὸς δέ].

1 D 20 τῶν εἰσφερομένων [σιτίων] αἱμάτωσιν. See 33 f.

1 D 22 τὸ ἀρχικὸν προ[σή]ρ[μοσε]. προνοεῖται [γοῦν].

1 D 25 f. ἰκτεριᾷ ἢ ὑδρωπιᾷ.

1 E 13 ὧν (η) τὸ τρίτον ὦμ. Here and again in 1 I 9 τὸ γὰρ ἀνάπαλιν (η) φαῦλον either η must be deleted or ἐστίν substituted, which in the latter place is less acceptable because of 1 H 24.

1 E 28 Ὀλύμπια should not be altered: στέφονται Ὀλύμπια is Horace's *coronari Olympia*.

1 E 35 κινουμέν[ου].

1 E 40 f. τὰ ἐμπρόσθια [τοῦ] ἀ[νδ]ρ[ιάντ]ος μέρη. See 1 B 34 f. cited at 1 A 8–11. Is the τ reported by Mr Robbins here and in 3 B 10 the first stroke of N?

1 F 14–18 κνήμας δὲ ἐμπεριέξει καί πως, ὁ[πό]τε ἴδωμεν ὄψιν ‖ ἐκπρεπῆ, ἐκπεριελθόντες εὐθὺ κνήμην ὁρῶμεν φύσει πά[ντε]ς, ἀγούσης ἐπὶ τοῦτο ὁμοζύγου μερίδος τῆς σεληνιακῆς ἡμᾶς. The Moon has two portions of the body, the face (ὄψις) in front (1 C 18–33) and the calves behind.

1 F 20–4 Κρόνου μέρος, [ἰγνύαι ?] καὶ μηρῶν ἄκρα, ἀεὶ ἐγκόπων [ἄνθρωπ]ων. εἶτα ἕως σοε Διός, μηροί. οἱ [οὖ]ν ἐ[π]έραστο[ι κα]ὶ εἰς χρῆσιν εὔθ[ετ]οι διὰ τοῦ Διὸς εἰς τοῦτο ἄγονται.

1 F 30–5 οἱ οὖν πάθος ἔχοντες αἰσχρὸν καὶ παρὰ φύσιν πάσχουσιν, εἰ μὲν βίᾳ καὶ ἀκουσίως, τούτων Ἀφροδίτη εὑρεθήσεται ἐν ταύταις ταῖς Ἑρμοῦ δαιμονιώδεσιν μοίραις κεκακωμένη, εἰ δὲ ἑκουσίως, καὶ τοῦ Ἑρμοῦ ἀστὴρ εὑρεθήσεται ἐν ταῖς αὐταῖς μοίραις κεκακωμένος. The meaning of τούτων Ἀφροδίτη is 'Venus in these men's genitures', and nothing is to be inserted; cf. Maneth. VI 216: δαίμονι...χαλεπῷ κείνης, 'the twelfth place in the wife's geniture', 220 f., Doroth. 158 f. (*CCAG* VI 104), Firm. *Math.* VI 29 17.

1 F 36 τένων in Graeco-Latin glossaries answers to *ceruix*. Man is here distributed among the planets as follows (I inclose within brackets those apportionments which the papyrus omits and we are left to infer): 'Before: top of head Sun, face Moon, shoulders Saturn, breast stomach liver Jupiter [belly and arms Mercury], hands genitals thighs knees shins Mars, feet Venus. Behind: back of head Sun, shoulders and back Mars, buttocks Mercury, thighs Jupiter, hams Saturn, calves Moon [heels Venus].'

1 G 10 Mr Robbins' [εὐτό]ναις, which should at least be εὐτόνοις, is not a good contrast to δαιμονιώδεσι; perhaps [ὑγιει]ναῖς.

1 H 16f. Ἡλίου κα[ὶ Cελήνης. ἄρχ]ει δέ. A symbol was used for Cελήνης, as in 9.

1 I 15 The sixth place is called Δαιμονία in *CCAG* VIII iii, p. 101, 23, and the fifth *Daemonie* in Manil. II 897.

1 I 18 τὸ δὲ ῑᾱ ἀγαθὸς δαίμων, ⟨τὸ δὲ ῑβ κακὸς δαίμων⟩.

1 I 20–6 Here we have a fourth account of the *octatropos*[1] to add to those which I cited from Firmicus, Antiochus, and Thrasyllus at Manil. II 969 and III p. 69; and it contains a surprise. The three other authors, Firmicus apparently, Antiochus certainly, and Thrasyllus with the utmost explicitness, make the places in this system of ‖ eight identical with the first eight places in the system of twelve; they are numbered downward from the horoscope, and the eighth is the place next above the Occident. But this author says ἀπὸ τοῦ ὡροσκόπου τὰ περὶ ϟωῆς ϟητεῖται (this is ungrammatical and should probably be ϟητητέα, for ϟητεῖτε is not likely), ἀπὸ δὲ τοῦ ἄνω δευτέρου βίον, numbering upward, so that the second place in the *octatropos* is the twelfth in the *dodecatropos*, the third the eleventh, the γονέων τόπος leaps from the base to the summit of the universe, and only in the first and seventh places do the two systems coincide.

1 I 32–4 ἔκ τε πρεσβυτέρων περί[λει]μ[μα] κ[αὶ θαν]άτων μονιῶν ὠφελίαν, 'left property from old men and benefit from the decease of celibates', *orborum hereditates*. The phrase ἀπὸ θανάτων ὠφέλεια occurs more than once in Paul. Alex., fol. Μ 4 ⟦pp. 61–2 Boer⟧.

1 J 7f. γυναικείων προσώπ[ων], 'female persons'.

1 J 40f. καὶ ἐντὸς τῶν ῑε μοιρῶν εἰ γίνονται ἐγκρύψεις, συνῳδοί εἰσιν οἱ ἀστέρες τοῖς ἀποτελέσμασι. See 25 δέκα πέντε.

2 A 9 ἀπο[σ]χόντες, and in 6 and 7 either this participle or ἀποστάς.

2 A 30 Not μοῖραν but μοίρας, as in 31.

2 B 10f. [ἀριθμῆ]σαι εἰς ϟωὴν ὁ χρόνος [ἕκασ]τος ἰσχύει [ἔτος]. This doctrine I have set forth, citing authorities, in Manil. III pp. xxiv–xxvi.

2 B 11–14 τῶν δὲ ϟῳδίων ἃ μὲ[ν λέγομε]ν ἀκούοντα ἀλλήλων, ἃ δὲ ὁρῶντα ἄλληλα, ἃ δὲ αἰσθανόμενα ἀλλήλων. ἀκούει [δ’ ἄρ’] οὖν ⟨ἀλλήλων⟩ τὰ ἀπὸ τῶν ἰσημερινῶν ἀρχόμενα καὶ ἴσον ἀπ’ αὐτῶν διιστάμενα. The papyrus has ἴσον ἀπ’

---

[1] Mr Robbins writes *octotopos*, and also *dodecatopos*; and indeed Mr W. Gundel is the only scholar whom I have yet induced to discard those figments of Scaliger's.

ἀλλήλων διίσταται. This is absurd in itself, because any two things are necessarily equidistant from each other; apart from that, the things from which these signs are equidistant are the equinoctial signs; and further ἀλλήλων is required with ἀκούει, since in all this exposition the verbs ἀκούειν ὁρᾶν βλέπειν are nowhere used without their object. I suppose that a scribe, for lack of punctuation, fancied that the ἀλλήλων immediately before ἀκούει belonged to it, and therefore omitted the other; and that this, having been added in the margin, was wrongly substituted for αὐτῶν. If διίσταται is not changed to the participle, καί must be changed to ἅ. Perhaps I had better give the warning that in *CCAG* VIII ii p. 89 12 f., ἀκούει δὲ τὰ ἴσον ἀπέχοντα τῶν ἰσημερινῶν ἀλλήλων, the construction is ἀκούει ἀλλήλων. ||

2 B 16–19 ἐπεὶ γὰρ ἡ ἡμέρα νύκτα οὐχ ὁρᾷ διὰ τοῦ διάμετρος εἶναι αὐτῇ, ἀκούει δ' ἴσης ἡμέρας ἴση νύξ, ὅταν ἐπ' ἴσαις ὥραις τελῆται ἡμέρα ἡ νύξ, ἀκούουσιν τὰ ζῴδια καὶ ἀλλήλων. See 28.

2 B 21 Full stop after Ταῦρον; Mr Robbins perceives what is missing in the sentence which ends here.

2 B 22 f. ἐν Διδύμοις γὰρ [ὄντος] ἡ ἡμέρα ὡρῶν ιϛ; then no addition is needed in 24.

2 B 25–31 ὑπὸ δὲ τῆς γῆς μέσης οὔσης ἐ[ξαπωθο]ῦν[ται. ὁ δὲ] Λέων καὶ Τοξότης ἀκούουσιν ἀλλήλων, ⟨καὶ ὁμοίως Παρθένος καὶ Σκορπίος⟩. ὁ δὲ Ζυγὸς καὶ Κριὸς [οὔ]. βλέπει δὲ ἡ ἴση ἡμέρα τὴν ἴσην ἡμέραν, οὐκέτι ἀκούει. τὰ οὖν ι τῶν τροπικῶν ἀρχόμενα καὶ ἑκατέρωθεν ἴσον ἀφιστά[μενα, οἷον Λέων Δίδυ]μ[οί τε], ὁρῶσιν ἄλληλα. Lines 29–31 have to be corrected by the light of the corresponding lines, 13 f., which are themselves corrupt. ἴσον is necessary and the θᾶττον of the papyrus meaningless; I can only suppose that it comes from a scribe who was puzzled, as well he might be, by the η which I have altered into ι, and thought that it was ἤ and that it needed a comparative.

2 B 35 Ὑδροχόος· [ὁ δὲ] Αἰγόκερως.

2 B 38–44 καὶ ὅθεν ὁ Αἰγόκερως ἀνατέλλει, [ὅθεν δὲ] Καρκίνος, ἕτερον ζῴδιον [οὐ]κ ἀνατέλλει, [ὥστε οὐκ] ἔστιν ὁρῶντα ἄλληλα ἐκ τῶνδε τῶν τόπων, [ἢ οὐδενὸς ὁ]ρῶντος ἀνατέλλει. διόπερ [ταῦτα] μόν[α ἔκτο]σθεν σκιὰν βάλλουσιν τοῦ Ἡλίου [. . . . . τὰ] ἄλλα ζῴδια διερχομένου. διόπερ ὁμολόγ[ως τεθ]έν[τ]ος ὁρᾷ ἡ ἡμέρα τὴν ἡμέραν. Cancer rises farther north, and Capricorn farther south, than any other sign; and therefore the Sun in Cancer casts shadows more to the south, and in Capricorn more to the north, than anywhere else in the zodiac. The one sign, therefore, is the other's counterpart in position, and his day 'sees' the other's day, though the one is the longest and the other the shortest; and so the two signs ὁρατικὸν ἔχουσιν λόγον πρὸς ἀλλήλους (36 f.).

2 B 44–6 [ἄλλ]α δ[ὲ κατην]αν[τιω]μένα ἀλλήλων ἐστὶν τὰ δ[ιαιτή]μ[ατα? τ]ῶν [ἀσ]τέρων, οἷον Καρκίνος καὶ Λέων, Παρθένος [καὶ Δίδυμοι, Ταῦρος καὶ Ζυγός, Σκορπίος καὶ Κριός, Ἰχθύες καὶ Τοξότης, Αἰγόκερως καὶ Ὑδροχόος]. These are the ὁμόζωνα of Paul. Alex., fol. E 3 [p. 26 Boer], and Ludw. Maxim., p. 106,

ll. 3 f.; and as the one ‖ passage is a chaos of misprints and the other obscure for lack of punctuation I have written out the list in full. Paulus defines them, ὁμόζωνά ἐστιν ὅταν τοῦ αὐτοῦ ἀστέρος τυγχάνῃ τὰ ζῴδια; the pairs are the two houses of the several planets, except that the Sun and Moon have but one apiece.

2 c 15 f. and 24 f. [ἐκκεν]τρότητες.

2 c 34–6 ἔκκ[εντροι δ' οἱ κύκλοι] λέγονται ὅτι ἡ γῆ τοῦ μὲν κόσμου κέντρον ἐστὶν τῶν δὲ ζ πλανήτων [μέση].

2 D 7 Not [θηριό]μορφα but [δί]μορφα: CCAG v iii p. 97 4: δίμορφα Τοξότης Αἰγόκερως.

3 A 5–8 τοῖς δὲ συγκινουμένοις πέντε θεοῖς ἀπένειμεν ἡ φύσις ἀνὰ δύο οἴκους ἀρρενικόν τε καὶ θηλυκόν. Ἥλιος μὲν γὰρ ἡμέρας ἔχει ἀρχήν, Σελήνη δὲ νυκτός. See CCAG v ii p. 132 29. The planets have two houses apiece, a masculine and a feminine.

3 A 9–11 ἔστιν δὲ τοῦ [κόσ]μου σπλάγχνα τὰ ἐνοικούμενα. ['Ερμῇ] τὸ πρῶτον τμῆμα ἐδόθη. In Manil. III 61 f., the signs of the zodiac are figuratively said *mundi praecordia obtinere*.

3 A 19 κατ' Αἰγόκερων.

3 A 34 φυλακὴ δὲ [Παρθένου].

3 B 4–7 [ἐπὶ] Ταύρου Παρθένου καὶ Αἰγόκερω χαίρειν μὲν Σελήνην 'Αφροδίτην 'Ερμῆν, [μέρος] δὲ κ[αὶ "Αρη, μὴ] μέντοι γε ἀντεπιτροπεύειν. See Doroth. 66–9 (CCAG VI p. 94) Ταύρου Παρθενικῆς τε καὶ Αἰγόκερω κρατέουσιν | ἤματος 'Αφρογενής, νυκτὸς δέ τε δῖα Σελήνη, | καὶ τρίτατος μετὰ τοῖσι θεὸς πολέμοισιν ἀνάσσων· | ἐν δὲ νυ Παρθενικῇ Μαίης προσλάμβανε κοῦρον. Mr Robbins' χ[αίρειν], if he has rightly deciphered the χ, seems to be unavoidable; but it is not wont to be thus used for οἰκοδεσποτεῖν (δεσπόζειν, κυριεύειν), it does not harmonize with ἀντεπιτροπεύειν, and its regular construction is ἐν c. dat. The κρατεῖν of Dorotheus would give the right sense, but is rather poetical.

3 B 9–11 ἐπὶ Σκορπίου 'Ιχθύων καὶ Καρκίνου [ἄρχειν] "Αρη καὶ 'Αφροδίτην, μετέχειν δὲ καὶ τριγώνου [Σελήνην, μὴ] μέντοι γε ἀντεπιτροπεύειν καὶ ἡμέρας. See Doroth. 73–5: Καρκίνον αὖτε λάχεν καὶ Σκορπίον ἠδέ τε λοίσθους | 'Ιχθύας ἡματίη Κύπρις, Πυρόεις δέ τε νυκτός, | καὶ μετὰ τοὺς ἑλικῶπις ἔχει βασίλισσα Σελήνη; these three planets are assigned to this triangle also by Valens and Ptolemy. Δ is the regular ‖ symbol for τρίγωνον. Where I have written Σελήνην μή, the papyrus had four letters; these were σε μη, and the same abbreviation was used in 1 F 14.

3 B 13–19 ['Ερμῆς δὲ] ἐτήρησεν τοὺς ἀστέρας [τῶν τ] ξ ⟨τ⟩αῖ[ς ἀπὸ] πρώτης Λέοντος ἕως Ζυγοῦ [μὲν] προσθετικούς – φερομένους –, ἀπὸ δὲ τῆς πρώτης Σκορπίου – ἀφαιρετικούς.

6 17–20 οἱ κακοποιοὶ τετράγωνοι καὶ διάμετροι εὐτονώτατοί εἰσιν εἰς τὸ βλάπτειν [τὸ θέμα· τρίγων]οι δὲ ἀβλαβεῖς εἰσιν, οἱ δὲ ἀγαθοποιοί.

6 28 ὁ[ραθ]εῖσα.

144

PROSODY AND METHOD [I]*

In a paper on the application of thought to textual criticism which I read before the Classical Association at Cambridge in 1921 (*Proceedings* vol. XVIII pp. 67–84 [this edition pp. 1058–69]) I made some remarks which I abbreviate as follows:

'One of the forms assumed by thoughtlessness in textual criticism is the endeavour, now frequent especially among Continental scholars, to break down accepted rules of grammar or metre by the mere enumeration of exceptions found in MSS. That can never break down a rule: number is nothing; what matters is weight, and weight can only be ascertained by scrutiny. If I had noted every example I have met, I should now have a large collection of passages where *orbis*, which our grammars and dictionaries declare to be masculine, has a feminine adjective attached to it. But I do not therefore propose to revise that rule of syntax: for scrutiny would show that these examples, though numerous, have no force. In most of them the context proves that *orbem*, *orbis*, *orbes*, etc., are merely corruptions of the corresponding case and number of *urbs*; and in the rest it is natural to suppose that the scribe has been influenced and confused by the likeness of the one word to the other.'

I then pursued the subject in the field of grammar, and examined, with particular reference to Mr Rothstein's note on Prop. I 3 17, the alleged examples of the Latin pluperfect with a perfect sense (*exciderant* ἐκπεπτώκασι). I shall now turn to prosody, and examine certain attempts made in this century to upset rules established in elder times; attempts to supersede wide and orderly inductions by eager and short-sighted clutching at any and every exception which our MSS may present, or may falsely be reported as presenting.

MSS present exceptions to every rule; a rule to which they presented no exception would be no rule, but something too vague to be worth formulating. But it is not every rule that these reactionaries try to upset. If they did, I could respect them; they would at least be consistent, and they might profess a principle, if only a false one. But their attempts are sporadic and capricious and bewray their origin; they spring from prepossessions and from whim. In these circumstances we know what to expect: fresh and superfluous proof of the

* [*CQ* 21 (1927), 1–12]

[1

weakness of man's reason and the strength of his passions; 'mens bona ducetur manibus post terga retortis | et pudor et castris quidquid amoris obest.' The investigator equips himself with blinkers, permitting him to see nothing but the mere examples, and excluding all surrounding objects and all illumination from without. ||

Jerome at Isaiah viii 27 [XXIV p. 307 Migne] cites a verse, 'quo fugis, Encelade? quascumque accesseris oras', which Heinsius and others have referred to the lost end of Claudian's Latin *gigantomachia*. This, said Mr Birt on p. ccxi of his Claudian, no sober man will dare to do: 'neque illud *Encelade* producta ultima...quisquam sobrius ad Claudianum referre audebit'. But that was in 1892, since which date Mr Birt has had occasion to cry 'quo me, Bacche, rapis tui plenum?' In 1910, uelox mente noua, at Verg. *catal.* 9 60, and in 1913, on p. 72 of his *Kritik und Hermeneutik*, he attributes, not indeed this verse to Claudian, but similar lengthenings of short final vowels at caesuras to better poets and stricter versifiers. He is not the first to do so: examples from MSS had been cited long before by Gifanius Lucr. p. 299 and Cortius at Luc. II 272; and some examples are cited legitimately and constitute prima facie evidence to support the case. But Mr Birt has gone out into the highways and hedges and mustered as ragged a regiment as ever marched through Coventry; and the mad fellow who met Falstaff on the way and told him he had unloaded all the gibbets and pressed the dead bodies might say much the same to Mr Birt. Here is his roll-call:

Enn. *ann.* III [147 Vahlen] (Prob. Verg. *buc.* VI 31 [vol. 3 2 p. 341 Thilo–Hagen]): et densis *aquilā* pennis obnixa uolabat.

carm. epigr. Buech. 331 3: de incerto *certā* ne fiant si sapis caueas.

carm. epigr. Buech. 331 4: de uero *falsā* ne fiant iudice falso.

epigr. Plaut. [*PLF* p. 32 Morel] ap. Gell. 1 24 3: scaena est *desertā*, dein risus ludus iocusque.

catalept. 9 60: Cynthius et *Musā*, Bacchus et Aglaie (BH, *Musae* AR).

Verg. *Aen.* III 464: dona dehinc auro *grauiā* sectoque elephanto.

Verg. *Aen.* XII 648: sancta ad uos *animā* | atque istius inscia culpae.

Prop. II 13 25: sat mea sit *magnā* si tres sint pompa libelli.

Prop. II 29 39: dixit et *oppositā* propellens sauia nostra.

Prop. IV 5 64: per tenues *ossā* sunt numerata cutes.

Tib. 1 7 61: te canit *agricolā* magna cum uenerit urbe.

Ouid. *amor.* III 7 55: sed puto non *blandā*, non optima perdidit in me.

ciris 189: credere quam tanto *scelerē* damnare puellam.

el. in Maec. 1 139: Nestoris *annosā* uicisses saecula, si me.

Aetn. 6: seu tibi *Dodonā* potior, tecumque fauentes.

Mart. *spect.* 28 10: diues *Caesareā* praestitit unda tibi.

Iuu. x 54: ergo *superuacuā* | aut perniciosa petuntur.

Maxim. *el.* I 95: nigra *superciliā*, frons libera, lumina clara.

(Prop. III 11 46: iura *darē* statuas inter et arma Mari.)

The last example hides shyly between brackets, because Mr Birt is conscious that everyone else who accepts the reading will attribute the lengthening to the following *st*; so I say no more about it. But before going further I will present Mr Birt with a draft of recruits, all of whom have passed a medical examination much more rigorous than his own.

Verg. *Aen.* I 501: fert umero gradiensque *deā* super eminet omnes (MPR, *deas* F).

Tib. IV 6 [[III 12]] 19: sis iuueni *gratā*, ueniet cum proximus annus. ||

Prop. IV 1 101: Iunonis *facitē* uotum inpetrabile, dixi.

Aem. Mac. [[*PLF* p. 108 Morel]] ap. Isid. *orig.* XII 4 24: seu *terrā* fumat qua taeter labitur anguis.

Manil. IV 478: et sexta et *decumā* | et quae ter quinta notatur.

These five examples[1] are all legitimate, because nothing can be alleged against them except the violation of that metrical rule which is itself in question: they contain no fault of sense or grammar, and critics have assailed and altered them purely for their prosody. And some of Mr Birt's examples are no less legitimate. Such, needless to say, are the three which he has borrowed from Lachmann's note on Lucr. II 27, – Enn. *ann.* III *aquilā*, Verg. *Aen.* III 464 *grauiā*, XII 648 *animā*. Such too is the verse from the so-called 'epigramma Plauti' in Gell. I 24 3 with its *desertā*, and such are Tib. I 7 61 *agricolā*, Prop. II 13 25 *magnā*, *ciris* 189 *scelerē*, and even, at first sight, Ouid. *amor.* III 7 55 *blandā*. To these I will return; but I now go on to examine the rest.

No, not to examine all; for some are to be dismissed without examination. Mr Birt actually cites inscriptions, and pulls from the sortes of *carm. epigr.* 331 such a mock hexameter as 'de incerto certa ne fiant si sapis caueas'. Inscriptions are a garden of illiteracy where anyone who relishes violations of metre or accidence or syntax may fill his hands with nosegays of all the horrors dearest to his heart; they will lengthen any short syllable to please Mr Birt and shorten any long syllable to please Mr Lindsay; in *carm.* 422, apparently no later than Hadrian, Mr Birt might have found within the compass of 19 lines no fewer than 6 lengthenings of final short *a*, *saeuā*, *magnā*, *sacrā*, *inmensā turbā*, *omnigenā*.

Then he plunges down to the sixth century and dredges up what he supposes to be an example from Maximianus. He need not have dived quite so deep, for

---

[1] If we are to believe the *thes. ling. Lat.*, there is another in *anth. Lat. Ries.* 439 1 'quid saeuis, *Cyparē*? domiti modo terga iuuenci', for Mr Reisch says 'Cyparus *nom. uir. gr.*'. But *Cypare*, as usual, is feminine: the poem is addressed to a woman who has seduced a boy and finds him a backward lover; addressed to a man it would be absurd.

on p. 395 of Mueller's *de r. m.* ed. 2 he might have found '*discē* conponere' and '*labor et curā* mea sunt' from Ausonius and '*resignassē* sursum' and '*arguerē* iam' from Prudentius. But Maximianus' '*superciliā* frons' is not an example; it is no more an example than the '*populeā* frus' which he does not cite from Ennius or the '*seruarē* frustra' which he does not cite from Tibullus. Lengthening before a mute and liquid in the next word, rare in the classical age, grows frequent from Prudentius onward: a single poem of Sidonius, as good a versifier as Maximianus and earlier in date, provides five specimens of the licence, VII 13 '*emeritā* trabeis', 237 '*Sauromatā* clipeo', 276 '*exererē* gladium', 277 '*turbā* graue', 376 '*spatiā* princeps'.

And here I remark that two more of Mr Birt's examples are similarly invalid, even on the face of them. If Propertius did write '*oppositā* propellens...nostra' in II 29 39 and Martial '*Caesareā* praestitit' in *spect.* 28 10, everybody except Mr Birt and the docile youth of Marburg will explain those ‖ lengthenings in the same way. And these too, which Mr Birt would have cited if they had not escaped him:

Ouid. *met.* VII 569: nec sitis *extinctā* prius est quam uita bibendo (cod. opt. et plerique).

Manil. I 90: semper enim ex aliis *aliā* proseminat usus.

Aetn. 290: si *fortē* flexere caput tergoque feruntur.

Quint. Ser. 28: *inductā* prosunt et eodem balsama pacto.

Another example to be brushed aside as merely futile is the *Dodonā*[1] of *Aetn.* 6. Here again I can supply Mr Birt with matter which he has not found for himself. I recommend him to add *Priap.* 75 1 '*Dodonā* tibi, Iuppiter, sacrata est' and Manil. IV 634 'et genetrix *Cretā* ciuem sortita Tonantem', and I condole with him that the scribes have not similarly substituted the Latin form for *Dodonē* in Claud. III *cons. Hon.* 117 nor for *Cretē* in Ouid. *met.* VIII 118. And why does he neglect the five examples of *Hecubā* which are proffered him by the best MSS or by all MSS at Ouid. *met.* XIII 423, 549, 556, *Il. Lat.* 551, 1017? But now we come to something worse than mere futility.

When a metrical anomaly is in question, and examples are cited to vindicate it, those examples are illegitimate in which the anomaly does not stand alone but is accompanied by bad grammar or bad sense or both. Such verses are of necessity corrupt; to remove the corruption might reform the metre; and a competent and impartial critic, in seeking a correction, will take for his first hypothesis, not to be discarded till it has been tried, that the metrical anomaly is part and parcel of the corruption, not a casual and innocent bystander. Mr Birt, though he has written 240 pages on *Kritik und Hermeneutik*, does not know this,

---

[1] I accept, for the sake of argument, the assumption that Dodona was the place which the author named.

and has no intention of learning it from me; but among critics it is a common-place, and he may find it enunciated in his own tongue by a genuine metrist, Mr Paul Maas, *Griechische Metrik* § 142: 'eine Metrik, die. . . bei grammatischen Verderbnissen metrische Anomalien aufzeigt und dazu führt, beide zugleich zu beseitigen,. . . wird einleuchtender sein als jene, für die nur wenig darauf ankommt, ob ein Text heil oder verdorben, alt oder jung ist.'[1] When Mr Birt cites Iuu. x 54, he cites a sentence of which nobody has ever yet made sense, 'ergo *superuacuā* aut perniciosa petuntur | propter quae fas est genua incerare deorum'; and critics in whom a distaste for nonsense is not altogether over-powered by a taste for false quantities have proposed alterations which cure both ills at once and remove the metrical anomaly by the mere act of restoring coherency to the thought. He might almost as well cite the spurious verse found in most MSS between xiv 1 and 2,

et quod maiorum *uitiā* sequiturque minores,

without trying to construe it; he might quite as well cite, and certainly would have cited unless he had overlooked it, viii 105, ||

inde *Dolabellā* | atque hinc Antonius, inde,

where again the sense halts no less than the metre, and Lachmann's *atque dehinc* (**hinc one MS of the eleventh century), whether right or not, sets both together on a sound footing. But another of his examples deserves to be examined at greater length.

Prop. iv 5 64 is printed as follows not only by Mr Birt but by the last German editors Mr Rothstein and Mr Hosius:

his animum nostrae dum uersat Acanthis amicae
per tenues *ossā* sunt numerata cutes.

All three[2] adduce as parallel ii 13 25 'sat mea sit *magnā* si tres sint pompa libelli', and I have already signified that they might also adduce iv 1 101 'Iunonis *facitē* uotum inpetrabile, dixi'. Let it be assumed then that the verse is metrically correct. And now, how do they propose to interpret it? The bones of somebody or other were counted, not through his skin, but through his *skins*. What of this plural? Not a word from the defenders. The *thes. ling. Lat.* has reached *cutis*, so that if a parallel exists it ought to be found there. And there, to be sure, Mr Gudeman proffers us no fewer than fifteen parallels, or what he takes for such: 'pluralis legitur, Prop. iv 5 64, Mela ii 14, Plin. *nat.* vii 12' – and then Tertullian and Arnobius and the like. But if anyone took the trouble to read these passages, this is what he would find: Mel. ii 14 'Geloni *hostium*

---

[1] The truth is more fully stated in relation to a particular case at *Die neuen Responsionsfreiheiten* I p. 3.
[2] Only Mr Rothstein was likely to adduce iv 3 44.

cutibus equos seque uelant', Plin. *n.h.* VII 12 'Anthropophagos...ossibus humanorum *capitum* bibere *cutibusque* cum capillo pro *mantelibus* ante pectora uti', and so forth: they are passages where the plural form, as might be expected, has the plural sense. The only exceptions, the only parallels to Prop. IV 5 64, are one instance, III 25, from the *historia persecutionum* of Victor Vitensis at the end of the fifth century, and one[1] from the uncouth *mulomedicina Chironis* §707. But suppose we condone *cutes* as we have condoned *ossa*: what does the verse mean? who was skin and bone? According to the Latin it was either Acanthis or Cynthia. Cynthia it certainly was not; Acanthis, who afterwards died of a pulmonary complaint, may perhaps have been skin and bone already, but Propertius did not say so here, for in the next line he begins his account of her death with *sed*: 'sed cape torquatae, Venus o regina, columbae | ob meritum ante tuos guttura secta focos'. Everyone recognises that the words must refer to Propertius, which the text does not allow. And the lengthening of a short final vowel is to be established by such evidence as this, – a verse containing a barbarism and not containing sense. This is the frame of mind in which Tereus ravished Philomela: concupiscence concentrated on its object and indifferent to all beside. ‖

If anyone tries to amend an unsound reading, its friends immediately attack the correction in the belief that they are defending the text. But I shall not let that deter me from discussing this passage further, because most of the attempts to correct it reveal no more notion of scientific method than Mr Birt's ardent embracement of the corruption. More than one scholar has proposed to insert the interjection *a* after *ossa*. This does not even aim at mending anything but the metre, and fails to mend even that. In order to remove a false quantity it introduces a forbidden elision.[2] The only parallel that I know of in any classical poet later than Catullus is *cons. Liu.* 76 'ultima: sit fati haec summa querella tui', where the MSS are of the fifteenth century and *haec* is quite superfluous; though of course examples of this and of all malpractices may be found in inscriptions, as *carm. epigr.* 986 8 'linquentem uitae et commoda militiae' and 1136 6 'omnia mecum uno hoc composui tumulo'. Hertzberg paid some heed to the sense, and made the verse refer to Propertius by writing 'per tenues ossa *has* sunt numerata cutes'; but this commits the same offence, and *cutes* still sticks fast. The only conjecture which cures everything is Jacob's 'per *tenuem* ossa *mihi* sunt numerata *cutem*', and the change was easier than it may seem,

---

[1] One, not three; for in 220 the sense as well as the form is plural, and in 669, 'ut ipsa ponderi deprimatur ad spinam cutes', *cutes* is nom. sing., a form which Mr Gudeman neglects to register.

[2] The observation which forbids it, though made so long ago as 1861 by Lucian Mueller *de r. m.* p. 300, is not yet universally known; and just as Schneidewin had conjectured 'aut aperi faciem aut tu tunicata laua' at Mart. III 3 4, so did Friedlaender afterwards conjecture 'os hominis, mulsum et me rogat Hippocrates' ib. IX 94 2, and Dr Postgate 'miramur, facili ut temperat arte manus' at Prop. II 1 10. All three conjectures have a second vice, in that they end the first half of the pentameter with words which are not allowed to stand there.

ossa m̊, ossam, ossā, and *-es . . .-es* to restore some sort of metre. The rhythm, though not usual, is that of 66 'ob meritum ante tuos', and support is lent by the parallel of Ouid. *trist.* IV 6 42 'uix habeo tenuem quae tegat ossa cutem'. But when a good conjecture has been made, some would-be improver will often turn it into a bad one; and here Palmer removes from Jacob's reading the necessary *mihi* and substitutes a superfluous *suam*.

But with Prop. IV 5 64 we are not yet at the worst. Here Mr Birt merely shuts his eyes to the attendant vices of sense and grammar. In Mart. *spect.* 28 10 he admits that the text is corrupt, and alters it; but he is careful to exempt from alteration the metrical anomaly, and keeps it as the apple of his eye.

> quidquid et in circo spectatur et amphitheatro
> diues *Caesareā*[1] praestitit unda tibi.

His remarks are contained in a footnote on p. 111 of his *Jugendverse und Heimatpoesie Vergils*, and the following is the show of reason under which he gratifies his wishes. 'Dieser Martialvers bietet zweierlei Anstoss, da erstlich zu *tibi* ein Vokativ fehlt und zweitens der poetische Sprachgebrauch verbietet dass ein Substantiv (*unda*) zwei Epitheta erhalte.' – This, I must ‖ observe in parenthesis, is quite false: Catull. 4 9 'trucem Ponticum sinum', Verg. *Aen.* x 408 'horrida acies Volcania', Prop. III 3 9 sq. 'pugnam sinistram Cannensem' are exact parallels to 'diues Caesarea unda'; and the truth is that any noun can have two epithets provided that one is descriptive and the other possessive. – '*Caesarea* aber ist richtig; vgl. *Caesaris unda*, Spectac. 25 2. Also muss *diues* fallen, und es wird zu emendiren sein: *Diue, id Caesarea praestitit unda tibi*, wobei *diue* auf den Nereus (v. 7) zurückweist; ein *id* aber konnte sich Martial ebensogut gestatten wie ein *is* (14 145 u. 2 30 5).' On this score Mr Birt need not trouble his head, and if he had looked at the right page of Friedlaender's index instead of the wrong one he would have found there five examples of *id*. As for his conjecture, I pass over the point that the vocative *diue*, in contrast to *diua*, is extremely rare,[2] and that Martial, if Friedlaender can be trusted, uses no case of the masculine but the genitive plural, and I only call it a preposterous conjecture. Nereus has been casually mentioned, together with Triton and Thetis and Galatea, in this description of the naumachia, and Mr Birt pretends that he was the person for whom the pageant was displayed. We know that he was not, and we know who that person was. The metrically anomalous *Caesarea* contains the vocative which *tibi* requires and the only vocative which *praestitit*

---

[1] Lucian Mueller *de r. m.* ed. 2 p. 390 explains the lengthening as due to the following mute and liquid; and, if *Caesarea* made sense, it would not be incredible that Martial, who ventures on the lengthening '*Romanā* stringis' even ἐν ἄρσει, v 69 3, should here venture even on the lengthening '*Caesareā* praestitit'.

[2] But Ouid. *trist.* III 1 78 should be added to the list in *thes. ling. Lat.* v p. 1652 20 and deleted at 1655 7–9, where its place may be filled by *anth. Lat. Ries.* 423 3.

tibi admits; and while prejudice, trying to talk the language of an open and enquiring mind, says '*Caesarea* ist richtig' and appeals to *Caesaris unda* 25 2, a disinterested critic will recall other parallels: *spect.* 5 3 sq. '*Caesar,...quidquid* fama canit, *praestat* harena *tibi*', 9 1 sq. '*praestitit...tibi, Caesar,...*proelia rhinoceros', 21 1 sq. '*quidquid* in Orpheo Rhodope *spectasse* theatro | *dicitur, exhibuit, Caesar,* harena *tibi*', 1 14 1 sq. '*Caesar,...*hoc etiam *praestat* harena *tibi*'. Such a critic was Heinsius, and he conjectured *Caesar, io*; not rightly, but the difference between hitting and missing is a trifle compared with the difference between missing and never aiming. My own proposal was made in 1907, *Journ. Phil.* xxx p. 231 ⟦this edition pp. 712–13⟧.

Mr Birt, to do him justice, is by no means the only person who comports himself in this fashion on the territory common to metrical science and textual criticism; and the lesson, how not to treat an anomaly, can be learnt even better from another example. There is no dispute among prosodists that *mel* is short. Lucian Mueller *de r. m.* ed. 2 p. 391 cites Ouid. *ex Pont.* IV 2 9 'quis *mĕl* Aristaeo' and Appul. *apol.* 9 'meum *mĕl* et haec', and might have cited also G.L.K. VI p. 86 10 'apes legunt *mĕl* ex rosa', described by Apthonius as 'duas iambicas coniugationes'. But he overlooked a verse in which the sole MS and all editions present *mel* as long. *anth. Lat. Ries.* 458 is a poem with the title 'interdum et neglectam formam placere', perhaps by Seneca, certainly by a good writer of a good age; and it contains this couplet, 7 sq.,

uincula nec curet capitis discussa soluti
et coram faciem *mēl* habet illa suam. ‖

Now a critic and metrist ought to consider, before anything else, that this lengthening occurs in an ungrammatical and meaningless verse; he ought therefore to suspect it, and in correcting the verse he ought to remove it if he can. But all editors so correct the verse as to preserve the false quantity: they all write 'mel habet illa *suum*' (or *suom*), and are thus committed to further alterations, the least bad of which is Heyne's '*me* coram: *facies* mel habet illa *suum*'. Methodical emendation will emend everything, metre as well as sense and grammar, with much less change:

et coram faciem me lauet illa suam,[1]

'let her wash her face when I am by', which she will not do if it is painted. After I had been at the pains of making this correction I found, as usual, that

---

[1] Why not *faciem coram*? Perhaps to avoid rhyming a declinable with an indeclinable word (see Lachmann on Prop. 1 5 20); perhaps merely to obtain the regular equipoise of substantive and adjective; or perhaps this poet thought, though Ovid did not, that a preposition and its case cohere so closely when in contact as to interfere with the division of the verse. Their separation is often much wider, as in Tib. 1 6 30 '*contra* quis ferat arma *deos*?'

it had been made by Heinsius;[1] yet no editor accepts it, and the two last do not
⟦so⟧ much as mention it.

But to proceed. Mr Birt's 'Maecenaselegie I 139: Nestoris *annosa* uicisses
saecula si me' is a false citation. What the MSS really give is this,

Nestoris *annosa uixissem* saecula, si me
dispensata tibi stamina *nempe* forent;

and it is nonsense. Editors have restored *annosi, uicisses, nente*. The metrical
anomaly is not here indeed an integral part of the corruption of the sentence,
and there is nothing against *annosa* except its prosody; but when we are invited
to trust MSS in a place where they show themselves thus untrustworthy, the
net is spread in the sight of the bird.

In *catalept.* 9 60 'Cynthius et *Musā*, Bacchus et Aglaie' it is only half the
MSS, though the better half, that give *Musa* for *Musae*; and, to show of what
account the MSS are, they all give *egiale* or worse for *Aglaie*. Mr Birt says 'Im
Interesse der Konzinnität steht hier nun auch *Musa* im Singular', and I agree:
I think it was introduced by a scribe who shared Mr Birt's notion of concinnity.
Cynthius and *Bacchus* are singular because they are the names of individuals:
Aglaie is an individual name substituted by synecdoche for the plural *Gratiae*:
what concinnity requires is either a similar synecdoche, such as *Clio*, or the
plural *Musae*, usually found thus associated with Apollo. The requirements of
concinnity and of metre therefore coincide, as might be expected. And one word
more. These same MSS, not half of them but all, give Verg. *Priap.* 2 2 thus,

ego *aridā*, uiator, ecce populus.

But not even Mr Birt believes that the vowel can be lengthened in these circumstances; he calls it 'unmöglich', and inserts an *o* like other editors. Does this
teach him no lesson? ‖

I have said already that '*oppositā* propellens' in Prop. II 29 39, if the MS
reading of that verse were true, would admit another explanation than Mr
Birt's. But no editor accepts the reading, and no connoisseur will ever accept it.
Put aside all question of the quantity, and compare this, 'dixit et opposita
propellens sauia *nostra* | prosilit' (in which *opposita* is to be nom. fem.), with
the received text 'opposita propellens sauia *dextra*', and say which hexameter is
like Propertius and which is unlike him; and then confirm your judgment
with the parallel of Hor. *epod.* 3 21 'manum puella sauio opponat tuo'. *dextra*
(*destra*) and *nostra* are both much like *uestra* and therefore something like one
another: at Ouid. *trist.* I 7 36 the MSS vary between *nostra, uestra,* and *dextra,*
and at Stat. *silu.* v 5 83 editors cannot agree whether the *uestra* of M should be
changed to *dextra* (*destra* exc. Polit.) or to *nostra* (ed. princ.).

---

[1] At Ouid. *art.* III 216; but he quite mistook the sense and wrote *nec* for *et*.

Mr Birt's remaining citation from Propertius, II 13 25 *magnā*, brings us at last to the legitimate examples which on an earlier page I set apart for future consideration; examples in which nothing but the prosody is anomalous, and which cannot therefore be instantly challenged as invalid. What has to be considered and estimated is their weight.

Three of them are taken respectively from Propertius, Tibullus, and the *ciris*. The MSS of Propertius and Tibullus are late and bad, and those of the *ciris* are abominable. Such MSS cannot furnish strong evidence for anything: their readings, even when faultless, are often false. Those MSS of Horace which in *carm.* III 10 5 sq. give 'nemus | inter pulchra *situm* tecta' are far older and better than any of these, and there is nothing in *situm* to awake suspicion; it would now be standing in all texts if superior MSS did not tell us that Horace wrote *satum*. Much less then should anomalies be accepted upon such authority. All MSS of Propertius at III 8 37 give the anomalous form *tendisti* for *tetendisti*: by mere accident we learn from two grammarians that what Propertius wrote was *nexisti*. As better MSS become available, anomalies tend to disappear; and not anomalies only but even rarities. Lucian Mueller *de r. m.* ed. 2 p. 406 cites from Persius two examples of lengthening at the caesura, one of which is VI 26 'emole. quid *metuīs?* occa, et seges altera in herba est'; but the best MS has *metuas*. If at *ciris* 189 we had the help even of the twelfth century MS which contains 454–541, who can be sure that it would confirm the fifteenth century MSS in their 'tanto *scelerē* damnare puellam', when it convicts them at 481 of writing *uexauit et aegros* for *uexarier undis?* And if we are to trust their scansion of *scelerē*, why are we not to trust their scansion of 'inde *măgno* geminat *Iōuī*' in 374? The MSS of Tibullus which give *agricolā* at I 7 61 give also *medicandŏ* at III 6 3; but that is not the sort of false quantity in which Mr Birt takes pleasure, so instead of defending it with *uincendŏ* and *petendŏ* and *lugendŏ* from Seneca and *uigilandŏ* from Juvenal he rejects it as 'unmöglich' (*Krit. u. Herm.* p. 140).

In the examples from Tibullus and Propertius there is yet another element of weakness. To correct *tanto scelere* into *tanti sceleris* at *ciris* 189 may be called rough treatment, justified only by the known and proved badness of the || MSS. But the *agricolā* of Tib. I 7 61 and the *magnā* of Prop. II 13 25 can so easily be removed that they would carry little weight as evidence even if the MSS were better than they are. In Tib. I 7 61 the repetition of a letter, 'agricola *a* (Baehrens, *e* Itali) magna cum uenerit urbe', at once gets rid of the anomaly and gives a much more usual construction, and the verse then resembles II 4 21. In Prop. II 13 25 Baehrens' 'sat mea sic magna*st* si tres sint pompa libelli' is again a gentle change. It is insufferable that Mr Birt should say, as he does in *Jugend-verse* p. 111, 'schon der Konjunktiv im Konditionalsatz *si tres sint* erfordert auch im Hauptsatz das *sit magna*, das in den Handschriften steht; ein *magna est* trägt einen plumpen Fehler hinein': the construction is illustrated in the grammars, Cic. *de am.* 40 'turpis...excusatio est...si quis contra rem publicam se amici causa fecisse fateatur.' His objection to the present tense beside *sequēris* and other futures is equally dispelled by such passages as Cic. *Att.* XII 29 2 'si quid erit, magnum est adiumentum'. But when, after saying, as we have seen, that the conjunctive in the protasis requires *sit magna* in the apodosis too, he goes on to call this *sit* 'Optativ' and to compare the optatives of I 17 10 and IV 11 81, I cannot imagine what opinion he really holds. It is ridiculous to say that a conjunctive in protasis 'erfordert', and 'erfordert auch', an optative in apodosis.

The best authenticated of all the examples is Verg. *Aen.* III 464 'dona dehinc auro *grauiā* sectoque elephanto'. Not only is it presented by MSS of the fourth century, but the lengthening is noticed by Seruius. Yet Schaper's conjecture

> dona dehinc auro grauia *ac* secto elephanto

is more than plausible, because in removing the anomaly it brings the verse nearer to its Homeric model, *Od.* XVIII 196 and XIX 564 πριστοῦ ἐλέφαντος. If *ac* were absorbed by *grauia*, a scribe inserting the necessary conjunction would be quite as likely to write *sectoque* and remove the hiatus as to write *et secto* and avoid the lengthening.

Aen. XII 648 'sancta ad uos *animā* atque istius inscia culpae' has almost equal authority from the MSS, but Seruius neither remarks upon the lengthening, though in combination with hiatus it is doubly remarkable, nor cites it at III 464 as a parallel to *grauiā*, which he treats as unique: it may be however that he elided the *-a* and lengthened the *-us*. His lemma, so far as it goes, agrees with Virgil's MSS, and the verse appears in the same form at Macr. *Sat.* III 3 6; but this may possibly be due to that interpolation from the current text of classics which in Seruius' citation of Hor. *carm.* II 18 30 at *Aen.* VI 152 has substituted (except in one MS) the *fine* of Horace's vulgate for the *sede* which Seruius wrote. The conjectures of Lachmann and Munro are not worth mentioning; the *nescia* of certain later MSS, adopted by several editors, is rather high-handed, because it is hard to say why any scribe who found *nescia* should alter it to *inscia*; though on the other hand it is no less ‖ hard to say why Virgil, having it in his power to write *nescia*, should write *inscia* instead. But an easier change will set the metre right:

> sancta adque istius ad uos anima inscia culpae
> descendam.

The form *adque* is frequent in Virgil's MSS and is here given by R: a scribe glances from the first to the second *ad* and writes

> sancta ad uos anima inscia culpae,

adque istius is added in the margin and then inserted in the wrong place. The lengthening of short final *us* in caesura is well established: the closest parallel is *georg.* IV 453 'non te *nulliūs* exercent numinis irae'; and Seruius, who makes no comment on the scansion there, would naturally make none here. Neither *istĭus* nor *istīus* occurs elsewhere in Virgil, but *illius* and *ipsius* have their penultimate long or short as required.

The most stubborn, in external appearance, of all the examples is that furnished by the good or at least respectable MSS of Ouid. *amor.* III 7 55, 'sed, puto, non *blandā*, non optima perdidit in me | oscula'. The transposition of Heinsius and many editors, 'sed non blanda, puto', fails for two reasons: *puto* in Ovid, who uses it more than thirty times, invariably has its final syllable short, and its proper place is immediately after the conjuction, as in u. 2 'at, puto'. Later conjectures, *blanda haec* or *est* Riese, *blande* Ehwald, are contemptible. And all are gratuitous, for the supposed anomaly is an empty phantom. No short syllable is lengthened here. The passage runs thus, 53–6:

> a tenera quisquam sic surgit mane puella
>   protinus ut sanctos possit adire deos?
> sed, puto, non blanda: non optima perdidit in me
>   oscula, non omni sollicitauit ope.

blanda is abl. fem. in agreement with the *puella* of 53, and the sense is 'sed, puto, non blanda a puella sic surrexi'. The construction is loose, but quite natural, and resembles Cic. II *Verr.* II 174 'possumne magis rem iudicatam adferre, magis reum condemnatum in iudicium adducere? at quorum iudicio condemnatum?' that is 'at quorum iudicio condemnatum hunc adduco?'

There are now left, of Mr Birt's list, only the two archaic examples, *aquilā* from Ennius and *desertā* from the epigram on Plautus; and it is by no means incredible that Ennius, in imitation of such Homeric scansions as an anapaestic Βαλίε *Il.* XIX 400 or ὁπόσα XXIV 7, made *aquila* an anapaest in the verse cited by Probus, and that the epigrammatist followed his lead and made *deserta* a molossus, as ἄσπαρτα is a molossus in *Od.* IX 109; for Ennius ventured upon other injudicious experiments in metre which were not destined to succeed. Keil's insertion of *in* after *aquila* is improbable: in the epigram *deserta scaena est* would be easy enough. ||

My object has not been to controvert the opinion that short final vowels were lengthened; it has been to show how flimsy is the evidence arrayed in support of that opinion, and to reprobate the temper of mind which finds such evidence sufficient. What sort of evidence does suffice may be seen in that one class of such lengthenings which is proven and beyond dispute. That the conjunction *que* was lengthened ἐν θέσει in the 2nd and 5th feet of the hexameter is a conclusion established by thirty-four examples,[1] all unimpeachable. Half of them, being in Virgil, have the best possible MS authority. Not one of them is attended by any error in grammar or defect of sense. All of them are surrounded by severe restrictions: the preceding word must fill a whole foot, the following word must be a spondee or an anapaest, and a second *que* must be subjoined; and furthermore the lengthening is confined to a few authors. What a contrast! Look back upon the examples here passed in review: seldom strongly attested, often discovered in bad company, sparse in comparison yet not obeying similar rules, till one cannot but wonder why the poets were thus sparing and thus capricious in resorting to a licence which, if they indeed possessed it, must have been so very convenient and seductive, especially in words ending with three short syllables. A contention founding itself upon such evidence deserves worse names than unscientific and unmethodical; it is something remote from serious disputation and even from honest enquiry.

[1] 17 in Virgil, 12 in Ovid's *metamorphoses*, 5 in other poets; 22 with a double consonant or a mute and liquid following, 12 without.

145

AN AFRICAN INSCRIPTION*

In 1914 Mr Héron de Villefosse published in the *Comptes Rendus* of the Académie des Inscriptions, p. 599, the remains of twenty Latin hexameters from a broken and cemented stone at Souhilia in Tunis, with the warning that the squeeze taken is not a good one and that some letters, especially at the beginning and end of lines, are doubtful. The inscription was reproduced in 1923 by Messrs Cagnat and Merlin in their *Inscriptions Latines d'Afrique*, no. 485, and in 1926 by Mr E. Lommatzsch in the supplement to Buecheler's *carmina Latina epigraphica*, no. 2296. These reproductions do not faithfully preserve the dimensions of the gaps in the facsimile; and I should add that the facsimile itself, if trustworthy, shows that the left-hand margin of the verses was not a perpendicular line.

They are an epitaph on a gladiator who was cut off in a promising career at the age of 26, 'ui]xit an. xxvi men. v dies x[', and the dead man is himself the speaker. But the supplements of the three editors give no coherency to the whole nor even a just sense to all the parts; and I therefore offer this restoration, omitting four verses which are too much broken to be mended, except that the first of them seems to contain the man's name, 'Cloe[*lius*]'. My own supplements are in italics.

>]statuae donatus [honore
> *pal*]mas Agnus habet Karthaginis u[*rbe sacratas*:
> *sic ha*]bitum referunt, sic membra de[*centia, fortis* ‖
> *sic an*]imae rigidos imitantur marmo[ra uultus.
> *illum*] ego discipulus primis imita[tus ab annis   5
>
> .   .   .   .   .   .
>
> commerui nam primitias, et fortia [*ferro*   10
> *cla*]rueram nudus prosternens corp[*ora tecta*;
> *nec*, Ph]oebe, tibi, diua, queam reputare qu[*ot annos*,
> qu]ot raptus leto iuuenes, quot stamina [*donem*.
> pa]rua meae nimium durae torsere So[rores,
> . . .]ida nam leto tradunt ingloria t[15
> dec]reta et celeres rapiunt mihi mun[
> felix,] heu nimium felix, si munere in ip[so

* [[*CR* 41 (1927), 60–1]]

percussu]s pulchram peterem per uul[nera mortem.
nunc] genetrix complexa sinu hic corp[us *humauit*,
20   et di]cet titulo nomen per saecul[a saxum.

In verse 4 I have written *imae rigidos* for the unmetrical *ima frigidos*; in 13 I have retained *raptus*, tacitly altered to *raptos* in the two last editions; and in 19 I have adopted Mr Lommatzsch's *complexa* for *comnexa*.

1–5. He begins with a mention of his trainer, whose victories in the arena are commemorated by a life-like statue at Carthage. *Agnus* is the proper name better spelt *Hagnus*.

10 f. He was a retiarius, and had already killed more than one secutor.

12 f. He cannot tell how many men's lives and limbs his premature death allows the Moon to retain in her dominion; that is, how many more men he would have killed if he had lived longer. In popular astrology the Moon is parent and mistress of the body: Firm. *math.* v praef. 5 'Luna...humanorum corporum mater', Seru. *Aen.* xi 51 'cum nasci coeperimus, sortimur a Sole spiritum, a Luna corpus', Macr. *Sat.* i 19 17 'Luna τύχη, quia corporum praesul est, quae fortuitorum uarietate iactantur', Paul. Alex. fol. κ 3 [[p. 49 Boer]] (*C.C.A.G.* i p. 168 22–9) τῇ φύσει ἡ μὲν Cελήνη τύχη καθέστηκεν...καὶ ἡ μὲν τύχη σημαίνει τὰ περὶ τοῦ σώματος ἅπαντα καὶ τὰς κατὰ τὸν βίον πράξεις.

14. *parua* stamina. *meae Sorores* has a clumsy ambiguity, but means the same as Iuu. ix 135 sq. 'mea Clotho | et Lachesis'.

15 f. are perhaps best completed thus, '*call*]ida nam leto tradunt ingloria t[erga | dec]reta et celeres rapiunt mihi mun[era *Parcae*' ('celeres Parcae' Stat. *Theb.* viii 328 and 439), *decreta* then agreeing with *munera*. The word at the end of 15 must be a substantive and the object of *tradunt*; but Mr Lommatzsch's *texta* is impossible, if only because the Fates are spinners and not weavers. *callida terga*, if right, will refer, as *nudus* does, to the retiarius' fashion of fighting, Iuu. ii 144 'fuga', viii 206 'fugit', Isid. *orig.* xviii 55 'secutor ab insequendo retiarium dictus'. But *decreta* may be a substantive and the subject of *tradunt*, and the letters lost at the beginning of 15 seem to be three rather than four, so that another possibility is '*inu*]ida', that is 'inuida decreta leto tradunt ingloria terga'. I can think of no epithet having the right length and suiting *terga*, for *uiuida* will hardly do.

18. Several other words might be put in the place of *percussus*, but the *perculsus* of the three editors is not one of them.

19. The hiatus has plenty of parallels in Virgil and Juvenal and others, and Mr Lommatzsch in avoiding it has fabricated a horrid verse.

I add remarks on a few other inscriptions in Mr Lommatzsch's supplement to Buecheler.

2041 (*C.I.L.* VIII 24658) 1 f.

>]odeum g[.]o[. . .] atl[. .]t[. .]s
>]sum tollit[.]n a[. .]ra capu[

Buecheler writes

> miretur uetus ord]o deum, c[h]o[rus] Atl[an]t[eu]s,
> hoc opus ut cel]sum tollit [i]n a[st]ra capu[t.

But as this inscription was found 'Carthagine in colle qui uocatur odei', it would be strange if *odeum* were not what it seems; and anyhow 'ordo deum, chorus Atlanteus' is an impossible apposition, and 'chorus Atlanteus' could only mean the Pliades or the Hyades. The word indicated is 'g[l]o[bus]', and the theme of the epigram was probably an Atlas carrying on his shoulders a celestial globe, like the Farnese statue at Naples (Thiele, *Antike Himmelsbilder*, taf. II). The form of the sentence may have been something like

> condecorans ecce] Odeum globus Atlanteus
> cognata excel]sum tollit in astra caput.

2062 (*C.I.L.* IV 3932, Engstroem 286)

The pentameter will be completed by inserting the letters *re uolo* from *C.I.L.* IV 2210 (Buech. p. 824) and *Priap.* 38 3.

2292, p. 155, lately exhumed at Pompei.

> nihil durare potest tempore perpetuo.
> cum bene sol nituit, redditur oceano.
> decrescit Phoebe, quae modo plena fuit.
> Venerum feritas saepe fit dura leuis.

Mr Lommatzsch appends this note:

> '1 lege *nil.* u. 1–3 aliunde sumptos credas (ex poeta neoterico?), si reputes quam rudis iste fuerit poeta in u. 4. *Veneres* inuenit Catullus.'

The first three verses show clearly how to correct the sense, language, and metre of the fourth. What the man meant to write was

> uentorum feritas saepe fit aura leuis.

146

REVIEW: F. BOLL, *STERNGLAUBE UND STERNDEUTUNG, ED.* 3*

In its first two editions this book was a sketch of the theory and history of astrology from the Babylonians to the present day, intended for the general public and printed in the German character. Boll died in 1924, and it now appears in Roman type with a page greatly enlarged and illustrations increased in number and improved in quality; and its length is much more than doubled by *Nachträge* and *Zusätze*.

The original portion is little altered, and some errors are repeated. P. 45: || 'Umlaufzeit durch den Tierkreis, von Frühlingspunkt zu Frühlingspunkt' is said to be 88 days for Mercury and 225 for Venus. This mistake is often made by scholars ignorant of the sky, but an astronomer like Boll should have avoided it. These are the times of the two planets' revolutions round the Sun in the Copernican system: the time of their passage through the zodiac is of course on an average the same as the Sun's, one year. P. 50: Jupiter is twice said to be moist, and is then included among the dry planets. P. 53: Sagittarius is said to be Chiron 'nach griechischer Deutung'. This identification is rare and heretical: in orthodoxy Chiron is the Centaurus Australis, and Sagittarius is not always even a centaur.

The additions, most of which are Mr Gundel's, have changed the scope and nature of the work, and it is now not merely a popular epitome but a repertory for students of the subject in detail, especially if they wish to know of things which have come to light since the publication of Bouché-Leclercq's *Astrologie Grecque* in 1899. But here also there are errors, as indeed a reader of Mr Gundel's writings might expect.

P. 120: that the fixed stars are not all on one plane is said to be 'als spezielle Doktrin der Stoiker überliefert (Diels Doxogr. S. 344)'. This is exactly contrary to truth. The Stoics held that the seven planets are on seven planes and all the fixed stars on an eighth. If the words πρὸ τῶν ἑτέρων (ἀστέρων) τοὺς ἑτέρους ἐν ὕψει καὶ βάθει (κεῖσθαι) required elucidation, they would receive it from Diels p. 466 (Chrysipp. ap. Stob.) τετάχθαι τὰ μὲν ἀπλανῆ ἐπὶ μιᾶς ἐπι-

* ⟦*Sternglaube und Sterndeutung*. By Franz Boll, 3rd edition by W. Gundel. Pp. xii + 211. Leipzig and Berlin: B. G. Teubner, 1926. *CR* 41 (1927), 70–1⟧

φανείας, ὡς καὶ ὁρᾶται · τὰ δὲ πλανώμενα ἐπ' ἄλλης καὶ ἄλλης σφαίρας; and when Manilius says at I 408 that Sirius (a fixed star) is further away than the Sun (a planet), that is no divergence. But this falsehood is pretty sure to be repeated, because it is needed for the defence of Manil. I 394. P. 129: 'Catal. cod. astr. VIII 3 S. 97, 8 aus Paulus Alexandrinus (die Stelle findet sich in den beiden Ausgaben Schatos nicht).' It is on fol. I 3 and 4 in the edition of 1586, and I have no doubt it is also in the other. P. 153: what is said of Prop. IV I 101 will deceive only those who do not read the passage. P. 193: 'der untere Halbkreis zeigt die Winterhälfte des Sonnenlaufes' is a statement which a glance at the figure (xv) will show to be false; but that is not so bad as the pretence of combining two unrelated things, the Sun's astronomical dejection at the winter solstice and his astrological dejection in Libra. P. 201: the citation of Luc. I 651 ff. is inappropriate, for Lucan says nothing about a σύνοδος of the planets; and Boll's 'Erklärung' in Sphaera p. 362, though it misrepresents him, does not misrepresent him thus.

147

REVIEW: A. BOURGERY, *LUCAIN I–V* *

This translation is not quite all that a translation should be.

The meaning of Latin words is not understood. I 442 *tonse* 'rasé', II 103 *stat cruor in templis* 'des mares de sang montent devant les temples', 430 *Sabello* 'sabin', 685 *salo* 'l'onde amère' (*sale*), 707 *ora* 'rivages' (*oras*), III 485 *perpetuam* (cratem) 'immense', 681 *pinguibus* (taedis) 'grosses', 687 *recipit fluctus* 's'engloutit dans les flots', 734 *distentis palmis* 'se tordit les mains', IV 241 *tument fauces* 'leur gosier se dilate', 664 *indulsit castris* 'installa son camp', V 132 *pressit deum* 'a chassé le dieu'. I presume that I 482 'antiques' and IV 598 'formes' are misprints (misprints are frequent), and that V 268 'du monde' for *arctois*, 570 'rivage' for *puppim*, and 768 'plus cher' for *tutius* are slips of the pen.

A word capable of two meanings is given the wrong one. I 87 *male concordes* (pestilent cabal) 'concorde peu sûre', 413 (and IV 435) *secundo* (second) 'favorable', 629 *micat* (throbs) 'brille', II 438 *cessere* (fell to the share of) *Peloro* 'se sont éloignés du Pélore', 691 *ultima* (Virgo) 'à son déclin' (she was rising), III 174 *inpiger* (Cephisos) 'diligent', 201 *sparsam profundo* (seabesprinkled) 'égarée dans les flots', IV 31 *prope* (close) 'presque', 72 f. *summus Olympi cardo* (the occident) 'le pôle de l'Olympe', 109 *medios* (zodiacal and therefore torrid) 'tempérées', 387 *frustra* (ill-advisedly) 'en vain', 496 *nostris fatis* (in our deaths) 'à nos destins', V 389 f. *nomen inane imperii* 'un titre sans pouvoir' (Caesar's consulship!). Add I 235 *tenuerunt*, II 585 *hinc* and *ad*, III 233 *post*, 465 *rapta*, 537 *summis*, IV 431 *cunctas*, V 380 *exit*, 709 *modum*.

Words are wrongly construed in the sentence. I 491 *urget* (quisque) with *impetus*, II 225 *multum* (maiore) with *coitur* (translated as *coit*), 494 *pauori* (latebras quaesisse) with *satis est*, 578 *pelagi* (metuens) with *fretum*, III 214 *desertus* (predicate) as epithet (of Orontes!), 646 *hac cum parte* (luctata) with *tulerunt*, 762 *primus* (addidit) with *uictor*, IV 371 *gurgite* (plenis) with *egens* (and *iam* rendered 'toujours'), 410 *tuta* (acc. plur.) with *fames*, V 8 *belli per munia* (uagos) with *elicit*, 125 *circum latices* (uagam) with *corripuit*, 194 f. *discriminis* (expers) with *minas* and *bellorum* (minas) with *expers*, 398 *tantum* (adverb) with

* [*Lucain: La Guerre Civile (La Pharsale)*. Tome I, Livres I–V. Texte établi et traduit par A. Bourgery. Pp. xxviii + 169 (really 338). Paris: Société d'édition 'Les belles lettres', 1926 (really 1927). *CR* 41 (1927), 189–91]]

tempus, 407 *Brundisii* (tecta) with *undas,* 720 *aquilonibus* (dative) as ablative. Particularly absurd is the translation of *incerta umbra* IV 725.

The sense and even the construction of the Latin is reversed. II 35 f. *nullis defuit aris | inuidiam factura parens* 'aucun autel ne manqua de mères, soucieuses de ne pas susciter de jalousie'; 260 f. *ne tantum...liceat feralibus armis, | has etiam mouisse manus* 'ne permettez pas...que ces mains aussi brandissent des armes funestes'; 503 f. *ingreditur pulsa fluuium statione uacantem | Caesar et ad tutas hostis* (nom.) *conpellitur arces* 'César chasse les défenseurs, entre dans le fleuve et se laisse entraîner jusqu'aux citadelles ‖ sûres de l'ennemi'; III 593 f. *nullam melius...carinae | audiuere manum* 'aucune carène n'écouta mieux la main'; IV 656–8 *sed maiora dedit cognomina collibus istis...Scipio* 'mais elle (l'antiquité) donna à ces collines un plus glorieux surnom...Scipion'; V 102–4 *hoc...numen ab humani solum* (nom.) *se labe furoris | uindicat* 'cette divinité ne s'écarte que de la souillure de la fureur humaine'; 149 f. *nullo confusae murmure uocis | instinctam sacro mentem testata furore* 'elle atteste d'une voix trop distincte que son esprit est poussé par un délire sacré'; 267 f. *fudisse cruorem | quid* (nos) *iuuat?* 'à quoi te sert d'avoir répandu le sang?'; 349–51 *quisquis mea signa relinquens | non Pompeianis tradit sua partibus arma, | hic numquam uult esse meus,* 'quand on abandonne nos enseignes même sans livrer ses armes au parti pompéien, c'est qu'on ne veut jamais être à moi' (the insertion of 'même' inverts the sense and ruins the point, as does 'seul' in IV 573); 458 f. *coepere...aequora classem | curua sequi* 'la flotte suivit les ondulations de la houle'; 546 f. *non...orbis medii puros exesa recessus* 'les pures lignes de sa courbe étaient rongées'; 694 f. *mundi iam summa tenentem | permisisse mari tantum!* 'abandonner à la mer celui qui tient l'empire du monde!' After these experiences one cannot feel sure that 'qui' at V 164 is a misprint for 'que'.

The French sometimes has hardly any relation to the Latin. In certain cases the error can be traced and analysed: II 489 f. *praecipitem cohibete ducem; uictoria nobis | hic primum stans Caesar erit* 'ici pour la première fois César restera immobile' (a whole verse skipped); III 664 *robora cum uetitis prensarent altius ulnis* 'ils cherchaient à saisir plus haut les aunes interdits' (*uetitis ulnis* translated as *uetitas alnos* and *robora* then thrown overboard); IV 22 f. *nam gurgite mixto, | qui praestat* (nomen) *terris, aufert tibi nomen Hiberus* 'car, y mêlant la masse de ses eaux, le roi de ces terres, l'Ebre, te ravit ton nom'; V 615 f. *quoties frustra pulsatos aequore montis | obruit illa dies!* 'combien de montagnes jusque-là battues des flots s'effondrèrent en ce jour!' (*quoties* mistaken for *quot* and *frustra* ignored). But oftener one is left to guess and wonder: II 126–8 *te quoque neclectum uiolatae, Scaeuola, dextrae...mactauere* 'toi aussi, Scévola, sans égard pour la main que brûla ton ancêtre, on t'égorgea'; 306 f. *utinam...deis...liceret | hoc caput...damnatum exponere* 'si seulement les dieux...me permettaient d'exposer ma tête condamnée'; III 132 *pacis ad exhaustae spolium non cogit egestas* 'la paix que tu as bannie ne t'a pas réduit à une pauvreté qui te force à nous dépouiller'; 183 *tresque petunt ueram credi Salamina carinae* 'et trois carènes gagnent Salamine qu'il faut pourtant croire véritable'; IV 34 f. *huc hostem pariter terrorque pudorque | impulit* 'dans cette ville la terreur comme la prudence à la fois saisirent l'ennemi'; 154 f. *donec decresceret umbra | in medium surgente die* 'jusqu'à ce que le jour, arrivé en son milieu, commence à décroître'; V 439 f. *nec peruia uelis | aequora frangit eques* 'le cavalier ne brise pas les flots qui lui livrent accès jusqu'aux voiles'.

Lest it should be thought that these specimens are exceptional, I will first give a bare list, itself only a selection, of other mistranslations, many of which are equally bad but cannot be exposed so briefly; and I will then examine the first page, containing only 12 verses.

I 91, 147, 451, 536, 596, II 52 f., 89, 95 f., 212, 214–17, 219, 410–12, 476, 712, 732–4, III 37, 115 f., 143, 194, 208, 251, 253 f., 259, 345 f., 524 f., 548, 624–6, 642, 670, IV 11 f., 60, 112 f., 137, 163 f., 168, 189, 243 f., 534, 615, 684, 733, 818, V 96, 355, 371 f., 385, 411, 483 f., 500–3, 505 f., 549, 602, 706 f., 746 f., 791 f.

I 4 *rupto foedere regni* (when the covenant of tyranny was broken, 86 *foedera regni*) is translated 'rompant l'unité de l'empire'. 8 f. are an exclamation in the Latin, an interrogation in the French, 10–12 an interrogation in the Latin, an affirmation in the French. The *que* of 10, being intolerable, is left untranslated, a refuge to which Mr Bourgery betakes himself again at I 681, III 78 and 327. I may also notice two annotations. '8 et 9 recte coniungi probat Sen. *n. q.* V 15 3': to say '8 et 9 recte disiungi probant Sil. || I 385, Stat. *Theb.* II 212 sq., Drac. *Rom.* V 1' would be equally false but less absurd. '11 *inulta*: -*te* Acro *carm.* I 2 51': this piece of misinformation is copied from Hosius, who took it in 1892 from some now obsolete edition of Acro.

Mr Bourgery often prints one reading or punctuation and translates another: I 397 f., 646 f., II 348, 387, 541, 595, 703, III 276, IV 217, 705, 740–2, V 211, 218, 300, 313, 576. Words, phrases, and even whole verses are left without translation at I 603, II 263 f., 462, 589, 726 f., III 35, 137 f., 320, 441, IV 58, 93, 303, 430, 633, 662, 696, 806, V 89 f., 227, 285, 380, 526, 714.

The few novelties in Mr Bourgery's text are mostly readings taken from the MS which he has made his pet, Z. One of these is *sequĕmur* II 320, which reminds me that III 722 *caecā tela manu...mittit* is rendered 'il lance de sa main...des traits aveugles'. He says on p. xvi that he has adopted Z's orthography: he does indeed adopt its false spellings *repulit, Sylla, sobole, littora, Aegeas,* but its true spellings *Suebos* and *nequiquam* he rejects. He has collated it more minutely than Hosius, and some new details, though not important, are interesting (*e.g.* V 257 *timorist*); but unfortunately his accuracy cannot be trusted. The dates of the MSS on p. xxvii disagree in four cases with those given in the preface. The explanatory notes on book I contain 28 references to other ancient authors, of which 11 are false. These notes, by the way, chiefly of a somewhat elementary nature, offer scraps of gratuitous misinformation: II 691 'en réalité Pompée partit au commencement...de l'été', III 272 *Croeso fatalis Halys* 'Crésus y fut vaincu par Cyrus', IV 322 'c'est sur l'Ida phrygien que les auteurs font habituellement pousser l'aconit', 552 'Jason sema les dents du dragon qui gardait la toison d'or', V 716 *littera* 'sans doute le lambda grec'.

In short, Mr Bourgery is not fully equipped for his task; and in consequence his numerous decisions and pronouncements on matters of interpretation and criticism, even when fortified with 'sans doute' or 'évidemment', carry no authority and are of little importance.

PROSODY AND METHOD II*

THE METRICAL PROPERTIES OF 'GN'

I choose the word *metrical* rather than *prosodical*, to make it plain at the outset that I am not concerned with the rule in Priscian – not *of* Priscian, for its irrelevance is sufficient proof of that – G.L.K. II p. 82 7–9 '*gnus* quoque uel *gna* uel *gnum* terminantia longam habent uocalem paenultimam, ut *regnum stagnum benignus malignus abiegnus priuignus Pelignus*', still less with the illegitimate inference sometimes drawn from it, that this pair of consonants, like *ns* and *nf*, lengthened a short vowel whenever they followed it. The present dispute is not about vowels but about syllables; the power of *gn* to *make position*, as they say, like *st* or *x*, and so to impede the flow of verse.

Sixty years ago it might have been thought that this question was settled. Lucian Mueller *de r. m.* pp. 315 f. said of *gn* in the body of a word 'semper porrigitur dactylicis correpta uocalis, si sequatur *gn*', and of *gn* at the beginning of a word '*gn* succedens longam efficit priorem'. Editors did not always obey this rule, but most of them obeyed it when they remembered it. Now, though some obey it still, others not only disobey it but try to overturn it; and before I go on to set forth the facts of the case and, as I hope, to reason upon them, I will give some examples of the strategy and tactics of the rebels.

I take for a starting-point H. Magnus's notes on Ouid. *met.* VI 468, where he prints with most MSS *ad mandata Prŏgnes* adding 'de positione *gn* cf. Comm. Cat. p. 193 sq. Friedrich', and on X 531, where he prints *piscosamquĕ Gnidon* adding 'cf. ad Catullum 36 13 Friedrich'. Since it thus appears that the country-men of Lachmann and Meineke regard Mr Gustav Friedrich as an authority on prosody, to that fount of doctrine let us go.

In his note on Catull. 36 13 *Anconā Gnidumque* (alternatively described as Comm. Cat. p. 193 sq.) Mr Friedrich has the following remarks.

'Das überlieferte *Gnidum* muss dem C. gelassen werden, ebenso wie *gnatis* in dem Hexameter 64, 298 *inde pater diuom sancta cum coniuge gnatisque*. Wenn man glaubt, *gn* mache im Unterschied von den andern Fällen der positio debilis stets Position, so irrt man.'

* ⟦*CQ* 22 (1928), 1–10⟧

He then rightly observes that the statement which I just now quoted from Priscian applies ostensibly only to the terminations *gnus gna gnum* and is not a statement that *gn* makes *position*, and he proceeds thus:

'Ob aber die Römer *īgnis* oder *ĭgnis* sprachen, ist nicht sicher. Jedenfalls finden wir bei Ter. *Eunuch.* 777 *quid ĭgnaue* und *CIG* I, 1060 ΚΟΓΝΙΤΟΥ.' ‖

This is very incautious, and damaging to his own case. If the vowel in *ignis* was short, the fact that in verse the syllable is always long must be due to *gn* always making position. The irrelevance of citing *quid ĭgnaue* from a scenic poet will be best exposed by citing *tibi ĕuenit* from Plaut. *merc.* 774.

'Natürlich machte *gn* noch viel weniger Position in Fällen wie *c. epigr.* 1076, wo sich unter lauter prosodisch tadellosen Versen der Hexameter findet: *paene immatura morte ereptam sibi gnatam.*'

I transcribe a few of these verses, that the reader may admire with Mr Friedrich their 'quite faultless prosody'.

> nam postquam et monumento hoc condecorauit.

That is an hexameter.

> heic sica quas rapit mortis acerba quis.

That is a pentameter.

> heu quantum mater in biciociost.

That is the pentameter belonging to Mr Friedrich's hexameter.

'Ebenso 986, 11 *quem uos inspicere et uestris ostendere gnateis.*'

Yes, in a piece which begins with the hexameter *qui legis et flores uiae carmina pia.*

'Selbstverständlich wird von der Regel Priscians auch das aus dem Griechischen stammende *cygnus* nicht getroffen, noch weniger *Progne.* Mart. 9, 103, 2 *quae capta est alio nuda Lacaena cÿgno.* So ist einhellig überliefert, –'

False: the oldest MS (E saec. x) and the family (γ) to which it belongs give *cycno*, as Lachmann at Lucr. III 7 required. But Mr Friedrich when he edited Catullus had never seen any edition of Martial but Friedlaender's, and did not know that Friedlaender's apparatus criticus was a snare and a delusion.

'– und so schreibt Friedländer, indem er anführt: *Fragm. Bobiense* (GL 7, p. 539 K): *l m n r liquidae uocantur, quia in metro saepe deficiant, ut – nuda Lacaena cygno.*'

This passage, G.L.K. VII pp. 538 f., from cod. Vindob. 16 (saec. VIII–IX), which Mr Friedrich copies out of Friedlaender with all Friedlaender's errors and omissions, really runs thus: '*l m n r* liquidae uocantur, quia in metro saepe deficiunt (not -ant): *l*, ut *neue flagella*, *m*, ut *distincta smaragdo*, *n*, ut *nuda Lacena cigno* (not *Lacaena cygno*), *r*, ut *ne desere frater*.' All therefore that the grammarian attests in the word is the *n*: it is only the MS which attests *g* for *c*, and the MS attests equally *i* for *y*, which nobody, not even Mr Friedrich, will accept, because nobody has a motive for accepting it.

He then transcribes from Friedlaender, without attempting to verify them, the following references: ||

'Auson. *epp.* 20, 8 *quid refert cornix non ideo ante cygnum*; *Mosella* 316 *măgnetis*; Petron. *c.* 131 *Prŏgne*; Val. Fl. 3, 34 *Prŏgnesson*';

which Friedlaender himself had similarly borrowed, verifying none and falsifying two, from Markland's note on Stat. *silu.* v 3 222.

What Ausonius wrote is no matter, and anyone who pleases may add *cўgnum* 410 8 to *noscerĕ* γνῶθι 320 19 and his many other misdemeanours; but let us do what neither Friedlaender nor Friedrich has done and try to find *măgnetis* in *Mosell.* 316. That verse is this:

spirat enim tecti testudine chorus achates.

A false reference, you may think. No, nothing so venial as a false reference. Tollius, and I daresay other editors of the 17th and 18th centuries, printed, instead of *chorus achates*, the conjecture of that great scholar and critic but imperfect metrist Gronouius, *uera Magnetis*; Markland, whose prosody was not that of a Bentley or a Dawes, accepted this without suspicion; Friedlaender, with the negligence natural to one engaged in so pleasant and easy a task as refuting Lachmann, copied it cheerfully down; and here it starts up again as fresh as a daisy in Mr Friedrich's note, which I will now pursue to its further figments. 'Petron. *c.* 131 *Prŏgne*.' *Progne* is, as you might expect, the reading of most of Petronius' MSS, which date from the 12th to the 15th century; but the best MS, which is of the 11th or 10th, had originally *Procne*, and the *c* was later altered into *g*. There is a lesson for those who can learn. Last comes 'Val. Fl. 3, 34 *Prŏgnesson*.' This, so far as I can discover, is a pure invention of Friedlaender's. Markland, from whom he took the reference, gave *Procnesson* (as he gave *Procne*); that is the reading of V, which virtually if not absolutely is our sole authority for the text of Valerius; and I can find no record of *Prognesson* as the reading of any MS or any edition.

'Unter diesen Umständen' proceeds Mr Friedrich, without suspecting the humour of the phrase, 'ist auch an dem einhellig überlieferten Ovid *met.* 10, 531 *piscosamque Gnidon grauidamque Amathunta metallis* nicht zu ändern; ebensowenig an 6, 468 *ad mandata Prognes et agit sua uota sub illa*': these are the two verses on which Magnus wrote the notes which are the text of my discourse. Mr Friedrich then adds Hor. *carm.* 1 15 17 *spiculă Gnosii* and Sen. *H.f.* 18 *sertă Gnosiacae*, and continues 'Ebenso hat Kiessling mit Recht Hor. *sat.* 2, 5, 28 *uiuet uter locuples sine gnatis, inprobus, ultro*'.

Not merely Kiessling but the best prosodists among Horace's editors, Meineke, Haupt, and Lucian Mueller, retain *sině gnatis*; and there is no doubt that they are right. But when Mr Friedrich proceeds to argue from Horace's satires to Catullus, –

'Es versteht sich von selbst, dass unter diesen Umständen auch 64, 298 *inde pater diuom sancta cum coniuge gnatisque* nicht zu ändern ist,'

– this sentence, which concludes his note, will serve very well to inaugurate my enquiry.

The enquiry has two parts and the examples fall into two classes, || according as the correption occurs within the body of one word or at the contact of two. The latter case, where a short final vowel is followed by an initial *gn* and the syllable remains short, is the more credible and shall be considered first. And first of all I will take the only native Latin word which enters into the discussion:[1] the *gnatus* which has just now cropped up for the fourth time.

When Horace's MSS give *sině gnatis* at *serm.* II 5 28, there is no shadow of a reason to doubt that Horace wrote it. Horace the satirist disregarded position even in pairs of consonants where the second is not a liquid: he wrote *fornicě stantem, uelatumquě stola, saepě stilum, quiă scilicet, mală stultitia, mihĭ Stertinius,* even *fastidirě strabonem* and *praemiă scribae*.[2] That was the tradition of satire, as may be seen in Lucilius; and if the correption were ascribed by their MSS to Lucretius or Propertius, who wrote *molliă strata* and *bině spondebant* and much else of the sort, it would be no less credible. Nay, since *gnatus* and *gnata* are the

---

[1] Terentianus Maurus 894 has *quandŏ 'Gnaeum' enuntio*, but that, as Lucian Mueller says *de r. m.* p. 386 ed. 2, 'exemplorum libertate excusabitur', like 887 *quandŏ* μνήμην *atquě* μνᾶσθαι *dicttatque* Μνεσθέα. There is however one more Latin word which I feel bound to mention, because it has been unaccountably overlooked by the reactionaries: unaccountably, for it is Magnus's own name. The paroxytone accent of Μάγνος ought to be a sign (though in fact it cannot be trusted) that the vowel itself was short; and that *gn* did not necessarily even lengthen it by position is proved by that sacred and indefeasible thing, the authority of MSS. I find two examples in Catullus, 90 1–3.

> nascatur *măgnus* ex Gelli matrisque nefando
> coniugio et discat Persicum haruspicium
> nam *măgnus* ex matre et gnato gignatur oportet,

and one in my favourite hexameter *ciris* 374,

> inde *măgno* geminat Iōui frigīdula sacra.

[2] To show the prevalent ignorance of this subject among scholars who set up for metrists, Vollmer, citing these examples on p. 344 of his Horace under the head *ad positionem notanda*, adds *tibi triplex* and does not add *uinosă glomus* nor *preců blandus*; and Jebb at Soph. *O.C.* 996, volunteering a needless note on the regular scansion περίβλέποις, adduces περιδρομή and περιγραφά as relevant to the question, and cannot even keep to himself the opinion that περιγράφεις is 'ambiguous' in Ar. *pac.* 879 οὗτος, τί περιγράφεις; τὸ δεῖν', εἰς Ἴσθμια. Did they never hear of a book entitled *Miscellanea Critica* and published in 1745?

regular forms of the substantive in the MSS of Horace's satires, the solitary exception should probably be corrected, and *Aulidĕ gnatam* restored with Keller and Mueller in II 3 199.[1]

Now turn to the alleged example in Catullus, 64 298,

> inde pater diuum sancta cum *coniugĕ gnatisque*
> aduenit,

and turn also from Horace's practice to his. Of all Latin poets Catullus is the most sensitive to position: he nowhere disregards it except in the traditional and unavoidable *undă Scamandri*; and not only has he *potē stolidum*, *modō scurra*, *nefariā scripta*, *gelidā stabula*, *nullā spes*, but even, in one metre, *Propontidā trucemue*, *impotentiā freta*, and *ultimā Britannia*. That is one test, a general one, by which to judge the likelihood of *coniugĕ gnatisque*; and here is another, a particular one. The usual spelling of the substantive in his MSS ‖ is with initial *g*: setting this verse aside there are ten examples of *gnatus* or *gnata* to eight of *natus* or *nata*. But, except in this single place, wherever the word follows a short vowel it is spelt without the *g*: 62 22 *auellere natam*, 64 324 *carissime nato*, 401 *funera nati*, 403 *impia nato*, 67 26 *semine natus*. What possessed Catullus not to write also *coniuge natisque* here?

When they realise that 'es versteht sich von selbst' does not quite suit the case, and begin casting about for something else to say, they will probably say this: that scribes were not likely to change the commoner form *natis* into the less common. But, not to mention that in Catullus the commoner form is *gnatus*, this argument, though often used, has little force. Scribes, unlike the imaginary scribe of scholars who do not read MSS, frequently alter commoner forms to rarer; but for the present occasion one example will be more than sufficient. The second-best MS of Ovid's *heroides*, G, is two centuries older than the principal MSS of Catullus and incomparably better; and at XII 187 it gives *respicĕ gnatos*. The best MS, P, has lost many pages, and if it had lost this page we should have this correption brandished in our faces together with Catull. 64 298. But it contains this page, and it gives *natos*, and so do the other MSS.

I will end this section with an act of showy generosity. In Sen. *Tro.* 246–8, 'placita nunc subito improbas | *Priamique natam* Pelei nato ferum | mactare credis', the best MS, E, has *patriamquĕ gnatam*, part of which at least should prove acceptable to some.

---

[1] When Mr Friedrich says of II 5 28 'auch klänge *sine natis* (ne-na) viel weniger gut', he displays that enviable fineness of ear which is peculiar to bad metrists. Neither Horace, who wrote not only *sine nascitur serm.* I 3 68 and *bene nata carm.* IV 4 36 but even *sine neruis serm.* II 1 2, nor any other Latin poet aspired to the fastidious elegance of Mr Friedrich. It would take a long time to count the examples in Ovid of *bene natus, ordine origine sanguine natus, Agamemnone Amazone Amythaone Andraemone Apolline Ixione Polypemone natus.*

All the other words involved in the controversy are Greek; and none of them is spelt in Greek with γυ. The Latin *g*, in every one of them, represents the Greek κ; and in every one of them we know that the Romans, often if not habitually, represented the Greek κ by *c*. When therefore, to take an instance, the MSS of Ovid at *met.* x 531 present *piscosamquĕ Gnidon*, a rational enquirer will want to know two things: why should Ovid choose to write *Gnidon*, with an unusual correption, when he indisputably might have written *Cnidon* without one; and what authority have medieval MSS in this detail of spelling. But those are just the questions which enquirers like Messrs Friedrich and Magnus never ask.

I will take this name Κνίδος first. The verses in which *Gnidus* is found with a short vowel before it and defended are Catull. 36 13 *Anconă Gnidumque* and Ouid. *met.* x 531 *piscosamquĕ Gnidon*. The oldest of Catullus' MSS are late in the 14th century, the oldest of Ovid's are of the 11th. Ovid's verse however is twice cited by Priscian, whose oldest MSS are of the 9th century, and at G.L.K. II p. 10 they too give *Gnidon*; but at p. 52 they give *Cnidon*, except one which has *Gnidum*. What Priscian himself wrote in these places we cannot learn from the context; but we do know what he regarded as the right spelling of the name, for on p. 42, where he is enumerating the various combinations of consonants, he has 'cn, *Cnidus*,...gn, *Gnaeus*', a piece of evidence which the *thes. ling. Lat.* does not record.

But why do not the allies cite a well-known verse where *Gnidus* follows a ‖ short vowel in MSS much older and better than Catullus' or Ovid's? For a very good reason. The verse is Hor. *carm.* 1 30 1, where *regină Gnidi* is given not merely by the vulgar crowd of Horace's MSS but by some of the most important, ACλl, the oldest of which is dated about A.D. 900. But unluckily a still more important company, BRδφψ, the oldest of which is dated about A.D. 800, give *Cnidi*, and so too the verse is cited in the cod. Par. 7530 of Seru. *de metr. Hor.* G.L.K. IV p. 469, which is of the 8th century, not to mention the cod. Pal. 1753 of Mar. Vict. *de metr. Hor.* ib. VI p. 175, which is of the 9th. If we had MSS of Catullus and Ovid as old and good as Horace's, do Messrs Friedrich and Co. think that they, unlike his, would all give *Gnidus*, or that, like his, they would lean to the side of *Cnidus*? The answer is that they think neither; they think nothing. There is no room left for thought in minds inhabited by a passion for false quantities.

Apart from the metrical witness borne by the three poets, it can be shown that in their times the regular if not the only spelling was *Cnid-*. I have already quoted Priscian, whose testimony is borne out by Martianus Capella 249 'C...consonantes quasdam praecedit, LTRMN, ut...*Cnidus*'. There exists on the other hand what looks at first like an earlier testimony to *Gnidus*: Ter. Maur. 890–2,

> tertia uda (N) sic uidetur posse G mutam sequi,
> Graia uerba quando in usum sermo noster suscipit,
> *Gnosios* si dicere arcus insulam aut *Gnidum* uelis.

But if the context is carefully read it will appear that Terentianus (of whom we have no MS, only editions from 1497 onwards) must have written *C mutam* and *Cnosios* and *Cnidum*; for he goes on to say that the praenomen written *Cn.* is pronounced *Gnaeus*, digresses to the similar case of *C(aius)* and to *amurca* pronounced *amurga*, and then proceeds, 902 f.,

> G tamen, mox tertia uda, rarius componitur,
> quando *gnatum* nominare dicere aut *gnarum* uoles.

The oldest MS in which I find *Gnidus* is the cod Moneus (saec. V–VI) at Plin. *n.h.* XIII 59. In the twelve inscriptions cited by the *thes. ling. Lat.*, one of which, *C.I.L.* IV 5533, is from Pompei, and another, X 1403 g 1 34, from Herculaneum, the spelling is always with C, *Cnidus Cnidius Cnidia*, except that in one, IX 4929, the letter is doubtful.[1] ||

From Caria let us now cross over to Crete, and see if Cnosus will be less inhospitable to the letter G than Cnidus was. It is; for the spelling *Gnosus* is as old as the reign of Augustus, and appears upon two Cnosian coins of that date, Svoronos no. 190 GNOS, 191 GNO. But *Cnosus* was still the usual form, and C(olonia) I(ulia) N(obilis) CN(osus) or C(nosus) appears not only on no. 180, which is earlier, but on 181–3, 188, 189, 192–4, some of which are later; and we also find COL. I. N. CN. in *C.I.L.* III suppl. 12041 and C. I. N. CNOS. in 14377, of the time of Claudius. Afterwards the true form was gradually superseded by that which the vulgar found easier to pronounce. Ter. Maur. 892 I have already dealt with; but in Virgil's text, where the adjective occurs six times, the majority of the capital MSS (saec. IV–VI) are usually for *Gnosius*. So now for the verses where a short vowel precedes.

In Hor. *carm.* I 15 17 it has long been customary to print *calami spicula Cnosii*; for Horace the lyrist has other principles than Horace the satirist, and in

---

[1] Before quitting Catullus I will let Mr Friedrich's competence to handle this matter be seen in the light of his dealings with 64 36 and 75 and his display of knowledge and consistency there. At 75 he prints, like most editors, 'iniusti regis *Gortynia* tecta' where the MSS have *cortinia*, but he thinks that the change needs justification and justifies it thus: 'die Schreibart *Gortynia* wird durch Claudian (*VI cons. Hon.* 634) gegen *Ciris* 114 *Cortynius* und Stat. *Theb.* 4, 530 *arbiter Cortynius* geschützt.' He has found these three examples in Baehrens's commentary and has searched no further; it does not occur to this student of orthography to enquire whether Virgil has the word, and how his MSS spell it. And then he proceeds 'G für griechisches K entsprach dem Genius der lateinischen Sprache; vgl. zu 11, 6' (*Sagas* for Σάκας): he does not know that the Greek word is Γορτύνιος. Now come to 36, where he prints, like everyone else 'Crannonisque domos', and writes no note. But instead of C the MSS give G, in accordance with the principle that G for Greek K 'entsprach dem Genius der lateinischen Sprache', and so do the older and better MSS of Cic. *de or.* II 352. Why then does he not print *Grannonis* at 64 36 as he prints *Gnidum* at 36 13? Because *Grannonis* would create no false quantity and therefore would afford Mr Friedrich no voluptuous sensation.

the odes there is no *saepĕ stilum* nor *sinĕ gnatis* but on the contrary II 18 28
sordidosque natos and III 5 42 *paruosque natos*. But when I saw that Kiessling's
edition was to be revised by Mr R. Heinze I knew that we should have *Gnosii*
back again, and also *palŭs* in *art.* 65; and we have. *Gnosii* is the reading of all
Keller's MSS excepting one; but that one is R, probably the best MS on the
whole, and certainly much the best in orthography. R has *Cnosii*; but R²
substitutes the vulgar form, and in the next copy the true spelling would have
vanished away.[1]

Naturally then it has vanished away from the later and inferior MSS of Ovid,
Seneca, and Statius: *met.* IX 669 *proximă Gnosiaco, H.f.* 18 'mundus puellae
sertă Gnosiacae gerit' (but *fert. a nobis lac e* cod. opt.), *silu.* V 1 232 *lucidă*
Gnosis.

The opinion that Seneca could write *sertă Gnosiacae* is not in itself preposterous. Though he writes *frigidā spatio* and *undiquē scopuli*, he does nevertheless write *enodĕ Zephyris, tranquillă Zephyri, tramitĕ ʒonas*, and *antră Zethi*,
and the form *Gnosiacus* did exist in his day. The question is whether after a
short vowel he would prefer it to the also existing form *Cnosiacus*, and whether
the evidence of MSS no earlier than the 13th century (for the spelling to which
E points is *Nosiacae*, not uncommon in MSS) is any proof that he did. That is a
question which can easily be answered, and answered right, by any unim-
passioned enquirer. Ovid was a more scrupulous metrist than Seneca, and
though the MSS of the *metamorphoses* are older than Seneca's they are not earlier
than the 11th century; so that *Gnosiaco* in IX 669 has no more likelihood.
lucidă Gnosis in Stat. *silu.* V 1 232 has even less. The *siluae* have ‖ survived only
in one MS of the 15th century, and Statius was a poet acutely sensitive to
position. His only violation of it is the unavoidable *ignĕ ʒmaragdos* of *Theb.*
II 276, and he lengthens a short final before *st* ib. VI 551 *agilē studium*. But stop:
I am overlooking the march of modern progress. P and some other MSS
represent this same poet as having written 'fas et *mihĭ spernere* Phoebum' in
Theb. VII 733, and the latest editors believe them. When zeal for a best MS joins
its voice to partiality for bad versification, neither the whispers of reason nor the
wails of Statius can be heard. The next stage in the gratification of appetite will
be to print *nihĭl transit amantes* with P in II 335 and *nihĭl foedere rupto* on 339.

Here ends the tale of supposed correptions before initial *gn*, and we come to
the still more difficult correption in the body of a word. And first in *cygnus*.

Horace, I hardly know why, is still allowed to write 'donatura *cycni*, si
libeat, sonum' in *carm.* IV 3 20, though C is the only one of Keller's MSS

---

[1] In *carm.* I 21 8 the MSS have *uiridis Gragi*, and this is the usual spelling of Κράγος in Latin MSS;
but Mr Heinze does not accept it, because it does not charm his ear with any illegitimate correption.
And at *carm.* I 3 6 he prints the *Vergilium* of R, not the *Virgilium* of R² and the other MSS, because
the false spelling does not redeem itself by being also a false quantity.

which preserves the spelling, and all the rest have *cygni* or *cigni* with the required false quantity. But in Mart. IX 103 2 we have already seen Friedlaender and Mr Friedrich upholding *cȳgno* against the incredulity of Lachmann. I said above that half of Martial's MSS give *cycno*, and that G.L.K. VII p. 539 1 gives not *Lacaena cygno*, which these metrists are resolved to write, but *Lacena cigno*, which they dare not.[1] But I now go further, and I raise the question whether *cygnus* is a form which Martial had ever seen or a sound which he had ever heard. Descend to the 4th and 5th centuries, to the capital MSS of Virgil: *cycnus* occurs there nine times and the proper name *Cycnus* once; and this is the invariable spelling except that M in three places has *cygnus*. Again in the palimpsest of Fronto we find *cycnus* twice and *cygnus* never. From inscriptions the *thes. ling. Lat.* cites no example of *Cygnus* or *cygnus* either, but one of *cycnus*, six of *Cycnus*, one of *Cicnus*, one of the adjective *cycneus*, and three of the derivative *cycnion*. To say that *cygnus* may have been the vulgar pronunciation in Martial's time, as *Gnosus* doubtless was, is to overlook the fact that the vulgar did not use the word. This name for the swan was exclusively literary and almost exclusively poetical. From all prose earlier than Fronto there are cited only nine examples, one of which does not count, for Mela I 110 is explaining why the town Cycnus was called so, and six of which are in Pliny's natural history. The vulgar called the bird *olor*, and when they began to try at its Greek name they pronounced it *cicinus*, preserving the *c*, so that it came into Italian as *cecino* and *cecero*. ‖

The next case, and the last, is *Prŏgne*, cited from Ouid. *met.* VI 468 *mandata Prŏgnes* and Petr. 131 8 7 *urbana Prŏgne*. The latter, as I have signified already, is not a prudent citation, and a true statement of the facts, '*procne* L, *procne* mutatum in *progne* B, *progne* ceteri,' teaches the same lesson as '*cnosii* R, *gnosii* R² ceteri' at Hor. *carm.* I 15 17. The MSS which give *Progne* in Ouid. *met.* VI are of the 11th century or later, and so are those which give that form in *fast.* II 629 and 855, *trist.* V 1 60, and *ex Pont.* III 1 119. But in the *fasti* we have also a MS of the 10th century, and it gives *prone* and *prome*, and at *ex Pont.* III 1 119 we have a MS of the 9th, and it gives *Procne*. The oldest MS in which I have found *Progne* is the cod. Salmasianus (saec. VII–VIII) at *anth. Lat. Ries.* 27 in the title of the poem. The absurd and unmetrical verse Plaut. *rud.* 604 'natas

---

[1] I note here, because Lucian Mueller *de r. m.* p. 385 ed. 2 overlooks it, that Martial does in one particular carry correption further than any other Latin poet of classical times. To neglect position before initial *gl* is quite regular; but Martial, sound pagan though he was, indulged in a licence which Mueller confines to Christians, and left a short vowel short at the junction of the compound *anăglypta* IV 39 8. For this he had the authority of Theocr. *epigr.* 4 2 (*anth. Pal.* IX 437) ἀρτῐγλυφές; but it is not to be inferred that either Theocritus or Martial would have shortened the first syllable of *Aglauros*. When Mueller adds 'at non credibilest auctorem peruigilii Veneris posuisse *peruiglanda* pro ditrochaeo [46], sed unice amplectemur quod habes libro Salmasiano *peruiclanda*', he disquiets himself in vain: the writer of the *peru. Ven.* allows spondees in the fifth foot of his tetrameter, and anapaests too.

ex Philomela atque ex *Progne* esse hirundines' is illegible in the Ambrosian palimpsest, and in that MS it was shorter; and if Plautus himself named the woman he called her neither *Progne* nor *Procne* but *Procina*. The earliest MS witness is in Verg. *georg.* IV 15, and it is instructive to those who admit instruction: all the capital MSS, MPR, have *Procne*, but *g* for *c* has already made its appearance in the 9th-century cod. Bern. 184. As for inscriptions, in the *C.I.L.* I find three examples (II 5392, III 2935, IX 405ᵇ) of *Procne*, one (IX 649) of *Prochne*, one (v 1323) of *Procine*; no trace of *Progne* unless in VI 135, where the reports of witnesses vary between *Caecilia Procne* and *Cecilia Progne*. The first business of those who pretend that Ovid and Petronius shortened the first syllable of *Progne* is to show reason for supposing that in their lifetimes *Progne* was even an existing form.[1]

But what I am arraigning is not misjudgment in any particular case but a vice of method. All the words cited to prove correption before *gn*, except where the citations are false, have one common feature: they are alternative spellings of words which were also spelt without the *g*. If there could be produced from classical poetry a single instance of *Polўgnotus* or *anăgnostes*, a single instance like the *Epĭgnomus* of Plaut. *Stich.* 464, it would constitute prima facie evidence and require consideration. But the instances produced are these: the Latin word *gnatus*, also spelt *natus*, and the Greek words *Gnidus, Gnosus, cygnus, Progne*, also, and originally, spelt *Cnidus, Cnosus, cycnus, Procne*: no others. These weigh no more than κατέγναψε from Eur. *Tro.* 1252 when κνάπτω exists, or the μᾶστεύων and ἄμπλακών and *potĭretur* and *dĕprehendo* which MSS proffer to all who crave them. They constitute evidence only for the intellectually or morally deficient; for those who do not know what evidence is, or for those who have set before themselves an end which they are determined to reach by fair means or foul. A competent enquirer and an upright man will ask two questions. First, did scribes introduce *g* into such words, or did they not; and the answer is that they did. Second, what motive had poets for spelling such words with *g*, when to do so involved a scansion ‖ not elsewhere admitted; and the only person who can answer that question is Echo.

If words which exist in alternative forms may be cited from MSS as evidence in matters of prosody, Mr Friedrich must be taken to task for corrupting with unnecessary alteration two verses of Catullus, 63 8 and 9, in both of which the consonants *mp* fail to make position and the first syllable of *tympanum* is short.

> niueis citata cepit manibus leue *tўmpanum*
> *tўmpanum* tubam Cybeles tu mater initia.

---

[1] I have already exposed their fiction that Valerius Flaccus has *Prŏgnesson* in III 34. They would dearly love to read *Tĕgmessae*, as many good MSS do, in Hor. *carm.* II 4 6, but unfortunately more and better MSS read *Tecmessae*.

This scansion recurs in Varro, Non. p. 49 ⟦70 Lindsay⟧,

tibi *tўmpana* non inanis sonitus matris deum,

and in Maecenas ⟦*PLF* p. 102 Morel⟧, G.L.K. VI p. 262,

ades et sonante *tўmpano* quate flexibile caput;

and at *Oxy. pap.* XIII p. 43 I collected from Greek poetry no fewer than five examples of τὔμπανον. There is therefore much more authority for *tўmpanum* than for either *cўgnus* or *Prŏgne*, and it surprises me that Mr Friedrich should accept Scaliger's conjecture *tўpanum*; or rather it would surprise me if one could expect to find even consistency, the humblest of the virtues, keeping house with this confederacy. But evidence for them is good or bad according as it may serve their turn: a short vowel before *mp* is not a false quantity on which they happen to have fixed their affections, and so they have no motive for believing that a vulgar scribal error is anything other than what it is.

149

OXYRHYNCHUS PAPYRI XVII. 2078*

Fr. 1 7–19 ⟦*GLP* p. 122 Page⟧ should be completed somewhat as follows.

θεὸς δέ μανία[ς ἀρτίως ἐλευθέρῳ
ἔπεμψεν ἄτη[ν· ἁρπάσας δ' ἠκασμένην
νεφέλην γυναικ[ὶ δυσσεβέστατον λόγον
ἔσπειρεν εἰς τοὺς Θεσσαλούς, ὡς δὴ Κρόνου
θυγατρὶ μίσγοιτ' ἐ[ν φυταλμίῳ λέχει.
τοιῶνδε κόμπω[ν δ' ὕστερον καταξίους
ποινὰς θεοῖς ἔτεισεν, [ὧν πάντων πατὴρ
μανίας τροχῷ περι[φερὲς ἐν δίναις δέμας
οἰστρηλάτοισιν ὤχ[μασεν, κᾆπειθ' ἑλὼν
ἄπυστον ἀνθρώποι[σιν αἰθέρος βάθει
ἔκρυψεν· ἀλλὰ βορε[άσιν πνοαῖς ἐκεῖ
διεσπαράχθη συμμ[έτρῳ κομπάσμασιν
πατὴρ ἁμαρτὼν εἰς θε[οὺς τιμωρίᾳ.

It is plain who speaks, and perhaps he continued

ἐγὼ δ' ἐκείνου πήματ' α[ἰνιχθέντ' ἔχων
[Περίθους ὀνόματι καὶ τύχας εἴληχ' ἴσας.]

Περίθους παρὰ τὸ περιθεῖν.
This account of Ixion's punishment, or something very like it, is given by some of the authorities collected in Rosch. *lex.* II pp. 766 f. Schol. Eur. *Phoen.* 1185 ὀργισθεὶς δὲ ὁ Ζεὺς ὑποπτέρῳ τροχῷ τὸν Ἰξίονα δήσας ἀφῆκε τῷ ἀέρι φέρεσθαι μαστιζόμενον, schol. Pind. *Pyth.* II 40 καὶ τὴν ἐπὶ τοῦ τροχοῦ δὲ κόλασιν αὐτῷ παρεγκεχειρήκασιν· ὑπὸ γὰρ δίνης καὶ θυελλῶν αὐτὸν ἐξαρπασθέντα φθαρῆναί φασιν, Philostr. *uit. Apoll.* VI 40 ἐκεῖνος μὲν τροχῷ εἰκασμένος δι' οὐρανοῦ κνάμπτεται. This εἰκασμένος accords well with these remains, which indicate no substantial wheel with nave and spokes and fellies, but rather what the Psalmist invokes on the enemies of Israel, ' O my God, make them like unto a wheel.'

Fr. 2 34 ⟦40 p. 124 Page⟧ λέξειν ἄν is the oldest piece of evidence yet forthcoming for this construction in Attic; but correction is as easy as usual. In Xen. *anab.* II 3 18 the ἔχειν preserved by Suidas and the best MS has become ἕξειν in the others. ἐρεῖν ἄν would be more of a nut to crack.

* ⟦*CR* 42 (1928), 9⟧

150

REVIEW: J.-L. PERRET, *LA TRANSMISSION DU TEXTE DE JUVÉNAL**

The author has collated 13 Florentine MSS, the best of which, Jahn's *a*, is of the 11th century, the rest later. None of them, not even *a*, is important, and, like most of Juvenal's MSS, they are not bound or severed into classes by the agreement or disagreement of their lections. But he classifies them by what he calls external signs: four, which are among the worse, differ from the others in numbering the satires continuously with no division into books, and in reversing the order of satires XV and XVI. He concludes (pp. 67 f.) that 'le texte de Ju-vénal nous est transmis par deux traditions distinctes dont l'une, la meilleure, est caractérisée par la division en 5 livres (et) par l'ordre normal des deux dernières satires,...tandis que la tradition inférieure est représentée par les MSS à un livre, avec interversion des deux dernières satires.' This second tradition he calls Z, and says on p. 86 'la présentation en un livre y concorde si absolument avec l'interversion...que je me sens justifié à affirmer que tous les MSS en un livre dérivent d'un seul et même ancêtre', which on p. 96 he dates 'au IXe siècle au plus tard', because, as he says on p. 74, the inversion appears in Jahn's *b*, 'qui est du IXe siècle'.

Mr Perret, whose whole treatise is distinguished by lucidity and sobriety, fully recognises that the importance of this conclusion is small, because the MSS concerned are of little or no value; but the conclusion is itself less solid than he thinks. First, Z cannot safely be dated so early, for, though Jahn assigned *b* to the 9th century, its true date, according to Beer *spic. Iuu.* p. 36, is the 11th; so that the 10th, the date of Jahn's *c*, will be the earliest century in which the inversion appears. Secondly, we are not informed that *c* (or *b* either) possesses the other feature of Mr Perret's Z, continuous numeration; and I can testify that in my T, also of the 10th century, though the two last satires are inverted, the division into 5 books is preserved. It appears therefore that the two changes were successive, or at least of separate origin.

* [*La transmission du texte de Juvénal d'après une nouvelle collation*. By Jean-Louis Perret. Pp. 99. Helsinki (Helsingfors): Suomalaisen Tiedeakatemian Toimituksia, 1927. *CR* 42 (1928), 43]

151

REVIEW: W. MOREL, *FRAGMENTA POETARVM LATINORVM**

The elder Baehrens, though an important figure in the history of learning, produced in his short life no book which can be called good without reservation; but he produced many books of great utility, and his *frag. poet. Rom.* was one of them. To young students it was a godsend. Mr Morel's revision of it is a better book so far as it goes, but is less useful and by no means supersedes it. Half the contents are missing, and for Ennius and Lucilius we are sent to Vahlen and Marx. Now Germany is always bewailing its poverty, and a young scholar in any country is usually poor: if he can scrape together a couple of pounds, is he to squander them on such hors-d'œuvres as Vahlen's Ennius and Marx's Lucilius? Mr Morel had no cause to fear the labour of recension, for it would not have been heavy if he had clung to Vahlen and Marx as fast as he clings to Leo throughout pp. 5–62.

Not that he has spared himself pains. He has examined each fragment anew, taking nothing on trust; and he has earned his readers' gratitude by subjoining the original Greek to the numerous translations. Among particular improvements the most noteworthy is the separation of the two Iliads of Ninnius and 'Neuius' on p. 51. He has made some 40 additions, most of which naturally are insignificant or doubtful. All that I had myself added is here, except Tert. *apol.* 25 8 'fato stat Iuppiter ipse'. But, since fragments of Ovid, Lucan, and Statius are included, why not of Catullus? Mr Morel has not Baehrens's reason for omitting them.

Beside Ennius and Lucilius, Varro Reatinus is ejected, with the irrelevant remark that his Menippean satires deserve editing by themselves. Such an edition would not contain fragments of the *imagines*, which apparently are to be left lurking in Gell. III 11 and Non. p. 528 ⟦848–9 Lindsay⟧. Scenic fragments are removed: well and good, if they are in Ribbeck's collection. But Naeu. *fr.* 36 and 61 and 63, which are not there, are consigned to limbo because Leo has pronounced them scenic; and if you want to know who wrote 'fato Metelli

* ⟦*Fragmenta poetarum Latinorum epicorum et lyricorum praeter Ennium et Lucilium post Aemilium Baehrens iterum edidit* Willy Morel. Pp. v + 190. Leipzig: B. G. Teubner, 1927. *CR* 42 (1928), 77–9⟧

Romae fiunt consules' you must enquire of the universe while Mr Morel sits clanking his chains. Baehr. p. 54 2 is banished as 'scenicus Acci uersus': this also is not in Ribbeck's last edition. For Laeu. 11ᵃ we are sent to Ribb. *trag. fr.* p. 4: fancy having to look for hexameters there! Cicero's translations from Greek dramatists disappear, but Chalcidius' remain. Baehr. p. 56 inc. 3, p. 304 14, p. 332 10, p. 376 Front. 2, are expelled as being prose, but pp. 268 f. 13–16 and p. 272 fin., though also declared to be prose, are kept, and Mor. p. 16 45 is actually inserted. Baehr. p. 405 inc. 1 is omitted as identical with 1490 in part 2 of Teubner's *anthologia Latina*, but p. 409 15 is not omitted, though identical with 786ᵇ in part 1 of the same. Certain verses of extant authors inadvertently included by Baehrens are cleared away; Licentius too is discarded, which is no loss, and also many verses from the metrical writers in *G.L.K.* vi, of which it is impossible to say whether they are citations or fictions, so that the lines drawn by Baehrens and Mr Morel are equally arbitrary.

There is an 'appendix quo de fragmentis a Baehrensio receptis, a me omissis ratio redditur', but it is incomplete as well as masculine, and does not tell us what has become of Liu. 33 and Acil. Glabr. 4 and 5. Some fragments, not omitted, are whisked out of sight, leaving no clue to their whereabouts, and anyone who tries to find Baehr. p. 37 inc. 2, p. 50 49, p. 138 4, p. 293 30, p. 303 9ᵃ, p. 329 13, p. 331 9, will have his work cut out for him. Mr Morel says 'numeros Baehrensianos cancellis inclusos meis addidi', but this he has often neglected, pp. 1–4, 35–40, 45, 73, 172, and a wrong number is given on p. 15 and p. 32. The continuous reference to Baehrens's pages is useful and apparently accurate. ‖

Baehrens often abandoned the MSS wrongly or needlessly, and Mr Morel has restored a great many of their readings; but he has also deserted them himself where Baehrens rightly adhered to them. The lections *qua* p. 46 6 4, *coniugio hanc* p. 111 fin. 2, *genio* p. 141 4 2, are true or at any rate faultless. Q. Cic. 17 f. 'squama sub *aeterno* conspectu torta Draconis ǀ eminet' is changed to *aetherio. sub aeterno conspectu* is ἀειφανής, just the right sense: *aetherio* has no propriety, being equally applicable to signs outside the arctic circle. Bibac. 1 3 'custodis uidet *hortulos Priapi*' (Prop. ii 34 61 *custodis litora Phoebi*) becomes 'custodes uidet *hortuli Priapos*'; but there would not be more than one Priapus in this tiny plot. In p. 123 fin. 2 *tantum* is not only right but necessary, and the conjecture *Tauri* inflicts two separate injuries, though that would take too long to explain. Iul. Val. 4 25 sq. '*una...metis* nostra...*Phaetonteis* ǀ regna* expli-cari' means that the realm is to be coextensive with the sun's course, and Iulius has this construction in i 44 *una seruitiis* and iii 25 *una Theodecto*: Mr Morel's *ultra...metas...Phaetonteas* is superfluous and improbable.

He has abolished Baehrens's *trăgica* at p. 119 14, but at p. 173 11 he praises the conjecture *măuis* as 'elegant'. At p. 50 16 he prints an iambic trimeter of

Leo's which ends with an anapaest, and at p. 52 2 he proposes another of his own which has no caesura, though at p.93 8 he says that this 'non licet'. Laeu. 24 in obedience to Leo is printed as a fragment of an epode (though Horace says 'Parios ego primus iambos ostendi Latio'), and its second verse is made by Mr Morel to begin with ∪ ∪ ∪ −. In Laeu. 22 an unmetrical *tuo* is tacked on to a catalectic Ionicus a maiore. For what concerns orthography, *paedicator* and *paedicem* are removed, but their place is more than filled by *Laerni*,[1] *Criseae*, *Berecynthius*, and *Burmann*.

The printer may be answerable for *infunditur* p. 35 4, *distantia* p. 36 13, *cum* p. 46 1 3, *irrunt* p. 58 14, *campos* p. 132 7, as he certainly is for *am* p. 87 1 3; but it can hardly have been the printer who substituted *este* for *fite* p. 51 Ninn. 1.

In defective verses Baehrens used to fill in the metre, as − ∪ ∪ − ∪ ∪ − *celerissimus aduolat Hector*. Mr Morel therefore determined that he would not, and kept his resolve till it broke down on p. 35, from which point onward he remembers and forgets it alternately, sometimes remembering and forgetting on the same page.

He says on p. IV that he has not recorded MS variants 'nisi ubi ad textum constituendum omnino necesse uidebatur'. In point of fact he has sometimes completely suppressed the readings of all MSS: his text gives *deum* p. 33 6 and *misit* p. 58 12 where the MSS give nothing; elsewhere *subito. . .mihi* for *m. s.*, *uerum ne ipsi* for *uerbum ne ipsiti*, *causa antiquitatis* for *a. c.*, *insolita plexit munera* for *insolito plexi munere*, *edens. . .uitans* for *euidens. . .uitas*, *infra* for *inter*, *uiribus ingerere ut* for *ui adingerere*, *rura domum nummos atque omnia denique* for *domum ruranum mostat* (or *durum rura nummos*) *denique omnia* without a word of warning; and, worse still, false readings silently substituted for true at p. 46 6 4, p. 111 fin. 2, p. 141 4 2.

There is some wrong attribution of conjectures, to be corrected as follows: p. 45 3 8 *Publio* not Ritschl but cod. Vrb., p. 52 3 *peperit* Maurenbrecher, p. 86 12 *Bistonis* not Baehrens but Munro (1878), Ouid. 1 2 *apparent* codd. and *sex. . .nube est* Grotius (*Arat.* p. 6) not Heinsius, p. 138 2 *undae* not Lachmann but Camerarius, p. 140 init. 17 *puerulum* not Buecheler but Hertz (1853), p. 142 6 7 *quo* not Weyman but codd. recc. and edd. uett., p. 144 2 2 *calentem* not Buecheler but L. Mueller (1861). These are mere mistakes: not so the substitution of Leo for Baehrens at p. 127 1 and the similar trick at p. 144 2 3. Leo is put forward in season and out of season. The reader of p. 35 4 who obeys the direction 'Cf. Leo *Lit. Gesch.* p. 391 2' will not be rewarded for his pains. At p. 59 17 *gracilenticolorem* we are told 'Leo. . . || *pudoricolorem* et *nocticolorem*. . . confert': those words are neither similarly formed nor similarly senseless. At p. 59 18 Leo conjectured *puella* for *illo*, and into the text it goes: I do not say

---

[1] Varr. Atac. 1 2, where Mr Morel has altered Baehrens's punctuation into Hagen's without looking at the Greek.

that it is wrong, but Mr Morel must know that if it were Baehrens's he would not even mention it.

Baehrens was a master of *Editionstechnik*; Mr Morel at present is not, and for want of skill or heed his notes on p. 34 3 5, p. 47 3 and 4, Laeu. 27 3, Cic. 11 50 f., p. 99 fin., p. 126 2, p. 154 7 6, p. 184 80 are marred by misstatement, omission, inconsistency, unintelligibility, or disorder. Seuius Nicanor is presented on p. 63 as one of the works of Laeuius, and there is another such negligence just below, and a third on p. 40. He has made one change for the better by attaching the notes to the several fragments instead of amassing them at the foot of the page; but this becomes an inconvenience in the longer pieces, where the reader must be turning the leaf to and fro.

Some false references in Baehrens are corrected, but others, which were not in Baehrens, are introduced, as at p. 4 15, p. 6 inc., Liu. 7, Naeu. 54, p. 30 2 and 3, Laeu. 32, Cic. 11, Q. Cic. p. 79, Varr. At. 17, Ouid. 4 and 12, p. 125 3, and Mueller's page of Festus is omitted at Acc. 2. In quoting Cicero Baehrens wasted ink and paper by giving chapter as well as section: Mr Morel deletes it in the *Brutus* but lets it stand everywhere else. He has amused himself by trying to change the numbers of books from Roman to Arabic, but has failed at Cic. 13 and 16. The commentary generally known as Seruius Danielis, 'Seru. auct.' in the *thes. ling. Lat.* and 'Seru.' by a harmless abbreviation in Baehrens, is cloaked under the ambiguous title 'schol. Verg.' or merely 'schol.'. It is therefore ignorance, not consideration for his readers, which prevents Mr Morel from substituting 'Apthon.' for 'Mar. Victorin.' on p. 97 and in many other places.

I should have written less harshly if Mr Morel had not taken measures to secure favourable reviews from his own countrymen. By duly disparaging Baehrens (in bad Latin) on his first page, and by ritual homage to Leo and Cichorius and other acceptable names,[1] he has done his best to create a friendly atmosphere and obtain commendation irrespective of desert; and he must not be surprised if smoke ascending from domestic altars draws in a current of cold air from abroad.

---

[1] 'Marx *Moloss. Wortf.*' and 'Boll *Sphaera*' are dragged in with almost comical irrelevancy on pp. 112 and 124 that Mr Morel may be given good marks for acquaintance with these esteemed works: if he were also acquainted with W. Schulze's *Orthographica* he would have earned more honestly another good mark on p. 75 instead of printing *Phthiae*.

152

THE FIRST EDITOR OF
LUCRETIUS*

The general and natural opinion that the *Cicero* named by Jerome as having corrected for publication the poem of Lucretius was Marcus and not the less celebrated Quintus may be confirmed, it seems to me, by certain slight indications hitherto latent.

Having told us how men adapted horses and elephants to the uses of war, Lucretius in v 1308–40 affirms that they also made trial of bulls and boars and lions in the same service, but found them ill to manage and no less dangerous to friend than to foe. Then follow these verses, 1341–9:

> si fuit ut facerent; sed uix adducor ut ante
> non quierint animo praesentire atque uidere,
> quam commune malum fieret foedumque, futurum.
> et magis id possis factum contendere in omni,
> in uariis mundis uaria ratione creatis,
> quam certo atque uno terrarum quolibet orbi.
> sed facere id non tam uincendi spe uoluerunt
> quam dare quod gemerent hostes ipsique perire
> qui numero diffidebant armisque uacabant.

The rational misgiving expressed in 1341–3, 'if they really did so; but I am hardly to be persuaded that they could not forebode and foresee the hideous general calamity before it came', is one which might well occur to our romancing historian; indeed it ought to have occurred to him and stayed his pen. But that he should have taken the trouble to dress it in verse and should then have set it over against his confident and circumstantial fiction, as if he were two persons instead of one, is not seriously credible. Munro therefore expels the three lines as foreign and dissentient, and nothing less will remove the discrepancy; neither the old change of *si* to *sic* adopted by Lachmann nor the verse inserted by Diels.

Now this elliptic use of *adducor*, 'adducor ut hoc ita sit' or 'hoc ita esse' for

* [[*CR* 42 (1928), 122–3]]

'adducor ut credam hoc ita esse', is not elsewhere to be found in Lucretius; and there are very few authors in whom it is to be found. Neither the *thes. ling. Lat.* I p. 602 33–8 and 59–68 nor Kuehner–Stegmann II i pp. 698 f. and ii p. 246 make any addition[1] to the examples collected by Madvig at Cic. *de fin.* I 14, so I suppose that his list is exhaustive. It has seven instances of 'adducor hoc ita esse': one is from Curtius, one from Columella, one from Festus, and all the rest from Cicero. It has only three instances of 'adducor ut hoc ita sit': one is this verse, and the others are Cic. *de fin.* I 14 and IV 55.

I therefore suspect that the author of this sceptical comment was M. Tullius, who amused himself by jotting it down in the margin when he was arranging Lucretius' manuscripts, and forgot to strike it out when they were handed over to the copyists. He was always ready to banter an Epicurean, and disastrously fond of scribbling verse; and these verses, even when improved by Lachmann's transposition of 1342 and 1343, are worthier of him than of Lucretius. The periphrasis *fuit ut facerent*, common in Lucretius, is rare in Cicero, but it occurs at *de diu.* I 128 'non est. . .ut mirandum sit',[2] and might easily spring up under the pen of one who was reading Lucretius through. The pleonasm *ante praesentire* is Ciceronian enough: he has *ante praedicere, praelabitur ante, ante praemuniat,* and *prouisum ante.*

The next three verses, 1344–6, as Madvig said in *opusc.* I p. 484 n., 'aliunde accesserunt'.[3] They are not, as Lachmann will have it, a derisive comment, even from a reader less intelligent than Cicero; as such, they are too completely pointless and too openly untrue. It is less incredible that men trained bulls and boars and lions for battle in one world, where those four animals are at least known to exist, than in other worlds, where they are ‖ not. The diction is thoroughly Lucretian, and indeed 1345 is 528.

But 1347–9 cohere with 1341–3. It is not satisfactory to strike out 1341–6 and let 1347 follow on 1340. As Giussani observes, 'non è facile intendere in *id*, non già l'ultimo pensiero, ma il pensiero fondamentale di tutto il paragrafo'; and whereas the author of these lines says that the men 'armis uacabant', Lucretius at 1311 had credited them with 'doctoribus armatis'. The objection of 1341–3 was directed particularly against the statement of 1334 f. 'siquos ante domi domitos satis esse putabant | efferuescere cernebant in rebus agundis', – that the men fancied they had trained the beasts to steadiness and afterwards

---

[1] Except indeed that the *thesaurus* cites Afran. *fr. com.* 290 'adducor ferre (with the false information "fero *codd.*") humana humanitus' and Varr. *r.r.* II 7 9 'equus matrem salire cum adduci non posset', and supposes that these also are examples of 'acc. c. inf.'. ἄνθρακες ὁ θησαυρὸς πέφηνεν · ἐπὶ τῶν ἐφ' οἷς ἤλπισαν διαψευσθέντων καὶ ἐν ἄλλοις ἐντυχόντων.

[2] Of the three examples cited there by Mr A. S. Pease one, *pro Mil.* 35, is different (causal) and the two others are simply false.

[3] This is also the opinion of Diels, to whom therefore, and not to Madvig, it will henceforth be attributed. Editors of Lucretius neglect Madvig, and his corrections of III 793 and V 122 f. (published in 1843) and of V 979 are usually ignored or ascribed to others.

found themselves mistaken; and the objector now puts forward a more plausible suggestion of his own, that their essay was from beginning to end a counsel of desperation. And these verses too contain something which is not Lucretian and which is Ciceronian. In Cicero *uacare* with the ablative, in the sense of lacking, is frequent: Lucretius never constructs *uacare* or *uacuus* with any case, and never uses either except in the literal signification of emptiness.

153

PHIL. WOCHENSCHR. 1927 PP. 1434–40*

Versuum initia p. 1439 edita ea sunt quae p. 1437 desiderantur in Ouid. Trist.
V 1, 13–27.

* ⟦*PhW* 1928, 127⟧

154

CATULLUS LXVI 51–4*

abiunctae paulo ante comae mea fata sorores
lugebant, cum se Memnonis Aethiopis
unigena impellens nutantibus aera pennis
obtulit Arsinoes Locricos ales equos.

The rivalry between Zephyr and the ostrich for a place in Arsinoe's household is terminated by the publication in *Stud. ital. di fil. cl.* VII (1929) p. 9 of the Greek original [Callimachus fr. 110 52–4 Pfeiffer], γνωτὸς Μέμνονος Αἰθίοπο[ς] | ἵ[ε]το κυκλώσας βαλιὰ πτερὰ θῆλυς ἀήτης | [λάτρις] ἰο[ζ]ώνου Λοκρικὸς Ἀρσινόης. But the chief obstacle to Zephyr's appointment, and the chief recommendation of his competitor, still remains: remains at least in the current text of Catullus. *ales equos* describes an ostrich very well, and at Helicon there was a statue of Arsinoe riding on an ostrich. But the Winds are not horses but horsemen, Eur. *Phoen.* 211 f. Ζεφύρου. . .ἱππεύσαντος, Hor. *carm.* IV 4 43 f. *ceu. . .Eurus. . .equitauit*, or charioteers, Verg. *Aen.* II 417 f. *laetus Eois* | *Eurus equis*, Val. Fl. I 611 f. *Thraces equi* (the horses of Boreas) *Zephyrusque et nocti concolor alas. . .Notus*. It was not only useless but injudicious to adduce Hom. *Il.* XX 223 f., where Boreas puts on the shape of a horse for the purpose of deception, as Saturn also did, and as Jove put on many shapes.

The reading of the MSS however is not this but *alis equos*, and it is an ancient reading. Hyg. *astr.* II 24 *hanc Berenicen non nulli cum Callimacho dixerunt equos alere* is probably not from the pen of the mythographer, but is in MSS which are much older than Catullus's and whose archetype was also older. It appears that Catullus coined *alisequos* on the analogy of *pedisequos*, so signifying his agreement with the general opinion that this compound is of the same sort as *uentriloquus* and *ueliuolus* and *remiuagus*, the nominal element denoting the instrument, not the object, of the verbal action. *odorisequus* may be either *qui odorem* or *odore sequitur*.

Achilles Statius is now praised for having hit on the true correction *Locricos* for *elocridicos*. That was a lucky chance: he deserves much more credit for refusing to allow that Zephyr was a horse and conjecturing *alisequus*.

* [*CR* 43 (1929), 168]

155

REVIEW: H. BORNECQUE AND M. PRÉVOST, *OVIDE, HÉROÏDES**

Encounters between Ovid and the French Academy have not always been happy, and Anatole France's amended text of *trist.* IV 10 42 is dropped by common consent into the neighbouring stream of Lethe when the two authors sit down together in Elysium for a chat about the art of love. But Mr Prévost has not to wrestle with recension. His translation is true in general to his announcement of its purpose, that it 's'attache d'abord à être fidèle'; it is simple, straightforward, and manly, without amplification or paraphrase or sacrifices to conventional elegance. Twice at least he is right where most translators and commentators are wrong: II 12 *procellosos uela referre notos* 'que les orageux autans refoulaient tes voiles' and v 156 *non ego cum Danais arma cruenta fero* 'je n'apporte pas, moi, une guerre sanglante avec les Grecs'. If he is not always able to say as he desires 'j'ai mis le lecteur français en face du texte français, dans l'état où se trouvait le lecteur latin en face du texte latin', that is because fidelity must in the last resort depend upon knowledge, and his knowledge is imperfect.

Many of his renderings are mistakes in Latin which would draw down censure on a schoolboy. II 53 *quo* 'où sont', III 50 *pectora iactantem* 'laisser échapper ses entrailles', 79 *scindi capillos* 'qu'on me coupe les cheveux' ('signe d'esclavage' adds Mr Bornecque), 109 *nulla Mycenaeum sociasse cubilia mecum* 'aucun Mycénéen ne partagea mon lit', 126 *Pelias hasta* 'ta lance reçue de Pélée' (Mr Bornecque again agrees, 'Pélée l'avait reçue lui-même de Pallas'), IV 30 *tenui ungue* 'précautionneux', 72 *flaua ora* 'hâlé', 87 *incinctae* 'à la tunique flottante', 99 *arsit et Oenides in Maenalia Atalanta* 'sur le Ménale', VI 104 *aurea Phrixeae terga reuellit ouis* 'arracha la toison d'or au bélier de Phrixus', 108 *patria Phasidis* 'Phase natal', 118 *me dotales inter habere* 'me ranger parmi les femmes bien dotées', VII 172 *eiectam ratem* 'l'élan d'un navire', IX 3 f. *fama factis infitianda tuis* 'une nouvelle contredite par tes prouesses', 9 f. (*nox una*) *non tanti* 'pas assez grande', 12 *humili sub pede* 'faible', X 44 *torpuerant molles ante dolore genae* 'la douleur jusque-là avait arrêté les larmes qui apaisent',

---

* [[*Ovide, Héroïdes*. Texte établi par Henri Bornecque et traduit par Marcel Prévost. Pp. xxiii + 164 (really 328). Paris: Société d'Édition 'Les Belles Lettres', 1928. *CR* 43 (1929), 194–7]]

[194

110 *illic, qui silices, Thesea, uincat, habes* 'là, Thésée, tu possèdes de quoi vaincre le caillou', XII 46 *deuota manu* 'docile', XIII 101 ⟦103⟧ *terris altior* (above the horizon) 'au plus haut, par-dessus la terre', XVI 58 *arbore nixus* 'ayant grimpé sur un arbre', 343 ⟦341⟧ *ecqua* 'laquelle', XVIII 187 *aestus* (warm weather) *adhuc tamen est* 'et encore n'est-ce en ce moment qu'un orage', XIX 113 *fallit* (opp. *nosse*) 'troublent', XX 123 f. ⟦121 f.⟧ *hostibus, et siquis...repugnat, | sic sit ut... solet esse mihi* 'et si quelque ennemi s'oppose', 228 ⟦226⟧ *amplius utque nihil, me tibi iungit amor* 'et, ce qui passe tout', 239 ⟦237⟧ *ponetur imago* 'que l'image soit présentée'. I have passed over others which are in fact no better, X 52 *exhibiturus*, XIII 23 *tenebris obortis*, XV 41 *etiam*. The following, if they are not downright errors, are extreme examples of licence: II 72 *pulsata regia* 'l'irruption dans les royaumes', VII 62 *bibat aquas* 's'engloutisse dans les flots', IX 35 *ipsa domo uidua* 'moi, veuve au logis', XVI 376 ⟦374⟧ *nomen ab aeterna posteritate feres* 'tu porteras ton nom à la postérité éternelle'. It is only fair to say that in some of his worst mistakes, even at X 110, Mr Prévost has predecessors.

Often, without actually violating the language, he misinterprets the author's words. I 10 *pendula tela* (*met.* IV 395 *pendens uestis*) 'inachevée', 26 *patrios* || *deos* (opp. *barbara*) 'de nos pères', II 30 *instar* (importance) 'apparence', III 32 *pondere et arte pares* (inter se) 'où le poids et l'art s'équivalent', 142 *sustinet hoc animae* (hanc animulam) *spes tamen una tui* 'ce qui le (*corpus*) soutient, c'est dans mon âme une espérance unique: toi', IV 118 *nati digna uigore* (digna uigore nati) *parens* 'mère digne de son fils par sa vaillance', 128 *quem* (tu quem) with *lectum*, V 77 *aperta aequora* (*thes. l. L.* II p. 220 42–56) 'faciles', IX 18 *Hercule supposito sidera fulsit Atlans* 'Hercule soutenait les astres quand Atlas les étaya', 123 *auerti* (que je me détourne) 'qu'on l'éloigne', XI 10 ⟦8⟧ *auctoris oculis exigeretur* (ἐξετασθείη) *opus* 'que l'acte fût consommé sous les yeux de l'auteur', XVI 71 *ne recusarem imperat* (forbids me to refuse) 'de peur que je refuse, il commande', 163 ⟦161⟧ *quae sit Paridi constantia* (quanta c. mea sit) 'ce qu'est la constance pour Paris', 200 ⟦198⟧ *cum dis potando nectare* (cum nectare dis potando) *miscet aquas* 'parmi les dieux mêle l'eau au nectar qu'ils vont boire', XVII 26 ⟦24⟧ *meum* with *crimen*, 129 ⟦127⟧ *laudibus istis* (laudatricis Veneris) 'tes louanges', XVIII 35 *inceptis iuuenalibus* (νεανικοῖς, vigoureux) 'ma juvénile entreprise', 148 *uector* (passager) 'passeur', XIX 45 *fere* (d'ordinaire) 'presque', XX 131 f. ⟦129 f.⟧ *ad limina* (hac illac eo) 'vers ta maison', XXI 203 f. ⟦201 f.⟧ *me infensam habet* (infensa sum illi, XVI 282 ⟦280⟧ *habeas faciles*, Liu. XXVIII 34 10 *iratos habere*) 'il me croit irritée', XXI 214 ⟦212⟧ *scriptis* (in malo) *eminus icta tuis* 'ta lettre m'a frappée de loin', 232 ⟦230⟧ *tu ueniam nostris uocibus* (pour mes paroles) *ipse petas* 'par ma voix' ('c'est-à-dire en mon nom' says Mr Bornecque). The sense of *eras ante* I 44, *prohibe* V 118, and *pacta* VI 5 is quite misunderstood.

Mr Prévost sometimes mistranslates under compulsion, because Mr Bornecque has given him a text which must be mistranslated if it is not to be nonsense. When at XIX 62 he renders *nostra* by 'ta', that is not ignorance but dire necessity; and presumably also when he takes II 109 *meae cui* as *tuas quae*, 115 *cui mea* as *cuius tibi*, and XI 48 ⟦46⟧ *dena* as *decima*. At XI 34 ⟦32⟧ he is obliged to pretend that he does not know *amans* from *amor* because Mr Bornecque has chosen to print *erat* instead of *eram*; and his absurd translation of XVI 77–9 is caused, though it cannot be excused, by an absurd punctuation. But now and again the interpreter loses patience and defies the editor: he has dared to translate the true readings VI 7 *signatur*, X 73 *tum*, XVI 145 ⟦143⟧ *crede*, XVII 173 ⟦171⟧ *relicta*, XX 76 ⟦74⟧ *parua*, XXI 64 ⟦62⟧ *iactas*, instead of what Mr Bornecque has put in their place.

Mr Bornecque's share of the work is much worse done. As he has collated no MS, he had only to report the witness of Sedlmayer or (for P) of Palmer; and this simple task he has been unable to perform without making more than 200 false statements, in which total I do not include transparent and corrigible misprints such as *ereandis* or *sribenti* or *fraximus*. Many of his notes are nonsense, like VI 144 *fuit* PG, *foret* P, where the second P should be E, or X 30 *tenta* G, *tenta* P, which should be *tenta* P, *tensa* G. Many of them exactly reverse the truth, as VII 12 ⟦10⟧ *quaeque* P, *quae* GE and 153 *quaeris* PG, *quaerit* E. P is so often substituted for P² and P² for P¹ that the printers are emboldened to such facetiousness as P' Pᵃ Pᵉ Pʳ. In Palmer's edition there is a photograph of the page of P containing VIII 30–57: Mr Bornecque contradicts it seven times. At XII 71 his note on the three words *noscis an exciderunt* contains five falsehoods, not reckoning a misprint. His note on VII 26, *Aenean* GE, *Aeneanque* P, is all false; the truth is *-an* P, *-anque* G, *-amque* E. At XVI 219 ⟦217⟧ P has *conuia* for *conuiuia*: he says it has *omnia* for *talia*. His antiquated text of VII 71 is *quicquid id est, totum merui; concedite, dicas*, in which the plural imperative is addressed, he says, to the phantom of Dido. The true note on this would be *Quidquid id* codd. recc., *quid id* E, *quid tanti* PG: *totum* P²G et corr. ex *tum* E, *tutum* P¹, *ut tum* Madvig: *dicas* P, *dices* GE. Mr Bornecque's is *Quicquid* PG, *quid* E: *merui* om. E: *quid tante est ut tum* codd. rec. Madvig et Palmes: one true statement, six false (but Sedlmayer is chiefly to blame for *merui* om. E), three suppressions of material fact, and a misprint. That all other editors since 1871 have printed *quid tanti est ut tum* 'merui, concedite' *dicas* the reader ‖ must find out for himself. A true note on VIII 77 *flebat auus Phoebeque soror* would be *Phoebeque* Mezeriacus, *phoebique* P, *flebatque* G: Mr Bornecque's is *Flebat* P, *flebatque* G, which he means for a note on the first word in the verse and doubtless fancies that he has copied from his authorities. For he has not learnt to read an apparatus criticus, and some of his mistakes are due less to negligence than to ignorance of his trade. Sedlmayer, though not a model of neatness and precision, is seldom ambiguous or unintelligible; but Mr Bornecque contrives to misunderstand him. At 1 85 he says that G has *ille tu* for *ille*: the meaning of Sedlmayer's note is that it has *tu* for *tamen*. At II 15 he says that E has *necdum* for *interdum*: Sedlmayer said that it had *necdum* for *ne dum*. At VII 59 he says it has *amor et mater* for *mater Amorum*: Sedlmayer said it had *et* for *quia*. Where his authorities have committed errors, Mr Bornecque will make them worse: Sedlmayer's reports of E at II 137 and IV 169 are false, but less false than what Mr Bornecque has substituted; and probably he is quite unaware that he has made any substitution. For he is no more skilful at framing an apparatus than at using one, and does not know how to say what he wants to say. Take III 67: text *reditusque placent*, note *reditus* PG, *redditus* E: *placent* PG, *placeant* E: this means either that all three MSS omit *que* or that all present it; and neither is true. His note on VII 65, though he does not guess it, means that P and E have *te*, which they have not: the lemma should have been *age te* G. XVII 53 [[51]] *et* P², *eea* P¹, *quod* G is both false and unintelligible, for there are two *et*'s in the verse and it refers to neither: it should be *Et* P²G, *ea* P¹. Similarly his notes on XIII 7 and 21 leave the reader not merely in ignorance but in conscious and aching ignorance. His note on XIII 29, *Vt* P, *utque* G, is not false, but no falsehood could be more deceitful, and a reader who finds out the truth will be somewhat indignant. At one moment he will record such utterly insignificant variants as *acerua* for *acerba* or *dii* for *di*; at another he will print *petendo* (XIV 61) without saying that the MS lections are *tinendo tenendo timendo*, silently substitute *est* for *et* (VII 19 [[17]]) or *cum* for *quo* (XIV 86) or *tu* for *io* (103) or *sibi* for *tibi* (XX 244 [[242]]), or silently suppress a *dum* in VII 179.

The verses XVI 39–144 [[142]] are said on p. 1 to be preserved by the cod. Treuiranus (*i.e.* of Trèves) saec. XIII, and on p. xx by 'un manuscrit de Trévise, du XVIe'. Neither is ever mentioned in the notes, for the sufficient reason that the one does not contain the verses and the other does not exist. Mr Bornecque's delusions appear to spring from the fact that in Vat. Gr. 1480 saec. XVI the verses are rendered into Greek by Thomas *Triuisanus*.

A recension of Ovid by this scholar can have no importance. It is chiefly distinguished by its freedom in admitting conjectures, on condition that they are causeless and useless, and its readiness to expel verses as interpolated, provided that there is nothing against them. Among all that has been written on the *heroides* Mr Damsté's paper in *Mnem.* 1905 pp. 1–56 is conspicuous for shallowness and futility; but in him Mr Bornecque has found a kindred spirit, and uses nearly 30 of his conceits to disfigure or lacerate the text. His own proposals, which are fewer, might be mistaken for Mr Damsté's. Those at XII 151, XIV 49, and XVI 352 [[350]] are not bad, but that is because they are not his. Accuracy in the ascription of conjectures is not to be expected from him, and he wrongly assigns more than 20. Palmer in his 1st ed. adopted at III 48, instead of *mihi*, the much inferior *mea* which Keil had falsely reported from P:

in his 2nd ed. he abandoned it, but Mr Bornecque prints it still and attributes it
to Palmer. At XV 198 he gives *plectra dolore iacent, muta dolore lyra* and his note
is '*iacent* Housman, *tacent* codd.: *lyra* Housman, *lyra est* libri'. Bad as the verse
was already, this namesake of mine has made it worse, and Mr Prévost very
properly ignores his aimless and mischievous meddling. The fact is that Mr
Bornecque, who probably has never read anything that I have written, saw an
emendation of mine cited on p. lvii of Palmer's edition, but could not transcribe
it. His inadequacy to an ‖ editor's task is visible at every turn. At I 2 he prints
attamen, fourth word in its sentence, without saying or knowing that the
oldest authority gives *attinet*. At XX 223 〚221〛 he prints *Carthaeis* for *Coryciis*,
in evident ignorance of *papyr. Oxy.* 1011 u. 56 〚Callimachus fr. 75 56 Pfeiffer〛,
which has been before the world ever since 1910. At X 143, where the true sense
is yielded by the *ne* of the best MSS, he prints *nec*, which is not even Latin,
because Madvig's edition of the *de finibus*, though published in 1839, has not yet
come his way. Some of the misprints in the text, as at XI 38 〚36〛, XV 139, and
XVII 207 〚205〛, are formidable. One would suppose that *fluctuosa* II 121,
Sychaeeu VII 97, *Tegaeus* IX 87, *credes* XVI 145 〚143〛 were also misprints, did
they not recur in the notes or the index. Because Ovid says *Cressa puella* and
Thressa puella, the index has 'Cressus, a, um' and 'Thressus, a, um'; because
he says *geminas Leucippidas*, it has 'Leucippidae'; because he says *cum Minyis*
and *orat opem Minyis*, it has 'Minyi'. From the explanatory notes it may be
learnt that Neptune was the grandfather of Theseus and Jupiter the father of
Leda, that Arcas was turned into a bear along with his mother, that Troezen is
situate at the isthmus of Corinth, and that the Mygdonian marble came from
Macedon. At V 30 Oenone mentions Xanthus and evokes from Mr Bornecque
this comment: 'Rivière de Troade. Elle prenait sa source dans le Taurus et se
jetait dans la mer de Lycie.' There should be a companion note on *Paris* in the
same distich: 'Fils de Priam. Selon Henri IV il valait bien une messe.'

156

THE LATIN FOR *ASS**

In English, down to the 19th century, the beast which carried Balaam was generally and almost universally, both in speech and in writing, denominated the ass. It is so no longer: the name *ass*, except in metaphor as a term of contempt or insult, has disappeared from conversation and from most kinds of print, and survives only in serious poetry and in prose of some solemnity. The name *donkey*, first printed in 1785 in a dictionary of slang, has usurped its place.

It is possible that in Latin, in the 1st century before Christ, an analogous but contrary change befel the usage of *asinus*. It is not certain, because most of Ennius and the old tragedy has perished, and we cannot be sure that the word was ever thought fit company for a sublime vocabulary; but in the classical age, from Lucretius to Juvenal, it was excluded from elevated and even from refined poetry. There are of course many poets, Lucretius, Tibullus, Lucan, Valerius Flaccus, Silius, Statius, and others, who had no occasion to mention the animal. But it is mentioned by Virgil, Horace, Propertius, Ovid, Seneca, Martial, and Juvenal, and in the *Priapea* and the 10th book of Columella; and all these authors, even Virgil, so chary of diminutives, call it *asellus*. The exceptions are the lowly and pedestrian Phaedrus, whose spiritual home was the stable and the farmyard; one line, I 121, in Persius, who added the coarseness of diatribe to the coarseness of satire; one line of the grossest obscenity in Catullus, 97 10; and this distich of the *copa*, 25 f.,

> huc calybita ueni. lassus iam sudat asellus:
> parce illi, Vestae delicium est asinus,

a pretty piece of artificial rusticity, in which *asinus* matches *delicium*.

It is true that Ovid, who has a dozen examples of *asellus*, is once presented by his MSS with *asinus*. In *fast.* VI 319–44 he relates how Priapus was baulked in a nocturnal attempt on Vesta by the unseasonable braying of an ass: then follow these verses, 345–7,

> Lampsacos hoc animal solita est mactare Priapo
> apta asini flammis indicis exta damus;
> quem tu, diua, memor de pane monilibus ornas.

* [[CQ 24 (1930), 11–13: the paper is mentioned in *PCPhS* 1929, 10]]

But the pentameter has aroused lively suspicion in critics who had no suspicion of *asini*. It stands in no relation, grammatical or other, to its hexameter, and, if it refers, as it must, to the Romans, it is not only false in itself but contradicted by the next verse. Heinsius condemned the whole couplet: and when Burman pointed out that its removal would make the ‖ relative *quem* in 347 pertain to *ille* in 344, that is to Priapus, Bentley condemned 343 f. into the bargain. But 345–7 were found here in conjunction at the beginning of the 4th century by Lactantius, *inst.* I 21 26 ‘hac de causa Lampsacenos asellum Priapo quasi in ultionem mactare consuesse, apud Romanos uero eundem Vestalibus sacris in honorem pudicitiae conseruatae panibus coronari’; and the seat of the evil is in 346, which must be bound to 345 by a participle agreeing with *Lampsacos.* Bergk *opusc.* I p. 664 proposed *domans* for *damus*, though acknowledging that the phrase *exta dare* was both appropriate and Ovidian; but Ovid never ends a pentameter with a present participle unless it has resigned its participial force and become an epithet, as in *ex Pont.* II 9 46 *cruoris amans.* Madvig therefore *adu.* II p. 108 did better to retain *damus* and write

> *fata* ‘asini flammis indicis exta damus’;

but it would be hard to find an example of *fatus* thus used, and there certainly is none in Ovid. Suspicion now converges from two quarters upon *asini*; and I believe that this un-Ovidian and superfluous word is a gloss on *indicis* which has ousted the necessary participle.

> Lampsacos hoc animal solita est mactare Priapo
> ‘apta’ ⟨canens⟩ ‘flammis indicis exta damus.’

I have said that *asellus* is the regular substitute, but there is also another. Manilius V 350–2 thus describes the character and pursuits of the man born under the Centaur:

> aut stimulis agitauit onus mixtasque iugabit
> semine quadripedes aut curru celsior ibit
> aut onerabit equos armis aut ducet in arma.

agitauit M, *agitauit aut* L, *agit aut* GL². *onus* M, *omnis* (i.e. *oṁis*) GL. Here, as often, it appears that the reading preserved by M, the least interpolated MS, has been corrupted and then corrected in the MSS of the other family; and such a conjecture as Mr P. Thomas’ *aget ante boues* begins at the wrong end and stands on a treacherous foundation. *agitauit*, if that is the right verb, must of course be altered with Jacob to *agitabit*, which is no more than a change of orthography. But his pretence (p. 215) that ‘stimulis agitabit onus’ can mean ‘agitabit iumenta onus ferentia’ is a characteristic piece of impudence.

The man born under the Centaur, says Manilius, will yoke mules and drive or ride horses. In a series where the horse comes third and the mule second, what animal should come first? The very animal which Manilius mentions. In 'stimulis agitabit onus' *onus* is the Greek ὄνους, for which spelling of Greek accusatives plural in Latin see *C.Q.* XIII p. 70 ⟦this edition p. 984⟧, where the reference to Naber's Fronto should be p. 146. Virgil *georg.* I 273 had said ‖ 'tardi...agitator aselli'; Manilius, like him, cannot stoop to *asinus*, but uses the creature's Greek name instead; and that he would not stick at this may be inferred from his use of *sybotes* instead of *subulcus* at V 126. I mention in conclusion, because the dictionaries omit it, that the emperor Commodus bestowed *onos* as a nickname on one of his favourites, *uit.* 10 9.

157

DRAVCVS AND MARTIAL XI 8 1*

The definitions of *draucus* in Forcellini and Freund and Georges and Lewis and Short may best be described as lurid moonshine; and the care of Benoist and Goelzer to conceal the very existence of the word from the Gallic nation reminds one of Miss Prism superintending Cecily Cardew's study of political economy and directing her to omit the chapter on the Fall of the Rupee. There ought surely to have been similar silence for the French and similar mis-information for the rest of us on an earlier page: '*comoedus, i,* m., moechus, Iuu. VI 73 soluitur his magno comoedi fibula || (379 sq. si gaudet cantu, nullius fibula durat | uocem uendentis praetoribus), Mart. XIV 215 dic mihi simpliciter, comoedis et citharoedis, | fibula, quid praestas? carius ut futuant.' *Draucus* is as innocent a word as *comoedus,* and simply means one who performs feats of strength in public. In two passages no other interpretation is possible:[1] Mart. VII 67 4–6 'harpasto quoque subligata ludit | et flauescit haphe grauesque draucis | halteras facili rotat lacerto', XIV 48 'HARPASTA. haec rapit Antaei uelox in puluere draucus, | grandia qui uano colla labore facit.' But partly because of the common though false opinion that muscular strength and sexual vigour go together, and partly because these men, being *infibulati* to prevent them from impairing their stamina, might be expected, when *refibulati,* to exhibit ardour, they were also in request for another purpose and could now and then earn pocket-money in their spare time. This, nothing more, is signified by Mart. I 96 12, IX 27 10, XI 72 1. The old citation '*gloss. Philox.* draucus κατοπύγων' has prudently been dropped by Georges, for the MSS have 'depugis', – not to mention that κατοπύγων means exactly the opposite of what *draucus* is supposed to mean; and it is hardly worth relating that *draucus* has been conjectured for *raucus* in Iuu. XI 156.

But neither with its true nor with its imaginary meaning can this word main-tain itself in Mart. XI 8 1. Its incongruousness in the one sense and its hideous incongruousness in the other cannot fully be displayed without printing the greater part of the poem.

> lassa quod hesterni spirant opobalsama drauci,
> ultima quod curuo quae cadit aura croco,

* [[CR 44 (1930), 114–16]]

[1] I spoke in haste: all things are possible. In Pauly-Wissowa VII p. 2407 the genitive *Antaei* is detached from *puluere* and attached to *draucus,* 'der Liebhaber des Antäus'.

poma quod hiberna maturescentia capsa,
   arbore quod uerna luxuriosus ager,
de Palatinis dominae quod serica prelis,   5
   sucina uirginea quod regelata manu,
amphora quod nigri, sed longe, fracta Falerni,
   quod qui Sicanias detinet hortus apes,
quod Cosmi redolent alabastra focique deorum,
   quod modo diuitibus lapsa corona comis: 10
singula quid dicam? non sunt satis: omnia misce,
   hoc fragrant pueri basia mane mei.

In all Martial there are no verses of more choice and elaborate refinement. The image, in such a poem, of an *hesternus draucus*, supposed to mean 'qui heri pathicum subegit', was naturally revolting to Gronouius and is not suffered to pollute the text of Schneidewin, Friedlaender, Gilbert, or Mr Duff. Two editors of our golden age retain it, and without an obelus; for if conservative critics had not strong stomachs they would not be conservative critics.

Gronouius found in an interpolated MS the reading

lapsa quod *externis* spirant opobalsama *truncis*,

and recommended it in a learned note, *diatr.* c. XVI, pp. 165 f. ed. Hand. The words *lapsus* and *lassus*, *externus* and *hesternus*, are much confused, and balsam is in fact the exudation of a shrub foreign to Italy. The conjecture nevertheless is false, and neither *lassa* nor *hesterni* can be altered; they harmonise too perfectly with the '*ultima*...aura' of 2 and the *longe* (spirat) of 7, all three verses suggesting a faint waft of distant or evanescent fragrance.

I have known for years and years that *drauci* is here a corruption of the name of some vessel used for holding the unguent: but probably I should never have discovered the name itself if it were not for the 9th edition of Liddell and Scott's Greek lexicon. It is *dracti*. Information about this word will be found in Dittenberger's *Orientis Graeci inscriptiones selectae* vol. II p. 83, where seven examples of it are collected from inscriptions: for instance θεὶς δρακτῷ τὸ ἔλαιον and ἀλείψασαν δὶς δρακτοῖς καὶ ἐπιρύτοις and ἔλαια δρακτοῖς πολλάκις τεθεικότα. Other Greek words used by Martial and, so far as can be learnt from the dictionaries, by no other Latin author are *ascaules*, *chersos*, *copta*, *eschatocollion*, *gelasinus*, *hexaclinon*, *opthalmicus*, *orthopygium*, *pityon*.

It will not be out of place to add that the obscene sense discovered by lexicographers and editors in *strangulare* || at Cic. *fam.* IX 22 4 is another hallucination. What Cicero says is that we are absurd in treating parricide as more mentionable than sexual intercourse, not that *strangulare* was ever used in the latter connexion. The text (*aliquid*) actually forbids that interpretation; and it has therefore lately been proposed to alter it.

158

REVIEW: A. BOURGERY AND
M. PONCHONT, *LUCAIN VI–X**

Since the appearance of the first half of this edition, reviewed in *C.R.* 1927 pp. 189–91 ⟦this edition pp. 1132–5⟧, it has been thought advisable to make some change in the editorship, and the last three books have been put into the hands of Mr Ponchont. The former review was much too long for the importance of the work, though all too short for the number and the nature of its mistranslations. In this second half the errors are fewer and less formidable, but to notice them adequately would still need too much room; and instead of sorting them into classes I will first give a general list of the worse among them and then exhibit a single specimen from each book.

VI 139, 226 f., 301, 311, 319 f., 385, 535 f., 716 f.; VII 132, 205 f., 249, 253, 325, 365, 375 f., 395, 418, 463, 467 f., 484, 501, 518 f., 537 f., 580, 603, 705, 842, 856 f.; VIII 40 f., 52 f., 236, 246 f., 402 f., 462, 512 f., 619, 646 f., 748, 792; IX 83, 153 f., 219 f., 245, 283, 346, 365, 369, 387, 390–2, 405 f., 434, 457, 520 f., 559, 580, 593 f., 616, 667 f., 684, 852 f., 983, 992 f.; X 9 f., 184, 203, 272, 369 f., 449, 472, 502.

VI 385 *Magnetes equis, Minyae gens cognita remis*. Having mistaken a nom. plur. for a gen. sing. the editor translates *Minyae gens* 'les descendants de Minyas', bolsters up his error with the fiction 'Minyas était un des compagnons de Jason', and puts this imaginary person into his index.

VII 375 f. *haec* (populus futurus) *libera nasci,* | *haec* (qui nunc est populus) *uult turba mori* 'libre cette foule veut naître, libre elle veut mourir'.

VIII 792 *inscripsit* (saxo) *sacrum semusto stipite nomen* 'il grave sur un pieu à demi consumé le nom auguste'.

IX 369 *haud ultra Garamantidas attigit undas* 'ne s'avança point au delà des eaux des Garamantes'.

X 9 f. *fertur securus in urbem* | *pignore tam saeui sceleris sua signa secutam* (which had pledged by Pompey's murder its adhesion to his cause) 'il entre, sûr du gage offert par un crime si cruel, dans la capitale, qui fait escorte à ses enseignes'.

* ⟦*Lucain: La Guerre Civile* (*La Pharsale*). Tome II, Livres VI–X. Texte établi et traduit par A. Bourgery et Max Ponchont. Pp. 225 (really 432). Paris: Société d'édition 'Les belles lettres', 1929. *CR* 44 (1930), 136⟧

I have chosen these rather than such blunders as VII 395 *nocte coacta* 'à la nuit noire' or 468 *percussā* mistaken for *percussă* because they better display the editors' incompetence as interpreters and make it the more surprising that they should so often venture to offer their own opinions in places where interpretation is the subject of dispute. Mr Bourgery even thinks that he can amend the text. X 314 'hoc fere modo restituit Bourgery: *qua iter est nostrum ad rubri commercia ponti*'. VII 156 *typhonas*: 'on pourrait lire *pithias*'. VII 309 f. 'il me verra percer mes entrailles, lui qui, vainqueur, n'avait pas jusqu'ici pitié de l'ennemi': 'what is he mistranslating now?' asks the astounded reader; but the French is faithful to the absurdity of the Latin, for the Latin is Mr Bourgery's and is this: *fodientem uiscera cernet | me mea, qui nondum uictor respexerat hostem.*

In the notes my reference at VII 156 to 'Olympiod. in Ar. *met.* p. 13 14–16 ed. Berol.' has become 'Olympiodore (*Métam. d'Aratus* p. 13, 14, 16 éd. de Berlin)', and at 161 my 'Cassius Dio XLI 61 2' is transformed into 'Dion Chrysostome'.

159

REVIEW: W. MOREL,
POETAE LATINI MINORES, VOL. I*

The late Friedrich Vollmer, after an unpromising start, became in the course of his life a considerable scholar and even something of a critic, and so far as concerns the investigation and collation of MSS and the structure of an *apparatus criticus* he was almost the model of what an editor should be; but he remained to the end of his days the most incapable and insensible of conjectural emendators, and the simplest way to improve his very bad text of the *appendix Vergiliana* would be to eject nearly all his innovations. This volume ‖ however is not a new edition but an anastatic reprint, and the changes made, though more than Mr Morel enumerates in his three pages of 'supplementa', are necessarily few and small.

Mr Morel is not master of the subject. He has paid attention to what has been written on these poems since 1909, but shows no great knowledge of anything earlier; and the new conjectures which he singles out are far inferior to dozens of old ones which Vollmer neglected or suppressed. For example, when *Cir.* 48 'impia prodigiis ut quondam *externit amplis*' has been corrected by Heinsius and Schrader to *exterrita miris*, who wants to be bothered with such things as *pro Stygiis . . . exterrita ⟨te⟩mplis?* Mr Muenscher's *rhoezo* at *catal.* 5 2 is excellent, Mr Reitzenstein's *moles, frustra* at *Aetn.* 489 ⟦488⟧ is satisfying, and there is something to be said for one or two of Mr Morel's own, *Cul.* 243 *quod* for *qui* or *de, Aetn.* 380 ⟦379⟧ *conualuere mora*; but on the whole it is a wretched show. Mr Birt's *Centaurum* at *catal.* 11 2 is the very type of a thoughtless conjecture: if Virgil had written this he could no more have added *pocula* than Callimachus added οἶνος.

The following notes will fill some gaps in Mr Morel's knowledge.

Cul. 141 '*monent* Sillig.' He took it from one of the codd. Vossiani.

Cul. 269 '*poenane* Schenkl.' Karl or Heinrich? The former, *Zeitschr. f. d. oesterr. Gymn.*, 1867, p. 783.

Cul. 301 '*sociatae* Klotz cum *v.*' Bembus, Scaliger, Heinsius, Ribbeck, Ellis cum V.

* ⟦*Poetae Latini minores.* Post Aemilium Baehrens iterum recensuit Fridericus Vollmer. Volumen I, Appendix Vergiliana. Exemplar anastatice iteratum curauit adnotationis supplemento auxit denuo emendauit Willy Morel. Pp. xii + 208. Leipzig: Teubner, 1930. *CR* 44 (1930), 234–5⟧

Cul. 326 '*alma* Fr. Marx, *Moloss... Wortformen* p. 225.' It was the vulgate for 300 years and more.

Copa 4 '*ad...calamos* coniungendum esse recte monuit Bannier *Thes. l. L.* III 124 24.' It was Leo *Cul.* pp. 44 f.; whether 'recte' is another matter. Those who obey Mr Morel and turn to Weege *Der Tanʒ in der Antike* p. 127 tab. 181 will be disappointed of their expectations.

Cir. 53 '*pro patria* Leonem secutus scripsi.' Et Hauptium secutus Leo.

Priap. 3 17 '*huic* Ribbeck.' This conjecture is unmetrical, and Ribbeck, having proposed it in 1868, abandoned it in 1895 for *tot.*

Aetn. 152 '*crusta est* nescioquis apud Gerckium – locum nunc non inuenio.' An editor of the *app. Verg.* ought to know of Haupt.

The coinage *reimpressionis* on p. ix is presumably a reverent imitation of Vollmer, who explained *rēnauit* in Manil. V 609 as *reenauit.*

I see that corrections which I sent to Vollmer have been embodied in the apparatus at *Cul.* 9, 57, 90, 231, 232, 353. His reports of V at 71, 98 f., 191 are not quite exact, but it does not matter.

160

REVIEW: H. J. IZAAC, *MARTIAL I–VII**

In the text of this edition there are few novelties, and only one, the interrogative punctuation of VII 36 6, is acceptable; but the choice of readings has been made with considered and independent judgment and the general result is good, though Schneidewin's cure for the metre of III 3 4, being itself illegitimate, should have been rejected. Mr Izaac is the second editor to adopt my *tristities* for *tristitia et* at VII 47 6; but I have now defended the MS lection in Manil. vol. v ⟦ed. 1, 1930⟧ p. 123. In the apparatus criticus, which on the whole is carefully constructed, sundry omissions are due to oversight, as at *spect.* 22 12, I 78 8, 107 7, III 82 2, 18, IV 53 6, 64 19, 66 17, VII 14 7, but many more are capricious and arbitrary, as at II 8 7 and VII 86 7. There are positive errors at *spect.* 12 1, I 29 4, 59 4 ('*lauer* α' is a fiction of Mr Lindsay's, and so is '*subigi* α' at VI 67 2), II 60 3, 61 7, IV 64 34, V 44 1, 60 4, 78 32, VII 35 7, 53 6, 54 8, 64 3, 69 2, 70 1, 72 3. The worst is VI 27 2 '*Ficelias* edd., *Ficuleas* [dubitanter] Friedlaender' with nothing said of the MSS, where the truth is '*Ficelias* β, *Ficetias* γ, *Ficuleas* Brodaeus'. One nuisance demands particular notice. The sign ω, defined as meaning 'consensus codicum omnium qui praesto sunt praeter eos qui nominatim citantur', is used not only when it serves a purpose, as at II 29 10 '*leges* ω, *legas* XV' or VI 74 1 '*imus* ω, *unus* PQFf', where the families β and γ split up, but often without any rule or consistency as a casual substitute for α or β or γ or αβ or αγ or βγ, so that the reader must halt and consider which of the six is meant. Take p. 15 '4 *scribit* γ, *scripsit* β. 5 *latine loqui* ω, *latina eloqui* β.' If Mr Izaac were asked why he calls the same MSS γ in the one note and ω in the other, he could not answer; but I can. It all depends on Mr Lindsay. The first note is copied from his; but in the second, to save space, he omitted the lemma and gave only the variant of β: Mr Izaac, inserting the lemma (for which the reader will thank him), could not be at the pains of ascertaining and specifying its ‖ authority, but used the vague ω for the precise γ; and the trouble which he would not take once for all must now be taken hundreds or thousands of times over by one reader after another. The inconsistencies of notation are sometimes ridiculous. V 1 1 '*hoc* βγ, *haec* α', 4 '*plana* ω, *plena* T': ω means the same as βγ and T the same as α. III 16 5 '*corio* αγ, *satis est* β; *te* ω,

---

* ⟦*Martial: Épigrammes*. Tome I (Livres I–VII). Texte établi et traduit par H. J. Izaac. Pp. xxxix + 272 (really 510). Paris: 'Les Belles Lettres', 1930. *CR* 45 (1931), 81–3⟧

tu R': to match the first note the second should be '*te* βγ, *tu* α'; to match the second the first should be '*corio* ω (or Rγ), *satis est* β'.

The translation is clear and fluent: mistakes are not many, and none is disgraceful; but Mr Izaac sometimes prints one reading or punctuation and translates another, as at II 14 7, III 81 4, IV 55 21, VII 19 2–5, 72 6, 87 7. He acknowledges obligation to Mr W. C. A. Ker's version in the Loeb series, and some of his false renderings, as at III 20 12 *delicatae sole*, IV 71 2 *siqua*, VII 15 1 *absistit*, 80 2 *tetricae*, appear to spring from that source; others may be due to Nisard, III 4 1 *requiret*, 65 5 *trita*, VII 17 9 *munere dedicata paruo*, 95 15 *recentem*, 16 *sensus*. The following words and phrases are mistranslated, some of them very strangely, though rendered aright by others: I 41 16 *qui*, 88 10 *mando*, 90 8 *Venus*, 108 5 *migrandum*, II 7 8 *ardalio*, 17 5 *tondet* (and 62 2 *tonsa*), 19 3 *Aricino...cliuo*, 49 2 *pueris* (and III 23 1), III 15 2 *caecus amat*, 36 7 f. *hoc, ut sim*, 55 3 *placeas tibi*, 63 14 *pertricosa*, IV 86 6 *si te pectore, si tenebit ore*, V 37 7 *uicit*, VI 13 5 *ludit*, 18 3 *reliquit*, VII 1 1 *crudum*, 18 6 *inguinibus*, 67 2 *mariti*, 80 11 *famulus. Memphitica templa* in II 14 7 is rendered 'le temple des deux déesses de Memphis', and these two goddesses are said to be Isis and Serapis. In the following errors Mr Izaac may have more companions. I 106 6 *certae fututionis* is not 'victoire certaine': the substantive is 'jouissance', the adjective has the force which he renders by 'nette' at VI 73 5 and by 'précise' at VII 84 6: compare Shakespeare *Tr. and Cr.* III 2 26 f. 'I do fear...that I shall lose distinction in my joys' and Loti *Pêcheur d'Islande* IV 7 'Lui, Yann, connaissant l'effet du vin sur les sens, ne buvait pas du tout ce soir-là.' II 71 1 the notion of *candidus* is not 'naïveté' but 'bienveillance' or even 'générosité', as again in IV 86 5 and VII 99 5. III 50 4 *oxygarum* evidently is not 'sauce pour le poisson' but an hors d'œuvre. V 16 9 *nunc* is not 'pour l'instant' but 'au lieu de cela', and also in V 20 11, where Mr Izaac does not translate it. VII 18 14 *disce uel inde loqui* is not 'apprends à parler même par là' but 'apprends au moins de là à parler'; and *et* is not 'ou' but 'et'. VII 35 7 f. *ecquid lauaris* is not 'est-ce que tu te baignes' but 'baigne-toi donc'. VII 49 2 *faucibus oua tuis* could not possibly mean 'pour ta faim': what it does mean may be learnt from Plin. *n.h.* XXIX 42 'prodest...luteum (ouorum)...faucium scabritiae'. VII 92 9 *subito sidere* is not 'coup du destin' but paralysis; 95 9 *dulcior* not 'plus agréable que moi' but 'qu'elles'; 97 12 *aedes* not 'maisons' but 'temples'.

Some misunderstandings which the translation itself does not betray are indiscreetly revealed by the explanatory notes. They are very wide of the mark at *spect.* 16 4, 28 7 f., II 60 3, 78, III 83, V 30 5, VI 16 1. In II 17 5 there is no 'jeu de mots obscène', and *radit* is incapable of the sense which Messrs Ker and Izaac attach to it. II 28 6 *res duas* is explained by two verbs, one of which is utterly wrong: two nouns are meant, and they will be found in XII 59 10. IV 61 16 *quod uelimus audire* is not 'le récit d'un cadeau fait avec ces richesses' but a piece of bad luck. VI 2 6 *et spado moechus erat* has not the remotest connexion with V 75 or II 60. VI 3 1 *Dardanio...Iulo* (the father of the Julian house) is safely translated 'au troyen Iule', but then the note blurts out 'c'est-à-dire au peuple romain'. III 14 3 *sportularum fabula* 'à savoir que les patrons affamaient leurs clients'; then 'cf. III 7', where the true explanation is given. III 42 2 *non mihi labra linis* 'qui sentent tes rides (dans un baiser)': they are *rugas uteri*. VII 45 5 *per Siculas...undas* 'le détroit de Messine (pour aller en Afrique)': what a route!

The notes indeed are the weak part ‖ of the book, for much in them is purely fictitious or definitely false. *spect.* 7 4 'le rôle de Lauréolus fut tenu...par un acteur qui, au moment du châtiment, disparaissait pour faire place à un criminel'. *spect.* 27 5 f. 'l'hydre de Lerne avait cent têtes qu'il fallait abattre d'un seul coup, sans quoi elles renaissaient'. I 76 11 *Permessus* 'fleuve de Thessalie'. II 80 *Fannius* 'Fannius Caepio'. II 86 2 *nec retro lego Sotaden cinaedum* 'il avait notamment composé des vers qui, lus de droite à gauche, donnaient un sens obscène: on les appelait κίναιδοι'. III 20 10 *porticum templi* 'sans aucun doute le temple d'Isis et Serapis'. III 68 8 'au mois d'août, les dames romaines fidèles au culte d'Isis apportaient solennellement un phallus au temple de Vénus Erycine'. V 5 2 'Domitien...avait composé un poème lyrique.' V 61 5 'les élégants avaient des bagues d'été et des bagues d'hiver. Cf. Juvénale *Sat.* I 28.' V 65 12 *est tibi qui possit uincere Geryonen* 'Carpophore'. VII 13 3 'Hercule était le fondateur mythique de Tibur.' VII 44 6 'Caesonius avait antérieurement été en Afrique comme proconsul.' VII 97 8 *Turni nobilibus libellis* 'poète inconnu'. VII 99 1 *Crispine* 'riche affranchi, très en faveur auprès de Néron'.

I have observed misprints in the French at I 62 2 and 103 5, in the Latin at VI 25 5, 74 3, VII 14 3, 72 2, 87 4, and in the apparatus at III 47 12, 86 3, 93 20, VI 50 3, VII 71 2. Endeavour to make the translation face the text translated has either been lacking or has signally failed at pp. 4 f., 172 f., 189 f., 196 f. The printers have indulged immoderately in their favourite sport of dropping letters on the floor and then leaving them to lie there or else putting them back in wrong places; and at the top of p. 113 of the text their merriment transgresses the bounds of decorum.

161

PRAEFANDA*

Catull. 56 5–7

deprendi modo pupulum puellae
trusantem: hunc ego, si placet Dionae,
protelo rigida mea cecidi.

Catullus amicae puerum delicatum, quem masturbantem deprehenderat, opportunitate data percidit; quod a bubus ex ordine iunctis arcessito uerbo, de quibus Cato orig. v ap. Non. p. 363 [[576 Lindsay]] 'protelo trini boues unum aratrum ducent', *protelo* se fecisse dicit, hoc est ita ut rem ueneriam patrantium series non triplex, ut Suet. Tib. 43 1 et anth. Pal. XII 210, sed tamen duplex continuaretur; nec multo aliter Lucretius IV 190 'quasi protelo stimulatur fulgure fulgur' (alio aliud pone sequente). nam quod 'eodem tractu et tenore' interpretantur, temporali sensu, id si omnino eo uerbo significari posset, certe longius a proprio translatum esset nec tam uiuidam exprimeret imaginem; qui autem *pro telo* (ita sane libri) aut recipiunt aut obtuso acumine simul cum altero intellegi uolunt, admonendi uidentur telis pueros ob delicta non caedi.

Priap. 21

copia me perdit: tu suffragare rogatus
  indicio nec nos prode, Priape, tuo.
quaeque tibi posui tamquam uernacula poma
  de sacra nulli dixeris esse uia.

ficta a Buechelero opusc. I p. 337 narratiuncula non praestat aliorum explicationibus quas suo iure reicit. accipe carminis argumentum. horti dominus tanta pomorum inopia conflictatur ut aliunde emenda sint etiam quibus Priapum muneretur; cuius inopiae causa inuenienda est quae in copia alicuius rei posita sit et non nihil habeat pudoris. ista copia uidelicet furum fuit, quibus salax dominus eam legem dixerat quam puero fertur dixisse Priapus 5 3 sq. 'quod meus hortus habet sumas inpune licebit | si dederis nobis quod tuus hortus habet', 38 3 sq. 'pedicare uolo, tu uis decerpere poma: | quod peto si dederis, quod petis accipies'; qui quoniam et ‖ multi fuerunt et singuli ei copiam sui non grauate fecerunt, stupri mercedem totum pomorum prouentum abstulerunt.

* [[*Hermes* 66 (1931), 402–12]]

quod hic domini, id Priapi culpa factum est Mart. VII 91 'de nostro...agello...
mittimus...nuces: | cetera lasciuis donauit poma puellis | mentula custodis
luxuriosa dei.'

Priap. 37 3–12

cum penis mihi forte laesus esset
chirurgamque manum miser timerem,
5   dis me legitimis nimisque magnis,
ut Phoebo puta filioque Phoebi,
curandam dare mentulam uerebar.
huic dixi 'fer opem, Priape, parti
cuius tu, pater, ipse pars uideris;
10   qua salua sine sectione facta
ponetur tibi picta, quam leuaris,
parue et consimilisque concolorque.'

12 *parue et* cod. opt., *parua et* ceteri, in quo cum *parua* paene ineptum esset et
ineleganter abundaret coniunctio Scaliger utrumque uitium sustulit *compar*
scribendo; deteriora alii coniecerunt, nam Antonii *parque* legi metricae ad-
uersatur. detracta una littera, aliarum ordine mutato fit, quo nihil aptius, 'picta,
quam leuaris, | uerpae consimilisque concolorque'; datiuus enim, quamuis non
necessarius, melius tamen et usitatius adest quam abest. uide praeterea 34 4 sq.
'quot nocte uiros peregit una | tot uerpas tibi dedicat salignas.'

Priap. 52

heus tu, non bene qui manum rapacem
mandato mihi contines ab horto,
iam primum stator hic libidinosus
alternis et eundo et exeundo
5   porta te faciet patentiorem.
accedent duo qui latus tuentur
pulcre pensilibus peculiati;
qui cum te male foderint iacentem,
ad partum ueniet salax asellus
10   nilo deterius mutuniatus.
quare, si sapiet, malus cauebit,
cum tantum sciet esse mentularum. ||

9. quod uulgo pro *partum* editur *partem*, recte Buechelerus plurale, quod
coniecit Salmasius, ponendum fuisse monet; nec nimis inter se distare *partis* et
partū adnotauit Vollmerus. *pastum* Burmanni commentum non satis apparet id
quod significandum est significare posse: potest, opinor, *pratum*, hoc est
λειμῶνα, aptum asello uocabulum, quod cum Euripides Cycl. 171 pro feminae

natura posuisset, hunc poetam ad marem transtulisse non incredibile est, sicut
5 4 pueri *hortus* commemoratur, cum κῆπος Graece γυναικὸς αἰδοῖον sit.

aselli in hac re mentione admonitus dicturus eram de Catull. 97 9 sq. 'hic
futuit multas et se facit esse uenustum | et non pistrino traditur atque asino',
ubi quae asini partes futurae fuerint editores etiam obscaenitatis studiosissimi
se ignorare ostendunt: nunc uideo recte uersum intellectum esse in thes. ling.
Lat. II p. 791 60. restat igitur ut huc referam C.I.L. IV 2887 'Quintio siqui
recusat, assidat ad asinum', hoc est conquiniscat ut clunem summittat asello.

Priap. 69

cum fici tibi suauitas subibit
et iam porrigere huc manum libebit,
ad me respice, fur, et aestimato
quot pondo est tibi mentulam cacandum.

cacandum male interpretantur *concacandum*, quod et cottidie a minutissimis
auiculis fiebat nec quicquam incommodi habiturum erat, siquidem rei quam quis
concacet pondus aut mensura nihil momenti facit. quid uerum esset uiderat
Scioppius. scilicet accusatiui ea ratio est quae in Graeco σησαμίδας χέζειν, Eupol.
colac. frag. 163 3 ed. Kock., Athen. pp. 630a et 646f, habetur; cuius modi est
Pelagon. 308 'sanguinem...cacant' et Isid. orig. XII 7 71 in prouerbio 'malum
sibi auem cacare' de turdela ex cuius stercore uiscus nasci putabatur; nam in
Phaed. IV 19 25 non plane certa lectio est. cacat, hoc est merdae modo emittit,
mentulam cui eam finito opere extrahit pedicator; quae si iusto maior sit, cum
dolore id fieri consentaneum est. eodem modo explicanda sunt tria huius uerbi
exempla non rectius in thes. ling. Lat. III p. 8 54–8 collocata. C.I.L. X 8145
'hanc (mentulam supra pictam) ego cacaui' scripsit impudicus εὐρυπρωκτίᾳ sua
gloriatus. Nouius Bucculo frag. 6 ed. Ribb., Non. p. 507 [815 Lindsay], 'quod
editis nihil est; si uultis quod cacetis, copia est', hoc est si pedicari uultis.
Pomponius prostibulo ‖ frag. 151 ed. Ribb., Non. p. 84 [118 Lindsay], 'ego
quaero quod edim, hi (*has* libri) quaerunt quod (*quos* libri) cacent: contrarium
est.' ultimi duo loci dubitationem excludunt, nam edendi et concacandi uerborum notiones inter se contrariae non sunt.

Priap. 80

at non longa benest, at non bene mentula crassa
et quam si tractes crescere posse putes?
me miserum, cupidas fallit mensura puellas:
non habet haec aliud mentula maius ea.

4 *ea* (hoc est mensura) Barthius, *eo* libri. sic sublato sermonis uitio cetera
sanissima sunt. Buechelerus enim (qui etiam in eo fallitur quod Priapum loqui

putat) cum dicit opusc. I p. 361 'uerum praeter mensuram non modo *maius* sed omnino utile nihil dei mentula habebat' non intellegit illa *non habet*, ut *non uult* et οὔ φησιν, in unum uerbum coalescere, ut sit *desiderat*, et hoc dici, 'est aliud mensura maius quod haec mentula non habeat'. ceterum *eum* pronomen in fine pentametri posuerunt Propertius II 29 8 et Martialis V 47 2.

<h3 style="text-align:center">Sen. nat. quaest. I 16 7</h3>

'simul' inquit 'et uirum et feminam patior, nihilo minus illa quoque super-uacua mihi parte alicuius contumelia marem exerceo; omnia membra stupris occupata sunt.'

uerba *alicuius contumelia marem exerceo* coniecturis partim ineptissimis temptata, a Gerckio autem obelo notata, interpretationem solum quaerunt. nimirum Hostius pedicatori substratus et feminam lambens pene tamen marem, hoc est uirilitatem, exercet; quo modo Horatium locutum esse serm. II 8 15 'Alcon... *maris* expers' (euiratus) docui C.Q. VII p. 28 [[this edition p. 862]], quem et intellexit et imitatus est Persius VI 38 sq. 'sapere... *maris* expers', hoc est interprete Casaubono, 'sapientia ἄρρενος οὐδὲν ἔχουσα': similia sunt Manil. V 150 sq. 'pumicibus... horrentia membra polire | atque odisse *uirum*', Catull. 63 6, Luc. X 134, Lucian. Demon. 15 αὐτίκα σοι μάλα τὸν ἄνδρα (uirilitatem meam) δείξω, nec dissimilia Verg. Aen. II 591 'confessa *deam*' et Ouid. met. XII 601 'fassus... *deum*'; Cicero autem et *uires* et *crudelitatem exercere* dixit. iam *contumelia alicuius* uirilitatem exercet qui uiri feminaeue ore abutitur ‖ uel ut ait Suetonius Tib. 45 *capiti illudit*.[1] uide anth. Pal. V 48 ἡ τρισὶ λειτουργοῦσα πρὸς ἓν τέλος ἀνδράσι Λύδη, | τῷ μὲν ὑπὲρ νηδύν, τῷ δ᾽ ὑπό, τῷ δ᾽ ὄπιθεν, | εἰσδέχομαι φιλόπαιδα, γυναικομανῆ, φιλυβριστήν, ubi φιλυβριστής irrumator est, cum ὑπὲρ νηδύν eodem spectet quo Mart. XI 46 6 *summa petas*.

<h3 style="text-align:center">Pers. IV 33–6</h3>

at si unctus cesses et figas in cute solem
est prope te ignotus cubito qui tangat et acre
despuat: 'hi mores! penemque arcanaque lumbi
runcantem populo marcentis pandere uuluas!'

feminam aliquo modo duas uuluas habere dici posse apparet ex Mart. XI 43 12: cinaedus si eadem ratione unam, at plus unam non habet. qui quas res pandere dicatur facile intellegitur ex Catull. 15 18 sq. 'quem attractis pedibus *patente porta* | percurrent raphanique mugilesque'. scripserat nempe Persius 'mar-

---

[1] Suetonii locus in thes. ling. Lat. III s. u. *caput* non p. 399 10 ponendus fuit sed obscaenis adiciendus quae p. 408 34–7 collecta sunt, ubi desiderantur etiam Cic. dom. 83 *capite demisso*, Catull. 88 8, Sen. n. q. I 16 4 *caput merserat*, Mart. II 61 3, VI 26 1 *periclitatur capite*, Iuu. VI 49 *capitis matrona pudici*: adde quod Caesaris dictum *insultaturum se omnium capitibus* obscaene interpretatus est qui hoc ulli feminae facile fore negauit Suet. Iul. 22 2.

centis pandere ualuas', quas uersu 40 *elixas nates* appellauit. iterum librarii Nemes. cyn. 168 *pandere uuluas* dederunt ubi poeta 'aut uexare trabes, laceras aut *mandere ualuas*'.

C.I.L. IV 2360

(carm. epigr. Buech. 45, Diehl. Pomp. Wandinschr. 582)

amat qui scribit, pedicatur qui legit,
qui auscultat prurit, pathicus est qui praeterit.
ursi me comedant et ego uerpam qui lego.

quod saepe in parietibus et postibus dealbatis scriptum conspicitur *whoever reads this is a fool*, id salsius et improbius hoc carmen exprimit, ne eis quidem parcens qui non legant. duplici uiatorum generi x 6616 commemorato, 'bene sit tibi qui legis et tibi qui praeteris', tertius accedit a priore non multum diuersus 'qui auscultat', hoc est qui animum aduertit, sicut carm. epigr. 121 lapis non solito more ut se legas precatur sed 'uiator, audi' inquit. hic autem probro reliquis conuenienti *prurire* dicitur, hoc est πασχητιᾶν, || ut Mart. VI 37 1–3 'secti podicis usque ad umbilicum | nullas relliquias habet Charinus | et prurit tamen usque ad umbilicum', IV 48 3 'paenitet obscaenae pruriginis': adde Ar. thesm. 133 ὑπὸ τὴν ἕδραν αὐτὴν ὑπῆλθε γάργαλος (Ionicos Agathonis modos audienti), Erotian. Γ 9 (p. 61 Kl. [[30 Nachmanson]]) γάργαλος...λέγεται ἐρεθισμός, ἀπὸ τῶν πασχητιωσῶν γυναικῶν εἰλημμένης τῆς λέξεως. iam tertio uersu, ubi pronomen relatiuum (quod praua distinctione fieri uetant) ad *me* non minus quam ad *ego* refertur, uiator legendo sensim in fraudem illectus sibi imprecatur ut deuoretur a feris et irrumationem patiatur. uide Catull. 80 6 'grandia te medii tenta uorare uiri' et 28 12 sq. 'uerpa | farti estis'. Buecheleri adnotatio plane inutilis est, quae autem de culi conuiuiis Mart. II 51 5 dicit alienissima.

Mart. II 83

foedasti miserum, marite, moechum,
et se, qui fuerant prius, requirunt
trunci naribus auribusque uoltus.
credis te satis esse uindicatum?
erras: iste potest et irrumare.

Mart. IV 17

facere in Lyciscam, Paule, me iubes uersus
quibus illa lectis rubeat et sit irata.
o Paule, malus es; irrumare uis solus.

interpretibus, quia utrobique irrumandi uerbum perperam accipiunt, neutrum carmen explicare contigit. quorum prius, collato ut oportuit III 85 'quis tibi persuasit naris abscidere moecho? | non hac peccatum est parte, marite, tibi. | stulte, quid egisti? nihil hic tibi perdidit uxor, | cum sit salua tui mentula Deiphobi', Farnabius sic enarrauit: '(moechus) ita foedatus desiderabit priorem formam, poterit tamen ad prius scelus *uel etiam aliud* recurrere, postquam illi intactam reliqueris partem qua peccauerat.' cuinam igitur moechum os conspurcaturum putamus? an adulterae?[1] aut cur omnino eius rei inicitur mentio? alterius autem carminis uel magis absona interpretatio est: 'malo animo et dolo facis hoc, ut me riuali excluso solus fruaris Lycisca.' immo ore eius; quae si fellatrix est, || ne Martiale quidem excluso, – quamquam quis umquam tali se dolo riualem amouere posse sperauit? – uni eam fidelem fore credibile est.

uerae interpretationis exordium ducam a duobus Catulli locis recte a Baehrensio[2] explicatis praeeunte Forcellino, qui s. u. *irrumo* 'est etiam ludibrio habere, contumelia afficere, bonis' – immo speratis lucris – 'aliquem defraudare. Catull. 28 9...*me*...*irrumasti*, h. e. sordide et illiberaliter mecum egisti: uerbis enim obscenis et imagine impudica ex triuio et lupanari petita rem non obscenam sed turpem et inhonestam expressit.' sunt autem hi: 10 9–13 'nihil... esse...cohorti | cur quisquam caput unctius referret, | praesertim quibus esset irrumator | praetor nec faceret pili cohortem', 28 9 sq. 'o Memmi, bene me ac diu supinum | tota ista trabe lentus irrumasti', 12 sq. 'nihilo minore uerpa | farti estis' (Pisonis comites, cohors inanis). Catullus et dulces comitum coetus Memmium in prouinciam secuti sociorum se rapinis diuites factum iri sperauerant et praetorem ad eam rem adiutorem habituros; qua spe deiecti illius neglegentiam et contemptum qui uidebatur grauiter ferebant seque deceptos et derisos querebantur, quae translato uerbo irrumatio est. ea metaphora imagine rem unde ducta est ob oculos proponenti exornatur 28 9 sq. *supinum* et *tota ista trabe*, 12 sq. *uerpa* | *farti*, similiter ac Persius IV 49 ad *puteal flagellas* adiecit *multa uibice*. eadem autem translatione qua qui cum contumelia decipitur et ludificatur Latine irrumari dicitur Graeci aliquem contemptus significandi causa λαικάζειν[3] iubebant, hoc est || fellare, ut Strat. Phoen. fr. 1 36 Kock.

---

[1] etiam absurdius Raderus pronum (nam *primum* typothetae mendum est) ad fellationem maritum finxit.

[2] nam quod alii *irrumator* 10 12 'Schweinhund' interpretantur, id nec rei accommodatum est nec illa uoce significari potuit; neque enim alios polluendo irrumator ipse pollui existimabatur, neque quicquam minus recte dici potuit quam quod uir alioquin doctus et prudens Guil. Krollius ad Catull. 16 1 adnotauit 'der *irrumator* gehört ebenso wie der *fellator* zu den αἰσχρουργοί (αἰσχροποιοί) oder ἀρρητοποιοί, d. h. er wird härter beurteilt als der Päderast und der Kinäde'; qui Catullum miro consilio, ut uirum se esse ostendat, obscaenitatis crimen suscepturum putat. scilicet non facile qui Pauli Tarsensis et Iudaeorum norma uti a pueris adsueuerunt opinionem mentibus comprehendunt quae, ut Catullo et Martiali, ita nunc cuiuis de plebe Siciliensi uel Neapolitana penitus a natura insita est, obscaenos fellatores et cinaedos, pedicones et irrumatores non obscaenos esse.

[3] de huius uerbi significatione non lexica adeunda sunt sed Heraeus mus. Rhen. an. 1915 pp. 38 sq., qui tamen et ipse fallitur cum cunnilingum λαικάζειν opinatur (nec minus cum uicissim λείχειν Ar. eq. 1285 pro *fellare* accipit), neque intellegere uidetur λαικάζειν nusquam omnino id quod *scortari* sonare (nam Ar. eq. 167 παρὰ προσδοκίαν ridiculi causa ponitur).

(Athen. p. 383a) οὐχὶ λαικάσει; Mart. XI 58 12 'λαικάʒειν...dicet auaritiae' (quod Catulli auaritiae dixerat Memmius), neque aliter Martialis III 83 2 'fac mihi quod Chione', parietes Pompeiani 'mentulam linge, oblinge, elinges'.

iam ut eo unde profectus sum redeam, Martialis II 83 moechum naso et auribus carentem nihilo setius uxorem permolere posse dicit atque eo ipso facto insuper maritum irrumare, hoc est uindicta ad irritum redacta ultro ei illudere. porro IV 17 Paulus non Lyciscam sed in primis Martialem irrumare, idque solus, hoc est eximie et unice, se uelle ostendit; qui si eius iussu probrosis carminibus in Lyciscam factis ruborem ferreo canis ore exprimere conatus esset, se ipse traduxisset et omnibus derisui fuisset, ut qui se laterem lauare non intellegeret. simili ueritatis supralatione *solus* ponitur Ter. Phorm. 854 'sine controuersia ab dis solus diligere, Antipho', Mart. III 26 1 sqq. 'praedia solus habes', IV 39 2 sqq., VI 50 4.

Mart. VI 36

> mentula tam magna est quantus tibi, Papyle, nasus,
> ut possis, quotiens arrigis, olfacere.

quantus αβ, *tantus* γ et ante Schneidewinum editores; qui cum codicum auctoritati rationem posthabere decreuisset, solus insequentium Duffius cogitare ausus est et secum quaerere num, si forte duae res eiusdem sint magnitudinis, continuo magnae sint.

Mart. VII 35 1–6

> inguina succinctus nigra tibi seruos aluta
>   stat, quotiens calidis tota foueris aquis.
> sed meus, ut de me taceam, Laecania, seruos
>   Iudaeum nulla sub cute pondus habet,
> sed nudi tecum iuuenesque senesque lauantur.
>   an sola est serui mentula uera tui?

4 *nulla* βγ, *nuda* ex insequenti uersu α et conglobato cuneo Schneidewinus, Friedlaenderus, Gilbertus, Lindsaius, Duffius, Heraeus. hoc dicit: seruus meus, qui Iudaeus est, mentulam, et eam quidem grandem, ne cute quidem tectam habet. *cutem* enim in huiusmodi loco praeputium esse, ut Tert. nat. I 14 'solo detrimento *cutis* Iudaeus', manifestum esse debebat: uide etiam schol. Iuu. XIV 104 ‖ 'uerpos: Iudaeos, qui sine *pellicula* sunt', Porph. ad Hor. serm. I 9 70 'curtos Iudaeos dixit quia uirile membrum uelut decurtatum habent recisa inde *pellicula*', Mart. VII 30 5 '*recutitorum*...inguina Iudaeorum'; quibus adicienda sunt, quia in thes. ling. Lat. IV p. 1578 73 sqq. frustra quaerentur, Cels. VII 25 2 'si glans ita contecta est ut nudari non possit, quod uitium Graeci phimosin appellant,...subter a summa ora *cutis* inciditur recta linea usque ad frenum,...

quod si parum sic profectum est...*cutis* ab inferiore parte excidenda est',
3 'eius (infibulandi) haec ratio est: *cutis*, quae super glandem est, extenditur,...
cutis acu filum ducente transuitur'; adde corp. gl. Lat. II p. 206 49 'uerpus...ὁ
λιπόδερμος', de *pondere* autem Priap. 69 4 'quot pondo...mentulam'. Iudaeus
quo sensu nuda sub cute pondus habere dicatur exputare non possum; nam *cutis*
pro glande colis accipi, ut *pondus* intellegatur testiculorum, prorsus nequit. ne
pro pene quidem (quod propterea dicendum est quia thes. ling. Lat. IV p. 1578 73
'sensu obscaeno, de praeputio uel pene' poni ait in Mart. VII 10 1 sq. 'pedi-
catur Eros, fellat Linus: Ole, quid ad te | de *cute* quid faciant ille uel ille sua')
quisquam usurpauit: neque enim aut pene aut praeputio suo Eros pedicari aut
Linus fellare dicitur. ibi quod ad Erotem attinet fortasse non inepte conferatur
Catonis *intercutibus stupris* (Prisc. G.L.K. II p. 271 5 [[*ORF* p. 28 Malcovati]])
et Paul. Fest. p. 110 23 [[98 Lindsay]] '*inter cutem flagitatos* dicebant antiqui mares
qui stuprum passi essent', sed aptius opinor prouerbium *de suo* uel *alieno corio
ludere*, sicut Mart. III 16 5 sq. in *corio* et *pellicula* iocatio est.

Mart. XI 58

cum me uelle uides tentumque, Telesphore, sentis,
 magna rogas (puta me uelle negare: licet?)
et nisi iuratus dixi 'dabo' subtrahis illas,
 permittunt in me quae tibi multa, natis.
5 quid si me tonsor, cum stricta nouacula supra est,
 tunc libertatem diuitiasque roget?
promittam; neque enim rogat illo tempore tonsor,
 latro rogat: res est inperiosa timor.
sed fuerit curua cum tuta nouacula theca
10 frangam tonsori crura manusque simul.
at tibi nil faciam, sed lota mentula lana
 λαικάζειν cupidae dicet auaritiae. ‖

11 pro *lana* Scaliger *laeua* sequente editorum parte multo maiore, qui collato
XI 73 4 (ubi puer hora locoque constituto nullus uenit) Martialem, cum Teles-
phorus nimis magna roget, potius masturbaturum esse uolunt. ergo nullam
usquam magis parabilem facilemque uenerem inuenire posse putandus est, ut
ad eam decurrere cogatur quam Herculis heredi Lemniam suasisse egestatem
dicit Ausonius? quid quod uersu 2 negare sibi non licere significat? aut quorsum
tot uerba de tonsore latrone et de promisso non seruando? nimirum promissurum
quidem se dicit quod rogatur sed post satiatam libidinem non daturum; quam
sententiam codicum lectioni a Lindsaio et Heraeo reductae inesse, quod ipsis
liquere minime confido (neque enim codicum lectionibus, ut editoribus
placeant, necesse est ut ullum intellectum habere credantur), ostendere aggre-

diar. igitur *lota lana*, ἔριον πεπλυμένον, cui contraria est *sucida*, ἄπλυτον (corp.
gl. Lat. II p. 314 21 ἔριον ἄπλυτον *lana sucida*: adde Paul. sent. III 6 82 '*lana...*,
siue *sucida* siue *lota* est', digest. XXXII 70 3 sq. '*lanae* appellationem eatenus
extendi placet quoad ad telam peruenisset. et sciendum *sucidam* quoque
contineri et *lotam*, si modo tincta non sit'), ad mentulam post opus tergendam
adhibetur. ablatiuus est qui dici potest comitatiuus, ut Verg. Aen. IV 517–19
'ipsa *mola* manibusque piis... *testatur* moritura deos', id est dum mola supplicat,
neque enim aut illic per molam aut hic per lotam lanam fit quod fieri dicitur.
amator, dum lana utitur, auarum puerum mercede pacta destitutum κλάειν et
οἰμώζειν iubebit, sed spurciore et rei unice apto uerbo.

Suet. Tib. 44 1

maiore adhuc ac turpiore infamia flagrauit, uix ut referri audiriue, nedum
credi fas sit, quasi pueros primae teneritudinis, quos pisciculos uocabat,
institueret, ut natanti sibi inter femina uersarentur ac luderent lingua morsuque
sensim adpetentes.

Suet. Dom. 22

libidinis nimiae, assiduitatem concubitus uelut exercitationis genus clino-
palen uocabat; eratque fama, quasi concubinas ipse deuelleret nataretque inter
uulgatissimas meretrices.

horum locorum neutro de natatione, quae proprie dicitur, agi perspicuum esse
oportebat: neque enim isto pacto mortem effugere potuerunt pueruli a Tiberio
instituti, neque, cum uiri et mulieres || una lauari solerent, aut insignitae libi-
dinis erat aut rumusculis tantum emanasset, si Domitianus eadem cum mere-
tricibus uel uulgatissimis piscina utebatur. unde colligo, ut equi et τοῦ κελητίζειν,
sic natandi uocabulum ad res uenerias translatum esse, significarique figuram
aliquam ob similitudinem quandam ita appellatam, quam ad perficiendam
plurium administratione opus fuerit; quales intellegi uoluerunt Seneca dial.
VI 17 5 et Lucanus VIII 397–404. ceterum hanc Suetonii dictionem parum
intellectam fraudi fuisse suspicor ei qui cum probra undique conquisita Helio-
gabalo adfingeret sic scripsit uit. 31 7, 'in balneis semper cum mulieribus fuit,
ita ut eas psilothro curaret'.

Suet. de gramm. 23 ⟦6⟧
(Reiffersch. p. 118 2–5 ⟦26 4–7 Brugnoli⟧)

(Q. Remmium Palaemona omnibus uitiis inquinatum et oris infamia fla-
grantem) dicto...non infaceto notatum ferunt cuiusdam qui cum in turba
osculum sibi ingerentem quamuis refugiens deuitare non posset 'uis tu', inquit,
'magister, quotiens festinantem aliquem uides, abligurrire?'

pro *festinantem* Reifferscheidius *haesitantem*, cuius dicti facetiae mihi non apparent. quanto satius erat uel ab hoc uno loco discere *festinare* uulgari sermone dici qui in certamine uenerio ad finem et seminis emissionem properat, 'iam cum praesagit gaudia corpus | atque in eost uenus ut muliebria conserat arua'. nec dissimile est Ouid. art. ii 727 'ad metam properate simul'.

Appul. Asclep. 21

si enim illud extremum temporis, quo ex crebro adtritu peruenimus ut utraque in utramque fundat natura progeniem, animaduertas ut altera auide alterius rapiat ⟨uenerem⟩ interiusque recondat, denique eo tempore ex commixtione communi et uirtutem feminae marum adipiscuntur et mares femineo torpore lassescunt.

obiectum uerbi suppleui ex Verg. georg. iii 135–7 'nimio ne luxu obtunsior usus | sit genitali aruo et sulcos oblimet inertis | set *rapiat* sitiens *uenerem inte-riusque recondat*': uulgo *semen* inserunt. '*peruenimus* ut. . .fundat natura', pro quo Hildebrandus *prurimus*, alter Vergilii tuetur locus, buc. ix 2–4 'peruenimus aduena. . .ut. . .diceret'.

162

DISTICHA DE MENSIBVS*

(ANTH. LAT. RIES. 665, POET. LAT. MIN.
BAEHR. I PP. 210F.)

The twenty-four lines of this poem have been preserved only by the cod. Sangallensis 878 (variously assigned to saec. IX or IX–XI or XI–XII), whence it was edited in 1863 by K. Schenkl *Sitzungsb. d. phil.-hist. Cl. d. kais. Akad. d. Wissensch.* (Vienna) XLIII p. 71. A single line, the last, exists also in the cod. Bernensis 108 saec. IX. Fifteen surive in a MS of the 17th century now divided into two parts, Barberinus (or Barberinianus) XXXI 39 and Vaticanus 9135, the former containing the hexameters 3, 5, 15, 17, 19, 21, 23 and a spurious hexameter in lieu of 1, the latter the pentameters 2, 4, 14, 16, 18, 20, 22, 24. The eight consecutive lines 6–13 are therefore missing from both; and in this imperfect and interpolated form the poem was edited by Mommsen with Haupt's assistance in *C.I.L.* I p. 411.

It may be read in *C.I.L.* I pp. 332 f. that the calligrapher Furius Dionysius Philocalus executed in A.D. 354 a manuscript calendar on twenty-four pages, two for each month of the year. On the first page of each pair was an emblematic picture of the month with a descriptive tetrastich in the margin; on the opposite page the fasti corresponding. At the foot, hexameter on the one page, pentameter on the other, were the distichs of which I am now to speak.

All the pictures and all the fasti, but with no verses accompanying, are extant in the cod. Vindob. 3146 written about A.D. 1480. A less complete MS was discovered at Arras in the 17th century by the great collector Peiresc, who assigned it to the 9th or 10th. It lacked the pictures of January, April, May, June, and July, and the fasti of March, April, May, and June; but on all the pages which it contained it preserved the verses proper to them. It is now lost again, but two copies of it were made before its disappearance and still survive. These are the cod. Bruxellensis 7542–8 and the MS now divided into Barb. XXXI 39 and Vat. 9135. Except for a spurious page in Barb., of which more anon, they agree with their lost original as described by Peiresc in possessing only seven pictures, Feb. March, Aug. Sept. Oct. Nov. Dec., and only eight tables of fasti, Jan. Feb. Jul. Aug. Sept. Oct. Nov. Dec.: Brux. further omits the

* [CQ 26 (1932), 129–36]

distichs, and the five tetrastichs which describe the missing pictures; Barb. and Vat. exhibit on each page the verse or verses belonging to it, the tetrastichs in minuscules, the distichs in capitals.[1] ||

Philocalus was a mere executant, and no part of his work, scientific or artistic or literary, originated with him. 'Auctor horum fastorum non fuit Philocalus, sed sunt uulgares eius aetatis publica auctoritate editi' says Mommsen *C.I.L.* I p. 332; Baehrens *poet. Lat. min.* I p. 204 denies with reason that either the distichs or the tetrastichs belong to so late an age, for their general purity and elegance are almost Augustan; and if the tetrastichs are older, so also must be the designs which they describe. But a limit to the antiquity of the distichs is fixed by the *concedŏ* of line 23. The first dactylic poet to make a palimbacchius out of a molossus by shortening a final *o* is Persius, who has *sartagŏ* and perhaps *accedŏ* (P, *accede* AB).

The whole series of tetrastichs, 48 lines, has found its way, whether from Philocalus' calendar or from an independent source, into many MSS, some as early as the 9th century, and is now *anth. Lat. Ries.* 395 (*poet. Lat. min. Baehr.* I pp. 206–9). The distichs, as appears from what has been said, have only the following authority.

B = Bern. 108, saec. IX: line 24.

S = Sangall. 878, saec. IX–XII: lines 1–24.

P = Barb. XXXI 39 + Vat. 9135, saec. XVII: lines 2–5 and 14–24.

January

1 primus, Iane, tibi sacratur et omnia mensis

2 undique cui semper cuncta uidere licet.

Attentive readers of *C.I.L.* I p. 411 must have been perplexed by a seeming contradiction. Mommsen there printed the first verse as 'Ianus adest bifrons primusque ingreditur annum', and not only did the silence of his apparatus criticus imply that it was in Barb. XXXI 39 but he expressly declared that this MS contains all the hexameters except for April, May, June, and July. But then he added that the hexameters are written under the pictures of the months; and on p. 333 he had told us that Peiresc's MS, of which he says Barb. is a copy, did not contain the picture of January. Light was cast on the puzzle a quarter of a century later by pp. 56 f. of Strzygowski's *Calenderbilder*, and Mommsen in *chron. min.* I p. 48 admitted that the facts are these. Barb. does contain a picture

---

[1] The seven figures of Feb. March Aug. Sept. Oct. Nov. Dec. were reproduced from Brux. by Bucherius in his *commentarius in Victorium Aquitanum* (1633) pp. 275–88, and the whole series of twelve from Vindob. by Lambecius in his *bibl. Caesarea append. comment. l. IV addit. I* (1671) pp. 271–303. Strzygowski in his *Calenderbilder d. Chronogr. v. Jahre* 354, *Jahrb. d. kais. deutsch. archaeol. Inst., Ergänzungsheft* I (1888) gives some examples from all three MSS. The fasti are edited from Vindob. and Brux. by Mommsen in *C.I.L.* I pp. 334–56 (ed. 2 pp. 256–78).

of January, and this hexameter beneath it; but both are spurious. Comparison with the genuine picture in Vindob. 3416 and the genuine hexameter in Sangall. 878 makes it clear that this page of Barb. has no earlier origin than the 17th century copyist. He knew the descriptive tetrastich – for the tetrastichs were accessible in many places – and he made a picture of January to suit it: the hexameter he besought and obtained from the too complaisant Muse.

et omnia is corrupt, and Schenkl's *ut* is no emendation: Baehrens's *eponyme* is thoroughly improbable in a poem whose vocabulary is otherwise classical. Buecheler's *nomine* satisfies the sense, but that can be satisfied with less alteration by

> primus, Iane, tibi sacratus it ordine mensis. ‖

Of *-tus* changed to *-tur* I can remember seven examples in Manilius alone, I 844, 874, II 138, 277, 494, IV 652, V 91, and Ribbeck cites six from the capital MSS of Virgil in *prol.* p. 253. Examples of *it* changed to *et* are too plentiful for counting, and the following could be multiplied many times over: Verg. *georg.* III 507, 517, *Aen.* IV 665, V 558, VI 448, VIII 557, XII 283, 452, *moret.* 101, Hor. *carm.* IV 5 7, *epist.* I 7 55, Luc. III 228, VI 372, 828, X 329, Val. Fl. III 3, 277, Sil. II 521, Stat. *Theb.* II 11, *silu.* I 1 43, IV 3 62, *peruig. Ven.* 29: in Verg. *georg.* III 517 and *Aen.* IV 665 the corruption is presented by the majority of the best MSS. Between *ordine* and *omnia* the half-way house may have been *omine*. The phrase is like Enn. *ann.* 424 Vahl. 'post acer hiemps it' and Verg. *buc.* IV 12 'incipient...procedere menses'.

February

> umbrarum est alter, quo mense putatur honore   3
> peruia terra dato manibus esse uagis.   4

March

> condita Mauortis magno sub nomine Roma   5
> non habet errorem: Romulus auctor erit.   6

6–13 om. P.   *errore* S, corr. Schenkl.

This can only mean that Rome was founded in the month of March and that Romulus will tell you so if you ask him. Then Romulus will lie; for we all know that Rome was founded XI kal. Mai., where *Roma condita* and *natalis urbis* stand in the fasti. Mommsen's *numine*, proposed before the pentameter was known, destroys the only connexion between the distich and the month.

What was here said about March ought not to be in doubt: Macr. *Sat.* I 12 3 'Romanos olim *auctore Romulo* annum suum decem habuisse mensibus ordinatum, qui *annus incipiebat a Martio*', Ouid. *fast.* I 27–39 'tempora digereret cum conditor urbis, in anno | constituit menses quinque bis esse suo...Martis erat primus mensis', III 97 f. 'Romulus...sanguinis auctori tempora prima dedit', Plut. *Numa* 18 5 μετεκίνησε δὲ καὶ τὴν τάξιν τῶν μηνῶν· τὸν γὰρ Μάρτιον πρῶτον ὄντα τρίτον ἔταξε, πρῶτον δὲ τὸν Ἰανουάριον, ὃς ἦν ἑνδέκατος ὑπὸ Ῥωμύλου. This tradition reappears at this place in other of the *carmina de mensibus*: *anth. Lat. Ries.* 394 3 'incipe, Mars, anni felicia fata reducti', 639 3 'Martius antiqui primordia protulit anni', 761ᵃ 'si nouus a Iani sacris numera- bitur annus, | Quintilis falso nomine dictus erit. | si facis, ut fuerant, primas a Marte kalendas, | tempora constabunt ordine ducta suo', Auson. 377 (p. 98 Peip.) 5 f. 'Martius et generis Romani praesul et anni | prima dabat Latiis tempora consulibus.' This meaning, that 'anni initium mensis est Martius' (Seru. *georg.* I 43) and that Romulus will be found to be the authority for the doctrine, was probably conveyed in these words:

Mauortis magno sub nomine tempora condi, ‖

first corrupted to *te roma condi* and then transposed and corrected as we see. I have collected many such progressions in error on pp. lxvi ff. of vol. I of my Manilius, and from Manilius himself might be added II 495 *in semet uertunt oculos, in semet uertitur oculis, uertitur in semet oculis* and III 353 'quaerentur medio *terrae* celata tumore', *tempore*, '*tempore* quaerentur medio celata tumore'. The year and its months are *tempora* not only in four of the passages cited above but often enough elsewhere, as in Luc. v 6 'ducentem tempora Ianum' and Stat. *silu.* IV 1 19 f. 'sic tempora nasci, | sic annos intrare decet'; *condere* is used as in Verg. *Aen.* VI 792 f. 'aurea condet | saecula qui rursus Latio', Stat. *silu.* IV 1 37 'altera saecula condes', Plin. *n.h.* VII 120 'a condito aeuo'.

April

7   Caesarem ut Veneris mensi, quo floribus arua
8   prompta uirent, auibus quod sonat omne nemus.

Schenkl proposed (for Riese reports him wrongly) '*Caesareae* (or *Caesaris et*) Veneris *mensis*'. I can think of no good reason why Venus in connexion with April should be called Caesarea, ancestress of the Iulii; but between April itself and Caesar there was once, though Schenkl does not mention it, a special link. This poem, as I have said, may belong to Nero's time, and Nero made this month his own: Tac. *ann.* XV 74 1 '(decernitur) ut...mensis...Aprilis Neronis cognomentum acciperet', Suet. *Ner.* 55 'mensem...Aprilem Nero- neum appellauit'. A poet writing in that reign might say '*Caesar inest* Veneris mensi'; but his verse would not have been perpetuated to the time of Philo- calus, and a better conjecture is Baehrens's *at sacer est Veneri mensis*. He assumes the stages *sacer ē, sa-ce-rem, ce-sa-rem*; and one of them is found in *anth. Lat. Ries.* 395 (*poet. Lat. min. Baehr.* I p. 206) 1 'hic Iani mensis *sacer est*' (*sacerem* cod. unus). This distich survives only in S, so that it is lawful to postulate minuscule corruptions.

For *prompta* Riese writes *compta*, which is indeed a less change than *picta* but not a natural word: the *thes. ling. Lat.* has nothing nearer than Ennod. *carm.* 1 5 48 'Eridanus claris radiabat comptus harenis'. For *quod* Schenkl writes *quo*, which may seem obvious but is far from certain. At Manil. II 380 I have cited errors such as *quod fieri* for *confieri* in the Mediceus of Virgil at *Aen.* IV 116, and '*consonat* omne nemus' is a Virgilian hemistich, *Aen.* V 149 and VIII 305.

May

> hos sequitur laicus toto iam corpore Maius　　　　　9
> Mercurio et Maia quem tribuisse Ioue.　　　　　10

Riese's *laetus* in the hexameter would not easily have been corrupted to *laicus* and is not as appropriate as one could wish to *corpore*; but I have nothing better to propose. In the pentameter Schenkl's *Maiae . . . iuuat* is no more convincing, for the change of dative to ablative, small though it is, was not likely to happen with *tribuisse* close by, and the change of *iuuat* to *ioue* is not very small. As *errore* in 6 is written for *errorem*, so *ioue* here would naturally || be *iouem*; and the ablative *Maia* suggests that *Mercurio* is a gloss on some such periphrasis as *genito Maia*: for instance

> ⟨fama sato⟩ Maia quem tribuisse Iouem.

Mercury is 'Maia satus' in Stat. *Theb.* II 1, and *fama* without *est* has an accusative and infinitive at Val. Fl. VI 137–9 'fama . . . Bacchum . . . Arabas fudisse' and in a relative clause, as here, at Stat. *Theb.* 1 699 f. 'ubi fama uolentem . . . umeris subiisse molares'.

This is not more than a possible remedy: but its possibility can be established by parallels. In Ouid. *art.* 1 683 f. 'iam dea laudatae dederat mala praemia formae | colle sub Idaeo uincere digna *duas*' the place of *duas* has been taken in most MSS by the marginal interpretation *Venus*. In Sen. *Oed.* 167 f., for the 'flumina seruat durus senio | nauita *crudo*' of the best MS, most of the others give *Charon*. In Ouid. *Ib.* 503 'quique Lycurgiden letauit et *arbore natum*' one of the chief MSS gives *Arcadem Ancaeum*, a correct explanation of *Lycurgiden*. In *pan. Mess.* 55 f. 'nec ualuit *lotos* coeptos auertere cursus, | cessit et Aetnaeae Neptunius incola rupis' it is only the frag. Cuiac. that preserves this reading: the rest have *Cyclops*, a correct explanation of *Neptunius incola* in the next verse. I said a good deal on this subject in *C.R.* XVI (1902) pp. 442–6 [[this edition pp. 577–82]].

June

> Iunius ipse sibi causam tibi nominis edit　　　　　11
> praegrauida attollens fertilitate sata.　　　　　12

July

13   quam bene, Quintilis, mutasti nomen! honori
14   Caesareo, Iuli, te pia causa dedit.

13 *quam* Riese, *nam* S, *iam* Buecheler. *honori* Schenkl, *honore* S. 14 redit P.
Caesareo Riese, *Caesare qui* P, *Caesari qui* (hoc supra scr.) S, *Caesaris o* Baehrens.
Iuli Mommseno praeeunte Buecheler, *Iulio* SP.

August

15   tu quoque, Sextilis, uenerabilis omnibus annis
16   numinis Augusti nomen in anno uenis.

16 *nomine* Riese, tum *notus* (*gratus magnus clarus*) *eris*; *in ora uenis* Buecheler;
nomina magna geris Baehrens.

The word *uenis* neither needs to be altered nor demands the alteration of
anything else, for 'uenerabilis uenis' will be 'uenerabilis es', like Prop. I 10 25
'irritata uenit', Ouid. *met.* VI 37, Manil. IV 382, 457, Sen. *H.f.* 45. If Riese's
nomine is right, the next word was probably a vocative, like 18 *uelate*, and the
slightest change would seem to be *magne*. *nomen* would require something like
adepte. ||

September

17   tempora maturis September uincta racemis
18   uelate, ⟨e⟩ numero nosceris ipse tuo.

17 *tempora maturis* Haupt, *temporis autumni* S, *temporibus autumnis* P. *uincta*
S, *uineta* P. 18 *e* Haupt, *iam* S P.

October

19   Octobri laetus portat uindemitor uuas,
20   omnis ager, Bacchi munere, uoce sonat.

20 *munera* Riese, *diues ouat* Baehrens.

I have shown by punctuation that the verse stands in need of no amendment.
The two ablatives are like Cic. *Tusc.* I 115 'Euthynous potitur, fatorum
numine, leto'. *munera* is of course possible, and may even be thought better.

November

21   frondibus amissis repetunt sua frigora mensem
22   cum iuga Centaurus celsa retorquet eques.

22 *retorque* P, *torquet* S. *eques* om. P.

The November of the Romans is φυλλοχόος μήν or μείς in Hes. [fr. 333 Merkelbach–West] ap. Polluc. I 231, Callim. *Hecal.* pap. Rein. VI col. I u. 12 [fr. 260 12 Pfeiffer], Apoll. Rhod. IV 217 and elsewhere; and it is annually accompanied by the return of seasonable cold. Q. Cicero (Auson. 383 [p. 107 Peiper], *frag. poet. Baehr.* p. 315, *Morel* p. 79) 10 f. 'ecfetos ramos denudat flamma Nepai, | pigra Sagittipotens iaculatur frigora terris': the leaves fall in the first part of the month, while the sun is still in Scorpius; the cold weather begins when he passes into Sagittarius. In Germ. *frag.* IV 18 ff. 'Scorpion ingrediens (Iuppiter) tua, Liber, munera condit | iamque Sagittiferum scandens sua *munera* reddit | numquam laetae hiemi', where *munera* has come from the preceding verse, I should again write *frigora*.

Centaurus eques is ἵπποτα φήρ, but this title, which in Arat. 664 describes the Southern Centaur, must here signify the zodiacal sign. In the table of fasti on Philocalus' opposite page the words *sol Sagittario* (*sagitari* Vindob.) stand against Nov. 19 (Vindob., 17 Brux. and P) with the figure of Sagittarius beneath them. But what is meant by saying that he 'iuga celsa retorquet'?

In *anth. Lat. Ries.* 874ª (= Drac. *de mens. P.L.M. Vollm.* V p. 236) the distich on December contains the verse 23 'algida bruma niuans onerat *iuga celsa* (high hills) pruinis'; but that is no more than a curious accident. Mommsen in *C.I.L.* I p. 411 suggested that *iuga* meant Libra or Ζυγός, invisible while the sun is in Scorpius but reappearing as a morning constellation when he enters Sagittarius. Libra however, which Cicero once calls Iugum, is nowhere called Iuga, though Manilius I 611 uses the periphrasis *iuga Chelarum*; and the epithet *celsa* would have no peculiar appropriateness || to this or any equatorial sign. *iuga celsa* as the name of a celestial object would most naturally mean *plaustrum septentrionale*; for Virgil in *georg.* III 140 has 'grauibus... *iuga* ducere plaustris' and the synecdoche *iuga* for 'currum' in *Aen.* X 594 'rotis saliens *iuga* deseris', and the Great Bear, which Martial VI 25 2 calls 'Parrhasio... Vrsa *iugo*' and of which Seneca *Tro.* 439 says 'clarum... septem uerterunt stellae *iugum*', is in a special sense *celsa* because near the north pole. Sen. *H.f.* 129 'signum *celsi* glaciale poli' is the same as 6 f. 'Arctos alta parte glacialis poli | sublime sidus': see too Germ. *phaen.* 23 'pars (axis) *celsa* sub horrifero aquilone', 324 f. 'sidera, quae mundi pars *celsior* aethere uoluit | quaeque uident borean', 459 '*celsior* ad borean qui uergit circulus'. Now the hour when men take most notice of the stars is nightfall; and the first constellation to come forth after sunset in northern latitudes is the Great Bear, 'quem septem stellae primum iam sole remoto | producunt nigrae praebentem lumina nocti', Manil. I 620 f. At Rome 1900 years ago on a November evening it made its appearance low upon the northern horizon, ceasing to descend and beginning to rise again: Centaurus iuga celsa retorquebat. Arabia in the course of the same month witnessed phenomena corresponding to the difference of latitude: Plin. *n.h.* II 178

'Septentrio...in Arabia Nouembri mense prima uigilia occultus secunda se ostendit.'

December

23   argumenta tibi mensis concedo December
24   quae sis quam uis annum claudere possis.

24 is contained in B, so that here we have three authorities. In all of them the end of the verse is thus corrupt and defective, but touching their variants at the beginning our information is contradictory. S, according to our only informant Schenkl, has *quae quamuis*. The reading of B is given by Mommsen 'über den Chronographen vom J. 354', *Abh. d. phil.-hist. Classe d. k. sächs. Ges. d. Wissensch.* vol. I (1850) p. 570, as *quae sis quam uis* on the faith of Albert Jahn (p. 558); but in *C.I.L.* I pp. 356 and 411 he gives *quae uis quam uis* and says of this fragment (p. 333) 'accurate descripsit mihi G. Rettig': Riese and Baehrens reproduce the latter testimony, Strzygowski pp. 3 and 81 the former. The reading of P is given by Mommsen *C.I.L.* I p. 411 as *quae sis quam uis*, which Riese and Baehrens repeat: Strzygowski p. 3 says that P has not *quae* but *quale*, and repeats this on p. 81 in the statement 'Das beigesetzte Distichon lautet *argumenta tuis festis concedo, December,* | *quale sis quamuis annum claudere possis*'; but this statement is so false and negligent as regards *tuis festis* (which is Baehrens's conjecture) that no trust can be put in it. Since *quae sis quam uis* was reported by one witness from B and by another from P, I suspect that it is in fact the reading of both.

Haupt in *C.I.L.* I p. 411 proposed with all due diffidence to write

quaeuis, quis annum claudere poscis ⟨ouans⟩

'i.e. concedo tibi quaeuis argumenta omnemque materiem Saturnaliciorum ‖ iocorum, quibus annum hilare claudere cupis'. Baehrens following in the same path altered *tibi mensis* to *tuis festis*, which was adopted by Riese; in the pentameter Baehrens wrote *quae quauis* leaving the end uncorrected, Riese *quis quemuis* and ⟨*iure*⟩ *potes*.

tuis festis, violent and unlikely though it is, is not inexcusable or causeless, for the addition of *mensis* to the vocative *December* is surprising: 'amnis Nilus' and 'mons Taurus' are familiar modes of speech, but not 'amnis Nile' nor 'mons Taure'. The vagueness and obscurity of *argumenta* is a difficulty common to all the readings. In the pentameter it is pretty clear that S has tried to correct the verse and that the unmetrical form of the corruption is the older.

The distich may be amended thus:

argumenta tibi mensis concedo Decemb⟨ris⟩,
qui squamis annum claudere piscis ⟨amas⟩.

That is 'tibi, Capricorne, concedo ut indices quae mensis Decembris natura sit'. As with Sagittarius in November, the figure of Capricorn and the words 'sol Capricorno' stand here in the fasti of the opposite page. Capricorn, the zodiacal sign in which the sun concludes the year, is a goat with a fish's tail, and accordingly in *catal. cod. astrol. Gr.* VII p. 208 it has the epithet λεπιδωτόν; *argumenta* is used as in *Aetn.* 143 'argumenta dabunt ignoti uera profundi'; and this poet, in saying that Capricorn's scaly tail is an apt symbol of December, has in mind what Isidore tells us in *orig.* III 71 31, 'Capricorni...posteriorem partem corporis in effigiem piscis ideo formauerunt ut pluuias eiusdem temporis designarent, quas solet idem mensis plerumque in extremis habere.'

At Nemes. *cyn.* 30 *qui squamosi* appears in the best MS as *quis quam osi*, and I suppose that here there was a like false division, *quis quamis*. If *uis* is rightly reported from B, its *ui* may be a relic of *qui*. It would be a great mistake to defend *quae* by adducing *anth. Lat. Ries.* 622 5 *pelagi capella* and 626 5 *Neptunia capra* (both missing in the *thes. ling. Lat.*), where the feminine gender is a concession to metre.

163

REVIEW: F. BOLL, *STERNGLAUBE UND STERNDEUTUNG, ED.* 4*

This fourth edition is for the most part a reprint of the third. I have observed small changes or additions on pp. 119 f. and 153 f., and there may be others. None of the errors pointed out ‖ in *C.R.* XLI pp. 70 f. ⟦this edition pp. 1130–1⟧ is corrected, though some of them are gross. Eight new pages giving a survey of the literature from 1926 to 1930 are subjoined; nine illustrations are added and one subtracted. The index is corrected, much enlarged, and divided into *Personen- und Sachregister*, *Stellenregister*, and *Autorenregister*.

* ⟦*Sternglaube und Sterndeutung*. By Franz Boll, 4th edition by W. Gundel. Pp. xiv + 230. Leipzig and Berlin: B. G. Teubner, 1931. *CR* 46 (1932), 44–5⟧

164

REVIEW: P. DE LABRIOLLE, *LES SATIRES DE JUVÉNAL**

This book does not call for much notice from a learned journal, being meant for readers who wish to hear that there are black swans in Australia and who need to be told that Quirinus was another name for Romulus and that *homo* is not the same as *uir*. M. Labriolle paraphrases Juvenal's satires and provides information, accessible elsewhere, about their subjects and circumstances, but communicates hardly anything that a scholar will thank him for unless it is the identification (which he attributes to W. M. Flinders Petrie, *Nagada and Ballas*, p. 65, 1896) of Juvenal's *Ombi* (which he calls *Ombos* because Juvenal mentions it in the accusative) with a *Nubt* actually adjacent to Tentyra and not, like the other *Nubt* (*Kom Ombo*), 120 miles away (p. 323). The attribution however should rather have been made to J. Duemichen, *Gesch. d. alten Aegyptens*, pp. 125 f., 1879. The imitations of Juvenal culled from the French poets are welcome for their literary interest.

Mistranslations occur too often. I 26 *uerna Canopi* 'un esclave de Canope', 60 *dum* (causal) 'qui', III 281 *ergo* 'mais non', IV 121 *Cilicis* 'du Cilicien', 128 *erectas in terga* 'qui se hérissent sur son dos', V 108 *modicis amicis* 'leurs moindres amis', VI 262 f. *quanta* (fascia) *poplitibus sedeat* 'comme elles restent ‖ fermes sur leurs jarrets', 299 *saecula* 'l'œuvre des siècles', VII 112 *conspuitur sinus* 'ils souillent de bave leur poitrine', 136 *conuenit illi* 'il lui plaît', 238 *cera uoltum facit* 'sculpte', XII 78 *igitur* 'oui' (the equally distressing *igitur* of XVI 18 is simply omitted), XV 90 *autem* 'puisque'. The verses XIV 50–3 are not recognisable in the translation on p. 308.

'Néron' on p. 107 is a misprint, '500' on p. 77 a slip of the pen, and 'incipe o Calliope! licet et consedere' on p. 98 perhaps a mixture of both; but there is no such excuse for 'de pierres' on p. 71 as a rendering of *latericiam*, nor for the statement on p. 210 that Naeuolus in *sat.* IX is a *cinaedus*.

On p. 330 it is said that 'on a repéré récemment une imitation, jusqu'ici inaperçue', in Tert. *adu. Marc.* IV 24, and reference is given to 'C. Weyman, dans le *Néo-Philologus*, t. VII (1922)'. This allusion by Tertullian to Iuu. III 231 was noted by Mayor in 1886, vol. I, p. 383. The statement on p. 331 that 'le fameux Heiric d'Auxerre composa sur les *Satires* tout un commentaire' is interesting if true.

* ⟦*Les Satires de Juvénal*. Étude et analyse par Pierre de Labriolle. Paris: Mellottée. Pp. 361. *CR* 46 (1932), 131–2⟧

165

THREE NEW LINES OF LUCAN?*

The three lines produced by Professor Souter in *C.R.* XLVI p. 114 from cod. Brit. mus. add. 14799 had already been cited, with the correct reading *quod*... *quod* in the second verse, by Cortius at Luc. VII 303 from the MSS which he called Guelf. 5 and Hamb. 1, and by Burman at VII 302 from Heinsius' collations of 'Hamb. sec.' (apparently the same) and a codex Langermanni.

That they are not required by the context may be thought to tell in their favour, since there would be no cause for inserting them; and when inserted they form an appropriate addition. The Caesarians have only two issues of the day to expect, reward if victorious, punishment if vanquished: a third, such clemency as was shown to the vanquished Pompeians in Spain, they must not hope for. Language and verse are quite like Lucan, and so is the exaggeration 'dedimus quod rura, quod urbes' representing IV 383–5 'miles...in urbes | spargitur' and 397 'non deductos recipit sua terra colonos'.

But on the other, the external side, the lines provoke suspicion. In the Hamburg MS they stand in a wrong place, before and not after 303, and in the cod. Langerm. they are added by a second hand; and these are frequent and familiar signs of interpolation. Moreover there is no apparent reason why, if genuine, they should have fallen out; for *parata...negatum* is not much of an homoeoteleuton.

* [[CR 46 (1932), 150]]

166

NOTES ON
THE *THEBAIS* OF STATIUS [I]*

I have not read the *Thebais* more than three times, nor ever with intent care and interest; and although in putting these notes together I have consulted a large number of editions – Bernartius, Tiliobroga, Geuartius, Cruceus, Gronouius, Barthius, Veenhusen, Beraldus (Delphin), ed. Bipontina, Lemaire (with Amar), Queck, O. Mueller (books I–VI), Kohlmann, Wilkins, Garrod, Klotz, and the translations of Marolles, Nisard, and Mozley (Loeb) – it may well be that profitable matter has escaped me and that some of my comments have been made before.

Systematic investigation and collation of the older and better MSS began with Otto Mueller in 1870, who separated P, Paris. 8051 saec. IX–X, from the company and kinship of the others, ω, and set it over against them as superior, which indeed it is. But this superiority was much exaggerated by his next successor Kohlmann, and even later the choice between P's lections and ω's has sometimes been made with obtuse partiality. Gronouius would not believe his eyes if he saw *numquam* in the text at IX 183 and 212, and he might sarcastically enquire why he did not see it also at XI 467. Another reason why neither recension nor interpretation has made strides proportionate to our increased knowledge of the MSS is that modern scholars are disadvantaged by their remoteness and estrangement from the ways of thinking and writing which were most fashionable and admired in the silver age of Latin poetry. Editors of the 17th and even the 18th century had more in common with Statius, and were quicker to catch his meaning.

I 85–7

da, Tartarei regina barathri,
quod cupiam uidisse nefas, nec tarda sequetur
mens iuuenum: modo digna ueni, mea pignora nosces.

Here is an example. 'modo, *dira*, ueni' Lachmann, *diua* or 'pignora *nosse*' Mueller, '*mea* digna, ueni *modo*, pignora nosces' Baehrens with one interpolated MS, 'cum hyperbaton non agnosceret' says Mr Klotz, who himself prints

* [CQ 27 (1933), 1–16]

'modo, digna, ueni, mea pignora nosces' with the same sense and construction, *digna* belonging to *pignora*;[1] and the *thes. ling. Lat.* v p. 1148 65 acquiescently transmits to future generations this specimen of Statian criticism at the beginning of the 20th century. ‖

Pope translated the first book of the *Thebais* at the age of fifteen: he saw the point that Statius was making, and his rendering is as good as a commentary:

> Couldst thou some great proportion'd mischief frame,
> They'd prove the father from whose loins they came.

digna ueni eis ad quos uenis, or as Barthius says 'tantae malitiae iuuenibus'. The use of the adjective is similar in I 73 'exaudi, si digna precor', explained by the next words 'quaeque ipsa furenti | subiceres', and in VI 37 f. 'maerentia dignis | uultibus Inachii penetrarunt limina reges'. The conceit that a fury from hell might not, without special effort, prove devilish enough to put the sons of Oedipus on their mettle was one which gave pride to Statius and joy to his contemporaries: *laetam fecit urbem.*

I 103 f.

> centum illi stantes umbrabant ora cerastae,
> turba minor diri capitis.

Lachmann's conjectures in the *Thebais*, never published by himself but extracted by Mueller and Kohlmann from the margin of an edition which he had bought when he was eighteen, are seldom happy and not always well-pondered; and here his *minax* for *minor*, though accepted by four editors, is quite mistaken. These hundred snakes were not 'turba capitis', only 'frontis': a fury is not bald behind. Mr Klotz, retaining *minor*, and ready to interpret even when not able,[2] says 'opposita est anguis quam manu Furia gestat' (not mentioned till 113 'uiuo manus aera uerberat hydro'), which is even less possible than the explanation of Barthius' 'glossographus', that the snakes on the back of her head were smaller than those in front. Statius says nothing about their size; what he mentions is their number, and that fixes the sense of *minor*, which was plain to more than one of the earlier editors: Marolles 'cent cerastes, la moindre foule de sa teste impitoyable', Beraldus 'qui minor numerus est crinium horrendi capitis', 'hoc denotat Tisiphonen innumerabiles serpentes in capite habuisse', Nisard 'c'est la moindre portion de sa chevelure'. A hundred is a good many snakes to have on one's forehead; but if one is a

---

[1] In I 246 f. 'neque enim *arcano* de pectore fallax | Tantalus...periit' Baehrens proposed *arcani*, 'quod quominus ad *fallax* referamus, impedimur collocatione uerborum' says Mr Klotz. One may steal a horse while another may not look over the hedge.

[2] Mr Klotz's kindly willingness to explain what he does not understand is less of a help than a hindrance. Examples follow at II 637 f. and IV 2 f.; and there are others at II 327, IV 318, V 702 (the most amazing of all), IX 19.

fury one harbours an even larger number in one's back-hair: at least 101, more probably several hundreds.

I 535 f.
Pallados armisonae pharetrataeque ora Dianae
aequa ferunt, terrore minus.

According to Mr Klotz on p. 508 of his index, *Dianae* is a genitive dependent on *ora*; but then *aequa*, whether it means 'aequa inter se' or whatsoever else, is an intolerable intrusion between 'Pallados Dianaeque ora' and 'terrore ‖ minus'. The *thes. ling. Lat.* I p. 1030 69 makes *Dianae* a dative dependent on *aequa*: this is not quite so bad, 'ora Pallados oraque Dianae aequa', but no one can call it good or even middling. And both interpretations, apart from their own demerits, are confuted by the parallel of *Ach.* II 134–6 [I 808–10] 'natis, | quas tibi sidereis *diuarum uultibus aequas* | fors dedit'.

The construction is 'ora aequa (oribus) Pallados Dianaeque', πρόσωπα τοῖς Παλλάδος καὶ Ἀρτέμιδος ὅμοια. I have cited many such ellipses in my note on Manil. II 269 and the addendum in vol. v p. 140,* among them Luc. I 446 'Taranis Scythicae non mitior ara Dianae', that is 'ara Taranis non mitior (ara) Dianae'. Here I will add one more example which perhaps may still escape others as it formerly escaped me. In Manil. vol. v p. 139* I said 'genetiuum cum *cognatus* adiectiuo coniunxit Plinius *n.h.* XXXV 179 (napthae) *ardens natura et ignium cognata*'. The *thesaurus*, in citing this passage at III p. 1482 60, signifies no opinion on its construction; but Pliny construes *cognatus* with the dative elsewhere, and this exception is illusory: he means 'ignium (naturae) cognata'.

I 716 f.
adsis o memor hospitii, Iunoniaque arua
dexter ames.

So the old editors; 'adsis, o memor' the new, making *memor* vocative. It is nominative and part of the prayer, like *dexter* in the next verse: compare *silu.* II 7 120 'adsis lucidus' and *Theb.* X 345 'uoti memor exige tauros'. *o* is no more to be detached from *adsis* than in Verg. *Aen.* IV 578 'adsis o placidusque iuues' or VIII 78 'adsis o tantum'.

In VII 775 f. 'uade diu populis promissa uoluptas | Elysiis' the comma now generally inserted after *uade* does less injury but is also better away, for *uoluptas* is no more vocative than *coniunx* in Val. Fl. VII 235 f. 'cui uadis Hibero, | ei mihi, uel saeuo coniunx non una Gelono?'

On the other hand, where vocatives are really present, they are apt to be

* [These references are to the first edition of Manilius v (1930): in the second edition of the whole work (1937) the addenda to volumes I–IV were incorporated in the places to which they pertain]

jumbled up with the sentence by unskilful and irrational punctuation. IV
238–40:

> depressae populus subit incola Pisae,
> qui te, flaue, natant terris, Alphee, Sicanis
> aduena, tam longo non umquam infecte profundo.

The three commas after *terris* and *Alphee* and *aduena* are superfluous: what is
needed, though I find it only in Walker's *corpus poetarum*, is a comma to separate
the verb *natant* from *terris* as it is separated from *flaue*; for *terris* depends on the
vocative *aduena*. IV 275 f.:

> Arcades huic ueteres astris lunaque priores
> agmina fida datis.

So W. E. Weber, Mueller, and Wilkins, which is perhaps the best punctuation,
for the apostrophe is merely formal, like Ouid. *fast.* 1 362 'quid placidae ||
commeruistis oues?' But if you insist on commas for the vocative there must
be three of them, 'Arcades, huic, ueteres astris lunaque priores, | agmina fida
datis'. Most editors give neither, but 'Arcades huic ueteres...priores, |
agmina...datis', in which the dative *huic* can have no construction, being
locked away from its verb.

II 629–39

	uos quoque, Thespiadae, cur infitiatus honora
630	arcuerim fama? fratris moribunda leuabat
	membra solo Periphas (nil indole clarius illa
	nec pietate fuit) laeua marcentia colla
	sustentans dextraque latus (singultibus artum
	exhaurit thoraca dolor nec uincla coercent
635	undantem fletu galeam), cum multa gementi
	pone grauis curuas perfringit lancea costas
	exit et in fratrem cognataque pectora telo
	conserit. ille oculos etiamnum in luce natantes
	sistit et aspecta germani morte resoluit.

637 *telo* is the reading of all MSS, and it is only by a slip of memory that the
scholiast at III 152 cites *ferro traicit* for *telo conserit*. A. Nauke proposed *leto*,
'cum subiectum mutari non sensisset' says Mr Klotz, '*conserit* enim auctor teli.'
The reason why conservative editors are so unsuccessful in explaining difficulties is that they are content to offer such explanations as this: explanations
which are only meant to soothe the ignorant, and which to an educated reader
are mere affronts.

At Manil. 1 539 and elsewhere I have largely illustrated the pleonasm or
tautology of which 'lancea pectora telo conserit' is an instance. *lancea* and

telum are one thing under two names, as are *Cithaeron* and *mons* in I 330 f. 'in plana *Cithaeron* | porrigitur lassumque *inclinat* ad aequora *montem*'. Other examples which I have not quoted before are Petr. 89 57 '*Danai* relaxant claustra et *effundunt uiros*' (sese), *Aetn.* 140 f. 'cernis...*antra*...demersas penitus *fodisse latebras*',[1] Luc. VI 134 '*nimbus* (telorum) *agens* tot *tela* peribat'.

Statius has a similar phrase in *Theb.* XII 58 f. 'Argiuus haberi | *frater* iussus adhuc atque *exule pellitur umbra*', where the *umbra* is none other than Polynices himself, and in *silu.* II 7 116 f. '*tu magna* sacer et superbus *umbra* | *noscis Tartaron*', where it is Lucan; and Lucan himself led the way in I 10 f. 'cum... foret Babylon spolianda tropaeis | Ausoniis *umbra*que *erraret Crassus inulta*'. ||

III 102–7

> quo carmine dignam,
> quo satis ore tuis famam uirtutibus addam,
> augur amate deis? non te caelestia frustra
> edocuit lauruque sua dignatus Apollo est,   105
> et nemorum Dodona parens Cirrhaeaque uirgo
> gaudebit tacito populos suspendere Phoebo.

107 '*suspendere* sollicitos facere'. 'sensus: otia habebunt oracula te mortuo, hoc est propter tuum interitum conticescent' schol. But 'Dodona gaudebit (*or* audebit) tacito populos suspendere Phoebo' is a hard nut for theologians to crack, however toothsome it might be found by conservative editors of the *Aetna*; and *et* is not a conjunction which can perform any such task as is here assigned it. 'These two last lines' says Jortin *Misc. Obs.* I p. 95 'have no connection with what goes before. I believe something is lost between the 105 and 106th verses. However it is easy to see what the poet intended to say; he speaks of the silence of the oracles of Dodona and Cyrrha, which was a mark of the concern of the Gods for the death of the Augur.' He compares the similar but much more elaborate lament over Amphiaraus in VIII 195–202; and when the two passages are put side by side it is easy to fill the gap with something very like its original contents.

> ⟨edere te rapto Delos responsa negabit⟩
> et nemorum Dodona parens, Cirrhaeaque uirgo
> gaudebit tacito populos suspendere Phoebo.

VIII 195 ff. 'quidquid es, aeternus Phoebo dolor et noua clades | semper eris mutisque diu plorabere *Delphis*. | hic Tenedon Chrysenque dies partuque ligatam | *Delon* et intonsi cludet penetralia Branchi,...quin et cornigeri uatis

---

[1] Wernsdorf proposes a change; Sudhaus imagines the expression to be a personification characteristic of 'our Stoic author', and is so completely at a loss for a parallel that he compares Iuu. x 193–5 'rugas, | quales...in uetula scalpit iam mater simia bucca'.

nemus atque *Molosso* | *quercus anhela Ioui* Troianaque Thymbra tacebit': add
IX 513 'rapto tacuerunt augure Delphi'.

Markland emended better than he knew when he altered *audebit* to *gaudebit*.
He explained 'gaudebit suspendere' as a circumlocution for 'suspendet'; but
Statius has before his eyes the narrative of Lucan V 71–224. The Pythoness had
good reason to be glad when the god withheld his inspiration: 114–20 'nec
uoce negata | Cirrhaeae maerent uates, templique fruuntur | iustitio. nam, siqua
deus sub pectora uenit, | numinis aut poena est mors inmatura recepti | aut
pretium; quippe stimulo fluctuque furoris | conpages humana labat, pulsusque
deorum | concutiunt fragiles animas.'

III 378 f.

ibo libens certusque mori, licet optima coniunx
auditusque iterum reuocet socer.

'*auditus* a me scilicet. ut obtemperans primum non isse. sic hoc dicit ut
intellegamus Polynicem ad Thebas ante ire uoluisse, sed prohibitum se ab ||
Adrasto queritur, ut prius legatio mitteretur' schol. In other words, the sense
is to be 'licet me socer, cui reuocanti ante oboediui, reuocationem iteret'. But
on turning back to II 364–9 we find that this does not represent the facts, which
were these: 'Tydea iam socium coeptis...socerumque adfatur tristis Adra-
stum. | fit mora consilio, cum multa mouentibus una | iam potior cunctis sedit
sententia, fratris | pertemptare fidem.' Dissatisfaction is eloquently expressed
by these conjectures: *Argiuus* Koestlin, *cunctatus* Baehrens, *adscitus* Deiter,
augustus Bury, *ambitus* or *grandaeuus* Slater, *adiutus* Klotz, *largitusque torum*
Lachmann, *suadeat usque torum* Garrod.

iterum belongs not to *reuocet* but to *auditus*, and the allusion is to I 431–73,
where the rebuke of Adrastus fell on the ears of Tydeus and Polynices and
composed their quarrel. On that occasion his words had weight; but if he now
a second time tries the effect of his voice, it will fail.

III 710

ei mihi, care parens, iterum fortasse rogabo.

parens P, *pater* ω and the latest editors. 'in caesura Statius hiatum syllabamque
ancipitem quamuis raro admittit: accedit quod non *parens* caritatis nomen est,
sed *pater*' Klotz. The first of these statements is too vague to be actually false,
but it is deceiving. The truth is that Statius, like Horace, lengthens a short final
syllable only if its last letter is *t*. Mr Klotz himself does not retain *tollīs* in *silu.*
I 3 102, and indeed it is ungrammatical. As for the second statement, *care parens*
is rarer than *care pater*, but occurs again in Val. Fl. II 293. In the 24 lines of this
speech Argia has called Adrastus *pater* four times: here she might at least for

once be allowed to call him *parens*, as she called him *genitor* in 689, especially when *pater* recurs in the very next verse 711. Then compare Cic. *Sex. Rosc.* 53 'incensus *parens*', *pater* codd. dett., 'uulgarius uoc. substitutum est exquisitiori' Orelli, Drac. *Orest.* 768 *parens* B (cod. opt.), *pater* A (apographus), Luc. IV 110 *parens* ω, *pater* Z. Hor. *carm.* II 13 5 is cited in Prisc. *G.L.K.* III p. 256 with *patris* for *parentis* even against metre.

IV 1–3

> tertius horrentem zephyris laxauerat annum
> Phoebus et angusto cogebat limite uernum
> longius ire diem.

This reading of P is probably true and certainly faultless, but Mr Klotz has accepted it in blind reliance on the MS without knowing what it means, for he says '*angusto limite* i. ab angusto initio'. The ablative is of comparison and depends on *longius*, and *angustus limes* is the narrow bound of the winter day, whose measurement in space is less than half the circle of the heavens, and in time less than twelve hours of the twenty-four, until extended by the vernal equinox. ‖

IV 168–71

> squalet triplici ramosa corona
> Hydra recens obitu: pars anguibus aspera uiuis
> argento caelata micat, pars arte reperta
> conditur et fuluo moriens nigrescit in auro.

All modern editors regard verse 170 as corrupt, and the cause of their opinion can be guessed from such conjectures as *recurua*, *retorta*, *reposta*, which last the *thes. ling. Lat.* II p. 672 fin. has adopted and Mr Klotz has placed in his text. It is apparently supposed that *arte* must signify the craftsmanship of the graver; but it is capable of quite another meaning.

Half of the Hydra still bristles with live snakes in bright silver, half is undergoing extinction and taking on as it dies the deeper hue of gold. And how comes this about? *arte reperta*, because Hercules and Iolaus have found out the way to do it. The Greek equivalent of the phrase appears in the account of Diodorus IV 11 5 δεύτερον δ' ἔλαβεν ἆθλον ἀποκτεῖναι τὴν Λερναίαν ὕδραν, ἧς ἐξ ἑνὸς σώματος ἑκατὸν αὐχένες ἔχοντες κεφαλὰς ὄφεων διετετύπωντο. τούτων δ' εἰ μία διαφθαρείη, διπλασίας ὁ τμηθεὶς ἀνίει τόπος· δι' ἣν αἰτίαν ἀήττητος ὑπάρχειν διείληπτο, καὶ κατὰ λόγον· τὸ γὰρ χειρωθὲν αὐτῆς μέρος διπλάσιον ἀπεδίδου βοήθημα. πρὸς δὲ τὴν δυστραπελίαν ταύτην ἐπινοήσας τι φιλοτέχνημα προσέταξεν Ἰολάῳ λαμπάδι καομένῃ τὸ ἀποτμηθὲν μέρος ἐπικάειν. In the age of understanding this was understood: Marolles 'une partie s'abaissoit pour exprimer l'invention qui fut trouvée pour vaincre cette Hydre', Beraldus 'inuento artificio', '(Hercules) admouit tandem ignem...sicque impediuit quominus (capita) repullularent'. Barthius at first had rightly said *arte reperta*: ambustione', but he then rambled away into the conjectures *repressa* and even *torre repressa*.

IV 520–4

> panditur Elysium chaos, et telluris opertae
> dissilit umbra capax, siluaeque et nigra patescunt
> flumina: liuentis Acheron eiectat harenas,
> fumidus atra uadis Phlegethon incendia uoluit,
> et Styx discretis interflua manibus obstat.

I wonder if the reader can even guess how this sentence is punctuated in the editions.

IV 699–704

> protinus Inachios haurit sitis ignea campos,
> 700   diffugere undae, squalent fontesque lacusque
> et caua feruenti durescunt flumina limo,
> aegra solo maci*es* [tenerique in ori*gine* culmi
> inclinata seg*es*], deceptum mar*gine* ripae
> stat pecus atque amnis quaerunt armenta natatos. ‖

702–3 *tenerique...seges*, omitted by Pω, is given by DN, two good MSS of the 10th century. The brackets are Mueller's, who is followed by Kohlmann, Garrod, and Klotz. The italics are mine, and their purpose is to remove the brackets. This was an uncommonly subtle interpolator if he provided both an homoeoteleuton and what I call an homoeomeson (ed. Luc. pp. xix f.) to make me think that two genuine hemistichs have been omitted for palaeographical causes.

Mueller's objection is this: 'interpolator nullam rationem habuit uersus 680 sqq., unde apparet hanc maciem immissam esse mediis aestatis caloribus, non eo anni tempore, quo proserpit seges teneri in origine culmi.' He seems to think, as the scholiast does, that those verses, 'tempus erat, medii cum solem in culmina mundi | tollit anhela[1] dies, ubi tardus hiantibus aruis | stat uapor atque omnes admittunt aethera luci', describe the time of year; but anyone who considers their place in the narrative must see that they describe the time of day, not midsummer but noon; and noon in the Peloponnese can be very hot even in the spring. Again, in 689 f. 'adiuuat ipse | Phoebus...summo...limite', *summo limite* can quite as well signify the meridian as the tropic of Cancer. A greater difficulty is pointed out by Mr Klotz *Herm.* 1905 p. 360 in verse 692 'aestifer Erigones spumat canis', for this expression ought to indicate August

---

[1] *anhela* with *tollit* is not, as the scholiast says, 'aestuosa', but pictures the day panting up the steep of heaven.

or late July, the dogstar rising about the 24th. But bad astronomy is at any rate less heinous in an epic[1] than in a calendar; and Ovid in *fast.* IV 904 makes the dogstar rise on April 25, which in truth was about the date of its vespertinal setting, and then in *fast.* V 723, by a less explicable blunder, makes it rise again on May 22. I should guess that Statius, having Verg. *georg.* IV 425–8 before him as a model for this description, borrowed the dogstar merely as a calorific, without considering or realising the inconsistency involved. As the gathering of the Argives and their allies began in the last days of March (IV 1 ff.), it may be supposed that they reached Nemea some while before the end of May.

VI 149–55

> narrabat seruatum fraude parentem
> insontesque manus. en quam ferale putemus   150
> abiurasse sacrum et Lemni gentilibus unam
> inmunem furiis! haec illa (et creditis ausae?),
> haec pietate potens solis abiecit in aruis –
> non regem dominumque – alienos impia partus,
> hoc tantum, siluaeque infamis tramite liquit.   155

In this lament of the queen Eurydice over the death of her infant son Opheltes by the fault of his nurse Hypsipyle the text of the earlier editors is ‖ right as far as *furiis* in 152. The construction is that of Cic. II *Verr.* I 93 'en cui tuos liberos committas!' and recurs, without this ironical force, in *Theb.* XII 690, 'en iterum qui moenia nostra lacessant!'. When Mueller makes 'quam putemus' a relative clause dependent on 'haec' or 'illa', he disregards the subjunctive: the mood and tense expected would be 'putauimus'. But from that point onward the old punctuation, 'haec illa, et creditis ausae? | haec pietate potens?' is obscure and incoherent, and Mueller's parenthesis, though he did not himself understand it (for he marked no interrogation, and paraphrased 'cui credere audetis', evidently mistaking *ausae*, as Lemaire's index also does, for the nominative plural), is nevertheless right, and likewise his abolition of the break in 153.

As conjectural alterations have been proposed, and as it is clear that no editor has understood the passage in its entirety, I give a paraphrase which will assist my punctuation in making matters plain. 'A likely woman to have kept herself exempt from the crime and frenzy of Lemnos! This heroine (and do you still believe her story, now that you see what she has dared?), this paragon of piety has cast away and abandoned – I do not say her king and master, though he was both,[2] – I say only another's child, no worse impiety than that!'

---

[1] Lucan's errors in this department, though not so many as Scaliger made them out to be, are sometimes monstrous, and one of them (X 210–18) involves the dogstar.

[2] Mr Klotz, with the old editors, reads *dominumue*, against the best MS; Mueller, Kohlmann, Wilkins, and Garrod are right.

The scholiast rightly interpreted *ausae* as 'quae fuerit ausa dominum proicere, linquere'. The two following lines are lucidly explained in the Delphin edition by an alien note, conflicting with the text and the paraphrase, which I cannot trace to its author: 'non objicio illi filium meum, quem in silua exposuit, ipsius et dominum et regem fuisse; id unum ingens scelus est, commissam sibi alienam prolem tam negligenter curauisse.'

VI 159–61

nec uos incessere luctu
orba habeo: fixum matri inmotumque manebat
hac altrice nefas.

For *habeo* one editor has proposed and two have accepted the inappropriate verb *aueo*. What Eurydice says is that she cannot blame the Argives for her child's death: it was inevitable so soon as Hypsipyle became his nurse. *habeo* is ἔχω, *possum*, as Barthius explained it, though he foolishly added *debeo*: he gave examples of the usage, and Gronouius others at Sen. *contr.* I 1 19; and a large though not complete collection was made by Ph. Thielmann *Arch. f. lat. Lexikographie* II pp. 50–64. The following are amply sufficient: Cic. *n.d.* I 63 'de diuis neque ut sint neque ut non sint habeo dicere' (= οὐκ ἔχω εἰδέναι Protagoras Diog. Laert. IX 51), *Sex. Rosc.* 100 'habeo...dicere quem...deiecerit', *ep. fam.* I 5ᵃ 3 'de Alexandrina re...tantum habeo polliceri me tibi...satisfacturum', Lucr. VI 711 'in multis hoc rebus dicere habemus', Hor. *epod.* 16 23 'an melius quis habet suadere?', Ouid. *ex Pont.* III 1 82 'nec te, si cupiat, laedere rumor habet', Sen. || *contr.* I 1 19 'quid habui facere?' But Mr Klotz, wishing to defend the text, could find none of these; only Varr. *r. r.* I 1 2 'cum...me...ut id mihi habeam curare roges, experiar', where *mihi habeam* means 'undertake'.

VI 355–64

355   interea cantu Musarum nobile mulcens
        concilium citharaeque manus insertus Apollo
        Parnasi summo spectabat ab aethere terras.
        orsa deum (nam saepe Iouem Phlegramque suique
        anguis opus fratrumque pius cantarat honores)
360   tunc aperit, quis fulmen agat, quis sidera ducat
        spiritus, unde animi fluuiis, quae pabula uentis,
        quo fonte inmensum uiuat mare, quae uia solis
        praecipitet noctem, quae porrigat, imane tellus
        an media et rursus mundo succincta latenti.

Such is the text and punctuation of 358 sq. in the editions. The construction then must be 'tunc aperit orsa deum, quis spiritus fulmen agat,...imane tellus an media'. And the sense? Apparently it is supposed that 'tunc aperit' can mean 'illo tempore aperiebat', and that 'orsa deum' can mean 'opera deum'. *orsa* is a word of which Statius is very fond, and it always signifies speech or writing; even if it could be stretched to mean *coepta*, it would still be far from meaning *opera*; and even 'opera deum' would be a ridiculous description of the contents of 360–4, which are questions about the causes of natural phenomena, 'quae pabula uentis', and even dubitations about fact, 'imane tellus an media'. Mr Mozley translates as if he had a comma at the end of 359, 'first he recounts the deeds of the gods...and then reveals what spirit drives the thunderbolt': this renders 'tunc aperit' correctly, but foists in a non-existent 'primum', and allows 'nam' no meaning; for to have sung a theme often can be no reason for singing it again.

In 358, instead of *deum*, P has *deo*; and 'orsa deo' is the remains of a sentence in which *orsa* had its proper sense of *carmen*. A verse has fallen out after 357. The first canto of Apollo's lay, hymning such things as the Gigantomachia, the slaying of the Python, the exploits of Bacchus and Hercules, was short, because he had often hymned them before; it was followed by a longer canto 'de rerum natura'. This supplement might serve:

> ⟨caelicolum meritas non longa sonantia laudes⟩
> orsa deo, nam saepe Iouem Phlegramque suique
> anguis opus fratrumque pius cantarat honores.
> tunc aperit quis fulmen agat, quis sidera ducat
> spiritus...

It may possibly be suspected that the *turbas* which is given by P instead of *terras* at the end of 357 was the last word of the lost verse, and that its loss ‖ was caused by homoeoteleuton. For my part, I cannot incorporate *turbas* in any verse which would properly suit the context or could fairly be imputed to Statius.

VI 404–13

> insonuit contra Tyrrhenum murmur, et omnes
> exsiluere loco. quae tantum carbasa ponto,   405
> quae bello sic tela uolant, quae nubila caelo?
> amnibus hibernis minor est, minor impetus igni,
> tardius astra cadunt, glomerantur tardius imbres,
> tardius e summo decurrunt flumina monte.
> emissos uidere atque agnouere Pelasgi,   405
> et iam rapti oculis, iam caeco puluere mixti
> una in nube latent uultusque umbrante tumultu
> uix inter sese clamore et nomine noscunt.

My business here is not with the question whether 409 is spurious, but only with interpretation, punctuation, and typographical arrangement. Gronouius and a few others print the passage virtually as above; but all modern editors tear it asunder by beginning a new paragraph with 410, and render that verse inapposite and intrusive by putting a full stop at the end of it. When the race began, the spectators saw and recognised the competitors, did they? Naturally they did: why say so?

Barthius understood and explained the connexion: 'hoc quoque' (praeter 405–9) 'ad summam celeritatem referendum. tantum enim uidere, tantum agnouere, uisi uix atque agniti ex oculis rapti sunt.' The verse is a protasis: *et iam* is used as in Prop. II 29 10 'dixit, *et* in collo *iam* mihi nodus erat', and the sense is 'uix uidere atque agnouere, cum rapti oculis latent'. At VI 469 f. Statius has left no room for mistake, '*uixdum* coeptus equis labor, *et iam* puluere quarto | campum ineunt', nor again at VII 300 f. '*nec longum, et* pulcher Alatreus | editus'. At Verg. *Aen.* III 8 f. 'uix prima inceperat aestas, | et pater Anchises dare fatis uela iubebat' Seruius says '*et*: haec coniunctio uelocitatem uidetur ostendere'.

VI 464–6

> audit et Herculeum Strymon Chromin, Euneon audit
> igneus Aethion, tardumque Cydona lacessit
> Hippodamus, uariumque Thoas rogat ire Podarcem.

On 465 Mr Klotz has this note. '*Aethion* Pω: *Aethalion* Schrader. ac sane -*i*- produci mirum. nam 7, 757. 10, 734 *Aetion*(*a*) (ab ἀετός) legendum idemque Ouidio restituendum Met. 5, 146 ubi epitheton *sagax* originem indicat. quod ne hoc quoque loco faciamus, impedimento est attributum *igneus*. itaque graeco accentu syllabam -*i*- produci censeo, sicut corripitur -*a*- in titulo Thebaidos propter graecum accentum sequentis syllabae' – on which last opinion I will speak at XII 812. The position of affairs is that at VII 757 || Pω have the proper name *Aetion* and two tenth-century MSS *Aethion*, at X 734 ω have *Aetiona* and P with a few others *Aethiona*, at Ouid. *met.* V 146 most MSS have *Aethion* but the two best *Ethion*: in our verse *Aethion* was read also by the scholiast, who says '*igneus Aethion*: iucunde Graeco nomini expositionem adiecit, quia Aethion dicitur de colore'.

Mr Klotz understands, what former editors and the *thes. ling. Lat.* have not understood, that Αἰθίων, whether from αἰθός or αἶθος, should by analogy be a cretic. But, instead of taking this for a token that the text is wrong, 'graeco accentu syllabam -*i*- produci censet'. I suppose that there will always be some scholars to nurse this idle fancy, and to take pleasure in defiling the first century with a vice of pronunciation which was rare even in the fifth. I have had to touch on the matter before, when dealing in *C.Q.* 1907 p. 276 [this edition

p. 699]] with Mr Birt's remarks on *pompīle* at Ouid. *hal.* 101,[1] and I will not a second time pay it serious attention. It should be treated humorously: some one should set up the opposite pretence, that what the Greek accent really did was to shorten long syllables, and should adduce in proof χορεία *chorĕa*, πλατεῖα *platĕa*, κρηπῖδα *crepĭda*, γυναικεῖον *gynaecĕum*, χορηγεῖον *choragĭum*, Κήριλλοι *Cĕrillae*, Ὕλη (– –) *Il.* II 500, *Hȳle* Stat. *Theb.* VII 267.

In spite of Mr Klotz and the scholiast I do not see in *igneus* any strong argument for *Aethion*. If the horse's name is to be significant, *Aetion* will suit *igneus* quite well. Whatever αἰετὸς αἴθων may mean in Homer, the eagle is 'fulminis ardens uector' in *Theb.* III 506 f., and *igneus* here is only what it is in IX 736 'circumuolat igneus' (Parthenopaeus), Verg. *Aen.* XI 718 'pernicibus ignea plantis' (Camilla), 746 'uolat igneus aequore Tarchon'. But there is no reason to expect a significant name. It is true that in the preceding sentence we had 'rapidum Ascheton' and 'meritum uocabula Cycnum'; but 'tardum Cydona' and 'uarium Podarcem' contain no etymology.

VI 571–3

> effulsere artus, membrorumque omnis aperta est
> laetitia, insignes umeri, nec pectora nudis
> deteriora genis, latuitque in corpore uultus.

In the last verse P has the corruption *aluitque in corpore uirtus*, and four modern editors print conjectures built on this, *patuitque*, which is less apt and pointed, or *ualuitque*, which is definitely inappropriate. Nothing could be better than the reading of ω. It is explained by the scholiast, 'latuit uultus comparatione membrorum; nudato enim corpore membrorum pulchritudo uenustatem uultus obnubit', and can be stoutly supported by Plat. *Charm.* 154d καὶ ὁ Χαιρεφῶν καλέσας με, τί σοι φαίνεται ὁ νεανίσκος, ἔφη, ὦ Σώκρατες; οὐκ εὐπρόσωπος; ὑπερφυῶς, ἦν δ' ἐγώ. οὗτος μέντοι, ἔφη, εἰ ἐθέλοι ἀποδῦναι, δόξει σοι ἀπρόσωπος εἶναι· οὕτως τὸ εἶδος πάγκαλός ἐστιν. The passage quoted || by Barthius from Aristaen. I 1, ἐνδεδυμένη μὲν εὐπροσωποτάτη ἐστίν, ἐκδῦσα δὲ ὅλη πρόσωπον φαίνεται, is a contrast rather than a parallel.

VI 598–601

> non aliter celeres Hyrcana per auia cerui,
> cum procul inpasti fremitum accepere leonis
> siue putant, rapit attonitos fuga caeca metusque
> congregat, et longum dant cornua mixta fragorem.

---

[1] What I then said against his explanation of Ovid's *Belīdes* and *Lycurgīdes* was afterwards confirmed by the emergence of Κοδρείδης and Λαγείδης from papyri of Callimachus.

The punctuation is ungrammatical, and requires *ceruos* for *cerui*. It ought to be 'non aliter, celeres Hyrcana per auia cerui | cum procul' etc.

VI 658–60

'illud cui non iaculabile dextrae
pondus?' et abreptum nullo conamine iecit
in latus.

To pick up something which is lying on the ground is not *abripere* but *adripere*; and *adreptum* is here given by B and b, MSS of the 11th century, and was conjectured, as you might expect, by Heinsius, though I wish he had not suggested *arrectum* as an alternative. In *thes. ling. Lat.* I p. 133 81 ff. this verse appears as one of seven alleged examples of '*abripio* fere id quod *ui arripio*'. In one of these, Plin. *n.h.* VIII 20 '(elephantus) repsit genibus in cateruas, abrepta scuta iaciens in sublime', the use of the verb is entirely normal. In Ouid. *her.* XIII 15 'incubuit boreas abreptaque uela tetendit' the sails, and the ship with them, are carried away from Phylace and Laodamia. In all the other places, Liu. II 33 7, Appul. *met.* IV 27, VII 28, IX 38, the best and the latest editors read *adripio*; and indeed 'temere abreptum' in the passage of Livy is an impossible combination. *adripio*, especially if so spelt, is easily changed to *abripio*, as it is by P at *Ach.* II 110 [I 784]; and half-a-dozen cases are noted in *thes. ling. Lat.* II pp. 639–42.

VI 925

tumulo supremum hunc addere honorem.

tumulo ω, *tumulis* P, 'quod reiciendum, nam Statius plurali poetico *tumuli* utitur aut propter metrum (*Theb.* V 679, *silu.* III 1 24, IV 4 55, V 3 106 et 243) aut propter euphoniam (*Theb.* IX 388)' Klotz. The picture of this superbly accomplished versifier reluctantly compelled to use a plural five times over because he could not find words beginning with consonants to follow the singular is more laughable than credible; and Mr Klotz's enumeration is faulty. *tumulos* in V 674 means what is meant here, the tomb of Archemorus, and is followed by *quanti*; *tumulos* in VII 179 means the tomb of Semele, and is followed by *siquid*. ||

VII 260

Ocalee Medeonque.

The variants of the MSS point to *Ocalee* or *Ocaleae*; the old editors wrongly chose the plural; Kohlmann restored the singular from *Il.* II 501, but in the form *Ocalea*. Mr Klotz's remark 'quamquam Ὠκαλέη non inauditum' is an irrelevant truism; it was of course the regular and the only form in epic and

Ionic: the pertinent question is whether Statius, in latinising Ὠκαλέην Μεδεῶνά τε, would necessarily also atticise; and the answer, according to the MSS of his *Thebais* and *Achilleis*, for the late MS of the *siluae* has little authority, is no. He has *Nemee* beside *Nemeā*, *Tegee* beside *Tegeā*, *Gargaphie Stratie Vranie* beside *Harmoniā Maleā Mideā Leucotheā Pasitheā*.

VII 500 f.

> tune ille exsilio uagus et miserabilis hospes?
> quem non permoueas?

Kohlmann and Mr Klotz give 'quem non permoueas!'. I should have supposed that this was nothing worse than a misprint left uncorrected by the one and inadvertently retained by the other, like the comma at the end of VIII 590, did I not find at *silu.* V 2 68 f. the parallel 'quem non corrupit pubes effrena nouaeque | libertas properata togae!' in both of Mr Klotz's editions.[1] The false punctuation therefore seems to be deliberate; and it brings me back to a subject which I illustrated in *C.Q.* 1923 pp. 170 f. [[this edition pp. 1082–3]] from Seneca's tragedies, the confusion existing in many minds between the interrogative and the exclamatory uses of words beginning with *qu*.

quis non? is a well-known equivalent for *nemo non*, *quis* asking a question to which *nemo* is the only answer; and it occurs in Statius about a dozen times. *quis non!* is something which I did not know to be Latin. There might be put up a pretence of explaining 'quem non permoueas!' as 'qualis homo sit quem non permoueas!', but for 'quem non corrupit pubes effrena!' I can fabricate no sense at all. And why not be thorough? why not print 'quid regnis non uile!' *Theb.* II 488, 'quid non ausa manus!' V 379, 'quas non in nomen credula uestes | urgebat studio cultusque insignia regni | purpureos sceptrumque minus!' VI 79–81, 'illud cui non iaculabile dextrae | pondus!' 658 f., 'quid non fata queant!' IX 309, 'diuum fortia quid non | tela queant!' 752 f., 'quis non in omni uertice Romuli | reptasse dulcem Septimium putet!' *silu.* IV 5 33 f.? Why not also, for instance, 'fecundi calices quem non fecere disertum!' Hor. *epist.* I 5 19 and 'cui non his uerbis aspergat tempora sudor!' Prop. II 24 3? Why not indeed 'solem quis dicere falsum audeat!' and a thousand more perversities? for the *non* can make no difference. ||

The commoner blunder is the reverse, to mistake exclamations for questions. All editors print rightly 'quis ardor!' in VIII 728; modern editors print rightly I 188 'quas gerit ore minas, quanto premit omnia fastu!' which used to be interrogative; yet all give I 165–8 thus:

---

[1] I do not add his punctuation of *silu.* II 1 129, which, though equally vicious, had more excuse until I analysed the sentence in *Class. Rev.* 1906 p. 41 [[this edition p. 645]].

> quis tunc tibi, saeue,
> quis fuit ille dies, uacua cum solus in aula
> respiceres ius omne tuum cunctosque minores
> et nusquam par stare caput?

Statius is putting no question to Eteocles: he is appraising what he thoroughly comprehends. In the passage of Lucan which he imitates, II 98–100, the punctuation was set right a hundred years ago, 'pro fata, quis ille, | quis fuit ille dies, Marius quo moenia uictor | corripuit, quantoque gradu mors saeua cucurrit!', and no mistake is made about *anth. Lat. Ries.* 415 36 f. 'o superi, quis fuit ille dies, | quo Marium uidit supra Carthago iacentem!' Most editors behave even worse at *Theb.* XII 698 f., where they print 'quis fuit ille dies? tanto cum sanguine Thebis | pax inuenta perit?', mistaking *cum* for the preposition in spite of I 166; and even those who recognise the conjunction retain the interrogation, 'quis...dies, tanto...perit?' There are four or five who understand how to punctuate *silu.* I 2 209–12 'quis tibi tunc alacri caelestum in munere claro, | Stella, dies, quanto salierunt pectora uoto, | dulcia cum dominae dexter conubia uultus | adnuit!', but the majority make 'quis dies' a question though they see that 'quanto uoto' is an exclamation. Neither *quis* nor *quantum* is understood in *Theb.* VI 513 f., where Polynices narrowly misses the good luck of being killed in the chariot-race, 'quis mortis, Thebane, locus, nisi dura negasset | Tisiphone, quantum poteras dimittere bellum!', though interrogation is there peculiarly absurd.

In *Theb.* XI 659 all editions have 'quid, melior Fortuna, potes?' or 'quid melior Fortuna potest?' The context is this:

	scandit fatale tyrannis
655	flebilis Aoniae solium. pro blanda potestas
	et sceptri malesuadus amor! numquamne priorum
	haerebunt documenta nouis? iuuat ecce nefasto
	stare loco regimenque manu tractare cruentum!
	quid, melior Fortuna, potes? iam flectere patrem
660	incipit atque datis abolere Menoecea regnis.

The Loeb translation is 'what availest thou, kindlier Fortune?', and that is what the words, so punctuated, mean; but then they are clean contrary to sense. Creon, lately bereft of Menoeceus, ascends the throne in tears; but the delights of sovereignty lay hold upon him, the father gives place to the tyrant, and the son is forgotten. The context therefore requires not 'quid potes?', that is 'nihil potes', but 'quid potes!', that is 'quantum potes!', or, if you prefer it, as Nisard translates, 'que *ne* peut sur nous la prosperité?', || 'quid *non* potes?'. I quote one parallel which is as good as a dozen, Sen. *Ag.* 512 ff. 'quid fata possunt! inuidet Pyrrhus patri, | Aiaci Vlixes, Hectori Atrides minor, | Aga-memno Priamo; quisquis ad Troiam iacet | felix uocatur.' The scholiast of Barthius, though the false interrogation is printed again in his paraphrase 'quantum, inquit, ualet Fortunae splendidioris accessio?', understood what was meant; and Lemaire compares Curt. III 2 18 'tu quidem licentia regni tam subito mutatus documentum eris posteris homines, cum se permisere Fortunae, etiam naturam dediscere.'

Again in *Theb.* IX 69 'qualis et ecce iaces!', where W. S. Walker and Mr Klotz are right, most editors give 'iaces?', which makes nonsense of 'ecce'. I foresee that trouble may arise in the future from some observant reader who is not observant enough unless I add a word on VII 172 f. 'unde tubas Martem-que pati, qui feruidus ecce | quanta parat?'. Here 'ecce quanta' is exclamatory, but the accepted punctuation is nevertheless correct, because the final stop of a sentence belongs to the sentence itself, not to any particular clause which may happen to come last, and this sentence is interrogative, 'unde pati?' To print 'unde tubas Martemque pati, qui feruidus ecce | quanta (!) parat?' would be to pay a high price for lucidity. In *Class. Rev.* 1906 p. 41 [this edition p. 645] I touched on a typographical difficulty of the same sort at *silu.* II 1 126–9, where 'quas uestes' is exclamatory, 'quae non gestamina' interrogative, and yet the sentence, being an affirmation, should end with a full stop, as does I 6 61, where the punctuation 'mortem sibi (qua manu!) minantur' is practicable and usual.

167

NOTES ON
THE *THEBAIS* OF STATIUS [II]*

VII 683–7

occidis audax,
occidis Aonii puer altera cura Lyaei.
685   marcida te fractis planxerunt Ismara thyrsis,
te Tmolos, te Nysa ferax Theseaque Naxos
et Thebana metu iuratus in orgia Ganges.

'altera cura' in 684 is supposed by some to mean a second cause of grief, the
first being the death of the two sacred tigers which after serving in the Indian
campaign were killed by Aconteus in 564–98. Others translate it 'one favourite
more' and say that the first favourite was the Phegeus mentioned in 603, who
however is merely described as 'Baccheus cultor'. The episode of Eunaeus,
649–87, is so elaborately polished, his youth and effeminacy are so fondly
depicted, and his death evokes such lamentation from the whole Bacchic world,
that neither of these explanations can be entertained, and a third spontaneously
presents itself. The reader of Statius must be on the look-out for mythological
allusions, which are not always obvious. The words 'ausum contraria Phoebo |
carmina *nec fida* gauisam Pallada buxo' in *silu.* v 3 88 were a puzzle for centuries
and only elucidated in 1892.[1] If we met anywhere such a phrase as 'puer altera
cura Alcidae' we should soon hit on the interpretation 'altera post Hylan': here
we are to remember a less famous personage and understand 'altera post
Ampelum'.

And now I find lurking unnoticed in Jortin's *Misc. Obs.* II p. 365 'Altera
cura post Ampelum, de quo uide Ouid. *fast.* II 409.' The reference however
should be 'III 409', though the error occurs also in the indexes to Riese's and
Guethling's editions.

* [[CQ 27 (1933), 65–73]]
[1] On the other hand *Theb.* II 664–6 'nebridas et fragiles thyrsos portare putastis | inbellem ad
sonitum maribusque incognita ueris | foeda Celaenaea committere proelia buxo?', intelligible to
everyone else, receives on p. 501 of Mr Klotz's index the extraordinary interpretation 'proelia
(*Apollinis et Marsyae*)': as if those 'proelia' were 'foeda' and 'maribus incognita ueris', and as if the
Thebans had anything to do with them.

VIII 65–8

sed quid ego haec? i, Tartareas ulciscere sedes,
Tisiphone; si quando, nouis asperrima monstris,
triste, insuetum, ingens, quod nondum uiderit aether,
ede nefas, quod mirer ego inuideantque sorores.

This of course is how verse 66 ought to be punctuated. Editors make no ||
mistake at *Ach.* 1 508 f. 'heia, inrumpe deos et fata latentia uexa, | laurigerosque
ignes, si quando, auidissimus hauri', but here they join 'si quando asperrima'
and say 'supple *fuisti*'. The *nunc* which Statius omits is expressed by Ovid *art.*
II 15 'nunc mihi, si quando, puer et Cytherea, fauete' and *amor.* 1 13 6 'si
quando, lateri nunc bene iuncta meo est'.

VIII 255–8

qualis post longae Phineus ieiunia poenae,
nil stridere domi uolucresque ut sensit abactas
(necdum tota fides), hilaris mensasque torosque
nec turbata feris tractauit pocula pinnis.

256 *uolucresque ut* D, *uolucres ut* P, *uolucres*(*que*) *et* ω. D is one of the better
MSS; but if it were quite the worst, or if its reading were in none of them, it
ought to be in every edition; and if Gronouius had read the epics as attentively
as the *siluae* it would be at least in one. It is in none,[1] P's is in all, and Barthius
interprets, as he must, '*nil stridere*, id est minime, prorsus non'. Phineus then is
said to perceive that the Harpies, having been chased from the house, are
making no noise there! *nil* is not object but subject,[2] and the participle is co-
ordinate with the infinitive as in 'magno misceri murmure pontum | emissam-
que hiemem sensit Neptunus'.

VIII 570–8

ac primum in facilis grassatus cuspide turmas
arma refert sociis et in agmina fida peracta
caede redit.   572
mox ignotum armis ac solo corpore mensus   577
Tydea non timuit.

570. Kohlmann's text is *primum in faciles* and his note '*primam facili* P pr.m.,
primam in faciles P m. sec., *primam faciles* BS', which implies that other MSS,
such as those which he denotes by the letter M, have *primum in faciles*, like his

---

[1] It stands in Bernartius' margin as a variant or emendation.
[2] If I compare Hor. *serm.* II 8 78 'stridere...susurros' it is only because C. F. W. Mueller
Synt. d. nom. u. akk. p. 11 makes the same blunder of taking the accusative for object.

text. The notes of the later editors are unskilfully framed and do not clearly inform us whether the MSS in general present *in* or omit it. As to P, Wilkins's report agrees with Kohlmann's, but Mr Klotz's note contradicts it, assigning the corrections to the first hand.

The *primam* of P points to *prima in*. *prima cuspide* is a pictorial equivalent for *primum*, resembling VI 469 f. '*puluere quarto* | campum ineunt', Verg. *Aen.* VII 148 *prima* (MP, *primo* R) *lampade*, Mart. X 93 5 *pollice primo*. Where poets use the adjective, scribes will sometimes substitute the adverb, as in *Theb.* IV 95 'ut *primae* (P, *primum* ω) strepuere tubae', VII 670 f. 'qualis ubi *primam* (*primum* cod. unus) leo mane cubilibus atris | erexit rabiem', ‖ III 552 *primus* (*primum* cod. unus), V 346 *primi* (P, *primum* ω), Verg. *buc.* VIII 24, *Aen.* IV 28, V 491, VI 819, IX 494, X 516, XI 238, XII 103 f. 'mugitus ueluti cum *prima* (P, *primam* M, *primum* R) in proelia taurus | terrificos ciet'.

IX 248–51

> talis agit sparsos mediisque in fluctibus heros
> frena manu pariter, pariter regit arma, pedumque
> remigio sustentat equum, consuetaque campo
> fluctuat et mersas leuis ungula quaerit harenas.

Hippomedon keeps afloat a large quadruped which can swim for itself by rowing with his feet. This impossible performance is mildly described by Jortin as 'very odd', and in *Misc. Obs.* I p. 186 he proposed 'pedum *se* | remigio sustentat *equus*': 'contra sensum non minus quam contra metricam Stati' says Mr Klotz, whose knowledge of Statius' metric is not what it should be.[1] Jortin cited the verse-endings I 625 *canum uim*, V 140 *agi rem*, and XI 490 *cadit Sphinx*, and might have added IV 87 '*riget Sphinx*', while *se* is the last word of VI 653. I suggested [[suggest]] as a slighter change 'pedum *quem*': a monosyllabic relative pronoun stands at the end of three verses of the *Thebais*.

But yet it must be recognised, as Madvig said, 'permulta sibi Statium permisisse quae apud alios incredibilia uiderentur', and there are indications that this is a case in point. *manu* and *pedum* might be expected to correspond, and the line 'fluctuat et mersas leuis ungula quaerit harenas' does not so well describe a swimming horse as a helpless poetical beast lifted off its legs by an almighty poetical rider whose horizontal motions counteract gravitation.

IX 462 f.

> non secus aequoreo iactat Teumesius amnis
> Hippomedonta salo.

---

[1] The *ergo hoc* at the end of XI 429, adopted by Mr Klotz from PN, would be 'contra metricam Stati' if it were a conjecture.

amnis ω and all editors before 1908, *ignis* P and Mr Klotz, 'quod explicat Vollmer [*mus. Rhen.*] 1896 p. 31, cf. 10, 685'. When Vollmer 'explicat' one is quite prepared to read as follows: 'Absichtlich spielt Statius mit den Worten, wenn er den Fluss umschreibt mit *Teumesius ignis* (*amnis* platt in BM); *ignis* steht für ardor, ira. Dasselbe Spiel mit dem Gegensatze findet sich *silu.* I 2 204 *amnis in externos longe flammatus amores, Theb.* VIII 17 *ustaeque paludes, silu.* IV 4 83 *tosto mari.*'

If *amnis* is 'platt', ποταμός is 'platt' wherever it occurs in the combat of Achilles and Scamander. But this term, in the lingo of German conservative critics (the English use 'weak' or 'tame'), means simply 'nicht absurd', and all good literature is in their private opinion 'platt'.

Now for *ignis. ardor* and *ira* are used in periphrasis, as at *Il. Lat.* 174 f. 'bis tricenis *Menelai* nauibus *ardor* | insequitur totidemque ferox *Agapenoris* || *ira*', and therefore *Ismenius ardor* is no more open to exception than βίη Ἡρακλείη. *Ismenius ignis*, being metaphorical, would be a long step further; and moreover its most natural meaning would not be *Ismenos iratus* but a person with whom Ismenos was ardently in love, on the analogy of 'meus ignis Amyntas'. But what we have is *Teumesius* (i.e. *Boeotius*) *ignis*: are we seriously asked to interpret that as *amnis Boeotius iratus*? And this brings us round to the enquiry, where is the 'Gegensatz'? It may exist in the '*amnis... flammatus*' cited from the *siluae*, but here no *amnis* has been left in the text, and Vollmer is trying to eat his cake and have it. As for Mr Klotz's reference to x 685, the best way to deal with that is to transcribe the sentence: 'uulgus euntem | auctorem pacis seruatoremque deumque | conclamat gaudens atque ignibus implet honestis.' If unthinking critics could know how much ashamed one is to answer what they write, they would begin to be a little ashamed of writing it.

The compilation known as *liber glossarum* or *glossarium Ansileubi* contains the gloss (Lindsay *gloss. Lat.* I p. 561 no. 699) *Teumesius: amnis est.* It appears to be a false interpretation of this line of Statius, and one of the MSS presenting it is nearly a hundred years older than P.

IX 788 f.

iamdudum hunc contra stimulis grauioribus ardet
trux Atalantiades; necdum ille quierat, et infit.

The *quierat et* of P was substituted for the *quieuerat* of ω by Kohlmann, but he did not alter the punctuation accordingly: he made 'necdum ille quierat' a parenthesis as 'necdum ille quieuerat' had been, and his successors have followed him. The construction is that of XII 609 f. 'necdum Atticus ire parabat | miles, et infelix expauit classica Dirce' and III 42–4 'necdum ora patent, dubiusque notari | signa dabat magnae longe manifesta ruinae | planctuque et gemitu'.

X 47 f.

quod superest, duris adfrangunt postibus ungues
pectoraque, et siccos minuunt in limine dentes.

I should have thought that this punctuation must be in some editions if not in all; but the only place where I have found it is Walker's *corpus poetarum*. Everywhere else the comma stands after *ungues*; and although the older editors, who revelled in commas, have another after *pectoraque*, those of them who translate join *pectora minuunt*, except only Nisard. Queck has no comma, which is correct but pusillanimous.

Walker's again seems to be the only text which punctuates XI 306–8 as the connexion of thought requires. ||

arma prius, famuli! coeant in proelia fratres;
uult gemitus lenire Creon. lucrare furorem:
uictori mihi cuncta lues.

Modern editors make two mistakes; some of their predecessors avoided one or other of them.

X 873–7

humilesne Amphionis arces,
pro pudor, hi faciles carmenque inbelle secuti,
hi mentita diu Thebarum fabula muri?
et quidnam egregium prosternere moenia molli
structa lyra?

873 *humilesne* Pω, *haene illae* N²r², 'manifesta interpolatione' says Mr Klotz, 'quam amplexi sunt Barthius et Garrodius'. Et Bentleius; because they, unlike Mr Klotz and most editors, were not perfectly satisfied with the sentence 'hine faciles muri sunt humiles Amphionis arces?'[1] Marolles was ashamed to translate *humiles*, and simply left it out; Nisard preferred to substitute 'horrible'. The true correction was found by Peyraredus, 'Amphionis *artes*': the corruption was partly caused by the *Amphionis arces* of IV 357, 611, VII 456. As no one has ever accepted this amendment, and as the last three editors do not even mention it, I conclude that it is not understood. The construction is 'hine muri qui faciles secuti sunt Amphionis humiles artes carmenque inbelle?' A third synonym follows, 'molli...lyra'.

X 897 f.

non tamen haec turbant pacem Iouis: ecce quierant
iurgia, cum mediis Capaneus auditus in astris.

[1] They ought also to have been disturbed by the co-ordination *faciles carmenque secuti*.

897 *quierant* P cum paucis, *queruntur* plerique: '*quierunt* Klotzius' says that editor. No: his own note informs us that this is a correction in Q, and in fact it is also in the text of Gronouius and the Delphin edition. The sum total of original conjectures which Mr Klotz has introduced into the text appears to be seventeen, half-a-dozen of which are merely orthographical; but he contrives to see his name in print at seventeen other places by attaching it to readings which are no conjectures of his. For instance at I 22 he says '*teque o*' Klotzius', but immediately divulges that this is the reading of P; and Mueller had told us that it was also the conjecture of Gronouius. Apparently he thus lays claim to honour for printing any MS lection which has not been printed by another editor. Suppose that all of us wooed fame so strenuously! When Mueller and Kohlmann similarly introduced, as they often did from P, a novel reading, they did not add 'Muellerus' or 'Kohlmannus'; and Mr Klotz does not extricate them from the dank shade of modesty by supplying *their* names. ‖

A considerable proportion of Mr Klotz's conjectures are useless changes or changes for the worse; and this '*quierunt*, cum Capaneus auditus' is one. *Lat. Gramm.* Stolz–Schmalz ed. 5 (Hoffmann) p. 750 'Im Hauptsatz steht meist ein duratives Tempus (Impf. oder Plqpf.), ganz selten das hist. Perf. seit Cic. *Phil.* II 73 al.' In Statius I have noticed only two examples of the preterite (*Theb.* v 89 and x 329) against twenty of the imperfect or pluperfect. I do not overlook the consideration that *quierunt* is nearer by one letter to *queruntur*; but on the other hand preterites (except of course when ending in -*ĕrunt*) are less often changed to pluperfects than pluperfects to preterites.

VII 567 'Liber in Aonios meritas dimiserat agros': meritas tigres, a pair which had drawn his car through his Indian campaign and to which on his return he had given their discharge and turned them loose to roam about the country. *dimiserat* ω, and that is the best possible word. No variant is commoner than *dimittere demittere*, and twenty examples are to be seen in Mr Klotz's apparatus, among them these: x 144 '*dimittunt* (ex *de-* M¹) ML', IX 499 '*di-* ex *demissa* Q', VI 696 '*dimisit* N . . ., *dẹm-* B¹b¹'. But when P in consequence here presents *diemiserat*, with the hypermetrical *di* underlined, Mr Klotz accepts the conjecture and attributes it to himself, '*emiserat* Klotzius'.

XII 408 'tempus erit lacrimis, accenso flebitis igne' Pω, and 'accenso flebitis igne' Seru. *Aen.* XII 156: '*igni* Klotzius'. Metre shows that Statius used both forms of the ablative, but *igne* often and *igni* seldom. At the end of the verse his MSS give *igni Theb.* v 194, XII 275, *silu.* II 1 216, v 3 204, *igne Theb.* VII 191, XI 483, XII 408. Mr Klotz, changing *igne* here, leaves it unchanged at VII 191 and XI 483.

XI 273–5

urbem armis opibusque grauem et modo ciuibus artam,
ceu caelo deiecta lues inimicaue tellus,
hausisti uacuamque tamen sublimis obumbras.

That *tellus* neither deserves the obelus usually affixed to it nor demands any
of the emendations proposed, and that 'caelo deiecta lues' supports the scholiast,
who interpreted *inimica tellus* of famine, rather than Barthius, who preferred
earthquake, would seem to me clear enough even without the parallel of Luc.
V 109–11 'sustulit *iras* | *telluris sterilis* monstrato fine, resoluit | aera tabificum'.

XI 329–37

quis furor? unde iterum regni integrata resurgit
330   Eumenis? ipsi etiam post omnia, comminus ipsi
stabitis? usque adeo geminas duxisse cohortes
et facinus mandasse parum est? quo deinde redibit
uictor? in hosne sinus? o diri coniugis olim
felices tenebrae! datis, improba lumina, poenas. ||
335   haec spectanda dies? quo, saeue, minantia flectis
ora? quid alternus uoltus pallorque ruborque
mutat et obnixi frangunt mala murmura dentes?

The punctuation of 334 f. should of course be this:

datis, improba lumina, poenas:
haec spectanda dies.

poenae quas dant Iocastae oculi, quod non, ut Oedipodis, excaecati sunt, eo
constant quod sic eis spectandus est dies mutua Eteoclis et Polynicis caede
funestus.

Again, 348–52 are to be punctuated thus:

sed pulsat muros germanus et impia contra
bella ciet. non mater enim, non obstat eunti
350   ulla soror. te cuncta rogant, hic plangimus omnes;
ast ibi uix unus pugnas dissuadet Adrastus,
aut fortasse iubet.

Modern editors disturb the connexion by placing a semicolon after *soror* and a
full stop after *omnes*, though Gronouius and his fellows made only the second
mistake. And yet again: this is the true punctuation of XII 491 f.

mite nemus circa cultuque insigne uerendo,
uittatae laurus et supplicis arbor oliuae.

The second line is an apposition to *nemus*, which is *mite* because of its olives and *cultu insigne uerendo* because of its *uittae*. Modern editors destroy sense and grammar by placing the comma after *circa*; their predecessors placed another after *laurus*, which they took to be genitive depending on *cultu*.

XII 661–4

> noctem adeo placidasque operi iunxere tenebras,
> certamenque inmane uiris, quo concita tendant
> agmina, quis uisas proclamet ab aggere Thebas,
> cuius in Ogygio stet princeps lancea muro.

How can 'quo concita tendant agmina' be an interrogation co-ordinate with 'quis proclamet' and 'cuius stet lancea'? How can it be an interrogation at all? How could the direction in which the Athenians were to march be a subject of competition? And what is the use of mock-translations like 'the warriors mightily strive how they may speed the army's march' and 'c'est une lutte ardente entre ces guerriers à qui l'emportera de vitesse'?

The reading of P is not *tendant* but *tendunt*: take this, and all is well. *quo* is relative with *certamen* for its antecedent, and ablative depending on *concita*. Emulous endeavour to catch the first glimpse of Thebes and lodge the first missile in its wall was what made their march so rapid. It would be also grammatical, but less natural and effective, to make *quo* the relative adverb and *Thebas* its postponed antecedent. ‖

XII 812

Thebai dactyl

Here I return to Mr Klotz's note on VI 465 and to these words in it: 'corripitur -a- in titulo Thebaidos propter graecum accentum sequentis syllabae.'

Suppose, for the sake of argument, that the Greek accent on the next syllable, which did exert this force in Latin in the fifth century and even at the end of the fourth (Mueller *d.r.m.* ed. 2 p. 444), had begun to exert it, though in Greek it had not, in the first. Then consider the thoughtlessness or hardihood of putting forward, to account for *Thebāi* in *Theb.* XII 812, an explanation which will not account for *Thebāicae* in *silu.* IV 9 26 and which *will* account for *Nerēis* in *Ach.* I 24. The accent of Θηβαϊκός is not on the next syllable. The accent of Νηρηΐs is; but Νηρεῖs is as old as Pindar.

If Mr Klotz's explanation of *Thebāis* were valid, it would be an equally valid explanation of *Nerēis*, and also of *Letōides* (beside *Letōis*) in *Theb.* I 663 and 695. But it would be a false explanation of both, as Νηρεῖs in Pindar and Λητοΐδηs in

Hesiod prove. Why then should it be thought a true explanation of *Thebăis*? merely because there is no Θηβᾱΐς forthcoming to give it the lie?[1]

And tell me, where is Θηβᾱΐς forthcoming, or *Thebāis*? for I do not know. On the other hand I know eleven examples of *Thebăis* in the classical age: two in Ovid, one in Seneca, one in Lucan, six in Statius (though Mr Klotz's index omits xii 812), and one in Juvenal. And what is wrong with it? why should anyone, even if *Thebăicus* did not exist, expect the vowel to be long? What parallels are there to an ἐθνικὸν θηλυκόν in -ᾱΐς from the primitive Θῆβαι? I know just one, Κωπᾱΐδων from Κῶπαι in Ar. *Ach.* 880; but that verse is spoken by a Boeotian, and everywhere else in Aristophanes (*pac.* 1005, *Ach.* 962 and even 883 where the Boeotian speaks again), and apparently in the rest of Attic poetry also, the form is Κωπᾱΐδ- or Κωπᾳδ-. The scansion of ʼΑθηνᾱΐς from ʼΑθῆναι seems to be perceptible only in *carm. epigr. Buech.* 1549 (a poem exhibiting no faults of prosody) 12, and there it is *Athenăidis*:[2] ʼΑθηναΐς, also found in inscriptions, is like Εὐβοΐς beside Εὐβοΐς.

It is further to be remarked that Mr Klotz's Greek accent is highly selective in its action, and does not affect any other of Statius' numerous feminines in -*is*. It does not make him say *Aenĕis*[3] or *Asŏpis* or *Bacchĕis* or *Brisĕis* or *Cebrĕnis* or *Maeŏtis* or *Nyctĕis* or *Persĕis* or *Scyrĕis* or *Titănis* or ‖ *Tithŏnis* or *Tritŏnis*; it confines its energy to the six examples of the single word *Thebais*, and in that narrow space it rages like a wild beast in a cage. Not one escapes.

Mr Klotz's frivolity invites banter; but now to be quite serious. For the prosody of the Greek word Θηβᾱΐς there could be no better authority than Statius; not Antimachus of Colophon himself. He was born and bred in a Greek city, he was saturated with Greek poetry by the poet and scholar who was his father, he knew how the Greeks pronounced the name of the cyclic poem and the other epics which they had written about Thebes, and you may be sure that he did not pronounce the name of his own epic otherwise. In short, Mr Klotz has brought a quack doctor to the bedside of a *malade imaginaire*.

[1] Mr Klotz will no doubt explain the *Phocăis* (from Φώκαια) of Lucan and Silius in the same way, and leave their *Phocăicus* to shift for itself. He would be well pleased if he could similarly explain the *Eubŏis* (from Εὔβοια) of *Ach.* 1 414 and *silu.* 1 2 263, similarly disregarding the *Eubŏicae* of *silu.* 1 2 177; but alas, though Sophocles has Εὐβοΐς, in Aeschylus and Euripides the word is Εὐβοΐδα or Εὐβοῖδα. For the *Edŏnis* of Lucan and Statius the explanation would have more plausibility, were not the false quantity assignable to the false analogy of *Bistŏnis* or *Sithŏnis*.

[2] Whence Georges and Lewis and Short got their 'Panathenāicus' I do not know, but it was not from Auson. 191 14 (Peip. p. 49) 'in *Panathenăicis* tu numerandus eris'.

[3] Though this is correctly formed from Αἰνέας and used by Ovid *ex Pont.* iii 4 84.

168

NOTES ON GRATTIUS*

137

After praising the natural straightness which makes the exotic *turea uirga* the best wood for spears, he proceeds, 136 f.,

> at enim multo sunt ficta labore
> cetera quae siluis errant hastilia nostris.

What is *errant*? 'postquam facta sunt hastilia et uenabula, passim geruntur ab errantibus in nostris siluis' said Rob. Titius: and that, however absurd, is an honest note and faces the difficulty: more than can be said for such misrepresentations as 'passim nascuntur' and 'temere inueniuntur'. Stern says '*errare uerbum de plantis passim crescentibus uidebis apud Maronem, Ecl.* IV u. 19'; but of course in that verse, 'errantis hederas', it means 'rambling', as in Catull. 61 34 f. 'hedera huc et huc...errans' (κισσοῦ...πολυπλανέος *anth. Pal.* VI 154 4). It can also be applied to branches which straggle or spread abroad, as in Calp. *buc.* I 11 f. 'fagus...ramis errantibus implicat umbras'; but it is repugnant to the very notion of *hastilia*, except that in an appropriate context it might signify waving to and fro, as at Stat. *Theb.* X 93 'ramos errare uetant'. The verb to suit this noun is *horrent*: Ouid. *met.* VIII 285 'saetae similes rigidis hastilibus horrent', Verg. *Aen.* III 23 'densis hastilibus horrida myrtus'; and in Ouid. *fast.* I 495 'nec fera tempestas toto tamen *horret* in anno' the oldest MS gives *errat*. But I should not be surprised if it were now to be contended that *errant* means 'curua nascuntur'.

228

> Thessalium quadriga decus.

Of this adjective *Thessalius* the dictionaries cite two more examples, Ouid. *ex Pont.* I 3 74 *Thessaliam humum* and Appul. *met.* I 25 *Thessaliae regionis*. Both are false, and now banished from our texts in obedience to the MSS. Some scholars of the 18th century took pride and pleasure in the whim of preferring *-ius* to *-icus* in geographical adjectives wherever they could find it in any MS however bad, or even where they could not. Cortius, if his diligence had been equal to his perversity and self-will, would have expelled *Thessalicus* from the text of Lucan,

* [[*CQ* 28 (1934), 127–33]]

where it is given invariably (24 times) by all MSS of any account (for *Thessalia* in VII 847 is the substantive); and the ridiculous Cunningham fell foul of Bentley for not having corrupted Horace with *puluerem Olympium, Laconias purpuras, Delphia lauro, curru Achaio, attagen Ionius*. But the only other instance of *Thessalius* which I have found in a MS of any authority is *Thessalio freno* at Val. Fl. I 424 in V (saec. IX), which nevertheless gives *Thessalicus* in all the 14 other places where the epithet occurs. In Appul. *met.* I 5 *Thessaliam* is better explained by Helm as substantive than by Oudendorp as adjective. From Greek authors Stephanus quotes only Eur. *Andr.* 1176, where ὦ πόλις Θεσσαλία is unmetrical, and metre is not more easily restored by omitting ς with Musurus than by transposing it with Hermann, ὦ πόλι Θεσσαλίας; 'nam etsi origine adiectiuum est Θεσσαλία' says he, 'tamen ita in substantiuum uertit ut exuisse adiectiui naturam uideatur.'

It seems to me that *Thessalium decus* in Gratt. 228 must stand or fall with *cannabias* ‖ *siluas* in 47. Neither form violates a law, but both are curious and apparently irrational deviations from usage. If Grattius wrote the one he may have written the other; but if Vollmer's *cannabinas* is to be accepted, as it is by the latest editor Mr Enk, *Thessalicum* should be written here.

287–300

tum deinde monebo,
ne matrem indocilis natorum turba fatiget,
percensere notis iamque inde excernere prauos.
290   signa dabunt ipsi. teneris uix artibus haeret
ille tuos olim non defecturus honores,
iamque illum inpatiens aequae uehementia sortis
extulit: adfectat materna regna sub aluo,
ubera tota tenens a tergo liber aperto,
295   dum tepida indulget terris clementia mundi;
uerum ubi Caurino perstrinxit frigore uesper
irreptat turbaque potens operitur inerti.
illius et manibus uires sit cura futuras
perpensare: leuis deducet pondere fratres.
300   nec me pignoribus nec te mea carmina fallent.

290 *teneris uix artibus haeret*. It was long supposed that these words, whatever they might exactly mean, described the bodily frame and aspect of the best sort of puppy. Vlitius 'incompactis et ἀσυμμέτροις prorsus membris optimae spei catuli plerumque sunt…*teneri* itaque artus sunt qui soluti et quasi luxati sunt'; Wernsdorf 'adeo teneris et fluxis membris est, ut uix se sustinere uideatur, inde et leuior ceteris praeferri uidetur u. 299'; Nisard has a different

rendering for *haeret*, 'peut à peine rester immobile, malgré la faiblesse de ses membres'. Vollmer, who read this poem with great care, was apparently the first to see that the clause is closely to be joined with *iamque* below, 'iam tum, cum uix...haeret, illum uehementia extulit', and that it describes no individual characteristic, but the early stage of growth at which the puppy begins to show its promise. But his rendering of *haeret* as 'inest' is mere nonsense, and Mr Enk's 'uix stare potest teneris adhuc artubus' is equally false to the sense of the word.

No editor of Grattius excepting Stern has observed that he is imitating Verg. *buc.* III 102; and Stern derives no benefit from the observation. Yet Virgil's *uix ossibus haerent*, 'their bones hardly stick together', is a clue to the meaning of *teneris uix artibus haeret*, and incidentally shows that *uix* does not, as Vollmer supposed, mean *uixdum*: the phrase describes the newly whelped animal, so frail and loosely jointed that you might almost think it would fall to pieces.

299 *leuis deducet pondere fratres.* 'loquitur tamquam catuli in libra appensi essent' said Barthius, rightly so far; but he took *leuis* to be nom. sing., and explained 'cum leuitate sua ipse adscendat, fratres pondere descendere cogit'. Vlitius understood that it was acc. plur., and that the stoutly built puppy is the promising one, as Nemesianus clearly and pointedly says in his imitation *cyn.* 138 f. 'pondere nam catuli poteris perpendere uires | corporibusque leues grauibus praenoscere cursu'; and he rendered *deducet* as 'uincet', which is roughly right but much too vague. Elucidation came from the learning and acumen of Gronouius, who in *obs.* II c. 13 pointed out and illustrated the illogical yet not altogether unnatural idiom by which *deducere* usurps the opposite sense of *eleuare* and means 'outweigh'. He quotes the parallel use of *deprimere*[1] from Cic. *de fin.* V 91 f. 'audebo igitur cetera, quae secundum || naturam sint, bona appellare nec fraudare suo uetere nomine, . . . uirtutis autem amplitudinem quasi in altera librae lance ponere. terram, mihi crede, ea lanx et maria *deprimet*' and *Tusc.* V 51 'quaero quam uim habeat libra illa Critolai, qui cum in alteram lancem animi bona imponat, in alteram corporis et externa, tantum propendere illam [boni lancem] putet, ut terram et maria *deprimat*', where Bentley in Davies's edition says 'nota locutionis genus ἰδιωτικόν. nam in bilance quae lanx praeponderat non *deprimit* oppositam uerum eleuat. sed uulgaris sermonis errore labi etiam sapienti et diserto concessum est.' There is a similar use of *grauare* in *anth. Lat.* Ries. 486 158 (the experiment of Archimedes) 'haec eadem puro deprendere possumus auro, | si par corrupti pondus lanx (*ita scripsi*, *om. cod.*, pars *in marg.*) altera gestet. | nam quotiens ternis pars inlibata *grauarit* | corruptam dragmis sub aqua, tot inesse notabis | argenti libras, quas fraus permiscuit auro.' The Greek καθέλκειν has the same force, not

---

[1] I lament that he adds *acad.* II 38 'necesse est lancem in libra ponderibus impositis deprimi', where the verb has its normal sense: he should have left this confusion to J. S. Reid ad loc. and the *thes. ling. Lat.* V p. 612 74 f., where there is no mention or recognition of the peculiar use.

indeed in Dem. *de pace* 12 (p. 60 Reisk.) which Gronouius adduces, but in a sentence cited by Stephanus s. u. from St John Chrysostom, *or.* 11 *in laud. Paul. apost.* pp. XLVIII f. ed. Valcken., τὸν κόσμον ἀντίθες ἅπαντα, καὶ τότε ὄψει καθέλκουσαν τοῦ Παύλου τὴν ψυχήν, and likewise in Callim. *aet.* pap. Oxy. 2079 fr. 1 9 f. ‖1 9 f. Pfeiffer‖ καθέλκει...πολὺ τὴν μακρὴν ὄμπνια Θεσμοφόρος; and so too has καταβρίθειν in Theocr. XVII 95 ὄλβῳ μὲν πάντας κε καταβρίθοι βασιλῆας.

383–93

<blockquote>

pluruma per catulos rabies inuictaque tardis
praecipitat letale malum: sit tutius ergo

385　antire auxiliis et primas uincere causas.
namque subit, nodis qua lingua tenacibus haeret,
(uermiculum dixere) mala atque incondita pestis.
ille ubi salsa siti praecepit uiscera longae
aestiuos uibrant accensi febribus ignes

390　moliturque fugas et sedem spernit amaram.
scilicet hoc motu stimulisque potentibus acti
in furias uertere canes. ergo insita ferro
iam teneris elementa mali causasque recidunt.

</blockquote>

388 *praecepit*] *percepit* Gronouius recte. *longae*] *longa* Sannazarius, *longe* Baehrens. 389 *uibrant*] *uibrans* Scaliger. *accensi*] *accensis* Pithoeus recte.

The subject of 383–93 is that of Plin. *n.h.* XXIX 100 'est uermiculus in lingua canum qui uocatur a Graecis lytta, quo exempto infantibus catulis nec rabidi fiunt nec fastidium sentiunt'; and through the corruptions of the text can be discerned the general sense that this worm, made uncomfortable by drought, shifts its seat in the body and by its irritating movements causes madness. Barthius and others absurdly referred *uibrant accensi* to the dogs, as did Vlitius the next verse also, despite the change of number; but at present the three lines 388–90 are generally given thus,

<blockquote>

ille ubi salsa siti praecepit uiscera longe (*or* longa),[1]
aestiuos uibrans accensis febribus ignes,
moliturque fugas et sedem spernit amaram,

</blockquote>

which is hardly less absurd: the worm originates thirst, to its own grave discomfort, and performs the impossible feat of darting fire. This is not a result for which it was worth while to make so many changes in the text.

What has really happened here can be learnt from two separate and converging indications: defective sense and defective syntax. First, the actions *siti*

---

[1] *longe* Baehrens, Vollmer; *longa* Postgate, Curcio; Mr Enk has *longe* in his text and *longa* in his note.

praecipere (or rather *percipere*) *uiscera* and *aestiuos uibrare ignes* and *accendere febres* must be those ‖ of some agent which is missing from the present text; and its nature can easily be inferred from common knowledge and from such passages as *Il.* XXII 29–31 κύν’ Ὠρίωνος…ὅ γε…φέρει πολλὸν πυρετὸν δειλοῖσι βροτοῖσιν and Verg. *Aen.* X 273 f. ‘Sirius ardor, | ille sitim morbosque ferens mortalibus aegris’. Secondly, the two words *longae* and *uibrant* are with-out grammatical construction; and since the attempt to correct them has proved so little satisfactory it appears that a construction should be found for them in a mention of the missing cause. In short everything points to the loss of such a line as this:

> ille, ubi salsa siti percepit uiscera longae
> ⟨sol lucis statione, Canis quo sidera mense⟩
> aestiuos uibrant accensis febribus ignes,
> moliturque fugas et sedem spernit amaram.

The words must be quite uncertain, but in part of the supplement I have had in mind Manil. 1 586 f. ‘longa stant tempora luce | uixque dies transit candentem extenta per aestum’, and in ‘sid*era*’ immediately below ‘uis*cera*’ I have pro-vided an occasion (see ed. Luc. pp. xix f.) for the omission of the verse. *Canis sidera* (the ancients counted 10 or 20 stars in Canis Maior) is like Verg. *georg.* 1 204 *Arcturi sidera*, where Arcturus is the constellation rather than the star; but the plural is used for the singular in Hor. *carm.* III 7 6 *Caprae sidera* and Ouid. *met.* XIV 172 *sidera solis*.

399–407

> quid, priscas artes inuentaque simplicis aeui
> si referam? non illa metus solacia falsi   400
> tam longam traxere fidem. collaribus ergo
> sunt qui lucifugae cristas inducere maelis
> iussere aut sacris conserta monilia conchis
> et uiuum lapidem et circa Melitensia nectunt
> curalia et magicis adiutas cantibus herbas,   405
> ac sic offectus oculique uenena maligni
> uicit tutela pax impetrata deorum.

These nine verses should constitute a paragraph by themselves, extricated from their present cohesion with the foregoing passage, which deals with madness, and the following, which deals with scab. That they continue the former, and deal with traditional charms against rabies, is the opinion expressed by Nisard, Curcio, and Enk, and shared, I surmise, by editors in general, though Vlitius on the other hand speaks of ‘morbos et maxime scabiem’.

The meaning and construction of 400 f. ‘non illa metus solacia falsi | tam longam traxere fidem’ is matter of wide dissent. Burman, followed by Nisard, Curcio, Vollmer, and Enk, construes *non* with *tam longam*, to which only

Vollmer assigns a possible sense. He says in Paul.-Wiss. R.-E. VII p. 1844 that the poet's 'epikureischer Standpunkt wird besonders u. 400 beleuchtet durch die Bezeichnung der religiösen Gebräuche als *metus solacia falsi*', and he takes the meaning to be 'the traditional belief in these alleviations of a groundless fear (fear of supernatural agency) is not so very ancient'. But this cannot be right: belief in *priscas artes* is necessarily ancient; and if Grattius were sceptically dismissing these *solacia* he would not proceed, with 'ergo', to the following enumeration. The connexion was understood by Johnson: 'quid si referam ueterum artes et reperta aeui imperitioris? operae pretium sane foret. non enim illa inuenta, si fuissent solummodo θέλγητρα δεισιδαιμονίας ad deliniendas superstitiosorum mentes fabricata, tam diu fidem apud omnes sustinuerant' (he should have said 'habuissent', *trahere* is *acquirere*); and similar explanations are given by Wernsdorf and W. E. Wagner. *non* belongs to *falsi*, and those ‖ two words are the kernel of the sentence, which is like Verg. *Aen.* III 42 f. '*non* me tibi Troia | *externum* tulit' and Hor. *epod.* 17 54 f. '*non* saxa nudis *surdiora* nauitis | Neptunus alto tundit hibernus salo'. metus, cuius illa solacia tam longam fidem traxere, falsus non est.

But still they do not rightly understand what this *metus* is. It is the evil eye. This, *fascinatio*, and neither *rabies* nor *scabies*, is the subject of this paragraph; and Grattius at the end of it explicitly states the effect which these 'inuenta simplicis aeui' produce: 'sic offectus oculique uenena maligni (*oculi maligni* depends on *offectus* no less than on *uenena*) | uicit tutela pax impetrata deorum'. Because enlightened persons regard the evil eye as a purely imaginary thing, he approaches the subject apologetically, with the argument that unless it were a reality the prophylactic measures prescribed against it would not have enjoyed credit with so many generations of mankind.

408–12

at, si deformi lacerum dulcedine corpus
persequitur scabies, longi uia pessima leti,
410   in primo accessu tristis medicina, sed una
pernicies redimenda anima, quae prima sequaci
sparsa malost, ne dira trahant contagia uulgus.

This punctuation, or a punctuation differing in no significant detail, having once been introduced by the first editor (for there is none in the MS), his successors have stuck in the groove. Yet I should think that any critic without a precedent to misguide him would punctuate thus:

in primo accessu, tristis medicina sed una,
pernicies redimenda anima quae prima sequaci
sparsa malost, ne dira trahant contagia uulgus.

415–19

tunc et odorato medicata bitumina uino
Hipponiasque pices neclectaeque unguen amurcae
miscuit et summam conplectitur ignis in unam.
inde lauant aegros; ast ira coercita morbi
laxatusque rigor.

It was Haupt who first restored in 418 the *ast* of the MS after the Aldine *est* had been printed and reprinted, with occasional hesitation and reluctance, for three centuries. But of late years *ast* itself has been giving difficulty. Vollmer's note is '*ast* A, uix recte; *est* Ald., *atque* Barth, *stet ut* Scaliger; an *sic*'? Mr Enk says 'uocabulum corruptum uidetur', and the *thes. ling. Lat.* II p. 944 7 f. has '*ast* (sic Vind., *est* uulgo, fortasse recte)'. Mr Curcio on the other hand gives the rendering 'ed ecco', which is quite correct and ought not to be slighted merely on account of its origin.

ast was supposed by the Augustan poets to be only another form of *at*; and *at* possesses a force insufficiently recognised by lexicographers and grammarians. It is used to express immediate consequence, 'thereupon'. So Verg. *georg.* IV 416 'haec ait et liquidum ambrosiae defundit odorem, | quo totum nati corpus perduxit; *at* illi | dulcis compositis spirauit crinibus aura | atque habilis membris uenit uigor', 471 'Taenarias etiam fauces, alta ostia Ditis, | et caligantem nigra formidine lucum | ingressus manisque adiit regemque tremendum | nesciaque humanis precibus mansuescere corda. | *at* cantu commotae Erebi de sedibus imis | umbrae ibant tenues simulacraque luce carentum', *Aen.* III 675 'clamorem immensum tollit, quo pontus et omnes | contremuere undae penitusque exterrita tellus | Trinacriae curuisque ‖ immugiit Aetna cauernis. | *at* genus e siluis Cyclopum et montibus altis | excitum ruit ad portus', Hor. *serm.* I 8 47 'pepedi | diffissa nate ficus; *at* illae currere in urbem', Ovid. *met.* V 448 'tectam stramine uidit | forte casam paruasque fores pulsauit; *at* inde | prodit anus', XII 278 'terribilem stridore sonum dedit, ut dare ferrum | igne rubens plerumque solet, quod forcipe curua | cum faber eduxit, lacubus demittit; *at* illud | stridet et in tepida submersum sibilat unda', XIII 567 'clade sui Thracum gens inritata tyranni | Troada telorum lapidumque incessere iactu | coepit; *at* haec missum rauco cum murmure saxum | morsibus insequitur.' This function is performed also by *ast*, as in Sen. *H.O.* 1752 'tunc ora flammis implet (Hercules); *ast* illi (Herculi) graues | luxere barbae', where the pronoun which so often accompanies *at* and *ast* is clearly not adversative and the conjunction cannot indicate contrast; and in Verg. *Aen.* XII 951 'hoc dicens ferrum aduerso sub pectore condit | feruidus; *ast* illi soluontur frigore membra' the sense is best given by the 'instantly' which I find in one translation.

437–41

te primum, Vulcane, loci, pacemque precamur,
incola sancte, tuam: da fessis ultima rebus
auxilia, et, meritis si nulla est noxia tanti,
tot miserare animas, liceatque attingere fontis,
sancte, tuos.

meritis in 439 has no interpreter but Mr Curcio, whose note '*meritis* "per le loro colpe"; ed ordina: si nulla noxia meritis tanti est' conveys no idea to me; neither do I understand Baehrens's *tanta*. The editors almost all agree in accepting the *meriti* of Sannazarius, but disagree very much in their efforts to expound the clause. Vlitius, the best of them, unworthily seeks refuge in silence; most take *meriti*, quite legitimately, as *peccati*, – Burman quoting Ouid. *trist.* II 546 and Liu. xxv 6 4, – but fail, and Burman admits his failure, to find an interpretation which shall be at once justifiable and satisfactory. Neither Wernsdorf's 'si nulla est culpa nostra quae tantum malum meruisse uideatur' nor Mr Enk's 'si canes tanti peccati, ut pereant, noxii non sunt' fulfils the duty of a translation and an explanation; and Barthius and Nisard are of still less use.

I understand 'if the great favour which we implore has no harmful consequence attached to it'. *meritum* is the beneficent act of the god, as in Prop. IV 5 65 f. 'cape torquatae, Venus o regina, columbae | ob meritum ante tuos guttura secta focos', and Grattius has two other examples, 368 and 461, of *noxia* in the sense of 'bane'. It appears from 447–56 that this was a formidable deity and a terror to unrighteous suppliants.

451–4

o quisquis misero fas umquam in supplice fregit,
quis pretio fratrum meliorisque ausus amici
sollicitare caput patriosue lacessere diuos,
illum agat infandae comes huc audacia culpae.

452 *quis*, a corruption probably due to *quisquis* overhead, was corrected in the Aldine to *qui*. In my notes on Manil. III 68 and 103, and in vol. v ⟦ed. 1, 1930⟧ p. 149, I collected instances of the relative thus used to avoid repetition of the longer words *quisquis* and *quicumque*. But Vollmer retains *quis*: 'at uidetur in hoc usu pro *quisquis* (cf. Mon. Germ. auct. antiq. xiv p. 438) forma *quis* proba esse'; and Mr Enk follows him and adduces in proof the same examples.

They are these: Drac. *laud. dei* III 90 'demere dum liceat *quidquid* dedit et *cui* confert', Verg. *catal.* 4 1 f. '*quocumque* ire ferunt nos tempora uitae, | tangere ‖ *quas* terras *quos*que uidere homines', Ciris 89 '*quidquid* et *ut* (= *utut*) quisque est tali de clade locutus'. From these four forms, *cui, quas, quos,* and *ut,* do two scholars infer a nominative singular *quis* in place of *qui*. Anyone who would rather seek truth by less peculiar methods will find it in my notes, where I cited Sen. *H.f.* 1163–5 '*quisquis* Ismeni loca, | Actaea *quisquis* arua, *qui* gemino mari | pulsata Pelopis regna Dardanii colis' and Luc. VII 346 f. '*quisquis* patriam carosque penates, | *qui* subolem ac thalamos desertaque pignora quaerit', together with two equally decisive examples, Tib. II 5 67 f. '*quidquid* Amalthea, *quidquid* Marpesia dixit | Herophile, Phyto Graia *quod* admonuit' and Luc. VII 755 f. '*quidquid* fodit Hiber, *quidquid* Tagus expulit auri, | *quod* legit diues summis Arimaspus harenis'.

482

supplicibus uocanda sacris tutela deorum.

To restore the metre Sannazarius inserted *que* after *supplicibus*; but this, in removing a metrical vice, imports a metrical singularity. It was observed by Lucian Mueller *de r. m.* p. 200 ed. 1 (p. 225 ed. 2) that hexameters thus divided, $- \cup \cup - \cup \mid \cup - \cup \mid \cup - \mid \cup \cup - \cup \cup - -$, with trochaic caesura in the 2nd foot as well as the 3rd, everywhere uncommon, are altogether eschewed by many poets, of whom Grattius, according to his MS, is one. Baehrens mentions this observation; Vollmer ignores it and adopts the conjecture, and goes out of his way to say in Paul.-Wiss. R.-E. VII p. 1845 'wegen der Caesur ist allein als weniger glatt bemerkenswert u. 240 *et tamen ut ne prima fauentem pignera fallant*'; and he is faithfully imitated in every respect (even the spelling *pignera*, which is not that of the MS) by Mr Enk (see vol. I p. 33). This opinion of roughness and smoothness is not borne out by the practice of Latin poets: thus Grattius' contemporary Manilius, in eight times as many verses, has only one of the former type, II 221 *sunt quibus esse diurna placet quae mascula surgunt*, but four of the latter, I 417, 493, II 213, III 411.

Of the modern conjectures, *uocitanda*, *socianda*, *captanda*, *reuocanda*, *uotanda*, *lucranda*, some are worse than others but none is plausible; and no word could in itself be better than the *uocanda* of the MS. I suspect therefore that only the order of words is to be changed:

supplicibus sacris tutela uocanda deorum.

Although transpositions often take place without any cause appearing (as in 356 *acer conprimat* for *c. a.*), it may here be possible to suggest one. Not only *cl* but *el* has sometimes a likeness to *d*, whence such corruptions as Mart. XIV 93 1 *caeli* β, *cadi* γ; so that *uocanda* might conceivably fall out after *tutela* by homoeoteleuton and then be inserted in a wrong place.

169

ENNIUS IN PERS. VI 9*

'Lunai portum, est operae, cognoscite, ciues.'
cor iubet hoc Enni, postquam destertuit esse
Maeonides, Quintus pauone ex Pythagoreo.

This verse was placed by Columna and again by Vahlen among the fragments of book I of the *annals* ⟦16 Vahlen⟧, in juxtaposition with fragments relating to the famous dream in which Homer appeared to Ennius and disclosed to him that the soul of the one had now passed into the body of the other. To this dream Persius alludes in his next verses, on which the scholiast writes '*cor iubet.* hunc uersum ad suum carmen de Ennii carminibus transtulit. uel merito ait *cor iubet hoc Enni postquam destertuit.* sic Ennius ait in annalium suorum principio, ubi se dicit uidisse in somnis Homerum dicentem fuisse quondam pauonem et ex eo trans- latam in se esse animam secundum Pythagorae philosophi definitionem, qui dicit animas humanas per palingenesian, id est per iteratam generationem, exeuntes de corporibus in alia posse corpora introire'; and Persius is supposed to have it again in mind at *choliamb.* 1–3 'nec fonte labra prolui caballino | nec in bicipiti somniasse Parnaso | memini, ut repente sic poeta prodirem', where the scholiast says 'tangit autem Ennium, qui dixit se uidisse somnium in Parnaso Homerum sibi dicentem quod eius anima in suo esset corpore': a third testimony is that of Porphyrion at Hor. *epist.* II I 51 'securus iam de prouentu suae laudis est Ennius, propter quam ante sollicitus in principio annalium suorum somnio se scripsit admonitum quod secundum Pythagorae dogma anima Homeri in suum corpus uenisset.'

What had Luna to do with this dream? Columna and Vahlen suppose that Ennius said he had dreamt it there, in which case, as Ribbeck remarks in *Rhein. Mus.* 1856 p. 270, the verse would more naturally introduce it, as in Columna's text, than follow it, as in Vahlen's. But, like Bergk *opusc.* I p. 264 and Lucian Mueller *Q. Ennius* p. 140, I cannot conceive why Ennius should mention or invent that detail nor why he should make it the occasion of such an advertise- ment. They assign the verse to some later book of the *annals,* where the poet's narrative of historical events had brought him to that district; but Vahlen p. cxlix has the right to object that this makes Persius' *postquam* less natural.

* ⟦*CR* 48 (1934), 50–1⟧

Supposing then that Vahlen's interpretation of *postquam* is correct, what is it that Persius says? The phrase 'postquam destertuit esse Maeonides' cannot mean 'when he had waked from his dream', and Vahlen's paraphrase 'postquam Ennius desiit esse Homerus qui sibi esse uidebatur per somnium et suam ueram naturam excusso somno repetiit' is no account of what happened when the dreamer awoke, and entirely stultifies the episode. Waking from the dream did not involve disbelief in its message; and Ennius would never have related it unless he had meant his readers to accept it as a true revelation and to regard his epic as though it were a new epic of Homer's.

That the scholiast of Persius assigns the verse to a place at the beginning of the *annals* was the belief of Columna and is repeated by Vahlen *Klein. Schr.* II p. 261. But there is no need so to interpret what the scholiast says: 'uel merito ait *cor iubet hoc Enni postquam destertuit*. sic Ennius ait in annalium suorum principio, ubi se dicit uidisse in somnis Homerum dicentem fuisse quondam pauonem et ex eo translatam in se esse animam secundum Pythagorae philosophi definitionem.' Although Vahlen and so far as I know all others refer 'sic Ennius ait' to the verse 'Lunai portum' etc., it can no less well be referred to 'esse Maeonides' etc. supplied after *destertuit*. Scholiasts often cite only the beginning of that to which their comment pertains; and this scholiast himself has done so in writing '*cor iubet*. hunc uersum ad suum carmen de Ennii carminibus transtulit': this scholium relates not to *cor iubet* but to the following and omitted word *hoc*, which indicates the preceding verse.

The verse therefore cannot on the scholiast's authority be assigned to the ‖ first book of the *annals*. The scholiast in fact does not assign it to the *annals* at all; he says 'hunc uersum...de Ennii carminibus transtulit'. And even if he or any other authority did assign it to the *annals*, we should be bound to disbelieve him. No such verse could form part of any epic poem. An epic poet does not apostrophise his readers, and vouchsafe them pieces of advice. The verse comes from some other work of Ennius, most likely his *satires*, where it would be quite at home; it belongs to the same world as Juvenal's 'ianua Baiarum est et gratum litus amoeni | secessus'. 'cor Enni' means the shrewd and sensible part of Ennius, Ennius as he was when writing with a cool head; and 'postquam destertuit' etc. is well enough rendered by Jahn 'postquam nimio poetico furore liberatus est', more precisely 'when he had left behind him his epic mood and its illusions, and no longer imagined that he was Homer come to life again'. For in his *Scipio* too he showed that he did not always nurse this fancy: Suid. I 2 p. 262 Bernh. [I 2 p. 285 Adler] Σκιπίωνα...ᾄδων...φησὶ μόνον ἂν Ὅμηρον ἐπαξίους ἐπαίνους εἰπεῖν Σκιπίωνος.

170

REVIEW: H. E. BUTLER AND E. A. BARBER, *THE ELEGIES OF PROPERTIUS**

Propertius certainly and urgently needs a new commentary; but this commentary has not that novelty of which his need is most extreme. The text on which it is written is better of course than Phillimore's, and better too than either Mr Rothstein's or Mr Hosius's; and the commentary itself, though it too often leaves the reader in the lurch, is the most useful and informative yet put together. To call it the most judicious is neither high praise nor praise which can be unreservedly given, for the editors' dependence on Mr Rothstein is excessive and unfortunate, and yet does not prevent them from deserting him in a number of places where he deserved to be followed. The best and most unusual feature of their work is the exposition of incoherencies caused by dislocations in the text. But they were not obliged to edit Propertius unless they had ambition and capacity for something more than they have attempted, and were prepared to face the effort of severe and resolute ἄσκησις. A new edition ought to raise itself high above the level of intelligence, attention, and scholarship to which we have been accustomed. One of the blackest marks against the poet's interpreters is their almost unanimous belief that *uerum* in II 5 1 means 'true', ‖ which renders the whole poem shameful and ridiculous: Messrs Butler and Barber translate as usual and betray no disquietude. My space is limited, and I must not illustrate this theme by examples which would involve arguing at length; so I confine comment in the main to notes in which they show that they are not good enough grammarians.

I 2 29 'The dative, *supposito campo*, may equally well depend on *proxima* or *contingens*.' If dative it were, which there is no need to suppose, it could not depend on *contingens*.

II 8 10 (p. 166) *Thebae steterant*. 'Here *steterant* by itself might stand as a preterite, but coming between *cecidere* and *fuit* must be changed to *steterunt*'. It could not anyhow stand as a preterite, for the sense must be 'Thebes is down'.

II 9 7 *uisura et quamuis numquam speraret Vlixem*. '*uisura*. Sc. *esse*. For this

* ⟦*The elegies of Propertius edited with an introduction and commentary by* H. E. Butler *and* E. A. Barber. Pp. lxxxiv + 407. Oxford: Clarendon Press, 1933.   *CR* 48 (1934), 136–9⟧

Greek use of nom. and infin. cp. III 6 40 [*iurabo integer esse*]; Cat. IV 2 [*ait fuisse celerrimus*] &c.' These examples, where an infin. in oratio obliqua is accompanied by an epithet in the nom. instead of an epithet in the acc. with a reflexive pronoun, are quoted to defend a reading where there is no epithet, no infin. (till the edd. supply one) and no oratio obliqua. *uisura speraret* will be Latin when ἐλπίζω ὀψόμενος is Greek.

II 18 9–14 '*quam prius = priusquam*. Cp. Tib. IV 7 8 *ne legat id nemo quam meus ante uelim*.' This note appeared in Mr Butler's ed. of 1905: in *C.R.* XIX pp. 318 f. [this edition p. 633] I tried to sharpen his discrimination, but in vain; and I presume that to Madvig's enquiry (Cic. *de fin.* pp. 771 f.) 'quis non intellegit *quam potius* pro *potius quam* non modo ab usu sermonis sed ab intima eius natura abhorrere?' he and his colleague can answer 'nos'.

II 19 5 f. *nulla neque ante tuas orietur rixa fenestras | nec tibi clamatae somnus amarus erit.* '*nulla neque*. A double negative, common in colloquial Latin, substituted for the more correct *neque ulla*; cp. III 13 23 *nulla puella | nec fida Euadne nec pia Penelope*; Virg. *E.* V 25 *nulla nec amnem | libauit quadrupes*; Tib. IV 7 8 *ne legat id nemo*.' Do they think that *ulla* would be correct in III 13 23? and why have they mutilated the passage of Virgil? There is nothing colloquial or incorrect in either; their Latinity is that of Cicero and Livy, abundantly illustrated by Hand *Turs.* IV pp. 131 f. Mr Rothstein's note might have dispelled this fog.

II 20 31 'It is tempting to read *adque iecur*.' No poet is known to have attached *que* to this preposition.

II 26 29 f. *seu mare per longum mea cogitet ire puella, | hanc sequar et fidos una aget aura duos.* '*cogitet...sequar...aget*. The futures express certainty as compared with the doubt expressed by the subjunctive in the *seu* clause.' Think: how can an apodosis express certainty if the protasis which conditions it expresses doubt? Certainty and uncertainty are notions which belong to another world than the forms of the conditional sentence.

II 33 2 '*est operata*. "Has offered sacrifice".' She had not; and *operatus* is not a past participle but an adjective formed from *opera*; the verb is later than Propertius.

II 34 21 *una tamen causa est, cur crimina tanta remitto.* 'For the indic. in indirect question after *cur*, see' etc. There is no question: *cur* is relative. Of this very common use, distinguished by Priscian, the *thes. ling. Lat.* knows only six examples: it jumbles up dozens among interrogatives.

II 34 31 'For the rare use of *satius* with a verb other than *sum* cp. Varr. *R.R.* 1 2 26 *satius dicas*.' Not a clear way of saying that they are among those who imagine that this adjective is here an adverb.

III 6 21 *ille potest nullo miseram me linquere facto.* 'Abl. abs. "Though nothing has been done"; i.e. either *sine causa* or *re infecta* ("without any act of love").

nullo = nihilo.' It means *nullum ob factum meum*: Lachmann devoted a note to the idiom at Lucr. 1 942.

III 9 34 *Maecenatis erunt uera tropaea fides.* 'The verb is attracted into the number of the predicate; cp. II 14 24; 16 46; IV 1 14; 9 20.' This construction is normal, nothing to write a note about, and they write none at IV 3 5 f. (their note at II 14 24 passes over a more noteworthy point). Propertius ‖ has only one clear instance of the opposite construction, IV 1 10, where the order of words necessitates it; for IV 4 13 is ambiguous, while in III 13 27 f. the reading *erat* is required, not by grammar, but by literary form, and the construction is *munus erat dare cydonia.*

III 22 3 *Dindymus* 'yields good sense, Dindymus being a hill above Cyzicus'. So I have often read in modern books, but never in any ancient; and they cite only passages where this form is not found.

IV 5 14 *sua nocturno fallere terga lupo.* 'For this use of *fallo* ("conceal") there seems no exact parallel; the nearest being perhaps Virg. *A.* 1 684 *tu faciem illius...falle dolo*, where it means "counterfeit".' Research has here gone no further than Lewis and Short's dictionary: I collected parallels in *C.R.* 1900 p. 259 ⟦this edition p. 521⟧ and at Manil. 1 240 (including Prop. III 14 5, which they misunderstand), and others are now to be found in *thes. ling. Lat.* VI 1 p. 187 69 ff., though the *thes.* puts Prop. IV 5 14 in a wrong place (p. 185 16 f.) and under a false heading, together with Ouid. *fast.* V 680, which it misinterprets even worse.

IV 6 63 f. *illa petit Nilum cumba male nixa fugaci,* | *hoc unum, iusso non moritura die.* '*hoc unum,* in apposition with the words that follow.' *unum* is precluded from such use by its meaning and demonstrative pronouns by the nature of language. How to extract from the text any such sense as translators find there, *hoc unum lucratura, ut iusso die non moriatur*, I cannot tell them; but this is not the way.

IV 10 31 *Veius.* 'The dactyl is preferable in sound [to *Veiens*], and *Veia* is found as a proper name in Hor. *Epod.* V 29.' The proper name is a trochee: the adj. recurs in *G.L.K.* VI p. 563 6.

Sometimes silence tells a tale. II 25 29 no note on *tamen*, which the ordinary inattentive reader is sure to misunderstand as Phillimore and Mr Butler himself did in their translations. III 13 33 no note on *furtiua*: does Mr Butler still construe it with *antra*, like the *thes. ling. Lat.*? IV 1 71 *quo ruis imprudens, uage, dicere fata, Properti?* no note on the construction, which was explained by Lachmann, though translators still tranquilly render *quo ruis dicere.*

It must already be doubtful whether these editors are competent to pronounce, so often as they do, that this or that 'presents no real difficulty' and that this or that is 'impossible'. Out of much acrimonious comment invited by their notes on matters other than grammatical I set down a little.

II 1 6 *hoc totum e Coa ueste uolumen erit.* '*hoc.* "This" as opposed to other *uolumina.*' That is just the absurdity which forced Lachmann to interpret the word otherwise and has provoked so many conjectures. Equally cynical are the translations of II 29 27 *hinc* and IV 3 49 *aperto in coniuge.*

II 15 25–6 'The repetition of *dies* at the end of the line in 24 and 26 points to the displacement of 25–6.' There are seven more such repetitions in Propertius, one of which, III 24 2–4, evokes a similar note. At IV 6 36 *lyrae* is said to be 'impossible following so soon after *lyrae* at the end of 32'.

II 20 15 *ossa tibi iuro per matris et ossa parentis.* '*parentis.* His father had died while he was very young; cp. IV 1 127.' Is that all? do they expect to have no reader whom the word *parens* will astonish, as it astonished even Hertzberg?

III 22 25 *Albanus lacus et socia Nemorensis ab unda.* This conjecture is defended by the statement 'they are both fed by the springs running down the Alban mount'. No springs run down the Alban mount into either: their springs are subterranean, and no doubt it will now be said that this is what *socia* means.

IV 6 21 *altera classis erat Teucro damnata Quirino.* '"Given over for destruction to the Trojan Quirinus." The name Quirinus...is here transferred to Augustus.' Will this crazy notion of Passerat's never be packed off to limbo? An editor who pretends that Quirinus does not mean Quirinus is in decency bound to allege a reason why. 'Antonii classis et Cleopatrae arma diuo Quirino ab Augusti partibus stanti damnata erant...contra Augustus habet postea *plena Iouis omine uela*' ‖ Lachmann. The dat. is of the agent, as also in Hor. *carm.* III 3 22 f. and Sil. IV 229.

IV 7 69 *mortis lacrimis uitae sanamus amores.* 'Tears shed in death heal the wounds dealt by life.' Apparently it is hoped that the audacity of the mistranslation – or is it a translation of Markland's *amara*? – will take the reader's breath away and leave him too faint to notice that *sanamus amores* is meaningless of Andromeda and Hypermestra and false of Cynthia.

IV 7 81 *ramosis Anio qua pomifer incubat aruis.* In a reader who is affected by this choice of epithets as Broukhusius and Bentley and Lachmann were the note which the edd. have borrowed from Mr Rothstein will create so strong a feeling of intellectual superiority as cannot be good for him. It shows that they have not even begun to apprehend his difficulties.

IV 9 59 f. *di tibi dent alios fontes: haec lympha puellis* | *auia secreti limitis una fluit.* '*una* in contrast with *alios.*' Unless they had shut their eyes for the sake of the MSS it would not escape them that the word in contrast with *alios* is *haec*; and a priestess ought not to tell a lie just for contrast.

Where it is a question between N and the other MSS impartiality is of course impossible. II 13 58 *qui* (N) is preferred to *quid* (cett.), though the only Augustan poet to use that adverb is Horace in his hexameters, and though N corrupts *quid* to *qui* at IV 1 86. III 14 19 'There is little or nothing to choose between *capere arma* [N] and *armata* in point of... probability. The loss of *capere* might result in the expansion of *arma* to *armata*, while alternatively the loss of *-ta* [before *ca-* or *pa-*] might cause the interpolation of *capere*.' So easily do they distract their own attention from the crucial question how the loss of *capere* took place.[1]

[1] Reviewing Mr Butler's earlier edition in *C.R.* 1905 p. 317 [[this edition p. 630]] I ought not to have blamed him for rendering I 11 11 '*tenui* unda' as 'shallow', a sense established for instance by Ouid. *met.* VIII 559 and Quint. *inst.* XII 2 11; though the sense found in Verg. *g.* IV 410, Ouid. *met.* VI 351, Manil. I 161 is equally appropriate.

171

REVIEW: H. J. IZAAC, *MARTIAL VIII–XIV* *

The first half of this respectable work was noticed in *C.R.* 1931 pp. 81–3 ⟦this edition pp. 1172–4⟧, and the second does not differ in ‖ general character. Mr Izaac persists in the unmannerly practice of saving himself trouble at our expense by making the letter ω stand for half-a-dozen different authorities or combinations of authorities, and laying upon his resentful readers the task, which is no simple one, of finding out for themselves what it means in each several case.[1] Sometimes the reward of their pains is misinformation. In VIII 33 12 '*parcos* ω' this sign, by Mr Izaac's definition, means βγ, and in IX 41 5 '*futuit* ω' it means β; but β in fact omits both verses, and Mr Izaac has neglected to say so. On the other hand at IX 63 1, where ω (short for βVX) would serve a purpose, β is inaccurately substituted.

The particular observations which follow confine themselves to books VIII and IX.

Apparatus criticus. VIII ep. 4 *mimicam...licentiam*: the MS reading is not mentioned. 28 18 *Gilbert* should be P or else ϛ. 50 (51) 21 *Lindsay* should be *Munro*. 73 1 *Heraeus* should be ϛ. 74 1 *edd.* should rather be R. IX 17 3 *domino* is not the reading of α. 45 6 *senis* should be *saxa*. 48 5 *interim* should be *interim q*. 54 1 *turtur* should be *tur*. 75 2 *edd.* should be *Lindsay*. 92 11 '*monstrum* α' is a groundless assertion of Mr Lindsay's: the sole extant member of the family has *non faum*, and the meaning of α in an app. crit. is the archetype of HTR, not any ancestor of that archetype. 93 8 *edd.* should be ϛ. 94 2 Friedlaender's *mulsum et*, mentioned also by Lindsay and Heraeus, should have been ignored, for the elision and the place of *et* are both illegitimate. 95 1 *Heraeus* should be P in the first place and ϛ in the second; *uulg.* in the second place should be T.

Translation. VIII ep. 3 *materia* (the subject, Domitian) 'l'abondance de la matière'. 57 2 and 6 *Picens* 'Picus'. 80 6 *casa tam culto sub Ioue numen habet* 'tous les hommages que reçoit Jupiter n'empêchent pas' etc.: Jove is Domitian and *culto* means magnificent. IX 3 14 Mr Izaac prints the *quod* of the MSS but

---

* ⟦Martial: *Épigrammes*. Tome II 1re Partie (Livres VIII–XII). 2me Partie (Livres XIII–XIV). Texte établi et traduit par H. J. Izaac. Pp. xii + 354 (really 508). Paris: 'Les Belles Lettres', 1933. *CR* 48 (1934), 187–9⟧

[1] The spaced saved is negligible, for though ω fills less room that αβ or αγ or βγ it fills more than α or β or γ; and moreover Mr Izaac is so little economical of space that at VIII 4 3 and 6 1 and IX 6 (7) 4 he prints twice words which ought not to be printed at all.

translates Mr Duff's *quo* (so too 45 3 he prints *Promethei* but translates *-ae*, 46 3 prints *que*, translates *ue*). 7 (8) 10 *quoque* not translated. 27 5 *purgent. . .cana labra uolsellae* 'tes lèvres exsangues' (so Ker). 36 5 *iam mihi prima latet longis lanugo capillis* 'mon premier duvet disparaît sous mes longs cheveux': nonsense, the sense is 'pousse inaperçu'. 36 7 *puer o dulcissime* 'O le plus cher à mon cœur de mes serviteurs': the point of the epigram is that he has no others. 37 9 *promittis sescenta* (sestertia) 'tu me promets des joies infinies' (so too Nisard and Ker). 38 1 *uelox*, though nominative by punctuation, is rightly translated as vocative; and so I punctuated in Manil. vol. v p. 22. 61 17 *deiecta est herba coronis* 'jonché'. 65 8 *Lichas* 'Lycas' (and again in note). 72 2 *quatis uerbera* (see *Culic.* 219) 'portes des coups', and in note 'il est question d'un pugiliste'. 101 2 Mr Izaac mistakes *fama* for vocative and renders *uiae* as *uiarum*; but so do all the other translators I have consulted. 101 4 *Libyn* (Antaeum) *domuit* 'il conquit la Libye'.

Explanatory notes (pp. 255 ff.). VIII 14 1 *Cilicum pomaria* (and 8 *arboris*): 'il s'agit du safran'. 28 13 Paphos is said to be an island. 28 16 *Parthenio candidiora*: 'allusion à l'étymologie grecque du nom', and the same idle and incongruous fancy at IX 49 10. 55 (56) 24 *Marsus ero*: 'entendez (cf. IV 29 8) un *mauvais* poète épique'. This in face of 21 *Varios Marsosque*! Entendez (cf. II 71 3, 77 5, V 5 6, VII 29 8, 99 7) un épigrammatiste de premier ordre. 78 10 *spectatas feras* (les animaux de l'arène): 'pigeons, tourterelles, lièvres, etc.'. IX 12 (13) 7 Mr Izaac's note is taken from Mr Ker, and everything in it is false or irrelevant. 35 7 *Phario Ioue* (the sky of Egypt: the gossip always knows when a shower falls at Syene, which is once in a blue moon): 'le Nil identifié avec Osiris–Jupiter', as if Syene were inundated, and as if the rising of the Nile were not annual and regular. 92 11, which means 'that ‖ you are not cursed with two of your master's vices', is marvellously misinterpreted. The above notes on VIII 55 24 and IX 35 7 are by Mr Izaac's coadjutor Mr H. Frère.

172

REVIEW: J. WIGHT DUFF AND A. M. DUFF, MINOR LATIN POETS*

This is a volume containing Grattius, Calpurnius, Nemesianus, Auianus, Rutilius, the *sententiae* of Publilius Syrus, the *Aetna*, the *disticha Catonis*, and a dozen shorter works, in all about 7400 verses. As I soon saw that it would invite more comment than its importance would justify I have read through only Syrus, who comes first, and the slenderer authors: from the bulkier I have taken samples of 50 lines or more apiece. Since translation is the chief feature of this series I will say nothing of the recension or any subsidiary matter, and in the versions themselves I shall not notice a few places where words are omitted or where the reading translated is not that of the text, nor the rather more frequent cases where a sense has been invented for Latin which possesses none. Mistranslations proper will occupy me sufficiently; for not only are they numerous, but many of them are such as would not have been expected, and some are quite astounding.

In a miscellaneous collection of authors with some of whom the editors were not familiar a certain amount of stumbling was inevitable. To translate *Phoen.* 90 *uitali toro* as 'life-giving couch', though that is not the meaning of the term, was in view of the context a seductive error; but the rendering of 84 *mixto balsama cum folio* as 'balsam with its blended leaf' ought to have been dissatisfying and suspicious; and for mistranslating 54 *caput* as 'prince' and 49 *putetur* as jussive there was no excuse.

Imperfect knowledge of the meaning of words and phrases will account for much false rendering, as at Syr. 30 *delicias facit*, 70 *bonus animus*, 83 *tenebris*, 492 *paelicis*, 658 *summissum, el. in Maec.* I 135 *candoris*, II 5 *integer aeuo*, Calp. I 3 *feruentia*, 31 *sequaci, laud. Pis.* 96 and 229 *excusso*, 103 *fluidum*, 242 *gracilis*, *Aetn.* 244 [243] *tenax*, Nem. *buc.* I 78 *tractabit*, Pentad. II 19 *iucundat*, Tiberian. IV 13 *mundo*, 20 *premis*; but the translations of Syr. 152 and 196 *quo*, 374 *decipitur*, 453 *solus*, 492 *nuptae*, 518 *crimen quaerere, laud. Pis.* 136 *summoto uulgo*, Nem. *cyn.* 65 *nostrum* show obtuseness to the requirements of sense; and to misunderstand in their context *el. in Maec.* I 24 *bene praecinctos*, 30 *durior*,

* [*Minor Latin Poets* with introductions and English translations by J. Wight Duff and Arnold M. Duff. Pp. xii + 838. (Loeb Classical Library) London: Heinemann, 1934. *CR* 49 (1935), 78–9]

Gratt. 80 *alterna res*, Aetna 16 *melius*, 21 *mendacia*, Flor. IX 2 *rex* needed remarkable inattention or perversity.

From words we come to sentences. I append the true renderings, though I am sometimes ashamed to do so, and at Syr. 319 *iratus nihil non criminis loquitur loco* 'an angry man has nothing but accusations to utter' I cannot bring myself to it.

Syr. 52 *aegre reprendas quod sinas consuescere* (it is hard to check what you allow to grow habitual) 'reproof comes ill for a habit you countenance'.

414 *mansueta* (domestic animals, see Phaed. III 7) *tutiora sunt sed seruiunt* 'the tame way is safer but it's the way of slaves'.

505 *peiora multo cogitat mutus dolor* (resentment, when mute, meditates much worse revenge) 'dumb grief thinks of much worse to come'. *cogito* is again misunderstood in 410 and 388 and 560.

537 *peccatum extenuat qui celeriter corrigit* (prompt amendment of an offence diminishes it) 'the quick corrector weakens sin'.

559 *quod timeas citius quam quod speres euenit* (fears are sooner fulfilled than hopes) 'the dreaded thing happens sooner than you might expect'.

607 *quam miserum est, ubi te captant, qui defenderent* (when those who should defend you seek occasion against you) 'when your supposed defenders take you prisoner'.

656 *secunda in paupertate fortuna est fides* (honesty is a second patrimony) 'faith is fortune renewed, *i.e.* if a man reduced to poverty retains a faith in better times to come, that is in some degree a restoration of fortune'.

el. in Maec. I 131 f. (*Hesperon*) *quem nunc in fuscis placida sub nocte nitentem* | *Luciferum contra currere cernis equis* (*in fuscis equis contra Luciferum*) 'thou canst see him now as Lucifer gleaming in the dark 'neath the stilly night and || charioting his steeds on an opposite course'.

II 7–10 'Alas' says Maecenas 'that I did not die before Drusus'; and then '*discidio uellemque prius*' – *non omnia dixit* | *inciditque pudor quae prope dixit amor,* | *sed manifestus erat: moriens quaerebat amatae* | *coniugis amplexus oscula uerba manus.* Even if the matrimonial fortunes of Maecenas were as completely unknown as they are unhappily notorious, could the context permit a doubt about the sense of *discidio?* It is translated 'our civil strife', with the note 'Maecenas recalls the hostilities between Octavian Caesar and Mark Antony'.

laud. Pis. 233 f. *forsitan illius nemoris latuisset in umbra* | *quod canit* (he might have stayed obscure in the shadow of that grove which he celebrates) 'his poem (*illius quod canit?*) might have lurked obscure in the shadow of the grove'.

Nem. cyn. 57 f. *implicitumque sinu spinosi corporis erem* | *ferre domum* (carry home the prickly hedgehog wrapped in one's bosom) 'the hedgehog entwined in the convolution of its prickly body'.

Auian. V 13 f. *rusticus hunc* (the ass in the lion's skin) *magna postquam de-*

prendit ab aure (having detected him by his length of ear) 'after catching him by his long ear'.

A singular fatality by which the editors are pursued is an impulse to believe that sentences mean the opposite of what they do mean. Nem. *cyn.* 33 *miratum-que rudes se tollere Terea pinnas* 'Tereus' wonderment *that he could raise wings as yet untried*'. Syr. 301 *iratus etiam facinus consilium putat* (the angry man thinks even a crime a sage proceeding) 'takes (hostile) intention as an actual deed'. 397 *multorum calamitate uir moritur bonus* (a good man's death is a misfortune to many) 'the affliction of many is death for the good man'. *el. in Maec.* I 28 *num tibi non tutas fecit in urbe uias?* (did he not enable you to walk the streets in safety?) 'did he make the streets of Rome unsafe for you?' Rutil. I 52 *sospes nemo potest immemor esse tui* (none enjoying safety can forget thee) 'none can be safe, if forgetful of thee'. Grammatical construction, and consequently sense, is again mistaken in *el. in Maec.* II 15 *contingat* and *iaceam, laud. Pis.* 169 f. *cum exultent*, buc. Eins. I 12 *damnato pignore*, Repos. 2 *flamma militat*, Auian. III 3 *hunc procedere*, Rutil. I 5 (*totiens*) *beatos quotiens numerare possum*.

In literary form the versions do not generally fall short of what it was reasonable to expect. Syrus is least adequately rendered, not so much because he is the best literature in the book as because of the difficulty inherent in rendering apophthegms.

173

FRAGMENTA POETARVM*

Ennius

Non. p. 472 5 [757 Lindsay] luctant pro luctantur. Ennius lib. ix

uiri a (*al.* uaria) ualidis uiribus luctant.

There is more MS authority for *uiri a* than for *uaria*, and most editors follow the ed. princ. in writing *uiri*. But this is not an easier change than *uaria*, even if *uaria* is merely conjectural, which a reading so obviously defective in sense and syntax is not likely to be. Vahlen Enn. *ann.* 300 accordingly writes '⟨fortuna⟩ uaria ualidis ⟨cum⟩ uiribus luctant', where the *cum* which Ianus Dousa supplied to prop the metre is certainly an apter preposition than the *a* which others transfer to this spot. But such piecemeal amendment is not craftsmanlike or economical: is there no word of two morae which is also a substantive for *uaria* to agree with? The demands of metre and syntax will both be satisfied by

uiri uaria ualidis ⟨uice⟩ uiribus luctant,

which further provides a palaeographical explanation of the error and a feast of alliteration congenial to the author of 'o Tite tute Tati tibi tanta tyranne tulisti', who was perhaps also the author of 'machina multa minax minitatur maxima muris'. Seneca in *Med.* 287 has 'Fortuna *uaria* dubia quos agitat *uice*', and Ennius himself *alterna uice* (*Atham.*, 110 Ribb., 126 Vahl. [123 Jocelyn]], Char. p. 241 G.L.K. I, p. 314 Barw.).

Lucilius

Non. p. 278 5–8 [427 Lindsay] delenitus, delectatus...Lucilius lib. xxx
[1004 Marx]   praeseruit, labra delicit, delenit amore.

For *delicit* Turnebus proposed *delingit*, which is generally adopted by the editors both of Nonius and of Lucilius. This verb has for its object in Plautus *salem*, in Celsus medicine administered in the form of a linctus, in the *interpretatio Itala* the blood of Naboth and Jezebel; and the *thes. ling. Lat.* cites from Lampr. *uit. Diad.* 5 6 'leo...puerum delinxit et inuiolatum reliquit'. But *labra delingere* is the blandishment of a four-footed beast, Mart. 1 83 1 'os et

* [CR 49 (1935), 166–8]

labra tibi lingit, Manneia, catellus'; and furthermore there is prosody to be considered. The pyrrhic scansion of *lăbră* cannot indeed be pronounced impossible, but I can adduce no example of it, and there is nothing like it in the remains of Lucilius. Even where the consonant before *r* is a tenuis the only trochaic words so treated with any frequency are *pătrĭs* and *pătrĕ*; *săcră* is very rare, and everything else of the sort much rarer. For *lăbră* I can call to mind no parallel but *Tĭgrĭs* in Manil. IV 806, for I will not dredge up *nĭgră* from Ven. Fort. *carm. app.* 22 14 and the sixth century.

Kisses are evidently meant, and the whole verse has a curious likeness to the passage of Ephippus' *Empole* ⟦fr. 6 2–7 Kock⟧ cited ‖ by Mr Marx from Athen. p. 363 c, ἐκολάκευσεν ἡδέως, | ἐφίλησεν οὐχὶ συμπιέσασα τὸ στόμα | ὥσπερ πολέμιον, ἀλλὰ τοῖσι στρουθίοις | χανοῦσ᾽ ὁμοίως, ἦσε, παρεμυθήσατο | ἐποίησέ θ᾽ ἱλαρὸν εὐθέως τ᾽ ἀφεῖλε πᾶν | αὐτοῦ τὸ λυποῦν κἀπέδειξεν ἵλεων. I suspect therefore that DELICIT is DFLIGIT and that 'labra ⟨a⟩dfligit' should be read: so Lucretius IV 1080 f. 'dentes inlidunt saepe labellis | osculaque adfligunt (O, adfigunt Q)'. But these two verbs are perpetually interchanged, and perhaps the latter, though less to the purpose of Lucretius, will be more natural here.

'Numitorius'

Donat. *uit. Verg.* ed. Brummer p. 10 (Reifferscheid Suet. p. 65) obtrectatores Vergilio numquam defuerunt, nec mirum: nam ne Homero quidem: prolatis bucolicis Numitorius (*Ribbeck and Woelfflin,* numinatoris *and* -rus *codd.*) quidam rescripsit antibucolica, duas modo eclogas sed insulsissime παρῳδήσας, quarum prioris initium est ⟦*PLF* p. 104 Morel⟧

> Tityre, si toga calda tibi est, quo tegmine fagi?

The parallels by which it was once sought to defend the construction of Verg. *Aen.* IV 98 'sed quis erit modus aut quo nunc certamine tanto?' have one by one fallen away, and ablatives have everywhere given place to accusatives in obedience to the witness of MSS. The authentic reading of Ouid. *amor.* III 4 41 is 'quo tibi formosam', not 'formosa'; of Mart. V 53 2 'quo tibi uel Nioben... uel Andromachen', not 'Niobe' and 'Andromache'; and even in Hor. *epist.* I 5 12 the most and best of the MSS are found to give 'quo mihi fortunam', not 'fortuna'. Only this fragment remains; and this is not in reality a parallel. It is not corrupt, and the *tegmina* of Gronouius is refuted by Virgil's own text, 'Tityre, tu patulae recubans sub tegmine fagi'; but the ablative case has no grammatical connexion with the interrogation. If the parodist had used modern print, we should be reading

> quo 'tegmine fagi'?

that is 'what point has the phrase *tegmine fagi*'?

Ouidius

Quint. *inst.* XII 10 75 euanescunt haec atque emoriuntur comparatione meliorum, ut lana tincta fuco citra purpuras placet:

> at, si contuleris eam (*Heinsius,* etiam *codd.*) lacernae,
> conspectu melioris obruatur,

ut Ouidius ait ⟦*PLF* p. 113 Morel⟧.

lacernae is indefinite and pointless, and to remove this reproach by placing the comma after *eam* is to incur another, for both *contuleris* and Quintilian lead one to expect the dative or its equivalent, as in the parallels to be quoted below from Ovid and Horace. My supplement is only meant to adumbrate the context, but my correction I think necessary:

> ⟨arridet tibi tincta lana fuco,⟩
> at, si contuleris eam *Lacaenae,*
> conspectu melioris obruatur.

Ael. *nat. an.* XV 10 Λακαίνης πορφύρας, Hor. *carm.* II 18 7 f. 'Laconicas... purpuras', Plin. *n.h.* IX 127 'Tyri praecipuus hic (sucus purpurae) Asiae,...in Laconia Europae', XXI 45 'purpuras Tyrias...ac Laconicas', XXXV 45 '(purpurissum) Tyrium aut Gaetulicum uel Laconicum, unde pretiosissimae purpurae', Ouid. *rem.* 707 f. 'confer Amyclaeis medicatum uellus aenis | murice cum Tyrio: turpius illud erit', Hor. *epist.* I 10 26 f. 'qui Sidonio contendere callidus ostro | nescit Aquinatem potantia uellera fucum'. The same corruption, *lacerna* for *Lacaena,* appears at Mart. IX 103 2 in cod. Paris. 8067 Lat. saec. IX–X.

Gaetulicus

[Probus] *comm. in Verg. georg.* I 229 ⟦vol. 3 2 p. 360 Thilo–Hagen⟧ Bootes est stella in Arctophylacis, ut plerique putant, balteo, ut alii iudicant, in umero, dicta a bubus. nam Septentriones, quos Graeci duas Vrsas uocant, Helicen et Cynosuram, in barbarica sphaera plaustrum esse, quod ducatur a bubus iunctis. cuius rei testis est Gaetulicus, cum ait de Britannis ⟦*PLF* p. 123 Morel⟧

> non Aries illum uerno ferit aera cornu
> Cnosia nec Geminos praecedunt cornua, tantum
> sicca Lycaonius resupinat plaustra Bootes.

1 *ferit* Keil, *ferat* codd.　*aera* scripsi, *aere* codd.

These lines, exaggerating the prevalent errors concerning the latitude of Britain, ‖ describe phenomena which are in fact observable only within the arctic circle or rather indeed under the north pole; and what they say is this: 'The Ram does not butt that clime in spring, nor do the Cretan horns come before the Twins; Bootes keeps his Wain supine and shifts it to no other position.' The Ram, that is, in which the sun rises at our vernal equinox, never rises at all, because he is above the horizon all the year round. The rising of the Bull does not, as with us, precede that of the Twins, because those two constellations also are permanently situate in the visible hemisphere. The Great Bear, instead of ascending and descending, is invariably overhead. Manilius III 358 f. designates this region as 'orbem...prona Lycaoniae spectantem membra puellae'; and in such a connexion *pronus* and *supinus* have the same sense, as Horace *carm.* III 4 23 says 'Tibur supinum' and Juvenal III 192 'proni Tiburis' with no difference of meaning: moreover, as Scaliger observes at Manil. I 393, astronomers are not agreed whether the constellations turn their fronts or their backs to us.

The last two lines are generally printed (Hagen *append. Seru.* p. 360, Boll *sphaer.* p. 389, Morel *frag. poet. Lat.* p. 123)

> Cnosia nec Geminos praecidunt (*cod. unus*) cornua Tauri (*Keil*),
> sicca Lycaonius resupinat plaustra Bootes.

What *praecidunt* is supposed to mean I cannot imagine; and not only is *Tauri* redundant but *tantum* is indispensable. *Cnosia cornua* designates Taurus as plainly as *Thessalicas sagittas* in Luc. IV 528 designates Sagittarius; and a choice of reasons for the epithet is given in schol. Arat. 167 [p. 368 25–9 Maass] τοῦτον οὖν οἱ μὲν τὸν τὴν Εὐρώπην διαγαγόντα ἐκ Φοινίκης εἰς Κρήτην διὰ τοῦ πελάγους φασίν, οἱ δὲ τοῦτον οὗ Πασιφάη ἠράσθη, οἱ δὲ τὸν ἐκ Κρήτης εἰς Μαραθῶνα παραγενόμενον, ὃν Θησεὺς κατηγωνίσατο. *tantum* belongs to *resupinat* and *resupinat* requires *tantum*. Even in the latitude of Rome the Wain is overhead once in the twenty-four hours, and more perpendicularly overhead than it ever is at the north pole; but only in the neighbourhood of the pole is that its only position.

Vagellius

Sen. *nat. quaest.* VI 2 8 f. quid habeo quod querar si rerum natura me non uult iacere ignobili leto, si mihi inicit sui partem? egregie Vagellius meus in illo inclito carmine [*PLF* p. 124 Morel] 'si cadendum est' inquit 'mihi, e caelo cecidisse uelim.' idem licet dicere: si cadendum est, cadam orbe concusso, non quia fas est optare publicam cladem, sed quia ingens mortis solacium est terram quoque uidere mortalem.

Seneca is urging us not to be frightened in earthquakes. *mihi*, which is recalcitrant to metre, stands before and not after *inquit* in one family of MSS, and Gercke transfers it to the next sentence, where it seems to be required, 'idem ⟨mihi⟩ licet dicere'. The sense even so is faulty, for 'e caelo' and 'orbe concusso' are not *idem*: to write '⟨mihi⟩ *item* licet dicere', without entirely removing the fault, would diminish it, and *mihi* would more easily have fallen out between *m* and *i*. The metre is still defective, and 'e caelo cecidisse' conspires with palaeographical probability to suggest

si⟨cunde⟩ cadendum est.

174

REVIEW: N. VIANELLO, *D. IVNII IVVENALIS SATIRAE**

This book must have cost its author considerable pains, but he has not spent quite enough of them upon thought and accuracy.

In the first satire the reports 16 *Sullae dedimus* Paris. 8072, 70 *rubetā* Paris. 8072, 86 *farrago l.e.* Fl. Sang., 108 *reductas* A, 131 *meiere* Paris. 8072, *mingere* L, 145 *it* GOT are false; which is the less excusable because he has made no original collations and his task was only to repeat correctly the statements of others. The apparatus, though he says on p. lxv 'curaui ne...superuacuis lectionibus laboraret', is loaded with such lections, 5, 11, 18, 19, 21, 51, 95–6, 102, 117, 119, 125, 133, 156, 160, 168: variants intrinsically insignificant, like *Thelephus* for *Telephus*, or offered only by insignificant MSS. At 85 *quidquid* he says '*quicquid* O': if this is true, it is beneath mention; but he has in fact no means of knowing the reading of O, and is heedlessly copying Hosius, whose O is a sign with a different meaning; and at 134 '*caules* O' he repeats the mistake. He professes to give the readings of F at 99, 110, 119, 159: F does not contain this satire; he has again rambled off into a notation not his own. He will not use, as others do, a compendious designation for the mass of vulgar MSS: he prefers to enumerate some half-dozen of them, not sticking to the same, nor picking out the best, nor confining himself to those about which he really possesses information. P¹, which was Leo's sign for the first hand of P, is chosen by Mr Vianello to signify the second.

I have made no search for faults in the other satires, but so many have caught my eye that the total must be very great, and some are very grave. The note at VI 614 on p. 92 is an assemblage of almost all imaginable blunders. That at III 109, though so chaotic that it must bewilder everybody, is so incredible that it can deceive nobody. Lack of skill and circumspection has disordered the notes on VII 96, VIII 7, X 359, XIII 4, 179, and at XV 75 his clumsiness has betrayed him into a false statement. In VIII he says that the vulgar MSS have *nasumque* for *nasoque* at 5 when the fact is that they have *nasumque* for *umerosque* at 4, and he neither records that 7 is given by the chief MS nor mentions its reading. At

---

* [*D. Iunii Iuuenalis satirae*: recensuit Natalis Vianello (corpus scriptorum Latinorum Parauianum). Pp. lxxix + 227. Turin: Paravia, 1935.   *CR* 50 (1936), 26–7]

VI 65 he attributes four different readings to O and two to P. Neither in prosody nor in syntax is he much at home: he mentions the conjecture *concīlia*, says that *Psĕcăs* is Ψηκᾶς, and imputes *quodcumquē* to Buecheler; he cites Ouid. *met.* VI 312 *lacrimas manant* as parallel to *animas caluerunt* at I 83, and X 46 *defossa in loculos* as parallel to IV 128 *erectas in terga sudes*.

The notes extend beyond the limits of an app. crit. and contain much matter taken from others, with or without acknowledgement. He sometimes falsifies quotations by unmannerly alteration, as when at VII 169 f., where I wrote 'ingrati reus est', he inserts 'animi', being ignorant of the technical term. Of his conjectures some are unprovoked and some violent; the best have no positive merit or claim to preference (for what he says of *laesi irae* X 313 is not true), and the worst (as III 42 and VI 511) are terrible. VI 64–6 he reduces to incoherency and shows that he has no conception of what is meant. Indeed, speaking generally, he does not think enough. Here are two ‖ straws to show how the wind blows: VI 57 'concedo et in agro castam fuisse* Σ unde Leo: ⟨ego⟩ cedo'; XIV 71 'ciuis* Housm. cl. Σ *ciuem bonum'*. It would surprise him to learn that these are calumnies: the bad logic which he imputes to Leo and me is not shocking to him and does not even penetrate his consciousness. It follows that he does not always argue well, and is apt to miss the point on which he ought to be disputing. Nor is he precise in the use of words. He applies the term 'glossa' to *firma* I 115, *pauperes* 119, *scutum et gladium* VIII 123, which, whatever they may be, are neither glossae nor glossemata. On p. xii he employs 'fortuna' as an abusive substitute for both cause and motive, and thereby vitiates his argument.

APPENDIX

1

〚AESCHYLUS, *PERSAE* 674 SQQ.〛*

The phrase 〚πόρι Δαρείου, conjectured at Ar. *Ran.* 1028 by R. Y. Tyrrell, *CR*
1 (1887), 130〛 plainly is one which a comic writer would hardly himself invent;
and, if Aristophanes did employ it, the surmise would be natural that Aeschylus
in the Persae had actually called Xerxes πόρις Δαρείου as a variation on πῶλος.
I think perhaps he had.

The epode Pers. 677 sqq. 〚674 sqq.〛 is handed down in this nonsensical form:

> ὦ πολύκλαυτε φίλοισι θανών,
> τί τάδε δυνάτα δυνάτα
> περὶ τᾶ σᾶ δίδυμα διαγόεν δι' ἁμάρτια
> πάσᾳ γᾷ τᾷδε
> ἐξέφθινται τρίσκαλμοι
> νᾶες ἄναες ἄναες.

Blomfield suggested τί τάδε δυνατὰ δυνατὰ παιδὶ τῷ σῷ; perhaps Aeschylus
wrote πόρει τῷ σῷ, which would explain the alteration τᾶ σᾶ by a scribe unfamiliar with πόρις masculine. The rest of the passage might possibly run thus:
δίδυμα διὰ γοέδν' ἁμάρτια πάσᾳ γᾷ τᾷδε ἐξέφθινται τρίσκαλμοι νᾶες ἄναες, λαὸς
ἄλαος, which would make sense of δίδυμα.

* 〚*CR* 1 (1887), 313: the note was published, with Housman's permission, by R. Y. Tyrrell〛

2

⟦NOTES ON FRAGMENTS OF EURIPIDES⟧*

235 πλουτεῖς · ὁ πλοῦτος δ' ἀμαθία δειλόν θ' ἅμα. Wealth and witlessness are often found together, but they are not one: write perhaps ἀμαθίᾳ δειλὸν θαμά, 'is often rendered a sorry thing by the thick-wittedness of its owner', comparing frag. 163 χρυσὸς ἀμαθίας μέτα | ἄχρηστον. It would also be possible to read ἀμαθίαν δηλοῖ θαμά. ‖

298 οὐκ ἂν γένοιτο τραῦμ', ἐάν τις ἐγξέσῃ | θάμνοις ἑλείοις, οὐδ' ἂν ἐκ μητρὸς κακῆς | ἐσθλοὶ γένοιντο παῖδες εἰς ἀλκὴν δορός. For ἑλείοις it is usual to write ἑλείοις, but the image is ludicrous, and since wounds really can be inflicted by θάμνοι, the comparison comes to naught. Write θαλλοῖς ἐλαίας, the regular name for the pliant shoots of young olive woven into wreaths at festivals.

330 ἐς ταὐτὸν ἥκειν φημὶ ταῖς βροτῶν τύχαις | τόνδ' ὃν καλοῦσιν αἰθέρ', ᾧ τάδ' ἔστι δή. | οὗτος κτλ. It is impossible to construe ᾧ τάδ' ἔστι δή intelligibly, nor after these words could the next sentence proceed as it does. βροτῶν above and θνητῶν in v. 6 below suggest αἰθέρ' ἑστίαν Διός, for which compare frag. 487 αἰθέρ' οἴκησιν Διός and the αἰθέρα Διὸς δωμάτιον imputed to Euripides at Ar. Ran. 100 and 311. ἔστι ΔΗ being written for ἑστίΑΝ, the compendium of Διός might be absorbed by δή.

495, 34 ὄρεος ὑλίμῳ φόβῃ. This verse of the fragment published by Blass in 1880 supports ὕλιμος (given in Christ. pat. 2260) against εὔλειμος in Eur. Bacch. 1084. The adjective is not in Liddell and Scott, and συοφόνος, found in v. 29 of this fragment, seems to be in no lexicon.

793 μακάριος ὅστις εὐτυχῶν οἴκοι μένει · | ἐν γῇ δ' ὁ φόρτος, καὶ πάλιν ναυτίλλεται. For πάλιν write ποδοῖν, which is easily confused with πόλιν, and πόλιν with πάλιν. The two halves of the verse then correspond: 'his "freight" is on dry land and his "voyages" are performed on two legs', i.e. he has nothing to do with either freights or voyages: for this form of expression compare Soph. Ant. 716 sq.

860. Etym. magn. p. 797, 14 πρότερον οἱ Φοίνικες ᾤκουν πρὸς τῇ ἐρυθρᾷ θαλάσσῃ, καὶ ἐντεῦθεν αὐτοῖς τοὔνομα · φοινικοῖ γὰρ τὴν χροίαν, ἀπὸ τῶν παρακειμένων αὐτοῖς πετρῶν πορφυρῶν οὐσῶν · διὸ καὶ ἐρυθρὰ λέγεται. καὶ παρ'

* ⟦*PCPhS* 1890, 10–11: summary of a paper⟧

Εὐριπίδη Φοινίσσαις 'ἅλμη' εἴρηται. Write, as the context demands, παρ' Εὐριπίδη 'φοίνισσα (or Φοίνισσα) ἅλμη' εἴρηται.

897 παίδευμα δ' Ἔρως σοφίας ἀρετῆς | πλεῖστον ὑπάρχει. Since either σοφίας or ἀρετῆς must go, perhaps the simplest change is to alter the latter to ἐρατῆς, so that love is said to lesson men in lovely wisdom. The same error occurs in Tyrt. frag. 10 [7 Diehl], 28.

996 σύμμεικτον εἶδος κἀποφώλιον τρέφος: a description of the Minotaur, which was by no means ἀποφώλιον, *empty*, *idle*. There is a MS variant καὶ ἀπόφημον: write κἀποφύλιον, i.e. *sui generis*, a word which is corrupted into ἀποφώλιος at Aesch. frag. 287 [493 Mette]. Compare the use of φῦλον in Aesch. Eum. 57, and also Lucr. v 839 'androgynum, interutrasque nec utrum, utrimque remotum' as a parallel to the whole verse.

1088. Suidas sub uoc. παλαιγενές· τοὺς γὰρ εὐήθεις ἀρχαίους καὶ παλαιοὺς ἔλεγον . . . Εὐριπίδης 'ἀρχαῖον εἴρηκας' ἀντὶ τοῦ εὔηθες. This should probably be removed from among the fragments: anyhow it enables us to emend I. T. 740 δίκαιον εἶπας· πῶς γὰρ ἀγγείλειεν ἄν; where δίκαιον is absurd, the required sense is εὔηθες, and ἀρχαῖον, a very easy change, should be written.

3

[EURIPIDES, *BACCHAE* 837]*

If we were shown this snatch of dialogue –

Π. I could not bear to put on women's clothes.

Δ. . . . .

Π. Well said: we must first go and spy them out,

and were asked to give the sense of the missing verse, I think we should do so without much trouble: 'if you are recognised you will be in jeopardy', or the like. Even if Ion 1225, 1260, I. A. 1418, and Or. 833 would altogether justify αἷμα θήσεις, which I do not think they will, still we should never insert any such remark as 'But you will cause bloodshed'. To cause bloodshed Pentheus is steadfastly purposed: 796, θύσω, φόνον γε θῆλυν, ὥσπερ ἄξιαι, | πολὺν ταράξας ἐν Κιθαιρῶνος πτυχαῖς; at 809 he has finally rejected Dionysus' offer to bring home the Bacchants peaceably; and the πρῶτον of 838 shows that he is still resolved on fighting, only he consents to a preliminary journey of observation. I do not see that the words can possibly mean 'shed *your own* blood', and indeed it does not seem to have been suggested that they can. Therefore I think the verse was this: ἀλλ' εὐμαθὴς εἶ συμβαλῶν Βάκχαις μάχην; 'What! will you go and be recognised and join battle with them?' a reminder of the danger already pointed out in 823, μή σε κτάνωσιν ἢν ἀνὴρ ὀφθῆς ἐκεῖ. 'Ah, you say well', returns Pentheus, 'I must defer that; we must reconnoitre first: afterwards I will go with my army.'

* [R. Y. Tyrrell, ed., Eur. *Bacchae* (1892), p. 111]

4

CORRECTIONS*

I am sorry to find that on p. 367 *b* ⟦this edition p. 524⟧ I have incidentally misrepresented Mr Heinze as neglecting to say who first invented the explanation of Lucr. III 420 which he adopts. Mr Heinze, on the contrary, says explicitly 'mit Wakefield'.

This is a good opportunity to retract another slander which I have long had on my conscience. In vol. IV of this Review, p. 107 *a* ⟦this edition p. 122⟧, I accused Mr Tucker of having invented a fable about Opis and Orion. This was sheer ignorance on my part: the story is duly told by Apollodorus bibl. I 4 5.

And further I will withdraw two conjectures in Ovid's metamorphoses which I published in 1890 in the Transactions of the Cambridge Philological Society, vol. III pp. 142 and 145 ⟦this edition pp. 163 and 166⟧, and which have led others into error. At met. I 632 I adopted Mr Riese's objection to '*amara* pascitur *herba*' and proposed '*amaro . . . eruo*' (*erui* is corrupted to *herbe* in med. fac. 55). This is wrong: Ovid is imitating the verse of Caluus ⟦*PLF* p. 85 Morel⟧ quoted by Seruius at Verg. buc. VI 47, 'herbis pasceris amaris'. At met. VI 63 I objected to 'ab imbre . . . percussis solibus' on the ground that it ought to be 'a solibus percusso imbre'. But though Juvenal I 54 has 'mare percussum puero' Lucan II 155 sq. can still write 'hic, se praecipiti iaculatus pondere, dura | dissiluit percussus humo'.

* ⟦*CR* 14 (1900), 413⟧

5

⟦THE MANUSCRIPTS OF JUVENAL⟧*

The textual criticism of Juvenal, since the middle of the 19th century, has suffered from two causes: firstly a tendency to follow the best MS, P, wherever its readings are tolerable, without impartially considering whether they are probably right; secondly a tendency, when its readings are intolerable, to fall back, not upon the best of the other class ω, but upon one of the worst, the second hand of P itself. This, P², ought to be excluded from the apparatus criticus: in its stead should be included at least six MSS, – Monacensis 408, Leidensis 82, Parisiensis 7900, Vrbinas 661, Bodleianus Canon. class. Lat. 41, and Trin. Coll. Cant. O. iv. 10, – which at present are almost unknown or almost ignored. ‖ Thus at III 109 editors read 'praeterea sanctum nihil *est neque* ab inguine tutum', though *est neque* has no authority but P²: P omits the words, most of the other MSS have *aut*, the Vienna fragment *auct*: write *aut* ⟨*tibi*⟩.

Although P has been unduly exalted, there still remain places where its true readings are neglected, such as XI 151 'pastoris duri hic filius', or XIII 49, where it omits *aliquis*, and the passage should be written 'nondum ⟨imi⟩ sortitus triste profundi | imperium Sicula toruos cum coniuge Pluton'. But the text is now more in need of help from the other MSS. These sometimes preserve the original reading of P, now obliterated by P², as at VIII 148 *sufflamine mulio* (Par. and Vrb. as well as the florilegium Sangallense), XV 75 *praestant instantibus Ombis* (Bodl.), 145 *pariendis* (Bodl. and Vrb.); sometimes the true form, or a less corrupt form, of the reading indicated by P, as at XII 54 *reccidit* Leid. Par. Vrb., *recidit* P, *decidit* al., XIV 217 *longae* Mon., *longe* P, *longi* al., XV 7 *aeluros* Juvenal (Brodaeus), *elu..s* Vrb., *aeruleos* P, *caeruleos* al.; sometimes an antique spelling, as XVI 5 *epistula*, X 189 *uoltu*, VI 644 *Procne*, modernised in P; sometimes true readings which modern critics have recovered by conjecture, as VIII 51 *hinc*, 78 *desideret*, IX 55 *lassas*, XIII 5 *homines*; sometimes readings no less true but universally disregarded, as X 155 '*acti*' inquit 'nihil est', with which compare Sen. Med. 993, Livy XXXII 37 5, Hor. carm. I 3 37. In short the recension, quite apart from the emendation, of Juvenal is not yet completed; and its completion will require both the collation of MSS and the exercise of thought.

* ⟦*PCPhS* 1904, 4–5: summary of a paper⟧

6

[A SUPPOSED ANOMALY OF
SCANSION IN STATIUS]*

There are in the Thebais of Statius five places where the compounds *deesse*, *praeire*, *deire*, are so scanned that the first element neither coalesces with the second nor becomes short instead of long. In the two latest German editions these scansions are adopted without other defence than a mere enumeration of the instances. The paper did not controvert the opinion that Statius himself used these scansions; but it set forth the facts and considerations by which any opinion on the subject ought to be determined, and without which no opinion can be formed which is anything more than a prejudice.

* [*PCPhS* 1911, 12: summary of a paper]

7

⟦NOTES ON MANILIUS⟧*

Manil. IV 6

  pauperiorque bonis quisque est, qui (*codd.*, quo *edd.*) plura requirit.

This is one of a string of questions introduced by the interrogative *quid* of *v.* 1 and ending only at *v.* 11; but neither the MS reading (which means 'why are all greedy men the poorer?') nor the vulgate text (which means 'why are all men the poorer the greedier they are?') is a question resembling the rest of the series and admitting the same reply; for the rest are enquiries why men distress themselves with toil and care and longing, and the answer is that they have no reason, inasmuch as everything is ordained by fate. Most editors therefore break the series and make *v.* 6 an affirmation; but thus to attach an affirmation to an interrogation by means of *que* is not even grammatical. Bentley changed *requirit* to *pararit*; Barthius expelled this verse and also the next, which cannot be detached from it. But it is enough to write *quia* for *qui*, understanding *bonis* as abl. not of respect but of cause (Hor. *carm.* III 5 40 'altior Italiae ruinis'), *bona quemque pauperiorem faciunt*: 'why is every man the poorer for his possessions because of his desire for more?' i.e. 'why does every man crave for more, so that his riches make him poorer?' This *quia* does not answer the question *quid*, but states the impelling cause; *quid* asks for the justifying reason, which is not forthcoming. ‖

  A similar ablative of cause will set right V 404 sq.

> censibus aequantur conchae, rapidumque notori
> uix quisquam est locuples;

where Salmasius proposed *lapidumque nitori*, but the dative yields no sense. *Nitore* might easily pass through *nitoro* to *notori*, and 'lapidum nitore uix quisquam est locuples' means 'lapidum nitor efficit ut uix quisquam locuples sit', i.e. all our rich men beggar themselves to buy pearls. For the fact see Plin. *n. h.* XII 84, Tac. *ann.* III 53 5 ⟦4⟧.

IV 53   cum iam etiam posset alium componere Magnum.

  This is the reading of LM: the *posses* from which commentators have failed to extort any tolerable sense is the reading of GL², which are prone to metrical

* ⟦*PCPhS* 1913, 16–17: summary of a paper⟧

interpolation. The lengthening of -*et* is not like Manilius, for IV 280 is corrupt; but if *possent*, which Barthius quite by accident proposed, is substituted, an appropriate subject and sense can be supplied in this way:

> cum iam etiam possent alium componere Magnum
> ⟨Pellaei uicina loco monumenta tyranni⟩,

'when now was the time for Alexander's tomb to inter a second Magnus at the side of the first.' See I 770 'Magno maxima Pella', Luc. IX 58 'membra... componere Magni', anth. Lat. 455 'diuerso terrarum litore Magnos...compositos' (Pompey and his sons), and especially ib. 438 'iunxit *magnorum* casus fortuna uirorum: | hic paruo, nullo conditus ille loco est. | ite, nouas toto terras conquirite mundo: | nempe manet *magnos* paruula terra duces', where the two conquerors signified are Alexander and Pompey.

IV 124 sq.   diues fecundis Aries in uellera lanis
              exutusque nouis rursum spem semper habebit.

nouis depends neither on *exutus* nor on *spem habebit* but on *diues*: 'diues fecundis in uellera lanis et, postquam exutus est, nouis rursum lanis diues.'

IV 133–5 will best be punctuated:

> quis sine non poterant ullae subsistere gentes
> uel sine luxuria. tantum est opus, ipsa suismet
> adseruit Pallas manibus dignumque putauit.

See Hor. *serm.* I I 13 sq. 'cetera de genere hoc adeo sunt multa, loquacem | delassare ualent Fabium'.

8

⟦OVID, *HER.* VI 110⟧*

Ovid her. VI 110

                    cur tua polliciti pondere uerba carent?

polliciti is not a neuter substantive but a masculine participle, and the construction is that of amor. I 8 108 'ut mea defunctae molliter ossa cubent'.

    * ⟦*PCPhS* 1915, 16: summary of part of a paper, of which the other items were published in full in 'Ouidiana' (this edition no. 112)⟧

9

⟦*SECVRICELLA*⟧*

Professor Housman remarked that this word ⟦*celtis*⟧ and an equally fictitious by-form *celta* have been foisted into the text of the Mulomedicina Chironis and thence received into the Thesaurus Linguae Latinae. The passages are 26 *percutiuntur trauerse securi, celle* (*celte* Buecheler) *uel flebotomo* and 693 *sanguinem ...emittito de securi cella* (*uel celta* Oder). But *securi celle* and *securi cella* are nothing but *securicella*, a diminutive of *securis* related to *securicula* as *cistella* to *cistula* and denoting a surgical instrument serving the purpose of a fleam; and this new word may perhaps console lexicographers for the loss of *celtis*.

* ⟦*PCPhS* 1916, 12: report of a discussion⟧

10

⟦STATIUS, *SILV.* II 7 73–4⟧*

Professor Housman read a paper criticising a recent attempt (Classical Quarterly x pp. 225–8) to make Stat. silu. II 7 73–4 'haec primo iuuenis canes sub aeuo | ante annos Culicis Maroniani' agree with the reading of most MSS in Donat. uit. Verg. 17 (28) 'fecit... Culicem cum esset annorum XVI' by special translations or paraphrases of *haec, canes ante, primo aeuo* and *coepta iuuenta* (64), and to set aside or modify the statements of Suetonius (uit. Luc. init.) touching the date of Lucan's works.

* ⟦*PCPhS* 1916, 16: summary of a paper⟧

11

⟦HORACE, *CARM.* I 31 17–20⟧*

frui paratis et ualido mihi,
Latoe, dones at precor integra
cum mente nec turpem senectam
degere nec cithara carentem.

The scholia once ascribed to Acro, and those editors who retain the text, explain 'at integra cum mente' as a restrictive parenthesis; but this would require *sed* instead of *at*, so that most editors read *et* with Lambinus or *ac* with one or two unimportant MSS. One of the oldest MSS, λ, Paris. 7972, has *adprecor*, a verb which recurs in *carm.* IV 15 28, and which in Appul. *met.* VI 3 is intransitive, like the similar verb *adoro* in Prop. I 4 27 'maneat sic semper adoro': the construction will be 'adprecor, Latoe, dones mihi frui paratis et ualido integra cum mente senectam degere nec turpem nec cithara carentem.' This reading is preferable to *et precor* or *ac precor* as involving no change, for *adprecor* and *atprecor* are only two ways of spelling the same word. Neue's examples of *at* for *ad* in compounds with *p* (*Formenl.* II p. 792 ed. 3) can be much augmented, for instance by *C.I.L.* x 6460 *atpeti*, palimps. Front. p. 156 l. 11 ed. Nab. ⟦150 l. 5 Van Den Hout⟧ *atpositas*, palimps. Plaut. *Epid.* 21 *atportas*, BCD Plaut. *rud.* 566 *atpotus*, 735 CD *atprime*, Lucr. V 221 *atportant*. In Hor. *epod.* 1 21 the unmetrical *ut sit* of half the MSS for *ut adsit* or *ut assit* may have arisen from the loss of *at* after *ut* in *ut atsit*.

* ⟦*PCPhS* 1918, 22: summary of a paper⟧

12

NOT LIVY*

Sir, – In to-day's *Illustrated London News* there are reproduced in facsimile the four lines which Dr Max Funke says that Dr di Martino-Fusco allowed him to copy from the MS shown to him. When a few slight and necessary corrections have been made, they will run as follows: –

> Vbi multitudo hominum insperata occurrit audire Gallum de sancti Martini uirtutibus locuturum.

This reference to Dr di Martino's patron saint cannot plausibly be assigned even to the prophetic books of Livy. The Provost of Eton may know where the words come from – I do not; but clearly they are an abridgment of what Sulpicius Severus relates in his Dialogus II (III) 1, 5:

> Quid, inquam, tam subito et *insperati* tam ex diuersis regionibus tam mane *concurritis?* Nos, inquiunt, hesterno cognouimus *Gallum* istum per totum diem *Martini* narrasse uirtutes, et reliqua in hodiernum diem, quia nox oppresserat, distulisse: propterea maturauimus frequens auditorium facere de tanta materia *locuturo.*

German scholars, who have had the facsimile before them ever since September 12, must have found out this more than a week ago.

Sir, – I can now complete the identification of the supposed excerpt from Livy. In vol. XXXII of the 'Mémoires de l'Institut National de France (Académie des Inscriptions)', at the end of a paper (pp. 29–56) read in 1884 by Léopold Delisle, there is printed a facsimile (Plate III) of a page from a manuscript now at Quedlinburg, but written early in the ninth century in St Martin's own abbey at Tours. There may be seen the four lines transcribed by Dr Funke: the hand is very similar, the divisions identical, the text a trifle more correct. They constitute the first item in a table of contents prefixed to the dialogue of Sulpicius, which I quoted in my former letter.

* ⟦*The Times*, 22 and 23 Sept. 1923⟧

13

[ARTHUR PLATT]*

Arthur Platt (1860–1925), growing up in an age when Greek scholarship in England was generally under the influence of Hermann, himself continued the line of his countrymen Dawes, Porson, and Elmsley, with whose turn of mind he probably had more in common than any Englishman of the last hundred years, not excepting Badham or Headlam. He united great critical refinement with an instinct which went straight to the point. That he did not write much was directly owing to the extraordinary width of his range and capacity. His chief love was not for Greek, but for great literature: in that air he dwelt, whether the tongue were Greek, Latin, English, French, Italian, Spanish, German, or Persian; and in Platt's company one felt that one was not an educated man. His work was most esteemed by the few who could best appraise it, but he was so gay and unpretentious that vulgar judgments underrated him; and academic honours tend rather to those whose levity lies nearer the centre. We have lost as genuine and straightforward a mind and character as can ever have been born into the world, and a delightful creature whom it is a precious treasure to have known.

* [*CR* 39 (1925), 49]

14

⟦NOTES ON FRONTO⟧*

Fronto, *ad M. Caes.* III, 12 (Naber, p. 49 ⟦45 Van Den Hout⟧). Read 'itaque deberem etiam gratias agere tibi si uerum me dicere ⟨*tantum docere*⟩*s*: *at tu* simul et audire uerum me doces.' *dicere satius* cod.

ib. 13 (p. 51 ⟦47 Van Den Hout⟧). 'haec *oratio amantibus* (*amanti plus* Orelli) decuit et melior et salubrior fuit.' Read *ratio*, and perhaps also *amandi*.

ad M. Ant. imp. I, 5 (p. 102 ⟦95 Van Den Hout⟧). 'ama me ut *amas*, inquis.' The context requires *amasti*, and Marcus in I, 4 had in fact said 'ama me quomodo amasti'.

ad L. Ver. imp. I, 1 (p. 115 ⟦133 Van Den Hout⟧). Supply 'an tu [censes Epictetum] consulto uerbis usum [sordidis]?' and later 'tam facile ille ‖ [pedum incolumitatem quam eloquentiam potuit comparare]', and in the marginal summary 'sed ita eloquentia caruit ⟨ut⟩ pedum incolumitate'.

de orationibus (p. 158 ⟦151 Van Den Hout⟧). Read '*septimum* de Aiacis scuto corium'. *septima* cod.

ad amic. I, 1 (p. 173 ⟦165 Van Den Hout⟧). 'neque forte aut temere necessitudine ista sumus copulati, *nec* ultro me amicitiam Corneliani adpetisse fateor.' Read *sed* or *nam* (*na* is erased after *fateor*).

ibid. (p. 174 ⟦165 Van Den Hout⟧). Supply 'sollicitudo animi me a[rcet] multis eum uerbis commendare; sed fidum amorem nostri spondet [spes subuenturum et, quid]quid postulem, orationem uobis unum meum uerbum uisum iri.'

* ⟦*PCPhS* 1926, 21–2: summary of a paper⟧

15

[PREFACE TO *NINE ESSAYS* BY ARTHUR PLATT]*

The author of the papers collected in this volume was one whose published writings, though they show the rare quality of his mind, do not portray the range of his studies and the variety of his accomplishments. Nor do these papers themselves complete the picture; but they have been recovered and put together that the world may know a little more of an uncommonly gifted man who was not much before its eye, and whose reputation was highest within the narrower circle which knew him well enough to admire him rightly.

It is not certain that he would have consented to their publication, for he must have felt that they bear some traces of the circumstances which called them forth. University College London, like many other colleges, is the abode of a Minotaur. This monster does not devour youths and maidens: it consists of them, and it preys for choice on the Professors within its reach. It is called a Literary Society, and in hopes of deserving the name it exacts a periodical tribute from those whom it supposes to be literate. Studious men who might be settling *Hoti*'s business and properly basing *Oun* are expected to provide amusing discourses on subjects of which they have no official knowledge and upon which they may not be entitled even to open their mouths. Platt, whose temper made him accessible, whose pen ran easily, and whose mind was richly stored, paid more of this blackmail than most of his colleagues, and grudged it less; but the fact is not to be concealed ‖ that these unconstrained and even exuberant essays were written to order. The only one which he allowed to be printed, and that only in a college magazine, is *Aristophanes*. Two however have a different origin and were composed with more deliberation. *Science and Arts among the Ancients* is an address delivered before the Faculties of Arts and Science in University College on a ceremonial occasion, the opening of the Session in October 1899; and the Prelection is one of those read in public by the candidates for the Cambridge Chair of Greek when it fell vacant in 1921.

John Arthur, eldest of the fourteen children of Thomas Francis Platt, was born in London on the 11th of July 1860 and died at Bournemouth on the

---

* [Cambridge University Press 1927]

16th of March 1925. He was sent to school at Harrow, whence he went up to Cambridge in 1879, winning a scholarship at Trinity College. In the first part of the Classical Tripos of 1882 he was placed in the second division of the first class, a position which may have disappointed himself but did not surprise those friends who, whenever they went into his rooms, had found him deep in books which had no bearing on the examination. In the second part a year later he obtained a first class in Literature and Criticism and also in Ancient Philosophy. In 1884, like his father and grandfather before him, he was elected a Fellow of Trinity. This Fellowship he lost under the old statutes by his marriage in 1885 with Mildred Barham, daughter of Sir Edward Bond, K.C.B., sometime Librarian of the British Museum, and granddaughter of R. H. Barham, the author of the *Ingoldsby Legends*. Their children were one son and one daughter. For the next eight years he taught at the coaching establishment of || Wren and Gurney in Bayswater; in 1894 he was chosen to succeed his friend William Wyse as Professor of Greek in University College London, and soon after took up his residence about a mile away on the edge of Regent's Park. He held his Professorship more than 30 years. In 1921, when Henry Jackson died, he was persuaded to become a candidate for the Chair of Greek at Cambridge, to which few or none of the competitors had a juster claim; but he was relieved when he was not elected, and it is certain that Cambridge would have been less to his taste than London as a place to live in. He would have vacated his office at University College by reason of age in July 1925, but in 1924 he was attacked by illness, and did not live to complete his term.

At the time of his appointment some feared that they were yoking a racehorse to the plough and that his duties might be irksome to him because they could hardly be interesting. Much of the teaching which he was required to give was elementary, and he seldom had pupils who possessed a native aptitude for classical studies or intended to pursue them far. But he proved assiduous, patient, and effective: only an oaf could help learning from him and liking him; and with his best students he formed enduring ties, and would inveigle them into reading Dante or Cervantes with him at his house of an evening after they had taken their degrees. Outside his own class-room he was a centre and fount of the general life of the College, most of all in the Musical Society and among his colleagues in the smoking-room after luncheon. Nearer to his house he made another circle of friends. He was a Fellow of the Zoological Society, frequented its Gardens, and inspired || a romantic passion in their resident population. There was a leopard which at Platt's approach would almost ooze through the bars of its cage to establish contact with the beloved object; the gnu, if it saw him on the opposite side of its broad enclosure, would walk all the way across to have its forelock pulled; and a credible witness reports the following scene.

'I remember going to the giraffe-house and seeing a crowd of children watching a man who had removed his hat while the giraffe, its neck stretched to the fullest capacity, was rubbing its head backwards and forwards upon the bald crown. When the object of this somewhat embarrassing affection turned his head, Platt's features were revealed.'

In youth he had poetical ambitions, and his first book was a volume of verse; a smaller one on a personal theme was printed privately, and so was a collection, made after his death, of sonnets, very personal indeed, with which he had entertained and striven to ameliorate his colleagues. He early produced recensions of the *Odyssey* and the *Iliad*, in which it was his aim to restore, so far as might be, the original language of the poet or poets, and thus to pursue further that special line of Homeric study which began with Bentley and his digamma, engaged the acute but undisciplined minds of Payne Knight and Brandreth, and has left as memorials of its progress the editions of Bekker and of Nauck. Nothing could be more different, or could better display his versatility, than his other chief work, the translation of Aristotle's *De generatione animalium* with its multifarious notes on matters zoological. A slighter performance was a free rendering of the *Agamemnon* of Aeschylus into the prose of King James's Bible. ‖

Among the Greek scholars of his country Platt belonged to that company of explorers whose leading figures, after the universal genius of Bentley, are Dawes, Porson, and Elmsley. Minute and refined observation for the ascertainment of grammatical and metrical usage was his chosen province; and his early investigations of Homeric practice were his most characteristic work, and probably surpass in value his later and more various contributions to interpretation and textual criticism. Metrical science, upon the death of Elmsley, had deserted its native isle and taken flight to the Continent: Platt was one of the very few Englishmen who in the last hundred years have advanced the study, and among those few he was the foremost. In conjectural emendation, like Dawes and Elmsley, he was shrewd and dexterous enough, but not, like Bentley and Porson, eminent. In literary comment he did not expatiate, although, or rather because, he was the most lettered scholar of his time. He stuck to business, as a scholar should, and preferred, as a man of letters will, the dry to the watery. He knew better than to conceive himself that rarest of all the great works of God, a literary critic; but such remarks on literature as he did let fall were very different stuff from the usual flummery of the cobbler who is ambitious to go beyond his last.

If his contemporaries rated him, both comparatively and absolutely, below his true position in the world of learning, the loss was chiefly theirs, but the blame was partly his. He had much of the boy in his composition, and something even of the schoolboy. His conversation in mixed company was apt to be flighty, and his writing, though it was not so, carried jauntiness of manner to some ‖ little excess. Those who judge weight by heaviness were perplexed and deceived by a colloquial gaiety, much less unseemly indeed than the frolic sallies of Dawes, but striking more sharply on the sense because not draped like them in the Latin toga; and it was disturbing to meet with a scholar who carried his levity, where others carry their gravity, on the surface, and was austere, where he might without offence or detection have been frivolous, in conducting the operations of his mind.

That he wrote little was the direct and natural consequence of his extraordinary capacity and the variety of his interests and attainments. He would rather improve himself than instruct others. He wrote on subjects where he could make definite and original contributions to the advancement of learning: otherwise he preferred to read. Greek was his trade, but the home in which he dwelt was great literature, whether its language were Greek, Latin, English, French, Italian, Spanish, German, or Persian. The best authors were his study, but his reading ran far beyond them; his curiosity invaded holes and corners, and his taste ranged from the *Divine Comedy* to *Jorrocks's Jaunts*. He followed his inclinations and read for his own delight, with a keen and natural relish, not a dutiful and obedient admiration of the things which are admired by the wise and good. Nor were his studies warped and narrowed by ambition. A scholar who means to build himself a monument must spend much of his life in acquiring knowledge which for its own sake is not worth having and in reading books which do not in themselves deserve to be read; *at illa iacent multa et praeclara relicta.*

Music was a rival of literature in his affections, and his ‖ knowledge of the art and its history was almost an expert's. He followed with interest and understanding the progress of discovery in the natural sciences, and his acquaintance with zoology in particular was such as few laymen can boast. In conclusion it is proper to mention his vices. He was addicted to tobacco and indifferent to wine, and he would squander long summer days on watching the game of cricket.

His happy and useful life is over, and now begins the steady encroachment of oblivion, as those who remember him are in their turn summoned away. This record will not preserve, perhaps none could preserve, more than an indistinct and lifeless image of the friend who is lost to us: good, kind, bright, unselfish, and as honest as the day; versatile without shallowness, accomplished without ostentation, a treasury of hidden knowledge which only accident brought to light, but which accident brought to light perpetually, and which astonished us so often that astonishment lost its nature and we should have wondered more if wonders had failed. Yet what most eludes description is not the excellence of his gifts but the singularity of his essential being, his utter unlikeness to any other creature in the world.

16

*[SYRACOSIVS/-CVSIVS]**

When Cυρακούσιος became commoner than Cυρακόσιος it tended to oust that form from texts, and it is found in half of Pindar's MSS where the metre proves that he did not write it. *Syracŭsius* is retained by Birt in Claud. 68 6 and Auson. Mosell. 304 and by Mohr in Sidon. carm. II 372, and they impute the false quantity to the poets. It is true that, though Claudian has very few false quantities, Ausonius and Sidonius have many; but even against them the testimony of their MSS can have no weight, for *Syracŭsius* is also the spelling of Ovid's MSS and, from the 9th century onward, of Virgil's. Virgil's capital MSS give correctly *Syracosius*; it was in capital MSS, not in MSS of the 9th century, that Claudian and Ausonius and Sidonius read Virgil; and it should be easy to judge whether *Syracŭsius* is more likely to be their spelling or the spelling of their MSS, none of which is older than the 9th century.

* [*PCPhS* 1927, 31: summary of a paper]

17

⟦OVID, *TRIST.* III 2 23–4⟧*

The reading of almost all the better MSS in Ouid. trist. III 2 23 f. is

> ei mihi, quod totiens nostri pulsata sepulcri
> ianua sub (*not* sed) nullo tempore aperta fuit.

This means 'at no time', and *sub* adds nothing to the simple ablative. It is equally superfluous to the sense and of service only to the metre in Manil. V 396 *tali...sub tempore*, 634, 699, laud. Pison. 68 *luce sub illa*, Ouid. met. XII 183, XIII 596, Luc. X 510, Val. Fl. VII 338, anth. epigr. Buech. 1167 3. It makes more difference, and sometimes distinctly signifies inclusion or comprehension, when prefixed to substantives of temporal meaning in Lucr. VI 413, 416, Ouid. fast. V 491, Manil. III 245, 249, 488, 671, IV 821, Val. Fl. VIII 288, Stat. Theb. XI 577, silu. II 3 63. Dictionaries and grammars have not registered these passages, and not many of the similar examples of *sub* local, Ouid. trist. I 3 19, Prop. III 9 36, Manil. III 338, Luc. IX 435, X 66, Stat. silu. V 3 94.

* ⟦*PCPhS* 1927, 31: summary of a paper⟧

18

⟦OVID, *FAST.* V 73-4⟧*

Cicero has several examples of the brachylogy found in *De diuin.* I. 35 *nec adducar* (ut credam) *totam Etruriam delirare*; and I do not think it incredible that a poet should extend the usage to *tangor*, 'I am influenced (to believe that)'. Somewhat analogous is Tac. *Ann.* IV. 57 ⟦1⟧ *permoueor* (ut quaeram) *num ad ipsum referri uerius sit.* Such at any rate seems to be the sort of sense required.

* ⟦J. G. Frazer, *The 'Fasti' of Ovid* (1929), vol. 4, p. 7⟧

19

⟦PROPERTIUS IV 1 150⟧*

I think it much most likely that Propertius had no definite idea what he meant; but in view of *time* the verse ought to have reference to κατάρχαί and to mean that for him it will be dangerous to set out on a journey, or to marry, or to undertake any other piece of business when the Moon is in Cancer. *terga Cancri*, i.e. *testudo Cancri*, is probably a periphrasis for the whole sign, and *sinistra* means 'ominous' without any reference to such subdivision of the back as you find in Firmicus (VIII. 4).

* ⟦H. E. Butler and E. A. Barber, *The Elegies of Propertius* (1933), p. 333⟧

20

DR FRAENKEL'S APPOINTMENT*

Sir, – I have been asked by scholars at Oxford to answer a note by 'Atticus' on p. 13 of the *Sunday Times* of the 16th inst. concerning the election of Dr Eduard Fraenkel to the Corpus Professorship of Latin, where he makes the shade (which he represents as indignant) of Conington (whom he describes as a great Latinist) inquire: 'Is, then, Oxford so barren in Latinity that she has to choose an ex-professor from Freiburg University to fill the chair and occupy the rooms which once were mine?'

The question is invidiously put, and would not have been put by Conington, who was a modest man; but 'Atticus' gives the answer in his next words: 'Herr Fraenkel is a Latinist of European reputation.' I do not know who the other candidates were, but they cannot have been Latinists of European reputation; for no Englishman who could be so described was young enough to be eligible.

* [*The Sunday Times*, 23 December 1934]

LIST OF CLASSICAL PAPERS

VOLUME I

1882

1	Horatiana [[I]]	*JPh* 10 187–96

1883

2	*Ibis* 539	*JPh* 12 167

1887

3	On Soph. *Electr.* 564, and Eur. *I.T.* 15 and 35	*CR* 1 240–1

1888

4	On certain corruptions in the *Persae* of Aeschylus	*AJPh* 9 317–25
5	Isocr. *Paneg.* §40	*CR* 2 42
6	Schol. on Aesch. *P.V.* 488 [[472]]	*CR* 2 42
7	CΩΦPONH	*CR* 2 242–5
8	Emendationes Propertianae	*JPh* 16 1–35
9	The *Agamemnon* of Aeschylus	*JPh* 16 244–90
10	Note on Emendations of Propertius	*JPh* 16 291
11	Horatiana [[II]]	*JPh* 17 303–20

1889

12	Notes on Latin Poets [[I]]	*CR* 3 199–201
13	Persius III. 43	*CR* 3 315

1890

14	Conjectural emendations in the *Medea*	*CR* 4 8–11
15	*Review*: T. G. Tucker, *The Supplices of Aeschylus*	*CR* 4 105–9
16	*Review*: I. Flagg, *Euripides' Iphigenia among the Taurians*	*CR* 4 160–2
17	Horace, *Carm.* IV. 2, 49	*CR* 4 273
18	Notes on Latin poets [[II]]	*CR* 4 340–2
19	Horatiana [[III]]	*JPh* 18 1–35
20	Emendations in Ovid's *Metamorphoses*	*TCPhS* 3 140–53

1891

21	The new fragment of Euripides	*Academy* 259, 305
22	Adversaria orthographica	*CR* 5 293–6

1892

23 The *Oedipus Coloneus* of Sophocles   *AJPh* 13 139–70
24 Sophoclea   *JPh* 20 25–48
25 Remarks on the Vatican Glossary 3321   *JPh* 20 49–52

1893

26 Soph. *Oed. Col.* 527   *CR* 7 449
27 The manuscripts of Propertius [I]   *JPh* 21 101–60
28 The manuscripts of Propertius [II]   *JPh* 21 161–97

1894

29 *Review*: K. P. Schulze, *Catulli Veronensis liber*   *CR* 8 251–7
30 The manuscripts of Propertius [III]   *JPh* 22 84–128
31 A note on Virgil   *TCPhS* 3 239–41

1895

32 The manuscripts of Propertius [IV]   *CR* 9 19–29
33 *Review*: J. P. Postgate, *Sexti Properti carmina*   *CR* 9 350–5

1896

34 Cicero *Pro Milone* c. 33 §90   *CR* 10 192–3

1897

35 Ovid's *Heroides* [I]   *CR* 11 102–6
36 Ovid's *Heroides* [II]   *CR* 11 200–4
37 Ovid's *Heroides* [III]   *CR* 11 238–42
38 Ovid's *Heroides* [IV]   *CR* 11 286–90
39 Ovid's *Heroides* [V]   *CR* 11 425–31

VOLUME II

1897

40 Lucretiana   *JPh* 25 226–49

1898

41 [Notes on Bacchylides]   *CR* 12 68–74
42 [Bacchylides] Ode XVII   *CR* 12 134–40
43 [Critical notes on Bacchylides]   *CR* 12 216–18

1904

69	Owen's *Persius and Juvenal* – A caveat	*CR* 18 227–8
70	Tunica retiarii	*CR* 18 395–8

1905

71	*Review*: R. Ellis, *Catulli carmina*	*CR* 19 121–3
72	Virgil *Aen.* IV 225	*CR* 19 260–1
73	*Review*: H. E. Butler, *Sexti Properti opera omnia*	*CR* 19 317–20

1906

74	The *Siluae* of Statius	*CR* 20 37–47
75	Corp. Inscr. Lat. II Suppl. 5839, Anth. Lat. Epigr. 1113	*CR* 20 114
76	Bacchylideum	*CR* 20 115
77	Notes on Phaedrus	*CR* 20 257–9

1907

78	Luciliana [[I]]	*CQ* 1 53–74
79	Luciliana [[II]]	*CQ* 1 148–59
80	Versus Ouidi de piscibus et feris	*CQ* 1 275–8
81	The Madrid MS of Manilius and its kindred	*CQ* 1 290–8
82	Corrections and explanations of Martial	*JPh* 30 229–65

1908

83	Dorotheus of Sidon	*CQ* 2 47–63
84	On the new fragments of Menander	*CQ* 2 114
85	Manilius III 608–17	*CQ* 2 313–15
86	On the *Paeans* of Pindar	*CR* 22 8–12
87	Martial III 93 18–22	*CR* 22 46–7
88	*Review*: F. Vollmer, *Q. Horati Flacci carmina*	*CR* 22 88–9
89	The apparatus criticus of the *Culex*	*TCPhS* 6 3–22

1909

90	*Sincerus* and Lucretius III 717	*CQ* 3 63–5
91	Vester = tuus	*CQ* 3 244–8
92	*Review*: G. Némethy, *Ciris epyllion pseudo-uergilianum*	*CR* 23 224–6

1910

93	Αἴτια Καλλιμάχου (Pap. Oxyrhynch. vol. VII, pp. 24–7)	*BPhW* 476–7

VOLUME III

1924

138   *Review*: E. T. Merrill, *Catulli Veronensis liber*   *CR* 38 25–7

1925

139   *Review*: A. C. Pearson, *Sophoclis fabulae*   *CR* 39 76–80
140   *Review*: W. Heraeus, *M. Valerii Martialis*   *CR* 39 199–203
     epigrammaton libri

1926

141   Martial XII 59 9   *CR* 40 19
142   *Review*: U. Knoche, *Die Überlieferung Juvenals*   *CR* 40 170–1

1927

143   The Michigan astrological papyrus   *CPh* 22 257–63
144   Prosody and method [[I]]   *CQ* 21 1–12
145   An African inscription   *CR* 41 60–1
146   *Review*: F. Boll, *Sternglaube und Sterndeutung*,   *CR* 41 70–1
     ed. 3
147   *Review*: A. Bourgery, *Lucain i–v*   *CR* 41 189–91

1928

148   Prosody and method II   *CQ* 22 1–10
149   Oxyrhynchus Papyri XVII. 2078   *CR* 42 9
150   *Review*: J.-L. Perret, *La transmission du texte de*   *CR* 42 43
     Juvénal
151   *Review*: W. Morel, *Fragmenta poetarum*   *CR* 42 77–9
     Latinorum
152   The first editor of Lucretius   *CR* 42 122–3
153   Phil. Wochenschr. 1927 pp. 1434–40   *PhW* 127

1929

154   Catullus LXVI 51–4   *CR* 43 168
155   *Review*: H. Bornecque and M. Prévost, *Ovide*,   *CR* 43 194–7
     Héroïdes

1930

156   The Latin for *ass*   *CQ* 24 11–13
157   *Draucus* and Martial XI 8 1   *CR* 44 114–16

158 *Review*: A. Bourgery and M. Ponchont,   *CR* 44 136
     Lucain vi–x
159 *Review*: W. Morel, *Poetae Latini minores*,   *CR* 44 234–5
     vol. i

1931

160 *Review*: H. J. Izaac, *Martial i–vii*   *CR* 45 81–3
161 Praefanda   *Hermes* 66 402–12

1932

162 Disticha de mensibus (Anth. Lat. Ries. 665,   *CQ* 26 129–36
     Poet. Lat. min. Baehr. 1 pp. 210 f.)
163 *Review*: F. Boll, *Sternglaube und Sterndeutung*, *CR* 46 44–5
     ed. 4
164 *Review*: P. de Labriolle, *Les satires de Juvénal* *CR* 46 131–2
165 Three new lines of Lucan?   *CR* 46 150

1933

166 Notes on the *Thebais* of Statius [[I]]   *CQ* 27 1–16
167 Notes on the *Thebais* of Statius [[II]]   *CQ* 27 65–73

1934

168 Notes on Grattius   *CQ* 28 127–33
169 Ennius in Pers. VI 9   *CR* 48 50–1
170 *Review*: H. E. Butler and E. A. Barber, *The*   *CR* 48 136–9
     elegies of Propertius
171 *Review*: H. J. Izaac, *Martial viii–xiv*   *CR* 48 187–9

1935

172 *Review*: J. Wight Duff and A. M. Duff,   *CR* 49 78–9
     Minor Latin poets
173 Fragmenta poetarum   *CR* 49 166–8

1936

174 *Review*: N. Vianello, *D. Iunii Iuuenalis satirae* *CR* 50 26–7

LIST OF ITEMS
INCLUDED IN THE APPENDIX

INDEX OF PASSAGES

INDEX OF WORDS

[Vol. I = pp. 1–422; vol. II = pp. 423–902; vol. III = pp. 908–1277.]

GREEK

ἀνέτως, 805
δυσ-, compounds with, 1096–7
εὐφρόνη, 26–8
καθέλκω, καταβρίθω = 'outweigh', 1225–6
λαικάзω, *lingo*, 1180–1
πατέομαι, πέπαμαι, πᾶμα etc., 78–80
πέλαγος κακῶν et sim., 207

πότμος, meaning of, 594
προφήτης, meaning of, 64–5
σωφρόνη, 24–8
τίθημί τινα ποιεῖν τι, 25
χρονοκράτωρ and ὡροσκόπος, 852–4
ὥρη = ὡροσκόπος, 812

LATIN

abripio, alleged virtually to = *ui arripio*, 1210
accingor, with accusative or with preposition, 584
adducor, in elliptic expressions of the form *a. ut hoc ita sit* or *a. hoc ita esse*, 1153–4
aliquid esse, et sim., 317–18
alisequus, 1157
alius . . . alius, 570
Allobroga, 1085–6
Amicius, 1087
annus = circuit of a planet, 957
anthias, scansion of, 700
antra = 'valleys', 1035
Arctos, sometimes a bear, sometimes a wain, 719
asinus, asellus, 1163–5
at, ast = 'thereupon', 1229
attamen, 1052–5
attinet, with subjunctive, 1052–5
auctor esse, certior esse + accus. = *suadeo, scio*, 473
aut (*uel*) . . . *seu* = *aut* (*uel*) . . . *aut* (*uel*): a dubious irregularity, 853
audire, legere with accus. (of a person) = 'hear, read the name of', 724–5

bis consul, iterum consul et sim., 728–9

caco = *merdae modo emitto*, 1177
Caesar = 'emperor', 929
candidus, candor, of those who think well of others' work, 733–4
caput, with obscene reference, 1178
casus, as abstract verbal substantive of *cadere*, 520
causa tua (*mea*) for *tua* (*mea*) *causa*, 579

celsus, of stars near north pole, 1191
celta, celtis, 1263
chelidon barbata, 482, 539–40
Cinyphius, 1034–5
colere, of friendship, 911–12
collatus, equivalent to protasis of conditional sentence, 922
Colo, 994
colocyntha, 482, 539–40
condere urbem, conditor urbis, etc., applied to emperors and others, 871–2
crudus dolor, and similar expressions, 641–2
cutis (*-es*), 1118–19
cutis = *praeputium*, 1181–2

decipio = *dissimulo, celo, occulo*, 521–2
deducere, deprimere, grauare = 'outweigh', 1225
defigere uisu/*lumine*, 590
denus, 953–4
destringo/*distringo*, 476–7
detersus/*tersus* = *serenus*, 637–8
Dexithea, 1029–31
Dexius, 993
dimissui esse, 844
dracton, 1167
draucus, 1166–7
duellum, Horace's use of, 2
duplico, multiplico, etc.: latent metaphor of folding occasionally developed, 866

ego, tu omitted though emphatic, 884
et iam or *et*, of swift consequence, 1208
et, -que, uel joining notions parallel in force, though not in form, 858

eum, eius, etc., used instead of *se, sui*, etc., 650
eumpse, et sim., 873–4

fallere = dissimulare or *simulare*, or *celare*, 1236
fastigia = 'extremities', 'outlines', etc., 432–3
fateor, parenthetic, 642–4
forsitan, Juvenal's use of, 967

galli, regarded as *ore impudici*, 722–3

habeo = ἔχω, *possum*, 1206
habeo, of sexual relations, 735
hactenus = non amplius, 1081
Hellespontus = 'the Aegean', 593
hora = horoscopus, 812

igne/igni (ablative): Statius' use of, 1219
incolumis/integer/sincerus, 788–9
intentio aeris, etc., 533–4
intestatus = 'unattested', 491
irrumatio, the threat of: commonly used as a rough pleasantry, 732–3
irrumatores and *pedicones* not regarded as *obscaeni*, 1180 n. 2
irrumo = ludibrio habere, contumelia afficere, 1180–1
ita = 'as follows', with verb of speech, 865
iugum, for training vines, 730
Iuppiter
    applied to other gods or to emperors, with epithet to indicate who is meant, 984–5
    oblique cases of used by Ovid to denote Augustus, 912

lamosus, 168
lana lota, lana sucida, 1182–3
limes signorum (et sim.) = 'zodiac', 595
logi = 'fables', 595
lunatus (noun), 506
lureo, 162

Macelo, 1029–31
maris pontus, 437–8
mas, uir = 'virility', 861–2, 1178
mergo = obruo, affligo, perdo, etc.: various uses of, 915–16
miluus, scansion of, 698–9
mulceo = 'sweeten', 642
muneris auctor, 990–1
municeps, of inanimate objects, 516
muratus/immuratus, 168
Mussetius, 995

nascor, meaning of in astronomy, 508
natum esse non putare, et sim., 731–2
nec = et 'non . . .', et sim., 413–14, 726
nego = 'prohibit, preclude', etc., 716

nihil and *nil*, in same verse or successive verses, 1003
Nili caput, 650–2
non secus ut, 133–4

Ombi, in Juvenal, 1195
opis, ope, opes, meaning and use of, 273, 913–14
os impurum, 732–3

Pallas/Tritonis = oliuum, 580
parua loquor/queror, 593–4
Passer, as proper name, 937
pinguis = 'stupid', 715
pipulum, -us, glossed by *conuicium*, 578
pomifer annus = anni pars pomifera, et sim., 951
potens, of a land or region, 734
praecurro, perhaps = *praetercurro*, 319
profundum (noun), 966, 1016–17
pronus and *supinus*, used indifferently in some contexts, 1247
protelum, 1175
prurio, 1179
punicus, -eus, 1035

qua licet, et sim., 917–18
-que attached to ĕ in Propertius, 269
-que, linking disparate members, 1079
qui, use to avoid repetition of *quisquis* and *quicumque*, 1230–1
quicumque, referring back to a list of possibilities, 511
quis, qualis, quantus, etc., exclamatory and interrogative, 1083, 1211–13
quīs = quibus, use of by Latin poets, 1084
quo = cur (only in the sense 'to what end?'), 919–20
quod = 'as for the fact that', in Martial, 538

retorridus, 877–8
reuincere, 382

securicella, 1263
seu (*siue*) *= uel, si*, 853
sic, standing for *talis*, 985
sidera, used for the singular, 1227
sincerus, 787–9
Sinti, 923–4
siparum (*sipharum*), 996–9
si pudor est, 334–5
solus = 'eximie et unice', 1181
spe, fide maior, 1039–40
stella, 906–8
stellare = καταστερίξειν, 596
sub + abl., temporal and local, 1274
succipere, use of, 263–4

INDEX OF SUBJECTS

coordination, by means of *et* or *-que*, of active verb and a deponent or passive participle without its auxiliary verb, 504
coronis, confused with smooth breathing, 130, 1097–8
criticism of Latin texts: danger of fanciful interpretations, 547

Dawes, R.: Housman's judgement of, 1005
disjunctives, often without disjunctive force when coupling interrogatives, 1077
Dobree, P. P.: Housman's judgement of, 1006

Ehwald, R.: Housman's judgement of, 582
Ellis, R.: his unreliability as a collator, 704–10, 776–9, 1019–22
Elmsley, P.
    G. Hermann's judgement of, 1005–6
    Housman's judgement of, 1005–6
Enyo, 409–10
Euripides: dramatic merits of *Hipp.* and *IT*, 129–30
exclamations, in Latin texts, mistaken by editors for questions, 1083, 1211–13

fire, supposed in some myths to immortalize, by destroying mortal elements, 960–1
Fraenkel, E.: his appointment to the Corpus Professorship of Latin, 1277
Friedlaender, L.: some errors in his commentary on Martial, 715

genitive
    latent, adjectives in agreement with, 570, 785
    of quality: adjective found with noun to which this gen. is attached, 615; without epithet, alleged examples of, 519–21
    with adjectives in *-ax*, 521
genitive singular
    -i for *-ii*, 710, 943
    of proper names and common nouns in *-ius* which are tribrachs, 671, 943
Germanicus, *Aratea*
    editing of, 495–501
    manuscripts of, 497–501
gladiators
    retiarii: costume of, 621–2; disrepute attached to certain of, 540; *retiarii tunicati* regarded as *impudici*, 619–22
Grotius, H.: his work on Germanicus, 495

hendiadys, necessary limitations of, 490–1
Hercules, his mortal nature eliminated by means of fire, 960–1
Heyne, C. G.: Housman's judgement of, 521
Horace
    manuscripts of, 772
    Porphyrion's commentary on, 137
    transmission of his text, 96
hyperbole, in Latin poets, especially Vergil, 349–50

Ibis, identification of, 1040–2, 1049–51
Ibis, of Callimachus, 1042, 1049–51
Ixion, punishment of, 1147

Juvenal
    interpolations in, 608
    manuscripts of, 603–5, 609–10, 814–15, 1106–8, 1258; fragmenta Ambrosiana, 814–15; fragmentum Oxoniense, 481–3, 539–42, 608–10; fr. Ox.: its relation to its context, 542; Oxoniensis, 604, 608–10; certain inferior manuscripts, 1148

word-order (*cont.*)
  ἀπὸ κοινοῦ construction, 938–9; postponement to second clause of noun or verb affecting con-
    struction of first clause, 581; some examples in Martial, 718; with preposition *in*, 585
  combination of two or three artificial dislocations in one clause, 938–9
  διὰ μέσου construction (Latin), 729
  hyperbaton: some examples in Germanicus, 514; some examples in Latin poetry, 139–41, 416–17,
    640–1, 659–60; some examples in Martial, 724
  non separated from adjective to which it belongs, 1228
  noun and adjective with intervening conjunction, 570–1
  postponement of conjunction, 938
  postponement of preposition, 938
word-play: same word in two senses (Latin), 695

zeugma, certain notable examples of, 545
Zmyrna, of Cinna, 9